Human Trafficking Is a Public Health Issue

Makini Chisolm-Straker • Hanni Stoklosa

Editors

Human Trafficking Is a Public Health Issue

A Paradigm Expansion in the United States

Springer

Editors
Makini Chisolm-Straker
Department of Emergency Medicine
Icahn School of Medicine at Mount Sinai
New York, NY, USA

Hanni Stoklosa
Department of Emergency Medicine
Brigham and Women's Hospital
Harvard Medical School
Boston, MA, USA

ISBN 978-3-319-47823-4 (hardcover)
ISBN 978-3-319-83833-5 (softcover)
DOI 10.1007/978-3-319-47824-1

ISBN 978-3-319-47824-1 (eBook)

Library of Congress Control Number: 2016962639

Printed on acid-free paper

This Springer imprint is published by Springer Nature
The registered company is Springer International Publishing AG
The registered company address is: Gewerbestrasse 11, 6330 Cham, Switzerland

Hanni:
To My Survivor Friends and Colleagues,
You are a constant source of inspiration.
Together we will create a public health
anti-trafficking response, and heal the world
of trafficking.

Makini:
This is for my parents: Mommy, because you
showed me what love looks like, in action,
and Daddy, because you taught me that love
and justice are twins.

This is for Jill:
Thank you for sharing and teaching and still
believing.

This is for the all abolitionists:
Sigue luchando, sigue amando.

This is for anyone who doesn't belong:
We matter.

Foreword

Human Trafficking Is a Public Health Issue: A Paradigm Expansion in the United States

Human trafficking, the horrific practice of people being abducted or tricked into servitude and exploited for money, is a modern-day form of slavery. It is both a criminal act and a significant violation of human rights. Worldwide, more than 21 million people are estimated to be in bondage. This $150 billion criminal enterprise is dedicated to forcing people into labor and sexual exploitation. It affects people of all ages and genders and is a major source of child labor globally. The incidence of this practice in the United States is unclear, but human trafficking may affect at least hundreds of thousands of people. Like many criminal acts, the individual health implications associated with trafficking are profound for those involved. Also, as is the case with many individual health problems, there is a public health aspect to addressing the health concerns when considering trafficked persons on a population basis.

The health implications—both physical and behavioral—of human trafficking are enormous. In addition, those trafficked face unique barriers accessing adequate care for their health needs. Because of the magnitude of the related health impacts, this problem demands the involvement of the public health community.

Public health is defined by the Institute of Medicine as "what society does collectively to assure the conditions for people to be healthy." Public health does its work through a population approach, addressing broad societal issues that impact health at its core determinants. The field has a long and distinguished history of advancing social justice and fundamental human rights as a component of ensuring a healthy society. Public health approaches problems by first conducting an assessment; then defining the policies, procedures, and programs necessary to address the problem; and assuring that the measures are put in place to resolve the problem. Next come appropriate evaluations to measure the impact, necessary midcourse corrections, and, if needed, the design of new approaches based on what is learned over time.

The health problems linked to human trafficking include both physical and behavioral ailments. Some are obvious, such as the consequences of sexual abuse and physical violence. Others include diseases associated with living in crowded conditions such as tuberculosis, malnutrition, and infectious diarrhea. Injury is a significant problem, resulting from physical violence, torture, and unintentional injury that occurs during forced labor. Some injuries are more subtle, like the sequelae of manual labor causing back pain and repetitive motion injury. Mental health problems from recurrent physical and emotional abuse can cover the full range of complex trauma and include anxiety, depression, phobias, and panic attacks. Depression is a frequent occurrence, with suicide as the tragic end point for too many. Hopelessness and helplessness from humiliation and shame are prominent feelings that, combined with the shock of finding oneself in a strange location or incomprehensible situation, make it difficult to escape these bonds. Other common problems include substance or alcohol use, whether used as a controlling mechanism by the perpetrators or as a coping mechanism by those victimized to mentally escape trauma.

In addition to labor trafficking, people of all genders, adults and children, are sex trafficked, resulting in not only physical injury but the full range of sexually related infections that may go inadequately treated, if treated at all. Unplanned pregnancies, the selling of offspring resulting from these pregnancies, and forced—often unsafe—abortions further define the magnitude of these despicable acts.

We value health insurance coverage because it provides both a mechanism to pay for healthcare and, when done properly, a regular provider of care. Victims of human trafficking may not have health insurance. Their lack of a regular source of care results in the failure to access even the most basic care for chronic medical and dental conditions. This means basic preventive medicine measures like vaccinations and health screenings are not conducted. Care for chronic conditions like diabetes, hypertension, heart disease, and cancer is not adequately achieved, if such care exists at all. Such lack of care contributes to a steady decline in health among those who live with otherwise treatable, chronic health problems.

The public health community can play an important role in addressing this human trafficking tragedy: first, by doing the research and publishing on the health impacts and prevention strategies; second, by providing healthcare programs to those victimized and suspected victims; and, finally, by using our enormous communication capacity as trusted messengers to raise awareness and advocate for the full range of public health actions to bring this human rights violation to an end.

The editors of this text have the powerful firsthand experience of seeing trafficked individuals in their clinical emergency medicine practice. And they bring that view of the health impact of this problem from the front lines of medicine. They also have an important perspective to this abhorrent problem: Because of their training and work in public health, they can apply a population perspective to the subject. The editors have brought together a remarkable collection of experts to examine human trafficking through a comprehensive public health lens.

We must not ignore the topic, no matter how uncomfortable or how seemingly insurmountable. Information is power, and this text is a key to understanding how to address an issue that crosses age, gender, and cultural boundaries and to demand the attention of the public health community. This collection is an important contribution to the field and should be a required reading for anyone who may serve trafficked persons.

Georges C. Benjamin, MD, MACEP,
FACEP(E), FNAPA, Hon FRSPH, Hon FFPH
Executive Director
American Public Health Association
Washington, DC, USA

Preface

Ratified on December 6, 1865, the 13th Amendment to the United States Constitution made slavery and involuntary servitude illegal in the United States (US) and areas of its jurisdiction. While this amendment formally ended 246 years of legalized slavery in the United States, its practice has continued in nuanced and clandestine ways until today. Throughout the centuries, slavery has taken many forms and names in the United States, including "debt bondage," "peonage," "involuntary servitude," and, most currently, "human trafficking." The issue became a topic of global public concern in the 1990s, and in the early 2000s it became apparent that the United States was not only a destination country but also a country in which trafficking was occurring without the transnational movement of persons. In this book, chapter authors specifically discuss human trafficking in the United States and use the US federal definition of "severe forms" of trafficking:

(A) Sex trafficking: the recruitment, harboring, transportation, provision, obtaining, soliciting or patronizing of a person for the purpose of a commercial sex act (any sex act on account of which anything of value is given to or received by any person) using force, fraud, or coercion, OR involving a child less than 18 years of age;
    Or
(B) Labor trafficking: the recruitment, harboring, transportation, provision, or obtaining of a person for labor or services, through the use of force, fraud, or coercion for the purpose of subjection to involuntary servitude, peonage, debt bondage, or slavery [1, 2].

Given the US history of using exploited labor and forced sex to subjugate races and build and sustain the national economy, it is not difficult to understand why human trafficking is hard to eradicate here: It is woven into this great nation's foundational fabric. Supply chain transparency is shrouded in complexity, and consumers are driven to acquire more product for less cost. Communities of color and LGBT or queer communities are particularly at risk for victimization; boys and men are likely to be under-recognized as being victimized. Undocumented immigrants, who know of little recourse, are vulnerable to traffickers and exploitative business practices. Homeless youth who are US citizens and lawful permanent residents (LPR) are well documented as a large percentage of those trafficked in the United States. Human trafficking affects all communities in the United States, directly or indirectly, because the US economy touches us all, and we all participate in it. The US consumer, wittingly or not, perpetuates this egregious human rights violation via ignorance of worker conditions, commodification of sex, an insatiable desire for material acquisition, and the need for the basic, material necessities of life.

Human trafficking, in its variety of forms, negatively impacts the overall health of US inhabitants: Those trafficked suffer from myriad of short- and long-term physical and mental health outcomes. The poor health of the victimized impacts their ability to contribute to their families' well-being and participate in their communities. Communicable diseases are perpetuated in the unsanitary living and working conditions of those trafficked and by unsafe sex practices in the course of sex trafficking or the sexual assault of those trafficked. Furthermore, the inequities that trafficking exploits and magnifies tear at the fabric of our interconnected communities. Affecting multiple systems and the health of large groups, human trafficking is a public health issue. While the medical care system is primarily focused on the health of individuals, public health is concerned with the health and welfare of a people.

Until now, the anti-trafficking movement in the United States has largely been framed by law enforcement and the criminal justice system. Focused on retribution and punishment, there has not been a fully concerted effort to prevent human trafficking at its root causes or understand "victims" or "perpetrators" as whole persons. Given that human trafficking affects the health of large populations, directly and indirectly, and permeates US society and given that public health is especially concerned for the most vulnerable, it is only rational to conceive of human trafficking as a public health matter. Viewing other issues of public health from a purely criminal justice lens as such has not served us well. Examples abound and include the "war on drugs" and the D.A.R.E (Drug Abuse Resistance Education), and the "war on crime" and its "three-strikes" policy. Not conceptualizing these issues outside of criminal justice, anti-drug and anti-crime efforts were doomed, from the beginning, to inadequate successes.

In contrast, recognizing issues as being of public health concern facilitates a proactive, rather than reactive, attitude about rectifying a problem. Public health attacks a problem on multiple fronts, in an effort to prevent, intervene upon, and mitigate a problem's fallout. For example, public health methods were useful in drastically reducing malaria in the United States. Initially endemic to the United States, the infection was eradicated (as a naturally occurring infection) from the country by the 1950s. In addition to creating a surveillance program (secondary prevention) and treating infected patients (tertiary prevention), a Centers for Disease Control (now, Centers for Disease Control and Prevention) endeavor against malaria focused on primary prevention of the infection. Via large-scale and cooperative efforts between local, state, and federal agencies, homes and large areas of land were sprayed with insecticide, wetlands were drained, mosquito breeding sites were eliminated, and education campaigns were waged. An expensive undertaking, by

1951 the United States was declared malaria-free; now, nearly all cases of malaria identified in the United States are among international travelers. Public health efforts have similarly been made in the efforts against tuberculosis, HIV, and other infectious diseases. Like human trafficking, these infections disproportionately affect the nation's most vulnerable: those of color, the poor, the socially marginalized, the incarcerated, and the undereducated.

As a field, public health recognizes the value of all human life, not only the wealthy, the well-educated, or the well-connected. Public health understands health or access to contributors to a healthy life as a human right; to that end, the field frames its understanding of problems as complex and complicated. A public health problem finds systems interconnected and reliant upon each other: The public's health is not possible without high-quality education, access to safe drinking water and nutrient-rich food, a reliable sewage system, strong familial units, intersystem collaborations, and so on. People are not just patients. In fact, they are largely *not* patients. People rely on various systems and communities to be healthy, maintain health, and recover from illness or injury.

A socio-ecological model of understanding allows advocates to more fully comprehend a public health problem and the various modes of undertaking that can be useful in combating such a problem. The socio-ecological model respects the downstream effects of upstream determinants and the indirect but powerful connections of interpersonal relationships, community influences, and policies and societal regulations and norms; it requires a holistic approach of combining research, prevention, intervention, monitoring and evaluation, and rehabilitation to positively affect change. HEAL (Health, Education, Advocacy, and Linkage) Trafficking is a not-for-profit organization that unites and mobilizes interdisciplinary professionals in the effort to shift the anti-trafficking movement from one that is centered on the criminal justice system to a more inclusive paradigm, rooted in public health approaches. HEAL members penned the American Public Health Association's 2015 policy on domestic anti-trafficking efforts with this goal in mind. In early 2016, the federal government followed the APHA's lead, formally recognizing the need to take a broader view in its anti-trafficking efforts.

This book is another step toward properly approaching anti-trafficking with public health principles: It is a brief, but comprehensive, introduction to many of the United States' anti-trafficking movement's participants. This academic text broadens the conversation, as public health requires, to include trafficking survivors, communities of particular vulnerability, clinicians, and non-academician advocates. The authors of this book's chapters know trafficking well, but their voices have not always been heard and respected in academic or formal settings. Still, their experience and knowledge are crucial to the anti-trafficking movement. Without these voices, the "war on trafficking" will flounder. This book will be foundational for those new to the issue of human trafficking and informative to niche experts.

Here, we must pause as book editors to explain a few items about this book. Firstly, in an effort to respect the autonomy and strength of those who are trafficked, the term "victim" is only used when trafficking is discussed from a law enforcement or legal perspective. All "victims" are survivors, even while living through exploitation and abuse. In a public health conversation, we must move away from specifically criminal justice language that mainly views the issue in terms of "perpetrator" and "victim." Human trafficking is not binary; it is complex and nuanced, and the use of the term "victim" oversimplifies how trafficking is experienced, does not recognize the agency and capacity of those trafficked, and ignores the conditions that foster "perpetrators."

Further, as the demographics of those trafficked and at risk of being trafficked are still poorly known, this text uses gender-inclusive language, forgoing traditional use of pronouns. That is to say, instead of using "he/she" or "him/her," chapter authors use "they" and "their" instead. In this way, we wish to highlight that people with a transgender or gender nonconforming life experience are often left out of these conversations, despite the fact that many experts name this diverse group as particularly vulnerable to being trafficked.

Beyond language, discussions about human trafficking in the United States frequently center on sex trafficking (and that of women and girls, to be specific) and largely ignore labor and other forms of trafficking. As this book aims to broaden the anti-trafficking paradigm, any time "human trafficking" is mentioned, all forms of trafficking are meant to be inferred. Sex trafficking is one form of human trafficking; it is the most oft discussed and studied. But it is not the most common type of trafficking, and anti-trafficking conceptualizations and efforts must be broadened in this country. Moreover, one form of trafficking does not preclude another. People are labor and sex trafficked, in parallel and in series.

And lastly, of course, the views and opinions expressed by chapter authors are their own and do not necessarily reflect those of the editors, the book's publisher, or the chapter authors' organizations or employers. That being said, we, the book editors, are honored to have such a broad range of perspectives, experiences, and knowledge reflected in this text. We are grateful for the participation of all the authors, who took on this work because it is important to them and to this country; their varying opinions reflect their passion about anti-trafficking work. We wholeheartedly believe that, with a public health approach and long, hard, intelligent, collaborative, caring work, a world without trafficking is someday possible.

> Let us have love and more love; a love that melts all opposition, a love that conquers all foes, a love that sweeps away all barriers, a love that aboundeth in charity, a large-heartedness, tolerance, forgiveness and noble striving, a love that triumphs over all obstacles. — Abdu'l Bahá

New York, NY, USA   Makini Chisolm-Straker
Boston, MA, USA   Hanni Stoklosa

References

1. United States Government. Trafficking Victims Protection Act of 2000.
2. United States Government. Justice for Victims of Trafficking Act of 2015.

Endorsement

"Thank you, Drs. Chisolm-Straker and Stoklosa for compiling what must be the most complete, compelling, and informative collection on human trafficking as a public health issue to date. At times poignant, at other times hopeful, and at all times enlightening—this will be considered a required reading for anyone interested in a comprehensive review of the public health implications of human trafficking."

George L. Askew, MD, FAAP
Former Chief Medical Officer
Administration for Children and Families
US Department of Health and Human Services
New York, NY, USA

Acknowledgments

Many people contributed to the success of this arduous work of love, and we must thank them, here. We are deeply indebted to Janet Kim, MPH, our editing publisher, and Dr. Georges Benjamin, our foreword author.

Hanni: My loving husband; Drs George Askew, J. Stephen Bohan, Annie Lewis-O'Connor, Ron Walls, Cathy Zimmerman; my Brigham and Women's hospital family, especially the Connors Center and Department of Emergency Medicine; HEAL Trafficking; and my cat, Hansel.

Makini: Drs. Lynne D. Richardson, Kaushal Shah, Bret Nelson; Tiffany D. Joseph, PhD; Cynthia W. Pong, JD; HEAL Trafficking; Jill Brenneman; all my friend-family; and my family-family.

Contents

Authors' Biography

Erin Albright, JD has worked in the anti-trafficking field since 2008. Her experience includes working for the Boston Police Department's Human Trafficking Unit managing a network of service providers in New England, participation in and leadership for Freedom Network USA and providing consultation and leadership for Task Forces in New England and across the country. She specializes in building organizational capacity and service collaboration through training and consultation with service providers, law enforcement, task forces, and lawmakers. Albright has a BA in international affairs from the University of Mary Washington and earned her JD at Boston College Law School.

Nina Aledort, PhD, LMSW has more than 25 years of experience working with youth with significant vulnerabilities, including LGBTQ, runaway and homeless, incarcerated/court-involved, and HIV-positive youth. Over the course of her career, Dr. Aledort has created and evaluated programs to serve these youth and has focused the last few years on key policy challenges at the intersection of child welfare, juvenile justice, child sex trafficking, and runaway and homeless youth. She is the author of several peer-reviewed articles and has presented nationally and internationally. She has a particular interest in the needs of young women in child welfare and juvenile and criminal justice settings. Dr. Aledort has an MSW from Hunter College School of Social Work, City University of New York (CUNY), and a PhD in social welfare from the Graduate Center of the City University of New York.

Elaine J. Alpert, MD, MPH trained in internal medicine and public health, is an internationally respected scholar and independent consultant in family violence, sexual assault, and human trafficking, with a focus on curriculum design and delivery, writing and editing, strategic planning, policy formulation, advocacy, and leadership development. Dr. Alpert contributes both expertise and experience in inter-professional education, distance (online) learning, trauma-informed care, and strengthening the health sector's role in the coordinated community response to violence and abuse across the lifespan. She currently focuses her energies as an independent curriculum design and strategic planning consultant in all forms of violence prevention and also teaches communication skills at the University of British Columbia School of Medicine.

Susie Baldwin, MD, MPH is a Los Angeles-based preventive medicine and public health physician whose career has focused on women's health, sexual and reproductive health, and epidemiology. She began working with human trafficking survivors in 2005. Dr. Baldwin has engaged in human trafficking research and advocacy, has trained hundreds of healthcare professionals in victim identification and response, and ran a survivor clinic for 7 years as a volunteer at a community health center, in cooperation with the Coalition to Abolish Slavery and Trafficking. Dr. Baldwin is a member of the LA County Interagency Steering Committee that is developing a large-scale response to commercially sexually exploited children (CSEC) and received the CSEC Champion Award from the County. Dr. Baldwin has received Freedom Network USA's Wellstone Award for her dedication to US anti-trafficking efforts, as well as LA County Department of Public Health's Award for Excellence and the Physician Recognition Award for Health Equity. Dr. Baldwin is cofounder and president of the board of HEAL Trafficking.

Dr. Baldwin attended Columbia University in New York City, the Downstate College of Medicine in Brooklyn, and the Arizona College of Public Health. She completed a National Cancer Institute-funded research fellowship in cancer prevention and control, focused on HPV infection in women and men, and a women's health services research fellowship at UCLA and the VA, where she studied access to emergency contraception in California and also began her work on human trafficking.

Wendy J. Barnes is a human trafficking survivor, survivor advocate, and author. She was trafficked by a "Romeo pimp" for over 13 years, starting at the age of 17. Her trafficker, who is the father of her three children, is now serving life in prison without the possibility of parole after his third conviction of promoting prostitution. Wendy's freedom from her trafficker cost her dearly: She was incarcerated for almost 2 years and lost parental custody of all her children. Fifteen years post-prison, Wendy is now able to live her genuine life. She volunteers for anti-trafficking activities and shares her story with law enforcement, faith-based groups, and service organizations. She has published her story, *And Life Continues: Sex Trafficking and My Journey to Freedom*, with the goal that it will help others understand the life of trafficking victims and that it will give hope to other survivors.

Jeffrey Barrows, DO, MA is an obstetrician/gynecologist who in 2005 began working with the State Department's Trafficking in Persons Office to study the health consequences of human trafficking. In 2006, he began teaching healthcare professionals how to recognize potential human trafficking victims, and in June of that year, he has consulted for the State Department on the health needs of trafficking victims in Sierra Leone and Liberia. In May 2008, he published the article "Human Trafficking and the Healthcare Professional" in the *Southern Medical Journal*. Also in 2008, Dr. Barrows founded Gracehaven, an organization assisting victims of domestic minor sex trafficking in Ohio through outreach, case management, and residential rehabilitative care. In 2014, he became a member of the Technical Working Group on health and human trafficking under the Department of Health and Human Services' Administration for Children and Families, and Dr. Barrows is a founding board member of HEAL Trafficking.

Cyril Bennouna, MPH is the technical lead for research at the Center on Child Protection at Universitas Indonesia (PUSKAPA UI), where his research informs the development of national policies and programs that strengthen access to basic services and social protections for Indonesia's hardest-to-reach populations. He is currently working on a project to identify children that have been trafficked in Indonesia's fishing industry. Bennouna is also a senior research associate at the CPC Learning Network, where his research focuses on children's protection and women's empowerment in humanitarian settings. In his previous work at the Program on Forced Migration and Health at Columbia University, Bennouna developed methodologies for documenting and estimating grave violations against children in complex emergencies, such as the recruitment and use of children in armed conflict, abduction of children, and sexual and gender-based violence. He received his Master of Public Health degree with a certificate in public health humanitarian assistance from Columbia University Mailman School of Public Health.

Kimberly Caceres, MSW has supported programs to identify and provide services to exploited and trafficked children and participated in a number of task forces and multidisciplinary efforts to serve this population. Her interest in human rights and social justice developed during her undergraduate studies at Skidmore College where she made the dean's list while earning a Bachelor of Arts. Ms. Caceres went on to earn a dual master's degree in criminal justice and social welfare from SUNY Albany in 2016 she also completed a certificate in public sector management with a concentration in homeland security.

Kimberly S.G. Chang, MD, MPH is a family physician at Asian Health Services (AHS) in Oakland, California. She spent 2014–2015 as a Commonwealth Fund Mongan Fellow in Minority Health Policy at Harvard Medical School, where she completed a policy practicum addressing the role of Federally Qualified Health Centers in caring for victims of human trafficking, with the Association of Asian Pacific Community Health Organizations. Prior to her fellowship, Dr. Chang was clinic director at the Frank Kiang Medical Center, Asian Health Services, directing the start-up of this family practice clinic, from assisting with design, developing programming, growing it to full capacity in less than 2 years, and expanding patients' language access to ten Asian languages. In addition, she provides care for many commercially sexually exploited children (CSEC) and is a cofounder and executive board member of HEAL Trafficking. She has trained thousands of front-line multidisciplinary professionals on the healthcare intersect with human trafficking across the United States and internationally to the Compact of Free Association nations in the Western Pacific, as well as coauthored several journal articles on the topic. She serves on a Technical Working Group for the Administration for Children and Families, to develop a pilot training for healthcare professionals on human trafficking. She currently serves as second vice chair of the National Association of Community Health Center's Committee on Service Integration on Behavioral Health and HIV. Her presentations and publications have focused on cultural competency, human trafficking issues, underserved populations, and global health issues, and in December 2015, she provided invited expert testimony for a congressional briefing for the US Helsinki Commission on "Best Practices in Rescuing Trafficking Victims." In 2011, she was nationally recognized with a Physician Advocacy Merit Award from the Institute on Medicine as a Profession.

Dr. Chang attended Columbia University for her undergraduate studies, received her MD from the University of Hawaii, John A. Burns School of Medicine, completed her family medicine residency at San Francisco General Hospital, University of California, San Francisco and received her Master of Public Health from the Harvard T.H. Chan School of Public Health, where she was awarded the Dr. Fang-Ching Sun Memorial Award for demonstrated commitment to promoting the health of vulnerable people.

Sharon E. Chin, MPH is a program evaluation and data quality specialist who monitors and implements continuous quality improvement measures in a range of state-level community-based child abuse and neglect prevention programs. She received her Master of Public Health degree from Rutgers University's School of Public Health, where her thesis covered the evaluation of the youth trafficking in persons prevention program My Life My Choice.

Katherine Y. Chon, MPA is the director of the Office on Trafficking in Persons (OTIP) within the Administration for Children and Families (ACF) at the US Department of Health and Human Services. She advises the assistant secretary by providing subject matter expertise and overall leadership of anti-trafficking activities under the purview of ACF. OTIP is responsible for the development of anti-trafficking strategies, policies, and programs to prevent human trafficking, build health and human service capacity to respond to human trafficking, increase victim identification and access to services, and strengthen health and well-being outcomes of survivors of human trafficking. OTIP collaborates with federal partners and other government and nongovernment stakeholders to raise public awareness, identify research priorities for ACF's anti-trafficking work, and make policy recommendations to enhance anti-trafficking responses.

Prior to government service, Chon was the cofounder and president of Polaris, establishing the global organization's innovative programs to assist victims of trafficking, expand anti-trafficking policies, and fundamentally change the way communities respond to modern slavery. Chon received her ScB in psychology from Brown University and MPA from John F Kennedy School of Government at Harvard University.

Shaylin Chock, MD is boarded by the American Board of Psychiatry and Neurology (ABPN) in adult, child and adolescent, and forensic psychiatry and is an assistant professor at the University of Hawaii, John A. Burns School of Medicine. She works with high-risk youth at the largest inpatient child and adolescent unit in the state and frequently works with victims of trafficking providing therapeutic psychiatric interventions. Additionally, Dr. Chock is an active participant with the Hawaii Coalition Against Human Trafficking (HCAHT) and has been a participant in the Hawaii Commercially Sexually Exploited Children (CSEC) Response Protocol Development Workgroup.

Kate D'Adamo, MA is a National Policy Advocate working on policy and social advocacy at the state, federal, and cross-regional level on issues impacting those engaged in the sex trade, including human trafficking and HIV. Prior to joining the Sex Workers Project, Kate was the lead organizer with the Sex Workers Outreach Project-NYC and Sex Workers Action New York, two constituent-led organizations supporting those trading sex in the NYC area. In this role, D'Adamo developed programming to promote community building, curated peer-support spaces, supported leadership development, and advanced community-directed advocacy. She has also worked on varying issues including human trafficking, labor rights, international solidarity, and migration at the International Commission for Labor Rights, the Global Workers Justice Alliance, the Open Society Foundation, and Freedom Network USA. D'Adamo has a BA in political science from California Polytechnic State University and an MA in international affairs from The New School.

James L. Dold, JD is a human rights lawyer who currently serves as advocacy director for the Campaign for the Fair Sentencing of Youth (CFSY) in Washington, D.C. Prior to joining the CFSY, Mr. Dold served as senior policy counsel for Polaris Project where he led successful state legislative campaigns that resulted in the passage of 40 new anti-human trafficking laws across the country. These laws ranged from criminalizing labor and sex trafficking to providing needed victim assistance and services to survivors. He received the inaugural 2013 Professor Louis Henkin Award by Rightslink at Columbia Law School as well as the 2013 Josephine Butler Award for his efforts in advancing human rights protections for victims of human trafficking.

Mr. Dold is a survivor of child labor trafficking/exploitation and sexual abuse which began when he was 13 years old. After returning home, Mr. Dold was able to finish high school and went on to become a first-generation college graduate.

While in law school, Mr. Dold served as a law clerk at the ACLU of Maryland where he worked on defending the First Amendment rights of street performers and religious groups. He also spent time working for Delegate Dana Stein in the Maryland State Legislature and in the United States Senate for Senator Ben Cardin. Mr. Dold received dual baccalaureates in criminal justice and psychology from the University of Nevada, Las Vegas, and graduated cum laude from the University of Maryland School of Law. He is licensed to practice law in the state of Maryland and is a member of the US Supreme Court Bar.

Dustin Dwiggins, MD is an emergency medicine resident physician at Mount Sinai Beth Israel in New York City. During his residency, he has helped to create educational materials regarding LGBT barriers to care, to educate other medical professionals on this particular population's unique health needs. Dr. Dwiggins' interest in these issues arose in medical school during his work in global health and while volunteering in free clinics for the underserved.

Sandra Gasca-Gonzalez, MS is director of the Annie E. Casey Foundation's Jim Casey Youth Opportunities Initiative since 2015 and leads national, state and local efforts to improve policies and practices to help ensure all young people have the opportunity to successfully transition from foster care to adulthood. She is known for addressing deep-rooted system challenges and understands the importance of working with diverse stakeholders across the communities being served. With deep professional roots in child welfare agency administration, Gasca-Gonzalez has worked with systems across the country to address sex trafficking of young people in foster care, including in the Midwest region and urban areas such as Washington, D.C. Her expertise includes operationalizing trauma-focused practices at a systems and community level by understanding the social determinants and risk factors that lead to human trafficking. In her work with the Jim Casey Initiative, she leads a team that is striving to help states effectively implement key provisions in the federal Preventing Sex Trafficking and Strengthening Families Act to keep young people in foster care safe and make sure they have equitable opportunities to learn, grow and thrive as they transition into adulthood.

An alumna of Casey's Children and Family Fellowship program, Gasca-Gonzalez has also served as executive vice president of practice and leadership integration for KVC (formerly Kaw Valley Center) Health Systems, where she led nationally recognized initiatives to transform child welfare systems with clinical best practices, change management skills and results-based measurement.

Before this, she was on assignment from KVC to one of the most embattled public child welfare systems in the USA—the Washington, D.C., Child and Family Services Agency—where she implemented best practices and championed a culture shift, achieving dramatic outcomes for the children and families served by the agency. Gasca-Gonzalez has also served as president of KVC Nebraska and worked for Youthville, where she led the implementation of privatization for the South Central area of Kansas.

Gasca-Gonzalez is a graduate of the National Hispanic Leadership Institute, a recipient of an Executive Leadership Certificate from Harvard University and has been recognized by business journals in two states as a "40 Under 40" leader. She earned a master's degree in psychology from Emporia State University and a bachelor's from Southwestern College.

Donna Gavin, JD is a 30-year veteran and lieutenant with the Boston Police Department. She has spent much of her career investigating cases involving violent crimes against women and children including domestic violence, sexual assault, and most recently human trafficking. She is presently the commander of the Boston Police Department's Human Trafficking and Crimes Against Children Units.

Lieutenant Gavin is a steering committee member of the Suffolk County Children's Advocacy Center's *SEEN* (Support to End Exploitation Now) Coalition. She has given testimony at the National Academy Institute of Medicine regarding commercial sexual exploitation of children and given trainings on sex trafficking and prostitution to various groups including law enforcement officers, school nurses, and hospital and hotel staff throughout New England. Lieutenant Gavin was an active participant in the World Symposium on Human Trafficking held at the Jimmy Carter Center in Atlanta, Georgia, in 2015. She presently serves as cochair of Boston's *CEASE* (Cities Empowered Against Sexual Exploitation) Network.

Lieutenant Gavin is a graduate of Suffolk University Law School and a member of the Massachusetts Bar Association. She is also a member of the Massachusetts and National Associations of Women in Law Enforcement. In 2014, she received the My Life My Choice *Turn on the Light Award*. In 2015, she was awarded the 3 Generations Malone Prize for Vision and Leadership in Law Enforcement.

Holly Austin Gibbs is a survivor of child sex trafficking and an activist against all forms of human trafficking and exploitation. She receives requests on a regular basis to provide testimony and input to law enforcement officials, legislators, social service providers, human trafficking task forces, and journalists. Gibbs has testified before the Congress and consulted for numerous organizations, including the Office for Victims of Crime, the National Center for Missing and Exploited Children, and the AMBER Alert Program. In 2014, Gibbs published an academic book titled *Walking Prey: How America's Youth Are Vulnerable to Sex Slavery*. In 2015, she joined Dignity Health, the fifth largest health system in the nation and the largest hospital provider in California. As Patient Care Services Program director, Gibbs is overseeing a new program to recognize and respond to at-risk and actual victims of human trafficking in the healthcare setting.

Jordan Greenbaum, MD is a child abuse physician at the Stephanie V. Blank Center for Safe and Healthy Children at Children's Healthcare of Atlanta. She obtained her medical degree from Yale Medical School and is board-certified in anatomic and forensic pathology. She has spent the majority of her career working as a child abuse physician, providing clinical evaluations for suspected victims and education and training for professionals, and engaging in program development. Dr. Greenbaum served on the board of the American Professional Society on the Abuse of Children, as secretary and as president. She co-chairs the Human Trafficking Committee for the Helfer Society and the Education/Training Committee for HEAL Trafficking, an organization of multidiscplinary professionals working on human trafficking issues. Dr. Greenbaum is also the medical director of the Global Initiative for Child Health and Well-Being at the International Centre for Missing & Exploited Children.

Madeline Hannan, MSW has worked on issues related to child welfare and human trafficking for more than 5 years at a variety of nonprofit and government agencies, including the International Organization for Adolescents (IOFA), Polaris Project, and International Bureau for Children's Rights. Ms. Hannan's work is grounded in her direct experience serving trafficking survivors and youth in foster care in New York City. She earned her MSW from McGill University and a BSW from SUNY—University at Albany.

A. Seiji Hayashi, MD, MPH is executive vice president for transformation and innovation at Unity Health Care, Inc., one of the largest health centers in the United States. Prior to coming to Unity, Dr. Hayashi served as chief medical officer for the Bureau of Primary Health Care at the Health Resources and Services Administration, US Department of Health and Human Services. He oversaw the clinical quality strategy for the federal Health Center Program that cares for 23 million people across the United States. He also spent many years teaching and directed the Master of Public Health program in Community Oriented Primary Care at George Washington University. Dr. Hayashi is a family physician and continues to care for patients. Dr. Hayashi graduated from Vassar College and received his medical degree from the Albert Einstein College of Medicine. He completed his family and community medicine residency program at the University of California at San Francisco and received his Master of Public Health degree from the Harvard School of Public Health while serving as a fellow for the Commonwealth Fund/Harvard University Fellowship in minority health policy.

Elizabeth K. Hopper, PhD is a licensed clinical psychologist at the Trauma Center at Justice Resource Institute (JRI), one of the nation's leading agencies in the study and treatment of the psychological impact of exposure to trauma. She is the director of Project REACH, a program that offers trauma-informed assessment and intervention for trafficking survivors throughout the United States and provides training and consultation to cross-discipline professionals. The mission of Project REACH is to increase trafficking survivors' access to trauma-informed care across legal, healthcare, and social services systems. Dr. Hopper conducts trainings nationwide in the areas of human trafficking, complex trauma, and cultural and developmental adaptations to assessment and intervention. She has written about psychological coercion, psychological impacts of human trafficking, body-based intervention, and the treatment of complex trauma. Dr. Hopper is also a staff psychologist and supervisor at the Trauma Center at JRI.

Sarah Ingerman, BA currently serves as the executive project coordinator and administrator for HEAL (Health, Education, Advocacy, and Linkage) Trafficking as well as a project manager for Brigham and Women's Hospital's (BWH) Center for Community Health and Health Equity (CCHHE). In her role at the CCHHE, Ingerman has assisted with the development of a human trafficking framework for healthcare institutions in the Boston area and the development of a BWH-wide interpersonal violence policy. Sarah is also seeking her master's in social work at Boston College. Previously, Ingerman worked in public health research and program evaluation in Philadelphia, PA. As a project manager for Public Health Management Corporation, Ingerman oversaw the evaluations of programs serving survivors of human trafficking, foreign-national survivors of torture, and immigrant and refugee communities in the Greater Philadelphia area.

Robyn Jordan, MPH is a public health professional, and currently a medical student in New York. She previously worked with marginalized populations and on harm reduction strategies at the New York City Department of Health and Mental Hygiene in the Bureau of Alcohol and Drug Use Prevention, Care and Treatment. Jordan is a graduate of the University of Pennsylvania where she earned a BA in health in societies. She then earned her Master of Public Health in epidemiology from Columbia University Mailman School of Public Health. Jordan is currently enrolled at the Icahn School of Medicine at Mount Sinai.

Smitha Khorana, MS is a journalist who focuses on human rights, citizenship, and public policy. She is a fellow at the Tow Center for Digital Journalism at Columbia Journalism School and has contributed to *The Guardian*, *The Intercept*, *BuzzFeed*, and *Columbia Journalism Review*. She is a coeditor of the volume *Journalism After Snowden: The Future of the Free Press in the Surveillance State*. The anthology, published with Columbia University Press, addresses the legal protections of journalists and whistleblowers in the post-Snowden era.

Khorana attended the Icahn School of Medicine at Mount Sinai as an MD candidate and as part of the humanities and medicine program, before realigning her career path to journalism and academia. Her focus was on HIV/AIDS, and as a medical student, she worked in HIV/AIDS clinics, taught sexual health education in Providence, Rhode Island schools, and worked at UNAIDS. Khorana was a Fulbright Scholar to India and is a graduate of Columbia Journalism School. At Brown University she studied international development and literary arts. Khorana also studied in the Forced Migration and Refugee Studies Department at the American University in Cairo.

Laura J. Lederer, JD founded and directed The Protection Project at John F Kennedy School of Government at Harvard University in 1997 and moved it to Johns Hopkins University School of Advanced International Studies (SAIS) in the year 2000. From 2001 to 2009, she served as senior advisor on trafficking in persons to the Under Secretary of State for Democracy and Global Affairs. She serves as subject matter expert for the US Department of Defense and investigator on a US Department of Justice project on the link between organized crime and human trafficking, as well as subject matter expert for the US Department of Health and Human Services SOAR to Health and Wellness Training. Lederer was an expert consultant for "The Day My God Died," a feature-length documentary that casts a spotlight child sex trafficking from Nepal to India. She also served as an advisor for *The New York Times* article that served as the basis for "Trade," a feature-length drama based on real cases of international sex trafficking, and starring Kevin Kline. Currently, she is serving as special advisor on a Worldwide Documentaries film in progress entitled "The Heart of the Matter," on trafficking inside the refugee crises in Europe and America. From 2010 to the present, Lederer has served as president of Global Centurion, an NGO fighting human trafficking by focusing on demand.

Annie Lewis-O'Connor, PhD, NP-BC, MPH, FAAN is a dually board-certified nurse practitioner in pediatrics and women's health. She is the founder and director of the C.A.R.E (Coordinated Approach to Recovery and Empowerment) Clinic which provides patient-centered and trauma-informed healthcare to people who have been intentionally harmed by violence. Dr. Lewis-O'Connor is committed to addressing violence from a research, policy, education, and clinical perspective. Her current research is focuses the use of tablets and virtual appointments for patients experiencing violence and abuse, patient-centered outcomes research, and implementing trauma-informed care models. Since 2012, Dr. Lewis-O'Connor has served as one of the tri-chairs of the Partners Health Steering Committee on Trauma-Informed Care. She is a past chair of the National Health Collaborative on Violence and Abuse. Since 2010, she has served on the executive board of Casa Myrna Vazquez, the oldest and longest standing shelter in Massachusetts for women and children. She received her master's in nursing from Simmons College in Boston, a master's in public health from Boston University, and her PhD from Boston College.

Nicole Littenberg, MD, MPH is an internal medicine physician at Kokua Kalihi Valley Comprehensive Health Services, a Federally Qualified Health Center (FQHC) in Honolulu, Hawaii, that serves a predominantly low-income Asian and Pacific Islander immigrant population. She is the cofounder of the Pacific Survivor Center, a nonprofit organization dedicated to advancing health and human rights in the Hawaii-Pacific region, and serves as the clinical director of the High-Risk Victims Clinic at the Sex Abuse Treatment Center, through which she provides forensic evaluations for high-risk survivors of sexual assault, including those impacted by domestic violence and sex trafficking. Over the past decade, Dr. Littenberg has provided forensic evaluations and medical care for hundreds of survivors of human trafficking, domestic violence, sex assault, and torture. She has conducted trainings on the evaluation and treatment of trafficking and torture for judges, attorneys, and healthcare providers locally and internationally. Dr. Littenberg is a cofounder and executive board member of HEAL Trafficking and is currently researching the healthcare and social service needs of labor trafficking survivors in Hawaii.

Michelle Lyman is a medical student in the MD SELECT (Scholarly Excellence, Leadership Experiences, Collaborative Training) Program at the University of South Florida Morsani College of Medicine. She is also an active student member of the American Medical Women's Association and the 2015–2017 advocacy student chair for the Physicians Against the Trafficking of Humans. Beginning in 2015, Lyman has worked with Dr. Hanni Stoklosa to research international trends in human trafficking and methods of anti-trafficking education within medical education. Lyman seeks to advocate for the rights of trafficked persons through direct service, research, and policy.

Zheng B. Ma, MD is a native of Houston, Texas, and attended the University of Texas at Austin (UT-Austin) where he first learned about the alarming reality of human trafficking through personal interactions with survivors. During his time at UT-Austin, Dr. Ma helped lead the largest campus events specifically focused on bringing awareness to trafficking and mobilized hundreds to join in the fight against this crime. He then attended Baylor College of Medicine where he designed and implemented the first educational courses in the healthcare providers' role in recognizing and caring for victims of trafficking. These courses have since become incorporated into the medical school curriculum. As a medical student, Dr. Ma was crucially involved in multiple community aide organizations as well as advocacy organizations. He also partnered directly with the local district attorney and state representatives' offices to combat trafficking in Texas. Dr. Ma is now training in the Harvard Affiliated Emergency Medicine Residency where he is still learning about the intricacies and challenges of this complicated issue from international leaders at Massachusetts General Hospital and Brigham and Women's Hospital in Boston, Massachusetts. Dr. Ma hopes to one day use his emergency medicine training to continue teaching healthcare providers and, more importantly, care for those personally affected by the crime.

Wendy Macias-Konstantopoulos, MD, MPH is a board-certified practicing emergency physician at Massachusetts General Hospital (MGH) and assistant professor of emergency medicine at Harvard Medical School. An Master of Public Health graduate from the Harvard School of Public Health, Dr. Macias-Konstantopoulos completed a Global Health Fellowship at the MGH Center for Global Health and was instrumental in the development of anti-trafficking work as a core program of the MGH Emergency Department's Division of Global Health and Human Rights. She is cofounding director of the MGH Human Trafficking Initiative and founding medical and executive director of the MGH Freedom Clinic. The Clinic is an innovative primary and preventative healthcare clinic for human trafficking survivors and won the 2014 Partnership for Freedom national competition. Previously, Dr. Macias-Konstantopoulos worked with the International Organization for Migration's Counter-Trafficking Unit in Indonesia and represented MGH at the 2008 UN Global Forum to Fight Human Trafficking in Vienna. She is active in policy advocacy efforts on behalf of trafficked individuals as a member of the New Hampshire Attorney General's Commission to Combat Human Trafficking, the Massachusetts Attorney General's Interagency Human Trafficking Task Force, the Leadership Advisory Board for the federal Massachusetts State Child Welfare Trafficking Grant, and the SOAR to Health and Wellness Training National Technical Working Group for the US Department of Health and Human Services. Dr. Macias-Konstantopoulos also serves as chair of the Massachusetts Medical Society Committee on Violence Intervention and Prevention and chair of the Trauma and Injury Prevention Section's Human Trafficking Task Force at the American College of Emergency Physicians.

Kathryn Martin, MPH is a 2016 Mirzayan Science & Technology Policy Graduate Fellow with the National Academies of Sciences, Engineering, and Medicine. In this role, she works on the Innovate to Incubate (i2I) and Forum for Investing in Young Children Globally (iYCG) teams. Martin's research interests span a wide range of issues, including child and adolescent well-being, school-based health centers, nutritional health in adverse conditions, and child trafficking. She received her Bachelor of Science in Foreign Service from Georgetown University and a Master of Public Health degree from Columbia University Mailman School of Public Health.

Cathy L. Miller, RN, PhD has worked with anti-human trafficking organizations for over 10 years with over 20 years' experience caring for victims and survivors in the emergency department and as a critical care flight nurse. She is currently on the Department of Health and Human Services SOAR to Health and Wellness Training Working Group for human trafficking education for healthcare providers as well as the healthcare consultant for Shared Hope International. Dr. Miller presents and trains nationally and internationally on all forms of human trafficking. She has multiple published works on child and adolescent complex trauma and child sex trafficking and coauthored the policy statement on human trafficking for the American Public Health Association which was officially adopted in November 2015. Dr. Miller teaches public health nursing, health policy and advocacy, leadership, and research at the undergraduate, graduate, and doctoral levels.

Brendan Milliner, MD is a resident physician in the Department of Emergency Medicine at the Icahn School of Medicine at Mount Sinai in New York City. Throughout his training, he has been involved in conducting medical evaluations for asylum seekers through the Libertas Center for Human Rights at Elmhurst Hospital, a public health facility serving a large immigrant population. During medical school, he was a member of the Student Advisory Board of Physicians for Human Rights and was involved in educating other medical professionals about the importance of human rights work. Dr. Milliner maintains an active interest in the issues facing victims of social injustice, including human trafficking and other types of forced labor.

Lennon Moore, JD has been a staff attorney for Covenant House since 2010. Moore earned his law degree from CUNY School of Law in 2003. In working with the Outreach Team at Covenant House, Moore works closely with young adult trafficking survivors on a daily basis.

Clydette L. Powell, MD, MPH is an associate professor of pediatrics at the George Washington University School of Medicine and Health Sciences. She currently serves as a medical officer and a division director, with the US Department of Health and Human Services (HHS), based in Washington, D.C. For the last 15 years, Dr. Powell worked as medical officer within the Bureau for Global Health at the US Agency for International Development (USAID). In that capacity, she also was the agency point of contact for matters pertaining to public health and human trafficking. Dr. Powell contributed to the USAID strategy for Counter-Trafficking in Persons (C-TIP), the Field Guide for USAID missions on C-TIP, and training materials for new USAID employee orientation on the C-TIP Code of Conduct. She served as mentor to the US Department of State's Virtual Student Foreign Service program for health and human trafficking projects. She was on the Federal Advisory Committee to HHS for training healthcare providers on human trafficking. Dr. Powell served on the Expert Group on Health and Human Trafficking for the International Organization for Migration (IOM), which published IOM's handbook for healthcare providers caring for trafficked persons. Dr. Powell is a national speaker and published author on the intersection of health and human trafficking. As a practicing physician, Dr. Powell has taken care of marginalized and underserved populations both in the United States and abroad. She is a graduate of the Johns Hopkins School of Medicine and holds a Master of Public Health from the University of California at Los Angeles. She is board-certified in pediatrics, child neurology, and preventive medicine/public health.

Valerie Schmitt, MSW, LSW is an advisory services manager for Polaris, a leading anti-trafficking organization. In this role, she provides trainings and consultations to government and nongovernmental organizations that are seeking to improve their anti-trafficking response infrastructure. She regularly speaks and trains on topics ranging from social service coordination and systems improvement for programs serving trafficking survivors to service needs for specific at-risk populations. Schmitt is also responsible for the development of educational resources and tools on human trafficking for Polaris and the National Human Trafficking Resource Center. She works with partner agencies and external stakeholders to evaluate service processes, improve outcomes for survivors of trafficking, and increase employee competency in engaging with individuals who have been trafficked. Schmitt has previously served as the outreach and survivor care coordinator for the Indiana Protection for Abused and Trafficked Humans (IPATH) task force.

Erin Shanley, JD is a licensed attorney in the State and US District Courts in Montana and North Dakota. She is also licensed to practice in the Standing Rock Tribal Court, Fort Peck Tribal Court, and Pascua Yaqui Tribal Court. Ms. Shanley is an enrolled member of the Cheyenne River Sioux Tribe and has an extensive background in the practice of Indian law. In 2007, she established the Fort Peck Tribal Public Defender's Office and served as the supervising public defender for 3 years. In this capacity, she represented defendants in the Fort Peck Tribal Courts on civil and criminal cases. In 2011, Ms. Shanley accepted a position for the Pascua Yaqui Tribe in Arizona as an assistant prosecutor handling child welfare and Indian Child Welfare Act (ICWA) cases. In 2013, Ms. Shanley returned to her home state of North Dakota to work as an assistant prosecutor/special US attorney for the Standing Rock Sioux Tribe and the districts of North and South Dakota, focusing on the prosecution of domestic violence cases at the tribal and federal levels. Ms. Shanley also served as the judicial administrator for the North Dakota Indian Affairs Commission. Working for the North Dakota Indian Affairs Commission provided Ms. Shanley with an opportunity to enhance cooperation and coordination between state and tribal officials in the area of justice, law enforcement, and public safety. Currently, Ms. Shanley is an associate chief judge for the Standing Rock Sioux Tribe. She has also served as an adjunct professor at Sitting Bull College and United Tribes Technical College, teaching classes in federal Indian law, trial techniques, business law, and criminal justice ethics. Ms. Shanley is a graduate of Brown University where she earned a BA in community health with a focus on policy and administration and from the University of Montana, School of Law, where she earned her *juris doctorate*.

Carol Smolenski is the executive director and one of the founders of ECPAT-USA, a children's rights organization that has worked for the protection of children from commercial sexual exploitation since 1991. At ECPAT-USA she has developed projects against the trafficking of children in New York City, Mexico, Belize, and Brazil. Smolenski is a subject matter expert on sexual exploitation of children for the Department of Health and Human Services Family and Youth Services Bureau and the Runaway and Homeless Youth Training and Technical Assistance Center, a winner of New York's Union Square Award, and a national expert on child sex trafficking. Smolenski has spoken at numerous conferences and has presented testimony in venues ranging from the New York City Council to the United States Congress to the United Nations.

Cassandra Thomson is an incoming law student focused on issues of health and human rights. She graduated from Harvard College in 2013 in social studies with a focus on global health and health policy, particularly on issues of women's health and human rights. After graduating, Thomson worked at the international law firm White & Case as a legal research assistant on their international arbitration and litigation teams. She then spent 2 years working at Boston Children's Hospital in the Center of Excellence for Pediatric Quality Measurement focused on improving quality of care for children through directing a national policy response from Medicaid and other payers.

Dianna L. Walters, MPP is the director of the Maine Learn and Earn to Achieve Potential (LEAP) initiative. In this role, Walters provides leadership, coordination, and oversight of the Maine LEAP initiative. LEAP is a partnership between many organizations that are working together in new and better ways to ensure young people transitioning from foster care to adulthood are successful in achieving their education and career goals.

Before joining the Muskie School, Walters served as a member of the Jim Casey Youth Opportunities Initiative's policy team, where she led efforts to educate key stakeholders across a variety of sectors about the implications of adolescent development on child welfare policy and practice. In her prior role at the Jim Casey Initiative, Walters co-managed *Success Beyond 18*, a multi-state policy campaign to extend foster care beyond age 18 and advance youth engagement policies and practices. She has also focused on national and state foster care policy issues, including older youth permanency, education, psychotropic medications, trauma-informed services, and healthy adolescent development.

Walters has spent more than a decade engaged in child welfare reform efforts in partnership with the Youth and Community Engagement Team at the University of Southern Maine's Muskie School of Public Service. She also worked in direct service with homeless and at-risk youth at New Beginnings' programs and has published on topics that include conducting transition planning with young people in foster care, permanency for older youth, and the importance of maintaining biological family connections.

A graduate of the University of Southern Maine, Walters earned a master's degree in public policy and management from the university's Muskie School of Public Service and a bachelor's degree in social and behavioral sciences. She also serves as a board member of Camp to Belong International, a program that reunites siblings separated by foster care.

Kathryn Xian is the executive director of the Pacific Alliance to Stop Slavery in Honolulu, Hawaii. She is responsible for inciting the reform of her state's promoting prostitution statute, which began in 2005, as well as the introduction and passage of Hawaii's first survivor-centered anti-sex trafficking law (HB1902 of 2016). In 2004, with the help of New York-based NGO, Equality Now, she led a focused campaign involving public action and legislative advocacy resulting in the passage of Act 82, the first state law in the nation to outlaw sex tourism. From conducting street outreach in the early 2000s to her present direct advocacy with adult and child survivors of trafficking, Xian has been involved in every aspect and stage of the healing process with survivors of both labor and sex trafficking in Hawaii. Xian is an out, non-gender-conforming, Korean-American lesbian and the great-granddaughter of celebrated national Korean hero Won Kiu Ahn.

The original version of this book was revised. An erratum to this book can be found at DOI: 10.1007/978-3-319-47824-1_25

Chapter 1
Introduction to Human Trafficking: Who Is Affected?

Jordan Greenbaum

1.1 Introduction

In addition to a fundamental violation of human rights, human trafficking has been viewed as a legal and a social problem. Until 2015, there had been little consideration of the phenomenon as a public health issue. Relatively little attention has been paid to the health consequences associated with exploitation and the complex economic, social, and cultural determinants of health that contribute to human trafficking.

According to the US federal law [1, 2], severe human trafficking involves:

(A) Sex trafficking: the recruitment, harboring, transportation, provision, obtaining, soliciting, or patronizing of a person for the purpose of a commercial sex act (any sex act on account of which anything of value is given to or received by any person) using force, fraud, or coercion, OR involving a child less than 18 years of age;
Or
(B) Labor trafficking: the recruitment, harboring, transportation, provision, or obtaining of a person for labor or services, through the use of force, fraud, or coercion for the purpose of subjection to involuntary servitude, peonage, debt bondage, or slavery.

The exact incidence and prevalence of human trafficking in the USA and worldwide remain unknown [3, 4]. Calculation is hampered by the lack of a common database for case tracking [3, 5–8], differences in definitions of key terms (such as "commercial sexual exploitation of children"), differences in sampling methods used in research [4], underreporting by trafficked persons [9], and lack of victim recognition by authorities [10]. Various databases may overlap or exclude cases; their variable definitions or software platforms may not allow comparison or merging of

J. Greenbaum (✉)
Stephanie V. Blank Center for Safe and Healthy Children,
Children's Healthcare of Atlanta, Atlanta, GA, USA
e-mail: Jordan.greenbaum@choa.org

© Springer International Publishing AG 2017
M. Chisolm-Straker, H. Stoklosa (eds.), *Human Trafficking Is a Public Health Issue*, DOI 10.1007/978-3-319-47824-1_1

data. However, using a complex sampling methodology, the International Labor Organization (ILO) conservatively estimated that 20.9 million people are trafficked for forced labor around the world. This estimate includes victims of labor and sex trafficking, as well as other forms of trafficking that do not fall under the US federal definition. Within this group, it is estimated that approximately 4.5 million people are subjected to forced sexual exploitation, and approximately 14.2 million suffer forced labor exploitation in the private economy [11]. According to the statistics published by the Polaris Project in January 2016, well over 25,000 trafficking cases had been reported through the National Human Trafficking Resource Center hotline and Polaris's BeFree Textline since December 2007 [12]. This number likely represents a significant underestimate of true cases given the reluctance of trafficked individuals to self-identify and the relatively low level of training of first responders on human trafficking recognition [13]. In fact, a study of labor trafficking in San Diego county estimated that over 38,000 people were trafficked in that geographic area, alone [14].Language and culture strongly affect the public health sector's views and professionals' ability to identify trafficked people. Traditional Western cultural beliefs support viewing those involved in commercial sex and sex trafficking as *choosing* to engage in this activity and therefore deserving of whatever adverse events may occur. Many assume that adolescents involved in these activities "make bad decisions," that they possess the emotional and cognitive maturity to give informed consent to sex, and the capacity to weigh the risks and benefits of their actions. They simply choose to engage in illegal behavior, thus they are not victimized at all, but drivers of their own destiny. These views prevail despite neurobiological research on adolescents showing an incompletely developed prefrontal cortex, with a comparable immature ability to consistently engage in appropriate executive decision-making; adolescents also have an increased tendency to take risks and indulge impulses [15]. Similarly many assume that adults involved in labor and sex trafficking are either gullible or reluctant to "get a real job." Factors such as extreme poverty, lack of education and opportunity, a history of violence in the home, and manipulation at the hands of skilled traffickers are ignored when these assumptions are made.These cultural attitudes are reflected in the language often used to describe the trafficked, especially the sex trafficked. Minors and adults involved in commercial sex are often seen as "prostitutes," "bad kids," or "nothing but a 'ho'"—their character being defined by their activities. This has an impact not only on the self-image of the person involved but also on the way they are treated by society. Those experiencing human trafficking may be viewed as adult criminals or juvenile offenders [10] rather than victimized persons. As a result, they may be prosecuted for crimes committed during their period of exploitation rather than offered the assistance they need. They may be seen as undeserving of the public's concern and attention. They may be deported or placed in the criminal justice system rather than being offered counseling services and job skills training.

Further, blaming the trafficked ignores the complex interplay of risk and resilience factors that combine to make some persons particularly vulnerable to trafficking. These factors are found at the individual, family, community, and societal levels. The socio-ecological model so often used in public health challenges cultural attitudes and biases, and prompts one to look beyond these attitudes and beliefs for objective information that will transcend blame and help prevent and intervene in human trafficking.

1.2 Discussion: Who Is Affected by Human Trafficking?

1.2.1 Trafficked Persons

People trafficked for labor and sex may be of any age, gender, ethnicity, socioeconomic background, or citizenship [16, 17]. In a global study of human trafficking, persons identified as trafficked originated from 152 countries [17]; in 2014, the top 3 origin countries for federally identified trafficking survivors in the USA were the USA, Mexico, and the Philippines [16]. According to the US Human Trafficking Reporting System, of the confirmed survivors identified between Jan 2008 and June 2010 in cities with federally funded human trafficking taskforces, 94 % of the sex trafficking survivors were female, and 84 % were US citizens or permanent legal residents. Nearly 26 % were Caucasian, while 40 % were African American; 55 % were minors. These demographics varied from confirmed labor trafficking survivors, among whom 68 % were female, and less than 2 % were US citizens or legal residents; 56 % were Hispanic/Latino and 15 % Asian/Asian American. Ten percent of labor trafficking survivors were minors [18]. Other studies show a predominance of males in labor trafficking [19, 20].

Trafficking for sexual exploitation may involve prostitution, pornography, massage parlors, or involvement in a sex-oriented business [21]. Common industries involved in labor trafficking include agriculture, construction, manufacturing, hospitality, food service, sales crews (especially magazine sales [22]), health and elder care, salon services, and domestic service [14, 16, 19]. Foreign national trafficking victims may enter the USA with a valid visa (71 % in one study [19]) or without such documentation; those entering with a temporary visa may be forced by their traffickers to stay longer than the visa permits so that they become vulnerable to deportation [19]. Traffickers may then use this vulnerability to coerce or manipulate people into compliance.

While any person may be trafficked, certain factors render some people more vulnerable. Age is a major risk factor, as children are at a stage of development when risk-taking and impulsive behavior are more common than a deliberate, cautious, and reasoned approach to decision-making [15, 23, 24]. They lack the life experience and executive functioning capabilities to understand and defend themselves against the psychological manipulations of savvy adults. Among both children and adults, those with a history of abuse or neglect, intimate partner violence, substance use, and untreated mental health disorders and those who are runaways or homeless are at increased risk for human trafficking [4, 9, 25–29]. Those who are marginalized are at increased risk [30], especially those who are identified as a sexual or gender minority [31]. Family factors such as financial stressors, interpersonal violence, criminal behavior and incarceration, as well as caregiver or partner substance use may contribute to the risk of human trafficking. At the community and societal levels, persons fleeing poverty, social upheaval and violence, corruption, gender discrimination and gender-based violence, war, and natural disasters are also at increased risk [8, 16, 32]. Of 404 unaccompanied and separated children from El Salvador, Guatemala, Honduras, and Mexico seeking asylum in the USA, 48 % indicated that they fled because of regional violence in their homeland related to organized criminal networks or state actors; 21 % reported abuse and violence in their homes [33]. Such children migrating alone are vulnerable to sex and labor trafficking [34].

People may be recruited for trafficking through a variety of means involving force, fraud, coercion, *or* abuse of power, although in cases of commercial sexual exploitation of minors [1], these conditions are not necessary. Typically, those seeking to escape the factors described in the paragraph above fall prey to false promises of love, acceptance, excitement, money to support themselves or their families, education, or "a better life" [29, 35]. Fraudulent employment agencies may promise well-paying jobs with free transportation and housing that will allow people to support their impoverished families [19, 35]. Traffickers may offer love to those craving acceptance, or drugs to those with substance use disorders (SUDs) [9]. Intimate partners or relatives may encourage, pressure, threaten, or intimidate people into participating in activities in which they are exploited [26, 35, 36]. Importantly, force may or may not be used during the recruitment process. In many cases, traffickers use false promises, deception, and high-pressure techniques to trick or coerce people [19]. Debt may be incurred during the process of recruitment and is often used to control an individual during the exploitation phase [16]. In short, recruitment techniques are intimately tied to risk factors and give the illusion of meeting the needs of those at risk.

Before, during, and after their period of exploitation, trafficked persons may experience myriad adverse physical and emotional conditions [20, 37, 38]. For those with preexisting poor health and limited access to medical care, chronic conditions (e.g., asthma, diabetes, bipolar disorder, and depression) may go untreated. During the recruitment, travel,[1] and exploitation phases of the trafficking experience, they may be subjected to violence, degradation, psychological abuse, isolation and deprivation, unsafe working conditions resulting in injury or toxic exposure, sexual assault, pregnancy and related complications, sexually transmitted infections (STIs) including HIV/AIDS, posttraumatic stress disorder (PTSD), depression and suicidality, irritability and aggression, somatic complaints, and other problems [13, 36, 39–42]. Many conditions, especially pain complaints and emotional problems, persist after the exploitation ends [39] and may lead to chronic disability. Some conditions may be lethal, such as untreated HIV/AIDS, certain physical injuries, and severe pregnancy-related complications. In one study of women and adolescent female sex trafficking survivors, 99 % reported at least one physical health problem during their period of exploitation, 98 % reported at least one psychological issue,

---

[1] If travel is involved in the trafficking experience.

and 95 % reported abuse/violence. Common reported problems included STIs (67.3 %), severe weight loss (42.9 %), depression (88.7 %) with attempted suicide (41.9 %), self-reported PTSD (54.7 %), and physical assault (strangulation 54.4 %, punched 73.8 %, and kicked 68 %) [40]. In a study of labor trafficking survivors, 40 % reported physical violence during their period of exploitation, 81 % reported at least one physical health symptom, and 57 % reported at least one posttraumatic stress symptom [20].

1.2.2 Families

Families of trafficked persons may be impacted in a number of ways. Guardians/parents, other relatives, or intimate partners may act as traffickers, or may participate in a trafficking network [26, 36, 43], and intentionally exploit a child or adult. Thus, they may profit from the transaction, and suffer the consequences if law enforcement investigates the case. In other instances, family members may be completely unaware of the trafficking scheme and be manipulated by the trafficker to give up a child or a spouse in an effort to alleviate severe poverty. They may trust the trafficker who promises money and a better life for their child or spouse, especially if the trafficker is a relative or respected member of the community [44]. Other families may be aware of the danger of trafficking but feel they have no choice but to give up a member in order to save the rest of the family. Families may put up their homes as collateral to pay the fees to traffickers, sell their valuables, or incur debt from others so that one member can seek a "better life." Families may never obtain any money from the trafficked relative, or they may receive a fraction of their earnings [19]. Adults may initially decide to engage in commercial sex to support children but later become trapped in a trafficking situation. Children may engage in commercial sex (with or without a third-party trafficker) in order to support their family.

On the other hand, family violence, dysfunction, bias, and discrimination may drive a child or adult out of the home and serve as the major risk factor for subsequent exploitation [45, 46]. Many lesbian, gay, bisexual, transgender, and queer (LGBTQ) youth are made to leave their homes because guardians will not tolerate their sexual or gender identity; these youth are at very high risk of engaging in "survival sex" when homeless [47]. Such youth, if under the age of 18, are considered sex trafficked by federal law. Similarly youth with behavior challenges or who experience major conflict with parents may be forced to leave, or may run away from home, and subsequently be recruited by a trafficker [48, 49].

Threats against families are an effective means of control and traffickers may prevent attempted escape by threatening harm to the trafficked person's family or their property [16, 19]. These are not empty threats as criminal networks use members in the origin country or area to inflict violence or even recruit another family member in retaliation for perceived wrongdoings by the initial victimized person. An adult or child trapped in sex or labor exploitation may not try to escape for fear of shaming the family, especially if they have yet to pay back the debt they believe they owe the trafficker or if the trafficker has threatened to disclose their activities while being sex trafficked [19]. Trafficked individuals may fear ostracism or even "honor killing" by a relative if word of their sexual exploitation reaches the family [43]. And family members may, indeed, view the sex trafficking survivor as bringing shame to the family and humiliating them in the eyes of the community.

Children and spouses left behind by individuals striving to help the family out of poverty or other severe distress may themselves experience tremendous loss and related traumatic grief. They may never see their loved one again and children may be raised by relatives or unrelated individuals. If a trafficking survivor does return, family members may experience considerable challenges adjusting to the change and rebuilding relationships, especially if the time away has been extended. In summary, human trafficking has a profound impact on the family and may engender feelings of fear and uncertainty, loneliness and traumatic grief, guilt, or humiliation and shame. Moreover, these consequences may fundamentally change the structure and functioning of the family to impact the next generation.

1.2.3 Traffickers

Just as there is no profile of a trafficked person, there is no stereotype of a trafficker/exploiter. Husbands, fathers, mothers, and other relatives may play this role [26, 43, 50]. Acquaintances may wittingly or unwittingly introduce someone to a trafficker [19]. Those who exploit others may do so alone (e.g., an individual subjects their intimate partners to sex trafficking) or they may work in small or large groups or networks [26, 48, 51]. Importantly, traffickers may also come from disadvantaged or troubled backgrounds, similar to the experiences survived by those they exploit. Some may even perceive that they are helping those trafficked, by providing a job, shelter, protection, and care to people otherwise ignored by society [36, 52].

Traffickers may be juveniles or adults, and may be of any gender; they may come from the same or a different country than the person(s) trafficked [50, 53]. Some traffickers have legitimate jobs outside their trafficking organization; they may be physicians, lawyers, politicians, or members of law enforcement. Some are highly educated, while others have had little formal schooling [50].

While identified traffickers are typically men, women may be involved in trafficking in a leading or supporting role. In one global study, 28 % of convicted traffickers were female, a rate that is much higher than the 10–15 % average proportion of females convicted of most other crimes [8]. Women may recruit trafficking targets, manage them, serve as the "bottom girl" for a trafficker (the most trusted trafficked female in the group, who is given extra privileges) or they may be the lead trafficker [53]. In some cases, a female teen may exploit her peers. It has been suggested that women may more easily build trust and rapport and so are successful recruiters [8, 50].

The lure of being a trafficker comes from its relatively low risk-to-benefit ratio [53]. While laws are establishing increasingly severe punishments for offenders [54] and law enforcement and the judicial system are making great strides in learning how to effectively investigate and prosecute trafficking cases [16], the US legal system has considerably less experience with human trafficking than with other serious offenses such as drug trafficking and homicide. In 2014, the US Department of Justice charged only 335 people with human trafficking offenses (190 for sex trafficking and 18 for labor) and only 184 defendants were convicted [16]. Penalties incurred by the 184 defendants ranged from 5 years to life in prison. Admittedly these numbers omit cases that were prosecuted under non-trafficking statutes, but the number is nonetheless extremely low in comparison to even the lowest estimates of trafficked persons nationwide. On the other hand, the potential profits related to sex and labor trafficking are enormous. If, for example, a sex trafficked person is required to make $500 per night as a "quota" and forced to work 7 days per week, the trafficker may make $182,500 annually from one person, and avoid paying taxes. And while drug and weapon trafficking provide one-time profits related to the initial sale, human trafficking reaps continuous profits for as long as the individual can be "sold." This calculus applies to the sex trafficked child in Boston and the labor-trafficked adult in Nebraska. Such an opportunity for continuous and enormous profit, in the face of a relatively low likelihood of prosecution and severe criminal sentence, makes human trafficking appealing to individuals and organized networks alike.

Traffickers may work individually or in groups, and among groups the level of internal sophistication and organization varies [8, 26, 48, 50, 51]. Small groups may consist of family members, friends, or persons within a community or region. These smaller groups may exploit a few people and have few resources so that their business tends to involve domestic trafficking or small-scale cross-border activity with *relatively* limited profits [8]. A man and his two friends may force their girlfriends into sex trafficking or a family may lure a single victim to the USA and exploit them in domestic servitude. On the other hand, large, well-organized criminal networks may victimize large numbers of people for long periods, move them across borders, and, in some cases, transport them across the globe [8]. Sophisticated criminal organizations may also have simultaneous or past involvement with other illegal activities such as drug or weapons trafficking [19]. Numerous persons may be involved in these large organizations, including recruiters, transporters, guides, enforcers, informers, corrupt officials, debt collectors, money launderers, managers, leaders, and investors [48, 50]. Gangs are becoming increasingly involved in human trafficking [55, 56] and may work with each other or with other well-established criminal networks to engage in commercial sexual exploitation [57].

1.2.4 Buyers and Exploiters

The constant demand for cheap labor and sex drives the human trafficking industry. Those making the demands comprise a highly variable group. Exploiters of people who are labor trafficked may be supervisors or owners of farms, factories, hotels, restaurants, salons, or a variety of other business enterprises [19, 53]. Some oversee victims in domestic servitude within the home. Others manage staffing agencies and use foreign recruitment agencies to obtain people to victimize. The ultimate "users" of the trafficked—the supervisors and owners of organizations, or the patrons of businesses—may or may not be fully aware of the trafficking situation [19]. Millions of people living in the USA are unwitting supporters of labor trafficking through their purchase of products made or harvested by trafficked persons (e.g., rugs, seafood, strawberries, and smartphones); or patronage of small and large businesses staffed by trafficked people (e.g., nail salons, hotels, karaoke clubs, restaurants, and elder care institutions).

Studies of commercial sex buyers show age ranges from teens to octogenarians, diverse occupations and educational levels, and variations in marital status and number of children [26, 48, 51, 58]. While some buyers specifically seek children, others seek adults or people of any age. They may buy sex in order to feel a sense of power and control, to have sex without accompanying relationship commitments, to experience a sense of adventure, or to have a partner who will engage in activities refused by a traditional partner. Adolescent boys may view commercial sex as a rite of passage; commercial sex may be viewed as part of a ritual (e.g., bachelor party) or a component of a business deal. Some buyers are misogynistic, others are not [58]. In one analysis of commercial sex buyers, a number of different rationalizations were provided for engaging in the activity. Some buyers saw their patronage as "helping" poor children and women and their families. Others assumed that the trafficked persons enjoyed their work and saw it as "easy money" that was preferable to working in a factory or another low-income job. Some buyers even viewed themselves as the victims, exploited by the women and children providing sex [58].

1.2.4.1 Society

Numerous societal factors influence human trafficking by creating vulnerabilities among populations. Cultural practices, sociopolitical and economic factors facilitate conditions that support exploitation [16, 29, 32]. Prominent among these are gender discrimination, tolerance of personal and community violence, sexual objectification of women and girls, political and judicial corruption, poverty, and the limited rights of children [4, 43]. Historical acceptance of slavery and extreme labor exploitation involving Native Americans, Africans and African-Americans, Chinese, and other immigrants to support the cotton industry and American industrialization laid the groundwork for continued acceptance of human rights violations to obtain cheap labor today. Human trafficking in North America has been described as a "supermarket" business model that emphasizes low cost and high volume, with resultant high profits [59]. Indeed, such a model is the foundation of many US businesses, which thrive on high demand for products and abundant supply of labor.

Longstanding racial and ethnic biases contribute to human trafficking by marginalizing populations such as Native Americans, and limiting opportunities and resources that might help impoverished families and communities find safe ways to support themselves. Gay, lesbian, bisexual, and transgender adults and youth face widespread discrimination and ostracism, which too often lead to violence, limited educational opportunities, and lack of employment options. Members of sexual minority groups are at high risk for homelessness [47]. And homeless and runaway persons in general are ostracized, facing limited means of obtaining money and items necessary for survival. Thus they are at high risk for engaging in survival sex and becoming involved with a third-party trafficker [27, 31, 46, 49, 60–63]. Gender and socioeconomic class biases limit options for many US and foreign nationals, making them vulnerable to risky enterprises that lead to human trafficking. Finally, the pursuit of the elusive "American dream" remains a strong factor pulling immigrants to the USA and setting them up for exploitation by traffickers.

While society contributes to human trafficking, it is also profoundly harmed by it. From a practical standpoint, the financial burden of treating the physical and emotional health consequences suffered by trafficked persons, the cost of investigating cases of trafficking and prosecuting offenders, and the cost of incarceration of traffickers fall on the shoulders of the US taxpayers. The loss in productivity by the trafficked is also borne by society. Infants of trafficked women may have health effects from prenatal alcohol and drug exposure, adding to the overall financial burden and loss of productivity.

But perhaps the most important adverse impact of trafficking and exploitation is the corrosive effect it has on the philosophical framework of our society. A truly democratic society that values human rights and freedom cannot tolerate the gross exploitation and slavery of its inhabitants. To accept the presence of human trafficking condones the beliefs that human lives are expendable, that the ultimate possession of material goods justifies any means of obtaining them, and that the guarantee of basic human rights is conditional. It encourages the attitude that trafficked persons are responsible for their plight—that they are gullible, greedy, lazy, or bad. When public apathy replaces accountability, the vulnerable among us are ignored and the humanity of all suffers.

1.3 Conclusions

Human trafficking affects everyone, from the survivors who suffer physical and psychological harm to the families of those survivors who may experience guilt, shame, fear, and loss, as well as physical harm and financial catastrophe. It affects the traffickers and buyers who profit from the victimization of others. And it impacts our society in which the exploitation occurs. As long as widespread labor trafficking continues, most, if not all of us consume services and products resulting from it and thus contribute to its existence. And ultimately all are negatively impacted by the financial, social, and philosophical burden of human trafficking.

1.4 Recommendations

The complex interplay of cultural, social, political, and economic factors giving rise to and supporting human trafficking demands a comprehensive approach to prevention and intervention. The wide array of risk factors renders large numbers of persons vulnerable, involving those from all classes, cultures, and geographic regions. To effectively combat trafficking requires more than increased investigation and prosecution of offenders, though these activities play a critical role. It requires more than providing services to survivors, although such services are absolutely necessary and need to be increased.

- *To abolish human trafficking, it must be approached as a public health problem.* Such a focus allows us to employ a multidisciplinary approach to identifying and characterizing the vulnerabilities leading to victimization and enabling exploitation, and to designing and scientifically evaluating programs, strategies, and policies of prevention and intervention. A public health framework emphasizes that human trafficking affects a large population, directly or indirectly, and impacts the health and well-being of society.
  - It encourages the strategic use of resources to reach those at highest risk.
  - In addition, a public health approach encourages advocates to draw on what has been learned about related social problems such as domestic violence, poverty, homelessness, and SUDs. From these areas, a tremendous amount of accumulated academic and social knowledge can be brought to bear on the problem of human trafficking.
  - This approach, combined with sufficient social and political resolve, will, empower society to combat this assault on human rights.

Following the public health socio-ecological model, *efforts at prevention and intervention need to consider factors at the individual, the family, the community, and the societal levels.* Ignoring one or more of these levels fails to adequately appreciate the complex interplay of vulnerabilities and leads to efforts that are destined for failure, or that ignore large populations of at-risk individuals.

- A public health perspective recognizes that combating human trafficking cannot be done in a vacuum. We must simultaneously address other major problems that marginalize our community members and increase their vulnerability: poverty, substance use, mental health disorders, and community violence, to name but a few.
- *Methodologically rigorous and sound research and data collection are essential to developing effective methods of combating human trafficking.*
- Those working with trafficked persons need improved methods of data collection, a centralized database for identification and tracking, and sufficient funding to support high-quality research.
- To address gross labor violations, increased transparency in our global supply chains is needed to make the US citizens aware of exploitative practices and hold violators accountable.

In summary, an effective response to the enormous problem of human trafficking requires addressing the myriad factors driving the process at all levels of the socio-ecological model. It requires public awareness and accountability, as well as the political and social will to dedicate the resources needed for application of public health strategies to prevention, intervention, and survivor healing.

References

1. United States Government. Trafficking Victims Protection Act of 2000.
2. United States Government. Justice for Victims of Trafficking Act of 2015.
3. Stansky M, Finkelhor D. How many juveniles are involved in prostitution in the U.S.? In: Crimes Against Children Research Center UoNH, editor. 2008. http://www.unh.edu/ccrc/prostitution/Juvenile_Prostitution_factsheet.pdf. Accessed 7 July 2013.
4. Institute of Medicine and National Research Council. Confronting commercial sexual exploitation and sex trafficking of minors in the United States. Washington, DC: The National Academies Press; 2013.
5. Todres J. Moving upstream: the merits of a public health law approach to human trafficking. North Carol Law Rev. 2011;89:447–506.
6. Finklea K, Fernandes-Alcantara A, Siskin A. Sex trafficking of children in the United States: overview and issues for Congress. In: Service CR, editor. 2011. http://www.fas.org/sgp/crs/misc/R41878.pdf. Accessed 7 July 2013.
7. Quayle E, Taylor M. Child pornography and the internet: perpetuating a cycle of abuse. Deviant Behav. 2002;23:331–61.
8. United Nations Office on Drugs and Crime. Global report on trafficking in persons. http://www.unodc.org/documents/data-and-analysis/glotip/Trafficking_in_Persons_2012_web.pdf (2012). Accessed 7 July 2013.
9. Greenbaum J, Crawford-Jakubiak J, Committee on Child Abuse and Neglect. Child sex trafficking and commercial sexual exploitation: health care needs of victims. Pediatrics. 2015;135:566–74.
10. Mitchell KJ, Finkelhor D, Wolak J. Conceptualizing juvenile prostitution as child maltreatment: findings from the National Juvenile Prostitution Study. Child Maltreat. 2010;15:18–36.
11. International Labor Organization. Global estimate of forced labour: executive summary. http://www.ilo.org/wcmsp5/groups/public/---ed_norm/---declaration/documents/publication/wcms_181953.pdf (2012). Accessed 23 Dec 2014.
12. Polaris Project. National Human Trafficking Resource Center. https://www.polarisproject.org/. Accessed 2 Feb 2016.
13. Baldwin S, Eisenman D, Sayles J, Ryan G, Chuang K. Identification of human trafficking victims in health care settings. Health Human Rights. 2011. http://www.hhrjournal.org/2013/08/20/identification-of-human-trafficking-victims-in-health-care-setting/. Accessed 21 Sept 2013.
14. Zhang SX. Looking for a hidden population: trafficking of migrant laborers in San Diego County. United States Department of Justice, National Institute of Justice; 2012.
15. Smith AR, Steinberg L, Chein J. The role of the anterior insula in adolescent decision making. Dev Neurosci. 2014;36:196–209.
16. United States Department of State. Trafficking in persons report. http://www.state.gov/j/tip/rls/tiprpt/2015/ (2015). Accessed 10 Feb 2016.
17. United Nations Office on Drugs and Crime. Global report on trafficking in persons. https://www.unodc.org/unodc/data-and-analysis/glotip.html (2014). Accessed 30 Nov 2014.
18. Banks D, Kyckelhahn T. Characteristics of suspected human trafficking incidents, 2008–2010. Department of Justice, 2011.

19. Owens C, Dank M, Breaux J, Banuelos I, Farrell A, et al. Understanding the organization, operation and victimization process of labor trafficking in the United States. Washington, DC: Urban Institute; 2014.
20. Turner-Moss E, Zimmerman C, Howard LM, Oram S. Labour exploitation and health: a case series of men and women seeking post-trafficking services. J Immigr Minor Health. 2014;16:473–80.
21. Victims of Trafficking and Violence Protection Act. http://www.state.gov/j/tip/laws/61124.htm (2000). Accessed 14 July 2015.
22. Polaris Project. Knocking at your door: labor trafficking on traveling sales crews. https://www.polarisprojectorg/sites/default/files/Knocking-on-Your-Door-Sales-Crewspdf   (2015). Accessed 10 Feb 2016.
23. Luciana M, Wahlstrom D, Proter JN, Collins PF. Dopaminergic modulation of incentive motivation in adolescence: age-related changes in signaling, individual differences, and implications for the development of self-regulation. Dev Psychol. 2012;48:844–61.
24. Steinberg L. A dual systems model of adolescent risk-taking. Dev Psychobiol. 2010;52:216–24.
25. Stoltz JM, Shannon K, Kerr T, Zhang R, Montaner JS, Wood E. Associations between childhood maltreatment and sex work in a cohort of drug-using youth. Soc Sci Med. 2007; 65:1214–21.
26. Smith L, Vardaman S, Snow M. The national report on domestic minor sex trafficking: America's prostituted children. In: International SH, editor. 2009. http://sharedhope.org/wp-content/uploads/2012/09/SHI_National_Report_on_DMST_2009.pdf. Accessed 7 July 2013.
27. Bigelsen J, Vuotto S. Homelessness, survival sex and human trafficking: as experienced by the youth of Covenant House New York. 2013. http://www.covenanthouseorg/sites/default/files/attachments/Covenant-House-trafficking-studypdf. Accessed 30 Nov 2014.
28. Reid J. An exploratory model of girl's vulnerability to commercial sexual exploitation in prostitution. Child Maltreat. 2011;16:146–57.
29. Reid J. Exploratory review of route specific, gendered, and age-graded dynamics of exploitation: applying life course theory to victimization in sex trafficking in North America. Aggress Violent Behav. 2012;7:257–71.
30. Walk Free Foundation. The global slavery index. Hope for Children Organization, LTD Australia. http://www.globalslaveryindex.org/ (2014). Accessed 20 Feb 2016.
31. Walls N, Bell S. Correlates of engaging in survival sex among homeless youth and young adults. J Sex Res. 2011;48:423–36.
32. Macias KW, Ahn R, Alper EJ, Cafferty E, McGahan A, et al. An international comparative public health analysis of sex trafficking of women and girls in eight cities: achieving a more effective health sector response. J Urban Health: Bull NY Acad Med. 2013;90:1194–204.
33. United Nations High Commissioner for Refugees. Children on the run: unaccompanied children leaving Central America and Mexico and the need for international protection. http://unhcrwashington.org/children (2014). Accessed 19 Feb 2016.
34. Chester H, Lummert N, Mullooly A. Child victims of human trafficking: outcomes and service adaptation within the U.S. Unaccompanied Refugee Minor programs. 2015. http://www.usccb.org/about/anti-trafficking-program/upload/URM-Child-Trafficking-Study-2015-Final.pdf. Accessed 19 Feb 2016.
35. Raymond J, D'Cunha J, Dzuhayatin S, Hynes H, Rodriguez A, et al. A comparative study of women trafficked in the migration process: patterns, profiles and health consequences of sexual exploitation in five countries (Indonesia, the Philippines, Thailand, Venezuela and the United States. Coalition Against Trafficking in Women. 2002. http://action.web.ca/home/catw/attach/CATW%20Comparative%20Study%202002.pdf. Accessed 20 Sept 2013.
36. Raphael J, Reichert J, Powers M. Pimp control and violence: domestic sex trafficking of Chicago women and girls. Women Crim Just. 2010;20:89–104.
37. Zimmerman C. Stolen smiles: a summary report on the physical and psychological consequences of women and adolescents trafficked in Europe. London: London School of Hygiene and Tropical Medicine; 2006.

38. Oram S, Stockl H, Busza J, Howard LM, Zimmerman C. Prevalence and risk of violence and the physical, mental, and sexual health problems associated with human trafficking: a systematic review. PLoS Med. 2012;9:e1001224.
39. Zimmerman C, Yun K, Shvab I, Watts C, Trappolin L, Treppete M. The health risks and consequences of trafficking in women and adolescents: findings from a European study. London: London School of Hygiene and Tropical Medicine (LSHTM); 2003.
40. Lederer L, Wetzel C. The health consequences of sex trafficking and their implications for identifying victims in healthcare facilities. Ann Health Law. 2014;23:61–91.
41. Edinburgh L, Pape-Blabolil J, Harpin SB, Saewyc E. Assessing exploitation experiences of girls and boys seen at a child advocacy center. Child Abuse Neglect. 2015;46:47–59.
42. Farley M, Cotton A, Lynne J, Zumbeck S, Spiwak F, et al. Prostitution and trafficking in nine countries: an update on violence and posttraumatic stress disorder. J Trauma Pract. 2004;2:33–74.
43. International Centre for Migration Policy Development. Targeting vulnerabilities: the impact of the Syrian war and refugee situation on trafficking in persons: a study of Syria, Turkey, Lebanon, Jordan and Iraq. Vienna; 2015.
44. Shuteriqi M, Pippidou D, Stoecklin D. Transnational protection of children: the case of Albania and Greece: 200–2006. In: Trafficking TPTAAH, editor. Terre des hommes, ARSIS. 2006. http://tdh-cp-org.terredeshommes.hu/component/option,com_doclib/task,showdoc/docid,142/. Accessed 22 June 2013.
45. Curtis R, Terry K, Dank M, Dombrowski K, Khan B. The commercial sexual exploitation of children in New York City: volume 1: the CSEC population in New York City: size, characteristics and needs. National Institute of Justice, US Department of Justice; 2008.
46. McIntyre S. Under the radar: the sexual exploitation of young men- western Canadian edition. 2009. http://humanservices.alberta.ca/documents/child-sexual-exploitation-under-the-radar-western-canada.pdf. Accessed 16 Feb 2016.
47. Dank M, Yahner J, Madden K, Banuelos I, Yu L, et al. Surviving the streets of New York: experiences of LGBTQ youth, YMSM, YWSW engaged in survival sex. Urban Institute; 2015.
48. Estes RJ, Weiner NA. The commercial sexual exploitation of children in the U.S., Canada and Mexico. Center for the Study of Youth Policy, University of Pennsylvania. 2002. http://www.sp2.upenn.edu/restes/CSEC_Files/Complete_CSEC_020220.pdf. Accessed 7 July 2012.
49. Whitbeck LB, Chen X, Hoyt DR, Tyler KA, Johnson KD. Mental disorder, subsistence strategies and victimization among gay, lesbian and bisexual homeless and runaway adolescents. J Sex Res. 2004;41:329–42.
50. United Nations Global Initiative to Fight Human Trafficking. The Vienna Forum report: a way forward to combat human trafficking. http://www.unorg/ga/president/62/ThematicDebates/humantrafficking/ebookpdf (2008). Accessed 20 Feb 2016. p. 5.
51. Raymond J, Hughes D. Sex trafficking of women in the United States: international and domestic trends. Coalition Against Trafficking in Women. 2001. http://www.uri.edu/artsci/wms/hughes/sex_traff_us.pdf. Accessed 4 Aug 2012.
52. Broad R. 'A vile and violent thing': female traffickers and the criminal justice response. British Journal of Criminology. 2015;55(6):1058–75.
53. Harris KD. The state of human trafficking in California. 2012. http://oag.ca.gov/sites/all/files/agweb/pdfs/ht/human-trafficking-2012.pdf. Accessed 20 Feb 2016.
54. Shared Hope International. Protected innocence challenge: state report cards. https://sharedhope.org/what-we-do/bring-justice/reportcards/ (2015). Accessed 20 Feb 2016.
55. Lederer L. Sold for sex: the link between street gangs and trafficking in persons. Protection Project Journal of Human Rights Civil Society. 2011. http://www.globalcenturion.org/wp-content/uploads/2010/02/Sold-for-Sex-The-Link-between-Street-Gangs-and-Trafficking-in-Persons-1.pdf. Accessed 20 Feb 2016.
56. Shared Hope International. Domestic minor sex trafficking: intervene: resource package. Shared Hope International; 2013.

57. National Gang Intelligence Center. National gang threat assessment 2011: emerging trends. http://www.fbi.gov/stats-services/publications/2011-national-gang-threat-assessment/2011-national-gang-threat-assessment-emerging-trends (2012). Accessed 20 Feb 2016.
58. Malarek V. The Johns: sex for sale and the men who buy it. New York, NY: Arcade Publishing; 2009.
59. Shelley LI. Trafficking in women: the business model approach. Brown J Int Aff. 2003; 10:119–31.
60. Cochran BN, Stewart AJ, Ginzler JA, Cauce AM. Challenges faced by homeless sexual minorities: comparison of gay, lesbian, bisexual and transgender homeless adolescents with their heterosexual counterparts. Am J Public Health. 2002;92:773–7.
61. Greene JM, Ennett ST, Ringwalt CL. Prevalence and correlates of survival sex among runaway and homeless youth. Am J Public Health. 1999;89:1406–9.
62. Kohl A, Molnar B, Booth R, Watters J. Prevalence of sexual risk behavior and substance use among runaway and homeless adolescents in San Francisco, Denver and New York City. Int J STD AIDS. 1997;8:109–17.
63. Yates GL, Mackenzie RG, Pennbridge J, Swofford A. A risk profile comparison of homeless youth involved in prostitution and homeless youth not involved. J Adolesc Health. 1991;12:545–8.

Chapter 2
Sex Trafficked and Missed

Wendy J. Barnes and Holly Austin Gibbs

2.1 Introduction

Health care professionals are among the few frontline professionals who come into contact with persons who have experienced human trafficking; however, vulnerable patients are often missed in health care settings. In one study, nearly 88 % of sex trafficking survivors reported having contact with a health care system while being exploited. This study underscores that medical professionals are often "woefully unprepared" to identify and respond to trafficked persons [1].

Would you be able to identify a trafficked person? Of the following three case scenarios, which patient might you suspect to be at risk of human trafficking?

- Scenario 1: A 33-year-old female presents to the emergency department. The patient is bleeding and covered in bruises. She has a broken finger so swollen that she cannot remove her ring. She states that she got drunk and had a fistfight with her roommate, a 27-year-old female, who has accompanied her to the emergency department.
- Scenario 2: A 19-year-old female presents to the hospital, going into labor with her first child. She is accompanied by two young adults: a female, who is also pregnant, and a male, who identifies himself as the patient's boyfriend and the baby's father. The female companion remains in the patient's room and is supportive. The boyfriend frequently steps out of the room to speak on the phone or to meet privately with other female visitors.
- Scenario 3: A 25-year-old female accompanied by law enforcement presents to a mental health facility. The officers explain that the patient originally presented to an emergency department with claims of "going crazy." Under direction from the emergency department, law enforcement then transported the patient to the

W.J. Barnes • H.A. Gibbs (✉)
Dignity Health, 185 Berry St. #300, San Francisco, CA, USA
e-mail: andlifecontinues@yahoo.com; Holly.Gibbs@DignityHealth.org

© Springer International Publishing AG 2017   15
M. Chisolm-Straker, H. Stoklosa (eds.), *Human Trafficking Is a Public Health Issue*, DOI 10.1007/978-3-319-47824-1_2

mental health facility. The patient admits to suicidal thoughts and hearing voices but cannot remember what the voices say. Additionally, she has two children; she says that the father visits but is not in the picture consistently.

If you guessed the patient in the second scenario, you would be right. However, if you guessed the patient in the first or third scenario, you would also be right. All three are based on actual interactions between a health care system and a survivor of sex trafficking: Coauthor Wendy Barnes was trafficked for more than 10 years, beginning at age 17. These scenarios describe actual clinical presentations based on her experiences in which she was the patient or companion.

Trafficked persons can present in a number of ways. In order to be better prepared to screen for red flags, health care professionals must first be educated on what human trafficking really means and which patient populations might be at greater risk of exploitation. Key health care professionals like clinicians and social workers should also be educated on trauma-informed care. The authors propose this foundation of education as the first step in preparing professionals on how to identify and effectively respond to trafficked persons.

2.2 Discussion

2.2.1 Essential Knowledge

2.2.1.1 Overcome Misconceptions

For many people in the USA, the term "human trafficking" is associated strictly with images of exploitation overseas. However, every country is affected by human trafficking, including the USA [2]. Even among those who do recognize that trafficking occurs in the USA, the term often conjures an image of people being smuggled into the country or small children being chained to beds. If this is a health care professional's understanding of what human trafficking looks like in the USA, then that professional has likely missed, and will continue to miss, opportunities to intervene in human trafficking cases.

In 2000, the USA passed the Trafficking Victims Protection Act (TVPA), which outlaws two common forms of human trafficking: sex trafficking and labor trafficking [3]. Based on the TVPA's definition of human trafficking, the National Human Trafficking Resource Center (NHTRC) [4] identifies three "victim" populations associated with these federal crimes:

- Anyone *under age 18* who is induced *under any circumstance* to perform a commercial sex act[1]

---

[1] TVPA defines a commercial sex act as "any sex act on account of which something of value is given to or received by any person." This can include money, drugs, or survival needs like food and shelter.

- Anyone *over age 17* who is induced *through the use of force, fraud, or coercion* to perform a commercial sex act
- Anyone, *of any age*, who is induced to perform labor or services through the use of force, fraud, or coercion. Labor trafficking includes situations of *debt bondage, forced labor, and involuntary child labor*

It is critical that health care systems educate all of their staff—from security officers and registration staff to physicians, physician assistants, nurses, and social workers—on the realities of human trafficking. In order to ensure that all staff members have basic knowledge on the topic, the authors recommend several educational options, including in-person classes and self-study modules. For example, Dignity Health, the largest hospital provider in California, created a self-study basic education module and offered it as a resource to staff: *Human Trafficking 101: Dispelling the Myths* addresses ten untruths associated with sex and labor trafficking as well as a description of red flags in the health care setting with instructions for frontline staff to follow in the event red flags are recognized.

There are many misconceptions about human trafficking, many of which are perpetuated by the media. For example, one falsehood covered in Dignity Health's *Human Trafficking 101* module is that human trafficking and human smuggling are the same crime. The US Department of Homeland Security Office of Immigration and Customs Enforcement (ICE) defines human smuggling as "the importation of people into the United States involving deliberate evasion of immigration laws." [5] Human smuggling is a violation of these laws, whereas human trafficking is a violation of a person's basic human right to life, liberty, and the pursuit of happiness. It is also untrue that persons trafficked in the USA are always foreign nationals. In 2015, the NHTRC hotline received 5500 cases of reported human trafficking in USA, and at least 1660 cases involved US citizens or lawful permanent residents [6].

Another misconception covered in *Human Trafficking 101* is that trafficked persons will always reach out for help. The media often portray the most sensationalized scenarios of this crime. The public sees images or movies portraying children being abducted or people held against their will. The viewer consequently assumes that the "typical" trafficked person is not only waiting to be rescued but also that they will reach out for help at the first opportunity. However, more often than not, trafficked persons do not seek help for many reasons, including the following, highlighted in *Human Trafficking 101*:

- They may not self-identify as a victim, and may blame themselves for their situation.
- They may have trauma-bonded with the trafficker. As defined by Austin and Boyd [7], traumatic bonding is "a strong emotional attachment between an abused person and his or her abuser, formed as a result of the cycle of violence."
- They may not know their rights or options.
- They may fear retaliation against them or their families.
- They may fear authorities and the possibility of being charged with a crime and going to prison or being deported.

2.2.1.2 Recognize High-Risk Patient Populations

Clinicians must not rely on trafficked persons to self-identify. Basic education should include a description of vulnerable patient populations. Human trafficking is a crime based on exploitation. As such, traffickers often prey on those who are most vulnerable, like people with substance use disorders, young people struggling with homelessness or mental health issues, immigrant workers lacking adequate resources, and so on. Practitioners should screen all vulnerable patients for human trafficking victimization, especially if there are signs of abuse or assault.

2.2.1.3 Incorporate and Appreciate Survivor Perspectives

Dignity Health's education modules also include the voices of survivors. Without hearing from survivors, health care professionals are missing the most important perspective in a trafficked person's health care experience. Moreover, survivor stories help health care professionals see the humanity in patients often stigmatized by society. Survivors come in all ages, classes, races, genders, ethnicities, and sexualities; and their stories of labor and/or sex trafficking are all different. Some survivors are trafficked by pimps, gang members, or companies, while others are trafficked by family members, friends, and/or neighbors.

In this chapter, we share Wendy's story as one example of human trafficking in the USA. Wendy was trafficked by a violent man. He lured young women and girls into abusive "romantic" relationships—in fact, he is the father of Wendy's three children—and then he forced the women and girls into street prostitution and escort services. He was ultimately sentenced to life in prison.

In the first two scenarios outlined in the Introduction, Wendy was the companion; in the third, she was the patient. In the first scenario, Wendy did not assault the patient; rather, the patient's wounds were inflicted by the trafficker and the women were forced to fabricate a story to explain the injuries. In the second scenario, Wendy and the female companion were both pregnant by the same man. There have been many cases in which male traffickers have fathered children with women under their control. Oftentimes, the result is that the bond between the trafficker and the trafficked person is strengthened [8]. In the third scenario, Wendy was seeking refuge in a psychiatric ward to escape the cycle of violence and forced prostitution. She was discharged by the mental health professionals who did not identify the underlying cause for her presentation. Wendy's perspective can help medical professionals understand why a trafficked person might not explicitly reach out for help.

As a child, Wendy felt unloved and bullied, and she also experienced sexual abuse at the hands of her stepfather. Child protective services removed Wendy from the home, but Wendy's mother later moved Wendy back in with her stepfather because it was the only way her mother could provide a warm home for her two children. In her memoir, *And Life Continues: Sex Trafficking and My Journey to Freedom*, Wendy describes how she perceived the consequences of disclosing the abuse [9]:

I had destroyed my mother's life. Everything she had ever wanted was ruined because I had told the counselor what [my stepfather] had done…I was relieved and grateful when she moved out of [his] house so I could live with her again. When … [we] moved back into [our] cold house without any food or cable…[my mother] once again had to work a second job. I watched her grow more tired and angry with each passing day — and it was all because of me.

So, when Wendy's mother asked Wendy if she would be willing to move back into the stepfather's house, Wendy agreed. Acceptance of abuse became part of Wendy's understanding of love, family, and home. Abuse was so normalized in her life that Wendy had become the perfect target for a sex trafficker. And the lesson she had learned was that reaching out for help either created more harm or accomplished nothing.

Today, Wendy has rebuilt her life, published her memoir, and is a national speaker and advocate for current and formerly trafficked persons. Below, Wendy describes her initiation into sex trafficking and some of her interactions with health care:

I met my first boyfriend when I was 15. At 16, I was pregnant with his child. When I was 17, he convinced me to distance myself from my mother and move into a homeless shelter. I was naïve, shy, and desperate to be unconditionally loved. I wanted to believe his promise that our life would be "happily ever after," but he had other plans for me.

Neither of us had a job or a way to support our daughter. He was suave and convincing, excellent at calming my nerves and giving me hope for a bright future in what I believed would be "the perfect family." He didn't stay at the shelter with me and our daughter, and chose instead to stay with his grandmother a few miles away. At least that is what he told me, and what I believed.

It wasn't long before the diapers and formula ran out. What I didn't see then was that this was all part of his plan. By isolating me in the shelter, he knew I would be vulnerable and scared. He needed for me to be desperate. My daughter not having diapers and formula did, indeed, make me desperate. Then Greg revealed his plan for how "we" could make money to take care of our daughter. He had only one question for me: "How much do you love your daughter?" If I loved my daughter, he said, then I would do anything for her, including trade sex for money.

Two months after I entered the shelter, I received my first welfare check and was able to get my own apartment. A rundown, roach-infested studio room and a shared bathroom, the apartment had a pullout bed, couch, and kitchenette. It was "perfect" to me because it was where our family was going to start our journey to becoming a "happily ever after" family. The apartment was a few blocks from a medical center, which in turn was only two blocks from the track[2] where I worked. Our only income was my welfare check and food stamps, which were meant for one adult and one child, not the two adults and one child that made up my "family."

Greg again put the responsibility on me to provide for our daughter, insisting that if I didn't, I was a bad mother. I didn't turn tricks every day. It was usually a Friday night that Greg would talk me into going out, reminding me that I could "easily" make a hundred dollars doing a few tricks. I would bring home the money and hope I wouldn't have to go out again until the following Friday—but Greg always had other plans for the money. By Saturday night, we still had no food, no diapers, no formula.

Looking back, I realize Greg knew how to manipulate me. I yearned to be a good mother and wife, and that is how Greg presented the "work opportunity" to me. If I were a good mother, I would do anything for our child. If I loved them, I would make this sacrifice. I

---

[2] In the subculture of prostitution, a "track" is an area known for street prostitution.

didn't see myself as someone who had sex with men for money. I saw myself as a mother making sacrifices for her child. For this reason, I didn't identify with the idea of being a "prostitute." To me, a "prostitute" chose to do this work. Of course that begs the question: How many others involved in prostitution are like I was? How many others are performing commercial sex work due to coercion or a lack of options as opposed to an actual choice?

One day my bare foot caught the metal strip holding the carpet under the doorway. Blood spewed everywhere. Greg grabbed our daughter and we made our way to the medical center, where Greg bounced the baby on his knee as they sewed up and bandaged my foot. As I recovered at home over the next couple of days, Greg cared for our daughter and me, cooking the last bit of food and changing our baby with the last of the diapers.

I woke up the third morning with a throbbing foot. It was still bandaged; I was too scared to unwrap it. Greg took me back to the emergency department; when nurses removed the bandage, my foot was severely swollen and so black and blue I couldn't bear to look at it. The doctor came in, checked my foot, and admitted me to the hospital.

Greg assured me that he would take care of our daughter. I worried about them, but also was looking forward to not having to go out on the street Friday night. All day Thursday and Friday I had an IV drip. I was scared and worried because Greg did not visit. Just after the nurse removed the IV on Saturday afternoon, Greg walked in with our daughter. I was so happy to see them both! I hugged our daughter and held her close while I asked Greg why he had not visited me, but he turned the conversation to our daughter. What kind of mother was I that she was out of formula and diapers? Breaking me down with his "bad mother" manipulation, he told me his plan: We would wait until the nurse checked on me, and then I would go outside, hobble the two blocks to the track, and make some money for diapers and formula. I complied, then returned to the hospital and continued treatment.

I was treated at the emergency department when I cut my foot, but for several years I mostly saw doctors at the public health clinic to be treated for venereal diseases. Although Greg instructed me to refuse a trick unless a condom was used, he also told me to forego the condom if the trick paid extra money. When I did contract a venereal disease, I could always tell whether I got it from a trick or from Greg. Usually, it was Greg who gave me the diseases. He was constantly having sex with other girls[3] as he groomed them to be under his control.

Over the years, I never perceived the doctors to be people who care. In the typical visit, the nurses ask only the questions that complete blocks on the chart: weight, age, height. Then the doctor walks in, looking down at the chart, and asks, "What seems to be the problem?" I respond with the exact issue at hand, and no more. I was a naturally shy and quiet person; I didn't talk to people I did not know well, and Greg had taught me never to volunteer information. The doctor looks at the health issue, fixes it, prescribes medications, and leaves the room. I have always thought of doctors as "fixers." They fix the problem. They may care about the problem, but I have never had any reason to believe that they cared about me. That may not be true; that may be what Greg put into my head so that is what I saw. Or, maybe, it's a little bit of both.

In my late teens, I had two abortions at a private clinic. Nobody—neither the nurses nor the doctors—ever asked me if I really wanted the abortion. Nobody asked me if it was a trick baby.[4] I had three or four more abortions at nonprofit community clinics. All of them were the same as any other doctor visit. The nurse prepared me, and the doctor came in, 'fixed' the problem, and left.

---

[3] Wendy refers to the other victims under Greg's control as "girls" without regard to age. In Wendy's case, Greg trafficked both underage girls and adult women. Note that trafficked persons can be of any age or gender.

[4] A "trick baby" is a term often used in the subculture of prostitution to describe a baby fathered by a sex buyer, otherwise known as a "john" or "trick."

A year later, Greg and I moved to another state to make a new start. We moved in with his parents and, pressured by his father, Greg got a real job. I didn't have to turn tricks—mostly because he didn't want his mom to be suspicious and because, being new to the area, he didn't know where the track was.

I got pregnant again with Greg's baby and visited a gynecologist twice. The only thing I remember about that doctor is how uncomfortable he made me feel. I remember he performed a breast exam and seemed to linger over my breasts for an unusual amount of time. He also attempted to make small talk and made an inappropriate comment about the size of my breasts. He felt like a trick to me.

During my pregnancy, Greg lost his job, his parents lost their home, and again we were homeless. With Greg's blessing, I called my mom; she sent me a plane ticket and offered me a place to live until Greg and I could get on our feet. At that time, my mom lived in an upscale suburb, and I was able to go to a major medical center for my care. That was in 1989. "Human trafficking" wasn't yet a well-known term.

When I went into labor, I called Greg and asked him to drive me to the hospital. He arrived at my mom's with a new girl, who was 16 years old. He said he was only using her so he could get an apartment for us and our children. He blamed me, telling me he needed her since I wasn't able to make money. If I were a good mother, he said, I would already have a place for us to live. While I was in labor at the hospital, Greg dropped the new girl off on the track and went back and forth between my contractions to pick up her money.

After our son was born, Greg had all he needed to control me and other girls. He had learned from his mistakes and had honed his pimping skills. He could easily run more than one or two girls at a time. My life became a world of girls, tricks, and drugs by night; by day I tried to live a "normal" life. I took my kids to their regular appointments. Nobody asked why I moved around or changed doctors so much. I don't blame the doctors for not noticing that something was wrong. I rarely went to the same one twice. However, a patient's moving from city to city should be a red flag of potential exploitation, especially if there are indicators of vulnerability like poverty or drug use.

As Greg became even more skilled in the art of pimping, he was able to seduce more girls who would make him money. All of us believed we were there by choice. I was there because I loved him. I was there because I believed he was someday going to be my husband and a good father to our children. His verbal beatings manipulated and controlled me:

Nobody will ever love you but me.

You are pathetic.

You're a bad mother.

Your children don't love you.

Then he would embrace me and tell me how much he loved me even though I was so worthless. This tactic kept me tied to Greg—it was a cycle. I believed I was worthless. Greg confirmed I was worthless. I thought nobody could love me. Greg said he loved me despite my being worthless, which made me feel grateful.

He embedded other "truths" in us: People in the real world don't want you. You'll never make it in the real world. *Encounters with "real world" people almost always reaffirmed Greg's truths. We were only allowed to have contact with tricks, and there was no empathy or caring from them. Police officers would arrest us or sweep us off their streets like garbage. In our many visits to emergency departments, it wasn't that we were treated badly; rather, we put on the act that we were "normal" and no one ever seemed to notice signs to the contrary like frequent STIs, bladder infections, repeated abortions or pregnancies, pregnancy with little to no prenatal care, pregnancy with positive drug use, medical and physical neglect, etc.*

Suicide attempts should be another red flag. I cannot tell you how many times I have overdosed on pills and cut my wrists. Sometimes, I completely wanted and expected to die. Other times were cries for help. One time I took two bottles of sleeping pills over a four-

hour period. When I started hallucinating, I drove myself to the emergency department. They had me drink charcoal and then admitted me. When I woke the following day, I begged one of the hospital workers to admit me into the mental health ward. I told her that I needed a break. She thought that was ridiculous. Who needs such a drastic "break" from life? She told me that life is hard and we all need to learn how to handle it. Greg came to the hospital soon after that to tell me that he loved me. I was released from the hospital, back into the arms of my oppressor.

When our injuries were caused by Greg's beatings, we knew better than to ask him to let us go to the emergency department or doctor—we knew he wouldn't allow it. Beatings were common. Some of us were beaten more often and more severely than others, and the worst beatings fell to a girl I will call April. One time, he beat her beyond recognition. I had never seen a person's entire back so battered. Her finger had swollen around her ring and she couldn't stop crying. I begged Greg to let me take her to the hospital. Furiously, he refused. As April continued to cry and her finger got bigger, I begged again, asking him why he wouldn't let me take her. His response was twofold: How did we know she wouldn't tell them that he had beaten her? How would we explain her condition? I had a bright idea that addressed his concerns. April and I promised that we would not mention him at the hospital. To allay any suspicion, we could say that she and I were drunk and got into a really bad fight.

I drove her to the hospital and we told our story. The doctor came in, looking down at his chart. He saw the injuries, had the nurse cut the ring off April's finger, gave her medication, and sent her home. No one seemed to notice that she was half a foot taller and 75 pounds heavier than me. No one noticed that neither of us would look them directly in the eye—maybe because they never tried making eye contact with us. Any signs of abuse or assault should be a red flag, as well as any signs of fearfulness or submission.

Sometimes Greg would have as many as 15 girls working for him. Other times, it was just me. There were times that we would live a "normal" life, nurturing my dream that we would live "happily ever after" as husband and wife. Our living situation went from one extreme to another. Sometimes we were homeless, sleeping in his car or moving from one sleazy hotel room to another. Other times, I would have my own apartment and Greg would keep all the girls in hotels near the track.

If you are looking for one specific situation that describes every sex trafficking case, you will miss many opportunities to see trafficking right in front of you. We were in plain sight. We were not hiding ourselves; we were hiding the pain and suffering we endured. We went to the grocery store, we went to the movies, we went to the beach and played. A person can be forced or coerced into sex work while living in an expensive home, a college dorm room, or a homeless shelter. The only thing that trafficked persons have in common is our vulnerability, but you have to get to know us to see it. Anytime you see a patient (whether it's in the emergency department, clinic, or physician's office), it's an opportunity to ask questions.

2.2.2   Extended Education: Victim-Centered and Trauma-Informed Care

In addition to basic education, Dignity Health created an extended education module to be assigned to key staff like clinicians and social workers who will likely engage with trafficked persons. This module addresses a "victim-centered" approach and trauma-informed care as well as ways to engage patients and internal protocols.

As defined by the US Department of Justice Office for Victims of Crime, a victim-centered approach gives priority to a patient's "wishes, safety, and well-being … in all matters and procedures" [10]. If health care professionals remain focused on "the needs and concerns" of a patient, they can ensure a "compassionate and sensitive delivery of services in a nonjudgmental manner" [10]. As described in Dignity Health's *Human Trafficking 102* module, a victim-centered approach is important for all patients but especially for patients who have experienced a crime like human trafficking. Traffickers often make all decisions for persons under their control, including when to work, how long to work, and when and where to sleep and eat. To help a trafficked person recover, health care professionals must help to instill in the patient a sense of safety and personal agency *as soon as possible*.

Dignity Health's extended education module also stresses the need to maximize the patient's input in all decisions regarding care, *including if and when to contact law enforcement*. Patients who have experienced sex or labor trafficking are often fearful of law enforcement. Therefore, clinical education should emphasize that law enforcement *not* be contacted against the patient's wishes *unless* a report is mandated by law, there is a threat of serious harm to the patient or other individuals, or there is imminent danger in the clinical setting. Clinicians should offer to contact a survivor advocate or service provider when a patient does not want law enforcement involved. Recalling her own experiences, Wendy emphasizes the importance of an approach that maximizes a patient's decision-making abilities:

> People ask me what is needed when encountering a trafficked person and I tell them, first and foremost, a genuine caring about that person. There must also be a sense of respect for his or her choices, even if those choices differ from what is considered best for them.
>
> For those of us under Greg's control, our minds were scrambled; our thinking was not our own. We were trained not to make eye contact. Hearing a question as simple as "Are you okay?" was and is powerful—it plants a seed of dignity. For me, it planted a counter-narrative to what Greg was saying all along—that nobody in the world cared about me. A trafficked person may not respond at that moment, but each respectful, caring encounter encourages that planted seed to grow, which in turn creates a foundation for personal strength and hope.
>
> What you don't do may be as important as what you do. Don't expect to save a trafficked person, especially if they have been isolated from and stigmatized by society over time. If you "rescue" them, they may go back to the trafficker. You cannot save them—but you can offer them tools that will enable them to save themselves. Trafficked persons need to dig themselves out of the hole of trafficking; if you try to dig them out, they will never develop the muscles they need to live fully in the outside world.

At Dignity Health, one "tool" offered to suspected or known trafficked persons is the NHTRC hotline: 1-888-373-7888 or text 233733 (BeFree). The NHTRC hotline is available 24/7 to report potential cases of human trafficking and provide information on local, regional, and national resources. NHTRC hotline specialists speak both English and Spanish and can communicate with callers in over 200 additional languages using a 24-h tele-interpreting service. Dignity Health clinicians and social workers are equipped with plastic "shoe cards" with the NHTRC hotline printed on them. These cards, available in several languages, are small enough to be hidden in a patient's pocket or shoe if the patient chooses to take one. The patient can then contact the hotline at a later time when ready to seek help.

In the extended education module, Dignity Health also emphasizes the importance of trauma-informed care. It is essential that clinical staff understand trauma and how trauma can affect a trafficked person's response "to services and the criminal justice process" [10]. Clawson et al. [11] describe varying levels of trauma:

> Trauma exposure occurs along a continuum of "complexity," from the less complex single, adult-onset incident (e.g., a car accident) where all else is stable in a person's life, to the repeated and intrusive trauma "frequently of an interpersonal nature, often involving a significant amount of stigma or shame" and where an individual may be more vulnerable, due to a variety of factors, to its effects.... It is on this far end of the continuum where victims of human trafficking, especially sex trafficking, can be placed.

From a *trauma-informed care* perspective, health professionals understand that a trafficked person's response may be influenced by past trauma rather than a deliberate attempt to be difficult. For example, consider the third case scenario presented in the Introduction of this chapter. After years of victimization, Wendy turned to an emergency department for help. She claimed to be "going crazy" in order to gain a temporary escape. The health professional recognized that Wendy was lying; however, did she recognize that Wendy's lying might be a response to trauma, even a cry for help?

How would you respond? Would you and your staff see a difficult patient, a criminal, a "frequent flyer," a drug addict, a prostitute, a bad mother, an irresponsible wife? Or would you see a potential victim of abuse or exploitation, possibly human trafficking? If you did see red flags associated with human trafficking, what protocols are in place to guide staff on how to respond to a patient like Wendy? As you reflect on these questions, consider Wendy's perspective, as a trafficked patient, on her encounter with the psychiatric hospital.

> *Greg and I were living in the northwest and had been together for over a decade. By this time I had learned how to manage the relationship with Greg well enough that we were able to live in one place for a year or two. Greg seemed to realize that he had to have a 'normal-looking' face, and that was the face of a husband and father. I don't know what neighbors thought about all the girls who would come and go—some would stay only a short time, others for a couple of years, still others for a lifetime. I don't know what the difference was between the girls—why one had the nerve to leave and another would stay.*
>
> *At one point, I lived in one apartment with our two children and all the other girls lived in another apartment. I only had to turn tricks on Friday and Saturday nights, and this occurred at one man's home. This guy would have a 'party' and invite all of his friends. Twenty to 40 men would come and go during the evening, and five to eight of us girls would be prostituted to the men. As long as Greg felt he had complete control over all of us and everything that happened, he wouldn't have a reason to beat me. I was often beaten for reasons out of my control. Sometimes, he wouldn't come over for an entire week and I could live my fairy tale that I was a mother taking care of her children while her husband was overseas working. Those weeks were really wonderful, but I also knew that at any time, Greg could blow up and invent a reason to come over and torture me.*
>
> *As it always did, that evening came. I don't remember what triggered his rage; I just remember him coming over with all the girls and humiliating me in front of them. I remember the other girls making fun of me while Greg berated me and pushed me around the house, causing me to knock over lamps and break dishes. Then he yelled at me for breaking the dishes and told me what a horrible mother I was. I knew the only thing that would stop this was to go make money for him. Then I was out on the street, crying, not wearing any make-up, and realizing that it was going to take me forever to earn enough money to keep*

Greg from hurting me. My children were in the house with him and all the girls. Because over the years Greg had managed to convince me that my children would be happier without me in their lives, I pictured them all playing games and laughing and eating dinner together. That, of course, was a figment of my imagination. Abuse was the "normal" reality for my children—not fun and games.

I walked to the hospital emergency department. I kept my eyes to the ground because that is what Greg had programmed us to do. I quietly told them that I needed help. I needed to be admitted into the mental health ward. To me, this was a break from the insanity. I had been to a different hospital's mental health ward a few times over the years after suicide attempts or threats to attempt. I would stay there for three or four days and I would get rest, a break from the drugs and the violence.

Someone had me sit in a waiting room for what seemed like forever, but it was probably only a couple of hours. Someone finally called me and asked me all the typical questions: weight, age, height, address, emergency contact. My emergency contact was one of the other women under Greg's control. Then two officers put me in a police car and drove me about two miles down the road to another building, which I assumed was their mental health ward.

It was about nine o'clock at night. The police took me to a room where I waited until a lady came in and asked why I wanted to be admitted. I told her I was going crazy. She kept asking questions that I could not answer so I started making up answers.

"Do you hear voices?"

"Yes." I thought that would be my ticket into the hospital.

"What do the voices say?"

"I don't know." I hadn't realized I should have been prepared with more details.

"Do you want to kill yourself?"

"Yes." I didn't really want to kill myself. I wanted life as I knew it to end. I wanted a better life, but I believed there was no hope for a better life.

The woman prodded me with questions. There was no sympathy in her voice. I stared at the wadded up, tear-drenched tissues in my hands. She asked me where I lived and about my children. I gave her my 'look normal' story: I have an apartment with my two children. The kids' father visits sometimes but I don't know where he lives or is at most of the time—quickly adding, "He's a good father to our children."

The lady explained to me that the mental health ward is not a place for people to take a break from life. This was a hospital for seriously ill people. I started to feel really bad—I just wanted to leave. I informed her that I was feeling much better and I wanted to go home. She asked me again if I wanted to kill myself, and I said, "No." She asked me what my plans were; I told her I was going to go home and go to bed.

I walked out of the hospital around midnight, with no money and no transportation. I didn't need transportation where I was headed. I knew I couldn't continue this way, I believed I had to die. I walked a couple of miles in the dark and stood on the tallest bridge in the city. I was alone, crying. I wanted to jump, but I was too afraid—afraid that I wouldn't die and I would be left in the weeds and bushes at the bottom of the bridge with broken bones and no one to help me.

I walked back to the track to make the money that would make Greg happy.

2.3 Conclusion

To ensure that health care professionals do not miss trafficked persons in the health care setting, the authors recommend providing education similar to what has been implemented at Dignity Health. Basic education on sex and labor trafficking should explain what human trafficking really means, including legal definitions, descriptions of vulnerable populations, and red flags in the health care setting. Extended education should include a discussion on victim-centered, trauma-informed care as well as suggestions on how to engage patients and an in-depth review of internal protocols. Whether education is in-person or self-study, the modules should include survivor stories to help facilitate understanding of trafficked persons' perspectives and vulnerabilities. Armed with knowledge, tools, and protocols, health care professionals are in an extraordinary position to identify trafficked persons, initiate their return to safety, and instill a sense of personal agency necessary for recovery.

2.4 Recommendations

The authors encourage health care systems to implement staff education programs that provide the following:

1. Basic education on sex and labor trafficking that includes survivor stories, along with a deconstruction of misconceptions often associated with human trafficking, red flags in the health care setting, and instructions for all frontline staff in the event red flags are observed.
2. Extended education for key staff who will engage with suspected or known trafficked persons. These key staff should be clearly identified in internal protocols. Extended education should include a discussion of a victim-centered approach, trauma-informed care, and an in-depth review of internal protocols. Whenever possible, include survivor stories or perspectives.
3. Ongoing education, including case scenarios, should be part of staff training. For example, Dignity Health created a third module, *Human Trafficking 103: Case Scenarios*, which presents ten clinical scenarios based on experiences of sex and labor trafficking survivors. This module is meant to be used in a group setting for staff to discuss concepts covered in education, protocols, resources, and tools like the NHTRC shoe card.
4. An internal multidisciplinary team should meet regularly to debrief on clinical cases and discuss protocols, education needs, awareness events, and other projects.

References

1. Lederer L, Wetzel CA. The health consequences of sex trafficking and their implications for identifying victims in healthcare facilities. Ann Health Law. 2014;23:61.
2. United Nations Office on Drugs and Crime—UNODC. Human trafficking FAQs. http://www.unodc.org/unodc/en/human-trafficking/faqs.html#Which_countries_are_affected_by_human_trafficking (2016). Accessed 25 Apr 2016.
3. US Department of State. Victims of Trafficking and Violence Protection Act. H.R.3244, §103(8) and (9). http://www.state.gov/j/tip/laws/61124.htm (2000). Accessed 25 Apr 2016.

4. National Human Trafficking Resource Center—NHTRC. The victims. https://traffick-ingresourcecenter.org/what-human-trafficking/human-trafficking/victims (and incorporated links) (2016). Accessed 25 Apr 2016.
5. US Department of Homeland Security Office of Immigration and Customs Enforcement. Human smuggling. https://www.ice.gov/human-smuggling (2016). Accessed 25 Apr 2016.
6. NHTRC. Hotline statistics. https://traffickingresourcecenter.org/states (2016). Accessed 25 Apr 2016.
7. Austin W, Boyd MA. Psychiatric and mental health nursing for Canadian practice. Philadelphia: Lippincott Williams & Wilkins; 2010.
8. Breakey S, Corless IB, Meedzan NL, Nicholas PK, editors. Global health nursing in the 21st century. New York: Springer; 2015.
9. Barnes Wendy J. And life continues: sex trafficking and my journey to freedom. Self-published; printed by CreateSpace Independent Publishing Platform; 2015.
10. US Department of Justice Office of Justice Programs Office for Victims of Crime Training and Technical Assistance Center (OVCTTAC). Human trafficking task force e-guide: victim-centered approach. https://www.ovcttac.gov/taskforceguide/eguide/1-understanding-human-trafficking/13-victim-centered-approach (2016). Accessed 25 Apr 2016.
11. Clawson HJ, Salomon A, Grace LG. Treating the hidden wounds: trauma treatment and mental health recovery for victims of human trafficking. Washington, DC: Department of Health and Human Services, Office of the Assistant Secretary for Planning and Evaluation; 2007.

Chapter 3
The Lost Boy: How a Forgotten Child Became a Victim of Labor Trafficking

James L. Dold

3.1 Introduction

3.1.1 Definitions

Chattel slavery: a form of slavery in which a person owns another person as well as their children and their children's children as property.

Traumatic bonding, or trauma bonding: a strong emotional attachment between an abused person and his or her abuser, formed as a result of the cycle of violence.

Exploitation: the action or fact of treating someone unfairly in order to benefit from their work.

Labor trafficking: a form of modern-day slavery in which individuals perform labor or services through the use of force, fraud, or coercion.

Involuntary servitude: any type of slavery, peonage, or compulsory labor obtained through the use of force, threat, fraud, or coercion, including psychological harm.

Obsessive–compulsive disorder: a common, chronic, and long-lasting disorder in which a person has uncontrollable, reoccurring thoughts (*obsessions*) and behaviors (*compulsions*) that he or she feels the urge to repeat over and over.

J.L. Dold (✉)
Campaign for the Fair Sentencing of Youth,
1319 F. Street NW, Suite 303, Washington, DC 20004, USA
e-mail: jdold@fairsentencingofyouth.org

© Springer International Publishing AG 2017
M. Chisolm-Straker, H. Stoklosa (eds.), *Human Trafficking Is a Public Health Issue*, DOI 10.1007/978-3-319-47824-1_3

3.1.2   Background

To understand the story of my exploitation and abuse — to really understand human trafficking for that matter — it is important to understand the philosophical and legal history behind the current movement to end modern-day slavery. The USA made slavery illegal through the adoption of the 13th Amendment to the US Constitution in 1865 following the Civil War. According to the 13th Amendment: "Neither slavery nor involuntary servitude, *except as a punishment for crime whereof the party shall have been duly convicted*, shall exist within the United States, or any place subject to their jurisdiction" [emphasis added]. While slavery was technically outlawed, the exception for criminal punishment remained to keep African Americans who were newly freed in a state of perpetual slavery. Following the Civil War, state legislatures in the South passed what have been termed the "Black Codes," which allowed states to incarcerate and re-enslave blacks for minor infractions [1]. The slavery exception within the 13th Amendment and the accompanying Black Codes were not the only mechanisms created to keep slavery alive.

Harriet Tubman, a leader of the Underground Railroad, once said, "I freed a thousand slaves, I could have freed a thousand more if only they knew they were slaves." Ms. Tubman was referring to what we know today as *traumatic bonding*, which occurs when a person has dysfunctional attachment to their abuser. Traumatic bonding is misplaced loyalty, and is also found in situations of exploitative cults, incestuous families, or in hostage or kidnapping situations. Over the years, clinicians have referred to similar abnormal psychological attachments as "Stockholm Syndrome" and in the case of domestic violence, "Battered Person's Syndrome".

The importance of Ms. Tubman's observation and its relevancy today cannot be overstated. From a historical perspective, although many African Americans were technically freed following the ratification of the 13th Amendment, many remained enslaved in practice: These former slaves were born into and maintained in slavery through the persistent use of lashings, physical and sexual abuse, rape, torture, and complete denigration of one's sense of self. As Ms. Tubman pointed out, understanding the world only as it had been shown to them, some of the newly freed slaves had a traumatic bond with their former slave owners.

In the several years following the adoption of the 13th Amendment, Congress passed a number of laws aimed at criminalizing slavery and involuntary servitude [2]. The principal difference between the two is that involuntary servitude was considered to cover a much broader range of conduct outside of chattel slavery, which had largely occurred in the southern states. The most comprehensive set of laws the USA has on this issue are found in Chapter 77 of Title 18 of the US Code, where criminal laws are housed [3]. Sections 1581–1588 of Chapter 77 criminalize peonage, transportation of and aiding in the slave trade, and involuntary servitude [3]. The US Department of Justice prosecuted a number of cases throughout the twentieth century, when the courts started to determine what types of conduct Congress had declared illegal under Chapter 77. The work of the Department of Justice and the limitations placed on the existing laws against involuntary servitude are vital to understanding why the sections previously mentioned were inadequate to capture much of the activities we now refer to as human trafficking or "modern-day slavery." Those limitations were highlighted by a case of human trafficking in 1988.

The seminal moment came when the 1988 US Supreme Court decided a case called *United States v. Kozminski* [4]. In *Kozminski*, two men with intellectual developmental disorder (IDD) were found laboring on a farm in poor health, squalid conditions, and relative isolation from the rest of society. Evidence showed that the two men worked on the farm 7 days a week, often 17 h a day, initially, for $15 per week and eventually for no pay. Further, the defendant used various forms of psychological coercion to keep the men on the farm and threatened to re-institutionalize one of the men if he did not comply. The Department of Justice argued that the Court should adopt a broad construction of "involuntary servitude," which would prohibit the compulsion of services by any means that, from the victim's point of view, either leaves the victim with no tolerable alternative but to serve the defendant or deprives the victim of the power of choice [5].

However, the Court, in an opinion by Justice O'Connor, held that:

> *Absent change by Congress*, we hold that, for purposes of criminal prosecution under § 241 or § 1584, 'involuntary servitude' necessarily means a condition of servitude in which the victim is forced to work for the defendant by the *use or threat of physical restraint or physical injury* or by the *use or threat of coercion through law or the legal process*.... guarantee of freedom from involuntary servitude has never been interpreted to specifically prohibit compulsion of labor by other means, *such as psychological coercion*... far from broadening the definition of involuntary servitude for *immigrants, children, or mental incompetents*, § 1584 eliminated any special distinction among, or protection of, special classes of victims" [emphasis added] [6].

Kozminski decided once and for all a long-standing split amongst the lower courts, which had disagreed over the scope of conduct covered by involuntary servitude. In the wake of the decision, it was clear that an expansion of the definition of involuntary servitude would require Congress to pass a new law. A few years later, in the 1990s, the issue of labor and commercial sexual exploitation began to gain prominence as reports from around the world painted a grim reality: Millions of people still toiled in slavery and involuntary servitude [7]. Women and children were the most vulnerable to exploitation, particularly in the developing nations that lacked a basic law enforcement infrastructure. Responding to the newly recognized crisis, the international community, via the United Nations, adopted one of the Palermo Protocols: The Protocol to Prevent, Suppress, and Punish Trafficking in Persons, especially Women and Children to the Convention Against Transnational Organized Crime in 2000 [8].

In October of 2000, the USA passed the Trafficking Victims Protection Act (TVPA), which included many of the concepts from the Palermo Protocol [9]. The TVPA created new crimes consisting of "human trafficking," including forced labor (Section 1589), trafficking with respect to peonage, slavery, involuntary servitude, or forced labor (Section 1590), and sex trafficking of children or by force, fraud, or coercion (Section 1591) [10]. Of particular note, Section 1589 expanded the traditional definition of "involuntary" to also include obtaining labor or services by "means of serious harm or threats of serious harm." [11] The statute defines "serious harm" as:

> ...any harm, whether physical or nonphysical, *including psychological, financial, or reputational harm*, that is sufficiently serious, under all the surrounding circumstances, to compel a reasonable person of the same background and in the same circumstances to perform or to continue performing labor or services in order to avoid incurring that harm [emphasis added] [12].

The effect of this change in the law was to overturn *Kozminski* and recognize that certain individuals—like immigrants, children, and those with IDD—are particularly vulnerable to certain forms of exploitation and must be protected. Under the TVPA standards, prosecutors must show that psychological or other harm was serious enough to compel someone in the victim's situation to provide labor or services, or engage in commercial sex acts. But what exactly does this mean?

The victims in the *Kozminski* case and in other similar cases provide us with guidance in how to consider under what circumstances exploitation meets the legal definition of human trafficking. As the *Kozminski* Court acknowledged, there are special classes of victims who are particularly vulnerable that the law at the time did not provide special protection to. Minors, for example, are more susceptible to being psychologically manipulated and will frequently acquiesce to the demands of adults due to an inherent power imbalance. And those with IDD and other learning disabilities may also be susceptible to manipulation if they are isolated or dependent on others for food or shelter.

Children have an inherent vulnerability because their brains are not fully developed and they lack the maturity to appreciate the gravity of dangerous situations. This is even more pronounced in adolescence when youth are often at odds with their guardians and are searching for their own identity. It is during this phase of their lives that children are particularly vulnerable to predators who seek to exploit their insecurities and capitalize on familial difficulties. Children, with immature prefrontal cortexes, process information and respond to stimuli differently than adults [13]. They are more likely to engage in risky behaviors and are more susceptible to external pressure from both peers and adults. They are also much less likely to perceive an exploitative or abusive situation as such and instead will be more likely to see themselves or their guardians as being at fault.

3.2   Discussion

3.2.1   *My Vulnerability*

During my preteen and early teenage years, my two sisters, two brothers, two cousins, as well as my nephew, niece, and uncle all lived in a 4-bedroom house with my parents. Because there were so many children in the household, my mother became a full-time caretaker; hence, my father was the only one really contributing substantively to the household income. My parents received assistance from the state for having guardianship and custody over their grandchildren and my two cousins, but it was barely enough to get by.

Money was tight and with that many kids to feed my mother would often have to improvise. For example, she would frequently fill a gallon jug with half milk and half water to make it last longer; and macaroni and cheese with hot dogs were the norm for dinner. To ensure we had Christmas presents every year, my parents would go to the local pawnshop and use their wedding bands as collateral for a small loan. It was tough, but they made it work. My parents' show of grit and unconditional love for all of the children in their care would eventually influence my worldview and incite my passion of caring for others. However, what later became a guiding moral compass for me, at the time sowed anger, resentment, and a deep searching for love and belonging that I felt I was not getting at home. As a young teen, the difficulties of living in a low socioeconomic environment, in which my parents were unable to meet my emotional needs because of work and having so many other children to care for, exacerbated the way I felt about myself; this in turn negatively impacted how I felt about my parents.

This point bears emphasizing again: Preteens and teens are particularly vulnerable to abuse and exploitation because of mental and emotional immaturity [14]. This vulnerability is more apparent when children find themselves in stressful and trying circumstances. It is further exposed when they do not feel the love or attention they need. For me, it did not matter that my parents were working as hard as they could to provide for all of the children in their care. They were trying to keep the family together and the children out of the child welfare system. My dad worked weekends and graveyard shifts so I barely saw him, except on his way to work. My mother had to focus most of her energy on the younger kids when she was not working at a part time job. For the most part, I was left to my own devices in middle school; I felt empty and yearned for adult attention and affection, which made me vulnerable to exploitation.

My feelings of emptiness and anger were compounded by another complication—untreated trauma from childhood sexual abuse. When I was around 5 or 6, another child in the house sexually molested me; this sowed powerful feelings of guilt and shame in me. The child in question was not much older than I was, and in retrospect, had probably been abused as well. I have since reconciled and have forgiven this person: They too were only a child at the time and not aware of the consequences of their actions. But for many years, guilt and shame boiled up inside of me, until one day, when I was about 12 years old, I finally built up the courage to tell my mother what had happened. This made matters worse.

After I disclosed the experience, my mother never made mention of it again. To my knowledge, my mother never talked to this person about the incident. There were no consequences, and there was no resolution. It made me feel like none of it mattered—what had happened or the courage it took for me to finally tell her. This made me angry and resentful. Looking back now, it was a very difficult situation for my mother, or any parent for that matter, to be in. Both children were under the age of 10 when the abuse occurred. Legally and morally the other child was not culpable—if anything, they too needed treatment. But a 12-year-old does not see morality in shades of gray: Things are black and white. And the perceived response or lack thereof pushed me away from the attention and affection my parents did show.

It was the confluence of these factors—the history of abuse, low socioeconomic environment, lack of parental guidance and engagement, and the changes of puberty—that made me particularly vulnerable to exploitation. However, there were many points along the way where an adult with courage and moral conviction could have prevented me from becoming a victim in the first place. The institutions that were designed to protect children from predators failed to protect me.

3.2.2 My Victimization

As I came into adolescence with a mixture of emotions and still struggling with anger and resentment toward my parents, I wanted to meet new people. A friend of mine introduced me to a nice, church-going lady in our neighborhood who took many of the kids on our block to church every Wednesday evening. This was my first real exposure to Christianity. I did not like church very much, but I loved attending the youth group—mostly because of the girls. I went to different events with the youth group for about a year or so until I ended up meeting new friends who were a part of the Boy Scout troop associated with the church. I decided to join the Boy Scouts and I loved that too. I quickly progressed through the ranks, making my way up to Star Scout and becoming the leader of my troop. Our Scoutmaster was a wonderful man with an Eagle Scout son. Most of the individuals associated with the troop were great people, who deeply cared for children, particularly those who came from the inner city.

But sometimes wolves wear sheep's clothing. In my case, the wolf came dressed as a devoted wife and mother of another young Cub Scout from my troop. She was about 28 years old with two children—a 3-year-old and a 7-year-old. I had just finished 7th grade and was 13 when we met at a Boy Scout fundraiser. She and her husband took a particular interest in my cousin and me. We were both pretty talkative and acted out quite a bit. We were both searching for love and affection and we thought we could get it from strangers. And in the beginning, we did. We would often visit their house in the summer to help them clean up their yard and hang out. They seemed happy together and we were happy to be around them. But appearances can be deceiving, especially to children.

There was a lot of marital strife boiling beneath the surface that I simply did not recognize. Gradually, the mother started to become closer and closer to me. She would take me out for fast food, and laugh and play with me. It seemed innocent but as time went on, our time together became less and less appropriate. Of course, I did not see this. I was happy to be receiving attention, especially from an attractive woman. We would spend time together even when her husband was not around. I became comfortable with and trusted her. I began to share some of my private feelings and personal thoughts with her: The rage and bitterness I had toward my parents; how I hated living in my house with so many people; the molestation that happened to me as a younger child. And she did what every child predator does, she affirmed what I was feeling, and stoked the bitterness and resentment I felt toward my parents. From my perspective, she became my champion: She was the only person who understood what I was going through and the only person who truly cared. I became emotionally attached to her and even felt that I loved her.

At the same time that I was growing emotionally close to her, the physical barriers slowly began to erode, until one day she was touching me in inappropriate places and kissing me. Barely in the 8th grade, the adults in church and Boy Scout leaders began to take notice of the inappropriate behavior that was sometimes displayed in public. Whispers abounded and rumors developed but at first, nothing was done. After a few weeks, church members finally began to speak up. However, it is hard to imagine a worse possible way for them to have handled the situation.

Some members told "Emily" they thought the amount of time we were spending together was inappropriate. My Scoutmaster did the same with me. She used this to her advantage. She planted an "us against the world" idea in my mind. Here were these people, who simply did not understand. Her manipulations worked. I felt that they were trying to separate me from the only person who seemed to care about me. Soon after that incident, I left the Boy Scouts and stopped going to church. She did the same. No one called my parents. No one reported it to the police. It becomes quite easy to forget about issues when they are no longer in front of your face. For many of the adults who had spoken to us, our departures ended a troubling issue with which they were grappling. They no longer had to see us. For me, it was the beginning of one of the darkest and most troubling times of my life.

Over the next few months, I continued to spend more and more time with "Emily." I went to her house right after school or sometimes she would pick me up. We went to the movies or out to eat. Sometimes we would just hang out at her house. Emily's husband was usually asleep by the time I got out of school because he worked very early in the morning. The molestation and inappropriate behavior continued and progressed. All the while, she continued to encourage the antipathy I had toward my parents, and reinforced the love and affection I had for her, my champion. I had trauma-bonded with "Emily."

As a young boy without many material items, the thought of someone taking me to concerts and movies, finding me attractive, showing an interest in me, and providing what I perceived to be love created what I can only describe as a psychological prison. About half way through my 8th grade year, we had sex for the first time. Given our age difference, what "Emily" did was *statutory rape*. Statutory rape refers to sexual intercourse with a child who is below the age of consent—usually between 16 and 18 years of age, depending on the state. The law recognizes that children below the age of consent do not have the mental capacity or decision-making ability to make an informed decision about sexual intercourse with an adult. The act itself, in other words, is inherently exploitative because of the power imbalance and development differences between an adult and a child. I will never forget how nervous and scared I was the first time. I lay there motionless, not really knowing what to do or what to say. Emotionally and psychologically I was still a young boy, having just turned 14 a few months prior.

I continued to spend increasingly more time at "Emily's" house. She often requested small things of me: Sometimes, it was to help her clean the backyard or the living room, which I was happy to do. After all, this was the person who cared about and loved me when I felt no one else did. I thought to myself that it was the least I could do to help. The situation progressively got worse as I grew more and more attached to her. She continued to drive a wedge between my parents and I; she convinced me that it was terrible that they forced me to live in the same house as someone who had molested me. There was great irony in this, of course; it was if she was oblivious to her own actions or perhaps had convinced herself that because I was a teenager it was different. Nevertheless, the anger I felt about the familial molestation and the perceived lack of interest from my parents resulted in me finally running away from home my freshman year of high school. I moved in with "Emily" and her family, who I felt actually loved and cared for me.

The lies I had been fed quickly unraveled from there, but only after I endured severe psychological torment. The love that was first showed to me was slowly replaced by anger and mistreatment. It was sometimes emotional, sometimes verbal, and sometimes physical. I was called a "nigger" often as a means to degrade or punish me or inflict injury for some perceived slight. Sometimes the insults came from her, other times from members of their extended family. "Emily's" marriage was quickly disintegrating and they needed someone to blame. I became an easy scapegoat because of my dark skin color and because I was living with but not a part of the family. According to the adults in the house, it was my fault. It did not matter that I was 14 and functioning as their live-in servant.

I went to school during the day and went straight back to their home afterwards. From eighth grade through my sophomore year of high school, I took care of "Emily's" kids, washed dishes, cooked food, mopped floors, and cleaned every room in the house, whilst being belittled and abused, emotionally, physically, and sexually. I became even more socially withdrawn than I was during my 8th grade year. Not only did people around me hate me, but also I felt constrained by the bond I had with "Emily" and all of the work she asked of me. Nothing was ever "Emily's" fault. It was always my fault. No matter what happened, I felt the need to make up for it. So I would do what was asked of me in hopes of getting back into her good graces so she would love me again. And that is how I became a victim of child labor exploitation and trafficking. I was psychologically and emotionally trapped; I would do anything for the only person I believed actually loved me. It was a pain and a prison I felt I could not escape.

In the sex trafficking context, pimps often engage in "grooming" behavior similar to what "Emily" did to me in order to create a traumatic bond with the child. This trauma bond gives the child a misplaced sense of loyalty and they are willing to do anything for their abuser. The primary difference in my situation and pimp-controlled trafficking was that instead of being coerced into commercial sex, "Emily" asked or told me to perform labor and services. The process of abuse, manipulation, and exploitation is very similar.

At my lowest point, I remember feeling broken and helpless. I thought about killing myself. There was a handgun inside "Emily's" closet. After an incident in which

I was again denigrated, I went into the closet, took out the gun, and closed myself in. I was alone, breathing heavily, and sobbing uncontrollably. I remember quietly crying to God, and asking what I had done to deserve this. I looked at the gun and put it close to my head. I imagined pulling the trigger to feel the escape from the hell that I felt inside. I imagined what it would be like to be free from the pain and from feeling like I was living every day just to be someone's servant. I cried awhile longer and put the gun back. I would continue living in this hell a little while longer.

My bond with "Emily" was slowly broken over time. She had begun to openly see other men as she and her husband began to separate. She was spending more and more time away, which made me feel like I had again done something wrong. But it was a blessing in disguise, as it allowed my feelings for her to slowly erode away. My return home was an even longer and more gradual process that was only aided by the passage of time. The more I was away from "Emily," the stronger I became emotionally. As time went by, it became easier to be without her. One thing that really helped me was joining the junior varsity football team at my high school. It was a distraction. I was socially awkward around kids of my own age; I had not spent a lot of time with my peers. My innocence was gone and I had seen too much of the world at that point to be able to relate to kids of my own age. Even still, playing football—as terrible as I was that first year—was a refuge from the hell I had been through. But soon football season would end and I needed a new distraction. Thankfully, the freshman football coach recruited me to join the wrestling team and I did. I loved it. And in return, it gave me something I never would have expected: It helped me get my life back. I dedicated myself to the sport and made new friends. Instead of spending every waking hour outside of school cleaning or taking care of children, I started spending it on the wrestling mat or on the track, running laps.

After "Emily" and her husband separated, still feeling a misplaced sense of loyalty and belonging to her, I lived with her at her parents' house for a brief time. Eventually and near the end of my sophomore year of high school, I finally moved back in with my parents. They were relieved. I think they really struggled to understand and respond in a way that would have been helpful. They were working all of the time and taking care of a number of kids, which also complicated the situation. I had lied to them about the circumstances under which I had left: I told them that I could not stand to live in the same house as my cousin and with so many people. I told them that it would be easier for me to live with this other family. At one point, my cousin, who was aware of my real situation, told my parents the truth of what was happening to me. I denied it vehemently, of course. There is nothing I would not have done or said to ensure that I could continue to be around the only person I thought loved and cared about me. I was trapped in a psychological and emotional prison that I could not recognize. I did not understand that I was being exploited. I felt I was old enough to make my own choices and I wanted to help the person I thought loved me.

As I developed a plate of armor around my heart and became emotionally stronger, I came to the startling realization of what "Emily" had done to me and what she had stolen. It was my innocence to be sure, but it was also precious time. More than two years of my young adolescence were taken from me. When I should have been out playing ball in the streets, exploring new feelings with girls, and discovering who I was, I was instead quietly toiling away in abusive anonymity, cooking, cleaning, and taking care of young children. And this is how most children in the USA end up in exploitative or trafficking situations: Traffickers and abusers take the most precious thing we are given as children—our love—and they turn it against us. They use the idea and promise of love, to get children to do what they please. In my case, it was living in a state of domestic servitude and frequent sexual exploitation.

3.2.3   Struggle for Normalcy

In recounting her own story of being a rape survivor, Oprah Winfrey once said, "I weep for the lost innocence, I weep for that because you're never the same again." I think any survivor of child abuse, rape, or exploitation would affirm Oprah's comments (https://www.youtube.com/watch?v=o5Y9PrQirvA, Oprah's Final Farewell). Coming out of my situation, my perspective on the world and on life was radically altered: I did not know how to be around kids of my own age and I struggled to leave behind a very painful chapter of my past. No one really knew what had happened to me. So when I would act out in class, or do or say outlandish things, people simply presumed I was a bad kid. But the truth was I was hurting. I fought to understand what I had just lived through and why it had happened. There were the continued distractions of high school sports that kept me preoccupied, but there was nothing to heal the emotional and psychological wounds I had, and no one to tell.

This void manifested itself in immature and unfortunate ways. I acted out often, which many boys do during adolescence. But I frequently went to extremes to get attention or win the admiration of my peers, with whom I was unsure how to interact. "Emily" forbade me from speaking to girls and I was socially withdrawn from boys of my age. Once I was living back with my parents, I started hanging out with other teens in my neighborhood. I engaged in delinquent and self-destructive behavior like drinking alcohol, smoking marijuana, shoplifting, fighting, and causing whatever other mischief I could. In school, I was no better. I always managed to do reasonably well in my studies. But I often acted out, reveling in the role I took on as class clown. I told obscene and inappropriate jokes with classmates that made my friends laugh, and others look on uncomfortably. Part of this was simply the immaturity of a 17-year-old, but it was also connected to everything that I had experienced. Acting out, making people laugh, and being the center of attention was the one thing that made me feel somewhat normal because it was the one thing that made me feel like I mattered.

Transitioning back into a normal teenage life was hard, but it was made easier because of the wonderful teachers and coaches I had around me. None of them knew what I lived through, but all of them unselfishly cared and showed a belief in me that I had not felt in a long time. They became my true champions. They saved my life, though many of them could not have known it. To them, I am eternally grateful. My high school friends were also pillars of strength for me, simply because we were friends. There was a core group of about six or seven of us, some of whom

I had known since middle school; they always welcomed me. Those final two years of high school, we were the best of friends. And they helped save me too.

By the end of my junior year in high school, I had cut off all contact with "Emily," my former abuser, though she regularly tried to communicate with me. I was able to have a relatively normal senior year of high school, save for my continued immature behavior. I started my first healthy romantic relationship with a girl at my school and went on to become the captain of my varsity football and wrestling teams. I was given the Coaches' award in both sports and, after winning a regional wrestling championship in my weight class, I was named athlete of the year at my zoned high school. My old high school wrestling coach used to say, "It's not where you start, it's where you finish." I started high school in a really isolated and wretched place, but hope, love, friendship, and others' belief in me allowed me to win back part of my adolescence. And for that, I can be nothing but thankful.

3.2.4   Finding Meaning in the Suffering

I wish I could say that after I graduated from high school everything awful went away and life magically got better, but trauma does not work that way. It impacts us in ways we cannot even imagine. For me, it resulted in a number of different psychological and behavioral changes. In 8th grade, I developed a slight obsessive–compulsive disorder, for which I briefly took medication. I came to believe that my hands were constantly dirty and always had a need to wash them. I also obsessed over the cleanliness of dishes. This was, of course, directly related to what I was living through. If a dish turned up dirty or something was done incorrectly, I was yelled at and made to feel incompetent. So my natural solution to this was to make everything perfect. After escaping from my situation, the condition slowly receded. And today, I no longer feel the need to incessantly wash my hands until they turn red. Now, washing a dish once is enough for me to know that it is clean.

Many survivors of childhood sexual abuse or statutory rape often respond by either becoming hypersexualized or developing a severe aversion to intimate contact. I was the former, which helps to explain some of my more colorful commentary during my high school years. And, I had difficulty in trusting adults and girls of my age. It took me a long time to finally develop healthy relationships—platonic and romantic—with women. Into my mid-twenties, I found it difficult to come to terms with what I had experienced. It was mostly kept secret and hidden away from the world. But it festered and ate away at me. I often worried that my victimizer might be doing the same thing to another young boy and I beat myself up over not having the courage to go to the police.

Telling your story to the police is a terrifying prospect for survivors, especially for boys who are so often taught not to be victims. When a woman sexually abuses a boy, men usually respond with a, "Where was she when I was his age?" remark or joke. A cruel double standard about victimization exists, which minimizes and ignores the rape and abuse of boys when the perpetrator is a woman. This contributed to my hesitancy in coming forward. Instead, I quietly made my way through life. I went to college and then law school, keeping what had happened buried. When I started working at Polaris on human trafficking, I recognized my experience for what it was. I wondered whether I should report what happened to the local authorities. I was about a month shy of my 28th birthday, and I knew that many states had a statute of limitations capped at 10 years for child survivors of crimes. A mentor from my undergraduate years encouraged me to file a report with the police. I did. Unfortunately, at that time, the state of Nevada had a 3-year limit of reporting for child survivors once they turned 18. In other words, once I turned 21 without having reported the crime, there was nothing the police could do.

In the year that followed, I really grappled with what to do next. It took soul searching and talking with amazing anti-trafficking advocates for exploited and trafficked youth for me to finally feel comfortable in sharing my story. I decided to do so before the 2013 Nevada legislature in support of AB 146, which criminalized the involuntary servitude of a minor [15]. It was a bill I developed to ensure that other children who found themselves in similar situations to mine would be recognized as child victims of trafficking. This law gives prosecutors and law enforcement additional tools to crack down on the exploitation and abuse of children. The new law made it a crime for any person "in physical custody of a minor, allowing a minor to reside in his or her residence, or providing care to a minor to knowingly obtain labor or services from the minor by engaging in a pattern of conduct that results in the physical or sexual abuse or sexual assault of the minor." The intent of the law was to make it easier for prosecutors to prove a child labor trafficking case where the circumstances clearly demonstrate a strong power imbalance, a particularly vulnerable child, and an extremely exploitative situation. The bill passed into law unanimously with accompanying support from the Attorneys Generals Office and the entire law enforcement community.

(Nevada Governor Brian Sandoval signing AB 146 into law; pictured from left to right: James Dold, Michon Martin, Governor Brian Sandoval, and Assemblyman John Hambrick)

The passage of the law was a vindication that what I had lived through was not meaningless. Even if I could not get justice for myself, maybe I could get justice for other children in situations like mine.

I was able to find meaning and purpose in my suffering by transforming this great source of pain and darkness into a source of strength and light. I decided that I was not going to be defined by the worst thing that ever happened to me. Rather, I was going to define this dark event in my life on my own terms. I became driven by the desire to ensure that children grow up in a safe and loving environment and that they have every opportunity to fulfill their God-given potential. During the time I served as Senior Policy Counsel for Polaris, I worked to protect children in more than half of the states in our country and helped pass 40 new laws to combat human trafficking, including AB 146 in Nevada.

3.3   Conclusion

Today I still advocate for children and fight for those whose life circumstances have left them devoid of hope. It is an important thing, hope. It is what allows us to turn tragedy into triumph. It is what brings us from our darkest place to our greatest glory. Hope transforms us and sometimes, just sometimes, it helps us transform the world and the lives we touch along the way. Hope is everything because hope is love.

I am still healing from what I lived through. And the truth is that I will never be who I might have been had none of it happened at all. I also am who I am today because of what happened to me. Suffering is one of the unfortunate certainties of the human condition, but our suffering is only tragic if we let it be. Out of our suffering hope is born. At first, this hope is just for us, but we can use it to light the candle of hope for others and ease their suffering too. When enough candles are lit in the darkest and most forgotten places of this world and even those who were once forgotten can see, only love is left.

3.4   Recommendations

For those interested in additional readings on the issue of human trafficking and exploitation of children, I encourage you to read:

A Crime So Monstrous by Benjamin Skinner;
Walking Prey by Holly Smith; and
Restavec: From Haitian Slave Child to Middle-Class American by Jean-Robert Cadet.

References

1. The Editors of Encyclopaedia Britannica. Black Codes, U.S. History. http://www.britannica.com/topic/black-code. Accessed 31 May 2016.
2. 18 U.S. Code 1940 ed., §§ 444, 445 (Mar. 4, 1909, ch. 321, §§ 269, 270, 35 Stat. 1142). http://uscode.house.gov/statviewer.htm?volume=35&page=1142. Accessed 31 May 2016.
3. 18 U.S. Code §1581 - §1588.
4. United States v. Kozminski, 487 U.S. 931. 1988.
5. United States v. Kozminski, 487 U.S. at 932. 1988.
6. United States v. Kozminski, 487 U.S. at 948. 1988.
7. Bales K. Disposable people. Berkeley, CA: University of California Press; 1999. Original Edition.
8. General Assembly resolution 55/25. UN Website. 2000. https://www.unodc.org/unodc/treaties/CTOC/. Accessed 31 May 2016.
9. Victims of trafficking and violence protection Act of 2000. U.S. Department of State Website. 2000. http://www.state.gov/j/tip/laws/61124.htm. Accessed 31 May 2016.
10. 18 U.S. Code §1589 – §1591.
11. William Wilberforce Trafficking Victims Protection Reauthorization Act of 2008. 2008.
12. 18 U.S. Code §1589.
13. Steinberg L. Should the science of adolescent brain development inform public policy? Issues Sci Technol. 2012;28(3):67–78.
14. Kempthorne VJ. Sexual abuse and sexual assault of adolescence. In: Forensic emergency medicine, 2nd ed. Philadelphia, PA: Lippincott Williams & Wilkins; 2007. p. 130.
15. Nevada Revised Statutes (N.R.S.) 200.4631. Involuntary servitude of minors; penalties. Nevada Legislative Website. https://www.leg.state.nv.us/nrs/nrs-200.html#NRS200Sec4631. Accessed 31 May 2016.

Chapter 4
Sex Trafficking in the USA

Clydette L. Powell and Cyril Bennouna

4.1 Introduction

Human trafficking is the illegal recruitment, exchange, transportation, or harboring of human beings for labor or commercial sex acts by force, fraud, or coercion. It has been occurring for thousands of years, as human slavery,[1] in the forms of what we now label *labor trafficking* or *sex trafficking*. Injustice permits trafficking operations to persist, and the accompanying violence destroys lives worldwide. Trafficking's conditions have garnered attention from legislative bodies, nongovernmental organizations, law enforcement, and individuals, all concerned about the exploitation of one human being by another; each of these entities is motivated to break the cycle of captivity and bring justice and healing to bear.

This chapter focuses on sex trafficking in the USA, beginning by defining and distinguishing between key terms and types of sex trafficking, which are often used inconsistently in the discourse about human trafficking. The next section characterizes the populations affected by trafficking operations and considers the health consequences that survivors tend to experience. The geographic distribution, flow, and magnitude of this form of twenty-first century slavery are outlined, and important gaps and weaknesses in the available research literature are highlighted. Federal and

---

[1] Though currently illegal, human trafficking or slavery of persons has not always been illegal, and has even been historically state sanctioned.

C.L. Powell (✉)
The George Washington University School of Medicine and Health Sciences,
Washington, DC, USA
e-mail: oboedoc@gmail.com

C. Bennouna
Center on Child Protection and Wellbeing, University of Indonesia, Depok, Indonesia

CPC Learning Network, New York City, United States
e-mail: cyril@puskapa.org

© Springer International Publishing AG 2017   43
M. Chisolm-Straker, H. Stoklosa (eds.), *Human Trafficking Is a Public Health Issue*, DOI 10.1007/978-3-319-47824-1_4

state legislation in the USA are then summarized, detailing the ways in which these laws, focused largely on sex trafficking, have created the foundation for investigation and prosecution of alleged perpetrators as well as the basis for survivor services and immigration remedies. The growing recognition of the need for collaboration, coordination, capacity building, and exchange between departments and service delivery systems is reflected in The Federal Strategic Action Plan and the outflow of that plan, which is discussed briefly. Reporting about human trafficking and resourcing for federal, regional, tribal, and state jurisdictions and authorities remains a challenge. The chapter concludes with provisional recommendations which are built upon the findings outlined in the sections and which project likely directions for those working in this area.

4.1.1 Defining Key Terms

The language used to describe human trafficking (also called *trafficking in persons*) and the issues related to it can be highly inconsistent, with definitions differing according to who is speaking, where, and for what purposes. Whether in the courtroom, during a political rally, on the streets, or in a news article, an advocacy brief, or a scientific report, the choice of wording can determine who receives services and who is imprisoned, and it can tip the scales when measuring the magnitude of the problem or budgeting the government's response [1]. As such, it is helpful to clarify a few important terms.

In the legal US definition, *human trafficking* does not necessarily involve movement of people. According to the *2015 Trafficking in Persons Report*, "People may be considered trafficking victims regardless of whether they were born into a state of servitude, were exploited in their hometown, were transported to the exploitative situation, previously consented to work for a trafficker, or participated in a crime as a direct result of being subjected to trafficking" [2]. By contrast, *human smuggling* must involve the illegal transportation of people across international borders, with or without the person's willful consent.

Force in these cases refers to the use of physical violence or restraint of movement, while *fraud* is deliberate deception to induce people to surrender their rights or otherwise act against their own interests to the defrauder's benefit. *Coercion* is the attempt to persuade someone through the threat, explicit or implicit, of serious harm against the person or someone they care about. *Sex trafficking*, which by definition must involve a commercial sex act, is considered a *severe form of human trafficking* by the US government. A *commercial sex act* is any sexual action that is exchanged for something of value, be it money, gifts, drugs, debt forgiveness, or the removal of force or threats. A commercial sex act can involve prostitution, in which something of value is exchanged for any kind of sexual activity (e.g., sexual intercourse, oral sex) as well as "exotic" dancing, escort work, pornography, web camera work, or even marriage. It is important to note that these activities are not considered *sex trafficking* if all parties are adults willingly consenting to the act. However, if an adult withdraws consent, any subsequent use of force, coercion, or deception constitutes trafficking. In the USA, children under the age of 18 are considered minors, and a commercial sex act involving a minor is always considered an act of sex trafficking, even if the child enters into the act "willingly," and even if the child has been emancipated legally from guardian care [2].

People who have been trafficked are usually referred to as "victims," denoting that they have suffered criminal violations, not to mention physical and psychological injury. However, this can have a stigmatizing or disempowering effect, as it describes people by the actions that were done to them, and thereby focuses on their weakness rather than the fortitude and resilience that characterize their survival. Many people often prefer the word "survivor" for this reason. Others favor the words "victor" or "thriver," to emphasize that, beyond survival, they are able to lead healthy, quality lives.

This chapter will refer to those who have been trafficked as "survivors" and those who are still being trafficked as "trafficked persons" or "trafficked individuals." "Victim" will only be used when considering the legal aspects of a trafficking case, as that is the language currently used under the US legal regime.

4.1.2 Magnitude of the Problem

The illicit, often transnational, nature of sex trafficking makes it a difficult crime to monitor. The inconsistent use of language and the difficulty of operationalizing terms like "coercion" further complicate efforts to characterize the incidence and distribution of trafficking [3, 4]. The figures that are available vary widely, rarely distinguishing sex trafficking from trafficking for forced labor, and the authors typically do not report their methodologies. Neither the UN Office of Drugs and Crime's (UNODC) 2014 *Global Report on Trafficking in Persons* nor the US State Department's 2015 *Trafficking in Persons Report* (TIP) included global estimates of sex trafficking [2, 5].

One of the most commonly cited figures estimates that between 600,000 and 800,000 people are trafficked annually around the world, of which about half are children, though this estimate is from 2004 [6, 7]. In 2012, the International Labor Organization (ILO) estimated that there are 20.9 million forced laborers globally, of which 4.5 million are sexually exploited [8]. The most recent official figure, from the US Department of State (DOS), estimates that there are between 14,500 and 17,000 people newly trafficked into the USA annually, but this also dates back to 2004 and is likely a significant underestimate [6, 7]. For instance, a study published in 2015 estimated that between 8,830 and 11,773 people were trafficked per year in San Diego County alone, of whom only 1,766 came into contact with law enforcement [9].

Because the crude estimates of sex trafficking are unreliable, it can be difficult to glean meaningful insight into the characteristics of trafficked persons, such as age and gender. A frequently cited study approximates that between 244,181 and 325,575 children were at risk of commercial sexual exploitation between 1999 and 2000, though this study had a number of methodological limitations and may have been an overestimate [10, 11]. The latest UNODC report found that 20% of people identified as being trafficked into the USA between 2007 and 2012 were children

[5]. The UNODC study also found that less than 5% of people trafficked to the Americas for commercial sexual exploitation were male, and the ILO's global estimate is about 2% [8]. Some scholars have criticized the disproportionately little attention that has been paid to male survivors in enumeration studies as well as male victim identification and service provision, suggesting that the proportion of males trafficked is likely higher [10, 12].

Beyond the efforts by perpetrators to hide their crimes, accurate estimations are extremely difficult because service providers struggle to recognize signs of trafficking, and survivors underreport it. Trafficked individuals often do not know they are victims of a crime, or fear retribution by perpetrators, criminalization for commercial sex work, stigmatization, or deportation [13]. Inadequate resources and concerns over confidentiality also inhibit data sharing among government agencies and nongovernmental organizations (NGOs) that collect reports of trafficking, limiting the interoperability and completeness of datasets [1].

Anonymous hotlines can be a powerful complementary source of data to help identify or verify trends, though these are also limited in their dependency on self-report. In 2015, the National Human Trafficking Resource Center (NHTRC), an independent anti-trafficking hotline, documented 4,136 sex trafficking cases throughout the country, and Polaris, the operating organization, has documented 24,156 cases since 2007 [14].

4.1.3   Trafficking: Locations and Flows

In the USA, sex trafficking operations frequently concentrate around urban hubs along country borders, with Mexico and Canada serving as key transit points. Transnational traffickers smuggle people across porous borders by foot or car, by ship using coastal ports, and even by plane. California had the most cases of sex trafficking reported to the NHTRC in 2015, followed by Texas and Florida [14]. From cities such as San Diego, Dallas, Miami, Atlanta, and Washington, DC, trafficked individuals are made to work in commercial sex operations and private homes across the country [15]. Expansive interstate trafficking networks and domestic recruitment and abduction contribute to trafficking nationwide.

Persons who are trafficked transnationally tend to come from impoverished contexts and are brought to wealthier ones through elaborate commercial sex networks. The UNODC reports that between 2010 and 2012, over half of all detected trafficking movements to the Americas originated within the region [5]. Mexico, Honduras, Guatemala, and El Salvador, for example, are common sources of sex trafficking to the USA [2]. Outside of this region, Asia is the largest source of trafficking to North America, from places like India, Thailand, and the Philippines [5]. Indeed, the most common countries of origin among survivors of sex and labor trafficking identified by federal authorities in 2014 were the USA, Mexico, and the Philippines [2]. Central Europe is also a common source of trafficking to the USA, according to the UNODC report.

While transnational flows clearly account for a substantial proportion of trafficked persons in the USA, some evidence suggests that the majority of trafficked persons likely originate within the country, and researchers have argued that not enough government, research, and media attention has focused on domestic sources of trafficking [16]. In fact, one US Bureau of Justice Statistics study reported that 83 % of survivors in sex trafficking incidents confirmed by federally funded task forces between 2008 and 2010 were US citizens [17]. This statistic may simply mean that US citizen survivors are more likely to be identified by authorities, but it also indicates a need for greater efforts to understand, surveil, and disrupt domestic recruitment operations.

4.1.4 Recruitment and Types of Sex Trafficking

Traffickers have elaborate recruitment strategies, which can take many forms. They may scout potential trafficking targets through social media sites and approach them through online messaging, unsolicited emails, at school, the mall, or through social gatherings. Aside from direct force, individuals may be defrauded, blackmailed, or seduced. In a common seduction scheme, called "grooming," a younger girl is approached by an older "Romeo," who gains her trust by acting like her boyfriend. The perpetrator then manipulates her into depending on him, sometimes by inducing her into drug or alcohol use, or monetary debt [18]. The promise of access to drugs, to those with substance use disorders, can be the bait to lure individuals into sexual exploitation [13, 16]. While the large majority of sex traffickers are male, women also work as recruiters, especially when they are well positioned to gain the trust of their targets, such as in schools [9, 16].

To expand their recruitment operations, traffickers have increasingly exploited online tools. Live video conferencing, social media, SMS, and peer-to-peer servers, for instance, allow traffickers to groom multiple potential victims across large geographic distances, affecting emotional connections with them, while normalizing commercial sex through repeated conversation and sharing of images or videos [19, 20]. Platforms like *Backpage* enable traffickers to place classified advertisements for the people they have trafficked, where they are usually sold as escorts [21]. Other websites, like *Model Mayhem*, have been used to place duplicitous advertisements for models, who are then lured to a private place with the trafficker under the guise of an interview, and subsequently exploited [22]. A variant of this scheme is used in many parts of the world, where people, often in poor areas, are deceived into believing that they are being offered relatively lucrative, desirable jobs, and sometimes visas, in more affluent places [20]. In the case of transnational trafficking, visas and other related paperwork may be confiscated by the perpetrator upon arrival to render the trafficked person more dependent.

There are many kinds of sex trafficking operations. Perpetrators may act alone, or on the behalf of owners of commercial sex businesses. Organized crime syndicates, often called "trafficking rings," control much more expansive operations that tend to cross state lines and even national borders. Reports from 2011 to 2014 indicate that law enforcement and researchers have recognized that street gangs in the USA, such as the Bloods, the Crips, Hell's Angels, and MS-13, have also become involved in human trafficking [16, 18].

Persons trafficked into the commercial sex industry may find themselves working alongside consenting commercial sex workers in brothels, strip clubs, live-sex shows, pornography, or on the streets. Others may be forced into prostitution fronts, such as massage parlors, nail salons, and spas, or made to work out of motels or even five-star hotels, where trafficking crimes are less easy to detect [23]. Truck stops are another popular place for trafficking fronts and trafficker-led operations, as they can be difficult to police [24]. In addition to being sexually exploited, trafficked individuals may also be forced into labor, domestic servitude, or marriage.

4.1.5 Populations Affected and Consequences of Sex Trafficking

Although adults and children of all ages, genders, and socio-demographics fall prey to sex trafficking, perpetrators tend to target particular profiles of people, often favoring the economically and emotionally vulnerable and socially isolated [25]. Youth are thought to be at especially high risk because of customer demand: Younger girls and boys can be exploited by traffickers longer, making them especially profitable, and adolescent girls are considered easier to persuade and control [18]. Those trafficked for commercial sexual exploitation frequently have histories of previous sexual abuse, early sexual experience, and drug and alcohol use [10]. These histories may contribute to limited school involvement and school dropout, which are also associated with involvement in commercial sexual exploitation. Substance use disorders can draw youths away from their support networks towards criminal activity, where they sometimes turn to sex work to pay for substances. Traffickers tend to cultivate and exploit these addictions, taking advantage of women's incapacitated states to rape them, or using sex work as payment for drugs [10, 26]. Psychogenic factors, such as poor self-esteem and clinical depression—which are highly comorbid with substance use disorders—are also thought to increase vulnerability to trafficking by impairing decision-making; cognitive difficulties, like intellectual and learning disability, present a similar risk [10, 11, 25]. Traffickers are thought to target those with physical disabilities as well, preying on the social and political marginalization that often leaves people with disabilities vulnerable [27, 28].

Dysfunctional home lives, domestic violence, abandonment, parental substance use, and loss of a parent may predispose youth to trafficking, especially when this leads them to run away from home or to be forced out by their caretakers [13]. Homelessness is an especially powerful risk factor for trafficking, and those in homeless shelters and the child welfare system are also at increased risk [10, 25]. Homeless youth who are identified as lesbian, gay, bisexual, and/or have a transgender experience disproportionately report having been sexually exploited for commercial purposes.

Although the conditions of male victimization are not well studied generally, those who are identified as gay or bisexual and/or have a transgender life experience are thought to be at particularly high risk for being trafficked [25]. Adults involved with sex trafficking also sometimes recruit from younger members of their family, or pressure them into commercial sex [9].

Social and familial exclusion drive individuals away from supportive community systems, which could otherwise be drawn on to detect early warning signs of manipulation, interrupt recruitment, notify law enforcement, or access services. Due to a range of structural inequities, racial and ethnic minority youth face an elevated risk of economic and educational marginalization and are represented disproportionately in the US child welfare system [10]. While ethnic or racial minorities in the USA have not consistently been associated with increased risks of trafficking, some studies have found people of color to be overrepresented as survivors of trafficking [11, 25]. A US Bureau of Justice Statistics study found that a full 40 % of sex trafficking survivors confirmed by federal task forces were Black, while 26 % were White, 24 % were Hispanic, and 4 % were of Asian descent, though this study was not meant to be nationally representative [17]. Black and Native American women are also more likely to be arrested for sex work in a number of settings, increasing the chances that they are identified as survivors [13, 29]. Interestingly, a study focusing on the commercial sexual exploitation of children found that agencies tended to make conclusions about the representativeness of their service populations by referencing national rather than local demographics [11]. Thus, an agency might report that 36 % of its beneficiary population in New Orleans is Black and compare that to the national population (13 % Black) instead of the general New Orleans population (35 % Black). After reviewing agency data from a range of services across the USA, the study found that the demographics of children receiving services for commercial sexual exploitation were usually proportionate to those of the average child population [11].

While the literature is inconclusive about whether people of color are trafficked at disproportionate rates nationally, race and ethnicity can influence an individual's risk of being trafficked through interactions with other risk factors, like involvement with the child welfare system, or more directly. Native Americans have a long history of being targeted for sex trafficking operations, dating back to the beginnings of colonization, but enduring in a number of ways into the present day [30]. In Alaska, for example, the police and Federal Bureau of Investigation (FBI) found that sex traffickers systematically preyed upon Native American females who had left their rural communities to find work in the city of Anchorage [31]. The traffickers reportedly not only found them easier to traffic but also easier to advertise, owing to their "ambiguous" ethnicity. A long history of forced relocations, societal trauma, poor access to education and economic opportunity, and the proliferation of organized criminal activity in Indian Country resulting from a host of social and political factors make Native American youth particularly vulnerable to exploitation [29, 30]. The sociocultural and economic alienation often experienced by immigrants, refugees, and asylum seekers in the USA, including language barriers and indeterminate documentation status, may contribute to similar vulnerabilities among those populations [25]. In addition to being marginalized within the USA, those fleeing conflict and persecution may face multiple threats throughout their displacement, including armed forces at home, and criminal syndicates attempting to exploit their insecurity during flight [2, 32, 33].

Survivors can experience profoundly negative acute and long-term physical and psychosocial sequelae while being trafficked, though longitudinal outcomes have largely gone unstudied, especially in the USA [34, 35]. One European study found that trafficked sex workers typically had 10 to 25 clients a night, while some had 40 to 50 [36]. Many reported forced unprotected sex, exposing them to sexually trans-mitted infections and unwanted pregnancy. Facing these conditions, many turn to drugs or alcohol to cope with their exploitation, if they have not already been ren-dered dependent by their traffickers as a means of recruitment and control. Several studies have documented an increased rate of substance use disorders among traf-ficked individuals, which in turn creates additional risk for negative psychosocial outcomes, transmission of HIV, and arrest [13, 34–36]. One study, for example, found that more than 75 % of homeless youth experiencing commercial sexual exploitation "abused"[2] alcohol and drugs, and several other studies have reported similar trends [10, 13]. This not only makes it difficult to free individuals from cycles of sexual exploitation, as they are dependent on their traffickers for drugs, but it also complicates treatment and recovery.

Serious physical injuries are also common, with trafficked persons experiencing abuse by traffickers and customers alike, including confinement, gang rape, food and sleep deprivation, tooth loss, and/or repeated, forced abortions [36, 37]. Recurring exposure to physical and verbal abuse, disempowerment, and forced isolation are associated with increased psychosocial distress, clinical depression, post-traumatic stress disorder, and suicidal ideation, along with other somatic symptoms [30, 31]. Studies of trafficking survivors have also documented high rates of gastrointestinal complications, respiratory infections, dermatological problems, and weight loss [34, 37]. Infrequent health care seeking on the part of survivors and poor identification of trafficking signs by clinical providers often allow these symptoms to remain untreated, or incompletely treated, which in turn increases the likelihood of down-stream health complications [13, 38, 39].

4.2 Discussion

4.2.1 Federal Legislation and the Federal Strategic Action Plan

As we have seen, sex trafficking is a multifaceted crime affecting tens of thou-sands, if not hundreds of thousands of lives throughout the USA. Although move-ment is not required, sex trafficking's profiteers and clientele are often involved in

---

[2] This study was conducted prior to the DSM V adoption of "substance use disorder" terminology. The study found that 75 % of the study participants "abused" substances while "virtually all" "used" substances.

organized, interstate, and at times transnational crime. They exploit individual and family vulnerabilities and capitalize on systemic weaknesses in detection and enforcement to infiltrate schools, businesses, institutions, and, through the Internet, private homes. The scale, complexity, and enduring consequences of trafficking necessitate a vertically and horizontally integrated government and public health-focused response that cuts across administrative levels and sectors to address issues as disparate as prevalence assessment, trafficking prevention, trafficking identification, immigrant and refugee protection, child welfare, mental health care, substance use disorder treatment, medical care, along with criminal prosecution. The remainder of this chapter will provide a broad overview of the US government's response to human trafficking, including federal legislation and action plans, interagency partnerships, sector-specific initiatives, and state legislation. Importantly, many anti-trafficking efforts have been mainly focused on sex trafficking, though this form of trafficking is not the only, and possibly not the main, form of trafficking in the USA. As such, this chapter, focused on sex trafficking, will discuss the US anti-trafficking legislation, which was largely borne of anti-sex trafficking efforts. The chapter will also briefly detail the services available to US citizens as well as noncitizens and summarize recent progress towards achieving justice for trafficking survivors.

4.2.1.1 Federal Legislation

Although the US legislation on the criminal aspects of involuntary servitude and slavery has existed for many years, it was not until 2000 that specific legislation was enacted to protect survivors of human trafficking (HT). The Trafficking Victims Protection Act (TVPA) served three main purposes: (1) to prosecute traffickers, (2) to protect victims, and (3) to prevent crime. These functions are sometimes referred to as the "3 P's," with a fourth "P" added to represent partnerships. Since 2000, the TVPA has been reauthorized as the Trafficking Victims Protection Reauthorization Act (TVPRA) in 2003, 2005, 2008, and 2013. A key aspect of the Act is to define service eligibility of victims of "severe forms of HT". The TVPA of 2000 strengthened the tools of prosecution by increasing penalties for HT, coupled with mandatory fiscal retribution for victims. Since the initial TVPA, subsequent reauthorizations have mandated increased awareness efforts about HT, broadened grant assistance to victims who are US citizens and lawful permanent residents (LPRs), encouraged the development of public–private partnerships to combat sex tourism, and strengthened the means for investigation and prosecution. The TVPRA of 2003 required the US Attorney General to publish an annual report to Congress and allowed victims of HT to sue their traffickers in federal district courts. The William Wilberforce TVPRA of 2008 expanded T-visa protections (discussed below under "Immigration Remedies"). The TVPRA enhanced support for state, territorial, tribal, and local efforts to address HT investigation and prosecution, and increased support for victims of HT, especially minors.

The TVPRA was last reauthorized in 2013, during which time the Violence Against Women Act (VAWA) was also reauthorized. Additional features of the TVPRA 2013 included enhancing youth safety (Section 302); strengthening safety and justice for Native American women (Sections 901 and 902); reducing sexual abuse in custodial settings (Section 1101); unifying federal government hotline outreach (Section 1203); assisting domestic minor sex trafficking victims (Section 1241); strengthening the child advocate program for unaccompanied children (Section 1262); and providing benefits to certain holders of U-visas (Section 1263).

4.2.1.2 Federal Strategic Action Plan

Subsequent to the federal legislation, and in commemoration of the 150th anniversary of the Emancipation Proclamation in 2012, the Obama Administration asked federal agencies to provide clear guidance over a 5-year period, on the needed collaboration, coordination, and capacity among governmental and nongovernmental entities for improving victim services. As a result, the *Federal Strategic Action Plan on Services for Victims of Human Trafficking 2013–2017* (SAP) was published in early 2014 [40]. This was a multi-phase, collaborative process co-chaired by the Department of Justice (DOJ), the Department of Homeland Security (DHS), and the Department of Health and Human Services (HHS). The three federal department co-chairs were chosen because of their work in various capacities aimed at supporting victims of HT. HHS supports outreach efforts and victim services, helps communities build capacity through local coalitions, and funds grants, contracts, and certifications for foreign national victims. DHS operations handle the identification of human trafficking perpetrators and victims, provide immigration protection for victims, and set penalties for traffickers. DOJ supports the development of multidisciplinary task forces for investigation and prosecution of traffickers. All three agencies aim to support victims, educate the public, and provide funding directly or indirectly to victim-service organizations [40].

The development of the SAP received guidance from the President's Interagency Task Force to Monitor and Combat Trafficking in Persons (PITF), a Cabinet-level task force chaired by the Secretary of State and comprised of 17 departments, agencies, offices, and commissions. In addition, the process incorporated the input of survivors and stakeholders. The SAP lays out four goals, eight objectives, and more than 250 associated action items, with timelines, for victim-service improvement. The four goals are to: (1) align efforts across federal, regional, state, territorial, tribal, and local agencies, (2) improve understanding through research, and evidence-based practices in victim services, (3) expand access through outreach, training, and technical assistance, and (4) improve outcomes which are effective, culturally appropriate, and trauma-informed. Goal number one is particularly important: The federal, regional, state, tribal, and local authorities cannot work in isolation if human trafficking is to be effectively monitored and combatted. Collaboration, coordination, and capacity building are the foundations of the SAP. Prosecution and prevention do not fall within the scope of the Plan.

4.2.1.3   Federal Partnerships

In the USA, the national response to HT and the implementation of the SAP are reflected in the collaborative efforts of many different federal and nonfederal entities, sometimes in sequence and other times in parallel fashion. This national response to trafficked persons is a complex one and cannot be fully detailed here. Three US federal agencies stand out as the main actors in the efforts to monitor and combat human trafficking within the USA and are coordinated with the fourth, which is focused on foreign governments: HHS, DHS, DOJ, and DOS (Table 4.1).

Primary sources of federal funding for victim services come from the HHS Office of Refugee Resettlement (ORR) and the DOJ Office for Victims of Crime (OVC). Resources also originate from the DOJ's US Attorney General's Office, the FBI, and the DHS Immigration and Customs Enforcement (ICE) Homeland Security

Table 4.1 Federal agencies with responsibilities related to human trafficking

Agency	Oversees or provides services	Provides immigration benefits	Investigates and prosecutes alleged perpetrators	Monitors and reports on cross-border activities
Department of Health and Human Services	X			
Department of Homeland Security	X	X	X	X
Department of Justice	X	X	X	
Department of State	X	X		
Department of Labor	X	X		
Equal Employment Opportunity Commission		X		
Department of Immigration and Border Protection				X
Legal Services Corporation	X			
Office for Juvenile Justice and Delinquency Programs (DOJ)			X	
Federal Bureau of Investigation (DOJ)		X	X	
Office on Violence Against Women (DOJ)			X	
Office of Immigration and Customs Enforcement (DHS)				X
Immigration and Naturalization Services (DHS)				X

Investigation when victims assist in the investigation of the crimes. Federal agencies also encourage businesses, philanthropic organizations, and civic leaders to contribute resources to support these efforts. It is important to note that funds under the TVPA are for non-US citizens to access the benefits and services that otherwise would be prohibited; those funds may not be used for victims who are US citizens, because US citizens may access other benefit entitlement programs dedicated to federal crime victims. Unfortunately there are few data demonstrating how effectively US citizens access those programs.

Department of Health and Human Services HHS's response to HT in the USA is addressed through the Administration for Children and Families (ACF) and its Office on Trafficking in Persons (OTIP), which was created in 2015 (http://www.acf.hhs.gov/programs/endtrafficking). OTIP brings together the anti-trafficking efforts of the ORR (http://www.acf.hhs.gov/programs/orr), the Family and Youth Services Bureau (http://www.acf.hhs.gov/programs/fysb), and the Children's Bureau (http://www.acf.hhs.gov/prgrams/cb). OTIP is responsible for the Trafficking Victim Assistance Program and the Rescue & Restore campaign, which focuses on educating those who may encounter but not recognize an HT victim. The Rescue & Restore campaign created the NHTRC (http://www.polarisproject.org/what-we-do/national-humantrafficking-hotline/the-nhtrc/overview), which is operated by the NGO, Polaris. OTIP also has responsibility for domestic trafficking grants.

In 2012, the ACF formed a Working Group (WG) on HT. The WG is co-led by ACF and the Office of Women's Health. This WG has broad representation from other HHS agencies and was instrumental in the development of the SAP.

Department of Homeland Security The DHS is responsible for investigating human trafficking, arresting traffickers, and protecting victims. DHS also processes immigration relief through continued presence (CP), T-visas, and U-visas for victims of human trafficking and other designated crimes. Four key entities within DHS fulfill its anti-trafficking duties: (1) ICE's Homeland Security Investigation handles both domestic and international cases, and works with US and foreign partners. In addition, it provides victim assistance specialists in support of persons who have been trafficked while their case is under investigation; (2) the US Citizen and Immigration Services (USCIS) provides immigration relief and handles the process for T-non-immigrant visas and the U-non-immigrant visas; (3) Customs and Border Protection (CBP) monitors 7000 miles of borders and 327 ports of entry; and (4) the Federal Law Enforcement Training Center (FLETC) provides career-long training to law enforcement and others.

The Blue Campaign is the unified voice for DHS to combat HT as it works in collaboration with law enforcement, governmental and nongovernmental, and private organizations (http://www.dhs.gov/blue-campaign). DHS's Blue Campaign raises awareness about HT to the general public and health care professionals (particularly emergency medical service, or EMS, providers), leverages partnerships, and offers training to law enforcement and others. It applies a survivor-centered approach to investigation, with the aim of arresting traffickers and protecting survivors.

Department of State Created in 2000 as a result of the original TVPA, the Office to Monitor and Combat Trafficking in Persons (J/TIP) within DOS focuses on trafficking overseas and across borders. Leveraging its diplomatic role, and using targeted foreign assistance, DOS J/TIP partners with foreign nations and civil society to develop and carry out counter-trafficking strategies. DOS works in conjunction with the US Agency for International Development (USAID) and US embassies in countries around the world to mitigate and prevent HT at country level. Each year since 2001, DOS J/TIP has released the *Trafficking in Persons* (TIP) *Report*, which ranks countries, including the USA, on efforts to prevent and combat trafficking (http://www.state.gov/j/tip/rls/tiprpt/index.htm). DOS also chairs the PITF and the Senior Policy Operating Group (SPOG) (http://www. state.gov/j/tip/response/usg). The SPOG represents each of the federal agencies engaged in anti-human trafficking efforts and is headed by the US Ambassador for DOS/JTIP.

Department of Justice The DOJ's Bureau of Justice Assistance and the OVC support anti-human trafficking task forces. These task forces have representatives from state and local law enforcement, investigators, victim service providers, and other key stakeholders. The DOJ Executive Office for the US Attorneys disseminates information to the anti-trafficking task forces throughout the USA. Under the DOJ's leadership, the task forces investigate and prosecute human trafficking cases and provide comprehensive victim services. OVC's Training and Technical Assistance Center has a comprehensive Human Trafficking Task Force e-Guide on multisystem efforts to address trafficking and help victims (https://www.ovcttac.gov/taskforce-guide). OVC's webpage on HT provides information for victims, service providers, law enforcement, and allied professionals (http://ovc.ncjrs.gov/humantrafficking/index.html). Training for law enforcement resides largely in the FLETC, with some grants for training through the DOJ's OVC.

The Office of Justice Programs (OJP) houses the Office of Juvenile Justice and Delinquency Prevention. From this office emanate the Amber Alerts about possible child abductions; this service is managed by the National Center for Missing and Exploited Children (NCMEC). OJP also oversees the National Sex Offender Public Website. These are important to note because sex offenders are sometimes linked with missing children, either abducting or luring them from home for the purposes of sex trafficking. The National Institute for Justice and the Office of Legal Policy, which compiles the Attorney General's annual reports on HT efforts across the USA, also reside within the OJP. In addition to these, DOJ houses the HT Prosecution Unit, the National Criminal Justice Reference Center, and the Office on Violence Against Women.

In 2003, the DOJ established the Innocence Lost National Initiative, which tracks domestic sex trafficking of children. This initiative reflects collaboration between the FBI, the DOJ Child Exploitation and Obscenity Section, and the NCMEC (http://www.fbi.gov/about-us/investigate/vc_majorthefts/cac/innocencelost).

4.2.1.4 Reporting

Given federal and state legislation, guidance from the SAP, and activities to monitor and combat HT at the federal, regional, tribal, state, and local levels, the collection and synthesis of data and information is a daunting task. Each year, the DOJ US Attorney General's Office publishes and disseminates *The Attorney General's Annual Report to Congress and Assessment of the US Government Activities to Combat Trafficking in Persons*. This report, compiled by the DOJ Office of Legal Policy, contains an annual status update with outcome data. The report, detailing the work of many federal agencies and partners, is presented to and reviewed by the SPOG and then formally submitted to the PITF. In addition, data and information are generated by the NHTRC and its hotline. Local task forces provide reports to DOJ, and nongovernmental organizations collect data on their program and project activities, but these are not collated into federal reports. Organizations such as The Protection Project, ECPAT,[3] and Shared Hope International have conducted an inventory and evaluation of shelter and services to domestic minor sex trafficking survivors [41]. Plans are underway to include within the international classification of diseases (ICD) specific coding that would facilitate capture of information about suspicion of trafficking experiences and clinical services to HT survivors who present to health facilities; however, a systematic data collection process through electronic medical records is, at the time of this writing, a distant goal.

4.2.1.5 State Legislation

To complement work at the federal level, states have responded with their own legislation. In 2003, Washington and Texas were the first states to develop anti-HT laws. Since then, all 50 states have developed similar laws over the following 10 years [42]. The National Conference on Commissioners' Uniform Law Commission's Uniform Act on Prevention of and Remedies for HT, passed in 2001, serves as a potential blueprint for state law and provides immunity to minors, victim assistance (access to services and legal aid), case-worker support, civil remedies, and vacates convictions for forced criminal activities [43].

In addition, legislative efforts have further developed in 34 states leading to safe harbor laws, which protect and assist minors who are sex trafficked [44]. The intent of safe harbor laws is to treat children and youth as victims who were exploited through acts of commercial sex by their traffickers, rather than as criminals who merit prosecution. The law provides them legal protection from the justice system and access to services through child welfare. Safe harbor legislation and its protections vary widely across states, and some laws have been viewed as failing to provide for substantive needs, including supporting programming with concrete funding. In some instances, a jurisdiction without adequate funding for safe harbor

---

[3] End Child Prostitution, Child Pornography and Trafficking of Children for Sexual Purposes.

will seek funds elsewhere for their anti-trafficking efforts, such as through grants from the US DOJ.

Both Polaris and the National Conference of State Legislatures provide information on states' safe harbor laws (http://www.polarisproject.org/what-we-do/policy-advocacy/national-policy/stateratings-on-human-trafficking-laws; http://www.ncsl.org/research/civil-and-criminal-justice/human-traffickingoverview.aspx). As an early and successful example, Minnesota enacted its safe harbor law in 2011, with full implementation in 2014. The state also allocated funds for training law enforcement on trafficking of youth and housing for survivors, and created regional coordinators of services for commercially sexually exploited youth. A guidebook from Minnesota's Department of Public Safety Office of Justice Programs provides information on this emerging approach to working with survivors of trafficking: *No Wrong Door: A Comprehensive Approach to Safe Harbor for Minnesota's Sexually Exploited Youth* (https://dps.mn.gov/divisions/ojp/forms-documents/Documents/!2012%20Safe%20Harbor%20Report%20%28FINAL%29.pdf). In 2015, Minnesota also published its first evaluation of the safe harbor policy, providing lessons for other states [45].

4.2.1.6   The Crosswalk Between Child Welfare and Human Trafficking

As mentioned above, youth who come from troubled families, have experienced neglect and abuse or have been involved in child welfare services, can be at risk for trafficking. The ACF and the Children's Bureau, both at the HHS, have attempted to address these vulnerabilities with the implementation of the 2011 Child and Family Services Improvement and Innovation Act as well as the 2014 Preventing Sex Trafficking and Strengthening Families Act. The 2011 Act requires states with health care oversight of child welfare services to include a plan for screening and treating emotional trauma secondary to maltreatment and subsequent placement in foster care. The 2014 Act provides new requirements to foster care and adoption assistance programs regarding at-risk youth and survivors of sex trafficking who are identified through the child welfare system. In 2013, ACF published its *Guidance to States and Services on Addressing Human Trafficking of Children and Youth in the United States*. ACF has partnered with the Assistant Secretary for Planning and Evaluation (ASPE) to develop and validate a screening tool and protocol that will identify trafficked persons among child welfare and runaway and homeless youth populations.

For child trafficking survivors who meet state eligibility requirements, many services are available through the following: Temporary Assistance for Needy Families (TANF), Medicaid, state Children's Health Insurance Program (CHIP), Substance Abuse and Mental Health Services Administration (SAMHSA) programs, Supplemental Nutrition Assistance Program (SNAP), Special Supplemental Nutrition Program for Women, Infants, and Children (WIC), medical screenings, and public housing programs. Some of these programs such as TANF, Medicaid/CHIP, and SNAP may have eligibility criteria related to citizenship or immigration status. HHS's ORR can help foreign national trafficking survivors to access similar benefits and some services, to the same extent as a refugee. A foreign national child survivor of human trafficking with no available parent or legal guardian in the USA and who holds an eligibility letter qualifies for ORR's Unaccompanied Refugee Minors (URM) program, even if the child does not have refugee status [46].

The Preventing Sex Trafficking and Strengthening Families Act was passed in 2014 and that year the Children's Bureau released an Information Memorandum (IM) on sex trafficking to inform states and tribes of the new federal legislation and its connection to child welfare (The IM is available at https://www.acf.hhs.gov/programs/cb/resource/im1403). In 2015, in an effort to build further support for implementing the Act, the Children's Bureau partnered with the White House to host the National Convening on Trafficking and Child Welfare, which gathered representatives from 52 states and jurisdictions.

4.2.1.7 Immigrant Assistance

Immigrant survivors of HT in the USA may have many needs: freedom from fear and protection for their families; access to medical care (including mental health services and treatment for substance use disorders), legal assistance, and certified translation services; shelter and housing; and an alternative form of employment. Part of the pathway to receive such services is the determination of their eligibility for a T-visa. The applicant must be or have been a victim of a severe form of trafficking and must be physically present in the USA due to being trafficked. Importantly, the latter clause excludes immigrants who came to the USA via other means but were trafficked once here. Additionally, a survivor applicant must be 18 years of age and older, must comply with any reasonable (not explicitly defined in the statute) request for assistance in the investigation of the crime or prosecution of the trafficker, and must provide evidence that they would suffer extreme hardship involving unusual and severe harm if removed from the USA. There is a "trauma exception" for this burden of proof offered to those who are unable to cooperate due to physical and psychological trauma or trauma-related psychiatric diagnoses.

The T-visa confidentiality provisions limit the trafficker's ability to influence the survivor's immigration case. Those provisions also prohibit the DHS and DOJ from making an adverse determination of admissibility or deportability based solely on information furnished by the trafficker. All the proceedings and filings are to be kept confidential. The benefits of the T-visa include a government sanctioned status and work authorization for 4 years as well as eligibility for public benefits as a refugee. The visa also allows the survivor to petition for family members, who may face danger of retaliation from the trafficker, to come to or stay in the USA. In addition, a survivor with the T-visa can apply to adjust their status to LPR (or "green card") after 3 years or upon conclusion of the investigation and prosecution of the criminal case. DHS can grant "continued presence" (CP), or temporary immigration relief to remain in the USA in order to aid the investigation and prosecution of their case. CP is commonly used when a survivor only wishes to remain in the USA for a brief period of time (e.g., to receive medical care). CP can only be requested by a federal law enforcement agency and it is granted at DHS discretion. More information about these visa types and DHS resources for survivors of trafficking and other crimes is available on the DHS website (http://www.uscis.gov/humanitarian/victims-human-trafficking-other-crimes).

Although the number of T-visas is capped at 5000 per year, the DHS issued only 447 T-visas to trafficking survivors in 2010 and 613 T-visas in 2014 [2]. These figures do not include LPR and US citizenship nor do they include derivative T-visas offered to family members of survivors, which are not included in the limit. This means that only about 10 % of the allotted T-visas are being issued; this resource under-utilization is thought to be largely due to the shortage of applications filed, though a significant percentage of applications are also denied [4, 47]. For example, 5202 T-visa applications were filed between 2002 and 2011, and of these only 3267 (63 %) were granted (http://www.state.gov/j/tip/rls/tiprpt/index.htm). Barriers to application include lack of awareness of the visas among trafficked persons; low identification of survivors among service providers and law enforcement; fear of deportation; the complexity of eligibility criteria, including the general requirement to be involved with the investigation and prosecution of the perpetrator; and the linguistic and literacy capabilities needed to complete the applications [2, 4, 47].

Another remedy is the U-visa: a non-immigration status for victims of certain qualifying crimes who have suffered mental or physical abuse and are able to contribute to a criminal investigation or the prosecution of the perpetrator(s). The crime must have occurred in the USA or violated US laws. The applicant is admissible to the USA under the current US immigration laws and regulations. Those who are not admissible may apply for a waiver. For example, trafficking might not be the only criminal trauma the victim endured. The victim may have initially been an asylum seeker and then became trafficked or victims may have previously been in abusive marriages. In the latter circumstance, the VAWA is applicable.[4] For U-visas, there is a statutory maximum of 10,000 visas issued each fiscal year (FY). In FY 2014, there were 17 approved principal applications in which trafficking was the qualifying crime. In 2015, DOL also expanded its U-visa program to consider certification requests for three additional qualifying crimes: forced labor,[5] fraud in foreign labor contracting, and extortion. However, NGOs report that trafficking victims continue to face difficulties obtaining U-visas, citing increased processing periods in some cases and overall demand that exceeded the annual statutory cap [2]. Between 2009 and 2012, there were 59,111 applications for U-visas, of which 36,108 were approved (61 % approval) [4].

According to the TVPRA, in order for human trafficking survivors to access the legal protection and services outlined above, the exploitative and commercial nature of the trafficking act must be demonstrated. This is especially important for foreigners who are trafficked within the USA and may want to access immigration relief. If

---

[4] VAWA protects partnered victims of all genders and sexual orientations.

[5] The Department of Labor recognizes forced labor as similar to trafficking but does not explicitly provide a legal differentiation in the Field Assistance Bulletin No. 2011–1—Addendum, Department of Labor, Wage and Hour Division April 2, 2015 Under 8 C.F.R. § 214.14(a).

a foreign national victim of sex trafficking cannot meet these burdens of proof and is thus not provided immigration relief, there are some possible alternatives. For example, they may apply for asylum consideration under the Refugee Act of 1980. This can be difficult, as individuals must apply within one year of entering the country, and must prove their "well-founded fear" of repatriation due to the likelihood of persecution based on race, religion, nationality, membership in a particular group, or political opinion [3]. If the applicant is unable to meet the one-year deadline, or a judge deems the applicant ineligible, they may also apply for withholding of removal, which provides fewer protections and demands a higher burden of proof, but prevents the individual's repatriation, and is not subject to a deadline or a judge's discretion. Similarly, the Convention Against Torture (CAT) protects against removal for those who are able to establish a high probability of being tortured if removed, and injury or abuse sustained during trafficking may constitute torture [48].

4.2.1.8   Justice for Trafficking Survivors

The essential question that remains for trafficking survivors is: How do we "repair" the lives of those who have been trafficked? Achieving "wholeness" is not just an emotional state but involves financial independence as well. Criminal restitution is mandatory in federal cases, but the first query is whether there is a federal criminal case, and if not, how might the case be reclassified as such. In some locales, police authorities may not view a case of domestic sex trafficking as a federal case. When the US government brings a trafficking prosecution under the TVPRA, 18 U.S.C. § 1593 states that the defendants (i.e., the traffickers) must pay the Criminal Restitution Order and/or civil judgment to the victims, as there are no federal funds available for this. The subsection of this statute defines this as the "full amount of the victim's losses" as restitution for back wages. Appropriately, restitution is not taxable. This amount may be more easily determined in the case of labor trafficking but is not so clear-cut in cases of sex trafficking: While labor activities have a legitimate market value in the USA, commercial sex does not [49].

It is worth noting that if prosecutors withdraw a criminal charge for the case, the victim still has the federal right to file a civil action. These civil action cases require a lower burden of proof and may recover damages and attorney fees beyond what is possible in a federal criminal case under the federal restitution statute. Civil litigation cases can be referred for pro bono counsel for T-visa applications. In addition, victims can sue under a pseudonym to avoid naming family members who may have been their traffickers. In sum, a civil trafficking suit still allows the victim their day in court, so to speak, and to hold unindicted perpetrators and co-conspirators accountable. Moreover, it provides a chance for greater economic independence [49].

In fiscal year 2014, 3,073 investigations related to human trafficking were opened by the various relevant federal government bodies, including ICE (987 investigations), the FBI (835), DOJ's Enhanced Collaborative Model task forces (1,083), the DOS (154), and the Department of Defense (14) [2]. During this time, the DOJ initiated 208 federal human trafficking prosecutions against 335 defendants. Of these prosecutions, 190 predominantly involved sex trafficking, though there was overlap with labor trafficking in several cases. That same fiscal year, 184 traffickers were convicted, of which 157 cases involved sex trafficking predominantly, though again there was overlap with labor trafficking [2].

4.3 Conclusions

The nature, scope, and magnitude of sex trafficking in the USA have catalyzed federal and state authorities to institute legal and systematic changes to address the problems faced by vulnerable populations within these borders. Importantly, this approach has not fully conceptualized trafficking as more than a problem of criminal justice: Anti-trafficking efforts must take into account trafficking's critical implications for population health and social welfare. Progress is also hampered by larger needs for collaboration, cooperation, and capacity building—important components identified by the Federal Strategic Action Plan. Moreover, human and fiscal resources are needed if initiatives are to be implemented effectively. A major challenge also lies in the fact that the demand for sex trafficking and the lucrative nature of this illicit business currently outpace interventions.

More comprehensive, accurate, and reliable sex trafficking data and a broader awareness of the problem can help authorities and service providers target their resources. This depends on a standardized vocabulary and indicators that can be shared among government bodies, nongovernmental entities, and the news media. Earlier identification of vulnerable individuals within families, communities, and institutions can mitigate the risk of exploitation, while public outreach can diminish the fear of stigma and discrimination that keep survivors from vital services. Improved identification and reporting would generate a virtual cycle, feeding a more sophisticated evidence base. More research about successful and unsuccessful interventions and prevention efforts, coupled with broad dissemination, can inform those who are poised to make a difference in legislatures, in service delivery systems, and in communities.

4.4 Recommendations

4.4.1 Research Needs

Based on the available literature, further research is needed on the following aspects of sex trafficking in the USA:

- The incidence and prevalence of sex trafficking. To enable further analysis and inform response, it would be ideal to collect data disaggregated at least by trafficking type, location, age, ethnicity, and gender of survivor

- The incidence and prevalence of the US-sourced sex trafficking compared to sex trafficking sourced from foreign countries
- The proximate and distal consequences of sex trafficking, and the ways these differ according to demographic characteristics of survivors, type of perpetrator, type of trafficking, and length of victimization
- The specific risk factors for and protective factors against the sex trafficking of males, and information on gender-related outcomes
- The specific risk factors associated with physical and cognitive disability, and outcomes related to these conditions
- The patterns of sex trafficking associated with street gang activity

4.4.2   Outreach, Community Engagement, and Basic Services

To better care for sex trafficking survivors, it would be advisable to:

- Improve public outreach to reduce stigma associated with being a sex trafficking survivor, to encourage care seeking, and to educate the public in recognizing signs of sex trafficking to improve identification
- Build capacity within the health, social services, and education workforce, as well as neighborhood associations and civil society, to identify survivors and vulnerable individuals early, and to refer them to appropriate care
- Support the use of electronic health systems, innovations in technology, and new classification systems, including ICD codes, to improve data capture and analysis
- Integrate symptomatology associated with trafficking within diagnostic tools as well as incorporate these into medical school curricula, and professional and specialty training programs [50]
- Monitor and evaluate interventions and prevention efforts to create a reliable evidence base with the ability to inform policy
- Improve capacity of medical, behavioral health, and social service sectors to respond to acute and long-term health needs of survivors

4.4.3   Legislation, Policy, and Justice

- Track the implementation of safe harbor laws as to long-term impact for sex trafficked minors
- Inform trafficked persons that if criminal proceedings fail to progress, civil action cases can be filed as a federal right and that in some circumstances *pro bono* services may be available [49]
- Document how effectively the US citizens access other benefit entitlement programs for federal crime victims and adapt policies and programs accordingly

4.5 Acronyms

Acronym	Full name
ACF	Administration for Children and Families
AFCARS	Adoption and Foster Care Analysis and Reporting System
ASPE	Assistant Secretary for Planning and Evaluation
CAT	Convention Against Torture
CBP	Customs and Border Protection
CHIP	Children's Health Insurance Program
CP	Continued presence
DHS	Department of Homeland Security
DOJ	Department of Justice
DOS	Department of State
ECPAT	End Child Prostitution, Child Pornography and Trafficking of Children for Sexual Purposes
FBI	Federal Bureau of Investigation
FLETC	Federal Law Enforcement Training Center
FY	Fiscal year
HHS	Department of Health and Human Services
HIV	Human Immunodeficiency Virus
HT	Human trafficking
ICD	International Statistical Classification of Diseases and Related Health Problems
ICE	Immigration and Customs Enforcement
ILO	International Labor Organization
IM	Information Memorandum
J/TIP	Office to Monitor and Combat Trafficking in Persons
LPR	Lawful Permanent Resident
NCMEC	National Center for Missing and Exploited Children
NHTRC	National Human Trafficking Resource Center
OJP	Office of Justice Programs
ORR	Office of Refugee Resettlement
OTIP	Office on Trafficking in Persons
OVC	Office for Victims of Crime
PITF	President's Interagency Task Force to Monitor and Combat Trafficking in Persons
SAMHSA	Substance Abuse and Mental Health Services Administration
SAP	Federal Strategic Action Plan on Services for Victims of Human Trafficking 2013–2017
SNAP	Supplemental Nutrition Assistance Program
SPOG	Senior Policy Operating Group
TANF	Temporary Assistance for Needy Families
TIP	Trafficking in Persons
TVPA	Trafficking Victims Protection Act

Acronym	Full name
TVPRA	Trafficking Victims Reauthorization Act
UNODC	United Nations Office on Drugs and Crime
USA	United States of America
USCIS	US Citizen and Immigration Services
VAWA	Violence Against Women Act
WG	Working Group
WIC	Special Supplemental Nutrition Program for Women, Infants, and Children

References

1. Clawson HJ, Layne M, Smalls K. Estimating human trafficking into the United States: development of a methodology: final phase two report. Fairfax, VA: ICF International; 2006.
2. US Department of State. Trafficking in persons report. Washington, DC: US Department of State; 2015.
3. Nawyn SJ, Birdal NBK, Glogower N. Estimating the extent of sex trafficking: problems in definition and methodology. Int J Sociol. 2013;43(3):55–71.
4. Siskin A, Wyler LS. Trafficking in persons: US policy and issues for congress. Washington, DC: Congressional Research Service; 2012.
5. United Nations Office on Drugs and Crime (UNODC). Global report on trafficking in persons. Vienna: United Nations; 2014.
6. United States Department of Justice. Assessment of U.S. Government activities to combat trafficking in persons. 2004.
7. US Department of State. Trafficking in persons report. Washington, DC: US Department of State; 2004.
8. International Labour Organization (ILO). ILO global estimate of forced labour: results and methodology. Geneva: International Labour Office; 2012.
9. Carpenter A. Measuring the nature and extent of gang involvement in sex trafficking in San Diego: executive summary. San Diego, CA: University of San Diego; 2015. https://www.sandiego.edu/peacestudies/documents/Executive%20Summary%20Human%20Trafficking%20Study%202015.pdf. Accessed 26 Feb 2016.
10. Clayton EW, Krugman RD, Simon P, editors. Confronting commercial sexual exploitation and sex trafficking of minors in the United States. Washington, DC: National Academies Press; 2013.
11. Estes RJ, Weiner NA. The commercial sexual exploitation of children in the US, Canada and Mexico. Philadelphia, PA: University of Pennsylvania, School of Social Work, Center for the Study of Youth Policy; 2001.
12. Lillie M. Invisible men: male victims of sex trafficking. Human Trafficking Search. 2014. http://humantraffickingsearch.net/wp/invisible-men-male-victims-of-sex-trafficking. Accessed 26 Feb 2016.
13. Clawson HJ, Dutch N, Solomon A, Grace LG. Human trafficking into and within the United States: a review of the literature. Washington, DC: Office of the Assistant Secretary for Planning and Evaluation, US Department of Human and Health Services; 2009.
14. National Human Trafficking Resource Center. Hotline statistics. http://traffickingresourcecenter.org/states. Accessed 26 Feb 2016.
15. Dank M, Khan B, Downey PM, et al. Estimating the size and structure of the underground commercial sex economy in eight major US cities. The Urban Institute (Ed.): The Urban Institute. 2014.

16. Lederer LJ. Sold for sex: the link between street gangs and trafficking in persons. The Protection Project Journal of Human Rights and Civil Society. 2011;1–20. http://www.global-centurion.org/wpcontent/uploads/2010/02/Sold-for-Sex-The-Link-between-Street-Gangs-and-TraffickinginPersons-1.pdf. Accessed 7 November 2016.
17. Banks D, Kyckelhahn T. Characteristics of suspected human trafficking incidents, 2008–2010. Washington, DC: US Department of Justice, Office of Justice Programs, Bureau of Justice Statistics; 2011.
18. Stolpe KE. MS-13 and domestic juvenile sex trafficking: causes, correlates, and solutions. Va J Soc Policy Law. 2014;21:341.
19. Kunze EI. Sex trafficking via the Internet: how international agreements address the problem and fail to go far enough. J High Tech Law. 2010;10:241.
20. Sykiōtou A. Trafficking in human beings: internet recruitment: misuse of the internet for the recruitment of victims of trafficking in human beings. Directorate General of Human Rights and Legal Affairs, Council of Europe. 2007.
21. Latonero M. Human trafficking online: the role of social networking sites and online classifieds. Center on Communication Leadership and Policy, USC Annenberg School for Communication and Journalism. 2011.
22. Conti A. The rape victim who is challenging one of the fundamental laws of the internet. Vice News. 2015. http://www.vice.com/read/how-a-rape-lawsuit-against-model-mayhem-turned-into-a-free-speech-case-826. Accessed 14 May 2016.
23. Polaris Project. Human trafficking in hotels and motels victim and location indicators. 2012. http://www.twolittlegirls.org/ufiles/Hotel%20and%20Motel%20Indicators%20AAG.pdf. Accessed 26 Feb 2016.
24. Polaris Project. Sex trafficking at truck stops. 2012. https://traffickingresourcecenter.org/sites/default/files/Sex%20Trafficking%20at%20Truck%20Stops%20AAG.pdf. Accessed 26 Feb 2016.
25. Reid JA. Exploratory review of route-specific, gendered, and age-graded dynamics of exploitation: applying life course theory to victimization in sex trafficking in North America. Aggress Violent Behav. 2012;17(3):257–71.
26. Gibbons P, Stoklosa H. Identification and treatment of human trafficking victims in the emergency department: a case report. J Emerg Med. 2016;50(5):715–9.
27. US Department of State. Trafficking in persons report. Washington, DC: US Department of State; 2012.
28. Yea S. Human trafficking: a geographical perspective. Geodate. 2010;23(3):2–6.
29. Sweet V. Trafficking in Native communities. Indian Country Today Media Network. 2015. http://indiancountrytodaymedianetwork.com/2015/05/24/trafficking-native-communities-160475. Accessed 14 Mar 2016.
30. Deer S. Relocation revisited: sex trafficking of native women in the United States. William Mitchell Law Rev. 2009;36:621.
31. DeMarban A. FBI-APD sex trafficking ring targets rural girls new to Anchorage. Alaska Dispatch News. 2010. http://www.adn.com/article/20101007/fbi-apd-sex-trafficking-rings--target-rural-girls-new-anchorage. Accessed 15 May 2016.
32. Acharya AK. The dynamic of internal displacement, forced migration, and vulnerable to trafficking in Mexico. J Hum Ecol. 2009;27(3):161–70.
33. Townsend M. 10,000 refugee children are missing, says Europol. The Guardian. 2016. http://www.theguardian.com/world/2016/jan/30/fears-for-missing-child-refugees. Accessed 26 Feb 2016.
34. Lederer LJ, Wetzel CA. Health consequences of sex trafficking and their implications for identifying victims in healthcare facilities. Ann Health Law. 2014;23:61.
35. Oram S, Stöckl H, Busza J, et al. Prevalence and risk of violence and the physical, mental, and sexual health problems associated with human trafficking: systematic review. PLoS Med. 2012;9(5), e1001224.

36. Zimmerman C, Yun K, Shvab I, et al. The health risks and consequences of trafficking in women and adolescents. Findings from a European study. London: London School of Hygiene & Tropical Medicine (LSHTM); 2003.
37. Raymond JG, Hughes DM, Gomez CJ. Sex trafficking of women in the United States. Amherst, MA: Coalition Against Trafficking in Women; 2001.
38. Dovydaitis T. Human trafficking: the role of the health care provider. J Midwifery Womens Health. 2010;55(5):462–7.
39. Richards K, Lyneham S. Help-seeking strategies of victim/survivors of human trafficking involving partner migration. Trends Issues Crime Crim Justice. 2014;468:1–10.
40. Coordination, Collaboration, Capacity: federal strategic action plan on services for victims of human trafficking in the United States 2013–2017. Washington, DC. 2014
41. National Colloquium. National Colloquium 2012 final report: an inventory and evaluation of the current shelter and services response to domestic minor sex trafficking. 2012.
42. Polaris Project. State laws and issues brief. 2016. https://polarisproject.org/state-laws-issue-briefs. Accessed 5 Apr 2016.
43. National Conference of Commissioners on Uniform State Laws. Prevention of remedies for human trafficking. 2011.
44. Polaris Project. Human trafficking issue brief: safe harbor, Fall 2015. 2015. https://polarisproject.org/sites/default/files/2015%20Safe%20Harbor%20Issue%20Brief.pdf. Accessed 12 Mar 2016.
45. Atella J, Schauben L, Connell E. Safe harbor: first year evaluation report. Wilder Research. 2015. https://www.documentcloud.org/documents/2514953-safe-harbor-first-year-evaluation-final-9-15.html. Accessed 5 Apr 2016.
46. Office of Refugee Resettlement. URM eligibility and application: state letter 15–07. 2015. http://www.acf.hhs.gov/programs/orr/resource/state-letter-15-07. Accessed 12 March 2016.
47. Okech D, Morreau W, Benson K. Human trafficking: improving victim identification and service provision. Int Soc Work. 2012;55(4):488–503.
48. Gott L, Bagder E, Hwang D, Kantemneni S. Guide to establishing the asylum eligibility of victims of human trafficking and forced marriage. Washington, DC: Human Rights USA; 2011.
49. Vandenberg ME. TVPA/Statutory Overview (Civil) and Labor. Presented at the Conference on Human Trafficking, American Bar Association/Section on Litigation, Washington, DC. 2013.
50. Stoklosa H, Grace AM, Littenberg N. Medical education on human trafficking. AMA J Ethics. 2014;17(10):914–21.

Chapter 5
The Ignored Exploitation: Labor Trafficking in the United States

Nicole Littenberg and Susie Baldwin

5.1   Introduction

A recent International Labor Organization (ILO) Report estimated that approximately 21 million people are trafficked at any given point in time, generating an estimated $150 billion in illegal profits per year [1]. This 2012 report found that 90 % of these individuals were trafficked by private enterprises or individuals (versus by nation states as prison labor or by state or rebel armed forces). Of people trafficked for private enterprise, 68 % of these, or 14.2 million individuals worldwide, were trafficked for forced labor in industries such as agriculture, construction, domestic work, and manufacturing [2]. In the United States, trafficked individuals are found in these sectors as well as in a variety of other legitimate and illegitimate businesses, including restaurants, hotels, janitorial services, nail salons, food processing, forestry, the fishing industry, peddling rings, and the drug trade. Notably, some forms of human trafficking fall outside the definition of forced labor, including forced marriage or adoption, and trafficking for the purposes of organ removal [3].

The hidden nature of this crime makes it very difficult to obtain reliable prevalence data [4, 5]. The US Department of State Trafficking in Persons (TIP) Report of 2004 estimated that between 14,500 and 17,500 people are trafficked into the United States annually, and this number has been widely repeated despite a lack of clarity about the methodology used to attain it [6, 7]. Free the Slaves in that same year reported that at

The original version of this chapter was revised. An erratum to this chapter can be found at DOI: 10.1007/978-3-319-47824-1_25

N. Littenberg (✉)
Pacific Survivor Center, P.O. Box 3535, Honolulu, HI 96811, USA
e-mail: NLittenberg@PSCHawaii.org

S. Baldwin
HEAL Trafficking, P.O. Box 31602, 3001 North Broadway, Los Angeles, CA 90031, USA
e-mail: SBaldwin@healtrafficking.org

any given time there are at least 10,000 forced laborers working in the United States adding that "it is likely that the actual number reaches into the tens of thousands [8, 9]." A 2006 study funded by the National Institute of Justice (NIJ), the research arm of the US Department of Justice, examined prevalence methodologies and estimated that 46,849 individuals are trafficked for labor into the United States across the Southwest border [7]. Another NIJ funded study in 2013 found that approximately 31 % of unauthorized[1] Spanish-speaking migrant workers in San Diego county experienced conditions that met the legal definition of human trafficking [10].

While most survivors of trafficking in the latter NIJ study entered the country without documentation, other people are trafficked following entry on temporary work, student, tourist, diplomatic, and other visas. A study of 122 labor trafficking survivors at four victim service agencies around the United States found that 71 % had entered the country on temporary visas, most commonly "H-2A visas for agricultural work and H-2B visas for jobs in hospitality, construction, and restaurants" [11]. Regardless of their means of entry, people trafficked in the USA are often absorbed into unregulated, poorly regulated, or underground sectors of the economy, where wage, safety, and health violations routinely occur [8]. The large service industry that drives much of the US economy also places many workers here at risk for exploitation [12].

Immigrants trafficked into or within the United States come from all different parts of the globe, with large numbers originally hailing from Mexico, Central America, Asia, and Africa. US citizens and lawful permanent residents, including children, also experience labor trafficking within US borders. Labor trafficking survivors have also been identified in American Samoa, Guam, the Commonwealth of the Northern Mariana Islands, and the Commonwealth of Puerto Rico [13]. The underlying social and economic conditions that drive human trafficking are fundamentally the same regardless of the region of origin or the industry into which people are trafficked: Upstream determinants of health such as lack of educational and employment opportunities, poverty, racism, and violence can lead people to accept work in dirty, dangerous, demeaning, or low-paying jobs or to migrate from their homes in search of a better job or a new life [14].

This chapter provides a brief history of labor trafficking in the United States, examines why sex trafficking receives more attention than labor trafficking, and argues that a public health and labor rights approach to trafficking, with improved conditions and augmented protections for all workers, will ultimately serve to reduce exploitation and trafficking. We review examples of modern day cases of labor trafficking and highlight existing successful programs that address the issue from a public health perspective, creating safer conditions for workers in industries rampant with exploitation and abuse. We urge US policy makers and anti-trafficking advocates to support strategies that prevent human trafficking and to provide resources that allow for a more robust, interdisciplinary approach that supports the role of the health care system and health care providers in prevention and redress.

---

[1] The term "unauthorized" reflects the characterizations used in the referenced study and does not reflect the opinions of the chapter authors or book editors.

5.2   Discussion

5.2.1   The Ignored Exploitation

Despite the greater prevalence of labor trafficking on a global basis, in the public policy, criminal law, research, health care, and public awareness arenas there remains a greater emphasis on sex trafficking than labor trafficking [15–18]. Educational initiatives, advocacy campaigns, and media portrayals disproportionately emphasize sex trafficking, and the majority of human trafficking cases identified and prosecuted in the United States have involved sex trafficking [15, 19]. In 2014, the US Department of Justice filed 208 cases of human trafficking, of which 18 involved labor trafficking and 190 sex trafficking, with 335 individual defendants, 45 in labor cases and 290 in sex trafficking cases. These prosecutions resulted in 184 convictions, of which 27 were for labor trafficking [20]. The law enforcement and criminal justice focus on sex trafficking case finding and prosecution at federal, state, and local levels results in official statistics that skew perceptions of trafficking, perpetuating the notion among both professionals and the lay public that only a small percent of trafficking cases in this country involve labor other than commercial sex work. In a vicious cycle, lack of awareness and response to labor trafficking means that fewer cases are identified, prosecuted, and publicized.

The emphasis on sex over labor trafficking dates back to the beginnings of the anti-trafficking movement, with the United Nations White Slavery Conventions of 1904 and the United States "White-Slave Traffic Act" of 1910, both of which intended to protect white women from recruitment into the commercial sex trade [19]. In 1921, the League of Nations renamed the crime with the adoption of the "Convention for the Suppression of the Traffic in Women and Children" [21]. This new code removed the racial and ethnic emphasis of earlier laws and expanded legislation to include international victims; later conventions, including the 1949 Convention for the Suppression of the Traffic in Persons and of the Exploitation of the Prostitution of Others, finally included men, but still focused solely on the sex trade [22]. It was not until decades later that the term "trafficking" began to also refer to forced labor.

Even with this official incorporation of labor trafficking into US and international protocols, preferential interest in and attention to sex trafficking persists. One basis for this has been a conflation of trafficking with commercial sex. Anti-trafficking, women's rights, and faith-based groups have increasingly become involved in anti-prostitution efforts, frequently deploying educational and media campaigns that portray commercial sex and trafficking with false equivalence [18]. Furthermore, the "innocent victim" narrative, of a naïve helpless female who needs to be rescued from the sex trade by a savior, drives many people into anti-trafficking advocacy and contributes to disproportionate interest in sex trafficking as a moral cause. While this narrative may make media headlines and help NGOs raise funds, it perpetuates stereotypes about trafficking, diverts resources from effective prevention and intervention strategies, and ignores underlying vulnerabilities. The focus on rescue of innocents suggests that "complicit" victims, such as those who initially consented to an interaction with their trafficker, have violated laws during the course of their trafficking, escaped trafficking on their own, or are unwilling to cooperate in the prosecution of their trafficker, are less deserving of protections [23]. Public discourse around trafficking in the United States rarely touches upon complex underlying economic and political issues, such as the role that our demand for cheap products and labor plays in enslaving people around the world, and the protection and enforcement of immigrant rights and worker rights.

Despite the lack of focus on labor trafficking in the United States, it is a serious human rights violation that has a devastating impact on the health of individuals and communities [24]. Labor trafficked individuals are exposed to infectious diseases, unsanitary living conditions, unsafe working conditions, inadequate nutrition, threats, and physical and sexual violence. Traffickers (often referred to by survivors as "employers," despite the exploitative nature of the relationship) also utilize a diverse range of nonphysical coercion tactics to entrap and manipulate their workers, including deception and psychological manipulation [25, 26]. The physical, sexual, and emotional abuse inflicted upon people trafficked for labor often results in significant acute and chronic medical conditions and mental health disorders [27, 28]. While more research is needed on the public health effects of human trafficking, studies of survivors demonstrate that they experience many of the same physical, mental, emotional, and sexual health consequences, regardless of the type of trafficking they experience [28].

The current US approach to labor trafficking has proven ineffective in the prosecution of perpetrators, the provision of relief for survivors, and in reducing the prevalence of the crime [9, 16]. Diversion of resources into ineffective anti-trafficking strategies, such as "john stings," in which police employ decoy operations to ensnare purchasers of sex, prevents serious consideration of other, more effective means to protect US workers, reduce human trafficking incidence, and support survivors [29–32]. For example, US agencies tasked with protecting worker safety, such as the Occupational Safety and Health Administration, remain perpetually underfunded and lack sufficient state and local counterparts to support inspection and enforcement in most jurisdictions [33, 34].

5.2.2   History, Definitions, and Laws

Although the term "human trafficking" only came into favor in the past century, slavery was first documented as early as 2000 B.C.E. in Sumer and has persisted in various forms in most civilizations since that time [35]. The Transatlantic Slave trade began in the 1400s when the Portuguese began importing slaves from the west coast of Africa [35]. The first slaves were brought to the this land, now known as the United States, in 1619, and over the ensuing centuries over 12 million people of all ages were victimized. Despite the theoretical emancipation of slaves through the Civil War, many former slaves were re-enslaved in the South in the decades following the Emancipation Proclamation, and indentured servitude persisted well into the twentieth century, through sharecropping, peonage, and convict leasing.[2] Various groups were impacted by these practices, including immigrant laborers, blacks, poor whites, Native Americans, and Native Hawaiians. Indentured servitude of Chinese immigrants was specifically authorized by law in 1852 by California Senate bill #63, "An Act to Enforce Contracts and Obligations to Perform Work and Labor" commonly known as the "Coolie Bill" [36].

Federal statute 18 US Code 444 criminalized peonage in 1867, but this statute was rarely used and forced labor remained common and rarely prosecuted until the Second World War. In 1939, the Civil Rights Section of the Department of Justice was created, with a focus on labor rights. In 1941, Attorney General Francis Biddle, with Circular No. 3591, issued a directive to the Department of Justice which strengthened criminal penalties related to the practices of involuntary servitude, slavery, and peonage [37].

Since the 1990s, the term "human trafficking" increasingly began to encompass not only forced commercial sex but also all of these other various forms of exploitative and forced labor. The crime of "trafficking" was further defined at the fourth United Nations World Conference in 1995, and since that time several international and national laws have emerged to better define and address human trafficking: In 2000, both the United Nations Protocol to Prevent, Suppress and Punish Trafficking in Persons, Especially Women and Children, and the United States Trafficking Victims Protection Act (TVPA) were enacted. These instruments defined and criminalized human trafficking.

The TVPA defined labor trafficking as "the recruitment, harboring, transportation, provision, or obtaining of a person for labor or services, through the use of force, fraud, or coercion for the purpose of subjection to involuntary servitude, peonage, debt bondage, or slavery" [38]. The UN Protocol defined TIP as:

> the recruitment, transportation, transfer, harbouring or receipt of persons, by means of the threat or use of force or other forms of coercion, of abduction, of fraud, of deception, of the abuse of power or of a position of vulnerability or of the giving or receiving of payments or benefits to achieve the consent of a person having control over another person, for the purpose of exploitation. Exploitation shall include, at a minimum, …forced labour or services, slavery or practices similar to slavery, servitude or the removal of organs [39].

The Protocol goes on to state that the consent of the victim is irrelevant; the TVPA does not include a similar clause.

---

[2] Sharecropping involved landowners renting a plot of land to laborers in exchange for a share of the crops. The landlords often also rented or sold equipment and supplies to the worker on credit, prevented the worker from selling to others, and took an unpredictable and disproportionately large share of the crops, effectively trapping the worker through debt. Peonage involved poor whites and blacks being arrested for often minor or imagined violations, and then being forced to work for a local businessman to pay off the fines and court fees. In convict leasing, businesses could "lease" convicts from states and counties in exchange for feeding and housing them. Leased convicts were forced to work long hours and conditions were often deplorable. (Wagner, Nancy O'Briem. *Slavery by Another Name: History Background*. Bluestem Heritage Group. Twin Cities Public Television 2012. PBS.)

5.2.3 Labor Trafficking Case Studies

One of the first publicized cases of labor trafficking in the United States occurred in Southern California at the El Monte garment factory, in which apartments were turned into a sweatshop. In that case, 72 Thai workers, mostly impoverished farmers from rural Thailand, were approached with promises of legitimate jobs in the United States [40]. They took out loans to pay the recruitment fees, and upon arrival in California, their passports were confiscated and they were locked into the El Monte complex, which had the outward appearances of a typical apartment complex. In reality, it was comprised of two buildings surrounded by barbed wire and 24 h armed guards [40, 41]. The workers slept in filthy quarters, were forced to sew clothing for 16 to 18 h per day, had to buy all of their personal items at inflated prices at the complex store, and were never allowed to leave the compound or communicate freely with family back home [42]. They were threatened with deportation and harm to their families if they attempted escape.

In 1995, law enforcement raided the compound and rescued the workers, some of whom had been there for as long as 7 years. At the time, there was no specific federal law defining or outlawing human trafficking, and the workers were removed to an Immigration and Naturalization Service (INS) detention facility pending possible deportation [43]. A community based organization, the Thai Community Development Center, and other immigrant rights advocacy groups organized to campaign for the workers' freedom. Upon their release 9 days later, these groups provided the workers with housing, interpretation services, health care referrals, and legal assistance [44]. Law enforcement and criminal justice officials provided immigration relief by classifying the victims as material witnesses to a crime and offering them the opportunity to apply for the S-visa, typically used for criminal informants [40]. Several of the traffickers were convicted in criminal court, and the survivors prevailed in a civil settlement. As a result of this trafficking case and the media attention it received, the T-Nonimmigrant Status (T-visa) was established.

Another labor case involved trafficking for agricultural work into multiple states. In 2010, the US Department of Justice filed the largest human trafficking case in the US history: They asserted that approximately 400 Thai workers were brought to the USA from 2004 to 2005 under false pretenses by Global Horizons and its Chief Executive Officer Mordeai Yosef Orian [45]. According to the indictment, the workers had annual family incomes of approximately $1,000 and were recruited with false promises of high wages and up to 3 years of continued employment [45]. Despite their highly limited resources, they were charged recruitment fees ranging from $9,500 to $26,500 for their passage and employment. They borrowed money to pay the fees, often using family land as collateral, and were brought to the United States under the H-2A visa program. The indictment alleged that the workers were led to believe that serious harm or physical restraint would befall them or others if they did not perform physical labor or services. They were threatened with arrest, deportation repatriation, homelessness, and loss of family land as a result of debts unless they continued to work for their employer.

The indictment also alleged that 15 workers—who were sent to Lucedale, Mississippi to perform agricultural labor in December 2013—were told by a Global Horizons supervisor that if they left, they would be killed [45]. Supervisors coerced them to work more rapidly by pressing a stick to the back of their necks; they were told if they left the work site, they would be arrested and captured. They worked 7 days a week and were not allowed to leave their housing unescorted [45]. Similar groups of workers were recruited to Global Horizons farms in Bakersfield, California and Yakima, Washington [45]. Workers were told not to socialize with outsiders and threatened that if they complained they would be shot. A supervisor carried a small gun in the waistband of his pants where it was directly visible [45]. Ultimately, in 2012, the Justice Department requested dismissal of the Global Horizons prosecution, even though three of the eight persons originally indicted pled guilty. The cases were dismissed because the "government [was] unable to prove the elements of the charged offense beyond a reasonable doubt" [46].

Despite the failure of the criminal case, the US Equal Employment Opportunity Commission (EEOC) filed suits against Global Horizons for both Hawaii and Washington and prevailed in both. In 2014, a federal judge in Hawaii found Global Horizons liable for $8.7 million due to its treatment of the farmworkers. The EEOC described that the workers:

> had their movements monitored and passports confiscated; had production quotas imposed that did not apply to non-Thai workers; were denied adequate food and water; and forced into unsanitary, overcrowded living conditions. Those who complained of the pattern or practice of discrimination and harassment were retaliated against, with many forced to quit or flee as a result [47].

In 2016, another federal judge ordered Global Horizons to pay $7.6 million for its treatment of Thai workers in Washington State, commenting that their practices were "reprehensible" and caused the Thai farmworkers "fear, anxiety, anger, intimidation, humiliation, shame, and … an unrelenting sense of imprisonment" [48]. This case starkly illustrates challenges in the criminal prosecution of trafficking as well as the lack of justice for many of those victimized, despite their willingness to come forward. It also reveals the extraordinary pitfalls of the current H-2A visa system: Trafficked persons were indebted due to the recruitment fees and did not have the option to change employers due to their visa status [49].

Many cases of labor trafficking in the USA involve "mom and pop" operations, or trafficking of a single worker or a small group of workers. One example from California involved a retired teacher who was trafficked to the United States from a country in Asia [50]. She had incurred debt sending her children to college, and in an attempt to pay this down, she accepted a job as a caregiver and travel companion for an elderly woman, a position for which a relative recruited her. After arriving in the United States, she was told that she would actually be working as a housekeeper and was sent to Los Angeles. At the Los Angeles International airport, she approached a security guard for assistance finding her way, at which time her new employer arrived and angrily instructed her not to talk to anyone. Her passport was confiscated for "safekeeping," she was not allowed to call her family for a month, and after that could only speak with them under direct observation. She worked an average of 18 h a day and was paid $300 in 1 year. She experienced verbal and physical abuse, including insults, hair pulling, slapping, spanking, and having hard objects thrown at her. She was also denied food and had to eat the slices of chicken and vegetables that she fed the family dogs. She was only permitted to leave the condominium to walk the dogs and remove the trash. During these excursions, she befriended a 13-year-old neighbor and another neighbor's nanny. At one point, she showed these neighbors injuries that she had received at the hand of her "employer." These encounters led the neighbors to contact law enforcement for assistance. Police later came to the door of the home where she was trafficked, but she was unable to speak with them because her traffickers were present. After this encounter, the traffickers contacted Immigration and Customs Enforcement (ICE) in an attempt to deport her. However, when ICE and law enforcement returned to the house, they did so to free her, forcing the trafficker to return her passport in the process. The traffickers were tried and convicted of involuntary servitude, negligence, and fraud, and were ordered to pay financial damages. While the survivor in this case never received the money she was legally awarded, unlike many trafficked persons she earned the satisfaction of bringing the case against her exploiters to trial, and having a jury validate her complaints against them.

This case illustrates the circumstances that create vulnerability to trafficking among domestic workers, including a lack of labor protections, as described below. Many domestic workers are isolated, living in the home of their employer; they may speak a different language and have little or no social support in the community. This case also highlights that labor trafficking cases can be successfully identified by average citizens, disrupted by law enforcement, and ended through prosecution.

5.2.4   The Current US Approach to Human Trafficking and Its Limitations

The current US approach to human trafficking is largely based on a criminal justice paradigm, which focuses on the 3P's: Prosecution, Protection, and Prevention [51]. Although more recent versions of the TVPA have attempted to boost services for trafficking survivors, the primary federal focus remains on increasing prosecutions and sentencing for traffickers [16, 52, 53]. In fact, multiple observers have argued that the criminal justice approach has fallen short on all three of its stated goals [52]. From a prosecution standpoint, the Department of Justice pursued only 45 labor trafficking defendants in 18 cases in 2014, resulting in 27 convictions [20]. These numbers represent only a slight increase from prior years; for example, from 2009 to 2011, the DOJ brought an average of 24 labor trafficking cases annually [54]. Even including numbers from the Federal Bureau of Investigation (FBI) and ICE, who in 2014 had 84 and 828 convictions, respectively (including all sex, labor, domestic, and international cases), the number of prosecutions and convictions of labor trafficking offenses in the United States remains extraordinarily low in relation to the estimated number of trafficked workers in this country.

With regard to protection, the TVPA provides for shelter, health care, financial assistance, social and legal services for certified victims. Under the TVPA, the US Department of Health and Human Services (HHS) has the responsibility of certifying international victims of trafficking. As of 2015, the Department of Labor (DOL) Wage and Hour Division (WHD) can also certify victims [55]. The DOJ's Office of Justice Programs' Office for Victims of Crime (OVC) and HHS provide funding for services to survivors of trafficking, including sex and labor, immigrant and domestic victims. From July 1, 2013 through June 30, 2014, this program served 2,782 victims of trafficking nationwide, of whom 1,528 were foreign-born. Of those victims served, 1,065 survived solely labor trafficking and 157 survived both sex and labor trafficking [20]. Again, the number of individuals served is only a fraction of those estimated to be impacted.

In terms of immigration relief, the TVPA provides for T-non Immigrant Status (the "T-visa"), which allows temporary residency for 4 years and provides a path to legal permanent residency. The T-visa requirements stipulate that the applicant must: (1) have a physical presence within the USA, Samoa, the Commonwealth of the Northern Marianas, or at a port of entry, (2) be a victim of a severe form of human trafficking, (3) comply with any reasonable request to participate in the investigation or prosecution of the trafficker, and (4) demonstrate extreme hardship involving severe and unusual harm if removed from the USA [56].

According to the US Attorney General's Report, in FY 2014, 944 victims applied for T-visas, 613 were approved and 153 were denied (some applications are approved or denied in subsequent years) [20]. This number of approvals mirrors the yearly approvals from 2010 to 2014, with an average of 627 per year. This is far below the annual federal cap of 5,000 T-visas and the estimated tens of thousands of trafficked laborers in the United States, many of whom are foreign-born [5, 7, 10].

The T-visa is meant to provide relief for trafficked persons, but its accessibility has been limited for a variety of reasons. The administrative complexities of the T-visa application process require the assistance of an immigration attorney. Many trafficking survivors, even if they are no longer controlled by their trafficker, are afraid to come forward. Many feel guilty or ashamed, or fear detention or deportation. Most do not understand that their circumstances constitute "trafficking," while others are unaware that immigration remedies exist for them. Those that contemplate coming forward with their stories may fear that the authorities will not listen to or believe them, or that the facts and evidence in the case will not meet federal standards for a T-visa. Some survivors are unwilling or unable to apply for the T-visa due to the TVPA requirement that they comply with "reasonable requests" to participate in the investigation and/or prosecution of their trafficker(s) [57]. Notably, there exists an exception to this rule for those who are "unable to cooperate due to physical or psychological trauma" [58]. A medical professional, social worker, or victim advocate can attest to the survivors' mental state in a letter that accompanies the T-visa application [59]. Pursuing justice from one's trafficker can potentially bring relief and reward, but it can also create enormous emotional stress for survivors, resulting in anxiety, depression, nightmares, and signs of Post-Traumatic Stress Disorder (PTSD) as well as somatic symptoms such as headaches, abdominal pain, and anorexia [60]. Survivors who pursue prosecution, or who cooperate with the prosecution in any capacity, often face risks not only to their own lives and well-being but also to their families outside the USA [61]. Retaliation from traffickers is a real threat, and the US government has little to offer survivors and their families in terms of protection [62].

Not only has a criminal justice approach neither sufficiently punished perpetrators of this crime nor protected its victims, the third "P," prevention, has been neglected as a strategy under the TVPA. For example, in 2015, the US Congress passed and President Barack Obama signed the Justice for Victims of Trafficking Act (JVTA), which increases funding for prosecution of human traffickers and law enforcement efforts, and creates a fund to support services for survivors [63]. That same year, however, Congress failed to authorize the Runaway and Homeless Youth Act, which provides funds to keep runaway and homeless youth safe and housed [64]. The legislative branch thereby refused to fund a key preventive strategy to reduce child trafficking [65], despite public proclamations that they were making great strides to help trafficked children through the JVTA.

In fact, the entire framework of the TVPA is inadequate for prevention, as it ignores the underlying conditions that cause human trafficking, and labor trafficking in particular. As the socio-ecological framework of public health captures, vulnerability to exploitation results from an interplay of risk factors and a lack of protective elements, at the individual, family, community, and societal levels. Economic, legal, and social factors [66], including poverty, discrimination, inadequate educational and employment opportunities, and insufficient protections for workers, must all be addressed in order to reduce and eliminate human trafficking. As Lin Leam of the ILO has explained,

> The challenge we face is to address the real root causes of trafficking – the reasons why people migrate and are trafficked and the reasons why other people are able to traffic them. It is not enough merely to regulate the sex market; we need to address the areas of vulnerability [67].

Efforts to tackle trafficking must focus on the supply side of *all* industries in which people are trafficked, and as Lo notes, must address the social determinants of health "with measures aimed at addressing the conditions, in particular poverty and unemployment, that drive people to leave their home in the first place" [67].

5.2.5   Other US Labor Policies that Contribute to Trafficking

Not only have current approaches failed to prosecute, prevent, or protect, but many US policies, programs, and regulations inadvertently promote trafficking. For example, one US program that has been associated with severe labor abuses and labor trafficking is the H-2 Guest Visa Worker program. This program allows employers who are unable to fill positions with domestic workers to bring in foreign workers on a temporary basis. H-2A visas are used for agricultural workers, and H-2B are generally for workers in other industries such as forestry, seafood processing, hospitality, and construction. In 2012, over 55,000 H-2A and 75,000 H-2B visas were requested [68]. The number of workers actually employed in specific occupations, however, is not known [69].

With H-2 visas, the maximum length of stay is 3 years, after which time the worker must return to their home country. Workers are required to remain with the employer who arranged for the visa. Despite laws that give the workers federal rights and protections through the DOL, abuses of workers in this system are rampant. Some experience a range of abuses even during recruitment, such as being charged exorbitant fees or being recruited for jobs that do not exist [68]. Workers incur substantial debt in order to pay these fees in their home countries, as occurred in the Global Horizons case. They are routinely cheated out of wages, held virtually captive by employers or labor brokers who seize their documents, are forced to live in squalid conditions, and are denied medical benefits for on-the-job injuries [69, 70]. Between 2012 and 2013, service providers assisted 340 survivors of human trafficking who had been identified in typical H-2 industries [69].

Human trafficking also occurs in industries in which workers are specifically excluded from the standard US labor protections afforded those in other sectors. For example, agricultural workers in the United States are excluded from workplace protections under federal law, such as those provided by the National Labor Relations Act (NLRA), which guarantees the right to organize, and overtime protections under the Fair Labor Standards Act (FLSA) [71, 72]. Furthermore, agricultural workers in the United States receive low wages and often earn sub-poverty incomes [73]. More than half of all farmworkers in the United States are undocumented migrants, and about 4 % are brought into the country under the H-2A visa program [74]. Many of these workers are unaware of the rights they are afforded by the US law and may also fear deportation.

Domestic workers are also excluded from several key federal laws that provide labor protections. They are fully or partially excluded from: the NLRA; the FLSA, which sets federal minimum wage, maximum hours, and overtimes; the Occupational Safety and Health Act, which ensures "safe and healthful working conditions" [75, 76]; and civil rights laws including the Americans with Disabilities Act, the Age Discrimination in Employment Act, and Title VII, which bars employment discrimination on the basis of race, color, religion, sex, or national origin [77]. Compounding this lack of protections is that domestic workers are often hired without a work contract, through a private agreement between the individual employer and the worker. Individuals hiring domestic workers often do not consider themselves employers, and therefore may not think it is their responsibility to provide the people working in their home with a living wage and benefits.

It is no coincidence that two sectors of the economy with very weak worker protections, agricultural and domestic work, are also among the industries where trafficking is most commonly found [8]. These two industries share a common history in that these positions were typically filled by "lower caste" workers [78, 79]. These included poor whites, black slaves, and eventually immigrant workers from Asia, Latin America, and elsewhere. Although a full discussion of this history is beyond the scope of this chapter, these racial and class distinctions between the "employer" and the "employee" created an "otherness" over the centuries which facilitated mistreatment and abuse [79]. Current US laws and policies have only served to perpetuate this power dynamic, by denying workers in these two particular industries the protections that most other workers are afforded, thereby increasing their vulnerability to exploitation and trafficking. The "invisibility" of these workers, both culturally, as individuals lacking equal treatment, and physically, as many of them are isolated on farms and in private homes, further exacerbates the problem. In order to reduce the incidence of trafficking and exploitation, it is imperative that these loopholes be closed and these and all workers have access to the full spectrum of labor protections, rights, and remedies.

5.2.6   Health Impact of Labor Trafficking

Although the vast majority of research studies on the health impact of trafficking have focused on sexual exploitation, the impact of labor trafficking on physical and mental health can also be severe [80]. Pre-trafficking health issues may include chronic medical conditions such as diabetes and hypertension or infectious diseases that are endemic in the region of origin, such as tuberculosis, malaria, and hepatitis [81]. During the transportation phase (if movement is involved), trafficked individuals are at risk for violence, drowning, suffocation, starvation, and additional exposure to infectious diseases. At the destination stage, survivors may live and work in unsanitary, overcrowded conditions, lack adequate nutrition or clean water, be exposed to unsafe working conditions and chemicals without safety training or protective equipment, and have limited to no access to health care. Explicit or implicit threats to their families, uncertainty about immigration status, and risk for deportation all contribute to the psychological stressors on exploited laborers [82]. Physical abuse and sexual assaults are also common. In a recent case series report in the United Kingdom (UK), 40 % of the 35 trafficking victims surveyed had experienced physical violence while in the trafficking situation; 7 % witnessed violence against their family members; 40 % had been threatened with violence against themselves or their families; and 30 % reported being deprived of food and water [27].

The health consequences of labor trafficking can include progression of untreated chronic diseases and infections; neurological damage; dental infections and injuries; eye injuries, infections, and strain; respiratory and cardiovascular illness; gastrointestinal issues; gynecological infections and injuries; musculoskeletal conditions such as back and neck pain, tendon strains and injuries, and untreated skeletal fractures; and mental health disorders such as anxiety, depression, and PTSD. The same study from the UK found that 81 % of participants reported one or more symptom of poor physical health and 57 % experienced PTSD [27].

5.2.7 Role of the Health Care Provider

Although many trafficked laborers have limited access to health care while under the control of the trafficker, traffickers or their agents may take trafficked laborers to a health care provider when their injuries or illnesses are so severe that they are unable to work productively [50]. Even in the presence of a healthcare provider, however, many will not disclose the trafficking situation; they may be afraid of the trafficker, fear harm to themselves or their families, be unaware that they are victims of crime, or believe that the healthcare provider will report them to law enforcement and have them arrested, detained, or deported. It is thus imperative that health care personnel learn to recognize the situation and take appropriate steps. Many educational programs, websites, and publications describe the "red flags" and "questions to ask" of patients who may be trafficked. These "red flags" typically include lack of identification documents; submissive or fearful behavior; a third party insisting on being present and interpreting; unfamiliarity with the community in which they work or live; signs of malnourishment or physical or sexual abuse [83, 84]. Useful screening questions include those surrounding living and working conditions, possession of identification documents, freedom of movement, debts, threats, and physical and sexual abuse [85, 86].

Recognizing trafficked patients is not enough, however, nor is simply providing medical care. Health care providers should also learn about the resources available for trafficked people in their community. They must have an understanding of the risks trafficked persons face, both personally and to their families. If the patient presents in the clinical setting with the trafficker, care must be taken not to alert the trafficker of the suspicion of trafficking: This could lead not only to removal of the patient from care but also to more severe ramifications such as refusal to bring them for future care and even retribution. Most organizations and experts agree that finding a subtle way to separate the patient from the trafficker, talking to them with an appropriate health care facility provided interpreter if necessary, and providing them with information about available assistance are critical steps in the approach to a potentially trafficked person or trafficking survivor.

Contacting law enforcement must be weighed carefully with an awareness of potential unintended consequences and discussion of these with the patient. One danger is that if a foreign-born patient is identified as being trafficked but does not meet the criteria for a T-visa, and a health care provider contacts law enforcement in an attempt to "rescue" the patient, that action may actually lead to their deportation. Similarly, a call to law enforcement to assist a youth victim of trafficking could result in the arrest and detention of that youth for crimes previously committed, even crimes that occurred during a trafficking situation. Therefore, these authors recommend that one of the first points of contact for suspected trafficked persons identified in the health care setting be a local nongovernmental organization (NGO) or advocate and/or an immigration attorney who is familiar with this issue. The National Human Trafficking Resource Center has a 24-h hotline (1-888-373-7888) that can assist with suspected cases of trafficking. Local advocates or the national hotline can advise whether victim services specialists from the Department of Homeland Security or the FBI may be of assistance.

5.2.8   Forensic Evaluations

Forensic examinations are conducted by health care providers to document any signs or symptoms of trafficking, including histories of fraud, abuse, exploitation, deprivation, or unsafe working conditions as well as any physical or mental sequelae of the trafficking. In a forensic examination, all physical injuries are described, with photographs if possible and with patient consent, and with descriptions of the mechanism of injury. Patients are also screened for mental health disorders such as PTSD, anxiety, and depression [87].

Foreign-born trafficking victims who apply for a T-visa must supply documentation to support their histories of "severe forms of trafficking." Despite the flaws of the current systems that are described above, until the criteria are changed at a federal level, the health care provider can play a critical role in helping foreign-born survivors meet this threshold. Being available to write affidavits, submiting photographs and records, and even appearing in court can impact whether a survivor is approved for a T-visa and can impact the outcome of civil and criminal proceedings.

5.2.9   Resources

A patient who is undergoing the T-visa evaluation process ("pre-certified") may have access to medical care, social services, and financial assistance for a limited time in certain jurisdictions. Those who are able to meet the threshold and prove "severe form of trafficking" will become "certified," which allows them to work legally and access government-sponsored insurance (Medicaid). Unlike other immigrants, who must wait 5 years for these benefits, those who are awarded a T-visa have the same immediate benefits as refugees, without the waiting period. They will also be able to apply for a green card in 3 years, sponsor their families to the USA, and may pursue a path to citizenship, if desired [58]. For these patients, the health care provider's role is supportive: to meet the ongoing medical and mental health needs in a trauma-informed way, to communicate with the patient's attorneys to ensure that medical–legal needs are met, and to encourage the patient to follow up on a regular basis with medical care, behavioral health care, and their attorneys.

The stringent and challenging nature of the T-visa process as described above, however, means that most patients who have been exploited will not apply for or be granted a T-visa. It is incumbent upon the health care provider to have an understanding of appropriate labor practices and the legal and immigration ramifications of identifying and reporting exploitative practices. Even undocumented migrants have the right to report unsafe working conditions, have protections under OSHA, and have the right to remedies from the DOL. The DOL Wage and Hour Division (WHD) is responsible for enforcing federal labor laws on topics including the minimum wage, overtime pay, recordkeeping, child labor, family and medical leave, migrant and seasonal worker protections, and worker protections in certain temporary guest worker programs. WHD can investigate potential cases of wage and hour violations, seek back wages for those victimized, and identify if such cases qualify as human trafficking under law [88].

Although workers who are denied or who elect not to pursue immigration relief are likely to remain undocumented and uninsured, the health care system safety net, particularly federally qualified health centers (FQHCs) and migrant health clinics, can provide health care and social service assistance to these patients. Regardless of where a trafficked patient is first identified, it is imperative that they be referred to experienced service providers in the community for ongoing assistance.

5.2.10   Promising Practices

5.2.10.1   Example of a Health Care Response

An effective response to trafficking requires multidisciplinary collaboration at the community level. One example of an organization addressing trafficking locally is the Pacific Survivor Center (PSC), a nonprofit organization based in Honolulu, Hawaii. PSC's mission is to advance health and human rights in the Hawaii-Pacific region, and its primary patient populations include survivors of labor trafficking, sex trafficking, immigrant domestic violence, and torture. Since 2012, PSC has been the State of Hawaii sub-grantee on the Department of Justice, Office for Victim of Crime's Comprehensive Services for Human Trafficking Victims Grant. PSC's role under this grant is to provide and coordinate medical, dental, and mental health services for victims and survivors of human trafficking, and to provide training for health care and allied professionals.

PSC partners closely not only with prosecutors and local and federal law enforcement but also with numerous other NGOs in the community, including Kokua Kalihi Valley Comprehensive Health Services (an FQHC) the Sex Abuse Treatment Center at Kapiolani Hospital, Susannah Wesley Community Center (SWCC), and the Hawaii Immigrant Justice Center at Legal Aid (HIJC). With these partners, PSC is able to ensure that victims and survivors receive immediate medical and psychological evaluation and treatment upon identification, ongoing trauma-informed care for chronic medical conditions, and forensic evaluations when needed. Furthermore, these close collaborations allow for seamless, comprehensive services for patients and ensure that barriers to care are addressed and social service needs are met, including shelter, food, clothing, transportation, interpretation, and legal assistance.

PSC worked with HIJC and SWCC and other community agencies to serve many farmworkers from the Global Horizons case. Early on in assisting these survivors, a screening event was organized that included assessing each individuals' medical, legal, and social service needs and providing education about worker rights and additional available resources within the community. At this event, PSC provided health care-related education and triaged survivors' medical, psychological, and dental needs. Several workers were found to have acute medical problems during this routine screening, including advanced heart disease, and others were found to have chronic conditions such as diabetes, high blood pressure, and elevated cholesterol. Many of the workers faced significant transportation and communication barriers, and even those with potentially life-threatening conditions were unaware that they needed medical attention. Collaborating closely with legal and social service providers allowed PSC to overcome these obstacles and provide workers with appropriate trauma-informed care.

5.2.11 Organized Agricultural Workers

The Coalition of Immokalee Workers (CIW) is a worker-based human rights organization that has been fighting for better pay and working conditions for US agricultural laborers since 1993. By focusing on the underlying problems plaguing farmworkers, the organization has identified human trafficking on US farms and has developed programs that prevent forced labor. CIW has uncovered, investigated, and assisted in the prosecution of numerous multi-state farm slavery operations, helping to liberate over 1,200 workers held against their will [89].

CIW's Campaign for Fair Food and Fair Food Program are model programs that address worker exploitation and trafficking in the US agricultural industry. The Campaign for Fair Food, started in 2001, educates consumers about the causes of and solutions to farm labor exploitation and forges alliances between farmworkers and consumers [90]. The Campaign began with a Taco Bell boycott in 2001, which publicized the plight of tomato pickers in Florida [91]. Since then, it has won Fair Food Agreements with 14 multibillion dollar food retailers, including Yum! Brands, Walmart, McDonald's, Subway, and Whole Foods. These agreements establish more humane farm labor standards and fairer wages for farmworkers [92].

CIW's Fair Food Program addresses human trafficking at its roots by creating partnerships between farmers, farmworkers, and retail food companies to ensure humane wages and conditions for the workers who pick fruits and vegetables on participating farms [93]. The program requires participating retail food companies to pay a small premium on their produce purchases, which augments worker wages. By requiring Participating Buyers to only purchase tomatoes from growers who comply with the Fair Food Code of Conduct, the Fair Food Program harnesses retailers' immense purchasing power to enforce the most progressive labor standards in modern US agriculture. The program also prevents labor exploitation and trafficking program by empowering tens of thousands of workers to serve as real-time monitors who can identify and expose perpetrators of slavery [94].

5.2.12 Domestic Workers' Bill of Rights

Following organized campaigns by domestic workers and their allies, several states have begun to improve labor rights and conditions for domestic workers through expansion of labor protection laws [95]. New York State enacted the first US

Domestic Workers Bill of Rights in 2010, followed by Hawaii, California, Massachusetts, Connecticut, Oregon, and Illinois [96]. The protections offered by these laws and their enforcement mechanisms vary by state. For example, in New York, domestic workers have received, among other provisions: the right to overtime pay; a day of rest (24 h) every 7 days, or overtime pay for workers who agree to work on that day; 3 paid days of rest each year after 1 year of work for the same employer; and protection under New York State Human Rights Law [96]. While California law already required overtime for domestic workers, lawmakers did not include provisions that addressed the rights of live-in employees to 8 h of uninterrupted sleep, "adequate, decent, and sanitary" sleeping accommodations, meal and rest breaks, or paid days of rest after 1 year of work with an employer. Domestic workers and their supporters had advocated for these provisions to protect the health and safety of domestic workers [88, 97].

5.2.13 Supply Chain Accountability

One key aspect of human trafficking prevention is supply chain management. A supply chain is the network created among different companies producing, handling, and/or distributing a specific product, encompassing all the steps it takes to bring goods or service from the supplier to the customer [98]. As businesses have globalized in recent decades, the demand for cheap labor has grown, and supply chains increasingly have internationalized to gain access to the most poorly paid workers [99]. The US State Department notes that long and complex supply chains that cross multiple borders, which typically rely on an array of subcontractors, impede the traceability of goods. This makes it challenging to determine if people are trafficked for the production of a given product [100]. Trafficking may occur at one point or multiple points throughout a product's life cycle, from harvesting of raw materials, through manufacturing and transportation, and to the shelves where products are sold [101].

The growing complexity of supply chains and greater focus on concerns about forced labor and trafficking by regulators, human rights organizations, and some federal and state governments have brought increased corporate attention to supply chain issues. The Economist magazine has described the importance of slave-free supply chains to modern day corporations [102]. The Wall Street Journal has noted, "few things are worse for a company or an industry than to be associated with human trafficking or slave labor" [103]. As described by the Interfaith Center on Corporate Responsibility, protecting human rights through corporate social responsibility is beneficial to corporations as well as workers, because:

> awareness of these risks and knowledge of the ways that traffickers may use a company's products, services, or workplaces in connection with their trafficking activities can help companies avoid negative publicity, business interruptions, potential lawsuits, public protests, and a loss of consumer trust, all of which can impact shareholder value [104].

Attention to the issue of forced labor in supply chains has increased since the implementation of the California Supply Chains Transparency Act, which took effect in January 2012. This Act requires that companies annually report their efforts to eradicate slavery and human trafficking from their direct supply chains. The legislation applies to companies that do business in California and earn more than $100 million in yearly worldwide revenues [105]. Similar legislation has been introduced at the federal level in the 114th US Congress, through HR 3226 [106]. The process of eliminating human trafficking through supply chain advocacy requires attention to the issue by consumers, corporations, and civil society. As President Obama has stated, "Every citizen can take action by speaking up and insisting that the clothes they wear, the food they eat, and the products they buy are made free of forced labor. Business and nonprofit leaders can ensure their supply chains do not exploit individuals in bondage" [107].

5.3   Conclusions

The etiology of labor trafficking is complex and diverse and includes push factors such as poverty, lack of educational and employment opportunities, instability from conflict and natural disasters, marginalization, and violence. Pull factors include demand for cheap goods and labor, and race, class, and gender bias. Workers throughout the United States are exposed to long hours, inadequate pay, hazardous materials and conditions, intimidation, threats, and violence, and all of the resultant health risks.

An effective response to labor trafficking requires multidisciplinary collaboration, with an emphasis on public health and labor rights. It requires commitment at the policy level to strengthen protections for workers, improve oversight of working conditions, and increase outreach and education to workers; funding at the community level for education, capacity building, and health care services; awareness among consumers of the impact of their buying choices on the treatment of workers; and engagement among health care providers to learn about the issue, increase awareness of local resources, and identify and appropriately care for trafficked persons and trafficking survivors. We urge the US policy makers and anti-trafficking advocates to support strategies that prevent labor trafficking and to provide resources that allow for a more robust, interdisciplinary approach.

5.4   Recommendations

A. Public Health and Enabling Services:

- Enhance funding for shelters for labor trafficking survivors;
- Develop protocols with local law enforcement to ensure that trafficked individuals are referred for medical and mental health care immediately upon identification;
- Ensure that all immigrant workers who may have been trafficked have access to consultation with an experienced immigration attorney;

- Increase trafficking education for health care providers and allied personnel, including in schools, residency programs, hospitals, clinics, and private practice settings. Trainings should include basic dynamics of trafficking, identification of trafficked individuals, best practices for response, and available resources;
- Increase the capacity of health care providers to document abuses and write forensic evaluations when indicated;
- Increase pre-certification services funding to encompass more communities throughout the USA and allow local agencies to determine eligibility for these programs;
- Provide specific funding to community health centers to develop local programs that address exploitation and human trafficking, and increase local capacity to serve these populations;
- Develop funding streams for enabling services to allow survivors of human trafficking and other traumatic experiences better access to health and wellness services through interpreters, transportation services, case management, and health system navigators.

B. Policy and Labor Protections

- Amend labor laws that omit certain classes of workers from coverage;
- Increase DOL and OSHA funding, including funding for occupational safety, health, and labor protection agencies at the state and local levels; expand workplace inspections; and increase fines for employers who violate worker protections;
- Overhaul the H-2 visa program to increase oversight, allow workers in the United States to change employers, and monitor recruitment tactics for H-2 workers abroad;
- Improve protections for workers with laws that ban foreign labor contractors from charging workers recruitment fees and requiring full disclosure of employment conditions;
- Increase education about workers' rights for those in industries at high risk for exploitation and trafficking;
- Improve supply chain monitoring and develop enforcement mechanisms to eliminate exploitative labor practices and slavery from the production of consumer goods.

Acknowledgment   The authors would like to acknowledge Lowell Chun-Hoon, Esq., for his contributions to this chapter.

References

1. International Labor Organization. ILO global estimate of forced labor: results and methodology. Switzerland. 2012. http://www.ilo.org/wcmsp5/groups/public/@ed_norm/@declaration/documents/publication/wcms_182004.pdf. Accessed 16 Mar 2016.
2. International Labor Organization. Forced labor, human trafficking, and slavery: facts and figures. http://www.ilo.org/global/topics/forced-labour/lang--en/index.htm. Accessed 16 Mar 2016.

3. International Labour Organization. Questions and answers on forced labor. http://www.ilo.org/global/about-the-ilo/newsroom/news/WCMS_181922/lang--en/index.htm. Accessed 27 May 2016.
4. Farrell A, McDevitt J, Perry N, et al. Review of Existing Estimates of Victims of Human Trafficking in the United States and Recommendations for Improving Research and Measurement of Human Trafficking, Final report to ATEST, 2010, pg. vii and 9.
5. Clawson HJ, Dutch N, Solomon A, et al. Human trafficking into and within the united states: a review of the literature. 2009. https://aspe.hhs.gov/basic-report/human-trafficking-and-within-united-states-review-literature. Accessed 18 Mar 2016.
6. U.S. Department of State Office to monitor and combat trafficking in persons. Trafficking in Persons Report. 2004. http://www.state.gov/documents/organization/34158.pdf. Accessed 30 May 2016.
7. Clawson HJ, et al. Estimating human trafficking in the United States: development of a methodology. Submitted to the Department of Justice. 2006. https://www.ncjrs.gov/pdffiles1/nij/grants/215475.pdf. Accessed 12 Mar 2016.
8. Free the Slaves and Human Rights Center. Hidden slaves: forced labor in the US. Washington, DC and Berkeley, CA. 2004. http://www.freetheslaves.net/wp-content/uploads/2015/03/Hidden-Slaves.pdf. Accessed 30 May 2016.
9. Haynes, D. (Not) Found chained to a bed in a brothel: conceptual, procedural and legal failures fulfill the promise of the trafficking victims protection. Act. 21 Geo. Immigr. L.J. 3. 2007.
10. Zhang, S. Looking for a hidden population: trafficking of migrant laborers in San Diego County. San Diego State University. November 2012. https://www.ncjrs.gov/pdffiles1/nij/grants/240223.pdf. Accessed 4 May 2016.
11. Owens C, Dank M, Breaux J. Understanding the organization, operation, and victimization process of labor trafficking in the United States. Urban Institute. Northeastern University; October 2014. http://www.urban.org/sites/default/files/alfresco/publication-pdfs/413249-Understanding-the-Organization-Operation-and-Victimization-Process-of-Labor-Trafficking-in-the-United-States.PDF. Accessed 19 May 2016.
12. Milkman R, Gonzalez AL, Narro V. Wage theft and workplace violations in Los Angeles: the failure of employment law for low wage workers. Los Angeles, CA: UCLA Institute for Research on Labor and Employment; 2010.
13. De Vivero AG, Payne E, Ploski M, Santis M. Human trafficking: an invisible crime on the Isla del Encanto. Washington, DC: George Washington University Elliot School of International Affairs, Latin American and Hemispheric Studies Program; 2013.
14. United Nations Office of Drugs and Crime. What are root causes of human trafficking? In: Toolkit to combat trafficking in persons. https://www.unodc.org/documents/human-trafficking/Toolkit-files/08-58296_tool_9-2.pdf. Accessed 3 May 2016.
15. National Institute of Justice, Office of Justice Programs. The prevalence of labor trafficking in the United States. http://www.nij.gov/journals/271/pages/anti-human-trafficking-us.aspx. Accessed 22 Mar 2016.
16. Todres J. Moving upstream: the merits of a public health law approach to human trafficking. North Carol Law Rev. 2011;89(2):447.
17. Goździak EM, Bump MN. Data and research on human trafficking: bibliography of research-based literature. Final report to the National Institute of Justice. October 2008.
18. Grant MG. The truth about trafficking: it's not just about sexual exploitation. The Guardian Opinion. http://www.theguardian.com/commentisfree/2012/oct/24/truth-about-trafficking-sexual-exploitation. Accessed 22 Mar 2016.
19. Raigrodski D. Economic migration gone wrong: trafficking in persons through the lens of gender, labor, and globalization. Indiana Int Comp Law Rev. 2015;25(1):79.
20. Attorney general annual report to congress and assessment of U.S. government activities to combat trafficking in persons fiscal year 2014. https://www.justice.gov/ag/file/799436/download. Accessed 16 Mar 2016.

21. United Nations Human Rights Office of the High Commissioner. Convention for the suppression of the traffic in persons and of the exploitation of the prostitution of others. http://www.ohchr.org/EN/ProfessionalInterest/Pages/TrafficInPersons.aspx. Accessed 22 Mar 2016.
22. Convention for the suppression of the traffic in persons and of the exploitation of the prostitution of others, approved by general assembly resolution. 317 (IV) of 2 December 1949.
23. Haynes DF. Good Intentions are not enough: four recommendations for implementing the trafficking victims protection act. Univ St Thomas Law J. 2008;6(1):77.
24. Oram S, Abas M, Bick D, et al. Human trafficking and health: a survey of male and female survivors in England. Am J Public Health. 2016;106:1073–8.
25. Kim K. Psychological coercion in the context of modern-day involuntary labor: revisiting United States v. Kozminski and understanding human trafficking. Loyola Law School Legal Studies, Paper No. 2007-40. 2007.
26. Baldwin SB, Fehrenbacher A, Eisenman DP. Psychological coercion in human trafficking: an application of Biderman's framework. Qual Health Res. 2015;25(9):1171–81.
27. Turner-Moss E, Zimmerman C, Howard LM, Oram S. Labor exploitation and health: a case series of men and women seeking post-trafficking services. J Immigr Minor Health. 2014;16:273–80.
28. Kiss L, Pocock NS, Naisanguansri V, et al. Health of men, women, and children in post-trafficking services in Cambodia, Thailand, and Vietnam: an observational cross-sectional study. Lancet Glob Health. 2015;3:e154-61.
29. Center for Problem-Oriented Policing. Negative features of sting operations. http://www.popcenter.org/responses/sting_operations/5. Accessed 27 May 2016.
30. Crouch D. Swedish prostitution law targets buyers, but some say it hurts sellers. The New York Times. 14 Mar 2015. http://www.nytimes.com/2015/03/15/world/swedish-prostitution-law-targets-buyers-but-some-say-it-hurts-sellers.html. Accessed 28 May 2016.
31. Flynn J. The Myth of super bowl trafficking obscures real issues. San Jose Inside. 21 Jan 2016. http://www.sanjoseinside.com/2016/01/21/the-myth-of-super-bowl-sex-trafficking-obscures-real-issues/. Accessed 28 May 2016.
32. Ditmor M. The use of raids to fight trafficking in persons. Sex Workers Project. 2009. http://sexworkersproject.org/downloads/swp-2009-raids-and-trafficking-report.pdf. Accessed 30 May 2016.
33. Schwellenbach N. Austerity budgets threaten worker health and safety. Washington, DC: Center for Effective Government; 2013.
34. Krisburg K. The Pump Handle. Congressional budget proposals slash OSHA funding, push back on silica exposure standard: 'These cuts and these riders are unconscionable.' http://scienceblogs.com/thepumphandle/2015/08/18/congressional-budget-proposals-slash-osha-funding-push-back-on-silica-exposure-standard-these-cuts-and-these-riders-are-unconscionable/. Accessed 4 May 2016.
35. Davis DB. Inhuman bondage: the rise and fall of slavery in the new world. London: Oxford University Press; 2006.
36. Johnson S. Roaring camp: the social world of the California gold rush.
37. Blackmon DA. The World War II effect. Wall Street Journal Books. 28 Mar 2008. http://www.wsj.com/articles/SB120674498432473091. Accessed 21 May 2016.
38. Trafficking Victims Protection, 22 U.S.C. § 7102(9).
39. Protocol to Prevent, Suppress and Punish Trafficking in Persons Especially Women and Children, supplementing the United Nations Convention against Transnational Organized Crime Adopted and opened for signature, ratification and accession by General Assembly resolution 55/25 of 15 Nov 2000.
40. Rojas L. El Monte sweatshop slavery case still resonates 20 years later. KPCC News. 31 July 2015. http://www.scpr.org/news/2015/07/31/53458/el-monte-sweatshop-slavery-case-still-resonates-20/. Accessed 29 May 2016.
41. Congressional Record 109th Congress. Recognizing the 10th anniversary of the landmark El Monte garment slavery case. 2005–2006. https://www.gpo.gov/fdsys/pkg/CREC-2005-07-29/html/CREC-2005-07-29-pt1-PgE1733-3.htm. Accessed 29 May 2016.

42. Kimitch R. Thai community remembers shocking case of modern slavery in El Monte. The San Gabriel Valley Tribune. 28 July 2015. http://www.sgvtribune.com/social-affairs/20150728/thai-community-remembers-shocking-case-of-modern-slavery-in-el-monte. Accessed 29 Mar 2016.
43. Wallace B. 70 immigrants found in raid on sweat shop. SF Gate. 4 Aug 1995. http://www.sfgate.com/news/article/70-Immigrants-Found-In-Raid-on-Sweatshop-Thai-3026921.php. Accessed 29 May 2016.
44. Davis CS. Wage Theft, and LA's Global Labor Problem. Good. 17 Sept 2015. https://www.good.is/features/thai-cdc-el-monte-raid-twenty-years-later-labor. Accessed 29 May 2016.
45. U.S.A. vs Orian et al, 2011 United States District Court District of Hawaii, No. 10-00576. Superseding indictment, filed 12 Jan 2011.
46. The Associated Press. Human trafficking case against executives is dismissed. New York Times. 21 July 2012. http://www.nytimes.com/2012/07/22/us/human-trafficking-case-dismissed-against-global-horizons-officials.html?_r=0. Accessed 10 Apr 2016.
47. EEOC News Release. Sept 2014. https://www.eeoc.gov/eeoc/newsroom/release/9-5-14.cfm. Accessed 10 May 2016
48. EECO News Release. May 2016. https://www.eeoc.gov/eeoc/newsroom/release/5-2-16.cfm. Accessed 10 May 2016.
49. Davidson L. "'Slavery' case dismissal frustrates utah 'victims'". The Salt Lake Tribune. 31 July 2012. http://archive.sltrib.com/story.php?ref=/sltrib/news/54591213-78/case-company-dismissal-global.html.csp. Accessed 1 Aug 2016.
50. Baldwin SB, Eisenman DP, Sayles JN, Ryan G, Chuang KS. Identification of human trafficking victims in settings. Health Hum Rights. 2011;13(1):1–14 (Note: this case study was part of data collection for this study, transcript from survivor #7, September 19, 2007, but these case details were not published.).
51. Office to monitor and combat trafficking in persons. Fact sheet: the 3Ps: prosecution, protection, and prevention. U.S. Department of State. 2014. http://www.state.gov/j/tip/rls/fs/2014/233736.htm. Accessed 12 May 2016.
52. Dottridge M. Collateral damage: the impact of anti-trafficking measures on human rights around the world, introduction. Bangkok: Global Alliance Against Traffic in Women; 2007.
53. Dottrige, M. Editorial: how is the money to combat human trafficking spent? 2014. http://www.antitraffickingreview.org/index.php/atrjournal/article/view/62/60. Accessed 23 May 2016.
54. The United States Department of Justice. Human Trafficking Prosecution Unit (HTPU). https://www.justice.gov/crt/human-trafficking-prosecution-unit-htpu. Accessed 3 May 2016.
55. U.S. Department of Labor Fact Sheet. The department of labor's wage and hour division will expand its support of victims of human trafficking and other crimes seeking immigration relief from DHS. https://www.dol.gov/general/immigration/u-t-visa. Accessed 24 May 2016.
56. The Immigration and Nationality Act, 8 U.S.C. 1101(a)(15)(T).
57. Li P. Little-known visa for trafficking victims chronically underused. Cronkite News. 9 Dec 2013.http://cronkitenewsonline.com/2013/12/little-known-cumbersome-visa-for-trafficking-victims-is-chronically-underused/. Accessed 1 Aug 2016.
58. U.S. Citizenship and Immigration Services. Questions and answers: victims of human trafficking, T Nonimmigrant Status. https://www.uscis.gov/humanitarian/victims-human-trafficking-other-crimes/victims-human-trafficking-t-nonimmigrant-status/questions-and-answers-victims-human-trafficking-t-nonimmigrant-status-0. Accessed 5 Apr 2016.
59. National Human Trafficking Resource Center. T nonimmigrant status and the trauma exception. https://traffickingresourcecenter.org/resources/t-visa-and-trauma-exception/. Accessed 1 Aug 2016.
60. Baldwin SB. Health effects of human trafficking in the U.S. Survivor Voices, Survivor #7. 2007. Available from: https://www.researchgate.net/publication/309731374_Survivor_Voices_Survivor_7_2007. Accessed 06 November, 2016.
61. Kandasamy A. U.S. Visas help trafficking victims, if applicants can vault legal hurdles. San Francisco Public Press. 12 Feb 2012. http://sfpublicpress.org/news/2012-02/us-visas-help-trafficking-victims-if-applicants-can-vault-legal-hurdles. Accessed 1 Aug 2016.

62. Rieger A. Missing the mark: why the trafficking victims protection act fails to protect sex trafficked victims in the United States. Harv JL & Gender. 2007. p. 21.
63. S. 178. Justice for Victims of Trafficking Act 2015. Congress.gov. https://www.congress.gov/bill/114th-congress/senate-bill/178. Accessed 24 May 2016.
64. HR 1779. Runaway and homeless youth and trafficking prevention act of 2015. https://www.congress.gov/bill/114th-congress/house-bill/1779. Accessed 24 May 2016.
65. National Network for Youth. Fact sheet: the runaway and homeless youth and trafficking prevention act, S. 2646, will strengthen effective prevention of human trafficking. Washington, DC. 2014. http://www.nn4youth.org/wp-content/uploads/Fact-Sheet-RHYA-2014-Reauthorization.pdf. Accessed 29 May 2016.
66. Shamir H. A labor paradigm for human trafficking. UCLA Law Rev. 2012;60:76.
67. Lim, LL. Trafficking, demand, and the sex market. International Labor Organization. http://lastradainternational.org/lsidocs/334LinLeanLimTraffickingDemandSexmarket.pdf. Accessed 15 May 2016.
68. Wilson JH. Immigration facts: temporary foreign workers. Brookings Institute. 18 June 2013. http://www.brookings.edu/research/reports/2013/06/18-temporary-workers-wilson. Accessed 14 May 2016.
69. United States Government Accountability Office. Report to Congressional Committees. H-2A and H-2B visa programs: increased protections needed for foreign workers. http://www.gao.gov/assets/670/668875.pdf. Accessed 28 May 2016.
70. Bauer M. Close to slavery: guest worker programs in the United States. Montgomery, AL: Southern Poverty Law Center; 2013. https://www.splcenter.org/sites/default/files/d6_legacy_files/downloads/publication/SPLC-Close-to-Slavery-2013.pdf. Accessed 14 May 2016.
71. Human Rights Watch. Defenseless workers: exclusions in U.S. labor law. Washington, DC: Legal Obstacles to U.S. Workers' Freedom of Association; 2000.
72. U.S. Department of Labor Wage and Hour Division. Fact sheet #12: agricultural employers under the fair labor standards act (FLSA). Washington, DC. July 2008. https://www.dol.gov/whd/regs/compliance/whdfs12.pdf. Accessed 15 May 2016.
73. U.S. Department of Labor. Report to congress: the agricultural labor market—status and recommendations. Washington, DC. Dec 2000. https://migration.ucdavis.edu/rmn/word-etc/dec_2000_labor.htm. Accessed 13 May 2016.
74. Farmworker Justice. No way to treat a guest: why the H-2A agricultural visa program fail U.S. and foreign workers. 2011. http://www.migrantworkersrights.net/en/resources/no-way-to-treat-a-guest-why-the-h-2a-agricultural-v. Accessed 14 May 2016
75. U.S. Department of Labor. Occupational health and safety administration. regulations. https://www.osha.gov/pls/oshaweb/owadisp.show_document?p_table=standards&p_id=9632. Accessed 15 May 2016.
76. OSHA factsheet: update to OHSA's recordkeeping rule: who is required to keep records and who is exempt. https://www.osha.gov/recordkeeping2014/OSHA3746.pdf. Accessed 1 Aug 2016.
77. Domestic Workers United. Domestic workers under labor law. www.domesticworkersunited.org/index.../1_cb7fdb965d9b9d2c4965d2a8726bafca. Accessed 15 May 2016.
78. Hsu KS. Poverty, migration and trafficking in persons: NOTE: masters and servants in America: the ineffectiveness of current United States anti-trafficking policy in protecting victims of trafficking for the purposes of domestic servitude. Georget J Poverty Law Policy. 2007;14:489.
79. Todres J. Law, otherness, and human trafficking. Santa Clara Law Rev. 2009;49(3):605.
80. Oram S, Stockl H, Busza J, Howard LM, Zimmerman C. Prevalence and risk of violence and the physical, mental, and sexual health problems associated with human trafficking: systematic review. PLoS Med. 2012;9(5), e1001224.
81. International Organization for Migration. Trafficking of migrants—hidden health concerns. IOM Migration and Health Newsletter. Feb 2000.
82. Todres, J. Moving upstream: The Merits of a public health law approach to human trafficking. Georgia State Univeristy College of Law, Legal Studies Research Paper No. 2011–02. 89 N.C.L. Rev. 447 (2011)

83. Polaris Project. Recognize the signs. https://polarisproject.org/recognize-signs. Accessed 23 Mar 2016.
84. U.S. Department of State. Identify and assist a trafficking victim. http://www.state.gov/j/tip/id/. Accessed 23 Mar 2016.
85. National Human Trafficking Resource Center. Identifying victims of human trafficking: what to look for in a healthcare setting. http://traffickingresourcecenter.org/sites/default/files/What%20to%20Look%20for%20during%20a%20Medical%20Exam%20-%20FINAL%20-%202-16-16.pdf. Accessed 28 May 2016.
86. National Human Trafficking Resource Center. Human trafficking assessment tool for medical professionals. http://traffickingresourcecenter.org/sites/default/files/Healthcare%20Assessment%20-%20FINAL%20-%202.16.16_1.pdf. Accessed 29 May 2016.
87. International Organization for Migration. Caring for trafficked persons: guidance for health providers. http://publications.iom.int/system/files/pdf/ct_handbook.pdf. Accessed 4 May 2016.
88. United States Department of Labor Wage and Hour Division. We can help. https://www.dol.gov/wecanhelp/. Accessed 24 May 2016.
89. Coalition of Immokolee Workers. About CIW. http://www.ciw-online.org/about/. Accessed 14 May 2016.
90. Coalition of Immokolee Workers. Campaign for fair food. http://www.ciw-online.org/campaign-for-fair-food/. Accessed 12 May 2016.
91. Brabant M. Florida tomato pickers urge Taco Bell boycott. BBC News. 3 Mar 2001. http://news.bbc.co.uk/2/hi/americas/1200644.stm. Accessed 14 May 2016.
92. Alliance for fair food. http://www.allianceforfairfood.org/our-history. Accessed 14 May 2016.
93. Fair food program: consumer powered, worker certified. http://www.fairfoodprogram.org. Accessed 14 May 2016.
94. Greenhouse S. In Florida's tomato fields, a penny buys progress. New York Times. 24 Apr 2014. http://www.nytimes.com/2014/04/25/business/in-florida-tomato-fields-a-penny-buys-progress.html. Accessed 14 May 2016.
95. Boris E, Jokela M, Undén M. Enforcement strategies for empowerment: models for the California domestic worker bill of rights. UCLA Institute for Research on Labor and Employment. May 2015.
96. National Domestic Workerks Alliance. Campaigns. http://www.domesticworkers.org/campaigns. Accessed 19 May 2016.
97. Liss-Schulz N. California passes domestic worker bill of rights, sort of. Mother Jones. 27 Sept 2013. http://www.motherjones.com/mojo/2013/09/california-passes-domestic-worker-bill-rights-sort-of. Accessed 19 May 2016.
98. What is the supply chain. Investopedia. http://www.investopedia.com/terms/s/supplychain.asp. Accessed 19 May 2016.
99. Verifte. Corruption and human trafficking in global supply chains. White Paper. Dec 2013. https://traffickingresourcecenter.org/sites/default/files/WhitePaperCorruptionLaborTrafficking_0.pdf. Accessed 29 May 2016.
100. U.S. Department of State. Office to monitor and combat trafficking in persons. trafficking in persons report 2015. Preventing Human Trafficking in Global Supply Chains. http://www.state.gov/j/tip/rls/tiprpt/2015/243360.htm. Accessed 24 May 2016.
101. Global Freedom Center. Human trafficking in supply chains. https://traffickingresourcecenter.org/sites/default/files/LaborTraffickinginSupplyChains-GFC.pdf. Accessed 24 May 2016.
102. Modern slavery: everywhere in (supply) chains. The Economist. 14 May 2015. http://www.economist.com/news/international/21646199-how-reduce-bonded-labour-and-human-trafficking-everywhere-supply-chains. Accessed 24 May 2016.
103. Dipietro B. How companies face up to human trafficking risk. Wall Street Journal, Risk and Compliance blog. http://blogs.wsj.com/riskandcompliance/2014/01/07/how-companies-face-up-to-human-trafficking-risk-in-supply-chains/. Accessed 23 May 2016.

104. Effective supply chain accountability: investor guidance on implementation of the California transparency in supply chains act and beyond. The Interfaith Center on Corporate Responsibility, Christian Brothers Investment Services, and Calvert Investments. WP10009-201111. Nov 2011. http://www.calvert.com/NRC/literature/documents/WP10009.pdf. Accessed 19 May 2016.
105. Verite. Compliance is not enough: best practices in responding to Transparency in Supply Chains Act. http://www.verite.org/sites/default/files/VTE_WhitePaper_California_Bill657 FINAL5.pdf. Accessed 24 May 2016.
106. H.R.3226—Business supply chain transparency on trafficking and slavery act of 2015. https://www.congress.gov/bill/114th-congress/house-bill/3226/text. Accessed 24 May 2016.
107. The White House, Office of the Press Secretary. Presidential proclamation—national slavery and human trafficking awareness month. 2015. https://www.whitehouse.gov/the-press-office/ 2014/12/31/presidential-proclamation-national-slavery-and-human-trafficking-prevent. Accessed 1 Aug 2016.

Chapter 6
Trafficking of Children Within the United States

Carol Smolenski and Sarah Ingerman

6.1 Introduction

Trafficking of children for sex and labor happens in the USA to US citizens and permanent residents, as well as foreign-born children. It is a complex and hidden phenomenon that occurs in rural, urban, and suburban areas. Especially in the case of children, human trafficking is often difficult to detect. Some trafficked children are subject to both sex and labor trafficking. For example, a child who is trafficked for labor such as domestic work might also be subjected to sexual abuse and exploitation. A child who is trafficked for sex might also be forced to sell drugs or to perform other tasks.

Until recently, it was often assumed that it was only children from other countries brought into the USA who were subjected to trafficking. But this is not the case. When the federal Trafficking Victims Protection Act (TVPA) became law in 2000 its definition of human trafficking made clear that it applied to US citizens and permanent resident children as well as foreign-born children. The TVPA defines "a severe form of trafficking" as follows: (1) sex trafficking in which a commercial sex act is induced by force, fraud, or coercion, or in which the person induced to perform such an act has not attained 18 years of age; (2) labor trafficking: the recruitment, harboring, transportation, provision, or obtaining of a person for labor or services, through the use of force, fraud, or coercion for the purpose of subjection to involuntary servitude, peonage, debt bondage, or slavery [1].

Under federal law, any child under 18 years old "induced to perform" a commercial sex act is defined as a trafficked child. For a case of labor trafficking to occur,

C. Smolenski (✉)
ECPAT-USA, 30 Third Ave. Suite 800A, Brooklyn, NY 11217, USA
e-mail: csmolenski@ecpatusa.org

S. Ingerman
HEAL Trafficking, Los Angeles, CA, USA
e-mail: ingermas@bc.edu

© Springer International Publishing AG 2017
M. Chisolm-Straker, H. Stoklosa (eds.), *Human Trafficking Is a Public Health Issue*, DOI 10.1007/978-3-319-47824-1_6

the law, at the time of this writing, requires there to be evidence of force, fraud, or coercion. In both cases, the definition of trafficking does not require there to be movement of that person from one place to another.

While all children under the age of 18 engaged in commercial sex acts are, by federal law, trafficked, public perceptions of exploitation vary by the age of the trafficked. Children[1] are bought and sold for sexual purposes from a very young age, including infancy. At that young age, children are substantially removed from public scrutiny and more likely to be trafficked by family members or others close to the family, rather than unrelated adults. These younger children are commonly considered to be "abused" rather than "exploited," even if money or goods are exchanged; they almost universally are seen as sympathetic survivors. But children who are sex trafficked at the time they reach puberty are more likely to be viewed as "prostitutes" who behaved badly and need to be punished and reformed. Anecdotal evidence points to the fact that children are recruited into the sex trafficking industry at a very early age. There are no reliable data about the average age of entry, but a common time of entry is the beginning of puberty [2, 3].

6.2 Discussion

6.2.1 How Many Children Are Trafficked in the USA?

There is, as yet, no good, methodologically rigorous study quantifying the phenomenon of child trafficking in the USA. Some of the factors that stand in the way of gathering good statistics on child trafficking are the covert nature of the crime, inconsistent definitions of who is a trafficked person by different agencies and jurisdictions, and lack of self-identification especially by children themselves; many children do not even know they are being trafficked. This lack of a broadly accepted estimate has been a major barrier to the creation of public policies and the ability to measure the impact of policy and practice improvement efforts.

6.2.2 Sex Trafficking

Media and nongovernmental organizations (NGOs) have used a number of statistics to estimate the number of sex trafficked children but none of them stands up to rigorous critique. One of the most regularly cited studies, "The Commercial Sexual Exploitation of Children In the U.S., Canada and Mexico" by Richard J. Estes and Neil Alan Weiner is from 2001 [4]. It contains a detailed table with, among other things, an estimate that the number of children *at risk* for commercial sexual

---

[1] For this chapter we are defining "child" based on the UN Convention on the Rights of the Child, as a person under 18 years old.

exploitation in the USA is between 244,000 and 325,000. For this study, children "at risk" are defined as "runaways, thrownaways, victims of physical or sexual abuse, users of psychotropic drugs, members of sexual minority groups, illegally trafficked children, children who cross international borders in search of cheap drugs and sex, and other illicit fare" [4]. This estimate has been repeated and often mistakenly modified to say that 244,000–325,000 children *are* commercially sexually exploited in the USA. But even as an approximation of youth "at risk," the estimate has limitations that are documented elsewhere. One critique of this estimate is that it relies heavily on mere guessing as to the proportion of children who are at risk in various categories, for example, runaway and homeless youth, foster care youth, or foreign-born youth. The second major criticism is that it does not rigorously account for children who may fall into more than one risk category [5]. No other national estimates of the extent of sex trafficking of children exist in the USA.[2]

Some state and local level studies help to give a limited picture of the extent of child sex trafficking on a smaller geographic scale. In one New York City study, published in 2008, almost 4000 children were found to be sexually exploited [6]. In San Francisco, during the last six months of 2014, the Mayor's Task Force on Anti-Human Trafficking identified 104 sex trafficked children [7]. Another study by the Ohio Attorney General's office estimated that more than 1000 Ohio children are sex trafficked each year [8]. These studies have mainly identified US children, not foreign-born children, as trafficked.

6.2.2.1 The Gap in Identification of and Services for Sexually Exploited Boys

There is limited research about the sexual exploitation of boys, including trafficker recruitment methods and survivor characteristics, but it is clear that boys are also recruited into the sex trade. One study of sexual exploitation of children in New York City found that 50 % of the trafficked children were boys [6]. In 2014, Homeland Security Investigations (HSI), the investigative arm of the U.S. Department of Homeland Security, found almost as many trafficked boys as girls in their investigations of online child abuse imagery and sex tourism cases. They identified 288 girls and 264 boys in these investigations [9].

Boys are less likely than girls to self-identify or be identified as sex trafficking survivors. Law enforcement, outreach teams, and juvenile justice organizations and other service providers tend to have the notion that boys are not victimized by sex trafficking, and therefore do not ask questions of boys that would help identify them. And boys themselves are less likely to self-identify in a culture where boys are always supposed to be strong and girls are the victims. In addition, there are

---

[2]There have been attempts to use national arrest statistics, estimates drawn from subgroups such as street youth, and other ways of devising an estimate. Most of these are described and critiqued in the 2013 study by the National Academy of Sciences Institute of Medicine "Confronting Commercial Sexual Exploitation and Sex Trafficking of Minors in the United States."

fewer service providers able and willing to help boys who are survivors of sex trafficking. In a survey of twenty-five service providers around the country that work with sexually exploited children, only four answered that they would serve boys. Reasons for not serving them include: lack of capacity; boys are not identified or referred to them; and they need more training to serve boys [10].

6.2.2.2 Child Abuse Imagery

The commercial sexual exploitation of children includes the production and distribution of "child pornography" also called child abuse imagery (CAI). This form of exploitation of children has grown exponentially since the introduction of the digital camera and the internet. The children depicted are younger and the abuse has become more violent. Since 2010, the National Center on Missing and Exploited Children (NCMEC), which runs the national hotline for reporting child abuse imagery, has sent more than 110,000 notifications to electronic service providers regarding publicly accessible websites (URLs) on which suspected child sexual abuse images appeared [11].

ECPAT,[3] an international NGO working to end sexual exploitation of children, and law enforcement prefer to use the term "child abuse imagery" because it more accurately names the harm that is depicted. Most law enforcement agencies report an increase in the violence being used against children in these pictures: Gang rape, bestiality, and sexual torture of very young children are some of the practices recorded. They often show gruesome violence such as children being strangled while being sexually violated and children in bondage. NCMEC reported that in 2012, of the images reported to them, 24 % were of pubescent children; 76 % were of pre-pubescent children; and 10 % were of infants and toddlers [12]. Infants, some as young as 3 months old, have been depicted being raped. Despite the trend towards the depiction of much more violence and younger children the term "child pornography" is still used consistently, but inappropriately, in most laws and policies and in most news reports about arrests.[4]

Child abuse images are sold for a monetary amount. In the mid-2000s the sums of money involved were thought to be substantial. In response, 34 banks, credit card companies, electronic payment networks, third-party payment companies, and internet services companies came together under the guidance of the NCMEC to address the use of mainstream banking and payment systems for the buying and selling of child pornography [12]. Working together over the course of a few years these mainstream methods of payment have diminished. But there are signs payment may evolve to use different types of "e-money" or untraceable online cash [13].

---

[3] ECPAT is an international NGO originally known as End Child Prostitution in Asian Tourism. In 1996, the organization changed the name but kept the acronym. The new name is End Child Prostitution, Child Pornography, and Trafficking of Children for Sexual Purposes.
[4] Google alerts for "child pornography" result in multiple news and web articles daily.

The images are also often traded on an enormous scale among pedophiles and collectors so that they do not have a dollar amount associated with them, but rather they are used in a barter system. In this system, CAI is exchanged for other CAIs. In 2010, the FBI reported that they had interviewed a man who admitted molesting his 5-year-old daughter and videotaping the assaults. He stated that he had to molest his daughter because he needed "fresh" images to trade with others on the Internet before they would trade their own "fresh" images with him. That is to say, he wanted pictures he had not seen before and in order to get them he was required to provide images others had not seen [14].

6.2.3 Labor Trafficking

Child labor trafficking is almost wholly unquantified. There are no published estimates of the number of children from the USA who are labor trafficked within US borders. One older study examined the identified cases of children trafficked *into* the USA *from* other countries from 2000 to 2007. Investigators found that trafficking for sexual exploitation was the most prevalent form. Most (over 70 %) of the unaccompanied trafficked children were trafficked for sexual exploitation or a combination of sexual and labor exploitation. Twenty-four percent were trafficked solely for labor, primarily for domestic servitude [15]. Children are also documented to have been trafficked to the USA for work in beauty salons and agricultural labor [16, 17]. Since 2007, cases of children trafficked into the USA for labor continue to be identified.

One well-known industry in which domestic children have been labor trafficked in the USA is in the magazine sales industry: Vulnerable people, both adults and children, are recruited by companies to travel across the country peddling magazine subscriptions door-to-door. Between 2008 and 2015, the National Human Trafficking Resource Center received 419 reports of "likely" labor trafficking cases involving these traveling sales crews. Thirty-four percent were reported to be potential child trafficking cases [18]. Additionally, children and youth have also reported being forced to work as drug couriers [19].

In general, government-collected statistics about human trafficking are not disaggregated by age [20]. The 2016 submission by the US government to the UN Committee on the Rights of the Child describes the long-term plans of the US government to improve data collection, but this pledge's goals have not yet (at the time of this writing) been realized [21]. As such, data about child trafficking in the USA is limited to smaller scale studies by NGOs, and state and local agencies.

6.2.4 How Do Children End Up Being Trafficked?

Numerous risk factors make children vulnerable to human trafficking. Some of these factors are more prevalent in developing countries, but many of them span both low- and high-income countries. For children trafficked into the USA from less developed regions, there can be a number of characteristics in their environments that lead to recruitment. Children are most vulnerable to being trafficked when they are separated from their families and communities. There are many elements that can contribute to this separation: Changes in national economic and social policies can lead to the deterioration of families. For example, a shift in a government's development policies can make it more difficult for a family to farm their traditional land and force them to move into cities. In urban areas, adults obtain jobs working away from home and their children. In cities, poor children may need to help support their families, often through street peddling or other street-based economic activity. They therefore spend much more unsupervised time on the streets and therefore are at risk for recruitment for exploitation. Families may seek to rid themselves of such fiscally burdensome children by selling them or giving them away. And children with intellectual or developmental disabilities can be easier for recruiters and traffickers to control and manipulate [22, 23]. Countries with civil unrest, war, or drought have many more families that are forced to migrate. Forced migration separates families from their communities and frequently from each other, especially if the migration occurs under chaotic conditions. Unaccompanied children, lacking caring supervision, are much more vulnerable to being exploited [22].

Frequently, children are encouraged to seek work in the USA by their family members, who then place them into the hands of someone they believe will find them a safe place and well paid work. Sometimes they are told they will also be able to go to school. But they are ultimately forced to do something different from what they believed; unpaid, working, and living in poor conditions, with no friends or family to look out for them, they are not permitted to leave the "work" premises, much less go to school. Sometimes they are sexually abused or forced into the sex trade. In some cases a young girl has been married to a man who she believes loves her, but brings her to the USA to force her into sex work. In other cases, a child might be out-right sold by a family member [24–28].

In high-income countries like the USA, children are vulnerable to recruitment into sex trafficking, even in the absence of extreme poverty.[5] Children at high risk for trafficking include those with a family history of abuse (especially sexual abuse) and neglect, foster care youth, youth with a history of involvement in the child welfare and/or juvenile justice systems, and runaway and homeless youth. There is some evidence that lesbian, gay, bisexual, transgender experienced, and questioning youth are particularly at risk for trafficking, especially as they are over-represented in runaway and homeless youth populations [29]. Children are easier to coerce and control than adults, and although children from all socio-economic backgrounds can become targets, many factors can make youth particularly vulnerable to trafficking. For example, children in foster care often do not have a caring adult to protect them from predators. Traffickers use social media more and more frequently to recruit vulnerable children into the commercial sex industry. Runaway and home-

---

[5] The National Academy of Science's Institute of Medicine's report analyzes risk factors for US children in great depth.

less youth are vulnerable to an adult offering an exchange of sex for a place to sleep, a meal, or cash [19].

Vulnerable young people are recruited into the sex trade by traffickers who employ techniques of psychological coercion, often called "grooming devices" to make a child believe that the trafficker is their best friend; that the trafficker has their best interest at heart; that the trafficker loves and will take care of them [30]. Human trafficking can be part of an organized crime activity. But a trafficker can be a neighbor, a friend, a community leader, a small business owner, and even a family member. In fact, according to a 2013 Covenant House study, the majority of people who traffic youth are known to the youth [19]. Traffickers seek out vulnerable young people by frequenting places where they congregate, such as outside of schools, shopping malls, group homes, and parks. The basic strategy is simple and consistent: Win the trust and love of a young person, by presenting a caring and concerned façade, and become an important and indispensible part of their life. The trafficker may buy gifts for the young person and may offer promises of a wonderful life together. During this "grooming" period, the trafficker may tell the child that they are talented and beautiful; the trafficker may be the only person from whom the child has ever heard such praise. Then after having gained the youth's loyalty, the trafficker sells them online or on the streets [31, 32]. Two girls, interviewed in a 2005 ECPAT study, shared their grooming stories:

From a girl who was recruited at age 14 into sex trafficking:

> My mom took off with my sister, leaving me behind to live with my grandmother. I never felt like she wanted me. I always thought if I could find and convince my mom to let me live with her, everything would be ok. But when I got to Baltimore, she didn't want me. Then I met M, when I was 14. He loved me so much and I was always afraid he would leave me too. That's why he could ask me to do anything for him and I did. So when he asked me to go make us some money, I did [30].

From a girl who was recruited at age 16 into sex trafficking:

> I ran away. And I was gone for like a month or two and that's when I got into prostitution.… [I was] like 16.… I met a um, guy while I was on the run…I didn't know that he was a pimp and we were friends at first. And um, uh, he, he pretended to be my boyfriend for probably like 3 or 4 weeks and then…he um, took me shopping you know, bought me a, a new wardrobe, shoes and at that age that kind of like, fascinates you. So, but when…he actually took me out like on the track…I never, you know, experienced nothing like that. So I was nervous but I felt like I had no other choice so I did it [30].

6.2.5 Problems of Identification

Youth who are trafficked for sex or labor in the USA can be hard to see: The vast majority are almost always exploited off the streets, behind closed doors. Sex trafficked youth are found in escort services, massage parlors, dance clubs, and other technically legal establishments where sex is sold. The population of children who are on the street are more visible than others but they too are hidden, often in motels and hotel rooms. In a 2008 study about commercial sexual exploitation of children in New York, 45 % of street youth reported being sexually exploited in a hotel [6]. Similarly, labor trafficked youth toil in anonymity. Young people are labor trafficked through work in domestic servitude as nannies or housekeepers [27, 33]. These youth are literally unseen by anyone except the family who controls them, often not allowed to attend school or, in some cases, even leave the house where they live and work.

The psychological manipulation that leads to the recruitment of children into the sex trade makes it difficult to break the "trauma bond"[6] that is developed between the child and the trafficker [34]. The child is convinced that the trafficker is their best friend, their "daddy," and/or their lover. Fact sheets and "trafficking indicators" for service providers, educators, health care workers, and others emphasize this attachment between the youth and their trafficker. Trafficked youth are often resistant to offers of assistance. They can be angry at outsiders and very protective of their traffickers, whom they have come to trust.

Frequently, people who are trafficked do not know they are in an unsafe situation until after they arrive at their destination or are drawn into a situation that makes it difficult to leave. And even then, they do not usually know the legal term "human trafficking" describes their new predicament. For example, both adults and children smuggled across an international border might have paid someone to help them cross illegally; they expected to join family members or find work once they are on the other side but instead are trafficked: They were not aware that they would be deprived of their freedom and forced into the commercial sex industry, forced to do work for which they are not paid, or in which they are trapped. In some trafficking cases trafficked persons may be kidnapped and drugged and physically confined. But that is the minority of cases. Internationally trafficked people are additionally disadvantaged because they may not know the language of the country where they have arrived; they might not even know where they are. Traffickers have a host of methods for maintaining control of the trafficked person, ranging from physical abuse, threats of harm to them or their family in their home country, and threats of arrest and deportation.

Even in cases of domestic trafficking, youth do not know the term "human trafficking" or that what happened to them is not their fault or not normal. Because of the methods used by traffickers to recruit and maintain control over young trafficked persons, these youth are difficult to identify and help. Despite all these barriers, trafficked children do come into contact with people outside of their traffickers. Sometimes they are in school. Sometimes they are brought to health care professionals. They interact with customers or other people in the general public. While traffickers struggle to keep their "property" under control and under wraps, first responders or even good Samaritans may identify their exploitation and make a call that helps a trafficked child.

---

[6]The "trauma bond" is a strong emotional attachment between an abused person and their abuser, formed as a result of the cycle of violence.

6.2.6 Recognizing Trafficked Youth

Since the passage of the TVPA in 2000, government agencies and NGOs have published checklists for different segments of the community that can help determine whether a child is being sexually exploited. Common "red flags" include [35]:

- An inability to attend school on a regular basis and/or unexplained absences
- Frequently running away from home
- References made to frequent travel to other cities
- Bruises or other signs of physical trauma
- Withdrawn behavior, depression, anxiety, or fear
- Lack of control over a personal schedule and/or identification or travel documents
- Hunger, malnourishment, or dress inappropriate to weather conditions or surroundings
- Signs of a substance use disorder
- Apparently coached or rehearsed responses to questions
- A sudden change in attire, behavior, relationships, or material possessions (e.g., expensive items)
- Uncharacteristic promiscuity and/or references to sexual situations or terminology beyond age-specific norms
- A "boyfriend" or "girlfriend" who is noticeably older and/or controlling
- An attempt to conceal scars, tattoos, or bruises
- A sudden change in attention to personal hygiene
- Tattoos (a form of branding) displaying the name or moniker of a trafficker, such as "daddy"
- Hyperarousal or symptoms of anger, panic, phobia, irritability, hyperactivity, frequent crying, temper tantrums, regressive behavior, and/or clinging behavior
- Hypoarousal or symptoms of daydreaming, inability to bond with others, inattention, forgetfulness, and/or shyness

6.3 Conclusions

The trafficking of children for sex and labor in the USA is a phenomenon that is only recently being acknowledged. Even though the data is incomplete, it is important for all sectors of society to mobilize to prevent it and to identify and protect young people who are victimized. Our children are being trafficked.

Families, communities, and young people themselves should be educated about how to respond when cases of child abuse or exploitation are suspected. Older children should be educated about the recruitment methods used by traffickers. It is equally important that everyone, in a position to potentially identify a trafficked child, is trained to know the signs of trafficking and how to respond. There have been some important steps in prevention and protection in the USA but we still have much to do. We must mobilize young people to demand their right to grow up free of any form of exploitation.

6.4   Recommendations

- Ensure that survivor-centered, gender-sensitive services are available to all labor and sex trafficked children, both foreign and domestic.
- Ensure that high quality and comprehensive training is available for all frontline first responders who may be in a position to identify a sex or labor trafficked child. Frontline workers include criminal justice agents, health care professionals, social workers, teachers, child protective service workers, and others. Training should also include people in the private sector, especially those who work for internet service providers and in the travel and tourism industry.
- Conduct methodologically sound research to determine how many trafficked children there are, as a baseline against which to measure programming for the prevention of child trafficking.
- Raise awareness among the general public that trafficked children exist in the USA. Increased awareness will facilitate greater support for demanding greater public resources for training programs to identify trafficked children and service programs to protect them.
- Incorporate human trafficking information into school curricula for middle and high school children.
- Pass additional legislation in all 50 states to ensure that children who are identified as exploited are offered services and protection, not arrest and punishment.
- Address demand for labor trafficked children by educating consumers about child labor in supply chains. Similarly, buyers must be educated about the harms of sexual exploitation of children.
- Raise awareness about child abuse imagery and educate the public to demand greater accountability by internet service providers.

References

1. U.S. Department of State. Victims of trafficking and violence protection act of 2000. U.S. Department of State's Office of the Under Secretary for Civilian Security, Democracy, and Human Rights Office to Monitor and Combat Trafficking in Persons. 2000. http://www.state.gov/j/tip/laws/61124.htm. Accessed 20 May 2016.
2. Williams LM, Frederick, ME. Pathways into and out of commercial sexual victimization of children: understanding and responding to sexually exploited teens. The University of Massachusetts Lowell's Department of Criminal Justice Criminology. 2009. https://traffick-ingresourcecenter.org/sites/default/files/Williams%20Pathways%20Final%20Report%20 2006-MU-FX-0060%2010-31-09L.pdf. Accessed 19 Mar 2016.

3. Gibbs D, Walters JLH, Lutnick A, Miller S, Kluckman M. Evaluation of services for domestic minor victims of human trafficking: final report. RTI International. 2015. https://www.ncjrs.gov/pdffiles1/nij/grants/248578.pdf. Accessed 20 May 2016.
4. Estes RJ, Weiner NA. The commercial sexual exploitation of children in the U.S., Canada, and Mexico. The University of Pennsylvania's School of Social Work Center for the Study of Youth Policy. 2001. http://news.findlaw.com/hdocs/docs/sextrade/upenncsec90701.pdf. Accessed 26 May 2016.
5. Stransky M, Finkelhor D. How many juveniles are involved in prostitution in the U.S.? The University of New Hampshire's Horton Social Science Center Crimes Against Children Research Center. 2008. http://www.unh.edu/ccrc/prostitution/Juvenile_Prostitution_factsheet. pdf. Accessed 19 Mar 2016.
6. Curtis R, Terry K, Dank M, Dombrowski K, Khan B. Volume one: the CSEC population in New York City: size, characteristics, and needs. In: The commercial sexual exploitation of children in New York City. The Project of the Fund for the city of New York's Center for Court Innovation. 2008. https://www.ncjrs.gov/pdffiles1/nij/grants/225083.pdf. Accessed 2 Jan 2016.
7. The San Francisco Department on the Status of Women. Human trafficking report in San Francisco 2015. The City and County of San Francisco's Mayor's Task Force on Anti-Human Trafficking. 2015. https://sfgov.org/dosw/sites/default/files/HT%20Report_FINAL.pdf. Accessed 2 Jan 2016.
8. Williamson C, Karandikar-Chheda S, Barrows J, Smouse T, Kelly G, Swartz P, et al. Report on the prevalence of human trafficking in Ohio to Attorney General Richard Cordray. Ohio Trafficking in Persons Study Commission's Research and Analysis Sub-Committee. 2010. http://www.centralohiorescueandrestore.org/uploads/Ohio_Trafficking_in_Persons_Research_Sub-Committee_Report_2010_2-8_Final.pdf. Accessed 20 May 2016.
9. U.S. Immigration and Customs Enforcement. 552 victims of child sexual exploitation identified by ICE so far in 2014. ICE Press Release. 2014. https://www.ice.gov/news/releases/552-victims-child-sexual-exploitation-identified-ice-so-far-2014. Accessed 26 May 2016.
10. Friedman SA. And boys too: a ECPAT-USA discussion paper about the lack of recognition of the commercial sexual exploitation of boys in the United States. ECPTAT-USA. Available via ECPTAT-USA. 2013. http://www.ecpatusa.org/wp-content/uploads/2016/02/and-boys-to-report.pdf. Accessed 2 Jan 2016.
11. The National Center for Missing and Exploited Children. Key facts. 2016. http://www.missingkids.org/KeyFacts. Accessed 20 May 2016.
12. Collins M. Federal child pornography offenses. Testimony of Michelle Collins, National Center for Missing & Exploited Children. 2012. http://www.ussc.gov/sites/default/files/pdf/amendment-process/public-hearings-and-meetings/20120215-16/Testimony_15_Collins.pdf. Accessed 20 May 2016.
13. Financial Coalition Against Child Pornography. Technology challenges working group report 2008: trends in migration, hosting and payment for commercial child pornography websites. 2008. http://www.icmec.org/wp-content/uploads/2015/10/Trends-in-Migration-May-2008. pdf. Accessed 20 May 2016.
14. U.S. Department of Justice. The national strategy for child exploitation prevention and interdiction. A report to congress. 2010. https://www.justice.gov/psc/docs/natstrategyreport.pdf. Accessed 20 May 2016.
15. Gozdziak E, Bump MN. Victims no longer: research on child survivors of trafficking for sexual and labor exploitation in the United States. Institute for the Study of International Migration. 2008. https://www.ncjrs.gov/pdffiles1/nij/grants/221891.pdf. Accessed 19 Mar 2016.
16. Bronstein S, Lyon A, Poolos A. Held as slaves, now free. CNN. 2010. http://www.cnn.com/2010/CRIME/12/02/slave.labor.ring.busted/. Accessed 20 May 2016.
17. Zachariah H. Workers trafficked for Ohio egg farmers had little contact lived in poverty. The Columbus Dispatch. 2015. http://www.dispatch.com/content/stories/local/2015/07/12/. Accessed 1 Aug 2016.
18. Polaris. Knocking at your door: labor trafficking on traveling sales crews. Polaris. 2015. https://polarisproject.org/sites/default/files/Knocking-on-Your-Door-Sales-Crews.pdf. Accessed 19 Mar 2016.

19. Covenant House. Homelessness, survival sex and human trafficking: as experienced by the youth of Covenant House in New York. 2013. https://d28whvbyjonrpc.cloudfront.net/s3fs-public/attachments/Covenant-House-trafficking-study.pdf. Accessed 20 May 2016.
20. U.S. Department of State. Trafficking in persons report. U.S. Department of State's Office of the Under Secretary for Civilian Security, Democracy, and Human Rights. 2015. http://www.state.gov/documents/organization/245365.pdf. Accessed 19 Mar 2016.
21. U.S. Department of State. Combined third and fourth periodic report of the U.S. on the optional protocols to the convention of the rights of the child on the involvement of children in armed conflict and the sale of children, child prostitution, and child pornography. U.S. Department of State's Office of the Under Secretary for Civilian Security, Democracy, and Human Rights' Bureau of Democracy, Human Rights and Labor. 2016. http://www.state.gov/j/drl/rls/252299.htm. Accessed 20 May 2016.
22. Capaldi M. Unfinished business: ending child prostitution, child pornography and child trafficking or sexual purposes. ECPAT International. 2014. http://www.ecpat.org/wpcontent/uploads/2016/04/UNFINISHED%20BusinessReport_2015.pdf. Accessed 20 May 2016.
23. U.S. Department of State. Trafficking in persons report. U.S. Department of State's Office of the Under Secretary for Civilian Security, Democracy, and Human Rights. 2012. http://www.state.gov/documents/organization/192587.pdf. Accessed 20 May 2016.
24. Junkin V. Salisbury human trafficking event reveals harsh truths. Delmarva Now. 2016. http://www.delmarvanow.com/story/news/local/maryland/2016/02/01/salisbury-human-trafficking/79572918/. Accessed 26 May 2016.
25. Matloff J. Brothel state in Mexico is conduit for human trafficking in New York. Aljazeera America. 2015. http://america.aljazeera.com/multimedia/2015/6/sex-slavery-links-mexico-with-new-york-city.html. Accessed 26 May 2016.
26. Sherman T. N.J. man is sentenced to more than 24 years in prison for human trafficking, forced labor. NJ.com. 2010. http://www.nj.com/news/index.ssf/2010/07/nj_man_is_sentenced_to_more_th.html. Accessed 26 May 2016.
27. Free the Slaves, Human Rights Center. Hidden slaves: forced labor in the United States. Free the Slaves and the Human Rights Center, University of California. 2004. http://www.freetheslaves.net/wp-content/uploads/2015/03/Hidden-Slaves.pdf. Accessed 26 May 2016.
28. International Committee of the Red Cross. Inter-agency guiding principles on unaccompanied and separated children. Central Tracing Agency and Protection Division. 2004. http://www.unicef.org/protection/IAG_UASCs.pdf. Accessed 26 May 2016.
29. Clawson HJ, Dutch M, Solomon A, Goldblatt Grace L. Human trafficking into and within the United States: a review of the literature. U.S. Department of Health and Human Services' Office of the Assistant Secretary for Planning and Evaluation. 2009. https://aspe.hhs.gov/basic-report/human-trafficking-and-within-united-states-review-literature. Accessed 2 Jan 2016.
30. Friedman S. Who is there to help us? How the system fails sexually exploited girls in the United States. ECPAT-USA, Inc. 2005. http://www.ecpatusa.org/wp-content/uploads/2015/10/WHO-IS-THERE-TO-HELP-US-How-the-System-Fails-Sexually-Exploited-Girls-in-the-United-States-Examples-from-Four-American-Cities-.pdf. Accessed 2 Jan 2016.
31. Lloyd R. Girls like us: fighting for a world where girls are not for sale. New York, NY: HarperCollins Publishers; 2011.
32. Smith HA. Walking prey: how America's youth are vulnerable to sex slavery. New York, NY: Palgrave Macmillan; 2014.
33. Owens C, Dank M, Breaux J, Banuelos I, Farrell A, Pfeffer R, Bright K, Heitsmith R, McDevitt J. Understanding the organization, operation, and victimization process of labor trafficking in the United States. Urban Institute. 2014. http://www.urban.org/research/publication/understanding-organization-operation-and-victimization-process-labor-trafficking-united-states/view/full_report. Accessed 26 May 2016.
34. Austin W, Ann Boyd M. Psychiatric and mental health nursing for Canadian practice. Philadelphia, PA: Lippincott Williams & Williams; 2010.
35. American Institutes for Research. Risk factors and indicators. Safe Supporting Learning. 2016. https://safesupportivelearning.ed.gov/human-trafficking-americas-schools/risk-factors-and-indicators. Accessed 8 Apr 2016.

Chapter 7
Children at Risk: Foster Care and Human Trafficking

Madeline Hannan, Kathryn Martin, Kimberly Caceres, and Nina Aledort

7.1 Introduction

Since 2000, human trafficking has gained significant attention as a social issue impacting vulnerable populations globally; however, much of the spotlight has focused on adult survivors and those from outside the USA. Approximately 21 million people currently experience forced labor, including sexual exploitation, worldwide [1].

Recently enacted federal and state laws have addressed trafficking in children, recognizing that this population has specific vulnerabilities and that their status as minors requires varying responses from the legal, health, and human service sectors. Youth with child welfare involvement have been identified as particularly at risk for trafficking [2–5]. Federal legislation passed in 2014 requires all child welfare systems to effectively address sex[1] trafficking of youth in the care, custody, or under the supervision of child welfare systems [6].

---

[1] The law specifically addresses sex trafficking of minors, and does not comment on labor trafficking of children.

The original version of this chapter was revised. An erratum to this chapter can be found at DOI: 10.1007/978-3-319-47824-1_25

M. Hannan (✉) • N. Aledort
Rensselaer, NY, USA
e-mail: madelinehannan@gmail.com

K. Martin
Washington, DC, USA
e-mail: kathryn.p.martin@gmail.com

K. Caceres
SUNY Albany, 135 Western Avenue, Albany, NY 12222, USA

© Springer International Publishing AG 2017
M. Chisolm-Straker, H. Stoklosa (eds.), *Human Trafficking Is a Public Health Issue*, DOI 10.1007/978-3-319-47824-1_7

Child welfare systems differ from state to state and can cover an expansive number of programs and services affecting youth. This chapter will discuss the vulnerabilities of youth in foster care to human trafficking in the USA. In addition, system responses based in child welfare to identify, refer, and support youth survivors will be highlighted. Although this chapter focuses on children aged 0–17 years old, many states allow involvement in the child welfare system beyond the age of 18.

7.1.1 Definitions

The federal Trafficking Victims Protection Act (TVPA) [7] first defined *human trafficking*, in the USA in 2000. Most recently reauthorized in 2013, the TVPA defines victims of *child sex trafficking* as those under 18 years of age who participate in the exchange of a sex act for something of value [7]. *Labor trafficking* is defined as the use of force, fraud, or coercion to compel an individual to provide labor or services for the benefit of a third party [7].

Another term commonly used in anti-trafficking discourse is the *commercial sexual exploitation of children* (CSEC). A slightly broader term than "child sex trafficking," CSEC is an umbrella term used to describe any instance of a commercial sex act or performance involving a person under 18 years old. Examples of CSEC include child abuse imagery (often referred to as "child pornography"), stripping, dancing, or other forms of sexual performance, cyber interactions with commercial and sexual elements, and other forms of commercial sexual exchange with a minor.

7.1.2 Prevalence of Child Trafficking

Field expert Dr. Richard J. Estes refers to CSEC and child trafficking as "the most hidden form of child abuse in the United States and North America today," and "the nation's least recognized epidemic" [8]. Despite these significant concerns, data about this population is largely unavailable due to the concealed nature of the crime and the complex challenges in identifying survivors [9, 10].

Data on child trafficking is further limited by the stigma attached to child survivors. The pervasive and erroneous perception that these survivors are "child/teen prostitutes" or that they engage in commercial sexual exchanges of their own volition has complicated responses to this population [11]. Additionally, the anti-trafficking field has largely focused its attention on CSEC while applying very little attention to child labor trafficking [12]. As a result, much of the limited data focuses on child sex trafficking.

Estimates from researchers in the USA suggest that between 1,400 and 2.4 million children are at risk for CSEC each year [13]. The most widely accepted range, which has been supported by the Federal Bureau of Investigations (FBI) [14], suggests that 293,000 youth are at risk of trafficking in North America because they live on the streets or in particularly vulnerable situations [15]. The National Center for Missing and Exploited Children (NCMEC) estimates that one in six endangered runaways were likely trafficked for sex in 2014 [16]. Approximately 5544 cases of human trafficking were reported to the National Human Trafficking Resource Center from across the USA in 2015; of those cases an estimated 1621, or more than a quarter of reported cases, involved in the trafficking of a minor [17].

Many service providers assert that available data are gross underestimations [12]. In an effort to better understand the prevalence of child trafficking, federal legislation was passed in 2014 that requires each state approved to participate in the federal Title IV-E foster care program to collect data on the number of youth who have been trafficked or are at risk of being trafficked for sex; reports are to be sent to the Administration for Children and Families at the US Department of Health and Human Services beginning in 2017 [6].

7.2   Discussion

7.2.1   Child Welfare

7.2.1.1   Background

The child welfare system is a group of services designed to promote the well-being of children by ensuring safety, achieving permanency, and strengthening families to care for their children successfully [18]. The core responsibility of child welfare systems is to respond to allegations of child abuse, neglect, or maltreatment as defined by The Child Abuse Prevention and Treatment Act (CAPTA), originally passed in 1974 [19]. CAPTA applies to maltreatment caused by parents, guardians, or persons otherwise legally responsible for the welfare of the child. Child welfare agencies generally are not charged with responding to allegations of maltreatment at the hands of acquaintances or strangers [18]. Child welfare systems are comprised of government and service-providing agencies that prevent child abuse and neglect; protect children from further maltreatment; provide safe reunification of children with their families; and find permanent families for children who cannot safely return home [18].

7.2.1.2   Framework: Safety, Permanency, and Well-Being

The mission of child welfare systems is carried out using a framework of safety (preventing and responding to maltreatment of children), permanency (stabilizing children's living situations, and preserving family relationships and connections), and well-being (enhancing families' capacity to meet their children's physical, mental health, and educational needs) [20]. Emerging evidence reflects that this framework can improve both child- and system-level outcomes when fully integrated with trauma-responsive care in developmentally appropriate ways [21].

7.2.1.3 Population and Demographics

The national prevalence rate of child maltreatment was 9.1 per 1000 children in 2013 [22]. That year, approximately 679,000 children in the USA were found, by state and local child welfare systems, to have suffered at least one form of maltreatment, including occurrences of children that died as a result of maltreatment [22]. Of these youth, an estimated 255,000 children (approximately 38 %) were placed in *foster care* in 2013 [22]. Foster care is defined as providing safe and stable out-of-home care for children until the children can be safely returned home, placed permanently with adoptive families or placed in other planned arrangements for permanency. Foster care settings range from individual, certified family homes to large institutions [6]. On December 31, 2013, approximately 402,000 children were in foster care in the USA [22]. The number of youth in foster care in the USA has been consistent between 2008 and 2013 [22].

Race and Ethnicity Nationally, black, Hispanic or Latino, and youth of two or more races are placed in foster care at disproportionately high rates. Although representing an estimated 13 % of the US population [23], approximately 24 % of youth in foster care in 2013 identified as black or African American [22]. Similarly, persons of two or more races[2] represented 2.9 % of the US population in 2010 but 6 % of youth in foster care in 2013 [22]. Youth of Hispanic or Latino origin[3] represented 16 % of the US population in 2010, but 22 % of youth in foster care identified as Hispanic or Latino in 2013 [22]. The overrepresentation of ethnic and racial minority youth in foster care may be attributed to disparate treatment of racial and ethnic minority families, service bias, service availability by locality, and a number of other factors [24, 25] (Table 7.1).

Table 7.1 Race/ethnicity in percentages reflected in the USA and foster care population

Race/ethnicity	Percentage of US population (2010 census)	Percentage of foster care population (2013 AFCARS)
Total population	308,745,538	402,378
White (non-Hispanic)	72.4 %	42 %
Hispanic	16 %	22 %
Black/African American	13 %	24 %
Asian	5 %	1 %
Two or more races	2.9 %	6 %
American Indian/Alaskan Native	1 %	2 %

Sources: US Department of Health and Human Services, Children's Bureau (2014) Adoption and Foster Care Analysis and Reporting System (AFCARS) FY 2013 Data. US Department of Health and Human Services Children's Bureau, (ed.). pp. 6; Humes, K. J., Nicholas; Ramirez, Roberto (2011) Overview of Race and Hispanic Origin: 2010. in US Census Bureau, (ed.)

---

[2] "Two or More Races" refers to persons who reported more than one of the six race categories defined by the Census Bureau and persons who self-selected "multiple-race" on the 2010 Census.
[3] "Hispanic" or "Latino" refers to a person of Cuban, Mexican, Puerto Rican, South or Central American, or other Spanish-language culture or origin, regardless of race.

Fig. 7.1 Age of youth in foster care by the end of 2013. Source: US Department of Health and Human Services, A., Children's Bureau (2014) Adoption and Foster Care Analysis and Reporting System (AFCARS) FY 2013 Data. US Department of Health and Human Services Children's Bureau, (ed.). pp. 6

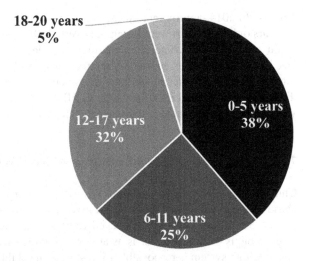

Age Of the approximately 402,000 youth in foster care at the end of 2013, an estimated 40 % were 5 years old or younger, 26 % were between the ages of 6 and 11, 33 % were between the ages of 12 and 17, and 5 % were between 18 and 20 years old [22] (Fig. 7.1).

Gender As of 2013, data on the gender identity of youth in foster care was reported on a male–female binary. Fifty-two percent of youth in foster care at the end of 2013 were male and 48 % were female [22]. Youth of a transgender or gender non-binary experience in foster care are frequently unable or not ready to disclose their gender identity to service providers, or are not asked [26].

Sexual Orientation Data on the sexual orientation of youth in foster care is not uniformly collected or reported. Approximately 66 % of youth in foster care are under 12 years old and still learning who they are, making system-wide extrapolations impractical. Lesbian, gay, bisexual, or questioning youth in foster care are frequently unable or not ready to disclose their sexual orientation to service providers [26]. Further, although gender identity and sexual orientation are unique aspects of one's identity, when data are available, figures on gender identity and sexual orientation are often reported together under the umbrella term "LGBTQ".[4] As a result, disaggregating foster care data specific to gender identity or sexual orientation is extremely difficult.

The limited data that is available suggests that LGBTQ youth are overrepresented in foster care. One study found that—out of 400 LGBTQ youth surveyed—65 % had lived in a foster or group home and 39 % were forced to leave their home because of their sexual orientation or gender identity [27]. When compared to the estimated 4–10 % of the American youth population that identifies as LGBTQ, it is plausible that LGBTQ youth are overrepresented in foster care [28].

---

[4] "LGBTQ" is an acronym inclusive of persons of lesbian, gay, bisexual, transgender, queer, or questioning experience.

Poverty In 2014, approximately 15.5 million children, or 21 %, of children under 18 years old in the USA were living in poverty [29]. Nationally, more than 50 % of youth in foster care come from families eligible for Temporary Assistance for Needy Families (TANF, commonly referred to as "welfare") funds [30]. Youth living in poverty experience higher rates of homelessness, incarceration, substance use disorders, and health conditions such as HIV that facilitate conditions in which youth are more vulnerable to experiencing child maltreatment [31].

7.2.1.4 Intersections of Child Welfare and Child Trafficking

Children who have experienced human trafficking often have significant histories of abuse and maltreatment at the hands of loved ones, trusted peers, as well as strangers [32–35]. In cases where a trafficked youth's parent, guardian, or person legally responsible is the trafficker or is aware of and unresponsive to the trafficking, the child welfare system is responsible for restoring the child's safety, enabling permanency, and empowering the youth to achieve well-being.

Previous and current child welfare involvement has been identified as a significant vulnerability for human trafficking [36, 37]. A New York study to identify the number of commercially sexually exploited youth found that 85 % of these youth had prior child welfare involvement [4]; 75 % reported foster care placement, and 69 % a child abuse or neglect allegation [4]. Similarly, data from a California sample found that between 50 and 80 % of commercially sexually exploited children were previously or at the time of the study involved with the child welfare system [38]. Testimony presented by NCMEC to the US House of Representatives Committee on Ways and Means Subcommittee on Human Resources asserted that 67 % of reported runaway youth who experienced sex trafficking had run away from their foster home [39].

Impact of Maltreatment While anyone can experience human trafficking, youth involved in the child welfare system have had specific adverse experiences and vulnerabilities that can be exploited by traffickers. Histories of familial violence [40, 41] and sexual abuse [11, 35, 42–45] make children particularly vulnerable. Studies have estimated that 70–90 % of women and children who were commercially sexually exploited were sexually abused prior to their trafficking situation [15, 40]. Additional risk factors include having a history of emotional abuse; being a runaway or abandoned child; having a substance use disorder; having problems at school; having been introduced to sexual activities at a young age; seeking independence; and looking for acceptance by adults during childhood [9, 46–48]. Survivors of child abuse and neglect often struggle with low school performance; depression; loss of self-confidence; speech disorders; complex trauma; and/or post-traumatic stress disorder (PTSD) [49–51]. Youth who have experienced trauma are more vulnerable to traffickers, and, in turn, trafficking often leads to high levels of traumatization resulting from experiences like repeated sexual assault, HIV/STI exposure, physical abuse, malnutrition, and forced abortions [3, 49, 50, 52].

Abuse, neglect, and maltreatment can become routine or normalized for youth who experience such traumas on a regular basis [53, 54]. Once youth view maltreatment as normal, it can be difficult for them to recognize or understand that they are being mistreated, or that they deserve respect and dignity. Traffickers who convince youth that they care for them, as a friend, caretaker, or romantic partner, exploit this vulnerability. Once a youth's trust has been secured, traffickers are experts at manipulating youths' behaviors, compelling them to engage in sexual or labor services for the traffickers' benefit [55]. This process of gradually exploiting a youth's trust while building controlling relationship dynamics is referred to as "grooming."

Community dynamics also play a substantial role in youths' vulnerability to trafficking. Risk factors in this dimension include community poverty and unemployment, police corruption, and the presence of violence, crime, drug use, adult prostitution, and trafficking in the neighborhood [9, 15]. Many of these factors at the familial and community levels parallel the individual vulnerabilities that contribute to youth entering the child welfare system.

Impact of Foster Care   Once involved in the child welfare system, children often have experiences that can exacerbate their previous traumas. For youth placed in foster care, the experience of being removed from home, even from abusive situations, is often an upsetting experience [56]. The trauma of a removal is compounded for youth who experience frequent changes in foster care placements [57]. Being moved may result in disruption of school attendance and a disconnection from mental or physical health care or social service providers [58–62]. Youth may also lose critical social and peer connections and supports as well as important identification documents, and personal mementos and belongings [63].

LGBTQ-identified youth in foster care often experience these traumas in addition to prejudicial treatment as a result of their LGBTQ status [26, 64]. Discrimination and abuse of these youth is both direct and indirect; some assigned caretakers physically or mentally abuse these youth [65].

Traumatic experiences in foster care create a sense of perpetual instability for youth. Children and young people may not be able to develop protective relationships with supportive adults and supportive institutions, or they may resist investing in relationships due to an overwhelming sense of vulnerability [66]. This can result in anxiety, depression, dangerous impulsive behaviors, or difficulty forming personal attachments [67, 68]. Often, these factors lead youth in foster care to leave without permission. Repeated instances of leaving can lead to restrictive placements, which can encourage the youth to run away again [69–73]. Youth who leave care, even for brief periods, are at great risk of CSEC and trafficking [5].

The Preventing Sex Trafficking and Strengthening Families Act of 2014 has only recently tasked child welfare systems with providing holistic approaches to the identification of and response to children trafficked for sex and their non-offending family members [6]. Youth who experience any form of trafficking benefit from coordinated, patient, and trauma-responsive care [74]. Youth survivors of trafficking often experience domestic violence, sexual assault, homelessness, and substance use disorders, and can benefit from best practice interventions from these fields [75].

Fig. 7.2 Youth-centered approach

Given the high levels of trauma inherent in being trafficked for sex or labor, trauma-centered and survivor-centered service approaches are recommended [76–78]. Trauma-responsive care addresses the widespread impact of trauma and potential paths for recovery; recognizes symptoms of trauma in survivors as well as those in their social networks; and responds to fully integrate knowledge about the survivor's trauma into a greater systematic approach, including policies, procedures, and practices [76]. Services that are client- or survivor-centered are tailored to provide the greatest form of support to the individual. Critical to this approach is empowering survivors to engage in their service planning and healing process [79]. Using this approach, service planning is responsive to survivors' needs and desires.

The youth-centered approach (see Fig. 7.2) is based on positive youth development (PYD) principles [80]; it is not based on the notion that youth need to be "rescued." PYD values youth's voices and input, which supports their ability to feel heard and respected, and provides a framework for youth to practice supported decision making. These are important, normative developmental tasks of young people that are frequently missed by trafficked youth [81]. Youth who have been in foster care and trafficked may have had very few opportunities to give appropriate input on critical life decisions. Rather, they have often been passive recipients of adult decisions.

In addition to serving young people from a youth-centered, trauma-responsive approach, caretakers, including foster parents and designated employees of childcare facilities, are now required by federal law to adopt a Reasonable and Prudent Parenting Standard ("the standard") [6]. The standard requires that decisions affecting the ability of youth in foster care to participate in normative experiences be made in a manner that permits them to participate in age- and developmentally appropriate normative experiences, while their health, safety, and best interests are maintained [82]. For example, the standard recognizes that experiences like school trips or sleeping over at a friend's house are critical for youth to connect to their communities, and to have the necessary experiences to thrive and grow into productive and well-rounded adults. When youth in foster care are not provided with these opportunities due to system barriers, they can feel isolated or stigmatized [83] or engage in risky, rebellious behavior. These missed opportunities for connection may leave youth vulnerable to traffickers [50, 84].

7.2.1.5   Spectrum of Services and a Multi-Disciplinary Approach

Building trust between youth and adults is critical to the success of any offered service; often, trust must be re-built with the very systems that youth have learned to doubt [78, 85]. Young people with foster care experiences and histories of trafficking present specific engagement challenges, and may be best approached through a *risk-tolerant* philosophy [86–88]. A risk-tolerant approach is one in which clients maintain ownership of their choices while receiving education and support from helping professionals. The goal of risk-tolerant interventions is to reduce the adverse consequences of clients' behaviors through the development of a supportive community [89–91].

A risk-tolerant approach recognizes youth can often be well served via wraparound services[5] in their community, and that young people—particularly those with histories of trafficking and exploitation—should not be detained by law enforcement or placed in locked settings for their own safety. Detention criminalizes youth and does not respond to their status as victims of often-brutal crimes. Placing and incarcerating youth for being trafficked reinforces their mistrust of institutions that are intended to support them [74].

No one service or service provider can meet all of the needs of each youth. The guiding principles described above should be embedded across a spectrum of services to meet the needs of youth in the community whenever possible. Designed as a spectrum, services range from those with low-thresholds of accessibility to those that require commitment from youth (see Fig. 7.3, below).

Figure 7.3 depicts a spectrum of services, with each threshold defined by the necessary level of youth's commitment to receive those services. For young people who are unable or unwilling to engage in service provision, low-threshold services should be offered. Low-threshold services are those that are available with few limitations, for example, drop-in centers, street outreach, and crisis shelters. Medium-threshold services

---

[5] Wrap-Around services is a series of services that address each of the youth's needs, including physical, mental, emotional, health, and educational supports [89].

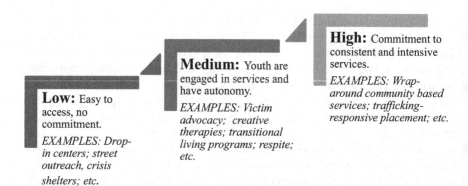

Low: Easy to access, no commitment.
EXAMPLES: Drop-in centers; street outreach, crisis shelters; etc.

Medium: Youth are engaged in services and have autonomy.
EXAMPLES: Victim advocacy; creative therapies; transitional living programs; respite; etc.

High: Commitment to consistent and intensive services.
EXAMPLES: Wrap-around community based services; trafficking-responsive placement; etc.

Fig. 7.3 Spectrum of services

should be offered to youth displaying some ambivalence toward service engagement. Medium-threshold services may include some engagement criteria, for example, participating in scheduled appointments, but can remain flexible. Examples of medium-threshold services include scheduled group or individual counseling services or programs for victims of crime. High-threshold services are appropriate for youth who express that they are ready to engage in services in an intentional and ongoing manner. These services may require high levels of commitment from youth, although they ideally remain flexible to a youth's potential relapse into a trafficking situation. A high-threshold service might include a care placement in which the foster parents or program is specifically trained to serve commercially sexually exploited youth.

Using a risk-tolerant approach that incorporates a spectrum of services is based on the Stages of Change model. This model conceptualizes behavioral change processes and interventions grounded in an understanding of a person's motivations, mindset, and goals [92]. Critically, the Stages of Change model anticipates barriers to successful change and relapse is recognized as a normative experience in the change process [93]. By incorporating services at a variety of thresholds, child welfare and allied systems can be appropriately responsive to trafficked youth with diverse needs [94].

7.2.1.6 Promising Practices: Multi-Disciplinary Approaches

Trafficked youth in foster care often have complex and overlapping service needs, including social services, physical health and mental health, and legal aid, among others. A multi-disciplinary approach is essential to coordinate and provide a youth-centered response.

Multi-disciplinary approaches have been successfully developed to respond to child trafficking across the country. As many youth who are at most significant risk to trafficking are in the care, custody, or supervision of child welfare, child welfare agencies are uniquely positioned to lead a multi-system response to such crimes. Further, child welfare systems have developed long-standing partnerships with the multi-disciplinary partners required to provide a robust spectrum of services to survivors.

7.2.1.7   Child Welfare: State Trafficking Response Examples

Case Example One

In some states, counties administer the child welfare system with state oversight. In one state with this structure, a multi-disciplinary approach to child trafficking is led by the state's child welfare agency and implemented locally. A *Critical Team* is a multi-disciplinary group of local partners formed and led by the local child welfare agency. Critical Teams are charged with identifying local assets as well as system gaps. They work collaboratively to address these gaps in order to best meet the needs of trafficked and at risk youth in their community. These teams incorporate many of the partnerships suggested previously, as well as child-serving community-based organizations, LGBTQ service providers, probation departments, Runaway-Homeless Youth Programs, refugee and immigrant services, legal services, and many others.

Additionally, Critical Teams are charged with bringing information about their work and child trafficking to the community through professional trainings, public awareness campaigns, and direct outreach to youth. The state child welfare agency maintains an active role in the work at the local level by providing coordination, training, and ongoing technical assistance. The state also offers trainings to each participating locality to disseminate information and provide space for practical skill-building.

Case Example Two

In another state, a child welfare response to child trafficking is led by the formation of regional multi-disciplinary teams [95]. A Leadership Committee coordinates the six regional teams, and is led by the state's child welfare system [96]. Local teams are inter-disciplinary and coordinate with the local Multi-Disciplinary Team (MDT) to ensure that survivors are offered all available resources to facilitate their recovery. Other efforts of regional teams include data collection, raising awareness, and promulgating training [97]. Critical to the success of these child welfare-based responses is commitment from inter-disciplinary partners and recognition that trafficked youth are victims of a crime and survivors of abuse, not delinquent children or criminals. This philosophy impacts the decisions made by each partner agency and creates responses that best serve youth at the individual and system levels.

7.3   Conclusion

Children in foster care have unique traumatic experiences that leave them vulnerable to human trafficking. State and federal laws are increasingly responding to the intersection between child welfare involvement and human trafficking risk, and child welfare systems are now charged with responding in a multitude of ways. Effective responses are those that adopt a multi-disciplinary approach grounded in positive youth development, trauma-informed care, and are responsive to the needs of each trafficked youth and their non-offending caretakers. Child welfare systems are uniquely positioned to lead these responses, as they have long-standing partnerships with many critical players and are responsible for the safety, permanency, and well-being of the youth in their state.

7.4 Recommendations

Although significant progress to address child trafficking through child welfare systems has been made, there continues to be room for improvement. First, much of what is known about child trafficking is rooted in practice developed with female survivors of sex trafficking. It is unclear if the information currently available is relevant for boys and LGBTQ experienced youth, and very little research or best practice data on child labor trafficking is available. These gaps in knowledge may have significant, yet unknown impacts on current child welfare practice.

- To expand the knowledge and current practices that are available, *new and stronger linkages between child welfare systems and community-based service providers who serve high-risk youth are needed.* Some of the necessary components include improved collaboration with sexual and reproductive health care providers; increased accessibility to services that prevent the spread of sexually transmitted infections, including HIV; and systematic identification and intervention training of staff in emergency departments, urgent care centers, and adolescent health clinics [98]. These all provide services to vulnerable children and adolescents, and each has a role to play in identifying and providing care to child survivors of human trafficking.
- To best serve the needs of youth identified as survivors of trafficking, *promising services need to be further developed and expanded.* These services span the spectrum referenced in this chapter, and include but are not limited to: crisis and long-term shelter; services for youth aging out of child welfare; educational and vocational supports; and survivor- and peer-led programming. Often, services are available to youth, however, very little support is offered to non-offending family members. This can cause great strain, particularly when underlying dynamics or histories that may have contributed to youth's vulnerability to trafficking are unaddressed and later resurface. The development of services for non-offending family members, including caregivers and siblings, is another area for future development.
- *Prevention programming is also necessary to prevent youth in foster care from experiencing human trafficking.* Several innovative curricula exist that can be delivered and evaluated in foster care and other group settings. In addition to programming designed to educate youth about trafficking and prevent their victimization, programming based in positive youth development principles can keep youth engaged and decrease their exposure to those who seek to exploit vulnerable youth.

References

1. International Labor Organization. Statistics and indicators on forced labour and trafficking. 2016. Available: http://www.ilo.org/global/topics/forced-labour/policy-areas/statistics/lang-en/index.htm. Accessed 17 Apr 2016.
2. US Department of State. Trafficking in persons report. Washington, DC: US Department of State; 2015.
3. Flowers RB. Runaway kids and teenage prostitution: America's lost, abandoned, and sexually exploited children. Santa Barbara: Greenwood Publishing Group; 2001.
4. Gragg F, Petta I, Bernstein H, Eisen K, Quinn L. New York prevalence study of commercially sexually exploited children. Rensselaer, NY: New York State Office of Children and Family Services; 2007.
5. US Department of Health and Human Services, Administration for Children and Families. Guidance to states and services on addressing human trafficking of children and youth in the United States. Washington, DC: US Department of Health and Human Services, Administration for Children and Families; 2013.
6. Preventing Sex Trafficking and Strengthening Families Act. in (2014): 113th Congress.
7. US Department of State (2000) Victims of Trafficking and Violence Protection Act of 2000. in State, U. D. o., (ed.) *H.R.3244*. Trafficking Victims Protection Act of 2000.
8. Lloyd R. Girls like us: fighting for a world where girls are not for sale, an activist finds her calling and heals herself. New York: Harper Collins; 2011.
9. Reid JA, Jones S. Exploited vulnerability: legal and psychological perspectives on child sex trafficking victims. Vict Offender. 2011;6(2):207–31.
10. Twill SE, Green DM, Traylor A. A descriptive study on sexually exploited children in residential treatment. Child Youth Care Forum. 2010;39(3):187–99.
11. Halter S. Factors that influence police conceptualizations of girls involved in prostitution in six US cities: child sexual exploitation victims or delinquents? Child Maltreat. 2010;15(2):152–60.
12. Child Welfare Information Gateway. Child welfare and human trafficking. Washington, DC: U.S. Department of Health and Human Services, Children's Bureau; 2015.
13. Mitchell KJ, Wolak J, Finkelhor D. The national juvenile online victimization study: methodology report. 2010.
14. Neubauer C. Sex trafficking in the US called 'epidemic'. *Washington Times*. 2011. Available: http://www.washingtontimes.com/news/2011/apr/23/sex-trafficking-us-called-epidemic/. Accessed 1 Aug 2016.
15. Estes RJ, Weiner NA. The commercial sexual exploitation of children in the US, Canada and Mexico. Philadelphia, PA: University of Pennsylvania, School of Social Work, Center for the Study of Youth Policy; 2001.
16. National Center for Missing & Exploited Children. National Center for Missing & Exploited Children 2014 annual report. Kansas City, MO: National Center for Missing & Exploited Children; 2014.
17. National Human Trafficking Resource Center. NHTRC hotline statistics. 2015. Available: https://traffickingresourcecenter.org/states2016. Accessed 1 Aug 2016.
18. Child Welfare Information Gateway. How the child welfare system works. Washington, DC: U.S. Department of Health and Human Services, Children's Bureau; 2013.
19. Child Abuse Prevention and Treatment Act. in (1974) Congress, U., (ed.) *S.1191*. Child Abuse Prevention and Treatment Act of 1974 (CAPTA).
20. Children's Bureau. What we do. 2015. Available: http://www.acf.hhs.gov/programs/cb/about/what-we-do. Accessed 23 Mar 2016.
21. National Resource Center for Permanency and Family Connections. Resources—well-being in the child welfare system. 2014. Available: http://www.nrcpfc.org/is/well-being.html. Accessed Mar 23 2016.

22. US Department of Health and Human Services, Children's Bureau (2014) Adoption and Foster Care Analysis and Reporting System (AFCARS) FY 2013 Data. US Department of Health and Human Services Children's Bureau, (ed.). p. 6.
23. US Census Bureau. QuickFacts: United States. In Bureau, U. C., editor. US Department of Commerce; 2015.
24. Summers A, Wood S, Donovan J. Disproportionality rates for children of color in foster care, Technical Assistance Bulletin. Reno, NV: National Council of Juvenile and Family Court Judges; 2013. http://www.ncjfcj.org/sites/default/files/Disproportionality%20Rates%20 for%20Children%20of%20Color%20in%20Foster%20Care%202013.pdf. Accessed 1 Aug 2016.
25. Wulczyn F, Lery B. Racial disparity in foster care admissions. Chicago, IL: University of Chicago; 2007.
26. Jacobs J, Freundlich M. Achieving permanency for LGBTQ youth. Child Welfare. 2006;85(2):299.
27. Berberet HM. Putting the pieces together for queer youth: a model of integrated assessment of need and program planning. Child Welfare. 2006;85(2):361–84.
28. Cray A, Miller K, Durso LE. Seeking shelter: the experiences and unmet needs of LGBT homeless youth. Washington, DC: Center for American Progress; 2013.
29. DeNavas-Walt C, Proctor B. Income and poverty in the United States: 2014. In Bureau, U. S. C., editor. Washington, DC: U.S. Government Printing Office; 2015.
30. Geen R. Short takes on welfare policy. Assessing the New Federalism. 2002.
31. McGuinness TM, Schneider K. Poverty, child maltreatment, and foster care. J Am Psychiatr Nurses Assoc. 2007;13(5):296–303.
32. Babatsikos G. Parents' knowledge, attitudes and practices about preventing child sexual abuse: a literature review. Child Abuse Rev. 2010;19(2):107–29.
33. Warf C, Clark L, Desai M, Calvo R, Agahi G, Hoffman J. Coming of age on the streets; survival sex among homeless adolescent females in hollywood. J Adolesc Health. 2010;46(2):S37–8.
34. Tyler KA, Hoyt DR, Whitbeck LB. The effects of early sexual abuse on later sexual victimization among female homeless and runaway adolescents. J Interpers Violence. 2000;15(3):235–50.
35. Walker K. Ending the commercial sexual exploitation of children: a call for multi-system collaboration in California. Sacramento, CA: California Child Welfare Council; 2013. p. 9–10.
36. Dank M, Yu L, Yahner J, Pelletier E, Mora M, Conner B. Locked In. Interactions with the Criminal Justice and Child Welfare Systems for LGBTQ Youth, YMSM, and YWSW Who Engage in Survival Sex. 2015.
37. Perry JR, Green ER. Safe & respected: policy, best practices, & guidance for serving transgender & gender non-conforming children and youth involved in the child welfare, detention, and juvenile justice systems. New York: New York City Administration for Children's Services; 2014.
38. Factsheet: Foster Care & Human Trafficking. 2013. Available: http://www.casre.org/our_ children/fcht/. Accessed 23 Mar 2016.
39. Hearing on Preventing and Addressing Sex Trafficking of Youth in Foster Care. in (2013) Subcommittee on Human Resources of the Committee on Ways and Means: U.S. House of Representatives.
40. Raphael J. Listening to Olivia: violence, poverty, and prostitution. Boston, MA: Northeastern University Press; 2004.
41. Wilson HW, Widom CS. The role of youth problem behaviors in the path from child abuse and neglect to prostitution: a prospective examination. J Res Adolesc. 2010;20(1):210–36.
42. Norton-Hawk M. The lifecourse of prostitution. Women, Girls Crim Just. 2002;3(1):7–9.
43. Estes JR, Weiner NA. The commercial sexual exploitation of children in the United States. Medical, legal & social science aspects of child sexual exploitation: a comprehensive review of child pornography, child prostitution, and Internet crimes against children; 2005. p. 95–128.
44. Brawn KM, Roe-Sepowitz D. Female juvenile prostitutes: exploring the relationship to substance use. Child Youth Serv Rev. 2008;30(12):1395–402.

45. Scott S, Skidmore P. Reducing the risk: Barnardo's support for sexually exploited young people: a two-year evaluation. Summary Report; 2010. Available: http://www.barnardos.org. uk/resources/research_and_publications/reducing-the-risk--barnardos-support-forsexually-exploited-young-people--a-twoyear-evaluation/publication-view.jsp?pid=PUB-1373. Accessed 1 Aug 2016.
46. Cusick L. Youth prostitution: a literature review. Child Abuse Rev. 2002;11(4):230–51.
47. Cobbina JE, Oselin SS. It's not only for the money: an analysis of adolescent versus adult entry into street prostitution. Sociol Inq. 2011;81(3):310–32.
48. Nixon K, Tutty L, Downe P, Gorkoff K, Ursel J. The everyday occurrence violence in the lives of girls exploited through prostitution. Violence Against Women. 2002;8(9):1016–43.
49. Silbert MH, Pines AM. Sexual child abuse as an antecedent to prostitution. Child Abuse Negl. 1981;5(4):407–11.
50. Farley M, Baral I, Kiremire M, Sezgin U. Prostitution in five countries: violence and post-traumatic stress disorder. Feminism Psychol. 1998;8(4):405–26.
51. Stanford Medicine. Signs & symptoms of abuse/neglect. 2016. Available: http://childabuse. stanford.edu/screening/signs.html. Accessed 18 Apr 2016.
52. Lepore G, Guinosso S. Human trafficking: implications for adolescent health outcomes. In: Bureau, F. a. Y. S., editor. Washington, DC: Administration on Children Youth and Families, Family and Youth Services Bureau; 2014.
53. Garbarino J. The human ecology of child maltreatment: a conceptual model for research. J Marriage Fam. 1977;39(4):721–35.
54. Dong M, Anda RF, Felitti VJ, Dube SR, Williamson DF, Thompson TJ, Loo CM, Giles WH. The interrelatedness of multiple forms of childhood abuse, neglect, and household dysfunction. Child Abuse Negl. 2004;28(7):771–84.
55. CAASE. Addressing misconceptions: Commercial sexual exploitation of children. Available: g.virbcdn.com/_f/files/d0/FileItem-150146-AM_Children.pdf.
56. Greeson JK, Briggs EC, Kisiel CL, Layne CM, Ake III GS, Ko SJ, Gerrity ET, Steinberg AM, Howard ML, Pynoos RS. Complex trauma and mental health in children and adolescents placed in foster care: findings from the National Child Traumatic Stress Network. Child Welfare. 2011;90(6):91.
57. Bruskas D. Children in foster care: a vulnerable population at risk. J Child Adolesc Psychiatr Nurs. 2008;21(2):70–7.
58. Hussey DL, Guo S. Characteristics and trajectories of treatment foster care youth. Child Welfare. 2005;84(4):485.
59. Ryan JP, Testa MF. Child maltreatment and juvenile delinquency: investigating the role of placement and placement instability. Child Youth Serv Rev. 2005;27(3):227–49.
60. Rubin DM, Alessandrini EA, Feudtner C, Localio AR, Hadley T. Placement changes and emergency department visits in the first year of foster care. Pediatrics. 2004;114(3):e354–60.
61. Rubin DM, Alessandrini EA, Feudtner C, Mandell DS, Localio AR, Hadley T. Placement stability and mental health costs for children in foster care. Pediatrics. 2004;113(5):1336–41.
62. James S, Landsverk J, Slymen DJ, Leslie LK. Predictors of outpatient mental health service use—the role of foster care placement change. Ment Health Serv Res. 2004;6(3):127–41.
63. Barber JG, Delfabbro PH. Placement stability and the psychosocial well-being of children in foster care. Res Soc Work Pract. 2003;13(4):415–31.
64. Sullivan C, Sommer S, Moff J. Youth in the margins: a report on the unmet needs of lesbian, gay, bisexual, and transgender adolescents in foster care. New York, NY: Lambda Legal Defense and Education Fund; 2001.
65. Child Welfare Information Gateway. Supporting your LGBTQ youth: a guide for foster parents. Washington, DC: US Department of Health and Human Services; 2013.
66. Singer E, Doornenbal J, Okma K. Why do children resist or obey their foster parents? The inner logic of children's behavior during discipline. Child Welfare. 2004;83(6):581.
67. Brantley N. Framing the issues of commercial sexual exploitation of children. Oakland, CA: Motivating, Inspiring, Supporting & Serving Sexually Exploited Youth (MISSSEY); 2009.

68. Miller P, Gorski P, Borchers D, Jenista J, Johnson C, Kaufman N, Levitzky S, Palmer S, Poole J, Rezin J. Developmental issues for young children in foster care. Pediatrics. 2000;106(5):1145–50.

69. Pardeck J. Multiple placement of children in foster family care: an empirical analysis. Soc Work. 1984;29(6):506–9.

70. Pardeck J. A profile of the child likely to experience unstable foster care. Adolescence. 1985;20(79):689–96.

71. Pardeck J, Murphy J, Fitzwater L. Profile of the foster child likely to experience unstable care: a re-examination. Early Child Dev Care. 1985;22(2–3):137–46.

72. Palmer S. Placement stability and inclusive practice in foster care: an empirical study. Child Youth Serv Rev. 1996;18(7):589–601.

73. Smith D, Stormshak E, Chamberlain P, Whaley R. Placement disruption in treatment foster care. J Emot Behav Disord. 2001;9(3):200–5.

74. Child Welfare Council CSEC Action Team (2015) Holistic needs of commercially sexually exploited children (CSEC).

75. Todres J. Taking prevention seriously: developing a comprehensive response to child trafficking and sexual exploitation. Vand J Transnat'l L. 2010;43:1.

76. SAMHSA. Trauma-informed approach. 2016. Available: http://www.samhsa.gov/nctic/trauma-interventions. Accessed 13 Apr 2016.

77. Goldman J. Creating trauma-informed systems. 2016. Available: http://www.nctsn.org/resources/topics/creating-trauma-informed-systems. Accessed 13 Apr 2016.

78. Ko SJ, Ford JD, Kassam-Adams N, Berkowitz SJ, Wilson C, Wong M, Brymer MJ, Layne CM. Creating trauma-informed systems: child welfare, education, first responders, health care, juvenile justice. Prof Psychol Res Pr. 2008;39(4):396.

79. Jim Casey Youth Opportunities Initiative. Issue Brief #5: Trauma-Informed Practice with Young People in Foster Care; 2012. Available: http://www.aecf.org/m/resourcedoc/jcyoi-IssueBrief5TraumaInformedPractice-2012.pdf. Accessed 1 Aug 2016.

80. Phelps E, Zimmerman S, Warren A, Jeličić H, von Eye A, Lerner RM. The structure and developmental course of positive youth development (PYD) in early adolescence: implications for theory and practice. J Appl Dev Psychol. 2009;30(5):571–84.

81. Williamson C, Baker LM. Helping victims of prostitution and trafficking. Groupwork. 2012;18(3):10–29.

82. Reasonable and prudent parent standard. (2016) *18 NYCRR 441.25*

83. Stott T, Gustavsson N. Balancing permanency and stability for youth in foster care. Child Youth Serv Rev. 2010;32(4):619–25.

84. Barnitz L. Effectively responding to the commercial sexual exploitation of children: a comprehensive approach to prevention, protection, and reintegration services. Child Welfare. 2001;80(5):597.

85. Mir T. Trick or treat: why minors engaged in prostitution should be treated as victims, not criminals. Fam Court Rev. 2013;51(1):163–77.

86. Slesnick N, Glassman M, Garren R, Toviessi P, Bantchevska D, Dashora P. How to open and sustain a drop-in center for homeless youth. Child Youth Serv Rev. 2008;30(7):727–34.

87. Slesnick N, Dashora P, Letcher A, Erdem G, Serovich J. A review of services and interventions for runaway and homeless youth: moving forward. Child Youth Serv Rev. 2009;31(7):732–42.

88. Rice E, Barman-Adhikari A, Milburn NG, Monro W. Position-specific HIV risk in a large network of homeless youths. Am J Public Health. 2012;102(1):141–7.

89. Leslie KM. Harm reduction: an approach to reducing risky health behaviours in adolescents. Paediatr Child Health. 2008;13(1):53–6.

90. Bellis MA, Hughes K, Lowey H. Healthy nightclubs and recreational substance use: from a harm minimisation to a healthy settings approach. Addict Behav. 2002;27(6):1025–35.

91. Parker H, Egginton R. Adolescent recreational alcohol and drugs careers gone wrong: developing a strategy for reducing risks and harms. Int J Drug Policy. 2002;13(5):419–32.

92. Prochaska JO, DiClemente CC. Transtheoretical therapy: toward a more integrative model of change. Psychother Theory Res Pract. 1982;19(3):276.
93. Prochaska JO, DiClemente CC, Norcross JC. In search of how people change: applications to addictive behaviors. Am Psychol. 1992;47(9):1102.
94. Zimmerman G, Olsen C, Bosworth M. A 'stages of change' approach to helping patients change behavior. Am Fam Physician. 2000;61(5):1409–16.
95. Human Anti-trafficking Response Team (HART). 2016. Available: http://www.ct.gov/dcf/cwp/view.asp?a=4743&Q=562654. Accessed 10 May 2016.
96. HART Leadership Committee. 2016. Available: http://www.ct.gov/dcf/lib/dcf/humantrafficking/pdf/HART_Leadership_Committee.pdf. Accessed 10 May 2016.
97. Connecticut Department of Children and Families (2014) Practice guide for intake and investigative response to human trafficking of children: for use with policy 31-10-6.1 Available: http://www.ct.gov/dcf/lib/dcf/policy/pdf/Human_Trafficking_PG.pdf. Accessed 1 Aug 2016.
98. Stoklosa H, Grace AM, Littenberg N. Medical education on human trafficking. AMA J Ethics. 2014;17(10):914–21.
99. Child Safety and Substantiation of Child Maltreatment. in (2008) ACTION for Child Protection, I., (ed.)
100. Humes KR, Nicholas AJ, Ramirez, RR. Overview of race and Hispanic origin: 2010. In: US Census Bureau, editor. 2011.

Chapter 8
Sex Trafficking in Indian Country

Erin Shanley and Robyn Jordan

8.1 Introduction

Although international sex trafficking has been a growing concern, literature on domestic trafficking in the United States (US) is comparatively limited, particularly for the Native American population. Lack of research on sex trafficking in Indian Country limits the evidence available to analyze the issue, even though anecdotal evidence has highlighted trafficking as an area of concern.

This chapter will focus on two geographical areas in particular, Minnesota and Oregon, where research has been conducted on Native American women involved in commercial sex. A large portion of this research has primarily focused on commercial sex in general; however, the authors recognize that a subset of these individuals are not engaging in commercial sex autonomously, and many are trafficked individuals [1].

8.1.1 Definitions

Sex trafficking: a commercial sex act which is induced by force, fraud, or coercion, or in which the person induced to perform such an act has not attained 18 years of age.
Commercial sex act: any sex act on account of which anything of value is given to or received by any person.

E. Shanley (✉)
Standing Rock Tribal Court, Fort Yates, ND, USA
e-mail: eshanley@standingrock.org

R. Jordan
Icahn School of Medicine at Mount Sinai, New York, NY, USA

© Springer International Publishing AG 2017
M. Chisolm-Straker, H. Stoklosa (eds.), *Human Trafficking Is a Public Health Issue*, DOI 10.1007/978-3-319-47824-1_8

Prostitution: exchanging the performance of sexual acts for money; a legal term, usually connotes a crime.

Native/Native American/Indian: an individual who is enrolled or self-identifies as a member of any of the Indian Tribes of the USA.

Indian country: all land within the limits of any Indian reservation; all dependent Indian communities within the borders of the USA; and "all Indian allotments, the titles to which have not been extinguished" [2].

Indian tribe: a separate and distinct community or nation of indigenous peoples in the USA.

8.1.2   Gaps in Knowledge

Although the International Labor Organization estimates that 4.5 million people are currently in forced sexual exploitation worldwide, statistics on the prevalence of those sex trafficked in the USA are limited [3, 4]. Of those that exist, most focus on children and adolescents. Moreover, there is not a uniform method of data collection or a compiled database with trafficking information to centralize the little data that is available. This lack of data is further exacerbated in the Native American population, as even fewer studies focus on this marginalized group [3]. The data on human trafficking in Indian Country is limited to a handful of research studies, which focused on commercial sex and sex trafficking (often without distinction) in Minnesota and Oregon involving Native American women. At the time of this writing, there is no research on labor trafficking or sex trafficking of males or transgender-experienced individuals in Indian Country.

The lack of data on human trafficking among Native populations is further compounded by underreporting. In reservation communities sexual violence is underreported beyond the extent seen in the general population due to the tight-knit, isolated nature of the populations [5]. Reporting can cause a survivor public shame and embarrassment, may place them in danger of harassment or retaliation, and can cause them to be shunned from the rest of the community [5]. Survivors may even feel a sense of loyalty to their abusers that prevents them from attempting to leave or getting help and further exacerbates mental health issues [6]. Moreover, a general distrust in law enforcement and their ability to respond prevents many survivors from reporting.

8.1.3   Characteristics of the Problem

The data that is available on sex trafficking in Indian Country reflects an overrepresentation of Native American women in the commercial sex industry [7–9]. In 2007, the Minnesota Office of Justice Programs (OJP) estimated that 345 Native American women and children were sexually trafficked in Minnesota in the previous 3 years

[10]. Approximately 25 % of women arrested for prostitution in Hennepin County, Minnesota, were identified as Native American, and 75 % of juvenile sex trafficking cases in Minneapolis in 2013 involved Native American trafficked persons, even though Natives only comprise approximately 2 % of the population [11, 12].

This overrepresentation is also found in other states with relatively large Native populations: In South Dakota, the United States Attorney's Office reported over a 5-year period, half of the survivors associated with prosecuted sex trafficking cases were Native American, though Natives comprise merely 9 % of the state's population [13, 14]. Likewise, in Alaska, 33 % of women arrested for prostitution were Native Alaskan, while Natives only make up 7.9 % of the Alaskan population [10, 12]. A subset of these women arrested for prostitution was likely trafficked, as law enforcement is only recently recognizing the distinction.

Native women are typically forced into sex trafficking at young ages, with 42 % being 15 years old or younger according to the Minnesota Indian Women's Resource Center (MIWRC) [9]. Other studies have corroborated this information, reporting the mean age of entry between 13 and 17 years, with 14 years being the most common [9]. Also disturbing is that, according to MIWRC's report, 71 % of sex trafficked girls were recruited by friends or family. An additional 19 % were recruited by then-boyfriends [9].

Effects of sex trafficking are not just physical or emotional, but also legal: The MIWRC found that 72 % of the women between 18 and 25 involved in sex trafficking had at least one related arrest [9]. One study in a county in Minnesota found that 24 % of the women on probation for prostitution were Native women, even though they constitute 2.2 % of that county's population [10]. No data were provided on the percentage of these women that were trafficked.

8.2 Discussion

8.2.1 Historical Context

It is necessary to examine contemporary sex trafficking in Indian country in the context of colonial practices of violence against Native American women. Sex trafficking of Native women is a deep-rooted phenomenon that started during the time of colonization when rape and sexual assault were used, by Europeans, as tools of imperialism [15]. Author Andrea Smith states, "...sexual violence does not simply just occur within the process of colonialism, but...colonialism is itself structured by the logic of sexual violence" [15]. Both colonization and the sexual violence employed were used to humiliate, dominate, and control Native people and continue to contribute to the marginalization of Native women today.

Documented accounts of sexual violence against Native American women during colonization reveal that whites commonly viewed Native women as being dirty and sexually promiscuous, and therefore not worthy of protection under the law [15–17]. Thus, the colonizers did not perceive nonconsensual sexual encounters with Native women as rape [18]. Even in the twentieth century, United States Congressmen and a Circuit Court of Appeals argued that violence against Native women should be punished differently than violence perpetrated against white women because of the belief that Native women were immoral [18]. At the time, society's understanding was that raping a woman who was considered dirty, impure, or sexually promiscuous could not constitute a criminal act, or was at least deserving of a lesser sentence [15]. Accordingly, the statistics on the actual number of Native women that were sexually assaulted or raped during this time period are unknown because it was not considered a crime to be quantified or punished.

Native American gender roles and status of women in society differed significantly from that of Europeans. Prior to European contact, and despite significant cultural diversity among Native tribes, Native women held respected positions within their tribes and communities. Research shows that Native populations were more egalitarian, in comparison to the patriarchal structure of European colonies, and Native women often enjoyed sexual autonomy as well [7, 15, 18]. Europeans viewed this sexual freedom, which was contrary to that of white women of the time, as devious and promiscuous. In contrast to their white counterparts' handling of Native female captives, Native men did not commonly rape or sexually assault white female prisoners captured in battle [18]. Brigadier General James Clinton of the US Continental Army stated, "Bad as the savages[1] are, they never violate the chastity of any women, their prisoners" [15].

Through the process of colonization and subsequent US policy targeted at assimilation and acculturation, the traditional cultural constructs of sexuality and gender roles in Native communities were replaced with European values [18]. This loss of traditional gender roles and identity has made Native women more susceptible to sexual violence, while instituting gender roles for Native men which are based in patriarchal control and domination. Other aspects of colonization, such as loss of land, culture, and all forms of self-determination, are also linked with Native women's exposure to sexual violence. Colonization and sexual violence share common goals, as well as common language: Both were used as a means of conquest and displays of power, and the abuses resulted in generations of socioeconomic marginalization and oppression of Native peoples. Law professor and scholar Sarah Deer provides various examples of the ways in which colonization has been described using sexual metaphors:

> Images of Native women were used to represent America, 'upon whose passive, receptive body European colonists could carry out their project of exploitation and domination' The language used to describe imperial conquest is often similar to the language used to describe sexual violence. The land itself was often referred to in feminine terms, often praised for its 'fertility' or 'virginity'. The Spanish explorers often wrote of having 'intercourse' with the land. Possession was also an integral part of the European discourse of 'discovery'. The dehumanization of Native peoples, which was used to justify the seizure of the land, is similar to the dehumanization of women, used to justify or minimize the harm of sexual violence [18].

---

[1] "Savages" is a derogatory term used by white colonists to refer to Native Americans.

In a 2011 qualitative study by the Minnesota Indian Women's Sexual Assault Coalition and Prostitution Research and Education, 62 % of interviewed Native women involved in prostitution in Minnesota reported a connection between the devaluation of women in colonization and present-day prostitution and sex trafficking [19]. These women related the subordination and subjugation of colonization to what they experienced in prostitution and sex trafficking [19]. They recognized the similar effects of colonization and prostitution, with both resulting in loss of their traditional values and practices, social status in tribal communities, and self-respect [19]. The same Minnesota study revealed that the majority of facilitators of sex trafficking are Native American, black, or multiracial men, often sharing similar backgrounds to the individuals being trafficked [19]. That the perpetrators shared racial and ethnic identity with those trafficked is indicative of internalized racism, whereby Native men have also taken on the colonial role of subjugating Native women. *Internalized racism* is racism from the dominant society that is internalized by the non-White group or individual and is directed inward toward the self or the group [20]. Again, it is important to point out that though prostitution, commercial sex, and sex trafficking are often conflated, they are not the same and are not always intertwined. In the Native population, data specifically about sex trafficking is severely limited. The authors of this study point out that approximately half of the participating women were sex trafficked, but do not disaggregate the remaining data specifically for sex trafficking versus prostitution. Unfortunately, this aggregation is the norm for the limited studies examining sexual exploitation among Native women [19].

8.2.2   US Government Policies

United States federal Indian policies of the nineteenth and twentieth centuries consisted of efforts to assimilate, terminate, and subjugate Native Americans. Centuries of violence and oppression have resulted in emotional trauma, poverty, substance use disorders (SUD), and internalized racism in Native American communities. These policies perpetuated cultural genocide, stripping Native Americans of their traditional means to cope and recover [21–23].

During the period of Removal, when whites' westward expansion pushed many Indian Tribes further from their homelands, there are several anecdotal accounts of US soldiers kidnapping and raping Native women [7, 24]. When Indian Tribes were placed on reservations, soldiers would exploit Native women who were dependent on government rations: These women were made to perform sexual favors in exchange for food or necessities [7]. Today, we would call such exploitation "survival sex," or depending upon the circumstance, "sex trafficking."

Although the large-scale removal of Indian Tribes from their ancestral homelands had ceased, in the nineteenth century the federal government began forcibly removing Indian children from their homes and placing them in boarding schools. These boarding schools strove to sever Native children's ties with their families, tribe, culture, religion, and language, and instill the values and belief system of the dominant, white, Christian society [5, 25, 26]. At these boarding schools, Indian children were not only culturally traumatized by being made to cut their hair and being forbidden to speak their language, but many also suffered physical and sexual abuse at the hands of administrators, teachers, and the clergy [27]. This abuse in boarding schools likely had downstream effects. In 2011, of the studied Native American women engaged in prostitution in Minnesota, more than two-thirds had a family member who had attended boarding schools, and 69 % of those who attended boarding school reported being physically or sexually abused [19]. These shared experiences illustrate how historical unresolved grief, or historical trauma, is "transposed" or transferred from family member to family member through generations because of the inability of a group of people to properly grieve and heal from major historical events [23, 28, 29]. Among Native women, this historical trauma is then compounded by current violence, abuse, and SUD, leading to increased vulnerability to trafficking [9, 30].

In the 1950s, the US federal government initiated the Urban Relocation Program, again removing Indians from their homes on the reservation and transporting them to urban centers under the guise of providing job opportunities. The purported goal of the Indian Relocation Act of 1956 was to move Native Americans to the cities and provide vocational training; the actual goal was to assimilate them into the general population. This federal policy was consistent with the ultimate aim of Indian eradication by diluting the Native American population into nonexistence. The number of Native people living in urban areas consequently dramatically increased during this time period. Often these Natives were living far from their support systems, and after they moved, the US government refused to provide them social services or educational training [19]. Thus, Native individuals living in urban areas were often economically marginalized, leaving them particularly vulnerable to victimization [7]. This created an urban Indian population who suffered all the issues of urban poverty, with the additional trauma of being disconnected from their home and support networks [31].

US federal Indian policy has a long history of systemic and pervasive marginalization contributing to the current disparities in income, health, well-being, and has led to victimization, via trafficking, in Native populations. Assimilation, relocation, and termination policies have left tribes with a dearth of resources and economic opportunities, resulting in widespread poverty and dire socioeconomic conditions on many reservations [5]. Sex trafficking in Indian Country is a complex issue clearly rooted in this legacy of widespread oppression and abuse.

8.2.3   Vulnerability

Researchers have identified a number of risk factors, including poverty, prior physical and sexual abuse, discrimination and substance use disorders, that are correlated with becoming involved in sex trafficking and commercial sex [7, 32]. Native

American women are particularly susceptible to sexual exploitation because, "Native [American] women and children 'are among the most economically, socially, and politically disenfranchised groups in the United States'," suffering from poverty, homelessness, racism, prior violence, and involvement in the foster care system, and substance use disorders at high rates [19]. These risk factors are interrelated, forming a vicious cycle; and these vulnerabilities are both caused from and exacerbated by the historical trauma rooted in colonization and racist and imperialist governmental policies to assimilate or eliminate Indian people [19].

8.2.3.1 Historical Trauma

Native American women are in a constant state of re-victimization because of the cumulative effects of historical exploitation and abuse. *Historical trauma* is the unresolved, collective, and cumulative grief from past experiences that passes to each new generation and is then compounded by further oppression [5]. A 2014 report by the International Human Rights Clinic at Willamette University in Oregon found that *generational trauma*, or historical trauma, was the single most influential factor in Native women's susceptibility to trafficking [5]. The long-term effects of Indian historical trauma include the factors that make anyone susceptible to sex trafficking: poverty, violence, substance use disorders, and unhealthy relationships [3, 5, 10]. Native adolescents trafficked in Minnesota also reported that constant exposure to abuse, exploitation, and violence as components of generational trauma increased their vulnerability to trafficking [10]. Additionally, having run away or being homeless, not completing high school, and the high visibility of trafficking of Native women in some communities also contributes to Native women's vulnerability to sex trafficking [10].

8.2.3.2 Rates of Violence Against Indian Women

Since colonization, Native women have experienced violent crime at an alarming rate. Today, the rates of rape, domestic and intimate partner violence, and murder of Native American women are higher than any other racial or ethnic group in the USA [33–35]. The number of Native women that are murdered is ten times the national average [35]. Native women are stalked at twice the rate of any other population [35, 36]. According to Amnesty International, one out of three Native women will be raped, and three of four will be assaulted in their lifetime [36]. A history of sexual assault has been correlated with a trafficking experience, making these high rates of sexual assault of Native women particularly concerning: Native women are more susceptible than women in all other racial/ethnic groups to a life experience of prostitution or sex trafficking [3, 7]. Minnesotan Native adolescents also reported high rates of exposure to violence as a contributing factor to their vulnerability to commercial sexual exploitation [10].

A substantial amount of literature links historical trauma with substance use disorders, child abuse, and violence in tribal communities, directly increasing risk of being trafficked [9, 37–40]. The 2011 Minnesota study revealed that 76 % of Native women in prostitution and sex trafficking had experienced three or four different types of violence (childhood sexual abuse, childhood physical abuse, or rape or physical assault in adulthood) in their lifetime [19]; most Native women who were involved with prostitution were sexually assaulted as children [19]. Seventy-nine percent of Native women survivors interviewed had been sexually abused as children by an average of four perpetrators, and 94 % had been raped as adults [19].

8.2.3.3 Gender Identity

Canadian studies have determined that some pimps will purposely seek Two-Spirit youth who have fled home to escape violence or abuse. *Two-Spirit* is a third gender that describes Native Americans who fulfill one of many mixed gender roles in indigenous groups. While Two-Spirit Indians were previously welcome in Native communities prior to colonization, imperialism and internalized racism have ostracized members of this group. Because these youths are marginalized by both their race and gender identity, they frequently encounter severe violence on the street, thus they are more vulnerable to accepting a pimp's offer of protection [29, 41].

8.2.3.4 Substance Use Disorders and Mental Health Diagnoses

Traffickers exploit Native women and youth with histories of substance use disorders, mental illness, and/or fetal alcohol spectrum disorder (FASD) [9, 10, 42–44]. Native Americans suffer from substance use disorders at disproportionately high rates [45]: 80 % of studied Native women involved in prostitution in Minnesota had previously used outpatient SUD services [19]. Sixty-five percent of studied Native women involved in prostitution in Minnesota had been diagnosed with a mental health disorder, most commonly depression, anxiety disorders, post-traumatic stress disorder (PTSD), obsessive-compulsive disorder (OCD), and bipolar disorder [19]. Forty percent of studied Native women in prostitution had been hospitalized in a psychiatric facility [19]. Research on Native survivors of sex trafficking shows a high percentage of previous sexual abuse as well as PTSD [5]. Service providers in Minnesota, working with trafficked Native adolescents, reported that addiction, emotional and mental vulnerability, and post-traumatic stress disorders were common risk factors to being trafficked [10].

8.2.3.5 Racism and Stereotypes

The attitudes about Native women that fueled sexual violence against them during colonization persist today. These stereotypes, established and perpetuated through colonization and indoctrination, increase Native women's susceptibility to sex trafficking: Sarah Deer states that "[t]oday, the eroticized image of Indian women is so commonplace in our society that it is unremarkable—the image of a hypersexual woman continues to be used to market any number of products and ideas" [7].

Native women in prostitution and sex trafficking reported that racism had a damaging effect on their lives and was an ongoing stressor [19]: Commodification of Native female bodies, rooted in colonization and capitalism, persists in today's societal sexual objectification of Native women [19]. Traffickers recruit American Indians, "because they can masquerade them as an exotic ethnicity—such as Polynesian, Asian or Native" [46]. Forty-two percent of Native sex trafficking survivors reported being racially insulted by sex buyers, pimps or traffickers, who were sexually aroused by making racist insults [19].

8.2.3.6 Poverty and Homelessness

Poverty, which often results in homelessness, is a major risk factor for being trafficked, and Native Americans are overrepresented in the homeless population in comparison to other groups in the USA [19, 47, 48]. Twenty-two percent of Native adolescents who were trafficked in Minnesota described themselves as homeless, and 35 % had run away from home at least twice in the past year, with an average of six runaway attempts per year [10]. Native adolescents who were homeless expressed being vulnerable to offers of affection, safety, and financial security from sex traffickers [10]. Of the Native women engaged in prostitution in Minnesota, 98 % were homeless at the time of the study or had been homeless at some time in the past; 77 % of the women had used homeless shelters [19]. Native populations in Alaska and Minnesota are disproportionately represented among the homeless. In 2008, 40 % of the young people served at Covenant House, Alaska's largest shelter for runaway and homeless youth, were Native [47]. And, in 2009, about 20 % of rural Minnesota's homeless youth aged 12–17 years were Native but Indians made up only 1 % of the region's overall youth population [48].

Native women also appear to disproportionately experience poverty. According to the Census Bureau's findings in 2012, one in three (34.4 %) Native American women lived in poverty [49]. Moreover, the poverty rate for Native American women increased from 27.1 % in 2011 to 34.4 % in 2012, while no other groups of adult women or adult men experienced a statistically significant change in poverty during this time period [36]. In 2012, the poverty rate for women of all races was 3.5 % higher than it was for men, and Native American women had the highest rate of poverty compared to all other groups [49]. Poverty has been named as one of the driving forces for traffickers themselves to enter into the sex trafficking world. Trafficking has become one of the fastest growing criminal industries in the world, with reported yearly revenues as high as 32 billion US dollars [3]. Thus, economics has dual roles of incentivizing people to traffic others, and making Native women, who are disproportionately impoverished, more vulnerable to be trafficked [36].

8.2.3.7 History of Child Welfare Involvement

Between 50 and 80% of survivors of sex trafficking have been in the foster care system at some point in their lives; Native American children are represented in foster care at 2.1 times that of the general population [12]. This overrepresentation of Natives in the foster care system also puts them at higher risk of becoming involved in sex trafficking [6]. Forty-six percent of women trafficked in Minnesota had been in foster care at some point of their childhood [19]. Half of these women experienced some form of abuse while in foster care, including verbal, mental, spiritual, cultural, physical, and sexual abuse [19].

8.2.3.8 Jurisdictional Loopholes and Sentencing Limitations

In addition to the above historical and consequent social factors, which increase Native women's susceptibility to being sex trafficked, the limited ability of judicial and law enforcement systems to protect this population also increases their vulnerability. Determining which entity or entities are responsible for the prosecution of crimes committed in Indian Country is a confusing and complex endeavor. Jurisdiction not only depends on the race of the perpetrator and victim, but also the type of crime that is committed. This complicated scheme of authority frequently undermines tribal power and impedes justice. Sex trafficking operations can span several reservations and state boundaries, leaving tribal law enforcement departments without jurisdictional authority and the necessary resources to pursue justice. A state jurisdiction on the reservation is limited to scenarios in which both perpetrator(s) and victim(s) are non-Indian. The federal government is able to pursue cases in Indian Country involving a Native American perpetrator, regardless of the race of the victim, and cases involving a non-Indian perpetrator when the victim is Native American, though it is unclear how frequently they actually intervene. The federal and tribal governments have concurrent jurisdiction in many cases in which the perpetrator is Native American. In addition to this lack of clearly delineated authoritative responsibility, the frequent involvement of multiple perpetrators, trafficked persons and geographic locations creates logistical confusion in the investigation and prosecution of sex trafficking crimes involving reservations [50].

Various studies reveal that most of the perpetrators of sexual violence against Native women, including those involved as consumers of sex trafficking, are non-Indian [19, 35, 36]: One study found that Non-Indians commit 88% of violent crimes against Native women [35]. Unfortunately, in *Oliphant v. Suquamish Indian Tribe*, the Supreme Court divested Tribes of their inherent authority to prosecute non-Indians for crimes committed on the reservation [51]. Without sufficient resources, or the right to prosecute, the 1978 ruling left Native peoples vulnerable and without recourse to non-Indian criminal predation. The Violence Against Women Reauthorization Act of 2013, reversed some of the 1978 ruling, broadening the scope of tribal authority to allow a Tribe to prosecute non-Indians for domestic violence, dating violence, and violations of protection orders [52]. But this expanded jurisdiction does not cover offenses for sexual assault, unless it is within the context of a violation of a protection order, and the expansion does not address crimes related to trafficking.

Furthermore, the 1963 Indian Civil Rights Act originally prohibited tribal courts from imposing sentences of more than one-year imprisonment and a $5000 fine, regardless of the crime committed [53]. In order to facilitate tribal public safety officials' ability to address the problems facing their communities and to empower tribal judicial systems, Congress passed the Tribal Law and Order Act of 2010: This law changed that sentencing limitation to 3 years and a $15,000 fine, with the ability to use consecutive sentences of up to 9 years [54]. Unfortunately, due to lack of resources, many Tribes have been unable to implement this increased authority, because Tribes must provide various procedural protections to defendants before being able to increase their sentencing authority. For example, many tribal courts do not have the means to provide counsel to indigent tribal members, or non-Indian defendants. Furthermore, many Tribes included the original one-year sentencing limitation within their tribal constitutions and these constitutions require a lengthy and expensive process to amend.

These jurisdictional complexities are also barriers to reporting and prosecuting of crimes. If a sex trafficked person does not trust that law enforcement will be able to adequately respond and tribal courts have limited ability to punish a perpetrator, they are less likely to report.

8.2.4 Intervention

8.2.4.1 Legal Interventions

Former US Attorney for the State of North Dakota, Tim Purdon, created a three-pronged approach to combatting sex trafficking: (1) treat trafficked people as victims, rather than arresting them for prostitution; (2) attack the demand and prosecute those who seek to exploit trafficked people; and (3) prosecute the traffickers [55]. In August of 2012, the North Dakota United States Attorney's Office successfully prosecuted the first sex trafficking case ever pursued on an Indian Reservation [56]. This case occurred on the Fort Berthold Indian Reservation and resulted in a 45-year sentence for the perpetrator. Subsequent policy changes, including the 2013 Violence Against Women Reauthorization Act explicitly added sex trafficking to the list of interpersonal violence facing Native communities, allowing for more legal avenues for prosecution of traffickers [6]. Additionally, the Administration for Native Americans Social and Economic Development Strategies offers grants for Native communities to address sex trafficking [6].

In 2014, the Fort Berthold Indian Reservation, located in North Dakota, implemented a new comprehensive anti-trafficking law, called "Loren's Law"[2] into their tribal code to allow the prosecution of human trafficking cases in tribal court [13].

---

[2] Loren's Law was named in memory of its primary author, Loren White Horne, a behavioral health specialist who treated sexual assault victims and co-authored the legislation.

The implementation of this law sets an important legal precedent for the country. Loren's Law identifies trafficked women and children as "victims" rather than criminals and outlines important culturally specific penalties like banishment from the reservation [56]. Banishment is a traditional sentence used by Plains Indian Tribes, which was akin to a death sentence during the pre-contact[3] period, when it would have been very difficult for an individual to survive on their own. Its use as a potential sentence warns traffickers that they are unwelcome. Furthermore, according to the new code, a Native American trafficker can have their oil payments[4] revoked and instead, awarded to survivors to fund counseling and treatment [56].

In 2015, the North Dakota Legislature passed a package of anti-trafficking laws to fund survivor services, increase punishment for traffickers, and provide training to anti-trafficking service providers. The Mandan, Hidatsa, and Arikara (MHA) Nation of the Fort Berthold Indian Reservation in northwestern North Dakota have been particularly affected by sex trafficking due to the 2006 "oil boom" in the area. The flourishing economy has attracted tens of thousands of people to the state, particularly young men, for high paying oil industry jobs [56]. The once impoverished Reservation, rife with jurisdictional complexities and loopholes, was a fertile environment in which organized crime, drug distribution, and sex trafficking could prosper [55]. However, the 2015 legislation has not had much impact on criminal prosecutions on the reservations in North Dakota because the state authorities only retain jurisdiction over cases involving non-Indian perpetrators and non-Indian trafficked persons and survivors. On the Fort Berthold Indian Reservation, for example, tribal authorities must collaborate with six different counties and the federal authorities to investigate non-Indian perpetrators.

Culturally Specific Interventions

Native women survivors, in the 2011 Minnesota study, stated that their involvement in commercial sex had disconnected them from their culture and traditional ways [19]. And 33% of those surveyed stated that their traditional practices were an important aspect of their identity [19]. These women stressed the importance of incorporating traditional values, practices, and healing ceremonies into treatment [5, 19].

There are more than 560 federally recognized tribes and Native Alaskan villages in the USA [57]. Traditional values, practices, and ceremonies vary greatly between each tribal nation, as well as each individual. Some individuals are very knowledgeable and philosophically connected to their tribe's traditions, while other individuals associate more with the dominant Western culture [57]. Incorporating culturally sensitive interventions should be specifically adapted based on the clientele [58]. Maria Yellow Horse Brave Heart, PhD and Lemyra M. DeBruyn, PhD give several examples of Lakota healing ceremonies they recommend to address historical

---

[3] "Pre-contact" refers to the time before Europeans made contact with Native Americans in the Americas.

[4] "Oil payments" are royalties paid to some Native Americans for allowing oil companies to drill for and extract oil from their land.

trauma among Lakota people [23]. For example, the *inipi* is a purification ceremony that assists individuals in personal healing and praying for the healing of others [23]. The *wasiglaki istamniuanpi wicakcepakintapi* is a "wiping of the tears" ceremony to acknowledge grief and connect individuals to extended family to develop support networks [23]. These ceremonies were used to address historical trauma and stimulate re-connection to traditional Lakota values [23]. The diversity of Indian Country is vast and it is outside the scope of this chapter to comprehensively outline culturally specific interventions for every Tribe. But, in consideration of the 2011 qualitative study in Minnesota, such efforts are important to Native healing, after centuries of trauma and vulnerability.

8.2.5 Consequences and Costs of Sex Trafficking

The effects of sex trafficking are not just limited to those trafficked, though they bear the most visible consequences. One cost to society as a whole is the increase in hospital and health care related costs, due to the many psychological, and physical injuries women sustain while sex trafficked [3, 37, 44, 59, 60]. Moreover, mental health treatment for survivors is long-term, meaning the general cost to society is ongoing instead of a one-off medical intervention that may be required due to physical violence [61].

Prolonged mental health issues can impact a woman's ability to maintain social relationships and work even after leaving the trafficking situation [62]. This negatively impacts the economic stability and growth of her society, community, and the security and health of her family. Women are more likely to invest more of their earnings in their families and communities, improving the health and economy of both the family and community [63]; thus if they are unable to work, potential gains for society are lost. Additionally, cost to society increases even more if the woman has to rely on social welfare programs to make up for her lack of income [61].

Women's overall health is tied to the health of their children, and a person's health in childhood heavily influences their health in adulthood: Healthy women and healthy mothers improve the health of the community's next generation [64]. Women use the health care system more than men, which contributes to better health outcomes for them, their families, and by extension, their communities [65]. The cost-saving and community building opportunities of trafficking prevention presents further motivation, beyond the ethical responsibility, for both tribal and state governments to eradicate the sex trafficking of Native women.

8.3 Conclusion

Native American women's susceptibility to sex trafficking is grounded in a wide array of factors cultivated over centuries, including: historical trauma; prior and systematic physical and sexual abuse; racism and discrimination; substance use disorders; mental health diagnoses; poverty; and jurisdictional loopholes. This increased susceptibility results in Native American women being disproportionately represented in the commercial sex trade. Sex trafficking prevention and intervention efforts must come from a culturally grounded perspective that understands that historical trauma and unresolved generational grief are the root causes leading Native American women to be more susceptible to sex trafficking.

8.4 Recommendations

The recommended solutions to sex trafficking in Indian Country are directly based upon the factors that make Native American women vulnerable to sex trafficking.

- Anti-trafficking groups must continue to raise awareness about human trafficking within Native American communities, both on and off the reservation.
- Communities at large, as well as service providers, educators, health professionals, social workers, and law enforcement agencies should be adequately trained on human trafficking identification and response in Native communities.
- Because trafficking does not abide by jurisdictional boundaries, it is important for tribal and state programs to build trusting, collaborative relationships with clear calls to action. Tribal courts must be empowered to protect those within their jurisdiction.
- Social workers, attorneys, and judges must be compliant with the Indian Child Welfare Act, and work to keep Native American children with their families and out of non-Native foster homes.
- Culturally competent and specific, comprehensive survivor services are needed and must include general health care, mental health services, substance use disorder treatment, homeless shelters, domestic violence and rape crisis centers and shelters, legal assistance, physical protection, and child care. Particularly important services are long-term individual counseling, peer support, vocational training, and housing.
- Historical trauma due to generations of abuse and oppression have made Native women more vulnerable to sex trafficking, while stripping them of their traditional means to prevent, protect, and heal themselves from tragic experiences. It is important that programs developed for Native survivors of trafficking incorporate traditional values and coping mechanisms.
- Researchers, using community-based participatory research methods, like the ones used in Minnesota and Oregon, should also explore (A) the prevalence of labor trafficking in Indian Country; (B) how other groups, including other Native American tribal groups not discussed in this chapter, as well as Native Americans of all genders, are affected by human trafficking in Indian Country; and (C) the effectiveness of culturally based and historically sensitive interventions to prevent and intervene upon trafficking among Native Americans populations [60].

References

1. Davidson JO. Prostitution, power, and freedom. Ann Arbor: University of Michigan Press; 1998.
2. United States Code. Indian Country Defined. 18 U.S.C. § 1151. 18 U.S. Code § 1151.
3. Gerassi L. From exploitation to industry: definitions, risks, and consequences of domestic sexual exploitation and sex work among women and girls. J Hum Behav Soc Environ. 2015;25(6):591–605.
4. International Labour Organization. Statistics and indicators on forced labour and trafficking International Labour Organization. 2016. Available online at: http://www.ilo.org/global/topics/forced-labour/policy-areas/statistics/lang--en/index.htm. Accessed 1 Aug 2016.
5. Weedn H, Scovel, J, Juran, J. Human trafficking & native peoples in Oregon: a human rights report. Prepared by International Human Rights Clinic at Willamette University College of Law. 2014. Available online at: http://www.doj.state.or.us/victims/pdf/human_trafficking_and_native_peoples_in_oregon_a_human_rights_report.pdf. Accessed 1 Aug 2016.
6. Administration for Children and Families. Recognizing and responding to human trafficking among American Indian, Alaska Native and Pacific Islander Communities. US Department of Health and Human Services. 2015. Available online at: http://www.acf.hhs.gov/sites/default/files/ana/ana_human_trafficking_im_2015_11_18.pdf. Accessed 1 Aug 2016.
7. Deer S. Relocation revisited: sex trafficking of native women in the United States. William Mitchell Law Rev. 2010;36:821. Available online at: http://open.mitchellhamline.edu/cgi/viewcontent.cgi?article=1157&context=facsch. Accessed 1 Aug 2016.
8. Farley M, et al. Prostitution and trafficking in nine countries. J Trauma Pract. 2004;2(3–4):33–74.
9. The Minnesota American Indian Women's Resource Center. Shattered hearts: the commercial sexual exploitation of American Indian women and girls. The Minnesota American Indian Women's Resource Center. 2009. Available online at: http://indianlaw.org/sites/default/files/shattered%20hearts%20report.pdf. Accessed 1 Aug 2016.
10. Pierce A. American Indian adolescent girls: vulnerability to sex trafficking, intervention strategies. Am Indian Alsk Native Ment Health Res. 2012;19(1):37–56. doi:10.5820/aian.1901/2012.37.
11. Pember MA. Mapping the market for sex: new report details Minneapolis sex trade. Indian Country Today. 2014. Available online: http://indiancountrytodaymedianetwork.com/print/2014/11/06/mapping-market-sex-challenging-attitudes-create-change-157664. Accessed 1 Aug 2016.
12. Sweet V. Trafficking in native communities. National Council of Juvenile and Family Court Judges Newsletter. Synergy. 2015;18(1). Indian Country Today (May 24, 2015). Available online: http://indiancountrytodaymedianetwork.com/print/2015/05/24/trafficking-native-communities-160475. Accessed 1 Aug 2016.
13. Dalrymple A, Lymn, K. Native American populations 'hugely at risk' to sex trafficking. Bismarck Tribune. 2015. Available online: http://bismarcktribune.com/bakken/native-american-populations-hugely-at-risk-to-sex-trafficking/article_46511e48-92c5-11e4-b040-c7db843de94f.html. Accessed 1 Aug 2016.
14. Pember MA. Living the life: sex abuse leads to sex trafficking. Indian Country Today. 2016. Available online: http://indiancountrytodaymedianetwork.com/2016/03/09/living-life-sex-abuse-leads-sex-trafficking-163681. Accessed 1 Aug 2016.
15. Smith A. Not an Indian tradition: the sexual colonization of native peoples. Hypatia. 2003;18(2):70–85.
16. Fischer K. Suspect relations: sex, race, and resistance in colonial North Carolina. Ithaca, NY: Cornell University Press; 2001.
17. Waselkov G, Braund K. William Bartrand on the Southeastern Indians. Lincoln, NE: University of Nebraska; 1995.
18. Deer S. Toward an indigenous jurisprudence of rape. Kans J Law Public Policy. 2004;14:121.
19. Farley M, et al. Garden of truth: the prostitution and trafficking of native women in Minnesota. St. Paul, MN: Minnesota Indian Women's Sexual Assault Coalition and Prostitution Research & Education; 2011.

20. Pyke K. What is internalized racial oppression and why don't we study it? Acknowledging racism's hidden injuries. Sociol Perspect. 2010;53(4):551–72. ISSN 0731–1214.
21. Palys T. Prospects for aboriginal justice in Canada. School of Criminology, Simon Fraser University; 1996. Retrieved from http://www.sfu.ca/~palys/prospect.htm. Accessed 1 Aug 2016.
22. Takaki R. A different mirror: a history of multicultural America. Boston, MA: Back Bay Books; 1993.
23. Yellow Horse Brave Heart M, Debruyn L. American Indian holocaust: healing historical unresolved grief. Am Indian Alsk Native Ment Health Res. 1998;8(2):60–82.
24. Brown D. Bury my heart at wounded knee: an Indian history of the American West. New York: Holt; 1970.
25. Kreisher K. Coming home: the lingering effects of the Indian adoption project, children's voices. Child Welfare League of America; 2002. Retrieved from http://www.cwla.org/articles/cv0203indianadopt.htm. Accessed 1 Aug 2016.
26. Johnston P. Native children and the child welfare system. Toronto: Lorimer; 1983.
27. Smith A. Soul wound: the legacy of Native American schools. 2007. Available at: http://www.amnestyusa.org/node/87342. Accessed 1 Aug 2016.
28. Evans-Campbell T. Historical trauma in American Indian/Native Alaska communities: a multilevel framework for exploring impacts on individuals, families, and communities. J Interpers Violence. 2008;23(3):316–38.
29. Kingsley C, Mark M. Sacred lives: Canadian aboriginal children and youth speak out about sexual exploitation. North York: Save the Children Canada; 2000.
30. Lynne J. Colonialism and the sexual exploitation of Canada's First Nations women. Paper presented at the American Psychological Association 106th Annual Convention, August 17. San Francisco, CA; 1998.
31. Canby Jr WC. American Indian law in a nutshell. 5th ed. St. Paul, MN: West Publishing; 2009.
32. Leidholdt DA. Prostitution and trafficking in women. J Trauma Pract. 2004;2(3–4):167–83. doi:10.1300/J189v02n03_09. Accessed 1 Aug 2016.
33. Greenfield LA, Smith S. American Indians and Crime (BJS, USDOJ, FNCJ 173386). 1999. http://www.bjs.gov/index.cfm?ty=pbdetail&iid=387. Accessed 1 Aug 2016.
34. Perry SW. American Indians and crime: a BJS statistical profile, 1992–2002. Washington, DC: Bureau of Justice Statistics; 2004. Retrieved from http://bjs.ojp.usdoj.gov/content/pub/pdf/aic02.pdf. Accessed 1 Aug 2016.
35. Brunner L. The devastating impact of human trafficking on native women in Indian reservations. 2013. Available at: http://www.vawnet.org/summary.php?doc_id=4232&find_type=web_sum_GC. Accessed 1 Aug 2016.
36. Amnesty International. Maze of injustice: the failure to protect indigenous women from sexual violence in the USA. Amnesty International USA. 2007. Available online at: www.amnestyusa.org. Accessed 1 Aug 2016.
37. Bohn DK. Lifetime physical and sexual abuse, substance abuse, depression, and suicide attempts among Native American women. Issues Ment Health Nurs. 2003;24(3):333–52.
38. Palacios JF, Portillo CJ. Understanding native women's health: historical legacies. J Transcult Nurs. 2009;20(1):15–27.
39. Kirmayer LJ, Young A, Robbins JM. Symptom attribution in cultural perspective. Can J Psychiatry. 1994;39(10):584–95.
40. Cole N. Trauma and the American Indian. In: Witko TM, editor. Mental health care for urban Indians: clinical insights from native practitioners. Washington, DC: American Psychological Association; 2006. p. 115–30.
41. Urban Native Youth Association (UNYA). Full circle. Vancouver: Urban Native Youth Association; 2002. Available at: http://www.unya.bc.ca/resources. Accessed 1 Aug 2016.
42. Benoit C, Millar A. Dispelling myths and understanding realities: working conditions, health status, and exiting experiences of sex workers. Victoria: Prostitutes Empowerment, Education, and Resource Society; 2001. Retrieved from: http://www.peers.bc.ca/pubs.html. Accessed 1 Aug 2016.

43. Boland F, Durwyn M. (1999). Fetal alcohol syndrome: understanding its impact. Correctional Service of Canada. Cited in Kingsley C and Mark M (2000), Sacred lives: Canadian aboriginal children and youth speak out about sexual exploitation. Save the Children Canada.
44. Farley M, Lynne J (2000). Pilot study of 40 prostituted women and girls in Vancouver, Canada. Cited in Farley and Lynne (2005), Prostitution of indigenous women: Sex inequality and the colonization of Canada's Aboriginal women. *Fourth World Journal* 6(1): 21–29.
45. Center for Behavioral Health Statistics and Quality, Data Spotlight. November 7, 2012. Available at: http://www.samsha.gov/data/. Accessed 1 Aug 2016.
46. Hansen T. Sex trafficking rampant in Indian country; pimps on prowl for native girls. Indian Country Today. 2012. Available online: http://indiancountrytodaymedianetwork.com/2012/01/17/sex-trafficking-rampant-indian-country-pimps-prowl-native-girls-72621. Accessed 1 Aug 2016.
47. Martin S, Meléndez A. Characteristics of homeless youth served by Covenant House Alaska. Anchorage: Institute of Social and Economic Research, University of Alaska Anchorage/Covenant House Alaska; 2009. Available online: https://d28whvbyjonrpc.cloudfront.net/s3fs-public/attachments/20100331-Youth-in-Crisis-CHA-Full-Report.pdf. Accessed 1 Aug 2016.
48. Wilder Research. Homelessness in Minnesota 2009: results of the wilder statewide survey. St. Paul, MN: Wilder Research; 2010. p. 14. Retrieved from http://www.wilder.org/download.0.html?report=2339. Accessed 1 Aug 2016.
49. Entmacher J., Lane A. Gallagher Robbins K. and Vogtman J., National Women's Law Center: Expanding the Possibilities. Insecure & Unequal: Poverty and Income Among Women and Families, 2000–2013. Insecure & Unequal: Poverty and Income among Women and Families 2000–2012.
50. Tatum M. Law enforcement authority in Indian Country. University of New Mexico School of Law Tribal Law Journal. 2003/2004;4.
51. *Oliphant v. Suquamish Indian Tribe*, 435 U.S. 191, 98 S.Ct. 1011 (1978).
52. Violence Against Women Reauthorization Act of 2013, Pub. L. No. 113-4, § 904. VAWA, 2013, § 904, P.L. 113–4.
53. The Indian Civil Rights Act of 1968 (ICRA), 25 U.S.C.§§ 1301–1304. ICRA, 25 U.S.C.§ 1302(a)(7)(B).
54. Tribal Law and Order Act amending ICRA, 25 U.S.C. § 1302(a)(7)(C)-(D) and 25 U.S.C. § 1302(b).
55. Michael J. Human trafficking: law enforcement says it's a problem, but stats lacking. 2014. Bismarck Tribune Available online: http://bismarcktribune.com/news/local/crime-and-courts/human-trafficking-law-enfrocement-says-it's-a-problem-but-stats-lacking. Accessed 1 Aug 2016.
56. Webley K, Hillstrom C. Sex trafficking on the reservation: one Native American Nation's struggle against the trade. Marie Claire. 2015. Available online: www.marieclaire.com/culture/news/a16028/native-american-sex-trafficking/. Accessed 1 Aug 2016.
57. Gray JS, Rose WJ. Cultural adaptation for therapy with American Indians and Alaska Natives. J Multicult Couns Devel. 2012;40. p. 82–92.
58. Williams R. Cultural safety: what does it mean for our work practice? Aust N Z J Public Health. 1999;23(2):213–4. doi:10.1111/j.1467-842X.1999.tb01240.x.
59. Robin R, Chester B, Goldman D. Cumulative trauma and PTSD in American Indian communities. In: Marsella A, Friedman J, Gerrity E, Scurfiled R, editors. Ethnocultural aspects of posttraumatic stress disorder: issues, research, and clinical applications. Washington, DC: American Psychological Association; 1996. p. 239–54.
60. Pierce A, Koepplinger S. New language, old problem: sex trafficking of American Indian women and children. Harrisburg, PA: VAWnet, a project of the National Resource Center on Domestic Violence; 2011. Available at: http://www.vawnet.org/Assoc_Files_VAWnet/AR_NativeSexTrafficking.pdf. Accessed 1 Aug 2016.
61. Kugel R, Murphy LE, editors. Native women's history in Eastern North America before 1900: a guide to research and writing native peoples. Lincoln, NE: University of Nebraska Press; 2007.
62. Martin L, Lotspeich R, Stark L. Early intervention to avoid sex trading and trafficking of Minnesota's female youth: a benefit-cost analysis. 2012. http://www.castla.org/templates/files/miwrc-benefit-cost-study-summary.pdf. Accessed 1 Aug 2016.

63. The OECD DAC Network on Gender Equality. Women's economic empowerment. 2012. Available at: https://www.oecd.org/dac/povertyreduction/50157530.pdf. Accessed 1 Aug 2016.
64. Cheng TL, Kotelchuck M, Guyer B. Preconception women's health and pediatrics: an opportunity to address infant mortality and family health. Acad Pediatr. 2012;12(5):357–9. doi:10.1016/j.acap.2012.04.006.
65. Breshears Wheeler J, Foreman M, Rueschhoff A. Improving women's health challenges, access and prevention. 2012. Available at: http://www.ncsl.org/research/health/improving-womens-health-2013.aspx. Accessed 1 Aug 2016.

Chapter 9
LGBTQ Youth and Vulnerability to Sex Trafficking

Kathryn Xian, Shaylin Chock, and Dustin Dwiggins

9.1 Introduction

Within our communities, there are individuals who take advantage of the vulnerability of youth for the most traumatizing ends: human trafficking. At highest risk, are children with one or more of the following qualities: being lesbian, gay, bisexual, having a transgender experience, or questioning their sexual orientation (LGBTQ); having a gender nonconforming identity, a history of surviving sexual abuse or a substance use disorder; being a member of a low-income family; being an ethnic minority, or having immigrant status [1].

In this chapter, we focus on LGBTQ or queer youth, who by no other act than self-identifying as LGBTQ, are often consequently categorized outside the definition of a "good child." As a result, they fall victim to myriad societal and interpersonal abuses, making them disproportionately vulnerable to sex trafficking. In the

The authors of this chapter include an Asian American, lesbian-identified, masculine-presenting victim advocate; and a mixed-race Native Hawaiian, heterosexual, feminine-presenting pediatric psychiatrist, who both work directly with sex trafficked youth; and a white, gay, masculine-presenting emergency medicine resident physician.

K. Xian (✉)
Pacific Alliance to Stop Slavery, 4348 Waialae Ave. #248, Honolulu, HI 96816, USA
e-mail: kathy@passhawaii.org

S. Chock, M.D.
Department of Psychiatry, John A. Burns School of Medicine, University of Hawaii, 1356 Lusitana St., 4th Floor, Honolulu, HI 96813, USA
e-mail: Schock@dop.hawaii.edu

D. Dwiggins
Icahn School of Medicine at Beth Israel Mount Sinai, 10 Nathan D Perlman Pl, New York, NY 10003, USA
e-mail: ddwiggins@chpnet.org

© Springer International Publishing AG 2017
M. Chisolm-Straker, H. Stoklosa (eds.), *Human Trafficking Is a Public Health Issue*, DOI 10.1007/978-3-319-47824-1_9

sections that follow we explain how these multi-layered vulnerabilities lay the foundation for trafficking of queer youth and provide recommendations for government action [2].

9.2 Discussion

9.2.1 Layers of Vulnerability to Trafficking Using the Socioecological Model

9.2.1.1 Society

Societal Norms The higher risk of trafficking among LGBTQ youth in part results from the downstream effects of a society requiring children to demonstrate particular behaviors in a hierarchy controlled by adults. By definition, "good behavior"—an adult construct—supports the ideal of a functional nuclear family where parents are caring and children are obedient. This aspiration of idyllic behavior creates more problems and harm than we realize, to both the family unit and to society as a whole. When youth do not act according to the "good behavior" paradigm, they are more vulnerable to exploitation and abuse than their obedient counterparts. Unfortunately, instead of recognizing the responsibility of society to widen its definition of "good" or acceptable behavior, youth that exist outside of societal ideals are often misidentified, abused, criminalized, condemned, incarcerated, and re-victimized [1].

Safe Expression Safe gender expression for gender nonconforming children is rarely possible on school campuses with anti-LGBTQ environments. Queer youth, regardless of gender identity, often seek other venues within which they can experiment with and express their sexual or gender awareness. Unfortunately, these alternate venues tend to be enveloped in adult nightlife at "clubbing" and "raver" events, where the use of illicit drugs often occurs. The popularity of drugs such as 3,4-methylenedioxy-methamphetamine or MDMA ("ecstasy" or "molly"), and methamphetamine, in adult LGBTQ clubs, dangerously expose queer youth to potential substance use disorders. Compounded with family abuse and a hostile school environment, LGBTQ youth experiencing these stressors may come to fully rely on substances to cope [3]. However, without supervision or self-moderation, which is rarely available, premature habitual exposure to alcohol and substance use increases a youth's risk for exploitation. Some traffickers provide drugs as a technique for controlling trafficked persons, including youth.

9.2.1.2 Community

Homelessness A very real and all too common potential result of a queer child's coming out experience to unaccepting guardians is homelessness. Once a child becomes homeless, they are immediately vulnerable to being trafficked due to:

1. the need for the basics of survival, including food and shelter;
2. lack of access to justice;
3. lack of access to physical or mental health care;
4. lack of access to education; and
5. the need for love and support.

To earn money to eat, be safely sheltered and clothed, and/or to sustain a chemical dependence, homeless children may resort to what has been inappropriately and imprudently termed *survival sex*. Survival sex is commercial sex engaged in by a person because of their extreme need. It describes the practice of people who are homeless or otherwise disadvantaged, trading sex for food, a place to sleep, or other basic needs, or for drugs [4]. Two problems arise when the label *survival sex* is attached to minors who endure commercial sexual exploitation: First, the term erroneously implies that a child victim of sexual exploitation has enough agency to choose to sell their body for money. According to the United States (US) Trafficking Victim Protection Act, in the case of minors, force, fraud or coercion is *not* a requirement in establishing the crime of sex trafficking [4]. That is to say, any child engaged in any type of commercial sexual activity, or receiving anything of value in return, is being sex trafficked. Second, by indirect implication, *survival sex* suggests that *johns*, or people who purchase these children for sex, are providing a benefit or integral need, not available by any other means. The term *survival sex* contributes to the misidentification of sex trafficked youth among service providers, health care professionals, and law enforcement officers. Applying *survival sex* to sex trafficked youth proffers a subversive misnomer that labels youth in need of services as willing prostitutes.

Additionally, risk of being trafficked for homeless youth is exacerbated by a timeframe of acute initial vulnerability. During this time of early homelessness, a trafficker may recruit youth independently selling sex for money, food, drugs, or basic needs. Trafficked children are desired commodities in the commercial sex industry, commanding upwards of several thousands of dollars per night based on their young age [5]. And, street life is highly territorial, with traffickers physically enforcing their borders. Homeless children recruited into sex trafficking are forced to *choose up*,[1] or join a trafficker and their *stable*,[2] or "family" of prostituted persons under their control. Refusal to do so can instigate a *breaking in*[3] process akin to constant sexual torture, or even death, belying the insinuation of liberty in the term "*choosing* up."

To be clear, and as per the Trafficking Victims Protection Act, anyone under the age of 18 years engaged in survival sex, regardless of emancipation status or third party involvement, is actually experiencing human trafficking. Understanding this differentiation is crucial to successfully identifying high risk and trafficked youth.

---

[1] Choose Up: the process in which one or more pimps force a person, who is independently engaging in commercial sex, to "choose" to be owned by a specific pimp.

[2] Stable: the group of people, controlled by a pimp, who are engaged in commercial sex.

[3] Breaking In: the process in which one or more pimps subject a person to fear, torture, and various forms of sexual, mental, and spiritual abuse to force compliance in commercial sex. This highly traumatizing period may last from a few days to a few weeks.

9.2.1.3 Systems

Transgender experienced or gender nonconforming (TGGNC) persons may have been assigned one gender at birth, but may physically present, via mannerisms, clothing, hairstyle, body language, or other means, in a way more traditional to another gender. TGGNC and lesbian, gay, and bisexual youth have a significantly more difficult experience obtaining services in physical health, mental health, education, and the juvenile justice system due to discrimination [6, 7]. This system-level marginalization puts LGBTQ individuals at even higher risk of being trafficked as the very organizational structures who should support them, contribute to their victimization [1].

Educational System Sixty percent of LGBTQ youth report feeling unsafe in school, 40 % experience physical harassment, and 18.3 % report being physically assaulted; queer students have a higher incidence of being bullied, threatened, or injured at school [8]. In this hostile learning environment, many queer youth feel justifiably afraid and are not able to benefit fully from their education system. In fact, many school health professional staff are ill-prepared to address the needs of these pupils: In a study published in 2014, nearly half of school social workers and counselors reported having no knowledge of available community resources for LGBTQ students in need [9]. This is particularly concerning because queer students are at particularly high risk for suicide, depression, and/or discrimination. These students may be isolated, suffer from problematic interpersonal relationships at school, or avoid school altogether. Children outside of the safe supervision of schools, caring guardians, and/or those emotionally unsupported are more vulnerable to being trafficked. Criminalized as truants, queer youth avoiding school may thus enter the juvenile justice system.

Criminal Justice System Some law enforcement officers have personal biases against LGBTQ individuals and may express their prejudice while functioning in an official capacity. LGBTQ communities report regular occurrences of police [10] harassment and have a history of enduring discrimination including verbal abuse, profiling, entrapment, neglect, and physical assault [11]. Police misconduct, neglect, or criminalization of homeless LGBTQ children occurs often, and may be due to homophobic bias [11]:

Compared to their heterosexual peers, perceived LGB youth are [12]:

- 53 % more likely to be stopped by police
- 60 % more likely to be arrested before the age of 18
- 90 % more likely to have had a juvenile conviction
- 41 % more likely to have had an adult conviction.

Compared to their heterosexual female peers, [gender nonconforming] lesbian or bisexual girls are [12]:

- 2.5 times more likely to be arrested before age 18
- Three times more likely to have a juvenile conviction
- Greater than four times more likely to have been arrested after the age of 18

- Twice as likely to have an adult conviction.

Given these experiences, LGBTQ youth have little recourse when they experience abuse or dangerous situations and queer youth who are trafficked are unlikely to view law enforcement as a viable means of help.

Physical and Mental Health Care System Many health care providers feel inadequately trained on how to care for LGBTQ patients: In a 2012 survey of 132 medical school deans across the USA and Canada, only 30% felt that their school's sensitivity and understanding of the unique needs of LGBTQ patients was "good" to "very good" [13]. According to a 2012 qualitative study, health care providers are inadequately trained to work with LGBTQ youth [11]. Thus, queer youth may have unmet psychiatric, psychological, and medical needs due to lack of provider training; these unfulfilled medical and mental health needs also place queer youth at increased risk for being trafficked.

Spiritual Health Systems Societal influences steeped in homophobic interpretation of religious tenets encourage familial maltreatment of LGBTQ children. *Spiritual wounding* results from the promotion of non-contextual religious doctrinal interpretation [14]. This misinterpretation not only convinces caretakers that their spiritual child abuse is justified, but also harms the child who believes that, in order to be truthful about their gender or sexual identity, they must either accept that they are categorically condemned or must defy the entire religion and the higher power associated with it. For a child raised in a religious household, spiritual wounding can be profoundly hurtful, injuring their *spiritual core* or spiritual self [14]. The stress and trauma of guardian and doctrinal spiritual wounding contributes to the child's feelings of rejection and frustration; it can rupture the development of the child's self-worth. Such rejection or abandonment puts queer youth at risk for various forms of victimization, including human trafficking, as they seek acceptance and belonging outside of the familial and religious homes.

Conversion Therapy The concept of *conversion therapy*, also known as "reparative" or "reorientation" therapy, is intended to change a person's sexual orientation from "other" to heterosexual; it is based on the belief that homosexuality is a mental illness or sinful in nature [15]. LGBTQ youth may respond to recommendations for or attempts at conversion therapy by running away from home, putting these children at higher risk for being trafficked. Historically, the desire for therapeutic alteration of sexual orientation was based on the fact that the Diagnostic and Statistical Manual of Mental Disorders (DSM) stated that a non-heterosexual identity was a mental illness [16]. Since 1973, the DSM no longer classifies non-heterosexual orientation as a disorder. The goal of conversion therapy is to help people develop their "heterosexual potential," thereby eliminating "unwanted same-sex attraction" [17]. Numerous researchers have confirmed that individuals who participate in these types of therapies have increased levels of depressive symptoms, suicidal ideation and attempts, isolation, and decreased self-worth [18]. In short, conversion therapy is destructive.

Furthermore, the American Academy of Child and Adolescent Psychiatry (AACAP) notes that, "there is no evidence that sexual orientation can be altered through therapy, and…attempts to do so may be harmful" [19]. The American Medical Association (AMA), "opposes, the use of 'reparative' or 'conversion' therapy that is based upon the assumption that homosexuality per se is a mental disorder or based upon the *a priori* assumption that the patient should change his/her homosexual orientation [20]."

Importantly, because sexual orientation and gender identity are often erroneously conflated, "conversion therapy" is also inflicted upon transgender-experienced and gender nonconforming individuals. In 2015, President Barack Obama called for an end to the practice of conversion therapy after the highly publicized suicide of a 17-year-old girl of transgender experience; she had been forced to participate in such a program. Several US states, including New Jersey and California, have made conversion therapy illegal [21]. Despite formal scientific opposition to this type of treatment, there is still no federal law banning these therapies, leaving LGBTQ youth vulnerable to another layer of re-victimization, and further increasing their risk for trafficking.

Due to systemic discrimination, queer children are at higher risk for victimization via human trafficking than their heterosexual or cisgender[4] peers [7]. Moreover, systemic mistreatment of this group retards, and may even prevent, the healing process for these survivors recovering from the trauma of human trafficking. Inadequate educational system support; poor, inconsistent training of health care professionals; rampant discrimination of law enforcement against queer youth; and the perpetuation of spiritual wounding and conversion therapy requires broad policy change, training, and LGBTQ specific services. Until these measures are in place, LGBTQ youth will remain a disproportionately represented group among children trafficked.

9.2.1.4   Interpersonal Relationships

Good parenting by at least one adult household member is essential in the prevention of risk factors leading to sexual exploitation. Unfortunately, youth frequently suffer serious danger from their own family members upon coming out as LGBT or Q. Survey results reflect that 68 % of self-identified queer youth became homeless due to family rejection and 54 % experienced physical or sexual abuse by a household member [6]. Alterations in attachment, rejection, abandonment, and abuse all contribute to an increased risk for trafficking among LGBTQ youth.

Effects of Attachment British psychologist, psychiatrist, and psychoanalyst, John Bowlby's attachment theory focuses on the persistence of dependency needs throughout a child's life, and the importance that attachment plays in relationships,

---

[4]Cisgender: denoting or relating to a person whose affirmed gender conforms to the gender they were assigned at birth; not transgender.

personality, and life functioning. Bowlby points out the import of a mother's (or caregiver's) empathetic responses to the infant in future self, personal, and age-appropriate development [22]. Attachment theory focuses on how one responds when emotionally wounded, separated from loved ones, or when a physical threat is perceived [23]. Successful attachment depends upon a child's ability to develop basic trust in their caregivers as well as in themselves. In infancy, the child seeks proximity with familiar caregivers who protect and provide emotional support [24]. The child learns to trust that the caregiver will be there to provide for their necessities. This caregiver becomes the child's "safe base."

There are four different attachment classifications: (1) secure attachment, (2) anxious-ambivalent attachment, (3) anxious-avoidant attachment, and (4) disorganized attachment. A *securely attached* individual feels that they can depend upon a caregiver to provide essentials. This is the ideal attachment class. The *anxious-ambivalent* individual will experience separation anxiety when removed from the caregiver and does not feel reassured when the caregiver returns. The *anxious-avoidant* individual avoids their caregivers and *disorganized attachment* describes a lack of any attachment at all [25].

Queer individuals often experience rejection or abandonment in their youth, leading to disruptions in attachments. If a child lacks a secure attachment at an early age, it is likely that they will struggle with personal development, the ability to manage highly emotional situations, and the ability to maintain relationships with others. Consequently, these youth may seek out care-giving support in unstable environments (e.g., streets or social media), which put them at risk for being trafficked.

Moreover, the processing of a traumatic event differs depending on the nature of the relationship between the "perpetrator" and the "victim"; this is known as the *theory of betrayal trauma*. In these instances, when the offender is someone that the victimized person trusts, relies upon, or cares for, the trauma is considered to be high in betrayal [26]. The rejection, abandonment, or abuse of queer youth exemplifies such betrayal. And individuals who experience trauma with betrayal early in life, like some LGBTQ children, are more likely to experience trauma with betrayal, like trafficking, as adolescents and adults [27]. Sometimes, to preserve and maintain the attachment bond between offender and victimized, the latter is less likely to remember the betraying events; this is known as *betrayal blindness* [28]. In these instances, it may be psychologically advantageous for the individual to forget the trauma and maintain closeness with the caretaker to ensure immediate survival. Given that many trafficked persons experienced trauma high in betrayal (e.g., being dependent upon their perpetrator), they may be less likely to take self-protective measures, such as leaving or seeking help.

Rejection, Abandonment, Abuse

In 2012, the U.S. Department of Health and Human Services documented 3.4 million referrals to child protective services, representing 686,000 children. Approximately 80 percent of the maltreatment was perpetuated by one or both parents…ELS [early life stress] was comprised of neglect (78.3 percent), physical abuse (18.3 percent), and sexual abuse (9.3 percent) [29].

While rejection and abandonment are problems applicable to both at-risk LGBTQ and heterosexual and cisgender youth, queer children may experience these forms of child abuse more frequently than their heterosexual and cisgender peers [30]. The effects of rejection or abandonment of any child by their parent can be more devastating than physical abuse [31]. LGBTQ youth who experience abuse have devastating long term neurobiological consequences that place them at high risk of being trafficked. Persistent abuse and trauma may have long term effects on brain development and mood regulation. Additionally, pervasive abuse creates alterations in endocrine function, genetics and epigenetics,[5] and in brain topography and physiology [32]. Long term abuse and neglect are associated with an increased risk for major psychiatric disorders and executive functioning may be permanently affected and possibly irreversible [23, 33]. Neglect, rejection, or abandonment, by at least one guardian, can make coming out intrinsically dangerous for queer youth. Thus, these youth may end up homeless, with poor self esteem, or with no support, making them prime targets for those looking to bring them into trafficking.

9.2.1.5 Individual

In general, LGBTQ youth are three times more likely to experience mental health conditions like major depression, generalized anxiety disorder, post-traumatic stress disorder (PTSD), thoughts of suicide, and substance use disorders than their heterosexual and cisgender counterparts. Specifically, LGBT youth are four times more likely to have attempted suicide; questioning youth are three times more likely to have attempted suicide, experience suicidal ideation, or engage in self-harm. Thirty-eight to forty-five percent of transgender-experienced youth struggle with suicidal ideation. Among LGBT individuals aged 10 to 24 years old, suicide is one of the leading causes of death [34]. These mental health problems have been associated with increased risk for trafficking among LGBTQ youth [35–37]. LGBTQ youth also report higher rates of experiencing violence and bullying than their heterosexual and cisgender counterparts [38]. Such bullying is often compounded by systemic discrimination or domestic abuse, which may lead to homelessness [7], and is considered a serious risk factor for sex trafficking.

Moreover, homelessness itself is strongly associated with increased risk of trafficking among queer youth [39–41]:

> Although LGBTQ individuals only account for three to five percent of the population, they account for up to 40 percent of the runaway and homeless youth population. It is estimated that 26 percent of LGBTQ adolescents are rejected by their families and put out of their homes for no other reason than being open about who they are [42].

---

[5] Epigenetics: refers to heritable changes in gene expression (active versus inactive genes) that does not involve changes to the underlying DNA sequence; it is a change in phenotype (appearance) without a change in genotype (genes). Epigenetics is also the study of changes in organisms caused by modification of gene expression rather than alteration of the genetic code itself.

Among homeless youth, sex trafficked youth in a 1991 study were five times more likely to be LGBT [43].

LGBTQ youth, in comparison to heterosexual and cisgender peers, are more likely to use illicit substances and alcohol, both experimentally and due to dependence [44]. This increased use is possibly related to the increased stress queer youth experience due to societal discrimination, frequent interpersonal microaggressions,[6] and fear of parental/guardian rejection. Gender nonconforming youth, who experience greater bullying in school than gender-conforming students, may feel unsafe with their classmates and therefore affiliate with a peer group more likely to misuse substances [44]. Twenty to thirty percent of LGBTQ youth abuse substances, compared to 9 % of their non-LGBTQ youth peers; 25 % of LGBTQ youth abuse alcohol compared to 5–10 % of their non-LGBTQ youth peers [34]. Substance use has been repeatedly linked to commercial sexual exploitation [46–51].

9.3 Conclusion

While, in general, sex trafficked minors suffer from a lack of resources, identification, and advocacy, self-identified LGBTQ youth are significantly more vulnerable to sexual exploitation than their gender-conforming or heterosexual peers. And due to systemic discrimination, these youth are at even higher risk for re-victimization and recidivism. All LGBTQ youth are at increased risk of being trafficked, and are disproportionately represented among the trafficked in the US. Without a full understanding of the underlying socioecological factors leading to the trafficking of youth, including the external factors negatively influencing a trafficked youth's sense of self-worth, the misidentification, neglect, and criminalization of sex trafficked children will continue.

9.4 Recommendations

To prevent child trafficking, curtail the vulnerability of children, especially LGBTQ youth, and protect our overall community from the rise of this crime against young people, the government must:

---

[6]Microaggressions: Microaggressions are the everyday verbal, nonverbal, and environmental slights, snubs, or insults, whether intentional or unintentional, which communicate hostile, derogatory, or negative messages to target persons based solely upon their marginalized group membership. In many cases, these hidden messages may invalidate the group identity or experiential reality of target persons, demean them on a personal or group level, communicate they are lesser human beings, suggest they do not belong to the majority group, threaten and intimidate, or relegate them to inferior status and treatment [45].

- Provide funding for services specific to LGBTQ children at risk and provide training to sensitize law enforcement, health care providers, and social services to the needs of queer youth. These needs include, but are not limited to: affordable and safe housing, mental health and health care, and education or skill building programs (http://www.polarisproject.org/sites/default/files/breaking-barriers-lgbtq-services.pdf).
- Implement and uphold policies to protect queer youth from discrimination, harassment, and neglect within the law enforcement, education, and health care systems.
- Fund LGBTQ-accepting outreach and survivor advocacy programs for the accurate assessment and identification of needs for this vulnerable population.

Without directly addressing systemic discrimination against queer youth and taking steps to protect these young people, the overall problem of commercial sex trafficking of children will continue to flourish.

References

1. Martinez O, Kelle G. Sex trafficking of LGBT individuals: a call for service provision, research, and action. Int Law News. 2013;42(4).
2. Clayton EW, Krugman RD, Simon P, editors. Confronting commercial sexual exploitation and sex trafficking of minors in the United States. Washington, DC: National Academies Press; 2013.
3. Mereish EH, O'cleirigh C, Bradford JB. Interrelationships between LGBT-based victimization, suicide, and substance use problems in a diverse sample of sexual and gender minorities. Psychol Health Med. 2014;19(1):1–13.
4. US Congress. Trafficking Victims Protection Act. HR 3244. 2000.
5. Flowers RB. Street kids: the lives of runaway and thrownaway teens. Jefferson, NC: McFarland; 2010. p. 110–2. ISBN 0-7864-4137-2.
6. Editorial staff at the Lancet. Ending LGBT conversion therapy. Lancet. 2015;385, p. 1478.
7. Durso LE, Gates GJ. Serving our youth: findings from a National Survey of Service Providers working with lesbian, gay, bisexual, and transgender youth who are homeless or at risk of becoming homeless. Los Angeles: The Williams Institute with True Colors Fund and The Palette Fund; 2012. p. 4.
8. Hughes D. The demand for victims of sex trafficking. Washington, DC: U.S. Department of State; 2005. p. 20.
9. Gay, Lesbian, & Straight Education Network. The 2011 National School Climate Survey. http://www.glsen.org/. Published 2011. Accessed 10 Mar 2016.
10. Dank M. Surviving the streets of New York: experiences of LGBTQ youth, YMSM, and YWSW engaged in survival sex. 2015.
11. Rutherford K, McIntyre J, Daley A, Ross LE. Development of expertise in mental health service provision for lesbians, gay, bisexual and transgender communities. Med Educ. 2012;46:903–13.
12. Mallory C, Hasenbush A, Sears B. Discrimination and harassment by law enforcement officers in the LGBT community. The Williams Institute, University of California at Los Angeles Law School. http://williamsinstitute.law.ucla.edu/wp-content/uploads/LGBT-Discrimination-and-Harassment-in-Law-Enforcement-March-2015.pdf. Published March 2015. Retrieved on 27 Apr 2016.

13. Madhi I, et al. Survey of New Mexico school health professionals regarding preparedness to support sexual minority students. J Sch Health. 2014;84(1):18–24.
14. Himmelstein K, Bruckner H. Criminal justice and school sanctions against nonheterosexual youth: a national longitudinal study. Pediatrics. 2011;127:49, 50, 53.
15. Haldeman D. Therapeutic antidotes: helping gay and bisexual men recover from conversion therapies. J Gay Lesbian Psychother. 2002;5(3–4):117–30.
16. Kruk E. Spiritual wounding and affliction: facilitating spiritual transformation in social justice work. Crit Soc Work. 2006;7(1).
17. Haldeman DC. Gay rights, patient rights: the implications of sexual orientation conversion therapy. Prof Psychol Res Pr. 2002;33(3):260–4. doi:10.1037/0735-7028.33.3.260.
18. Rosik CH. Motivational, ethical, and epistemological foundations in the treatment of unwanted homoerotic attraction. J Marital Fam Ther. 2003;29(1):13–28.
19. Adelson SL, American Academy of Child and Adolescent Psychiatry (AACAP) Committee on Quality Issues (CQI). Practice parameter on gay, lesbian, or bisexual sexual orientation, gender nonconformity, and gender discordance in children and adolescents. J Am Acad Child Adolesc Psychiatry. 2012;51(9):957–74.
20. McGeorge CR, Carlson TS. An exploration of family therapists' beliefs about the ethics of conversion therapy: the influence of negative beliefs and clinical competence with lesbian, gay, and bisexual clients. J Marital Fam Ther. 2015;41(1):42–56. doi:10.1111/jmft.12040.
21. AMA. AMA policies on LGBT issues. Available at: http://www.ama-assn.org/ama/pub/about-ama/our-people/member-groups-sections/glbt-advisory-committee/ama-policy-regarding-sexual-orientation.page. Accessed 1 May 2016.
22. SAMHSA. A provider's introduction to substance abuse treatment for lesbian, gay, bisexual, and transgender individuals. Rockville, MD: SAMHSA; 2012. p. xv–xvi.
23. Nemeroff CB. Paradise lost: the neurobiological and clinical consequences of child abuse and neglect. Neuron. 2016;89(5):892–909.
24. Alvy LM, Hughes TL, Kristjanson AF, Wilsnack SC. Sexual identity group differences in child abuse and neglect. J Interpers Violence. 2013;28(10):2088–111.
25. Herzberger SD, Potts DA, Dillon M. Abusive and nonabusive parental treatment from the child's perspective. J Consult Clin Psychol. 1981;49(1):81–90.
26. Hecker T, Radtke KM, Hermenau K, Papassotiropoulos A, Elbert T. Associations among child abuse, mental health, and epigenetic modifications in the proopiomelanocortin gene (POMC): a study with children in Tanzania. Dev Psychopathol. 2016;28(4)1–12.
27. Waters E, Corcoran D, Anafarta M. Attachment, other relationships, and the theory that all good things go together. Hum Dev. 2005;48:80–4.
28. Norman RE, Byambaa M, De R, Butchart A, Scott J, Vos T. The long-term health consequences of child physical abuse, emotional abuse, and neglect: a systematic review and meta-analysis. PLoS Med. 2012;9(11), e1001349.
29. Landa S, Duschinsky R. Crittenden's dynamic–maturational model of attachment and adaptation. Rev Gen Psychol. 2013;17(3):326.
30. Textbook International Association for Children and Adolescent Psychiatry and Allied Professions
31. Freyd J, DePrince A, Zurbriggen E. Self-reported memory for abuse depends upon victim-perpetrator relationship. J Trauma Dissociation. 2011;2(3):5–15.
32. Freyd J. Betrayal trauma: the logic of forgetting childhood abuse. Cambridge, MA: Harvard University Press; 1998.
33. Hocking E, Simons R, Surette R. Attachment style as a mediator between childhood maltreatment and the experience of betrayal trauma as an adult. Child Abuse Negl. 2016;52:94–101.
34. National Alliance on Mental Illness (NAMI). 2016. https://www.nami.org/Find-support/LGBTQ. Accessed 16 Mar 2016.
35. Stein JA, Leslie MB, Nyamathi A. Relative contributions of parent substance use and childhood maltreatment to chronic homelessness, depression, and substance abuse problems among

homeless women: mediating roles of self-esteem and abuse in adulthood. Child Abuse Negl. 2002;26(10):1011–27.

36. Swanston HY, Plunkett AM, O'Toole BI, Shrimpton S, Parkinson PN, Oates RK. Nine years after child sexual abuse. Child Abuse Negl. 2003;27(8):967–84.

37. Steel JL, Herlitz CA. The association between childhood and adolescent sexual abuse and proxies for sexual risk behavior: a random sample of the general population of Sweden. Child Abuse Negl. 2005;29(10):1141–53.

38. Shields JP, et al. Impact of victimization on risk of suicide among lesbian, gay, and bisexual high school students in San Francisco. J Adolesc Health. 2011;50(4):418–20.

39. Cochran BN, Stewart AJ, Ginzler JA, Cauce AM. Challenges faced by homeless sexual minorities: comparison of gay, lesbian, bisexual, and transgender homeless adolescents with their heterosexual counterparts. Am J Public Health. 2002;92(5):773–7.

40. Rew L, Whittaker T, Tylor-Seehafer M, Smith L. Sexual health risks and protective resources in gay, lesbian, bisexual and heterosexual homeless youth. J Spec Pediatr Nurs. 2005;10(1):11–20.

41. Whitbeck LB, Chen XJ, Hoyt DR, Tyler KA, Johnson KD. Mental disorder, subsistence strategies, and victimization among gay, lesbian, and bisexual homeless and runaway adolescents. J Sex Res. 2004;41(4):329–42.

42. Bean LJ. LGBTQ youth at high risk of becoming human trafficking victims. Administration for Children and Families, U.S. Department of Health and Human Services. http://www.acf.hhs.gov/blog/2013/06/lgbtq-youth-at-high-risk-of-becoming-human-trafficking-victims. Published 2013. Accessed 20 Mar 2016.

43. Yates GL, MacKenzie RG, Pennbridge J, Swofford A. A risk profile comparison of homeless youth involved in prostitution and homeless youth not involved. J Adolesc Health. 1991;12(7):545–8.

44. Blake SM, Ledsky R, Lehman T, Goodenow C, Sawyer R, Hack T. Preventing sexual risk behaviors among gay, lesbian, and bisexual adolescents: the benefits of gay-sensitive HIV instruction in schools. Am J Public Health. 2001;91:940–6.

45. Sue DW. Microaggressions: more than just race. Can microaggressions be directed to women or gay people? 2010. Retrieved 2 May 2016 from: https://www.psychologytoday.com/blog/microaggressions-in-everyday-life/201011/microaggressions-more-just-race. Accessed 1 Aug 2016.

46. Chettiar J, Shannon K, Wood E, Zhang R, Kerr T. Survival sex work involvement among street-involved youth who use drugs in a Canadian setting. J Public Health. 2010;32(3):322–7.

47. Edwards JM, Iritani BJ, Hallfors DD. Prevalence and correlates of exchanging sex for drugs or money among adolescents in the United States. Sex Transm Infect. 2006;82(5):354–8.

48. Estes RJ, Weiner NA. The commercial sexual exploitation of children in the U.S., Canada, and Mexico. Philadelphia, PA: Center for the Study of Youth Policy; 2001.

49. Greene JM, Ennett ST, Ringwalt CL. Prevalence and correlates of survival sex among runaway and homeless youth. Am J Public Health. 1999;89(9):1406–9.

50. Cusick L, Hickman M. "Trapping" in drug use and sex work careers. Drugs. 2005;12(5):369–79.

51. Stoltz J-AM, Shannon K, Kerr T, Zhang R, Montaner JS, Wood E. Associations between childhood maltreatment and sex work in a cohort of drug-using youth. Soc Sci Med. 2007;65(6):1214–21.

Chapter 10
The Multimodal Social Ecological (MSE) Approach: A Trauma-Informed Framework for Supporting Trafficking Survivors' Psychosocial Health

Elizabeth K. Hopper

10.1 Introduction

For many survivors, the human trafficking experience is one of the many lifetime experiences of stress and trauma. Traffickers take advantage of pre-existing vulnerabilities, such as poverty, a history of trauma exposure, lack of adequate supports and resources, and lack of opportunities. Victimized persons are treated as objects and are often subjected to emotional, physical, and/or sexual abuse while being trafficked. Even after they are able to get out of the trafficking situation, many trafficking survivors continue to struggle with a host of unmet needs, as well as the emotional aftermath of their experiences. In their report examining the health consequences of human trafficking, Zimmerman et al. reflected that "mental health is perhaps the most dominant health dimension in trafficking cases because of the profound psychological damage caused by (often chronic) traumatic events and the common somatic complaints that frequently translate into physical pain or dysfunction" [1]. Despite this, the mental health needs of trafficking survivors are often overlooked or not adequately addressed.

10.1.1 Commonly Identified Mental Health Symptoms in Trafficking Survivors

Not surprisingly, given the extent of stress and trauma typically associated with human trafficking, depression, anxiety, and post-traumatic stress disorder (PTSD) are commonly identified in survivors of human trafficking [2–5]. More than half of

E.K. Hopper (✉)
The Trauma Center at JRI, 1269 Beacon Street, Brookline, MA 02446, USA
e-mail: ehopper@jri.org

© Springer International Publishing AG 2017
M. Chisolm-Straker, H. Stoklosa (eds.), *Human Trafficking Is a Public Health Issue*, DOI 10.1007/978-3-319-47824-1_10

the trafficked women in one study met criteria for a mental health diagnosis, with PTSD, depression, and anxiety disorders being the most common diagnoses [6].

Depression Symptoms of depression are among the most commonly reported mental health consequences in trafficking survivors. One study found that the majority of trafficking survivors endorsed feelings of depression and intense sadness (95%) and hopelessness about the future (76%) [7]. In a review of multiple studies, 54.9–100% of trafficking survivors were found to be suffering from significant depressive symptoms [8]. Depressive symptoms may become chronic and can include safety concerns such as suicidal ideation or attempts. For instance, one study of female survivors of transnational sex trafficking found that more than 85% of these women continued to experience a depressed mood several years after they got out of the trafficking situation [9]. Similar rates of depression (79%) have been found in trafficked youth [10]. Suicidal ideation and attempts are also common [9]: A history of suicidal ideation was reported by 59% of trafficked youth in one qualitative study [10], while another study identified a history of suicide attempts in 41.5% of trafficking survivors [11].

Anxiety Depression is often found with comorbid anxiety among trafficking survivors. Across 16 studies in multiple countries, a significant portion (48.0–97.7%) of trafficking survivors struggled with severe anxiety [8]. Commonly experienced symptoms of anxiety in one European study included: nervousness or "shakiness" inside (91%), terror/panic spells (61%), and fearfulness (85%) [7]. High rates of anxiety have been found in survivors of both labor (87.5%) and sex (97.7%) trafficking [5].

Post-traumatic Stress Disorder PTSD is frequently identified as a consequence of trafficking across a range of ages and cultural contexts; many survivors struggle with intrusive memories and experiences, avoid traumatic reminders, and suffer from hyper-aroused states [3, 5, 10, 12–14]. There is considerable variability in estimates of PTSD among trafficking survivors; for instance, one review found that estimates of PTSD ranged from 19.5 to 77% across multiple studies [8].

10.1.2 Variability in Presentations

It is important to keep in mind that trafficking survivors are not a uniform population. There may be differences amongst trafficking survivors, with respect to age, sex gender identification, cultural background, trafficking history, experience of distress, reporting of symptoms, and/or help-seeking behaviors.

More research has been conducted on mental health impacts among female survivors of sex trafficking than other groups. Some evidence suggests that there may be differences in the psychological consequences of trafficking depending on gender and/or trafficking type. In a study of female trafficking survivors in Nepal, sex trafficking survivors had higher reported symptom levels than labor trafficking survivors, including anxiety (97.7 % vs. 87.5 %), depression (100 % vs. 80.8 %), and PTSD (29.6 % vs. 7.5 %) [5]. A labor trafficking study that included primarily male respondents (77 %) found that survivors more commonly reported physical symptoms than psychological symptoms such as symptoms of PTSD [15]. However, a large-scale survey, published in 2015, including male and female survivors of labor and sex trafficking did not find notable differences in mental health outcomes based on gender or trafficking type, aside from a slightly increased endorsement of depression in women [3]. Additional research is needed about the psychological aftermath of labor trafficking and about potential gender differences in the psychological response to human trafficking, as well as in reporting and help-seeking patterns.

The extent of trauma exposure in the trafficking context likely impacts mental health outcomes. Injuries and sexual violence during trafficking have been linked with higher levels of PTSD, depression, and anxiety [14]. A recent study found that, regardless of gender, age, and trafficking type, people who had experienced abusive overwork, restricted freedom, poor living conditions, threats, or severe violence were more likely to report symptoms of depression, anxiety, and PTSD [13].

10.1.3   Comorbidity

Further complicating the mental health picture, trafficking survivors often present with multiple inter-related symptoms and behavioral issues. An international study of over 200 trafficked girls and women in seven post-trafficking service settings found that 80 % of survivors met criteria for at least one mental health disorder, commonly including depression (55 %), anxiety (48 %), and PTSD (77 %). Even more notable, however, was the fact that over half of these survivors (57 %) showed comorbid depression, anxiety, and PTSD [14]. Other comorbid issues may include alcohol and substance use, dissociation, self-injurious behavior, guilt and shame, memory problems, anger and aggression, and somatic complaints [11, 16–18]. Trafficking survivors sometimes suffer from chronic mental illness, including conditions such as schizophrenia, schizoaffective disorder, or bipolar disorder. For instance, in a recent study of sex and labor trafficking survivors seeking mental health treatment, 15 % had diagnoses of schizophrenia [3, 8, 19]. In addition, the US State Department has identified people with physical and mental disabilities as "one of the groups most at risk of trafficking," and many cases have come to light involving the trafficking of individuals with a range of disabilities [20]. A recent analysis found that trafficked adults are more likely than their peers to be compulsorily admitted to inpatient psychiatric hospitals and have longer admissions, reflecting the severity of mental health symptoms experienced by some trafficking survivors [19].

Similarly, trafficked children and adolescents frequently struggle with a range of emotional, psychosocial, and behavioral difficulties [21]. These young people are often diagnosed with multiple comorbid mental health disorders. Data indicate that they may meet diagnostic criteria for mood disorders, substance use disorders, dissociative disorders, impulse control disorders, conduct disorder, attention-deficit/hyperactivity disorder, antisocial personality traits, and anxiety disorders like obsessive compulsive disorder and post-traumatic stress disorder [22, 23].

10.1.4 Complex Trauma in Trafficking Survivors

Although trafficking survivors often meet criteria for multiple diagnostic labels, many of their struggles could be better explained by a more unified construct called "complex trauma" or "Complex PTSD" [24]. Complex PTSD is a constellation of symptoms that is associated with repeated or chronic interpersonal trauma [25–27]. The complex trauma construct recognizes that chronic or repeated trauma impacts people in multiple areas, including emotional and dissociative responses, neurophysiology, cognition, behavior, relationships, self-concept, and future orientation [28–30].

Human trafficking has been identified as a type of traumatic exposure that is linked to Complex PTSD [16, 18, 26, 30–35]. Most trafficking survivors have experienced the type of chronic or repeated trauma that is associated with complex trauma. In many cases, their experience of deprivation, losses, and/or abuse began early in life, during pivotal developmental periods. High levels of pre-existing trauma exposure have been consistently identified amongst trafficking survivors [10, 13, 16, 18]. In addition to early physical and sexual abuse, emotional abuse and neglect have been highlighted as an early form of trauma exposure for some trafficking survivors [10, 36]. The traumatic exposures that occur within the context of human trafficking are also well documented and include threats, control, enforced isolation, verbal and emotional abuse, deprivation of basic necessities, physical abuse, sexual abuse, and torture [11, 18, 37–39]. Key signs of complex trauma have been found in trafficking survivors, including dysregulation of emotions, somatic states, cognition, and behavior; relational impacts; and impacted sense of self and future orientation [10, 16, 18].

10.1.5 Dysregulation of Emotions, Somatic States, Cognition, and Behavior

Dysregulation refers to impairments in awareness of, tolerance of, and/or ability to manage aspects of experience. Although the majority of health-related research on trafficking has not explored this area, intense and dysregulated emotions have been noted in trafficking survivors [10, 16, 21]. One report identified *affect dysregulation*, or difficulty managing emotions, in 88 % of trafficked youth [10]. Survivors of complex trauma often experience emotional distress through somatic symptoms.

Research has revealed a high prevalence of physical complaints in trafficking survivors that may have psychological contributors, including headaches, dizzy spells, exhaustion, nausea, weight loss, stomach pain, sleep disturbance, and immune suppression [1, 3, 8]. When trafficking survivors have difficulty tolerating intense emotions, they may cope through *dissociation*, or disconnection from feelings, sensations, or the surrounding environment. Trafficking survivors may dissociate in preparation for perceived threats, feel disconnected from their bodies, feel that they have different "parts" of self, be unable to recall certain aspects of their trauma, or have impacted memory in general [7, 8, 11]. Estimates of the extent of memory loss in trafficking survivors are quite variable, and have ranged from 15.6 % [3] to 63 % [7]. Memory loss may be a result of dissociation or due to other health-related concerns, including traumatic brain injuries resulting from physical assaults. Also related to affect dysregulation, survivors may struggle with a host of behavioral issues that involve maladaptive, often impulsive, attempts to cope with overwhelming experiences. For instance, self-injurious behavior, "running,"[1] and high-risk behaviors (such as engaging in unsafe sexual behaviors, driving while under the influence, or ignoring potential signs of danger) have been identified among sex trafficked youth [10, 12, 21]. Alcohol and substance use are means of coping with overwhelming emotions and memories for some trafficking survivors [40].

10.1.5.1   Relational Impacts

Because human trafficking is a form of interpersonal trauma that typically involves betrayal, exploitation, and injury, trafficking survivors often struggle with relational consequences. Some may struggle with establishing trusting relationships, feeling fearful or detached, or withdrawing from others [18]. Anger, defensiveness, and aggression are other forms of protection for people who have been repeatedly hurt by others. For instance, one study of sexually abused trafficked girls in India found that over a quarter of these young people were considered "highly aggressive" [41]. In another study, over half of trafficking survivors struggled with feeling irritable and having outbursts of anger [7]. In contrast, some survivors overlook potential signs of danger in interpersonal relationships, which can lead to continued exploitation [42]. In "*Stockholm syndrome*" or "*trauma bonding*," a survivor develops feelings of attachment or love to the perpetrator. This issue is a well-documented struggle for many trafficking survivors who have difficulty getting out of the abusive situation, despite available help. Re-victimization is not uncommon for trafficking survivors, and, even in non-abusive situations, some survivors have difficulty asserting their own wants and needs [7, 12].

---

[1] *Running* is a colloquial term that encompasses running away from home as well as elopement from treatment programs; it is a common concern for minors who have been trafficked.

10.1.5.2 Impacted Sense of Self and Future Orientation

After being treated like an object or a commodity, many trafficking survivors struggle to connect with a positive sense of self. Loss of important roles and community membership often occur with displacement. Survivors may feel stigmatized by others as a result of their experiences during trafficking and may blame themselves for getting into the situation [12]. Shame is an extremely common emotional consequence of trafficking, as survivors' identities are impacted by their experiences [16, 18]. In one study, over three quarters of trafficking survivors experienced feelings of worthlessness [7].

People who have been trafficked may also experience a sense of hopelessness and difficulties with future planning [10, 12]. In addition to concrete impediments to short- and long-term goals, a number of psychological issues may interfere with future orientation for trafficking survivors, including: negative self-concept, focus on immediate threats and rewards rather than longer-term outcomes, and the lack of belief in one's ability to influence the future [12, 21, 32]. The chronic trauma that many trafficking survivors experience can impact cognitive functioning, including attention, memory, and executive functioning skills such as problem-solving [21], further complicating life skills and future planning.

10.1.6 Accessibility of Mental Health Care for Trafficking Survivors

As survivors cope with the complex impact of trafficking on their physical, emotional, social, cognitive, and spiritual well-being, they need a range of supports to foster their recovery. Mental health services can be an important part of this supportive network. In a study of comprehensive services for trafficked persons within three communities, survivors often expressed a desire for counseling or therapy, particularly after they stabilized [43]. Survivors who received counseling reported "many positive outcomes, including a stronger sense of self and a feeling that they have grown stronger from having survived the trafficking experience and coped with its aftermath" (p. 20). Despite these reported benefits, trafficking survivors often face a range of barriers that prevent them from accessing effective mental health care [43, 44].

Some survivors are faced with concrete barriers that interfere with access to mental health services. Systemic and structural barriers include issues such as lack of identification documents or insurance; lack of linguistically matched or culturally sensitive services; social instability and legal concerns; basic impediments such as difficulties with transportation, childcare, or finances; and challenges with interagency collaboration [12, 43, 45]. For some trafficked people, survival-driven priorities such as the need to work long hours to support themselves and their families interfere with the ability to seek counseling; others are not connected with mental health care, even when they request emotional support, perhaps due to lack of available referral resources [43].

Beyond systemic and structural barriers, many trafficking survivors struggle with emotional responses that also interfere with accessing help. Alienation, mistrust of others, and social withdrawal can interfere with help-seeking in trafficking survivors. Shame can further increase their reluctance to disclose their experiences [46]. Many survivors have concerns regarding societal stigma about mental health struggles and mental health care. Some foreign national survivors come from communities with particularly strong stereotypes and pejorative attitudes about mental illness and thus may view the concept of mental health care as alien or frightening. Avoidance of traumatic memories and trauma-related emotions, a key symptom of PTSD, can also contribute to reluctance to seek mental health support, particularly when survivors perceive mental health services to be focused on the repeated recollection of painful memories. Finally, providers' difficulty establishing trusting relationships with survivors can prevent longer-term engagement in mental health care. When survivors have negative experiences with the mental health system, they may be more likely to avoid further contact [12, 45].

10.2   Discussion

10.2.1   Trauma-Informed Services for Trafficking Survivors

The complex mental health needs of trafficking survivors, along with limitations in current available services to address these needs, highlights the importance of improving services to support trafficking survivors' psychosocial health. Because many emotional barriers to help-seeking are associated with traumatic stress reactions, the availability of trauma-informed service systems and trauma-specific services may increase survivors' access to social assistance and mental health care and may be linked to improved outcomes [12, 18, 47].

10.2.1.1   Trauma-Informed Service Systems

The concept of *trauma-informed care* (TIC) offers guiding principles for service systems caring for survivors of violence, including trafficking survivors. Trauma-informed service systems acknowledge the widespread impact of trauma, understand potential means of recovery, recognize the signs and symptoms of trauma, integrate knowledge about trauma into policies and procedures, and actively work to avoid re-traumatization, or a triggered[2] relapse into the experience of trauma [48].

---

[2]A *trigger* is a term commonly used in the mental health field to refer to an internal experience or external stimuli that is a reminder of a traumatic experience and that precipitates an increase in trauma-related symptoms.

When the mental health system is not trauma-informed, it can repeat elements of trafficking-related trauma. Zhang Li*[3], a Chinese woman who had been held in a locked room for several years during her sex trafficking experience, was depressed and struggled with chronic suicidal ideation. Her case manager was finally able to convince her to access mental health services, but she was admitted to a secure psychiatric unit. Instead of being able to access help to support her mental health, Zhang Li was triggered by being "locked in"; she became extremely dysregulated and was eventually restrained and sedated by health care providers to calm her down. When she was finally discharged from the hospital, Zhang Li refused further contact with mental health providers. She was fearful of being hospitalized again and even more mistrustful of providers. Building culturally appropriate and trauma-informed mental health responses can decrease the likelihood of re-traumatization and increase the flexibility with which providers respond to the mental health needs of trafficking survivors.

Building collaborative relationships with clients, a key element of trauma-informed care, is based on providers' trustworthiness, transparency, mutuality, and respect for others [48, 49]. In addition to emphasizing physical and emotional safety, trauma-informed approaches recognize the cultural uniqueness of each person, highlight their strength and resilience, and support people's self-determination in their own recovery processes.

There are several frameworks available to aid organizations in becoming more trauma-informed or that offer an intervention framework to educate and guide professionals in working with survivors with complex trauma. For instance, the *Attachment, Regulation, and Competency (ARC)* treatment framework [50] has been implemented in residential treatment programs and youth outreach programs that serve trafficking survivors. Other frameworks that support the development of trauma-informed service settings include the *Sanctuary* model[4] [51] and the *Risking Connection* model[5] [52].

10.2.1.2 Supporting Resilience and Promoting Empowerment

Recognizing and supporting resilience are central elements of trauma-informed care for trafficking survivors. *Resilience* is "a dynamic process encompassing positive adaptation within the context of significant adversity" [53]. Resilience can be shown across many domains of functioning [54] and varies based on cultural and

---

[3] To better elucidate this complex issue, case examples from the author's professional experience with trafficking survivors are shared. All the names and any other identifying information have been modified to protect their identities. These clinical case examples are identified by asterisks throughout this chapter.

[4] Sanctuary is a model for clinical and organizational change that promotes safety and recovery from adversity through the active creation of a trauma-informed community.

[5] Risking Connection is a relational framework that focuses on the healing potential of RICH relationships (those based in Respect, Information Sharing, Connection, and Hope), that teaches skills for working with trauma survivors, and that emphasizes self-care for service providers.

contextual factors [55]. For instance, while "autonomy" or "self-sufficiency" are often valued in Western contexts, other cultural contexts may be more likely to prioritize family and community interconnectedness. In a study of resiliency in young female Cambodian trafficking survivors, qualitative analysis identified several qualities of resilience demonstrated by these girls and women. Qualities included perseverance, adaptability, self-preservation, interconnectedness, hope for the future, buoyancy, introspection, steadiness, and social awareness [56]. Along with cultivating these personal qualities, service networks should strive to encourage survivors' resiliency by strengthening their environmental supports.

Further, because people who have been trafficked have been disempowered as part of their victimization, an empowerment approach is essential in supporting them as they work to rebuild their lives. Empowerment refers to people's internal sense of efficacy and their ability to effectively take action to change their lives, communities, and/or larger sociopolitical environments. Respect for every person's expertise on their own life, recognition of each person's right to self-determination, and advocacy regarding the protection of these ideals are important aspects of promoting empowerment.

10.2.1.3   Trauma-Specific Services: Complex Trauma Treatment for Trafficking Survivors

Beyond trauma-informed service systems, trauma-specific services are designed to directly address the impacts of trauma and to facilitate healing. With mental health services for trafficking survivors in their infancy, there is a lack of consistency in the types of interventions that are being offered to trafficking survivors. Some programs offer "supportive" counseling for trafficking survivors that is not guided by any specific therapeutic framework. In an effort to provide structure and an empirical basis for the interventions offered, some reports have recommended the application of evidence-based treatments for a variety of specific disorders to trafficking survivors who present with these symptoms [17]. However, many symptom-focused treatment approaches do not address the complexity of the trauma response of many trafficking survivors. Even models that are empirically supported for "classic" forms of PTSD may lead to decompensation and avoidance in trafficking survivors with complex trauma who lack the prerequisite affect regulation skills to tolerate trauma processing [26]. In a study of trafficking survivors from three communities, one survivor engaged in counseling, but "ended up saying I wanted to stop...the more I took counseling, the more I [felt] depressed... [I] had to say the story over and over again" [43]. Additionally, some protocolized treatments that were developed for US populations may lack resonance with foreign national trafficking survivors.

In contrast to targeting individual symptoms, complex trauma treatment targets a wide range of affective and behavioral conditions that can result from chronic trauma exposure. Beyond simply targeting psychiatric symptoms related to trauma, complex trauma treatment models emphasize the development of key competencies, including: (1) increasing regulatory capacity, (2) developing the capacity to form healthy relationships, and (3) building positive self-identity and future orientation, along with the executive control and life skills necessary to make progress towards goals. It also emphasizes the importance of environmental systems, such as the family system or social service systems, in supporting the development of these competencies.

Increasing Regulatory Capacity *Regulatory capacity* refers to one's ability to tolerate and to exert control over thoughts, feelings, and behaviors. As described above, trafficked persons with complex trauma exposure often have difficulty regulating their emotions, somatic states, cognitions, and impulses. Some survivors may use unhealthy behavioral means to attempt to manage or cope with their emotions, including substance use disorders, self-injurious behavior, bingeing and/or restriction of food, enmeshment in relationships, creating ongoing chaos in their lives, and so on. Traditional behavioral treatments that focus solely on minimizing or eliminating damaging behaviors can be ineffective if they do not address underlying issues that are driving the behavior. Janae* described feeling "bored" and "lonely" when she was in her room alone and had a pattern of sneaking out of her foster home to meet boys and to "party" whenever she felt uncomfortable emotions. The more that her foster mother confronted her and established consequences for this behavior (such as the loss of her phone or other privileges), the more her "running" behavior escalated. Jorge*, a young man was sexually abused during childhood and then labor trafficked by a family member, described feeling more intense emotions after he stopped drinking. Although he remained sober, Jorge began binge eating to comfort himself, gaining over 50 pounds in less than a year. In this case, the removal of a maladaptive coping strategy without the development of alternative regulatory skills led one behavioral issue to be replaced with another. Instead of a behavioral focus, a complex trauma framework views such behaviors as regulatory efforts and encourages the development of a "toolbox" of alternative strategies for regulation [50].

Several treatment aims are involved in increasing regulatory capacity: increasing awareness of internal states (emotions, cognitions, somatic states, and behavioral impulses), building tolerance for discomfort or distress; strengthening the ability to share internal experience with others; and developing new skills to modulate emotional and somatic experience. Many trafficking survivors disconnect from their internal experience because they have had inadequate modeling or support in dealing with overwhelming emotions. Jorge (described above) had witnessed his father's use of alcohol as a coping mechanism during his childhood; he had grown accustomed to avoiding his emotions through alcohol and later through binge eating. So when he became more aware of his emotions, he was overwhelmed and felt panic and somatic symptoms such as nausea, dizziness, and excessive sweating. His therapist first used psychoeducation to help him understand his regulatory patterns and the role that alcohol and food had played in helping him manage his emotions. They worked to build a framework for treatment, including identifying Jorge's hopes for treatment: "not needing to rely on alcohol or food to feel ok," "not feeling so ashamed," "figuring out what kind of relationship I should have with my mother [his trafficker]," and "continuing in school." They also agreed on the importance of pacing the interventional efforts so that Jorge did not feel overwhelmed and revert to old coping strategies of binge drinking or eating. Jorge's therapist provided support around pacing by helping Jorge to address his feelings a bit at a time, emphasizing awareness of his internal states, noticing when he was becoming distressed, and coaching him in the use of regulatory tools. This often took the form of Jorge's therapist supporting him in using breathing, counting, or imagery to calm down. Gradually, they worked to increase his tolerance of emotions by being mindfully aware of his moods for longer periods of time, and by addressing more uncomfortable feelings such as shame and anger at his mother for her role in exploiting him. At the same time, Jorge's therapist continually supported and praised his commitment to education, his dedication and hard work, and his strength in confronting these difficult emotions. Jorge approached his therapy like a committed student and practiced and internalized a number of regulatory tools. He developed concrete behavioral plans for responding to his impulses to use food or alcohol to feel better, including reaching out to a friend, going to the gym, or playing basketball. He gradually began to lose weight, feel more confident about being able to manage his feelings, and address vulnerable feelings about his experiences.

Building Healthy Relationships Because human trafficking is a form of interpersonal trauma, its consequences often reverberate in other interpersonal relationships. It is not uncommon for trafficking survivors to leave a trafficking situation, only to later find themselves in another abusive or exploitative situation. Repeated or chronic interpersonal trauma, particularly that which begins in early development, can impact survivors' implicit assumptions about other people [26, 57], causing a ripple effect in later relationships.

Some trafficking survivors develop a hypervigilant stance towards relationships, being overly alert to signs of potential danger or aggression, boundary violations, criticism, or rejection. This can lead to social avoidance, mistrust, and difficulty entering into intimate, or even casual, relationships. Deanna*, a young woman who was the victim of early sexual abuse and later sex trafficking, described intense anxiety when riding public transportation with her daughter; she viewed every male around her as a potential predator. When family members are the traffickers, there is often a strong sense of betrayal, making trust even more difficult to cultivate: Miguel*, a boy who was labor trafficked by his grandparents on a farm, described withdrawing from potential sources of support, not trusting anyone enough to disclose the trafficking. Some trafficking survivors avoid sexual intimacy in relationships because any form of sexual contact triggers traumatic memories. Others react impulsively when triggered in relationships: Tony*, a young gay man who survived sex and labor trafficking by an older male, described a pattern of threatening to harm himself in response to conflict with romantic partners. When survivors are constantly alert for potential interpersonal threats, relationships with service providers and other anti-trafficking professionals are also often impacted. Because power was taken away from them in the trafficking situation, survivors may have negative reactions when they perceive they are being controlled, leading to difficulty engaging effectively with authority figures.

Conversely, other survivors have learned to cope through compliance; they are more likely to struggle with being easily manipulated or re-victimized. Aditi* had recently left a labor trafficking situation, where she performed domestic work and provided childcare, and was staying in a domestic violence shelter. She had a desire to please others and frequently offered to help the other residents. The other residents took advantage of Aditi by frequently using her to care for their children, provide meals, and perform other one-sided "favors." Some survivors feel compelled to engage in sexual behaviors or feel that their value is dependent on their sexuality. As Chantelle*, a woman who had been sex trafficked since adolescence, shared, "I had to learn how to go on a date; at first, I felt like I had to sleep with anyone who bought me a cup of coffee." In cases of trauma bonding, survivors may idealize the trafficker or justify the trafficker's behavior, which often leads to continued exploitation. Others feel dependent in relationships and believe that they need someone to protect or care for them. Juanita* married a former "John"[6] who helped her escape from her trafficker; although she did not feel attracted to him or love for him, she felt indebted to him for his assistance and was afraid to be on her own.

Many trafficking survivors also struggle with a sense of alienation—the feeling that "I'm alone" or "I'm different." In many cases, the traffickers have fostered this alienation, by cutting off contact between trafficked persons and their families or loved ones; verbal and psychological abuse leaves survivors feeling that they are somehow damaged or defective. Compounding this alienation, many trafficking survivors lack an adequate support network because of concrete impediments. For instance, they may have limited family supports as a result of physical distance, death of loved ones, or rejection by family members. They often struggle with insufficient community supports due to linguistic or cultural barriers, situational obstacles including frequent relocation, and lack of time and opportunity to make connections because of their extensive daily survival-based demands.

Because of these interpersonal struggles, complex trauma treatment with trafficking survivors requires a relational approach. Part of developing this therapeutic relationship involves the provider's ability to engage in an authentic and culturally sensitive way, to remain regulated, and to balance openness with consistency and clear boundaries. Some of the interpersonal patterns of trafficking survivors can lead to reactivity in providers. For instance, some survivors present themselves as tough, cynical, and/or angry; this self-protective stance can lead providers to underestimate the survivor's needs or to respond with their own cynicism or rejection. Providers who feel the urge to "save" or "rescue" trafficking survivors also commonly run into difficulties. Desiree*, a sex trafficking survivor, had been repeatedly abused and exploited. Her therapist, Barbara, had a strong protective reaction towards Desiree and felt a sense of pride that she had supported Desiree in getting sober and leaving "the Life." Desiree enjoyed the praise and wanted to please Barbara, whom she viewed as a mother figure. However, after a particularly stressful time in her life with mounting debts and unpaid bills, Desiree returned to her trafficker. Barbara was so disappointed and upset that she told Desiree she could not

---

[6] A colloquial term for a sex-buyer.

work with her if Desiree was not committed to getting better. Desiree responded with a mix of shame and anger; she soon relapsed and cut off contact with Barbara. Barbara ultimately made the decision that she could not work with sex trafficking survivors any longer because she "got too invested." This example highlights the importance of utilizing consistent and regulated providers for trafficking survivors with complex trauma [50].

Through complex trauma treatment, trafficking survivors can become more aware of their implicit *schemas*, or beliefs, about relationships and of their relational patterns. After receiving counseling that addressed her role in her family of origin, her domestic servitude, and her current relationships, Aditi reflected, "I realized that I never put myself first. I'm always taking care of other people." The therapeutic relationship can offer a place to practice reworking these relational schemas. Through a slow process of building trust and experiencing disappointments and repairs in the therapeutic relationship, trafficking survivors can have a healing relational experience. They can develop crucial relational skills such as assertion and boundary-setting. For survivors who are highly reactive in interpersonal affairs, the work may focus on recognizing triggered reactions within relationships. Alternatively, when a survivor's "radar" for potential threat is under-responsive, individual treatment may focus on increasing awareness of warning signals for dangerous or unhealthy relationships. This may begin by reflecting on choices that have led to unwanted outcomes, retrospectively noticing red flags that were overlooked or discounted. Over time, this reflective process will ideally occur earlier and earlier, until the person is able to avoid many of these negative outcomes by developing or restoring the capacity to distinguish safe from potentially unsafe situations.

Because many trafficking survivors have had to comply or shut down their own survival instincts to resist or fight back against perpetrators, there is often a learning process around boundary setting. Experiential learning could include exercises such as experimenting with personal space and learning about what feels comfortable, a common practice in a body-oriented treatment called *Sensorimotor Psychotherapy* [58]. Many trafficking survivors need experience paying attention to what they want or need, a skill that can be supported through the use of mindfulness. Communication, boundary-setting, conflict management, and assertiveness skills can be practiced in therapy or in real-life conditions. To develop these skills, trafficking survivors might practice expressing their thoughts and feelings, setting limits in verbal and nonverbal ways, negotiating differences of opinion, and calmly and confidently expressing their wants and needs.

Building a Positive Sense of Self and Future Orientation Because traffickers treat trafficked people as commodities rather than human beings, survivors' identities, self-esteem, and future orientation can be negatively impacted in many ways [59]. Complex trauma treatment supports the development of self-awareness, positive aspects of identity, future planning, problem-solving, cohesion in sense of self, integration of traumatic experiences into a larger life narrative, and transformation of trauma.

Because their time and activities were controlled during trafficking, survivors often have not had the opportunity to explore their own interests or goals. When people are separated from their communities and roles, particularly those from collectivist cultures, there is often a loss of an important part of their identity. Some survivors fear judgment from their families, communities, or from society in general, leaving them feeling alienated and alone. Survivors who have been tricked, manipulated, degraded, or repeatedly abused often experience a sense of shame and self-blame. Self-perception can be distorted if trafficked people view themselves as criminals rather than as survivors of human rights violations [60, 61]. Self-image can also be negatively impacted when people who have been trafficked view themselves as permanently damaged, leading to a decreased sense of empowerment, self-efficacy, and self-worth [24].

To address these impacts on sense of self, mental health intervention might focus on survivors' ability to identify and verbalize their own personal characteristics, interests, skills, and desires. Developing self-awareness and building connection to self also includes the identification of internal and external sources of resiliency for each person. For instance, Luis* was trafficked for many years in a restaurant and was forced to work every day, with no time off. When he finally got out of the situation, Luis did not know what to do with himself because he had no idea what he enjoyed doing or what he wanted from his life. In counseling, he began to learn simple things about himself, like that he enjoyed singing and drawing. He began going to church and, after joining his church's choir, started to feel that he was part of a community. He developed a view of himself as a person who was kind, giving, and who wanted to bring hope and faith to other people through music.

Problem-solving and future planning can be difficult for survivors of complex trauma [28]. While they are being trafficked, many people have difficulty seeing a way out of their situation. Even after getting out, goal-driven behavior can be interrupted by feelings of hopelessness, helplessness, and the impulse to feel better in the moment versus trying to overcome hurdles through a longer-term plan. For instance, after escaping from her trafficker, Bryanna* got a job as a waitress and began attending community college. She hoped to start working in social services with other survivors. However, she became frustrated with the comparatively lower wages and their impact on her lifestyle, so she returned to "the Life." This cycle of exiting and re-entry in commercial sexual exploitation is not uncommon [62], and urges to return should be anticipated and openly discussed in therapy. *Motivational interviewing* can be helpful in exploring ambivalence about exiting and other behavioral changes [63]. Executive functioning skills involving planning and problem-solving are important in supporting a future orientation. Many survivors could benefit from support in breaking longer-term goals down into short-term goals and identifying first steps towards those goals. Therapy can support the development of problem-solving skills, including slowing down initial behavioral impulses, identifying a range of potential responses to challenges, considering possible outcomes for each reaction, and making informed decisions about one's response. Life skills are also essential to future planning. Trafficking survivors may benefit from daily living skills, self-presentation and communication skills, career planning and job-related skills such as resume-building and interviewing, and financial literacy and financial planning.

Attempts to cope with the consequences of trauma can also interfere with identity. Some survivors of sex trafficking glamorize "the Life" and focus on external factors such as money or belongings to amplify their self-worth. Some try to find power through the use of their sexuality as a commodity. Although avoidance and dissociation are coping strategies that are protective against immediate distress, they tend to have complicated outcomes. When dissociation is chronic or extreme, survivors may experience fragmentation of their mental states into different "parts" of self. The lack of a unitary or coherent identity can lead to inconsistent presentations and behaviors, which may be misinterpreted as "manipulative" or "deceptive" in settings that do not understand complex trauma. Daria*, a girl who was abused and trafficked at an early age, often did not respond to others and indicated that she suffered from hearing loss. When her case manager attempted to schedule a hearing test, Daria protested that she did not have any problems hearing and denied ever implying otherwise. Dissociated "parts" of self can also be linked to repetition of traumatic situations. Jeanne* described her difficulty exiting sex trafficking due to her feelings of connection to her trafficker, who was also the father of her children. She would leave him and feel very confident about her desire to create a different life for herself. She referred to this part of her as her "strong self." However, when her trafficker repeatedly contacted her, another part of her that she called "the pleaser" would emerge. At these times, she would feel a strong appeal to go back to him and reunite their "family."

Because dissociation can interfere with self-awareness and/or lead to fragmentation in sense of self, complex trauma treatment often focuses on increasing awareness of "parts" of self and developing a more cohesive sense of self, despite strong emotions, variable external situations, or the opinions or demands of others. Jeanne's goals in therapy included building awareness of these various "parts" of herself and increasing the connection between these different parts. She worked to use her "strong self" as a resource to resist her impulse to return to her trafficker; instead, she tried to channel her desire for connection and belonging (a strength of "the pleaser") into developing healthier relationships.

Nonintegrated traumatic memories are isolated from a person's conscious awareness or kept separate from other memories; unintegrated memories are often re-experienced through triggered reactions, flashbacks, nightmares, or intrusive thoughts of the trauma. With less awareness of the role of trauma in their lives, many survivors unconsciously replay aspects of their trauma and are at increased risk of re-victimization. Perhaps because Tariq* had been emotionally abused and neglected by his family during childhood, he did not consider his employer's/trafficker's treatment as abusive, despite the belittling, name-calling, threats, control, and underpayment for his work. In another example of repeated victimization, Marcela* was trafficked by her "boyfriend" after fleeing her violent childhood home; she was subsequently physically and sexually abused by the "John" who helped her leave her trafficker. Because of the emotional and safety-related implications of unprocessed trauma, another mental health goal for trafficking survivors includes integration of the traumatic experiences into a larger life narrative. As traumatic memories become more integrated into one's consciousness, they lose some of the emotional intensity that comes from the phobic avoidance of these thoughts and feelings. Although they still are often painful, the memories are reframed as just one part of the person's experience and typically require less psychic energy to manage.

The complex trauma field has long-advocated a phase-oriented model of treatment, with safety and stabilization forming the groundwork for later trauma processing [24]. In approaching trauma-processing with trafficking survivors, it is important that the client has the requisite regulatory skills to manage the distress that often emerges when confronting detailed memories of the trauma. Given that these may be emerging skills, the therapist has an important role in supporting the survivor through co-regulation and effective pacing as they are processing traumatic memories. *Co-regulation* means that the therapist supports the survivor in their awareness of emotions, thoughts, somatic states, and behaviors; provides support so that they can tolerate moderately distressing feelings; and assists them in using regulatory skills during trauma processing. In complex trauma treatment that is well-paced, the trafficking survivor is challenged, is learning new skills, and is able to apply regulatory tools such that they do not become overwhelmed and in crisis or shut down and dissociate. Trauma processing may include methods such as Eye Movement Desensitization and Reprocessing (EMDR), narrative therapies, use of creative arts for trauma processing (visual arts, writing, theater, and music), or other similar methods [64–66]. Finally, because traumatic experiences are only a piece of the life of each trafficking survivor, trauma processing should be one aspect of the development of a larger life narrative which includes a focus not only on the past, but also on the present and hopes and plans for the future.

Many trafficking survivors withstand horrific experiences with remarkable strength, not only surviving but often thriving in many ways. "Post-traumatic growth" is a concept that refers to positive change following trauma and adversity [67]. A systematic review of the literature revealed several common themes of resilience in survivors of interpersonal violence, including post-traumatic growth in appreciation of life, personal strength, a sense of new possibilities, experience of relationships with others, and positive outlook on life [68]. *Transformation of trauma*, in which survivors use their experiences in positive ways such as educating the public or helping other survivors, is another means of post-traumatic growth. There are many potential opportunities for trafficking survivors to use their experience to build awareness or help others, including: public speaking, lobbying, participating in awareness events, writing about life experiences, sharing experiences through the creative arts, providing direct services for other survivors, holding leadership and/or program development positions within anti-trafficking programs, and combating trafficking within the criminal justice system. Mental health services can support trafficking survivors in considering or engaging in leadership opportunities. The anti-trafficking field has rapidly burgeoned with survivor-leaders who are involved in awareness-raising, public policy efforts, and direct services [69–71] (for example, the United States Advisory Council and survivor-led organizations such as Girls Educational and Mentoring Service (GEMS) and the Coalition to Abolish Slavery and Trafficking (CAST) National Survivor Network). Complex trauma treatment can support survivors in transforming the meaning of their trauma and using their experiences towards a greater external purpose.

Culturally Responsive Services Cultural differences can be understood broadly, including variability in worldview due to differences in race or ethnicity, class, sexual orientation, gender identity, disability status, socioeconomic status, religious beliefs, national origin, culture of one's family, and so on. Lack of cultural resonance may prevent trafficking survivors from accessing or engaging in mental health services [72]. Many foreign-born trafficking survivors lack an understanding of Western mental health services and fear having to retell their trafficking narrative repeatedly. Others experience mental health services as stigmatizing, only utilized by people who are "crazy." Mental health treatment approaches that are inflexibly rooted in a Western-centric framework may face particular difficulties in engaging foreign-born trafficking survivors. Many trafficking survivors, regardless of country of origin, feel alienated, different, and misunderstood by larger society. They are likely to have difficulty engaging with providers who are not able to step outside of their own worldview to try to understand another's perspective.

In a review of trafficking for mental health professionals, Yakushko emphasized that cross-cultural work with trafficking survivors should have a foundation in both trauma awareness and cultural empathy. Cultural empathy is possible when the therapist understands a diversity of worldviews, social/relational processes, and ethnic identity. The therapist should also have an awareness of political issues and immigration/resettlement policies. Treatment should include mental health education, psychotherapy, cultural empowerment, and a blend of Western and healing methods culturally relevant to the survivor [47].

In cross-cultural work, a primary focus of the therapist should be to try to understand the survivor's cultural context and unique worldview. A *culture-broker*—a person who bridges, links, or mediates between people of differing cultural backgrounds—can be helpful in offering providers with background on values, customs, and morays within a survivor's specific cultural context. Perhaps more importantly, the therapist can approach the survivor with genuine interest, working to understand their perspectives and priorities. For instance, Sanjay*, a Nepali man who was labor trafficked after coming to the USA in hopes of supporting his family, viewed the world with a collectivist lens, prioritizing his family system and role within his family over individualistic goals. To develop a good working relationship, his therapist engaged Sanjay in discussions about what "empowerment" meant from within his cultural framework and worked with him to develop goals that were culturally resonant.

10.2.2   The Multimodal Social Ecological Framework

Supporting the mental health of trafficking survivors requires a holistic and flexible approach, depending on the unique situation and preferences of each individual [18]. Research has suggested the importance of a continuum of aftercare services to address survivors' changing needs as they move from initial freedom to recovery and independence [73]. Trafficking survivors' psychological and behavioral

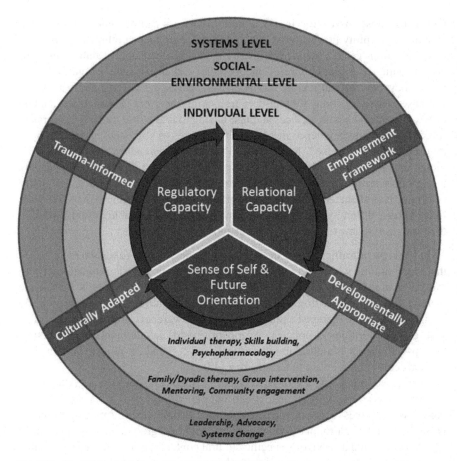

Fig. 10.1 The Multimodal Social Ecological (MSE) framework

reactions do not occur in a vacuum; each person affects, and is shaped by, multiple levels of influence within their social environment. *Social ecology* is a means of understanding the dynamic interrelationships between personal and environmental factors, including the social, institutional, and cultural contexts that impact each person. This theoretical concept has been the basis for numerous multi-level models, particularly in the social psychology and public health fields, and can be applied within the anti-trafficking field.

The Multimodal Social Ecological (MSE) framework offers an approach for addressing the mental health needs of trafficking survivors using varied modalities, at multiple levels of intervention, to support survivors' recovery and empowerment (see Fig. 10.1). This approach is informed by awareness of complex trauma and emphasizes development of competencies through the use of varied intervention modalities. Because of the important interaction of personal, social-environmental, and contextual systemic factors in trafficking survivors' mental health, intervention must take a comprehensive approach that addresses each of these levels. Incorporating services from multiple modalities supports trafficking survivors' mental health from different angles and increases the likelihood that survivors will find services that are a "fit" for them. All interventions should be trauma-informed, culturally adapted, developmentally appropriate, and should utilize an empowerment framework.

Potential healing methods within the MSE framework include interventions at the individual level, at the social-environmental level, and at the systems level. Individual-level modalities include individual therapy and counseling (including individual treatment for substance use disorders), psychopharmacological treatment, and psychosocial interventions such as improving nutrition, increasing physical activity, and teaching daily living skills. At the social-environmental level, interventions focus on building social support and improving close relationships. Interventions at this level may include family or dyadic therapies; group treatment; support groups; 12-step programs; and psychosocial interventions such as case management, mentoring, educational and vocational support, and increasing social and community connections. At the systems level, interventions include survivor leadership, advocacy, education, organizational change, and changes in larger social, economic, and political systems. Across these levels, interventions should be trauma-informed and culturally adapted and should emphasize empowerment. Expressive modalities and non-Western or folk healing methods can be integrated into various interventions across these levels. Psychosocial interventions can be implemented at each of these levels. The varying modalities of intervention can support the development of regulatory capacities, relational wellness, and/or a positive sense of self and future orientation.

Individual Therapy While there has not yet been any research in this area, complex trauma treatment is recommended for trafficking survivors due to the high incidence of repeated or chronic interpersonal trauma exposure within this population [18, 24, 26]. Historically, trauma treatment has focused on targeting traumatic memories, with the framework that repeated exposure to the memory would decrease trauma-related distress over time. However, for trafficking survivors who have been exposed to multiple layers of stress and trauma, disclosure is often not adequate to improve psychological health. In contrast, most complex trauma treatment models utilize a phase-oriented or sequenced approach to intervention with an early emphasis on safety and skill-building. This emphasis has emerged from Herman's (1992) phased model of complex trauma treatment, which described three stages of recovery: (1) re-establishing safety and a sense of self-care; (2) remembering and mourning, which involves integrating traumatic memories into one's life story; and (3) reconnection, a future-oriented phase which includes the development of new relationships and new belief systems [24]. Although recent work suggests that these phases are not discrete and often do not occur in a linear fashion, Herman's model is seminal in establishing two core concepts of complex trauma treatment: Trauma work is much more than simply talking about traumatic experiences, and the development of core regulatory capacities is a central element of recovery.

The first priorities for complex trauma treatment include safety (crisis management and safety planning, reduction of symptom acuity, and improvement in basic self-care), engagement in treatment, and development of a therapeutic relationship. Treatment supports survivors as they develop their capacity for emotional awareness, tolerance, and expression; address feelings of guilt and shame; build interpersonal competencies; and cultivate a positive sense of self. As the therapeutic relationship strengthens, regulatory tools are developed, and survivors' day-to-day functioning improves, trauma processing may become more central, contributing to a further reduction of trauma-related symptoms. Although no research has been conducted on the application of specific complex trauma treatment approaches with trafficking survivors, a variety of models are available that might be applicable to trafficking survivors, including: *Treatment of Complex Trauma: A Sequenced, Relationship-Based Approach* [74], *Components-Based Psychotherapy (CBP)* [75], the *Self-Trauma model* [76], *Skills Training in Affective and Interpersonal Regulation* (STAIR) [77], *Trauma Affect Regulation: Guide for Education and Therapy (TARGET)* [78], *Emotionally Focused Treatment for Complex Trauma* [92], and others. Individual therapy needs to be modified based on the developmental level of survivors. There are several modified versions of these models for children and adolescents, including: *Integrative Treatment of Complex Trauma for Adolescents* (ITCT-A, a modified youth version of the Self-Trauma model) [79] and TARGET-A and STAIR-A (both modified for adolescents). *Trauma-Focused Cognitive Behavioral Therapy* (TF-CBT) has been widely applied with trafficked children, although it should be noted that this model requires some adaptations to be appropriate for children with complex trauma [80]. Beyond providing larger organizational frameworks for systems serving young people with complex trauma, *Trauma Systems Therapy* (TST) [81] and the *ARC* model [50] also address clinical treatment with complexly traumatized youth.

Other targeted therapeutic models may be useful for specific goals or phases of treatment with trafficking survivors. For instance, *Sensorimotor Psychotherapy* [58] targets somatic experience and can be particularly beneficial when survivors are dissociated or highly defended against emotional experience. *Dialectical Behavior Therapy* (DBT) [82] is a skills-based approach that can support the development of regulatory and relational capacities. *Eye Movement Desensitization and Reprocessing* (EMDR) [83] is an intervention that focuses on trauma processing, incorporating "bilateral stimulation" through eye movements, sounds, or tactile sensations that occur on alternating sides of the body. There are also EMDR protocols that are designed to build internal resources, prior to trauma processing. Narrative therapy approaches, frequently used with refugees and torture survivors, may be helpful for trauma processing and identity development [66, 84]. The choice of any treatment approach should be matched to the unique needs and preferences of each client; these needs may change as each person progresses through their recovery process.

Psychopharmacology Although it is beyond the scope of this chapter to explore the potential role of psychopharmacological interventions with trafficking survivors, medication can play an important role in treatment for some trafficking survivors. For instance, medications are important for individuals with biologically based conditions such as schizophrenia or bipolar disorder; they can facilitate substance use disorder treatment for certain conditions such as physiological dependence on opioids; and they can help to stabilize individuals who have debilitating depression, anxiety, or dysregulation [64].

Family and Dyadic Therapies   Because of the relational consequences of trafficking, survivors may benefit from therapy involving family members or close relationships. When families are reunited after trafficking, there may be an extended period of adjustment, in which shame, anger, resentment, grief, and other emotional reactions cause conflict or other complications in the relationship [85]. Romantic relationships are also often impacted: Trafficking survivors may be triggered by sexual contact, or by physical or emotional intimacy in general, creating conflict or alienation within the relationship. For trafficked youth who had pre-existing family conflict that contributed to their vulnerability to trafficking, the family system requires intervention to ensure that reunification will not lead to dysregulation or re-victimization. Complex trauma exposure can also impact parenting; therefore, parenting support or parent–child dyadic therapies might be beneficial for trafficking survivors with children [18].

Group Treatment and Support   Group treatment provides the opportunity for trafficking survivors to share common experiences and to develop supportive peer relationships. Many elements of group treatment can be helpful in the healing process for trafficking survivors. By breaking the silence about trafficking and other forms of trauma, survivors can reduce their sense of shame through shared experience and can begin to reassign responsibility to the perpetrators. Psychoeducation can be helpful in normalizing post-trauma responses and can contribute to empowerment, as survivors are able to make more informed and conscious choices. Group treatment can provide a forum for learning and practicing new regulatory skills. Group members can provide interpersonal reflection, connection, and peer support. Relational capacity can be developed, as group members practice managing close relationships through the use of new coping skills. Group intervention is a promising model for working with survivors from non-Western cultures. Because identity in collectivist cultures tends to be based on role, family, and interpersonal connections, group work can be an important means of re-establishing a sense of connectedness and belonging for some trafficking survivors. Group modalities include group therapy but may also include more informal support groups, educational groups, or peer-led models such as 12-step programs.

It is important to note that, while group intervention can contribute important connections, the interpersonal dynamics are often complex. For instance, stigma can contribute to judgment by other group members over issues such as the type of trafficking or the length of the trafficking experience. Alienation may also occur if the experiences of group members are too disparate. Thus, thoughtful development of a group's composition is important to maximize the likelihood of group cohesion.

If conflict occurs amongst group members, facilitators can highlight commonalities among members by engaging the group in discussion about broad dynamics such as trust, coercion, secrecy, exploitation, psychological abuse, current struggles, and future planning [86].

There is very little literature regarding group intervention for trafficking survivors. Initial reports have suggested that trauma-informed groups focusing on psychoeducation, relational support, and coping skills can be beneficial for sex trafficked youth [86, 87]. The My Life My Choice (MLMC) program has developed an educational survivor-led model for girls who have been commercially sexually exploited or who are at risk of sex trafficking [88]. Several group treatment models have been developed for complex trauma, which may be useful for trafficking survivors. The *Trauma Recovery and Empowerment Model* (TREM) is a manualized[7] group intervention for trauma survivors that draws on cognitive restructuring, psychoeducation, and coping skills training. The STAIR and TARGET models have also been applied with groups. Group intervention should also be adapted to the developmental needs of survivors: *Structured Psychotherapy for Adolescents Responding to Chronic Stress* (SPARCS) is a group model for chronically traumatized adolescents who are experiencing problems across realms of functioning and who are often living with ongoing stress [89].

Substance Use Disorder Treatment Substance use disorder (SUD) treatment should ideally support the development of regulatory capacity through a decrease in the use of substances that block emotional experience. At the same time that the substance use is decreasing or being stopped, other coping tools need to be developed to replace the regulatory role of the substance. SUD treatment can be offered through individual modalities or through group treatment or group support. Chapter 12 provides a review of substance use issues facing trafficking survivors and a description of potential treatment modalities to address substance use disorders.

Expressive Modalities A number of trafficking programs have incorporated expressive modalities as part of their "menu" of healing opportunities. Some expressive modalities that have been used with trafficking survivors include: music (listening to music, singing, playing instruments, and composing), visual arts (drawing, painting, sculpting, and collage-, mask-, and mandala-making), movement-based modalities (dance, drama), and writing (journaling, poetry, and song-writing) [12, 65]. These types of expressive interventions should be offered by clinicians with particular training in expressive therapy [64]. Expressive therapies may be applied within individual or group treatment settings. In addition, expressive modalities may be used for systems change. For instance, documentary plays and films have been used to raise awareness of the issue of human trafficking and may normalize survivors' experiences.

---

[7]Manualized treatments are described in detail in a book or manual, with instructions for other clinicians wishing to offer the intervention.

Non-western Modalities As described above, culturally responsive services may include a blend of Western intervention methods and healing methods that are culturally relevant to the survivor. The field of complex trauma draws from non-Western healing traditions such as mindfulness, meditation, acupressure, and movement-based interventions such as yoga and tai chi. These modalities may be helpful for stress reduction and can contribute to self-awareness and regulatory capacity [90]. Research has shown that mindfulness practices are helpful with trafficking survivors from certain non-Western cultures [91]. However, with the increasingly broad application of Eastern healing methods with survivors of complex trauma in the USA, it appears that such interventions may be helpful for trafficking survivors regardless of cultural background. Some anti-trafficking programs offer these healing modalities as alternatives to, or adjunctive to, traditional therapy [12, 65]. In addition, as discussed above, clinicians may draw from folk healing practices or other methods that have particular cultural resonance for an individual and tailor the intervention to each person's unique needs [47]. Non-Western modalities can be used in individual treatment, with groups, and to support re-integration into a community; the increasing implementation of non-Western healing modalities into Western health care models is an important aspect of systems change in health care services for trafficking survivors.

Psychosocial Interventions Affect regulation, relational engagement, and developing a positive sense of identity and future orientation are goals that can also be supported outside of traditional therapy environments, through psychosocial interventions. These interventions may be focused on the individual, the person's interactions with their immediate environment, or on systemic issues.

At the individual level, psychosocial interventions can include encouragement and support regarding health-promoting behavior, such as maintenance of proper nutrition, engagement in physical activity, and sustaining regular sleep patterns. Building proficiencies in daily living, financial management, problem-solving, communication, and self-presentation skills may be important for some survivors.

Some psychosocial interventions, such as case management and mentoring, bridge the individual and social-environmental levels. Case management is a psychosocial intervention that can have important psychological benefits for trafficking survivors. Because unmet needs and concrete barriers can leave survivors stuck in a loop of re-victimization, environmental changes and an increased support network can be important prerequisites for change. Support in navigating complex systems such as legal, medical, or job market systems can enhance self-sufficiency and contribute to empowerment [34]. Research has suggested potential benefits of mentoring for trafficking survivors [60]. Particularly for survivors who feel alienated from others, trust-building may be facilitated when they feel that another person understands something about them through first-hand experience. After hearing their survivor mentor's story of transformation, survivors who are struggling to leave or have recently gotten out of a trafficking situation may be able to envision a future beyond their trafficking experience [59].

Intervention at the social-environmental level often focuses on building connections and community. Linking trafficking survivors to religious or spiritual communities can support culturally relevant coping methods, as well as increase a person's support network and sense of connectedness [12]. In addition to boosting mood, engagement in sports or group-oriented physical activities can also build community. Educational and vocational support can help survivors reconnect with important social roles and can facilitate empowerment and future orientation.

In terms of psychosocial interventions at the systems level, trafficking survivors can become active in influencing the systems with which they engage. Beyond the personal benefits of developing positive identity and building self-efficacy, survivor leadership is an important element of systems change by raising awareness and directly informing policy and practice [12, 59].

Advocacy, Education, and Systems Change Finally, some interventions focus at the macro level[8] to address systemic issues that impact trafficking survivors' mental and psychosocial health. This may include organizational change, such as creating trauma-informed systems for trafficking survivors. It can include advocacy to address systemic and structural barriers to services that may support survivors' mental health. Public education can change perceptions of trafficking survivors, and targeted education to different professional groups may improve the ability of law enforcement, health and mental health care, or social service systems to meet the unique needs of trafficking survivors. Finally, education and advocacy can be used to address disparities that increase trafficking survivors' vulnerabilities to further harm.

10.3 Conclusion

The anti-trafficking field is in its infancy in understanding the psychological impacts and mental health needs of trafficking survivors. The available literature points to a high incidence of depression, anxiety, and PTSD in people who have experienced trafficking. Many other mental health symptoms have been noted in trafficking survivors, with frequent comorbid symptom presentations. Despite these numerous impacts of human trafficking and the potential benefits of mental health intervention, structural and emotional barriers often interfere with access to services which could support psychological wellness in trafficking survivors. Given the extent of pre-trafficking trauma exposure and the often chronic and/or severe nature of trafficking-related trauma, complex trauma is a construct that may explain a range of psychological, social, cognitive, somatic, behavioral, and spiritual impacts of trafficking and that can offer guidance for intervention with trafficking survivors.

---

[8] Macro social work involves efforts to help people by intervening in large systems, such as lobbying to change health care laws, organizing large-scale activist or professional groups, or advocating for social policy change.

   The establishment of culturally appropriate trauma-informed mental health interventions is essential for trafficking survivors. Trauma-specific services should utilize a complex trauma lens, moving beyond a symptom focus to an emphasis on the development of key competencies in emotional regulation, relational engagement, and positive sense of self and future orientation. Because of the variability of experiences and needs among trafficking survivors and the importance of the social and contextual environments in survivors' wellness, a Multimodal Social Ecological framework can guide planning regarding trauma-informed, culturally appropriate interventions that may further trafficking survivors' mental health, supporting them as they move beyond recovery to empowerment.

10.4   Recommendations

The literature on human trafficking highlights the importance of holistic interventions to address the mental health needs of trafficking survivors. However, in order to develop interventions that are tailored to the specific needs of trafficking survivors, more information is needed. The current gaps in awareness and services regarding the mental health of trafficking survivors lead to a number of recommendations in research, policy, and practice.

Research

- There are many gaps in the literature on the mental health impacts of human trafficking. Research is needed to identify potential differences in the mental health impacts and needs of survivors of variable backgrounds who have experienced different patterns of human trafficking. There are particular research gaps regarding men, boys, and GLBTQ+[9] individuals who have been trafficked, and on mental health issues faced by survivors of labor trafficking. Beyond a focus on common psychiatric disorders, research on mental health impacts on trafficking survivors should include an examination of complex trauma. Longitudinal research may help to clarify changes in the mental health needs of trafficking survivors over time.
- Because of the range of systemic, structural, and emotional barriers to mental health services for trafficking survivors, research is needed regarding potential methods to increase access to and engagement with mental health care.
- Evaluation of the efficacy of various forms of mental health intervention with trafficking survivors is needed.
- Investigation into culturally informed adaptations of various forms of mental health support may help to clarify their cultural resonance with different subpopulations of trafficking survivors.

---

[9] GLBTQ+ refers to people who identify as gay, lesbian, bisexual, transgender experienced, queer/questioning, plus people of other nontraditional gender and sexual identities.

Policy

- Additional funding should be devoted to mental health intervention for trafficking survivors, supporting crisis *and* longer-term mental health support for all survivors of trafficking.
- Funding is also needed to support research related to mental health issues and services for trafficking survivors.
- Mental health care for trafficking survivors should be directly informed by survivors; survivor leadership is essential for high-quality policy development regarding mental health services for trafficking survivors.
- Training on human trafficking should be a standard part of the educational curricula for mental health professionals. And all health professionals should be trained on the effects of trauma on trafficking survivors and on a trauma-informed approach to service delivery.

Practice

- Mental health care should be made more accessible for trafficking survivors.

    - Service systems for trafficking survivors should systematically assess and address structural barriers to services supporting psychological wellness. For instance, offering mental health services and other comprehensive services in one centralized location, offering childcare, or providing transportation to therapy might help to mitigate some of these barriers.
    - Outreach and an early focus on engagement are essential for addressing emotional barriers such as mistrust, shame, and lack of cultural resonance with available healing modalities. Other trusted providers may serve as a bridge to mental health treatment by offering information about potential therapeutic opportunities, by eliciting survivors' motivation for change, and by facilitating personal connections with potential mental health providers. Available mental health services should be adapted to unique populations of trafficking survivors. In addition, providers should work directly with each survivor to develop an individualized plan for meeting unique mental health needs.

- Trauma-informed service networks need to be developed for trafficking survivors. All service systems for trafficking survivors, whether medical, legal, or social, should incorporate awareness of the impact of complex trauma in trafficking survivors and should be adapted to meet the unique needs of trafficking survivors.

    - Service providers, including mental health practitioners, should help to identify and support various forms of resiliency in the clients that they serve.
    - Providers should consider symptoms and behaviors through a trauma lens to understand their adaptive nature in coping with traumatic stress.
    - Services for trafficking survivors should employ an empowerment approach, helping survivors to develop their own right to self-determination.

- For trafficking survivors with complex trauma, mental health care should focus on the broad goals of increasing regulatory capacity, developing the capacity to form healthy relationships, and addressing issues of self-identity and future orientation.
- The mental health of trafficking survivors should be addressed using multiple modalities of intervention at the individual, social-environmental, and systems levels. The Multimodal Social Ecological framework may be beneficial in developing individualized plans to support each survivor's holistic psychosocial health.

Acknowledgements The author would like to express sincere appreciation to Jeff Nicklas for his administrative assistance in the production of this chapter.

References

1. Zimmerman C, Hossain M, Watts C. Human trafficking and health: a conceptual model to inform policy, intervention and research. Soc Sci Med. 2011;73(2):327–35. doi:10.1016/j.socscimed.2011.05.028.
2. Ottisova L, Hemmings S, Howard LM, Zimmerman C, Oram S. Prevalence and risk of violence and the mental, physical and sexual health problems associated with human trafficking: an updated systematic review. Epidemiol Psychiatr Sci. 2016;1–25. doi:10.1017/S2045796016000135.
3. Kiss L, Pocock NS, Naisanguansri V, Suos S, Dickson B, Thuy D, et al. Health of men, women, and children in post-trafficking services in Cambodia, Thailand, and Vietnam: an observational cross-sectional study. Lancet Glob Health. 2015;3(3):E154–61.
4. Clawson HJ, Dutch N, Solomon A, et al. Human trafficking into and within the United States: a review of the literature. Department of Health and Human Services, Office of the Assistant Secretary for Planning and Evaluation. http://aspe.hhs.gov/hsp/07/humantrafficking/litrev/. Accessed 25 May 2016.
5. Tsutsumi A, Izutsu T, Pouyal AK, Kato S, Marui E, et al. Mental health of female survivors of human trafficking in Nepal. Soc Sci Med. 2008;6(8):1841–7.
6. Abas M, Ostrovschi NV, Prince M., Gorceag VI, Trigub C, Oram S, et al. Risk factors for mental disorders in women survivors of human trafficking: a historical cohort study. BMC Psychiatry. 2013;13(204). doi:10.1186/1471-244X-13-204.
7. Zimmerman C, Hossain M, Yun K, Roche B, Morison L, Watts C, et al. Stolen smiles: the physical and psychological health consequences of women and adolescents trafficked to Europe. London: London School of Hygiene & Tropical Medicine; 2006.
8. Oram S, Stöckl H, Busza J, Howard LM, Zimmerman C, et al. Prevalence and risk of violence and the physical, mental, and sexual health problems associated with human trafficking: systematic review. PLoS Med. 2012;9(5):1–13. doi:10.1371/journal.pmed.1001224.
9. Raymond J, Hughes D. Sex trafficking of women in the United States: international and domestic trends. U.S. Department of Justice. 2001. https://www.ncjrs.gov/pdffiles1/nij/grants/187774.pdf. Accessed 25 May 2016.
10. Hopper EK (2016). Polyvictimization and developmental trauma adaptations in sex trafficked youth. Journal of Child & Adolescent Trauma. doi:10.1007/s40653-016-0114-z.
11. Lederer L, Wetzel CA. The health consequences of sex trafficking and their implications for identifying victims in health care facilities. Ann Health Law. 2014;23(1):61–91.

12. Clawson H, Salomon A, Goldblatt-Grace L. Treating the hidden wounds: trauma treatment and mental health recovery for victims of human trafficking. In: Study of HHS programs serving human trafficking victims. Health and Human Services. Available via HHS. https://aspe.hhs.gov/basic-report/treating-hidden-wounds-trauma-treatment-and-mental-health-recovery-victims-human-trafficking. Accessed 5 May 2016.
13. Farley M, Cotton A, Lynne J, et al. Prostitution and trafficking in nine countries. J Trauma Pract. 2008;2(3–4):33–74. doi:10.1300/J189v02n03_03.
14. Hossain M, Zimmerman C, Abas M, Light M, Watts C, et al. The relationship of trauma to mental disorders among trafficked and sexually exploited girls and women. Am J Public Health. 2010;100(12):2442–9.
15. Turner-Moss E, Zimmerman C, Howard LM, Oram S, et al. Labour exploitation and health: a case series of men and women seeking post-trafficking services. J Immigr Minor Health. 2014;16(3):473–80. doi:10.1007/s10903-013-9832-6.
16. OSCE Office of the Special Representative and Co-ordinator for Combating Trafficking in Human Beings in partnership with the Ludwig Boltzmann Institute of Human Rights and the Helen Bamber Foundation. Trafficking in human beings amounting to torture and other forms of ill-treatment. Occasional Paper Series No. 5, Vienna. 2013. https://www.osce.org/cthb/103085?download=true. Accessed 5 May 2016.
17. Williamson E, Dutch NM, Clawson HJ. Evidence-based mental health treatment for victims of human trafficking. U.S. Department of Health and Human Services. 2010. http://aspe.hhs.gov/hsp/07/humantrafficking/mentalhealth/index.pdf. Accessed 25 May 2016.
18. Task Force on Trafficking of Women and Girls. Report of the task force on trafficking of women and girls. Washington, DC: American Psychological Association; 2014.
19. Oram S, Khondoker M, Abas M, Broadbent M, Howard LM. Characteristics of trafficked adults and children with severe mental illness: a historical cohort study. Lancet Psychiatry. 2015;2(12):1084–91.
20. Langham M. Human trafficking of the mentally and physically disabled. 2013. http://aconspiracyofhope.blogspot.com/2013/04/human-trafficking-of-mentally-and.html. Accessed 25 May 2016.
21. Rafferty Y. The impact of trafficking on children: psychological and social policy perspectives. Child Dev Perspect. 2008;2:13–8.
22. Alexander MP, Kellogg ND, Thompson P. Community and mental health support of juvenile victims of prostitution. In: Cooper SW, Estes RJ, Giardino AP, Kellogg ND, Vieth VI, editors. Medical, legal, and social science aspects of child sexual exploitation, vol. 1. St. Louis: Medical Publishing Inc.; 2005. p. 397–421.
23. Basson D, Rosenblatt E, Haley H. Research to action: sexually exploited minors (SEM) needs and strengths. Oakland, CA: West Coast Children's Clinic; 2012.
24. Herman JL. Complex PTSD: a syndrome in survivors of prolonged and repeated trauma. J Trauma Stress. 1992;5(3):377–91.
25. Briere J, Spinazzola J. Phenomenology and psychological assessment of complex posttraumatic states. J Trauma Stress. 2005;18(5):401–12. doi:10.1002/jts.20048.
26. Courtois C. Complex trauma, complex reactions: assessment and treatment. Psychother Theory Res Pract Train. 2004;41(4):412–25.
27. Cloitre ME, Stolbach B, Herman J, van der Kolk B, Pynoos R, Wang J, Petkova E. A developmental approach to Complex PTSD: childhood and adult cumulative trauma as predictors of symptom complexity. J Trauma Stress. 2009;22(5):399–408. doi:10.1002/jts.20444.
28. Cook A, Spinazzola J, Ford J, Lanktree C, et al. Complex trauma in children and adolescents. Psychiatr Ann. 2005;35(5):390–8.
29. D'Andrea W, Ford J, Stolbach B, Spinazzola J, van der Kolk BA. Understanding interpersonal trauma in children: why we need a developmentally appropriate trauma diagnosis. Am J Orthopsychiatry. 2012;82(2):187–200.
30. Herman JL. Trauma and recovery. New York: Basic Books; 1997.

31. Cloitre M, Courtois CA, Ford JD, Green BL, et al. The ISTSS expert consensus treatment guidelines for complex PTSD in adults. International Society for Traumatic Stress Studies. 2012 Available via http://www.istss.org/ISTSS_Main/media/Documents/ISTSS-Expert-Concensus-Guidelines-for-Complex-PTSD-Updated-060315.pdf Accessed 8 May 2016.
32. Hopper EK. Trauma-informed psychological assessment of human trafficking survivors. Women Ther. 2017;40:1-2, 12–30. doi:10.1080/02703149.2016.1205905.
33. Choi H, Klein C, Shin M, Lee H. Post-traumatic stress disorder (PTSD) and disorders of extreme stress (DESNOS) symptoms following prostitution and childhood abuse. Violence Against Women. 2009;15:933–51.
34. Hardy V, Compton K, McPhatter V. Domestic minor sex trafficking: practice implications for mental health professionals. Affilia. 2013;28(1):8–18. doi:10.1177/088610991247517.
35. Kissane M, Szymanski L, Upthegrove R, Katona C. Complex posttraumatic stress disorder in traumatized asylum seekers: a pilot study. Eur J Psychiatry. 2014;28(3):137–44.
36. Williamson C, Prior M. Domestic minor sex trafficking: a network of underground players in the Midwest. J Child Adolesc Trauma. 2009;2(1):46–61. doi:10.1080/19361520802702191.
37. Baldwin S, Fehrenbacher A, Eisenman D. Psychological coercion in human trafficking: an application of Biderman's framework. Qual Health Res. 2014. doi:10.1177/1049732314557087.
38. Reid JA. Doors wide shut: barriers to the successful delivery of victim services for domestically trafficked minors in a southern U.S. metropolitan area. Women Crim Just. 2010;20(1–2):147–66. doi:10.1080/08974451003641206.
39. Hopper EK, Hidalgo J. Invisible chains: psychological coercion of human trafficking victims. Intercult Hum Rights Law Rev. 2006;1:185–209.
40. Ostrovschi N, Prince M, Zimmerman C, et al. Women in post-trafficking services in Moldova: diagnostic interviews over two time periods to assess returning women's mental health. BMC Public Health. 2011;11:1–9. doi:10.1186/1471-2458-11-232.
41. Deb S, Mukherjee A, Mathews B. Aggression in sexually abused trafficked girls and efficacy of intervention. J Interpers Violence. 2011;26(4):745–68. doi:10.1177/0886260510365875.
42. Hodgdon H, Kinniburgh K, Gabowitz D, Blaustein M, Spinazzola J. Development and implementation of trauma-informed programming in youth residential treatment centers using the ARC framework. J Fam Violence. 2013;28(7):679–92.
43. Aron LY, Zweig JM, Newmark LS. Comprehensive services for survivors of human trafficking: findings from clients in three communities. Washington, DC: Urban Institute; 2006.
44. Gibbs DA, Walters JLH, Lutnick A, Miller S, Kluckman M, et al. Services to domestic minor victims of sex trafficking: opportunities for engagement and support. Child Youth Serv Rev. 2015;54:1–7. doi:10.1016/j.childyouth.2015.04.003.
45. Domoney J, Howard L, Abas M, et al. Mental health service responses to human trafficking: a qualitative study of professionals' experiences of providing care. BMC Psychiatry. 2015;15. doi:10.1186/s12888-015-0679-3.
46. Dewan S. Patterns of service utilization among pre-certified victims of human trafficking. Int Soc Work. 2014;57(1):64–74. doi:10.1177/0020872813507592.
47. Yakushko O. Human trafficking: a review for mental health professionals. J Adv Counsel. 2009;31(3):158–67.
48. Substance Abuse and Mental Health Services Administration. Trauma-informed approach and trauma-specific interventions. 2015. http://www.samhsa.gov/nctic/trauma-interventions. Accessed 5 May 2016.
49. Elliot D, Bjelajac P, Fallot R, Markoff L, Reed B. Trauma-informed or trauma-denied: principles and implementation of trauma-informed services for women. J Community Psychol. 2005;33:461–77.
50. Blaustein M, Kinniburgh K. Treating traumatic stress in children and adolescents: how to foster resilience through attachment, self- regulation, and competency. New York: Guildford Press; 2010.
51. Bloom SL, Farragher B. Restoring sanctuary: a new operating system for trauma-informed systems of care. New York: Oxford University Press; 2013.

52. Saakvitne KW, Gamble S, Pearlman LA, Lev B. Risking connection: a training curriculum for working with survivors of childhood abuse. Baltimore, MD: Sidran Press; 2000.
53. Luthar S, Cicchetti D, Becker B. The construct of resilience: a critical evaluation and guidelines for future work. Child Dev. 2000;71(3):543–62.
54. Harvey M. An ecological view of psychological trauma and trauma recovery. J Trauma Stress. 1996;9(1):3–23.
55. Gray G. Resilience in Cambodia: hearing the voices of trafficking survivors and their helpers. Dissertation, George Fox University; 2012a.
56. Gray GG. Exploring resilience: strengths of trafficking survivors in Cambodia. Int J Adolesc Med Health. 2012b;24(4):363–71. doi:10.1515/ijamh.2012.053.
57. Janoff-Bulman R. Shattered assumptions: towards a new psychology of trauma. New York: Free Press; 1992.
58. Ogden P, Fisher J. Sensorimotor psychotherapy: interventions in trauma and attachment. New York: W. W. Norton & Company; 2015.
59. Lloyd R. From victim to survivor, from survivor to leader: the importance of leadership programming and opportunities for commercially sexually exploited and trafficked youth. 2011. Retrieved from http://www.gems-girls.org/from-victim-to-survivor-from-survivor-to-leader. Accessed 1 Aug 2016.
60. Kalergis K. A passionate practice: addressing the needs of commercially sexually exploited teenagers. Affilia. 2009;24(3):315–24. doi:10.1177/0886109909337706.
61. Kotrla K (2010) Domestic minor sex trafficking in the United States. Social Work 55(2):181–7. doi:10.1093/sw/55.2.181.
62. Hammond GC, McGlone M. Entry, progression, exit, and service provision for survivors of sex trafficking: implications for effective interventions. Glob Soc Welf. 2014;1:157–68. doi:10.1007/s40609-014-0010-0.
63. Miller WR, Rollnick S. Motivational interviewing: helping people change. 3rd ed. New York: The Guilford Press; 2013.
64. Foa EB, Keane T, Friedman MJ, Cohen JA, editors. Effective treatments for PTSD: practice guidelines from the International Society of Traumatic Stress Studies. 2nd ed. New York: The Guilford Press; 2010.
65. Polaris Project, Sanar. Promising practices: an overview of trauma-informed therapeutic support for survivors of human trafficking. POLARIS Project. 2015. Available via https://polaris-project.org/sites/default/files/Sanar-Promising-Practices.pdf. Accessed 30 Apr 2016.
66. Katona C, Robjant K, Shapott R, Witkin R. Addressing mental health needs in survivors of modern slavery: a critical review and research agenda. 2015. Available via The Freedom Fund. http://freedomfund.org/wp-content/uploads/2015-Addressing-the-Mental-Health-Needs-in-Survivors-of-Modern-Slavery.pdf. Accessed 4 May 2016.
67. Linley PA, Joseph S. Positive change following trauma and adversity: a review. J Trauma Stress. 2004;17(1):11–21.
68. Elderton A, Berry A, Chan C. A systematic review of posttraumatic growth in survivors of interpersonal violence in adulthood. Trauma Violence Abuse. 2015. doi:10.1177/1524838015611672.
69. U.S. Advisory Council. 2015. https://www.whitehouse.gov/the-press-office/2015/12/16/president-obama-announces-more-key-administration-posts. Accessed 4 May 2016.
70. Girls Education and Mentoring Services. 1998. www.gems-girls.org. Accessed 4 May 2016.
71. National Survivor Network. 2011. nationalsurvivornetwork.org. Accessed 4 May 2016.
72. Wilson B, Critelli F, Rittner B. Transnational responses to commercial sexual exploitation comprehensive review of intervention. Women's Stud Int Forum. 2015;48:71–80. doi:10.1016/j.wsif.2014.10.005.
73. Macy RJ, Johns N. Aftercare services for international sex trafficking survivors: informing U.S. service and program development in an emerging practice area. Trauma Violence Abuse. 2011;12(2):87–98. doi:10.1177/1524838010390709.
74. Courtois CA, Ford JD. Treating complex trauma: a sequenced relationship-based approach. New York: Guilford Press; 2013.

75. Hopper EK, Grossman F, Spinazzola J, Zucker M (under agreement) Across the abyss: components based psychotherapy for adult survivors of emotional abuse and neglect. New York: Guilford Press.
76. Briere J, Scott C. Principles of trauma therapy: a guide to symptoms, evaluation, and treatment. Thousand Oaks, CA: Sage; 2006.
77. Cloitre M, Koenen KC, Cohen LR, Han H. Skills training in affective and interpersonal regulation followed by exposure: a phase-based treatment for PTSD related to childhood abuse. J Consult Clin Psychol. 2002;70:1067–74.
78. Ford JD. An affective cognitive neuroscience-based approach to PTSD psychotherapy: the TARGET model. J Cogn Psychother. 2015;29(1):69–91.
79. Briere J, Lanktree CB. Integrative treatment of complex trauma for Adolescents (ITCT-A): a guide for the treatment of multiply-traumatized youth. 2008. National Child Traumatic Stress Network. Available via, http://www.johnbriere.com. Accessed 1 Aug 2016.
80. Cohen JA, Mannarino AP, Kliethermes M, Murray LA. Trauma-focused CBT for youth with complex trauma. Child Abuse Negl. 2012;36:528–41.
81. Saxe GN, Ellis BH, Brown AD. Trauma systems therapy for traumatized children and teens. 2nd ed. Guilford Press: New York; 2015.
82. Linehan MM, Dimeff L. Dialectical behavior therapy in a nutshell. Calif Psychol. 2001; 34:10–3.
83. Shapiro F. Eye movement desensitization and reprocessing: basic principles, protocols and procedures. 2nd ed. New York: Guilford Press; 2001.
84. Howard GS. Culture tales: a narrative approach to thinking, cross-cultural psychology, and psychotherapy. Am Psychol. 1991;46(3):187–97.
85. Brunovskis A, Surtees R. Coming home: challenges in family reintegration for trafficked women. Qual Soc Work. 2012;12:454.
86. Hickle K, Roe-Sepowitz D. Putting the pieces back together: a group intervention for sexually exploited adolescent girls. Soc Work Groups. 2014;37(2):99–113. doi:10.1080/01609513.2013.823838.
87. Arnstein E. A trauma-informed psychoeducation program for professionals treating adolescent female victims of human sex trafficking. Dissertation, Chicago School of Professional Psychology; 2014.
88. My Life My Choice. 2016. http://www.fightingexploitation.org/. Accessed 4 May 2016.
89. DeRosa R, Pelcovitz D. Igniting SPARCS of change: structured psychotherapy for adolescents responding to chronic stress. In: Ford J, Pat-Horenczyk R, Brom D, editors. Treating traumatized children: risk, resilience and recovery. New York: Routledge; 2008.
90. Emerson D, Hopper EK. Overcoming trauma through yoga: reclaiming your body. Berkeley: North Atlantic Books; 2011.
91. Villareal AG. Cultural competence in the trauma treatment of Thai survivors of modern-day slavery: the relevance of Buddhist mindfulness practices and healing rituals to transform shame and guilt of forced prostitution. In: Kalayjian A, Eugene D, editors. Mass trauma and emotional healing around the world: rituals and practices for resilience and meaning-making, vol. 2: human-made disasters. Santa Barbara, CA: Praeger; 2010. p. 269–85.
92. Pascual-Leone, A, Orrin-Porter Morrison, JK. Working with Victims of Human Trafficking. J Contemp Psychother. 2016;1–9. doi:10.1007/s10879-016-9338-3.

Chapter 11
Physical Health of Human Trafficking Survivors: Unmet Essentials

Wendy Macias-Konstantopoulos and Zheng B. Ma

11.1 Introduction

Human trafficking is an egregious human rights violation with significant impact on the physical, mental, and social health and well-being of individuals, communities, and society. In the United States (US), human trafficking cases have been reported in all 50 states and the estimated number of individuals *at risk* for trafficking per year number in the hundreds of thousands [1, 2]. According to US federal law, the Trafficking Victims Protection Act of 2000 (TVPA), "severe forms of human trafficking" include:

(a) sex trafficking in which a *commercial sex act*[1] is induced by force, fraud, or coercion, or in which the person induced to perform such act has not attained 18 years of age; or
(b) the recruitment, harboring, transportation, provision, or obtaining of a person for labor or services, through the use of force, fraud, or coercion for the purpose of subjection to involuntary servitude, peonage, debt bondage, or slavery [3].

The original version of this chapter was revised. The correction to this chapter is available at https://doi.org/10.1007/978-3-319-47824-1_26

[1] A commercial sex act is defined as a sex act performed in exchange for anything of value to any person.

W. Macias-Konstantopoulos (✉)
MGH Human Trafficking Initiative, Division of Global Health and Human Rights,
Department of Emergency Medicine, Massachusetts General Hospital,
125 Nashua Street, Suite 910, Boston, MA 02114, USA

MGH Freedom Clinic, Massachusetts General Hospital, Boston, MA, USA

Department of Emergency Medicine, Harvard Medical School, Boston, MA, USA
e-mail: wmacias@mgh.harvard.edu

Z.B. Ma
Harvard-Affiliated Emergency Medicine Residency, Massachusetts General Hospital/
Brigham & Women's Hospital, Boston, MA, USA

© Springer International Publishing AG 2017
M. Chisolm-Straker, H. Stoklosa (eds.), *Human Trafficking Is a Public Health Issue*, DOI 10.1007/978-3-319-47824-1_11

A US Department of Justice analysis of confirmed cases of human trafficking investigated by federally funded human trafficking task forces between January 2008 and June 2010 found that 82 % of cases were classified as sex trafficking, 11 % as labor trafficking, and the remaining 7 % as unknown [4]. Approximately four-fifths of confirmed sex trafficking survivors were US citizens (83 %), while the majority of confirmed labor trafficking survivors were either undocumented (67 %) or qualified[2] (28 %) immigrants [4]. Although the study was geographically diverse in that it pooled data from across the nation's human trafficking task forces, the authors acknowledge its limitations in the varying capabilities of different task forces to investigate cases and provide high quality data. These findings are nevertheless informative and the general trends are corroborated by country data from the National Human Trafficking Resource Center (NHTRC). Through the NHTRC hotline, 5544 potential cases of human trafficking were identified in 2015 with the distribution of 75 % sex trafficking, 13 % labor trafficking, 3 % both sex and labor trafficking, and 9 % non-specified [5]. Notably, recent years have seen an increased awareness of human trafficking in the US, and more than double the number of potential cases were reported to the NHTRC in 2015 as compared to 2011.

While myriad factors affect the nature of the exploitation, the adverse health outcomes of human trafficking are ubiquitous and often long-lasting. Consistent with the very nature and legal definition of their crime, traffickers often employ abusive and violent tactics to entrench and maintain control over those whom they force, defraud, and coerce into exploitation [2, 3]. As a result, trafficked persons may experience significant physical, emotional, and psychological trauma with serious short- and long-term implications for their health and well-being. Health outcomes, however, may differ from one trafficked person to another based on baseline health status and health risks prior to being trafficked; the type and duration of trafficking experienced; health conditions endemic to the geographic location of the exploitation; and stage of trafficking at which a health assessment is completed. One of the largest surveys to date on the health of trafficking survivors found that no single profile of a trafficked individual exists: Survivors differ by age, gender, country of origin, and exploitation experience. While this heterogeneity suggests that practitioners must treat each individual and their[3] experience as unique, common patterns of abuse and occupational risks are also present and can be predictive of certain health outcomes [6].

Although this chapter aims to provide a comprehensive review of the physical health needs of trafficking survivors, it is important to note that epidemiological studies on human trafficking and health have largely been conducted outside of the US. Thus, the potential limitations on the generalizability of findings to the US traf-

---

[2] Under Title 8 U.S. Code § 1641, the term "qualified alien" is defined as an immigrant who is lawfully admitted to the USA under one of several legal immigration categories, including permanent resident, asylee, and refugee status.

[3] The possessive adjective "their" will be used throughout the text instead of "his" or "her" so as to remain gender neutral and inclusive of gender non-conforming, intersex, and transgender-persons.

ficking context must be considered and parallels should be drawn with caution. Additionally, globally permeating cultural norms that define the male gender as strong and dominant, and hence less likely to be exploited, may actually impede efforts to accurately estimate the extent to which boys and men are trafficked. This limitation may falsely distort not only our understanding of the crime, but also of the needs of boys and men as they relate to both treatment and prevention. Indeed, there is consensus opinion that the prevalence of trafficked boys and men is largely underestimated and this should be noted when assimilating and applying the information contained in this chapter [7].

Similarly, research thus far has historically assigned "gender" as a dichotomous variable tied to the biological sex of individuals. This seemingly innocuous labeling trend severely limits our ability to develop a more inclusive understanding of the specific risks, experiences, and health outcomes among gender non-conforming, intersex, and transgender persons who are trafficked. In an effort to be inclusive of persons who are typically excluded by a historically two-dimensional understanding of gender, the authors have taken the liberty of using the possessive adjective "their" against the rules of traditional grammar at times. Findings from research studies, however, are reported with the conventional use of pronouns so as to accurately reflect the literature cited. Finally, in this chapter, the term "victim" is only used to signify a person who is actively being trafficked.

11.2   Discussion

11.2.1   Variation of Health Effects by Regional Geography

The push and pull factors of human trafficking vary geographically and give rise to regional variations in the types of trafficking that exist, the commercial industries into which persons are trafficked and, as a result, the physical health effects of trafficking. In parallel fashion, a region's burden of disease, population health profile, and public health infrastructure capacity also influence the physical health outcomes of trafficking and may further contribute to regional heterogeneity in health data. Countries and regions where widespread poverty exists, for example, are also areas where human trafficking may be the most overtly prevalent and where the health effects of poverty may become tightly intertwined with those that result from the living and working conditions of human trafficking (see Table 11.1).

Table 11.1   Health effects of poverty

Condition	Health outcomes
Food insecurity	Malnutrition (underweight or overweight)
Air pollution	Chronic respiratory conditions
Poor sanitation	Communicable diseases
Overcrowding	Communicable diseases
Lack of access to safe water	Dehydration, skin conditions, communicable diseases

Among international communities impacted by human trafficking, there are also regional variations in the level of understanding and acceptance of the use of exploitation in the various economic sectors into which people may be trafficked. A high level of acceptance of exploitation, for example, may give rise to labor industries completely devoid of policies and regulations that assure appropriate legal and social protections for its workers. The vacuum created by the lack of public and private sector incentives to enforce health and safety regulations and implement harm reduction strategies, in turn, directly influences workers' vulnerability to unique, industry-specific health risks and exposures. Such a lack of protective policies and regulations in both formal and informal labor sectors also facilitates and perpetuates exploitative labor trafficking across certain regions of the world, giving rise to industry- and region-specific health hazards and outcomes of human trafficking [2, 6, 8, 9]. Examples of such labor trafficking industries include the US domestic work industry, the extractive mining sector of Central and South America, the cocoa farms of West Africa, the construction industry in Middle East Gulf States, the agricultural sector of South Asia, and the fishing industry in South East Asia [2, 8, 10, 11].

Similarly, the level of understanding and acceptance of exploitation in the world's commercial sex industries is directly influenced by the religious beliefs, cultural norms, politico-economic forces, and legal environments of the regions in which these commercial sex industries exist. This, in turn, influences the degree to which trafficked individuals are at risk for industry- and region-specific health hazards and outcomes. In countries where the commercial sex industry is widely accepted or where international *sex tourism* (travel solely for the purpose of buying sex) supports a sizeable portion of the local and national economy, trafficked persons may receive periodic sexually transmitted infection (STI) testing and treatment, and may even possess greater condom-use negotiating power [12].[4] However, at times, a paradoxical effect on health occurs. Strong economic incentives may conversely prevent the enforcement of laws that attempt to regulate the commercial sex industry. For example, if the sex trafficking of minors accounts for a large proportion of the financial transactions supporting the economy, regulatory laws prohibiting the use of children under the age of 18 years in the legal commercial sex and sex tourism industries may fail to be enforced by authorities [13, 14]. Under these circumstances, children exploited in commercial sex lack protections and are less likely to benefit from harm reduction practices like periodic STI testing and increased condom availability, thus, directly and unequivocally impacting the health of children within the region. In other regions of the world, such as sub-Saharan Africa, a similar demand for and acceptance of children in settings of sexual exploitation may be fueled by an ill-conceived cultural belief that unprotected sex with a child carries less risk of human immunodeficiency virus (HIV) transmission, or even a cure for acquired immunodeficiency syndrome (AIDS). This again directly impacts health

---

[4]This practice is an example of the harm reduction strategy utilized in some communities to mitigate the negative health risks of high-risk activities without overtly criminalizing the activities.

by increasing the biological hazards to which children are exposed and potentially perpetuating high HIV transmission rates and prevalence [15, 16].

Trafficked individuals and survivors may also experience deleterious health consequences under other religious, cultural, and legal paradigms as well. In countries where participation in the commercial sex industry is socially unacceptable and/or punishable by law, trafficked persons—despite their victimization—may be subjected to legal charges and punitive treatment by authorities. They may suffer advanced disease states from delayed presentation and treatment of acute injuries and infections [17]. Moreover, sex trafficking survivors may face harsh judgment and disapproval from their families and communities for being *prostitutes* and *disease vectors*—carrying and spreading communicable diseases such as STIs [18]. Under such unwelcoming circumstances, the return of trafficking survivors into their communities can lead to repeated victimization, social ostracization, and decreased ability to access health care services [19, 20]. Unfortunately, the guilt and shame over their traumatic experiences—and perhaps a sense of complicity or self-blame—may inhibit survivors from advocating for themselves and dispelling misconceptions that they willingly chose to engage in commercial sex.

Despite the many contextual differences influencing the health outcomes of trafficked persons, a 2013 study conducted across several geographic regions found that although coordinated systems of health care for trafficked people are lacking, there is resounding support and desire for greater health sector participation in anti-trafficking efforts [21]. While the data extrapolated from one regional study may or may not be applicable to another region, common themes and experiences found within regional studies are invaluable to helping inform the approach to future research and clinical care in differing geographic locations. Understanding the diversity and complexity of health outcomes, as well as the context in which these are addressed, is key to the strategic design and implementation of more effective and multifaceted responses to the physical health needs of trafficking survivors.

11.2.2   Variations of Health Effects by States of Trafficking

The "Stages of Human Trafficking" model is based on the understanding that human trafficking, as it relates to health effects, can be understood as a process that a trafficked person undergoes rather than a single act (Fig. 11.1) [20]. This cycle is separated into chronological stages that include the *pre-departure/recruitment stage*, followed by the *travel/transit stage* towards the *destination/exploitation stage* during which people are exploited within their intended forced occupations and suffer repetitive abuse. The subsequent *reception/detention stage* is the time when the survivor exits the trafficking situation and is detained by authorities investigating the crime or executing their deportation. Finally, the *integration/reintegration stage* takes place if the survivor is supported by services through their integration into the

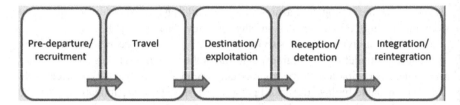

Fig. 11.1 Stages of trafficking health effects (Adapted from Zimmerman 2007 Findings from a European Study) [20]. Each stage poses a risk to an individual's health and an opportunity for health care professionals and others to intervene with information and assistance. Note that not all stages exist for each individual trafficking case and the final integration/reintegration stage may actually result in re-trafficking

local society or return home for reintegration into their society of origin. This conceptual model of trafficking is useful in identifying the unique health risks and health outcomes potentially experienced at each distinct stage of the process, thereby allowing the implementation of targeted strategies to reduce the adverse physical health effects at each stage where interventions are possible.

This model, while helpful in understanding the various health risks and outcomes based on the chronology of the trafficking process, is limited in its applicability as some cases of human trafficking, such as familial sex trafficking, do not involve transportation, or even a change of physical location, and thus may not have a discrete "travel/ transit" stage. Furthermore, many trafficked persons do not experience a "reception/ detention" or "integration/reintegration" stage. Instead, many may remain indefinitely in the "destination/exploitation" stage; re-cycle through stages multiple times before succumbing to fatal outcomes—accidental death, murder, or suicide; or leave their trafficking situation without any supportive integration or reintegration services [20].

The abusive and traumatic events suffered by trafficked persons frequently occur simultaneously across different stages rather than in distinct chronologic periods [22]. The process of being trafficked entails fluid movement forwards and backwards from one stage to another. It is therefore advisable to approach caring for trafficked persons' physical and mental health needs in a holistic manner with special attention to the important social, familial, and community factors that may have contributed to their initial exploitation and may further serve as barriers to reintegration. The challenging efforts for integration or reintegration require interdisciplinary collaboration among multiple health care providers, legal aid resources, law enforcement agencies, and community organizations [23, 24].

11.2.3 Variation of Health Effects by Type of Trafficking

11.2.3.1 Sex Trafficking

Human trafficking for the purpose of commercial sexual exploitation is arguably the most publicized form of trafficking and also the most studied. Adults and children alike fall victim to this crime. Adolescents and young adults are particularly vulnerable to manipulation and exploitation because of limited life experience and reduced ability to control impulses and critically analyze the risks and benefits of different situations and decisions [25]. Although results vary and outliers exist, studies generally indicate that the average age of entry for children into commercial sexual exploitation in the US is in the teenage years [1, 26, 27]. One study of domestically trafficked minors in the US described initial commercial sex experiences occurring between ages 10 and 17 years with a median age of entry into sex trafficking at 15 years [27].

Minors with heightened vulnerability to sex trafficking include those with predisposing individual, familial, and community risk factors. A history of childhood sexual abuse has been frequently correlated to an increased risk of sex trafficking due, in part, to the disruptive effects of sexual abuse on a child's self-esteem and relational boundaries [21, 23, 28–30]. Similarly, youth who have substance use problems, behavioral and mental health problems, or cognitive disabilities are also more vulnerable to trafficking [28, 30]. Research also shows that minors who self-identify as lesbian, gay, bisexual, transgender, or questioning (LGBTQ) are at elevated risk of trafficking due to an increased vulnerability conferred by their experiences of difference, isolation, and rejection [30–33]. Runaway, "thrown-away" (those who are expelled from their homes or not allowed to return), and homeless youth are at especially high risk of exploitation due to their lack of safe and stable housing, and their limited ability to meet their basic needs [1, 23, 28–30, 34]. Survival sex, commonly seen among displaced youth, is the exchange of a sex act to meet basic survival needs such as shelter or food, and qualifies as sex trafficking when it involves persons under the age of 18. Children from families with other dysfunctions (e.g., caregiver substance use, mental illness, intimate partner violence, and incarceration) also suffer from the same lack of reliable familial support [23, 28–30, 34]. Finally, children residing in communities with high levels of poverty, crime, gang violence, adult prostitution,[5] and predominantly male transient populations (e.g., military bases, truck stops, and convention centers) are also at heightened risk [16, 28, 30, 34].

In a study conducted in southern US, child trafficking survivors reported experiencing significantly greater degrees of violence, substance use, housing instability, and involvement with child protective services and/or law enforcement while being trafficked as compared to those who had been sexually abused or assaulted without commercial gain. These findings are particularly salient in that they highlight the significant health risks and exposures—beyond the act of sexual abuse itself—of sex trafficking [35]. A large study involving 387 minors, aged 10–17 years from the Greater Mekong Subregion, found that exploited children have remarkably high

---

[5] Prostitution involves exchanging the performance of sexual acts for money, is a legal term, and usually connotes a crime. Legally, the components of force, fraud, coercion, and/or exploitation distinguish trafficking from prostitution. However, a strong argument can be made that adult cases of prostitution (i.e., not involving such exploitative and coercive elements) often begin with commercial sex acts at an age younger than 18 years, qualifying them as trafficking at least at their inception. Nonetheless, even individuals who begin commercial sex work in adulthood often face coercive and exploitative factors that are not always clearly identified.

levels of both physical and mental health symptoms, and strong associations with self-harm and suicidal behavior [36]. Studies based in the US found similar trends of astonishingly high frequency of physical and psychological health problems during trafficking. In one such study, 99.1% of the survivors reported at least one physical health problem and 96.4% reported at least one psychological symptom [37]. In three major US metropolitan cities, structured interviews with highly experienced anti-trafficking stakeholders again confirmed the wide range of physical and mental health problems associated with the commercial sexual exploitation of adolescents and young adults. Injuries suffered stemmed from a wide range of perpetrators including traffickers, clients, other trafficked individuals, and even the trafficked persons themselves, in the form of self-harming behaviors or suicide attempts [21, 29].

Violence Physical and sexual violence, and the threat of future violence, are a major means by which traffickers exert control over those they victimize. These forceful and coercive methods may include repeated bodily strikes, forced substance use, rape and gang rape, and other forced submission tactics. One multi-country study found that 95% of sex trafficked women reported sexual violence, and more than half of the adolescent girls and women surveyed reported experiencing pre-trafficking physical or sexual violence [38]. Among female sex trafficking survivors, violence in the period immediately after entry to the commercial sex industry may involve especially high levels of sexual brutality, leading to anogenital[6] injuries with the potential for severe bleeding and, ultimately, increased vulnerability to STIs [39].

A US-based study found that 92.2% of sex trafficking survivors reported suffering at least one form of physical violence, most often involving direct blows to the head or face [37]. Despite agreement across different studies that sex trafficked persons experience high rates of sexual and physical violence, the reported prevalence of violence may be an underestimate of its true occurrence as a result of possible underreporting due to self-blame, fear of stigma, and varying perceptions of what constitutes sexual violence [38].

Communicable Diseases The nature of commercial sex requires close, personal contact with a litany of sex buyers, naturally predisposing trafficked individuals not only to sexually transmitted infections, but also to other communicable diseases. The use of violence leading to skin and mucosal breakdown further increases the risk of transmission of infectious organisms between individuals, creating a direct relationship between injury, exposure, and infection. Skin infestations, such as body lice and scabies, can spread from contact with buyers of commercial sex, as well as contact between trafficked persons living in close, crowded quarters [24].

Among infectious diseases affecting sex trafficked individuals, HIV has been the most well-studied. Though epidemiological data among US sex trafficked populations are lacking, HIV prevalence studies conducted internationally suggest that sex

---

[6] Anogenital: relating to or involving the genital organs and anus.

trafficked individuals carry higher likelihoods of HIV infection than the non-trafficked background population. Increased HIV incidence among sex trafficked populations is multifactorial. In addition to the forced nature of the sex, the vulnerability of sex trafficked individuals to HIV infection is also exacerbated by high levels of sexual violence, anogenital wounds, limited ability to negotiate the use of barrier protection, and restricted access to health care and other services [39–46]. The location of commercial sex also influences risk for HIV transmission. Individuals trafficked in regions with higher HIV prevalence in the general population are more likely to later test positive for HIV than those trafficked in lower prevalence regions. Some studies have found as much as a sixfold increased risk of HIV infection among trafficked individuals in high prevalence areas relative to those trafficked in low prevalence regions [42, 43]. Finally, younger age of entry into trafficking has also been associated with a higher likelihood of acquiring HIV. This increased risk is thought to be related to longer lengths of time in sexual servitude, increased number of clients served, greater biological susceptibility to infectious organisms in the less mature, fragile, and traumatized genital tract, and local beliefs (where they exist) that sex with a young, virgin child is a cure for HIV/AIDS [15–17, 42, 44–46].

Co-infection of HIV with other sexually and non-sexually transmitted infections is also commonly seen among sex trafficked individuals. In cases where sexual transmission of HIV occurs, other STIs such as gonorrhea, chlamydia, trichomonas, bacterial vaginosis, hepatitis B (HBV), hepatitis C (HCV), syphilis, and human papilloma virus (HPV) are generally also present and are more readily transmitted and acquired through unprotected sex than HIV [18, 47]. Non-sexual communicable diseases such as tuberculosis (TB) also occur and the risk of developing *active* TB dramatically increases among those co-infected with HIV [48].

Industry-Specific Reproductive Health Exposures Repeated sexual abuse, sexually transmitted infections, and a lack of access to contraception during trafficking are related to high risk of unplanned pregnancy and other gynecological symptoms. In one U.S. study, 63.8% of sex trafficking survivors reported at least one gynecologic symptom such as pain during sex or urinary tract infections. Of those who reported pregnancies, 71.2% reported at least one pregnancy during their exploitation, and 21.2% reported five or more pregnancies. Among those who responded to questions regarding termination of pregnancy, 55.2% reported at least one abortion and 29.9% reported multiple abortions [37]. While the study did not explore the availability of contraception, the findings are consistent with reports of decreased ability to negotiate condom use in commercial sex.

Many sex trafficking survivors, both internationally- and domestically-born, describe being beaten to induce spontaneous abortions ("miscarriages") and forced to undergo abortions during their exploitation [20, 49, 50]. In addition to any immediate medical complications of the procedure, the long-term consequences of forced, unsafe abortions on physical and reproductive health are numerous and include blood-borne diseases from inadequately sanitized tools; infertility; future high-risk pregnancies; and pregnancy-related deaths. In cases in which pregnant women and girls are allowed or made to carry their pregnancy to term, few may receive adequate prenatal care. High rates of maternal transmission of HIV, HBV, HCV, and congenital syphilis further lead to neonatal death and morbidity [17]. A recent US-based study identified that children born to sex-trafficked mothers were at particularly high risk for adverse health effects including fetal alcohol syndrome, blindness, neonatal abstinence syndrome,[7] physical and sexual abuse, and even death as a consequence of abuse [51].

Substance Use and Dependence Substance use has been frequently linked to sex trafficking in the US. Survivors describe the use of alcohol or other illicit substances as a means used by traffickers to "initiate" individuals into sex work and maintain control, and also, in some cases, as a means by which trafficked persons cope with their harsh reality and traumatic experiences [20, 39, 52]. One US study found that 84.3 % of trafficked survivors used alcohol, drugs, or both while trafficked. In this study, a multitude of illicit drugs were recorded with the most commonly used substances being alcohol (59.8 %), marijuana (53.4 %), and cocaine (50.5 %). Other substances identified include heroin, ecstasy, and phencyclidine (PCP) [37]. Intravenous drug use also carries additional health risks such as skin infections at injection sites and blood-borne infections from needle-sharing. A study conducted in Canada found that high rates of injection drug use among youth (age less than 18 years) entering commercial sex likely also contributes to the high prevalence of HIV in this population [45].

Other Health Issues Sex trafficking can also give rise to musculoskeletal strain, malnutrition, poor dentition, and chronic pain syndromes [20, 23, 24]. One study found 71.4 % of trafficked individuals suffered at least one diet and nutrition-related symptom including weight loss, malnutrition, loss of appetite, and/or an eating disorder. This study also highlighted the vast range of physical symptoms reported by sex trafficking survivors including neurological symptoms (91.7 %), cardiovascular and respiratory symptoms (68.5 %), gastrointestinal symptoms (62.0 %), and dental problems (54.3 %) [37]. It is likely that abuse, violence, and poor living and working conditions exacerbate pre-existing conditions while also creating new adverse health outcomes as described above.

Surveys conducted with sex trafficked individuals frequently detail physical symptoms including headaches, fatigue, dizzy spells, back pain, memory difficulties, and stomach pain, among other symptoms. These same studies routinely show the majority of survivors reporting more than ten concurrent physical health problems upon entering post-trafficking programs, highlighting the compounded pain and discomfort experienced by this population [38].

---

[7] Neonatal abstinence syndrome: a group of problems that occur in a newborn as a result of the abrupt discontinuation of chronic fetal exposure to substances that were used or abused by the mother during pregnancy.

11.2.3.2   Labor Trafficking

While the majority of research on human trafficking has focused on sex trafficking, data regarding the health risks and outcomes of labor trafficked persons are increasingly available. Low skilled labor sectors in which trafficking flourishes include, but are not limited to, agriculture, factory work (e.g., textile manufacturing, food processing, and brick kiln production), commercial fishing, extractive mining, construction, and domestic servitude [2, 8, 9, 53, 54]. The frequency with which these sectors exploit workers is largely based on geography, with specific labor industries being more prevalent in certain parts of the world. As with sex trafficking, labor trafficking is not limited to the developing world. Numerous workers are trafficked in developed countries for domestic servitude, agricultural, construction, landscaping, and other manual labor jobs. As in the recruitment for other forms of trafficking, trafficked individuals often believe they are accepting legitimate jobs only to find that their circumstances are closer to slavery and slave-like practices [2].

The health risks and outcomes of labor trafficking are multiple and are closely related to environmental and industry-specific occupational risks. Agriculture, construction, and extractive mining have high occupational death rates, whereas high non-fatal injury rates are common in occupations such as domestic servitude [2, 8, 9, 53, 54]. Many trafficked laborers work in unregulated or unregistered businesses where labor inspections may never take place. The lack of independent oversight facilitates the potential magnification of baseline occupational health risks [2, 8, 9, 54]. A study about the specific health problems of 35 labor trafficking survivors accessing post-trafficking services showed that physical health symptom levels were astoundingly high. Specifically, 81 % of labor trafficking survivors reported at least one symptom of poor physical health [55]. These findings were corroborated by an earlier study in 2012 that found headaches, stomach pain, memory problems, back pain, loss of appetite, and tooth pain to be the most commonly reported health symptoms amongst a cohort of women trafficked for labor exploitation [56]. Yet despite the profound deleterious physical health effects experienced by trafficked laborers, few labor trafficking victims receive medical care and most rely on self-treatment [6, 10, 54, 55].

Violence Similar to sex trafficking, physical violence is a frequent component of the exploitation and is liberally used by traffickers to keep victims under their control. While little actual data exist to detail the specific health hazards related to those trafficked in labor industries, there are global accounts of severe physical violence perpetrated by traffickers and abusive employers. Trafficked people are beaten, starved, threatened, intentionally wounded with knives and guns, forced to use drugs (e.g., amphetamines to help them work longer hours or barbiturates to make them more compliant), and sexually abused [6, 10, 53]. In one study of labor-trafficked survivors, 40 % of respondents expressed experiencing physical violence and 40 % expressed witnessing overt violence or threat of violence to their family or other workers [6, 55]. Among labor trafficked women, many have reported sexual abuse in addition to physical and verbal abuse; they often express constant fear and worry about sexual harassment from traffickers and even other trafficked co-workers [6, 54]. Relatively little is known about the health of children who have experienced violence in the context of child labor exploitation and even less about the health needs of children who survive both labor and sexual exploitation [36].

Crowding, Sanitation, and Malnutrition Crowded living quarters, poor ventilation, limited access to fresh water, and poor sanitation are common health risks described by survivors of labor trafficking [8, 54]. Survivors also frequently describe experiencing intentional deprivation of food, water, or other basic living needs. Prolonged duration in poor and hazardous conditions compounded with deficiencies in basic survival needs may further exacerbate chronic medical issues or cause acute health problems such as diarrheal illnesses and/or respiratory problems. Tuberculosis is of particular concern worldwide given its rapid transmission and frequently delayed diagnosis among workers who have limited access to medical care [54]. High levels of internal moisture due to overcrowding, inadequate ventilation, and leaks encourage the outbreak and growth of biological hazards including viruses, bacteria, molds, insects, and rodents. The emergence of such disease vectors is another well-known health complication of substandard living conditions and contributes to the spread of infectious diseases among labor trafficked persons [57].

Chronic Pain and Fatigue Injuries related to repetitive movements such as scrubbing, hammering, bending, and heavy lifting are a common theme across various labor sectors [41]. The repetitive motion injuries sustained by trafficked laborers from their physically demanding tasks result in prolonged musculoskeletal stress and strain. These simple acute injuries, while ordinarily self-limited in nature, become complex chronic conditions that are painful and exceedingly difficult to heal as trafficked persons have limited access to basic medical care and are rarely allowed to rest or recover from their injuries. Given their prolonged toil in physically arduous jobs and extended work hours with limited breaks, it is not surprising that labor trafficked persons struggle with profound levels of fatigue that are likely exacerbated by dehydration, malnutrition, anemia, and other conditions of poor health. Chronic pain and fatigue syndromes persisting beyond the trafficking experience may also represent somatic manifestations of the psychological distress experienced during their exploitation related to the threats, abuse, violence, poor living and working conditions, isolation, and outright lack of freedom [6, 53, 55].

Industry-Specific Environmental and Occupational Exposures Labor trafficked workers are likely to work in sectors with few health and safety protections and/or infrequent labor inspections. Exploited laborers are also unlikely to be offered adequate training (in a language they can understand) or personal protective equipment. The types of health risks and exposures affecting labor trafficked persons are largely industry-specific environmental and occupational exposures that are closely intertwined. For example, outdoor labor such as agricultural, farming, and construction work increase the risk of dehydration, heat exhaustion, and subsequent life-threatening heatstroke from prolonged exposure to the sun and extremes of heat. In addition to exposures to the elements, labor trafficked persons must contend with prolonged exposures to hazardous environmental factors without proper personal protective equipment. Examples of environmental exposures include the dust, loud noise, and dangerous heights that are characteristic of construction sites; the pesticide chemicals used in agricultural fields; the biological pathogens of livestock farms; and the dim lighting of extractive mines. Prolonged exposure to such health hazards may lead to chronic respiratory illnesses, noise-induced hearing loss, traumatic injuries, skin conditions, infections, and eye strain [2, 6, 8, 54, 58, 59].

Laborers in the fishing industry face unique health exposures, including extremes of cold and wind. In addition, trafficked fishermen[8] may suffer water immersions due to vessel capsize and collision; drowning due to lack of personal flotation devices; fall-related injuries due to rough sea waters or slippery wet floors; deep cuts and puncture wounds due to the use of sharp knives (and while on a moving vessel); hazardous chemical exposures (e.g., ammonia and chemicals used for insulation and refrigeration); and electrical shocks due to inadequate safety procedures and training [2, 6, 60–62].

11.2.3.3   Trafficking in Persons for the Removal of Organs

While, as of 2016, state and federal laws focus on the two major forms of human trafficking known to predominate in the US—sex and labor trafficking—human trafficking can take many forms. Trafficking in persons for the removal of organs (TPRO), more uniquely associated with low- and middle-income countries, has galvanized attention in the US due to concerns that the commercialization of human organs harms voluntary organ donation programs. In addition, survivors of this crime may seek asylum and medical care in the US.

The demand for human organs has increased in response to the worldwide shortage of organs for transplantation. As a consequence, transplant commercialism and tourism has become an increasing problem in many countries, particularly in impoverished nations where wealthy domestic or international organ tourists can exploit the vulnerabilities of financially insecure persons. While the majority of cases of exploitation of persons for the extraction of organs involve kidneys, cases of liver lobe explanation have also been described. Indeed, the World Health Organization estimates that organ trafficking accounts for 5–10% of kidney transplants performed annually throughout the world [63]. It is unclear how prevalent this problem is in the US; still, there is an outcry among some in the US anti-trafficking movement to include organ trafficking in the US definition of human trafficking [64].

---

[8]"Fishermen" includes people of all genders. While "fisher" is more commonly being used in academic circles, one study shows that North American men and women in the industry prefer to call themselves "fishermen" regardless of gender. For more information, see: Branch TA, Kleiber D. "Should we call them fishers or fishermen?" *Fish and Fisheries*, 2015 Sept. DOI: 10.111/ faf.12130.

One article synthesized the findings of a number of studies conducted with organ-trafficked individuals after their experience and highlighted three common themes:

Desperation, the participants' decision to sell their kidney was forced by poverty or the need to repay a debt or to fulfill a family obligation; despair (including subthemes of destroyed bodily integrity, shame and secrecy, dehumanization, dispiritedness, loss of livelihood, heightened sense of vulnerability, disappointment, and regret); and debasement (including subthemes of deception by brokers and recipients, victimization by hospital staff, stigmatization by community, and rejection by family) [65].

A 2002 study of individuals who had undergone paid kidney removal in India found that 86% of those exploited for organ removal reported deterioration in their health [66]. Factors identified as contributing to their decline in health included insufficient prior medical screening and pre-existing compromising health conditions. Commonly reported complications of organ removal included the development of chronic pain and cramping at the site of incision, inability to lift heavy objects or perform labor-intensive work, swelling of legs, hypertension, loss of appetite, insomnia, and considerable fatigue [66–69].

One study found that the vast majority (78%) of persons trafficked for organ removal did not receive medical follow-up care after kidney removal. Many cited hesitance in consulting a doctor due to the association of physicians with their exploitation and instead relied upon non-prescribed pain medicine from local pharmacies. Of the minority of those who did receive post-removal care, it was never by the medical professional(s) who performed the kidney removal, but rather by health care providers in local low-cost clinics. Additionally, 89% of those who disclosed the financial repercussions of their organ removal reported they could not return to their labor-intensive jobs, thus limiting their ability to generate future income and leading to further incurred debt. Finally, it is worth noting that all study participants unanimously regretted the commercial removal of a kidney and would advise others against it [67].

11.2.4 Untreated Chronic Medical Conditions

It is important to remember that in addition to acute injuries, illnesses, and infections occurring while exploited, trafficked persons may also have pre-existing health conditions worsened by their lack of access to medical care while trafficked. New medical conditions that arise during the exploitation and fail to be diagnosed and treated due to restricted access to health care create an additionally complex burden of disease for many trafficked individuals. Neglect of overall health certainly contributes to the long inventory of negative health outcomes associated with human trafficking [10, 20, 23–25].

11.2.5   A Brief Word on Mental Health

Any discussion on the health effects of trafficking is incomplete without mention of the profound effects of exploitation on the mental health of trafficked persons [6, 20, 29, 30, 36, 37]. While the immediate physical effects can take significant tolls on the health of trafficked individuals and indeed even lead to significant debilitation and death, the mental health effects are often concurrent and lifelong. This topic is covered in-depth separately in this book.

11.2.6   The Role of Health Care Providers

Given the expansive health effects of trafficking, health care providers are uniquely positioned to interface with trafficked persons at various stages of trafficking [20, 22, 29, 35, 37, 70–74]. Health care providers have the critical opportunity—and privilege—not only to treat the immediate health needs of patients, but also to participate in anti-trafficking prevention and intervention efforts to help break the cycle of violence and exploitation.

Patients who are being trafficked are often difficult to identify. The crime of human trafficking, and its physical health effects, may share similarities with other high-risk situations encountered in the health setting such as child maltreatment, intimate partner violence, elder abuse, sexual violence, and torture [25, 70–74]. While important legal distinctions exist between trafficking and other abusive relational conditions, there are frequent commonalities between the health risks and needs of people in these circumstances. For health care practitioners, distinctions in category of abuse should not affect the approach to or level of care provided for these patients [23]. These distinctions, however, become important when determining the type of care provided, the referrals needed, and the follow-up services required to continue to assist and reduce risk of further harm. It is, therefore, essential that health care providers not only understand the health effects of human trafficking, but also familiarize themselves with the resources and options available for their trafficked patients following the clinical encounter [23].

For trafficked persons who seek care, the stage of trafficking in which they find themselves may also determine the nature and scope of referrals and/or services needed [20]. The outcome of an isolated clinical encounter differs for a person in the midst of their exploitation seeking medical care for an acute condition, as compared to a survivor on the path of recovery and reintegration seeking to begin a therapeutic relationship. During the exploitation phase of human trafficking, a clinician interacting with a patient suspected of being trafficked has a vital opportunity to review a safety plan and provide resources for future assistance. Likewise, the health care provider can also assist in arranging emergency shelter, protection, and other support measures for those seeking immediate assistance in exiting their situation. A trafficking survivor in the integration/reintegration phase looking to reenter society, on the other hand, would benefit greatly from long-term primary and preventative health care. Clinicians engaging survivors at this stage should aim to perform a comprehensive assessment of the full scope of their physical and mental health, and social needs, and be prepared to provide appropriate referrals and case management [75]. Regardless, it is always important to be respectful of the patient's wishes and sensitive to the complexity of factors that may have increased their vulnerability to being trafficked in the first place.

The health care practitioner additionally has an important role and opportunity to provide anticipatory guidance to high-risk individuals. Many at risk of being trafficked or re-trafficked after exiting their exploitation would benefit from addressing particular vulnerabilities with their health care providers. This might allow for early intervention and connection to care and resources to mitigate the desperate circumstances upon which traffickers prey. Even if a medical professional cannot assist someone out of a trafficked situation, medical guidance may prevent disease and even save the trafficked person's life [16, 25, 73].

11.2.6.1 Provider Education and Training

Health care providers' ability to assist victims and survivors of human trafficking in the health care setting begins first with provider education about human trafficking, and training on the identification, evaluation, and the medical and social care of trafficked persons. Specific training on the proper evaluation of the complex physical and psychological needs of people in post-trafficking situations may also be appropriate. While historically, human trafficking has been poorly recognized by the health sector as relevant to clinical practice, increased efforts to gain support for the integration of human trafficking curricula into medical education and training continue to gain momentum [75–80]. Nevertheless, the lack of validated clinical screening tools for victim identification, proven care resources, and infrastructure specific for trafficked persons can make clinical intervention difficult to navigate. Resources and lessons learned from the successes of intimate partner violence, child maltreatment, and early adopter human trafficking programs are informative for future developments.

11.2.6.2 Approach to Care

Trauma-informed, survivor-centered, culturally competent care should be the goal of any health care provider's encounter with a potentially trafficked person. Several guiding principles may be helpful for the clinician in their initial encounter with a potential or self-identified trafficked patient [23–25, 29, 81, 82]:

- *Patient–Provider Encounter*: It is helpful to build trust and rapport with the patient before the physical medical evaluation to assure the survivor that questions asked are relevant to guiding the exam, determining health needs, and indicating appropriate referrals. Disclosure of a trafficking experience should *not* be the goal of *any* medical interaction.

- ***Patient Empowerment*:** A preliminary discussion about privacy, confidentiality (including any limitations due to state mandatory reporting laws), patient choice, and shared decision-making[9] can help give the patient a sense of balanced power and control over the patient–provider encounter and its outcomes.

- ***Minimized retraumatization*:** The physical examination and discussion of the patient's past or present situation may provoke intense stress and anxiety. It is important to monitor for signs of distress during the interview and minimize the risk of retraumatizing the patient. Clinicians should learn techniques for helping patients de-escalate when emotions are heightened. In general, the health care provider could make it a practice to always approach individual patients with the understanding that they may have suffered significant trauma, even if not disclosed and regardless of the presenting medical problem. Care should always be taken by the provider to be sensitive to this possibility so as not to re-expose the patient to the psychological anguish of their trauma.

- ***Informed Consent/Assent*:** Practitioners should obtain the patient's consent (for adults)/assent (for minors) to the medical evaluation, including the physical examination, diagnostic testing, consultations, and services engaged, and respect patients' right to decline services. Mandated reporting events, which vary by state, are not optional however, and limits to confidentiality of the patient–provider relationship should be carefully explained and all questions answered early in the clinical encounter.

- ***Patient Right to Privacy*:** All patients should speak with their provider privately (via a licensed interpreter, as needed) at least once during the encounter, as traffickers may accompany patients to care visits. A private discussion with the patient is important, because it is not always obvious when a visitor is the trafficker (see Chap. 2). Clinicians should avoid asking a patient in the presence of the person(s) accompanying them if they wish to speak privately. Health care providers may ensure privacy by stating that they need to speak with the patient alone or examine the patient in privacy, and requesting that others excuse themselves from the examination room. Alternatively, if the situation is more difficult or precarious, clinicians may need to create more subtle opportunities to speak to their patients alone and without the knowledge of those accompanying the patient.

- ***Thorough Physical Exam*:** Consider the presence of a staff chaperone during the evaluation and examination. The patient should be asked, in private, if they want the person accompanying them to be present as well. A thorough examination of the patient's body (with patient permission) can facilitate the identification of injuries or other clues of exploitation, such as ownership markings or brandings.

---

[9] Shared Decision Making (SDM): A collaborative process that allows patients and providers to make health care decisions together, taking into consideration the risks and benefits of a treatment plan with respect to the best scientific evidence possible and the patient's personal values, goals, and preferences.

When individuals report sexual violence, a forensic examination should be offered, regardless of gender, but performed only with the patient's permission. Though visible injury may be present, the absence of visible injuries is not unexpected nor does it disprove assault. Documentation should be clear and legible, and should employ body maps when available. When available, photographic documentation should be pursued, with the patient's consent, in a manner that satisfies the requirements for forensic photography.

- *Comprehensive Treatment for Illnesses and Injuries*: As medical conditions are identified, treatment plans must be devised. Particularly as it pertains to sex trafficked and sexually abused labor trafficked individuals, reproductive health care should be comprehensive and should make contraception methods, emergency contraception, STI testing and treatment, pre- and post-exposure HIV prophylaxis, safe termination of pregnancy, and prenatal care available to patients. Whenever possible, treatment plans should be straightforward and definitive, and should presume that medication and follow-up appointment compliance will be difficult for the trafficked or formerly trafficked patient. Similarly, treatment plans for substance use disorders, acute and chronic medical conditions, injuries, and mental illness may need to be developed and prioritized based on the patient's anticipated ability to follow through.

- *Follow-Up Plan*: As indicated and to the greatest extent possible, clinicians should provide the patient with a plan for follow-up care. Inviting the patient back for a follow-up appointment will cultivate the patient–provider relationship and allow the patient another opportunity to address their needs for physical, mental, and emotional health and well-being.

- *Multidisciplinary Team Approach and Referral to Services*: Because the circumstances leading to trafficking are often multifactorial, the approach to complete recovery should be multidisciplinary. With the understanding that local available resources are often limited, the multidisciplinary approach to care may involve the resources and efforts of various community service organizations, legal aid, victim of crime compensation, and other assistance programs.

Availability of Resources While there are limited resources available specifically for trafficking survivors, programs and services needed to address their unmet needs may overlap with the resources available for migrants and refugees; victims/survivors of child maltreatment, domestic violence, and sexual assault; and persons with mental illnesses or substance use disorders [23].

11.2.7 Limitations of Extant Evidence

Research on health and human trafficking is limited by numerous factors including the lack of common databases, the challenges of victim identification, definitional differences, small sample sizes, memory-based recollections of trafficking experiences, and aggregation of multiple types of trafficking. Frequently, the challenge is further exacerbated by the misidentification of survivors of exploitation and trafficking as perpetrators of crimes (e.g., prostitutes) rather than crime victims. Another particularly clear limitation is the disproportionate number of studies detailing experiences of sex trafficked women and girls, while trafficked boys, men, and gender non-conforming, intersex, and transgender individuals are rarely included. In similar fashion, labor trafficking has typically received less attention in medical and public health research, though there are growing efforts to expand investigations in this area.

A significant limitation in current studies is small sample size. While estimates of prevalence of trafficked persons routinely number in the millions worldwide, existing health-related studies often involve samples of survivors in tens to hundreds. One of the studies with the largest sample size involves approximately 1100 trafficked persons pooled across three geographic regions [6]; however, this study is an outlier among numerous others with more modest sample sizes. These small sample sizes limit the generalizability of even significant findings to the much larger population of trafficked persons across different geographic distributions. Yet despite these limitations, the information gained from the composite of all studies to date is extremely valuable as it gives health care providers much needed guidance to care for these patients of great complexity.

The majority of studies conducted on the health consequences of trafficking are qualitative, interview-based, and at the stage of post-trafficking integration and re-integration, involving survivors who seek post-trafficking services through non-governmental organizations. These studies, while extremely valuable in characterizing the poorly understood trafficking circumstances, suffer from selection bias,[10] small sample sizes, and lack of generalizability to different forms of trafficking, different stages of trafficking, and different geographic locations of exploitation. The results of these studies are further limited by their cross-sectional nature while longitudinal outcome-based data is almost nonexistent. Furthermore, these studies may also be limited in scope due to self-reporting bias and symptom-based understanding of health rather than actual diagnoses (e.g., headaches vs. post-concussive syndrome).

Clinically validated screening tools for victim identification in the health care setting are lacking. This, compounded with underreporting of physical symptoms, further limits the scope of research and the knowledge base. Because no instruments are, as of yet, validated for trafficking identification in a clinical health setting, studies often draw upon several different tools validated among trafficking survivor populations in non-clinical settings or among diverse populations exposed to high levels of trauma. However, these instruments may fail to fully capture the unique and extreme features of the physical and psychological trauma of human trafficking, and the culturally different ways in which exploitation is experienced or expressed by trafficked individuals [38].

---

[10] Selection Bias: The unintended selection of particular types of individuals, groups, or data for analysis without proper randomization, such that the sample obtained is not accurately representative of the population intended for analysis.

Lastly, there are ethical challenges associated with conducting health-related studies with individuals in active captivity. It would be ethically irresponsible for clinicians and researchers to obtain health-related data without addressing the egregious human rights violations and health outcomes suffered by their patients—and, unfortunately, many clinical sites do not have the necessary resources to provide for the complex needs of patients identified as being trafficked. Additionally, it can be logistically difficult for people in the midst of their exploitation to seek even single medical encounters with trusted health care providers, let alone follow-up assessments, both of which are crucial for health outcomes data collection. As a result, the majority of data on health effects are gathered from qualitative analyses of interviews and surveys of formerly trafficked persons. Meanwhile, those who are entrenched and unable to exit their exploitation are often the most difficult to identify and are not included in the research.

11.3 Conclusion

This discussion on the physical health effects of human trafficking is by no means exhaustive. There continues to be a dire need for further research that expands knowledge of the immediate and long-term needs of trafficked persons and survivors, and informs best care practices for this particularly vulnerable population. In addition to aggressive prevention strategies, a coordinated, trauma-informed, and survivor-centered approach to care seems promising in mitigating the physical health effects of human trafficking.

11.4 Recommendations

As with any emerging field, directions for future improvement are crucial for capitalizing and building upon the newfound momentum in caring and advocating for trafficked individuals. We recommend a few "next steps" for the health sector to participate meaningfully in anti-trafficking efforts.

- **Expansion of Education and Training**
  While the problem of human trafficking has gained a greater level of awareness among health care providers, significant gaps in knowledge continue to exist even on the academic forefront of medical education [83, 84]. *Health care providers, across the various disciplines of medicine, should receive basic education and training on the relevance of human trafficking to their practice, the intricacies of victim identification, trauma-informed care, and referrals for community and legal resources [75–79]. Furthermore, human trafficking curricula should be incorporated into health professional schools to educate the future generations*

of health professionals. Education about other forms of interpersonal violence is already standardized in the majority of health professional schools across the nation and it would likely be minimally disruptive if the topic of human trafficking is simply added to the established format and curriculum.

- **Development of Protocols for Providing Patient Care Specific for Human Trafficking**
  In conjunction with training for providers, *there is a strong need for evidence-based practice protocols and guidelines specific to this unique patient population* [82]. Informed by the extant knowledge on human trafficking, as well as experiences and lessons learned from the related fields of intimate partner violence, child maltreatment, and torture, numerous clinical care resources and protocols have been developed and are being utilized in clinical settings where trafficked persons and trafficking survivors are treated [23, 24, 81, 85]. While these may currently serve as promising practices, they must be implemented with a plan for monitoring and evaluation of impact and ongoing quality improvement efforts. *Trafficking survivors should be invited to participate in the process of defining best care practices.*

- **High Quality Health Research**
  While the scope and quality of research in the field of human trafficking continue to grow, *glaring deficiencies persist in the equal study of gender groups, as well as forms of human trafficking.* Improved research quality and impact would also be facilitated by standardization of definitions in trafficking across national, state, and local groups. The centralization and sharing of information among researchers would yield easy access to data and allow for expounding upon previously formed building blocks. Similarly, the inclusion of human trafficking and commercial exploitation as diagnoses in the forthcoming ICD-11 (International Classification of Diseases, 11th Edition) diagnostic code system would allow for an improved means of monitoring incidence and prevalence of health-related symptoms and conditions in trafficked persons and trafficking survivors. Finally, *the inclusion of survivor-informed research in the field is imperative to developing effective tools and answering questions* about issues of which non-trafficked researchers may be unaware.

- **Resources and Advocacy**
  The best-devised plan cannot advance when faced with the numerous practical and logistical challenges posed by a lack of resources. For the fight against human trafficking to achieve ultimate success, there must be a genuine commitment of financial means, intellectual capabilities, and human resources. These *resources need to come from governmental agencies, the business and health care sectors, philanthropic foundations, faith-based institutions, service and advocacy organizations, community groups, and individuals alike.* With regard to advocacy, a strong starting point would be for survivors to have a voice in shaping policy that pertains to them.

References

1. Estes RJ, Weiner NA. The commercial sexual exploitation of children in the US, Canada and Mexico. University of Pennsylvania, School of Social Work, Center for the Study of Youth Policy. Philadelphia: University of Pennsylvania; 2001.
2. Trafficking in Persons Report, 2015. United States Department of State.
3. Victims of Trafficking and Violence Protection Act of 2000, Public Law 106-386, 114 Stat 1470. Available at http://www.state.gov/documents/organization/10492.pdf. Accessed 1 Aug 2016.
4. Banks D, Kyckelhahn T. Characteristics of suspected human trafficking incidents, 2008–2010. U.S. Department of Justice, Office of Justice Programs, Bureau of Justice Statistics. Washington: U.S. Department of Justice; 2011.
5. Polaris Project. National Human Trafficking Resource Center 2015 Statistics.
6. Kiss L, Pocock NS, Naisanguansri V, Suos S, Dickson B, Thuy D, et al. Health of men, women, and children in post-trafficking services in Cambodia, Thailand, and Vietnam: an observational cross-sectional study. Lancet Glob Health. 2015;3(3):e154–61.
7. Oram S, Stöckl H, Busza J, Howard LM, Zimmerman C. Prevalence and risk of violence and the physical, mental, and sexual health problems associated with human trafficking: systematic review. PLoS Med. 2012;9(5), e1001224.
8. Ghaemi H, Whitson SL. Building towers, cheating workers: exploitation of migrant construction workers in the United Arab Emirates. Human Rights Watch (HRW). 2006;18(8)(E). Available at https://www.hrw.org/sites/default/files/reports/uae1106webwcover.pdf. Accessed 1 Aug 2016.
9. Andrees B. Forced labour and human trafficking: a handbook for labour inspectors. International Labour Organization (ILO). Geneva: ILO; 2008.
10. Owens C, Dank M, Breaux J, Banuelos I, Farrell A, Pfeffer R, et al. Understanding the organization, operation, and victimization process of labor trafficking in the United States. Urban Institute and Northeastern University; 2014.
11. Burnham L, Theodore N. Home economics: the invisible and unregulated world of domestic work. National Domestic Workers Alliance, Center for Urban Economic Development, and University of Illinois at Chicago DataCenter. New York: National Domestic Workers Alliance; 2012.
12. Gupta J, Reed E, Kershaw T, Blankenship KM. History of sex trafficking, recent experiences of violence, and HIV vulnerability among female sex workers in coastal Andhra Pradesh, India. Int J Gynaecol Obstet. 2011;114(2):101–5.
13. Macias-Konstantopoulos W, Palmer Castor J, Cafferty E, Ahn R, Burke TF. Sex trafficking of women and girls in Rio de Janeiro (p. 140–63). In: Sex trafficking of women and girls in eight metropolitan areas around the world: case studies viewed through a public health lens. Division of Global Health and Human Rights, Department of Emergency Medicine, Massachusetts General Hospital. Boston: Massachusetts General Hospital; 2010. Available at http://www.massgeneral.org/emergencymedicineglobalhealth/assets/IES.pdf. Accessed 1 Aug 2016.
14. Macias-Konstantopoulos W, Palmer Castor J, Ahn R, Burke TF. Sex trafficking of women and girls in Salvador (p. 164–85). In: Sex trafficking of women and girls in eight metropolitan areas around the world: case studies viewed through a public health lens. Division of Global Health and Human Rights, Department of Emergency Medicine, Massachusetts General Hospital. Boston: Massachusetts General Hospital; 2010. Available at http://www.massgeneral.org/emergencymedicineglobalhealth/initiatives/Human-Trafficking-Initiative.aspx. Accessed 1 Aug 2016.
15. Leclerc-Madlala S. On the virgin cleansing myth: gendered bodies, AIDS and ethnomedicine. Afr J AIDS Res. 2002;1(2):87–95.
16. Kloer A. Sex trafficking and HIV/AIDS: a deadly junction for women and girls. Hum Rights Magazine. 2010;37(2).
17. Willis BM, Levy BS. Child prostitution: global health burden, research needs, and interventions. Lancet. 2002;359(9315):1417–22.

18. Beyrer C, Stachowiak J. Health consequences of trafficking of women and girls in Southeast Asia. Brown J World Aff. 2003;10(1):105–17.
19. Williams TP, Ahn R, Cafferty E, Alpert EJ, Burke TF. Sex trafficking of women and girls in Kolkata (p. 117–39). In: Sex trafficking of women and girls in eight metropolitan areas around the world: case studies viewed through a public health lens. Division of Global Health and Human Rights, Department of Emergency Medicine, Massachusetts General Hospital. Boston: Massachusetts General Hospital; 2010. Available at http://www.massgeneral.org/emergency-medicineglobalhealth/assets/IES.pdf. Accessed 1 Aug 2016.
20. Zimmerman C. Trafficking in women: the health of women in post-trafficking services in Europe who were trafficked into prostitution or sexually abused as domestic labourers. London School of Hygiene and Tropical Medicine, 2007. Available at http://researchonline.lshtm.ac.uk/1343272/1/498767.pdf. Accessed 1 Aug 2016.
21. Macias Konstantopoulos W, Ahn R, Alpert EJ, Cafferty E, McGahan A, Williams TP, et al. An international comparative public health analysis of sex trafficking of women and girls in eight cities: achieving a more effective health sector response. J Urban Health. 2013;90(6): 1194–204.
22. Zimmerman C, Oram S, Borland R, Watts C. Meeting the health needs of trafficked persons. BMJ. 2009;339:b3326.
23. Alpert EJ, Ahn R, Albright E, Purcell G, Burke TF, Macias-Konstantopoulos WL. Human trafficking: guidebook on identification, assessment, and response in the health care setting. MGH Human Trafficking Initiative, Division of Global Health and Human Rights, Department of Emergency Medicine, Massachusetts General Hospital, Boston, MA and Committee on Violence Intervention and Prevention, Massachusetts Medical Society, Waltham. September 2014.
24. International Organization for Migration, United National Global Initiative to Fight Human Trafficking, and London School of Hygiene and Tropical Medicine. Caring for trafficked persons: guidance for health providers. Geneva: International Organization for Migration; 2009.
25. Greenbaum J, Crawford-Jakubiak JE. Committee on Child Abuse and Neglect. Child sex trafficking and commercial sexual exploitation: health care needs of victims. Pediatrics. 2015;135(3):566–74.
26. Gragg F, Petta I, Bernstein H, Eisen K, Quinn L. New York prevalence study of commercially sexually exploited children: final report. Rockville: Westat; 2007. Available at http://www.ocfs.state.ny.us/main/reports/CSEC-2007.pdf. Accessed 1 Aug 2016.
27. Gibbs D, Hardison Walters JL, Lutnick A, Miller S, Kluckman M. Evaluation of services for domestic minor victims of human trafficking: final report. Research Triangle Park: RTI International; 2014. Available at https://www.ncjrs.gov/pdffiles1/nij/grants/248578.pdf. Accessed 1 Aug 2016.
28. Institute of Medicine (IOM) and National Research Council (NRC). Confronting commercial sexual exploitation and sex trafficking on minors in the United States. Washington: IOM-NRC; 2013.
29. Macias-Konstantopoulos W, Munroe D, Purcell G, Tester K, Burke TF, Ahn R. The commercial sexual exploitation and sex trafficking of minors in the Boston metropolitan area: experiences and challenges faced by front-line providers and other stakeholders. J Appl Res Child. 2015;6(1):4. Available at http://digitalcommons.library.tmc.edu/childrenatrisk/vol6/iss1/4. Accessed 1 Aug 2016.
30. Macias-Konstantopoulos W, Bar-Halpern M. Commercially sexually exploited and trafficked minors: our hidden and forgotten children. In: Parekh R, Childs EW, editors. Stigma and Prejudice: touchstones in understanding diversity in healthcare. Current clinical psychiatry. Geneva: Springer; 2016.
31. Cochran BN, Stewart AJ, Ginzler JA, Cauce AM. Challenges faced by homeless sexual minorities: comparison of gay, lesbian, bisexual, and transgender homeless adolescents with their heterosexual counterparts. Am J Public Health. 2002;92(5):773–7.
32. Whitbeck L, Xiaojin C, Tyler K, Johnson K. Mental disorder, subsistence strategies, and victimization among gay, lesbian, and bisexual homeless and runaway adolescents. J Sex Res. 2004;41(4):329–42.

33. U.S. Department of Health and Human Services, Administration for Children, Youth and Families (ACYF). Guidance to states and services on addressing human trafficking of children and youth in the United States. Washington: Administration for Children and Families; 2013. Available at https://www.acf.hhs.gov/sites/default/files/cb/acyf_human_trafficking_guidance. pdf. Accessed 1 Aug 2016.

34. Smith L, Vardaman S, Snow M. The national report on domestic minor sex trafficking. Arlington: Shared Hope International; 2009. Available at http://sharedhope.org/wp-content/uploads/2012/09/SHI_National_Report_on_DMST_2009.pdf. Accessed 1 Aug 2016.

35. Varma S, Gillespie S, McCracken C, Greenbaum VJ. Characteristics of child commercial sexual exploitation and sex trafficking victims presenting for medical care in the United States. Child Abuse Negl. 2015;44:98–105.

36. Kiss L, Yun K, Pocock N, Zimmerman C. Exploitation, violence, and suicide risk among child and adolescent survivors of human trafficking in the Greater Mekong Subregion. JAMA Pediatr. 2015;169(9), e152278.

37. Lederer LJ, Wetzel CA. The health consequences of sex trafficking and their implications for identifying victims in healthcare facilities. Ann Health Law. 2014;23(1):61–91.

38. Zimmerman C, Hossain M, Yun K, Gajdadziev V, Guzub N, Tchomarova M, et al. The health of trafficked women: a survey of women entering posttrafficking services in Europe. Am J Public Health. 2008;98(1):55–9.

39. Gupta J, Raj A, Decker MR, Reed E, Silverman JG. HIV vulnerabilities of sex-trafficked Indian women and girls. Int J Gynaecol Obstet. 2009;107(1):30–4.

40. Huda S. Sex trafficking in South Asia. Int J Gynaecol Obstet. 2006;94(3):374–81.

41. Sen S, Nair PM. A report on trafficking in women and children in India, 2002–2003. Institute of Social Science, National Human Rights Commission, UNIFEM. New Delhi: National Human Rights Commission; 2003. Available at http://nhrc.nic.in/Documents/Reporton Trafficking.pdf. Accessed 1 Aug 2016.

42. Silverman JG, Decker MR, Gupta J, Maheshwari A, Willis BM, Raj A. HIV prevalence and predictors of infection in sex-trafficked Nepalese girls and women. JAMA. 2007;298(5): 536–42.

43. Wirth KE, Tchetgen Tchetgen EJ, Silverman JG, Murray MB. How does sex trafficking increase the risk of HIV infection? An observational study from Southern India. Am J Epidemiol. 2013;177(3):232–41.

44. Silverman JG, Decker MR, Gupta J, Maheshwari A, Pate V, Raj A. HIV prevalence and predictors among rescued sex-trafficked women and girls in Mumbai, India. J Acquir Immune Defic Syndr. 2006;43(5):588–93.

45. Goldenberg SM, Chettiar J, Simo A, Silverman JG, Strathdee SA, Montaner JS, et al. Early sex work initiation independently elevates odds of HIV infection and police arrest among adult sex workers in a Canadian setting. J Acquir Immune Defic Syndr. 2014;65(1):122–8.

46. Sarkar K, Bal B, Mukherjee R, Saha MK, Chakraborty S, Niyogi SK, et al. Young age is a risk factor for HIV among female sex workers—an experience from India. J Infect. 2006;53(4): 255–9.

47. Silverman JG, Decker MR, Gupta J, Dharmadhikari A, Seage 3rd GR, Raj A. Syphilis and Hepatitis B co-infection among HIV-Infected, sex-trafficked women and girls, Nepal. Emerg Infect Dis. 2008;14(6):932–4.

48. Dharmadhikari A, Gupta J, Decker MR, Raj A, Silverman JG. Tuberculosis and HIV: a global menace exacerbated via sex trafficking. Int J Infect Dis. 2009;13(5):543–6.

49. Raymond JG, Hughes DM, Gomez CJ. Sex trafficking of women in the United States: International and Domestic Trends. Coalition Against Trafficking in Women International (CATW). New York: CATW; 2001.

50. Decker MR, McCauley HL, Phuengsamran D, Surang J, Silverman JG. Sex trafficking, sexual risk, sexually transmitted infection and reproductive health among female sex workers in Thailand. J Epidemiol Community Health. 2011;65(4):334–9.

51. Willis B, Vines D, Bibar S, Ramirez Suchard M. The health of children whose mothers are trafficked or in sex work in the U.S.: an exploratory study. Vulnerable Child Youth Stud. 2016;11(2):127135.

52. Muftić LR, Finn MA. Health outcomes among women trafficked for sex in the United States: a closer look. J Interpers Violence. 2013;28(9):1859–85.
53. Zimmerman C, Schenker MB. Human trafficking for forced labour and occupational health. Occup Environ Med. 2014;71(12):807–8.
54. Buller AM, Vaca V, Stoklosa H, Borland R, Zimmerman C. Labour exploitation, trafficking and migrant health: multi-country findings on the health risks and consequences of migrant and trafficked workers. International Organization for Migration and London School of Hygiene and & Tropical Medicine; 2015.
55. Turner-Moss E, Zimmerman C, Howard LM, Oram S. Labour exploitation and health: a case series of men and women seeking post-trafficking services. J Immigr Minor Health. 2014;16(3):473–80.
56. Oram S, Ostrovschi NV, Gorceag VI, Hotineanu MA, Gorceag L, Trigub C, et al. Physical health symptoms reported by trafficked women receiving post-trafficking support in Moldova: prevalence, severity and associated factors. BMC Womens Health. 2012;12:20.
57. Krieger J, Higgins DL. Housing and health: time again for public health action. Am J Public Health. 2002;92(5):758–68.
58. Hribar C, Schultz M. Understanding concentrated animal feeding operations and their impact on communities. Bowling Green: National Association of Local Boards of Health; 2010.
59. Cameron L, Lalich N, Bauer S, Booker V, Bogue HO, Samuels S, Occupational health survey of farm workers by camp health aides. J Agric Saf Health. 2006;12(2):139–53.
60. Committee on Fishing Vessel Safety, National Research Council. Fishing vessel safety: blueprint for a national program. Washington: National Academy Press; 1991.
61. Matheson C, Morrison S, Murphy E, Lawrie T, Ritchie L, Bond C. The health of fisherman in the catching sector of the fishing industry: a gap analysis. Occup Med. 2001;51:305–11.
62. ILO, Asian Research Center for Migration, Institute of Asian Studies, Chulalongkorn University. Employment practices and working conditions in Thailand's fishing sector. Bangkok: International Labour Organization; 2013.
63. Budiani-Saberi DA, Delmonico FL. Organ trafficking and transplant tourism: a commentary on the global realities. Am J Transplant. 2008;8(5):925–9.
64. Budiani-Saberi D, Columb S. A human rights approach to human trafficking for organ removal. Med Health Care Philos. 2013;16(4):897–914.
65. Tong A, Chapman JR, Wong G, Cross NB, Batabyal P, Craig JC. The experiences of commercial kidney donors: thematic synthesis of qualitative research. Transpl Int. 2012;25(11):1138–49.
66. Goyal M, Mehta RL, Schneiderman MD, Sehgal AR. Economic and health consequences of selling a kidney in India. JAMA. 2002;288(13):1589–93.
67. Budiani-Saberi DA, Raja KR, Findley KC, Kerketta P, Anand V. Human trafficking for organ removal in India: a victim-centered, evidence-based report. Transplantation. 2014;94(4):380–4.
68. Naqvi SA, Rizvi SA, Zafar MN, Ahmed E, Ali B, Mehmood K, et al. Health status and renal function evaluation of kidney vendors: a reports from Pakistan. Am J Transplant. 2008;8(7):1444–50.
69. Zargooshi J. Quality of life of Iranian kidney "Donors". J Urol. 2001;166(5):1790–9.
70. Patel RB, Ahn R, Burke TF. Human trafficking in the emergency department. West J Emerg Med. 2010;11(5):402–4.
71. Gibbons P, Stoklosa H. Identification and treatment of human trafficking victims in the emergency department: a case report. J Emerg Med. 2016;50(5):715–9.
72. Chisolm-Straker M, Baldwin S, Gaigbe-Togbe B, Ndukwe N, Johnson P, Richardson LD. Health care and human trafficking: we are seeing the unseen. J Health Care Poor Underserved. 2016;27(3):1220–33.
73. Greenbaum VJ. Commercial sexual exploitation and sex trafficking of children in the United States. Curr Probl Pediatr Adolesc Health Care. 2014;44(9):245–69.
74. Macias-Konstantopoulos W. Human trafficking: The role of medicine in interrupting the cycle of abuse and violence. Ann Intern Med. 2016;165(8):582–88.

75. Titchen KE, Loo D, Berdan E, Rysavy MB, Ng JJ, Sharif I. Domestic sex trafficking of minors: medical student and physician awareness. J Pediatr Adolesc Gynecol. 2015;20:pii: S1083-3188(15)00210-7.
76. Stoklosa H, Grace A, Littenberg N. Medical education on human trafficking. AMA J Ethics. 2015;17(10):914–21.
77. Yankovich T. Human trafficking education and assessment for medical students. 143rd APHA Annual Meeting and Exposition (October 31–November 4, 2015). APHA 2015.
78. Tracy EE, Konstantopoulos WM. Human trafficking: a call for heightened awareness and advocacy by obstetrician-gynecologists. Obstet Gynecol. 2011;119(5):1045–7.
79. Grace AM, Ahn R, Macias Konstantopoulos W. Integrating curricula on human trafficking into medical education and residency training. JAMA Pediatr. 2014;168(9):793–4.
80. Ahn R, Alpert EJ, Purcell G, Konstantopoulos WM, McGahan A, Cafferty E, et al. Human trafficking: review of educational resources for health professionals. Am J Prev Med. 2013; 44(3):283–9.
81. Macias-Konstantopoulos WL. MGH Freedom Clinic: Clinical Operating Guidelines and Procedures. 2015.
82. Shandro J, Chisolm-Straker M, Duber HC, Findlay SL, Munoz J, Schmitz G, et al. Human trafficking: a guide to identification and approach for the emergency physician. Ann Emerg Med. 2016;pii: S0196-0644(16)30054-3.
83. Chisolm-Straker M, Richardson LD, Cossio T. Combating slavery in the 21st century: the role of the emergency medicine. J Health Care Poor Underserved. 2012;23(3):980–7.
84. Viergever RF, West H, Borland R, Zimmerman C. Health care providers and human trafficking: what do they know, what do they need to know? Findings from the Middle East, the Caribbean and Central America. Front Public Health. 2015;3(6).
85. Morrow K. Presumptive treatment of sexually transmitted infections and syndromic management of genitourinary infections in trafficked women and girls: short-term stay shelter protocol. Doctors of the World—USA. Kosovo, 2005.

Chapter 12
Trauma-Informed Treatment of Substance Use Disorders in Trafficking Survivors

Elizabeth K. Hopper

12.1 Introduction

12.1.1 Substance Use Problems in Trafficking Survivors

Human trafficking reports indicate that substance use issues are critical health concerns for many trafficking survivors [1–4]. However, there is a lack of research regarding the extent of substance use disorders (SUDs) in trafficking survivors. Most studies investigating health and/or mental health in trafficking survivors do not include an investigation of substance use. Investigations that have included questions about substance use show great variability in the self-reporting of participants, from minimal endorsement of alcohol and drug use [5] to acknowledgement of substance abuse issues in the majority of respondents [6].

Research linking trafficking and substance use has focused almost exclusively on sex trafficking. In a 2014 study of domestic girls and women who were sex trafficked, Lederer and Wetzel found that 84.3 % used alcohol, drugs, or both during their trafficking experience. The most common substances were alcohol, marijuana, and cocaine, each used by more than 50 % of the sample. Opioid use was also common, with 22.3 % of respondents acknowledging heroin use. More than a quarter of these girls and women (27.9 %) reported that they were forced to use substances during their trafficking experience [6]. Research comparing sex trafficked minors to sexually abused children identified substance use as a major difference between the two groups: Sex trafficked youth had a greater likelihood of having a history of drug use (69.6 % vs. 19.2 %) and more specifically, a history of using multiple substances (50 % vs. 5.8 %) [7].

The author would like to express sincere appreciation to Jeff Nicklas for his administrative assistance in the production of this chapter.

E.K. Hopper (✉)
The Trauma Center at JRI, 1269 Beacon St, Brookline, MA 02446, USA
e-mail: ehopper@jri.org

© Springer International Publishing AG 2017
M. Chisolm-Straker, H. Stoklosa (eds.), *Human Trafficking Is a Public Health Issue*, DOI 10.1007/978-3-319-47824-1_12

The extent of substance use issues in survivors of labor trafficking is unknown, due to the extremely limited research base. A recent historical cohort study included both sex and labor trafficked individuals who were in contact with mental health care systems in London and found that 34 % of trafficked adults acknowledged having a history of substance use problems; however, differences in the levels of substance use between sex trafficking and labor trafficking survivors were not provided [8]. A small study focusing on labor trafficking survivors resulted in low levels of self-reported substance use: Only two labor trafficking survivors (6 %) reported drug use (both cannabis) and only three (10 %) reported heavy alcohol use (drinking most days or everyday) [5]. However, it is likely that survivors of labor trafficking, who are often foreign nationals, are particularly reluctant to disclose substance use concerns. The criminalization of illicit drug use, the stigma of SUDs, and the isolation experienced by many labor trafficking survivors may discourage them from acknowledging or seeking help for substance use problems, for fear that their immigration status will be negatively impacted.

Because of the lack of available literature specifically on substance use and human trafficking, research on substance use in related populations may be informative, including individuals engaging in commercial sex, migrant worker populations, and people involved in drug trafficking culture. Research on these related groups may include trafficking survivors without identifying respondents as such. Finally, even without this overlay, there are commonalities between the experiences of these groups and people who have been exploited through various forms of human trafficking.

There is overlap between individuals involved in commercial sex and those who have been sex trafficked, and these blurry boundaries are reflected in the literature. Research on sexual exploitation clearly points to substance use as a primary concern for respondents. For instance, substance use concerns were prevalent in a small sample of women involved in commercial sex in Mexico, 60 % of whom described themselves as being forced or coerced into commercial sex, and all of whom were initially commercially sexually exploited as minors: 57 % of these women reported current alcohol use, including 25 % who endorsed heavy alcohol use, while 33 % of them reported recent use of "hard drugs"[1] such as crystal meth, heroin, crack, and so on [9]. A study that investigated the health consequences of sexual exploitation, including commercial sex and sex trafficking, found that, across nine countries, 52 % of respondents endorsed alcohol use, while 48 % acknowledged drug use [10].

Research on migrant labor populations may have some relevance to labor trafficking. Scholars have documented substance use issues in migrant labor populations; members of this group often live under chronic stress, in relatively isolated, often overcrowded housing conditions, and without familial- and community-based deterrents to heavy drinking and drug use [11, 12]. These risk factors for substance use are also common to many survivors of labor trafficking.

Finally, research on the impacts of narcotic-trafficking culture may have implications for both labor and sex trafficking. There is a clearly established link between drug trafficking and human trafficking, with intersections in the organized criminal

---

[1] "Hard" drugs are narcotics that are considered relatively strong and likely to cause addiction.

networks that profit by selling illicit drugs and people [13]. Numerous cases have been prosecuted that have involved charges related to both drug trafficking and human trafficking [14–16]. Drug cartel activities are contributing to the growing drug problems amongst transnational migrants [17]; more information is needed to understand potential implications for labor trafficking survivors. The director of one rehabilitation center in Tijuana, Mexico, estimated that about a tenth of the adolescents treated at the center, in addition to having SUDs, also were involved in the drug trade; many adolescents, some of whom may be trafficked, are made to sell drugs by drug cartels [18]. Similarly, adolescents and adults are labor trafficked as "mules," being forced to transport illicit substances into the USA [18, 19].

12.2 Discussion

12.2.1 The Relationship Between Substance Use and Trafficking

There is a complicated inter-relationship between substance use and trafficking. Pre-trafficking substance use problems or substance use exposure via one's caregivers can increase vulnerability to trafficking. Substances are often used as a form of coercion by traffickers, to induce compliance and to maintain control over trafficked people. Drugs[2] are sometimes used by people during trafficking to tolerate extensive trauma exposure. Finally, trafficking survivors may continue to struggle with substance use after getting out of the trafficking situation, with substances often serving as a tool for managing posttraumatic stress responses.

12.2.1.1 Substance Use as a Vulnerability Factor for Trafficking

Substance use problems may interfere with caregivers' ability to provide adequate physical and emotional care or to effectively maintain a safe environment for their children. This type of early developmental trauma is associated with an increased risk of re-victimization [20], including trafficking [21]. Karen*,[3] a woman in her 50s, struggled with addiction and multiple victimizations throughout her life, including being trafficked on several occasions by different perpetrators. Karen was exposed to substance use and drug trafficking beginning in early childhood: Her mother used heroin and sold drugs from their home in Karen's early life. Karen's mother's addiction interfered with her ability to parent effectively, leaving Karen

---

[2] Including illicit substances, alcohol and prescription drugs that are misused.

[3] To better elucidate this complex issue, case examples from the author's professional experience with trafficking survivors are shared. All the names, and any other identifying information, have been modified, to protect the identity of these individuals. These cases are denoted by asterisks throughout this chapter.

feeling emotionally abandoned and alone. Early exposure to caregivers' substance use problems can initiate a repetitive cycle that plays out in the child's adult life, in which the person develops substance use problems themselves or forms relationships with people who struggle with addiction. Karen's first trafficker was a man who sold drugs to her mother; he manipulated Karen's need for connection, providing her with attention, as well as with drugs. He used escalating violence and Karen's increasing reliance on drugs to coerce her into sex trafficking during her adolescence. After finally escaping from this violent man, Karen was re-trafficked by two other men, both of whom appeared to be intimate partners at first but used her addiction as a means of coercing her into commercial sex and drug trafficking, confiscating the money that she earned.

People with pre-existing substance use problems may be more vulnerable to manipulation and abuse by traffickers. Being under the influence of a substance can compromise a person's judgment, increasing the likelihood that they will ignore or fail to recognize signs of potential danger. Some may be drawn into a trafficking situation in order to financially support a substance use problem. Traffickers may target people who are vulnerable due to substance use problems and related issues like homelessness. For example, Mohammed Sharif Alaboudi, a trafficker in South Dakota, opened his home to girls and young women, many of whom were struggling with SUDs and homelessness. After offering them drugs and a place to stay, he used violence and control over their access to drugs to coerce them into performing commercial sex acts [22].

12.2.1.2 Use of Substances as a Form of Coercion

Although some trafficking survivors had pre-existing substance use issues, research suggests that the more common source of post-trafficking SUDs is the trafficking situation itself [7]. Traffickers use illicit substances as a means of coercion in the recruitment and initiation phases of trafficking [23]. For instance, while she was staying in a homeless shelter, Chantelle* was recruited by a neighbor who got to know her by offering her and her friends alcohol as they walked by his house every day. Gina* developed a relationship with a man online who introduced her to the use of illicit substances and then coerced her into sex trafficking. She recalled, "At first, we were just partying a lot. I was helping him sell, and we were rolling in dough. Then I started to need it." Some survivors report being drugged by their traffickers to facilitate their kidnapping and/or transit [2].

Traffickers may force or coerce drug or alcohol use in trafficked persons, to decrease their self-protective defenses and induce compliance. This may include moderate alcohol use to decrease inhibitions, severe alcohol use to block resistance or awareness of abuses, misuse of prescription drugs, and/or the use of traditional or unknown medications [2]. A study in India found that women who were sex trafficked were more likely to consume alcohol at the first episode of commercial sex, as well as in the subsequent months, than women who reported that they were not forced to engage in the commercial sex [24]. Traffickers may use substances to coerce victims into working longer hours, serving more clients, engaging in degrading or dangerous acts, and giving more money to the trafficker [7, 23]. As Lexi*, a survivor of sex trafficking, recalled, "He would hold it over my head... no coke unless I brought home my quota. I was desperate."

Some traffickers are opportunistic, exploiting others to meet their own immediate addiction needs. In a recent case of family controlled sex trafficking, a young woman described being traded by her father for drugs. She said, "My dad started to not be able to afford the stuff he was addicted to, so he started using me to pay for his drugs. [A] certain amount of time equaled certain amounts of whatever it was he was feeling that week. He was just a trash can addict and would use whatever he could get his hands on." She reported that he also provided her with drugs, leading her to develop an addiction herself [25].

In other cases, the coercive use of substances by traffickers is more systematic. For instance, in a high-profile trafficking case, Andrew Fields used prescription drugs, including oxycodone, Dilaudid, and morphine, to coerce a number of girls and young women into sex trafficking [26]. The survivors testified that Fields provided them with pills, escalating their use until they developed physiological dependence on the drugs. They indicated that he used their intense fear of withdrawal to coerce them to perform commercial sexual acts in exchange for another dose of the drugs. One young woman testified that Fields would watch her as she suffered through physical and psychological withdrawal, coercing her to serve another commercial sex buyer, saying, "I'll give you one pill. I'm not going to give you another until you get up and go to work. And you know you need another" [26]. In another similar case out of Wisconsin, Jason Guidry created and then manipulated heroin addictions in several women, manipulating their supply of heroin to manipulate them into performing commercial sex acts [27].

Although the majority of cases involving drugs as coercive factors have been sex trafficking cases, there have also been documented cases of labor trafficking in which the traffickers utilized substances as part of their coercive strategy to maintain control over the trafficked persons. For instance, in several cases in the southeastern USA, labor traffickers targeted homeless US citizens by providing shelter, food, cigarettes, cocaine, and alcohol on credit, leaving the otherwise homeless individuals "perpetually indebted" to their traffickers [28–30].

12.2.1.3 Use of Substance to Cope with Trafficking-Related Trauma

Some trafficked persons find themselves using substances during the course of trafficking to cope with the extensive trauma exposure. Janet* was sex trafficked by a man posing as a romantic partner and was coerced into degrading sexual acts. She reflected, "I drank to stay with my boyfriend, so I wouldn't think about the things he was making me do." Opioids in particular can block both physical and emotional pain [31, 32]. Daniella*, a sex trafficking survivor who was repeatedly physically assaulted, recalled, "I started using more and more heroin, to the point where I wouldn't even feel it when he'd beat me." With involvement of physicians who are well-versed in human trafficking, one emergency department in an urban setting is identifying trafficking survivors on a weekly basis and has identified opioid addiction in more than half of the trafficking survivors served [33].

12.2.1.4 Post-trafficking Substance Use

When some survivors finally exit their trafficking situation, substance use that began during the trafficking may persist. Survivors might continue using substances as a coping mechanism to manage trauma-related symptoms [1, 2, 7, 34]. Darlene*, an adult survivor of poly victimization including repeated trafficking, reflected on her use of substances to manage intrusive PTSD symptoms, noting, "Using drugs helped keep the memories away." Angelo*, a survivor of labor trafficking, used marijuana to control his insomnia; he said, "I need to smoke pot every night to fall asleep." Jia* perceived her substance use as life-saving, saying, "The choice was either to keep drinking or to kill myself."

Norma*, a transgender woman from Mexico, learned very early in her life that it was not safe to be vulnerable. As a result of her effeminate behaviors while living as a male child, she was rejected and abused by her family and harassed, bullied, and assaulted by peers and adults in her community. She ran away from home and lived on the streets of Mexico City as an adolescent, engaging in commercial sex to support her heroin addiction. After coming to the USA, she was repeatedly trafficked, and was in and out of jail as a result of drug- and prostitution-related charges. When she finally was able to seek help, she had been using drugs for over 10 years to avoid emotions and traumatic memories.

Labor trafficking survivors may also rely on substances to avoid trauma-related memories. Jose*, a 17-year-old boy, was targeted by a narcotic-trafficking ring that essentially controlled his town in El Salvador; he was forced to use drugs, sell drugs, and to witness and commit violent acts to prove his loyalty to the gang. The gang threatened to hurt him and kill his family members if he refused to comply. He eventually escaped when he was apprehended by US Border Patrol during an attempt to transport drugs across the border into the USA. After escaping his traffickers, Jose continued to struggle with addiction to alcohol and drugs, relying on these substances to avoid memories of the violence he had both witnessed and perpetrated. Substance use does not necessarily originate within the trafficking situation. Jorge*, a 63-year-old migrant laborer, was labor trafficked in an agricultural setting, where he was forced to pick tomatoes without pay. After he got out of the trafficking situation, he sought assistance for multiple medical conditions, including chronic back pain and Type II diabetes. However, he suffered from depression and struggled with his doctor's recommendations regarding diet, exercise, and medication. As a result, he increasingly relied on alcohol to manage his pain, depression, and sense of isolation.

12.2.2 Behavioral and Health Implications of SUDs in Trafficking Survivors

Substance use has a range of negative behavioral and health implications for trafficking survivors. In their conceptual model used to explore the health impacts of human trafficking, Zimmerman and colleagues (2011) described some of the potential health consequences of forced and coerced substance use during trafficking [23]. Physiological dependence on drugs is a health concern that often leads to increased use over time due to tolerance. Overdoses are another common concern with SUDs: A study of domestic women who were sex trafficked found that 26 % had overdosed at some point in the past [6]. Disordered substance use can increase high-risk activities, including involvement in dangerous criminal activities [23]: Trafficking survivors who have SUDs may also be at increased risk of arrests or convictions related to illegal substances, creating further stigma against survivors and preventing their reintegration into society [35, 36]. High-risk behaviors can also include unprotected and high-risk sexual activity [37], which is linked to health consequences such as sexually transmitted infections (STIs) [6]. More than a quarter of the girls and women in Lederer and Wetzel's 2015 study reported the use of injected drugs [6], which can lead to needle-introduced infections including HIV and hepatitis B and C [38] and associated brain or liver damage [23]. While research is not available on the extent of cigarette and marijuana use amongst trafficking survivors, cigarette smoking is a common correlate of substance use [23] and is the primary cause of lung cancer [39], while marijuana poses health risks to the lungs [40] and is associated with cognitive and neurological effects [41]. Problems with periodontal health [42], sleep problems [6, 43], and nutritional deprivation [44] are also associated with SUDs. Disordered substance use may interfere with preventative or proactive health care, resulting in the unnecessary escalation of treatable health and chronic medical conditions and in increased health care costs related to treatment in emergency care settings [45, 46]. Substance use can also pose safety concerns, increase the risk of re-victimization, and create barriers to services for trafficking survivors.

12.2.3 The Complex Needs of Trafficking Survivors with Trauma and SUDs

A government report suggested that substance use treatment may be under-utilized by trafficking survivors as a result of shame about their trafficking experiences, fear of discrimination based on a trafficking history, and shame about substance use itself [47]. Even when trafficking survivors acknowledge problems with substance use and desire treatment, appropriate substance use treatment may not be available or may not meet the unique needs of trafficking survivors. Faced with these barriers, survivors may lose motivation for trying to change or may lose contact with potential sources of assistance [48].

Trafficking survivors who struggle with comorbid drug use and trauma-related sequelae are likely to have a more complicated clinical picture and to have more difficulty accessing or making use of standard available services for trafficking survivors. A review study found that women with comorbid substance use and PTSD have more psychological symptoms, interpersonal problems, psychiatric diagnoses, medical problems, and inpatient admissions than women with PTSD or substance use alone; they also have other significant life problems, such as homelessness, HIV, a history of domestic violence, and loss of custody of children. Furthermore, they were found to have lower levels of functioning in general, and decreased motivation for treatment and compliance with aftercare [49].

12.2.4   The Need for Integrated Treatment for SUDs and Trauma

Despite the well-established link between trauma and SUDs [50–55] and the fact that trauma-related triggers can lead to relapse, traditional SUD treatment often does not address trauma-related issues early in recovery. Historically, the mental health and SUD fields developed and functioned separately. Providers are often not trained in both fields, resulting in poorly integrated treatment for people with comorbid mental health and SUDs [56].

In a monograph on the treatment of women with SUDs around the world, the United Nations emphasized the importance of acknowledging the link between addiction and all forms of interpersonal violence (physical, sexual, and emotional) in women's lives [57]; this recommendation is applicable to survivors of all sexual and gender identities. Theorists and clinicians have recently acknowledged the need to treat comorbid trauma and SUDs concurrently [56, 58], suggesting that treatment for trafficked persons who struggle with SUDs should focus on both traumatic impacts and the consequences of drug use. If treatment focuses solely on the substance-related issues without addressing the underlying trauma, treatment is likely to be less effective and is more likely to result in relapse [56, 59].

12.2.5   Trauma-Informed Care for Trafficking Survivors with SUDs

Given the common experience of trauma for many individuals in need of intervention for substance use concerns, treatment for SUDs should, at a minimum, utilize a trauma-informed framework [56, 60]. A trauma-informed model for substance use

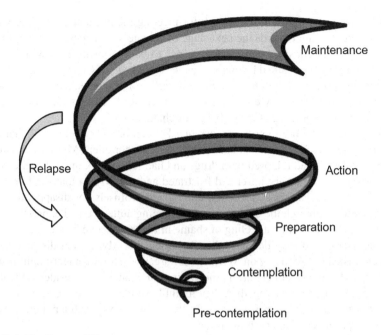

Fig. 12.1 The Stages of Change

issues considers the potential regulatory role of drugs for a user. Instead of a purely behavioral approach, which focuses solely on decreasing or eliminating use of the substance(s), trauma-informed treatment also highlights the importance of finding alternative means of meeting the regulatory need that is being fulfilled by the drug use. Recognizing an individual's place in the change process and respecting their right to ownership over their own path to recovery are important elements of providing trauma-informed care for SUDs. Given the control and esteem that is often stripped from trafficking survivors, trauma-informed care that is empowering is particularly important for trafficking survivors with SUDs.

12.2.5.1   Stages of Change

Prochaska and Norcross's Transtheoretical Model (TTM), also known as the *Stages of Change*, emphasizes that behavior change is a process that happens in stages [61] (see Fig. 12.1). The identified stages include:

1. *Pre-contemplation*: no acknowledgement of a problem and no intention of changing behavior
2. *Contemplation*: awareness that a problem exists, but no commitment to action
3. *Preparation*: considering taking action, thinking about steps towards change
4. *Action*: active modification of behavior
5. *Maintenance*: new patterns of behavior replace old ones, sustained change
6. *Relapse*: falling back into old patterns of behavior.

TTM offers an important framework for meeting the trafficking survivor where they are and working towards the next stage of change. For instance, if a trafficking survivor does not consider their substance use to be a problem, they will not successfully engage in sustained behavior change. The Stages of Change model emphasizes that relapse, or a return to previous behavior, is an expected part of the change process. Relapses are thus viewed as an opportunity for learning which can contribute to an upward spiraling effect of behavior change.

Professionals' failure to ground work in TTM can provoke feelings of shame in survivors with SUD: A case manager described how her client Myrna* reluctantly disclosed that she had relapsed with drugs and had fallen back into "the Life": The case manager became very upset and frustrated and told Myrna that she felt disappointed in her. Myrna was tearful and apologized profusely for disappointing her case manager. Although the case manager was being authentic and expressing concern, her response elicited a feeling of shame in Myrna. Shame can lead to feelings of hopelessness and may decrease the likelihood that Myrna will disclose future relapses. Instead of focusing on Myrna's "failure," her case manager might instead have helped her consider her current motivation for change and considered the lapse as a learning opportunity. Together, they might have identified some of the triggers that led to her impulse to use. They might then work to establish a plan for Myrna the next time she encounters these triggers.

12.2.5.2 Motivational Interviewing

Consistent with the Stages of Change model, *motivational interviewing* techniques are designed to help a person explore their own ambivalence about change [62]. Instead of providers encouraging change, this client-centered framework recognizes that the motivation for change must come from the individual. Although there has been no research examining the use of motivational interviewing with trafficking survivors, one study examined the use of motivational interviewing techniques with women involved in commercial sex who were also using illicit drugs such as cocaine and heroin. Four months later, participants showed reductions in the frequency (days) of drug use and commercial sex, with a corresponding increase in days of lawful employment [63].

12.2.6 Treatment Models that Offer Integrated Treatment for Trauma and SUDs

12.2.6.1 Seeking Safety

Lisa Najavitz's *Seeking Safety* model is a present-focused counseling model that addresses both trauma and drug use problems concurrently [58]. This model has the strongest empirical support base of any treatments for both trauma and substance use [64]. Safety is the overarching goal in this model, helping survivors to attain stability in their emotions, thinking, behavior, and relationships. Although it addresses trauma and addiction, it does not require that participants "process" their trauma, or recount detailed disturbing trauma memories. Instead, it focuses on cognitive, behavioral, and interpersonal aspects of survivors' current lives. In addition, case management is an integral part of the model, acknowledging the important role of a person's environmental context and resources in their recovery.

12.2.6.2   Other Models for Trauma and SUDs

Several other group treatment models have been utilized for trauma survivors with substance use disorders, including: *Trauma Recovery and Empowerment Model* (TREM), the *Addiction and Trauma Recovery Integration Model* (ATRIUM), *Trauma, Addiction, Mental Health, and Recovery* (TAMAR), and *Trauma Affect Regulation: Guide for Education and Therapy* (TARGET).

- Designed for survivors of physical and sexual violence, the TREM model integrates discussion of a variety of trauma-related topics with experiential exercises [65]. It has been implemented in criminal justice, mental health, and substance use settings.
- The ATRIUM model is a 12-session intervention that integrates peer support, psychosocial education, interpersonal skills training, meditation, creative expression, spirituality, and community action, with recovery groups as a starting point for healing from trauma and SUD [66]. It has been used in a variety of structured settings, including prison and jail diversion programs, programs for people with HIV/AIDS, and drop-in centers for trauma survivors.
- The TAMAR Education Project was developed as part of a major SAMSHSA study on female trauma survivors with co-occurring SUDs [67]. It is a structured, protocolized 10-week intervention that combines psycho-educational approaches with expressive therapies and has been implemented in a variety of residential systems, including detention centers and state psychiatric hospitals, as well as and in community settings. The TAMAR model provides psychoeducation[4] on trauma and its developmental effects on symptoms and current functioning; symptom appraisal and management; the impact of early chaotic relationships on health care needs; the development of coping skills; prevention of pregnancy and sexually transmitted infections; sexuality; and help in dealing with role loss and parenting issues.
- The TARGET model is a trauma-focused, present-centered model that was developed for concurrent treatment of posttraumatic stress disorder (PTSD) and substance use disorders. This model emphasizes emotional regulation and has been utilized in individual and group psychotherapy of co-occurring PTSD and addiction [68].

---

[4]Psychoeducation refers to the education offered to individuals and their families about mental health to help them understand their condition and to empower them in moving towards wellness.

Although there is not yet any research in this area, the effectiveness of these models with survivors of other forms of trauma suggests that they may have potential benefits for trafficking survivors with SUDs.

12.3 Conclusion

12.3.1 Tailored Treatment and Holistic Care

A variety of treatment modalities should be available to address SUDs in trafficking survivors. More intensive services include inpatient treatment and detoxification services, residential treatment, and medication (for instance, to enable a safe detoxification process and to support abstinence). Partial hospitalization programs and intensive outpatient programs can bridge between these intensive services and longer-term services. Ongoing supports may include individual counseling, group counseling, 12-step programs, case management, recovery support services, peer supports, and relapse prevention programs. Level of care is dependent on a person's individual needs, including the severity of their substance use disorder, potential health risks of removing the substance(s), and level of available environmental supports.

Treatment for SUDs should be one part of a holistic approach that includes emphasis on increasing environmental supports, promoting healthy lifestyles, developing skills for tolerating and managing emotions, improving family functioning, building competencies such as problem-solving and communication skills, developing a positive sense of self, and promoting empowerment.

12.4 Recommendations

Despite the extremely limited research base on SUDs in survivors of human trafficking, clinical experience and documented trafficking cases have highlighted substance use disorders as a health concern for many trafficking survivors. The relationship between trafficking and drug use is complex: early exposure to SUDs or pre-existing substance use problems may leave individuals at greater risk of being trafficked; perpetrators utilize substances to coerce people into trafficking; substance use may help trafficking survivors cope with extensive trauma exposure during trafficking; and substance use problems may continue after survivors leave the trafficking situation. Trafficking survivors with SUDs have complex needs and may struggle with extensive behavioral and health-related consequences of their addictions. Despite this, trafficking survivors often have difficulty accessing appropriate care. Trafficking survivors with SUDs are in need of trauma-informed care that concurrently addresses trauma and drug use concerns. A variety of models offer integrated treatment for trauma and substance use. However, more information is needed regarding the applicability of these models for trafficking survivors with SUDs. The following recommendations in research, policy, and practice will support the development of more effective service systems for trafficking survivors with SUDs.

12.4.1   Research

- More information is needed regarding the *extent of substance use problems* within various populations of trafficked people. In particular, research regarding substance use issues among survivors of labor trafficking is notably absent from the literature.
- Research may also help to clarify the *unique needs* of trafficking survivors with SUDs.
- Investigators should explore the efficacy of various *strategies designed to increase access to services* for trafficking survivors with SUDs.
- Research is needed regarding the *effectiveness of various treatment modalities* for different populations of trafficked people with varying types of substance use issues.
- Investigators should explore how *trauma-informed services* might improve service utilization and outcomes for trafficking survivors with SUDs.
- Researchers should examine effectiveness of available SUD treatments for trafficking survivors from different cultural backgrounds and investigate *culturally informed adaptations of SUD treatment* for these groups.

12.4.2   Policy

- More education is needed to *increase awareness of the intersection between drug use and trafficking*, and to increase competencies within cross-discipline professionals that allow them to work effectively with trafficking survivors with SUDs.
- Because of the potential role of SUDs in continuing the cycle of trafficking and re-victimization, *treatment for SUDs should be available as a standard element of comprehensive service models* for trafficking survivors.
- Specialized *trauma-informed substance use treatment services* should be developed for trafficking survivors at all levels of care, including detoxification or inpatient programs, residential treatment, partial hospitalization programs, intensive outpatient treatment, standard outpatient counseling, 12-step programs, and other peer supports.
- Treatment for drug use and mental health concerns in trafficking survivors should be integrated with comprehensive services in a *holistic model* that addresses psychosocial and environmental factors that may increase the risk of relapse and re-victimization.

- Forced or coerced substance use or manipulation of an SUD should be understood by law enforcement, legislators, funders, and service providers as a *method of coercion* utilized by traffickers. Additionally, these groups must recognize that some survivors use substances to cope with significant and complex trauma.
- Many shelter and housing placements have eligibility criteria that prevent service delivery to individuals with active substance use problems. When trafficking survivors relapse, they may be required to leave shelters or other housing, resulting in homelessness and increased vulnerability to re-victimization. The creation of more *service settings that are able to meet the unique needs of trafficking survivors with substance use issues* would address this gap in the safety net.
- Because people with SUDs disorders may be at increased risk for being trafficked, systems working with this population should provide *awareness-building* and *prevention* programming, particularly when there is a nexus of multiple vulnerabilities, including youth, poverty, homelessness, mental illness, and/or prior trauma exposure.
- Substance use treatment programs should standardize the *screening* of all clients for human trafficking experiences.
- Public education is needed to *decrease stigma* regarding treatment for SUDs.
- Policy efforts are needed to address *structural and systemic barriers to treatment for trafficking survivors with SUDs*, such as the difficulty accessing services without insurance. *Increased funding* is needed for specialized SUD treatment for trafficking survivors. Asset forfeiture from drug trafficking and human trafficking operations may be used to support these types of services.

12.4.3 Practice

- *Offer holistic care*: Treatment for SUDs should be one aspect of a comprehensive approach to wellness in trafficking survivors.
- *Increase access to services*: Logistical barriers, stigma, and cultural issues can prevent trafficking survivors from accessing treatment for drug use and mental health concerns. Therefore, programs serving trafficking survivors should implement practices that increase access to services and that improve engagement.

  – Providers can increase accessibility of services by helping survivors negotiate logistical barriers. For instance, providers may offer assistance with transportation, provide childcare during treatment, and/or house SUD treatment in settings that offer a range of services to trafficking survivors.
  – Providers should work to decrease the stigma of substance use for trafficking survivors by posting materials relevant to substance use, normalizing substance use concerns, and employing staff who are in recovery from SUDs.
  – Cultural viewpoints that prevent access to services (e.g., "I don't want anyone to know because drinking alcohol is shameful"; "I'm a man, and I can handle

it", "They will lock me up; I'm not crazy.") should be addressed individually. Cultural leaders may provide supports in navigating these types of barriers. Linguistically matched SUD treatment may also increase accessibility for trafficking survivors.

- *Increase environmental supports*: Many trafficking survivors who struggle with SUDs have physical and social environments that support ongoing substance use. As with any person who is attempting to address substance use issues, trafficking survivors will need to develop a support network that can aid them in their abstinence efforts. If survivors feel comfortable with 12-step programs, the sponsor model offers peer support that can be pivotal when survivors are struggling with urges to use. Other models involving group treatment can also offer essential peer support. Community engagement may also be pivotal in establishing healthy support networks.
- *Ground treatment in comprehensive assessment*: Assessment of trafficking survivors should include current drug use patterns and history of substance use. It should attempt to discriminate drug use from SUDs; and when necessary, referrals should be made to the appropriate level of trauma-informed substance use treatment.
- *Utilize Stages of Change Theory and motivational interviewing approaches*: Providers should assess survivors for their current stage of change. Motivational interviewing or motivational enhancement therapy might be used to help trafficking survivors with SUDs to build motivation and commit to specific plans to engage in treatment and seek recovery.
- *Normalize reactions*: Shame and alienation are common emotional responses to trafficking. Trafficked persons may blame themselves for their use of substances during their trafficking experience and for ongoing drug use problems. This shame is reinforced by the societal stigma of SUDs. Normalization of the use of substances as a coping strategy for trauma survivors can be an important step in addressing shame.
- *Offer psychoeducation*: Information can be a first step towards empowerment. Survivors should receive education about human trafficking as a form of interpersonal trauma, the potential impacts of trauma, and the role of substances as regulatory tools. Educating survivors about human trafficking can help them begin to appropriately place blame with their trafficker(s) instead of themselves. Psychoeducation about the potential traumatic impacts of human trafficking can normalize their responses, helping them to understand why they are experiencing certain emotional, somatic, cognitive, or behavioral reactions; it can also establish a framework for recovery. Information about alternative regulatory coping strategies can combat survivors' fears of giving up substances that they rely on to manage overwhelming emotions and memories. Harm reduction or controlled use models may be helpful for survivors when fears about abstinence prevent them from accessing help.
- *Build affect regulation skills:* Practitioners should help survivors build affect regulation skills. For many trauma survivors with SUDs, the substance serves as

a primary tool to regulate their emotions. Reduction or removal of this coping mechanism needs to be combined with the development of alternative coping tools. These skills include grounding tools, containment, mindfulness, self-soothing activities (such as self-massage or listening to calming music), anxiety management tools (such as breathing exercises), imagery, or other tools based on belief systems (e.g., prayer) or folk healing practices. If new coping tools are not developed, the risk of relapse is much higher. Trafficking survivors with SUDs may need support in recognizing that the development of new affect regulation tools is not a simple or linear process. Substances tend to be reliable, quick-acting, and to require less effort on the part of the user than other coping tools. Survivors are working to replace an immediate coping tool with something that is unfamiliar and generally less immediately effective, which requires patience and persistence. When survivors stop using substances, there is often an increase in emotional distress, and trauma-related thoughts and memories. There can also be physical and/or emotional distress associated with withdrawal from substances.

- *Identify triggers:* Providers should work with survivors to identify triggers for drug use or other maladaptive coping strategies. Early in treatment, trafficking survivors with SUDs may begin to identify common triggers that may lead to substance use. "HALT" is an acronym used by many substance use treatment programs to describe somatic or emotional states that are common triggers for relapse: feeling Hungry, Angry, Lonely, and/or Tired. Identifying one's own internal and external triggers is a precursor for minimizing and managing triggered responses.

- *Minimize triggers*: As survivors identify triggers that lead to urges to use, they can make plans to minimize exposure to these triggers. For instance, going to dance clubs had a strong association with drug use for one trafficking survivor with an SUD. She learned to advocate for her friends to spend time together in other ways, like going shopping and watching movies together. Other survivors may need to create new social networks that are not involved in substance use.

- *Develop a plan for coping with triggers*: Providers should help survivors develop coping plans for confronting triggers. Although survivors can try to minimize triggers, it is generally not possible to avoid all triggers. Trafficking survivors may benefit from establishing proactive plans when faced with triggers. For instance, one might write lists of coping strategies to use, supportive people to call, meetings to attend, inspirational messages to read, and so on.

- *Establish self-care plans*: Many trafficking survivors with SUDs would benefit from the development of an individualized self-care plan. Self-care plans include the healthy activities that survivors are involved in on a regular basis and the structure that they create in their lives. This can involve going to bed and waking up at regularly scheduled times, eating healthy foods, engaging in physical activity, being around friends, cultivating hobbies, engaging in relaxing activities such as taking a warm bath or getting a pedicure, and becoming involved in activities that provide a source of meaning. These regular activities provide the groundwork for a more balanced and grounded stance from which trafficking survivors are more able to respond to triggers and crises in an effective way.

- *Plan for relapse prevention*: Trafficking survivors with SUDs must develop plans for responding to relapses. As described above, relapse is an expected part of the change process. Survivors should work with their providers on plans for when they relapse, focusing on minimizing the length and intensity of the relapse, confronting shame, and reaching out for help. Concurrently, providers should focus on patience and persistence in working with trafficking survivors who are struggling with substance use issues and repeated relapses.

References

1. Clawson HJ, Dutch N, Solomon A, et al. Human trafficking into and within the United States: a review of the literature. Department of Health and Human Services, Office of the Assistant Secretary for Planning and Evaluation. 2009. http://aspe.hhs.gov/hsp/07/humantrafficking/litrev/. Accessed 23 May 2016.
2. Zimmerman C, Yun K, Shvab I, et al. The health risks and consequences of trafficking in women and adolescents: findings from a European study. London School of Hygiene and Tropical Medicine, London. 2003. http://www.lshtm.ac.uk/php/ghd/docs/traffickingfinal.pdf. Accessed 23 May 2016.
3. Williamson E, Dutch NM, Clawson HJ. Evidence-based mental health treatment for victims of human trafficking. U.S. Department of Health and Human Services. 2010. http://aspe.hhs.gov/hsp/07/humantrafficking/mentalhealth/index.pdf. Accessed 23 May 2016.
4. Task Force on Trafficking of Women and Girls. Report of the task force on trafficking of women and girls. Washington, DC: American Psychological Association; 2014. https://www.apa.org/pi/women/programs/trafficking/report.pdf. Accessed 23 May 2016.
5. Turner-Moss E, Zimmerman C, Howard LM, Oram S, et al. Labour exploitation and health: a case series of men and women seeking post-trafficking services. J Immigr Minor Health. 2014;16(3):473–80. doi:10.1007/s10903-013-9832-6.
6. Lederer L, Wetzel CA. The health consequences of sex trafficking and their implications for identifying victims in healthcare facilities. Ann Health Law. 2014;23:61–91.
7. Varma S, Gillespie S, McCracken C, Greenbaum VJ. Characteristics of child commercial sexual exploitation and sex trafficking victims presenting for medical care in the United States. Child Abuse Negl. 2015;44:98–105. doi:10.1016/j.chiabu.2015.04.004.
8. Oram S, Khondoker M, Abas M, Broadbent M, Howard LM. Characteristics of trafficked adults and children with severe mental illness: a historical cohort study. Lancet Psychiatry. 2015;2(12):1084–91.
9. Servin AE, Brouwer KC, Gordon L, Rocha-Jimenez T, Staines H, Strathdee SA, Silverman JG. Vulnerability factors and pathways leading to underage entry into sex work in two Mexican-US border cities. J Appl Res Child. 2015;6(1):3.
10. Farley M, Cotton A, Lynne J, et al. Prostitution and trafficking in nine countries. J Trauma Pract. 2008;2(3–4):33–74. doi:10.1300/J189v02n03_03.
11. Garcia V. Problem drinking among transnational Mexican migrants: exploring migrant status and situational factors. Open Anthropol J. 2008;67(1):12–24. doi:10.2174/1874912701104010003.
12. Garcia V, Gonzalez L. Participatory research challenges in drug abuse studies among transnational Mexican migrants. Open Anthropol J. 2011;4:3–11. doi:10/2174/1874912701104010003.
13. Grillo I. The Mexican drug cartels' other business: sex trafficking. 2013. http://world.time.com/2013/07/31/the-mexican-drug-cartels-other-business-sex-trafficking/. Accessed 23 May 2016.
14. Department of Justice, Office of Public Affairs. Maryland man sentenced on federal sex trafficking, drug and firearm charges. 2010. https://www.justice.gov/opa/pr/maryland-man-sentenced-federal-sex-trafficking-drug-and-firearm-charges. Accessed 23 May 2016.

15. Department of Justice, U.S. Attorney's Office. Madison county man charged with sex and drug trafficking. 2015. https://www.justice.gov/usao-ndfl/pr/madison-county-man-charged-sex--and-drug-trafficking. Accessed 23 May 2016.
16. Department of Justice, U.S. Attorney's Office. Three conspirators sentenced to a total of more than 40 years in prison for sex and drug trafficking. 2010. https://www.justice.gov/archive/usao/md/news/archive/ThreeConspiratorsSentencedtoaTotalofMorethan40Yearsin PrisonforSexandDrugTrafficking.html. Accessed 23 May 2016.
17. Garcia V, Gonzalez L. Labor migration, drug trafficking organizations, and drug use: major challenges for transnational communities in Mexico. Urban Anthropol Stud Cult Syst World Econ Dev. 2009;38(2–4):303–44.
18. Associated Press. Mexico drug gangs using more children as "mules." 2012. http://www.cbsnews.com/news/mexico-drug-gangs-using-more-children-as-mules/. Accessed 23 May 2016.
19. United Nations Office on Drugs and Crime. Drug mules: swallowed by the illicit drug trade. 2012. https://www.unodc.org/southasia//frontpage/2012/october/drug-mules_-swallowed-by-the-illicit-drug-trade.html. Accessed 23 May 2016.
20. Ports KA, Ford DC, Merrick MT. Adverse childhood experiences and sexual victimization in adulthood. Child Abuse Negl. 2016;51:313–22. doi:10.1016/j.chiabu.2015.08.017.
21. Wilson JM, Dalton E. Human trafficking in the heartland: variation in law enforcement awareness and response. J Contemp Crim Justice. 2008;24(3):296–313. doi:10.1177/1043986208318227.
22. Federal Bureau of Investigation, U.S. Attorney's Office. Sioux Falls man convicted in sex trafficking case. 2013. https://www.fbi.gov/minneapolis/press-releases/2013/sioux-falls-man-convicted-in-sex-trafficking-case. Accessed 23 May 2016.
23. Zimmerman C, Hossain M, Watts C. Human trafficking and health: a conceptual model to inform policy, intervention and research. Soc Sci Med. 2011;73(2):327–35. doi:10.1016/j.socscimed.2011.05.028.
24. Silverman JG, Raj A, Cheng DM, Decker MR, et al. Sex trafficking and initiation-related violence, alcohol use, and HIV risk among HIV-infected female sex workers in Mumbai, India. J Infect Dis. 2011;204(Suppl 5):S1229–34. doi:10/1093/infdis/jir540.
25. Johnson H. Edmond teen says dad pimped her for drugs. 2011. http://www.news9.com/story/15071353/edmond-teen-says-dad-pimpedher-for-drugs. Accessed 23 May 2016.
26. U.S. Department of Justice, Office of Public Affairs. Lutz, Fla., man convicted on drug distribution and sex trafficking charges. 2013. https://www.justice.gov/opa/pr/lutz-fla-man-convicted-drug-distribution-and-sex-trafficking-charges. Accessed 23 May 2016.
27. U.S. Department of Justice, U.S. Attorney's Office. Federal judge sentences Sheboygan sex and heroin trafficker to 25 years imprisonment. 2015. https://www.justice.gov/usao-edwi/pr/federal-judge-sentences-sheboygan-sex-and-heroin-trafficker-25-years-imprisonment. Accessed 23 May 2016.
28. Coalition of Immokalee Workers. Anti-slavery campaign. 2012. http://www.ciw-online.org/slavery/. Accessed 23 May 2016.
29. Michigan Law. Case view: Leroy Smith v. Bulls-Hit Ranch & Farm. 2012. http://www.law.umich.edu/clinical/HuTrafficCases/Pages/CaseDisp.aspx?caseID=775. Accessed 23 May 2016.
30. Michigan Law. Case view: United States v. Ronald Robert Evans Sr. 2007. http://www.law.umich.edu/clinical/HutrafficCases/Pages/CaseDisp.aspx?caseID=151. Accessed 23 May 2016.
31. Ribeiro SC, Kennedy SE, Smith YR, Stohler CS, et al. Interface of physical and emotional stress regulation through the endogenous opioid system and mu-opioid receptors. Prog Neuropsychopharmacol Bio Psychiatry. 2005;29(8):1264–80.
32. Washton AM, Zweben JE. Treating alcohol and drug problems in psychotherapy practice. New York: Guilford Press; 2008.
33. Chon K. Human trafficking and opioid abuse. 2016. http://www.acf.hhs.gov/blog/2016/05/human-trafficking-and-opioid-abuse. Accessed 23 May 2016.

34. Raymond JG, Hughes DM. Sex trafficking of women in the United States. International and Domestic Trends. 2001. https://www.ncjrs.gov/pdffiles1/nij/grants/187774.pdf. Accessed 23 May 2016.
35. Schauer EJ, Wheaton EM. Sex trafficking into the United States: a literature review. Crim Justice Rev. 2006;31(2):146–69. doi:10/1177/0734016806290136.
36. Wilson JM, Dalton E. Human trafficking in the heartland: variation in law enforcement awareness and response. J Contemp Crim Justice. 2008;24(3):296–313. doi:10.1177/1043986208318227.
37. Flom PL, Friedman SR, Kottiri BJ, Neaigus A, et al. Stigmatized drug use, sexual partner concurrency, and other sex risk network and behavior characteristics of 18- to 24-year-old youth in a high-risk neighborhood. Sex Transm Dis. 2001;28(10):598–607.
38. Fussa MJ, Paul SM. Medical implications of injection drug use. 2009. http://ccoe.rbhs.rutgers.edu/online/ARCHIVE/09hc09/index.htm. Accessed 23 May 2016.
39. Centers for Disease Control and Prevention. Lung cancer. 2015. http://www.cdc.gov/cancer/lung/basic_info/risk_factors.htm. Accessed 23 May 2016.
40. Tashkin DP. Effects of marijuana smoking on the lung. Ann Am Thorac Soc. 2013;10(3):239–47. doi:10/1513/AnnalsATS.201212-127FR.
41. Volkow ND, Baler RD, Compton WM, Weiss SRB. Adverse health effects of marijuana use. N Engl J Med. 2014;370:2219–27. doi:10.1056/NEJMra1402309.
42. Saini GK, Gupta ND, Prabhat KC. Drug addiction and periodontal diseases. J Indian Soc Periodontol. 2013;17(5):587–91. doi:10/4103/0972-124x.119277.
43. Substance Abuse and Mental Health Services Administration. Treating sleep problems of people in recovery from substance use disorders. 2014. http://store.samhsa.gov/shin/content/SMA14-4859/SMA14-4859.pdf. Accessed 23 May 2016.
44. Nabipour S, Said MA, Habil MH. Burden and nutritional deficiencies in opiate addiction-systematic review article. Iran J Public Health. 2014;43(8):1022–32.
45. Mertens JR, Weisner C, Ray GT, Fireman B, Walsh K. Hazardous drinkers and drug users in HMO primary care: prevalence, medical conditions, and costs. Alcohol Clin Exp Res. 2005;29(6):989–98.
46. National Institute on Drug Abuse. Drugs, brain, and behavior: the science of addiction. 2011. http://drugabuse.gov/scienceofaddiction/health.html. Accessed 23 May 2016.
47. Clawson HJ, Dutch N. Addressing the needs of victims of human trafficking: challenges, barriers, and promising practices. U.S. Department of Health and Human Services: Office of the Assistant Secretary for Planning and Evaluation. 2008. Retrieved from https://aspe.hhs.gov/basic-report/addressing-needs-victims-human-trafficking-challenges-barriers-and-promising-practices#2. Accessed 23 May 2016.
48. Gorenstein D. Identifying trafficking victims is just the start of health care's challenge. 2016. http://www.marketplace.org/2016/03/04/health-care/identifying-trafficking-victims-just-start--health-cares-challenge. Accessed 23 May 2016.
49. Najavits L, Weiss R, Shaw S. The link between substance abuse and posttraumatic stress disorder in women. Am J Addict. 1997;6(4):273–83. doi:10.1111/j.1521-0391.1997.tb00408.x.
50. Dube SR, Felitti VJ, Dong M, Chapman DP, et al. Childhood abuse, neglect, and household dysfunction and the risk of illicit drug use: the adverse childhood experiences study. Pediatrics. 2003;111(3):564–72. doi:10.1542/peds.111.3.564.
51. Kessler R, Sonnega A, Bromet E, et al. Posttraumatic stress disorder in the national comorbidity survey. Arch Gen Psychiatry. 1995;52(12):1048–60. doi:10.1001/archpsyc.1995.03950240066012.
52. Garner BR, Hunter BD, Smith DC, Smith JE, Godley MD. The relationship between child maltreatment and substance abuse treatment outcomes among emerging adults and adolescents. Child Maltreat. 2014;19(3–4):261–9. doi:10.1177/1077559514547264.
53. Kilpatrick DG, Acierno R, Resnick HS, Saunders BE, Best CL. A 2-year longitudinal analysis of the relationships between violence assault and substance use in women. J Consult Clin Psychol. 1997;65(5):834–47. doi:10.1037/0022-006X.65.5.834.

54. Kilpatrick D, Saunders B, Smith D. Youth victimization: prevalence and implications. Research in brief. Maryland: National Institute of Justice; 2003. https://www.ncjrs.gov/pdffiles1/nij/194972.pdf. Accessed 23 May 2016.
55. Kilpatrick D, Edmunds C, Seymour A. The national women's study. Arlington: National Victim Center; 1992.
56. Covington S. Women and addiction: a trauma-informed approach. J Psychoactive Drugs. 2008;40:377–85. doi:10.1080/02791072.2008.10400665.
57. Beckerleg S, Copeland J, Covington S, Ernst ML, et al. Substance abuse treatment and care for women: case studies and lessons learned. In: Drug abuse treatment toolkit. United Nations Office on Drugs and Crime. Available via UNODC. https://www.unodc.org/docs/treatment/Toolkits/Women_Treatment_Case_Studies_E.pdf. Accessed 23 May 2016.
58. Najavits L. Seeking safety: a treatment manual for PTSD and substance abuse. New York: Guilford Press; 2001.
59. Alexander MP, Kellogg ND, Thompson P. Community and mental health support of juvenile victims of prostitution. In Cooper SW, Estes RJ, Giardino AP, Kellogg ND, Vieth VI, editors. Medical, legal, and social science aspects of child sexual exploitation, Vol. 1. St. Louis: Medical Publishing; 2005. p. 397–421.
60. Elliot D, Bjelajac P, Fallot R, Markoff L, Reed B. Trauma-informed or trauma- denied: principles and implementation of trauma-informed services for women. J Community Psychol. 2005;33:461–77.
61. Prochaska JO, Norcross J. Changing for good: a revolutionary six-stage program for overcoming habits and moving your life positively forward. New York: William Morrow Paperbacks; 2007.
62. Miller WR, Rollnick S. Motivational interviewing: helping people change. 3rd ed. New York: The Guilford Press; 2013.
63. Yahne C, Miller W, Irvin-Vitela L, et al. Magdalena pilot project: motivational outreach to substance abusing women street sex workers. J Subst Abus Treat. 2002;23(1):49–53. doi:10/1016/S0740-5472(02)00236-2.
64. Najavits LM, Hien D. Helping vulnerable populations: a comprehensive review of the treatment outcome literature on substance use disorder and PTSD. J Clin Psychol. 2013;69(5):433–79. doi:10.1002/jclp.21980.
65. Fallot RD, Harris M. The trauma recovery and empowerment model (TREM): conceptual and practical issues in a group intervention for women. Community Ment Health J. 2002;38(6):475–85.
66. Miller D, Guidry L. Addictions and treatment recovery: healing the body, mind & spirit. 1st ed. New York: W. W. Norton & Company; 2001.
67. National Association of State Mental Health Program Directors. 2015. www.nasmhpd.org. Accessed 23 May 2016.
68. Ford JD. An affective cognitive neuroscience-based approach to PTSD psychotherapy: the TARGET model. J Cogn Psychother. 2015;29(1):69–91.

Chapter 13
The Development and Psychology of Young Minds: Communities Can Prevent Exploitation and Facilitate Rehabilitation

Sandra Gasca-Gonzalez and Dianna L. Walters

13.1 Introduction

Why are adolescents in the United States (US) at greater risk for poor life experiences and outcomes than their peers in other developed nations [1]? Why are adolescents here more susceptible to dangerous situations like human trafficking [2]? What has science and clinical experience contributed to our collective understanding about what young people need to avoid harm, thrive, and experience lasting well-being? Have strategies and interventions been identified to help our nation create a safe context for development that young people need to be protected and healthy? What role can communities play in protecting youth and ensuring they all have the connections and resources they need to develop resilience in the face of trauma? As US youth continue to fare more poorly than their peers in other developed nations, it becomes increasingly urgent to translate knowledge into improved policy and practices that better shape the experiences of this population. This chapter offers some answers to the above questions and discusses related advancements made in the fields of neuroscience, behavioral science, and clinical psychology. Interventions that arise from these developments have the potential to significantly enhance the well-being of young people in the USA, particularly adolescents at risk for and involved in sex trafficking.

S. Gasca-Gonzalez (✉)
Jim Casey Youth Opportunities Initiative, The Annie E. Casey Foundation,
Baltimore, MD, USA
e-mail: sgasca-gonzalez@aecf.org

D.L. Walters
Learn and Earn to Achieve Potential (LEAP) Initiative, University of Southern
Maine's Muskie School of Public Service, Portland, ME, USA
e-mail: dianna.walters@maine.edu

© Springer International Publishing AG 2017   231
M. Chisolm-Straker, H. Stoklosa (eds.), *Human Trafficking Is a Public Health Issue*, DOI 10.1007/978-3-319-47824-1_13

13.1.1 Scope of the Problem

Adolescence and young adulthood have long been viewed as particularly challenging times of development and equally troublesome for the adults trying to protect them from harm. Unfortunately, it is becoming increasingly apparent that many parents, educators, health professionals, and state and federal policy makers have yet to successfully create the environment needed to ensure young people safely transition to adulthood with their greatest social, emotional, cognitive, and neurobiological potential. Young people in the USA are struggling to secure the things necessary to be safe and successful such as education, physical health, mental health, and connections to healthy families and communities. The struggle of communities and families to build strong and secure psychological, emotional, economic, and physical attachments with adolescents can leave youth vulnerable to sexual exploitation or other forms of human trafficking. Due to unreported cases and differing definitions of what constitutes sex trafficking, an accurate estimate of youth being trafficked in the USA is, at the time of this writing, unknown [3].

13.1.1.1 Adolescent Outcomes

Studies on education show that high school students in the USA continue to perform more poorly than their peers in other industrialized countries [4]. College graduation rates are also on the decline here, moving the USA from a top achiever to one of the lowest among high-income nations [5]. The physical health of our nation's youth continues to decline as rates of adolescent obesity rise [6]. The USA is also a world leader, among developed nations, in teen alcohol use disorders, illicit drug use, pregnancies, and sexually transmitted infections [1]. Issues such as teen violence are also staggeringly high in the USA and the country carries the highest rate of violent teen deaths [7]. Mental health issues abound among our nation's youth and adolescent suicide attempts and ideation rates are on the rise [8]. More young people are on medications designed to alter their behavior than ever before and one study found that adolescents today have higher rates of mental health problems such as depression and anxiety than they did 75 years ago [9–11].

Collectively, young people in the USA are not faring well. When sub-populations of adolescents and young adults are considered, the disparities across different groups call for even greater urgency around prevention strategies to make young people in the USA safer, healthier, and more connected to supportive people. For example, young people who age out of foster care and are suddenly without family are at increased risk of homelessness, criminal involvement, early parenthood, unemployment, underemployment, mental health issues, substance use disorders, and low educational attainment [12]. Youth involved in other public systems are also faring more poorly than young people in the general population [13].

Youth detention centers have not only proven to be ineffective at rehabilitating youth, but they also expose them to more risk factors for poor life outcomes, including physical and sexual abuse while incarcerated [13]. Moreover, youth of color are particularly vulnerable as they are more likely to be involved in child welfare and juvenile justice systems, to experience poverty, and to be unemployed and undereducated as young adults [14].

As clinicians become more aware of trafficking, minor survivors of commercial sexual exploitation are being identified in hospitals across the nation [15]. But information to help explain the contributing factors to youth vulnerability is not fully delineated. The evidence that is available supports what anecdotal data suggests: Youth who have run away, been abandoned, or are otherwise homeless; survived sexual abuse; or live in group placement settings like foster care are most at risk of being sexually exploited [16]. Many youth who are survivors of commercial sexual exploitation become incarcerated or involved with public systems that fail to treat or may worsen the trauma that led them to become victimized in the first place [17].

13.1.1.2 Reform Efforts

Policy and practice have long sought to make the environments in which youth grow up safer and more conducive to healthy adolescent development. Yet, the health, safety, and well-being of young people in the USA appear to be worsening rather than improving [1]. Policy governing divisions between adolescence and young adulthood is inconsistent and perplexing: In most states an individual can drive a car at age 16, vote and join the military at age 18 but cannot buy alcohol until age 21. The relatively early age of legal driving exists despite the leading cause of death for teenagers in the USA being motor vehicle accidents; it does not seem logical for this to be the first area in the law in which teens are legally given greater freedom [18]. In short, US society appears to be confused about where to draw the line between childhood and adulthood.

While there remains a great deal to be done, it does appear that the scientific evidence, which has been growing since the mid-1990s, is making its way into policy and practice. The juvenile justice system, for example, has clear improvements, such as the abolishment of the juvenile death penalty in 2005. This legislative change was supported by evidence about adolescent brain development [19]. Another notable example is federal policy that now allows the definition of "child," used by the nation's foster care systems, to be extended from age 18–21. This change recognizes that young people are not fully neurobiologically developed until their mid-20s. Moreover, another policy requires child welfare agencies to provide developmentally appropriate experiences for youth in their care [12, 20].

13.2 Discussion

13.2.1 Overview of Adolescent Development

In light of poor outcomes and national tragedies, like the sexual exploitation and trafficking of youth in the USA, it becomes increasingly urgent for families, communities, service providers, and policy makers to understand adolescent brain development and human behavior. It is only through such an understanding that we will be able to respond effectively to the challenges that our nation's youth face and wrap youth, who have been traumatized, in healing and nurturing communities that promote their well-being and protect them from harm.

13.2.1.1 Experience Matters

Human brains can change, or adapt, in response to experiences in the environment throughout life [21]. This concept is called *neuroplasticity*. During the two major periods of developmental neuroplasticity, early childhood and adolescence, the brain is building itself and undergoes heightened levels of plasticity [22]. In early childhood, neuroplasticity is *experience expectant*, which means the types of experiences that shape brain development are anticipated during this time period [23]. While there are some exceptions, most infants and young children have things to see and people to hear to stimulate the development of vision and language functions in the brain. More complex abilities, such as being able to plan ahead or regulate emotions, are dependent upon there being an environment in which these abilities are fostered. This is the type of plasticity that occurs in the brains of adolescents and young adults, and is referred to as *experience dependent* [24]. During a person's mid-20s the brain becomes less malleable and the ongoing plasticity of the fully developed adult brain allows only minor modifications to the existing circuitry of the brain [21].

Experience matters throughout a person's lifetime but is especially important to the brain during these major periods of developmental plasticity. This is because, for better or worse, brain structure is most heavily shaped by all experiences a person has during these two windows of brain development. During early childhood, the parts of the brain that are most malleable are not the same as those being built and maturing during adolescence and young adulthood [25]. Due to the different location of brain plasticity in these developmental periods, there are important yet different implications for experiences' impact on the brain's physical development in early childhood and adolescence [1]. For example, one study found that sexual abuse in early childhood impacted a different part of the brain than sexual abuse that occurred in adolescence [26]. In general, childhood exposure to *toxic stress*, or stress that yields excessive activation of the stress response, can cause physiologic harm and consequences that last long past childhood: For example, adults with a childhood history of exposure to toxic stress, like sexual or physical abuse, can suffer from anxiety, difficulty with memory and learning [27]. And adolescents with a history of toxic stress are more likely to start using alcohol at a younger age and use alcohol as a stress coping mechanism. Because of the fundamental differences between them, each period of developmental plasticity is important in its own way [28].

To take full advantage of the brain's neuroplasticity during adolescence, experiences must be challenging enough that the brain is performing a task it has not yet mastered but not so difficult that the task cannot be accomplished. Ensuring young people have opportunities to make decisions, create their own plans while taking some risks is actually nurturing of the developing brain when there is a supportive environment. Such an environment should provide a safety net for youth to practice their newly forming executive skills. Ensuring the brain is being continually challenged to grow in positive ways during periods of developmental plasticity also helps keep open the window of opportunity to strengthen the brain for a longer period of time. This concept is called *metaplasticity* and means that stimulating brain development not only helps the brain grow in that moment but also facilitates enhanced capacity for brain growth in the future [29].

13.2.1.2   The Adolescent Brain

Defining the period of adolescence can be a difficult task as there are many milestones that can be used to differentiate this developmental period from others. For the purpose of this discussion, the landmark used to indicate the beginning of adolescence will be the physiological onset of puberty. A surge in sex hormones during this time triggers changes in the brain, causing some brain systems to begin maturing. Puberty triggers the changes in the brain that make it more plastic-like [30]. These changes in the brain cause the limbic system to become more easily aroused. The limbic system is the part of the brain that detects rewards and threats, and creates emotions that motivate people to react to the environment. One chemical that is heavily influenced by sex hormones is called *dopamine*. Dopamine's release in the brain causes excitation when a reward is possible and causes a sense of pleasure when the reward is received. These changes in the brain, triggered by puberty, are what make youth more bored or excited than those with a more developed brain. Adolescent risk taking can thus be explained by these changes in the brain's reward system: Adolescents must engage in increasingly exciting activities to feel even moderate levels of excitement (Fig. 13.1) [31, 32].

This medical illustration is provided courtesy of Alzheimer's Disease Research, a BrightFocus Foundation program [33].

Findings from neuroscience have also shown that the brain is not fully matured until the mid-20s, the same time at which many young people have begun to settle into adult life: completing college, getting married, beginning a career, and/or living independently [12]. Research suggests it may even be the transition to less novel and challenging environments that closes the window of increased brain plasticity [1]. Using these milestones and the knowledge about the developing brain,

Anatomy of the Brain

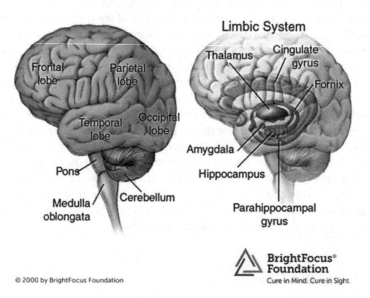

Fig. 13.1 Brain anatomy

adolescence will be defined in this chapter as ending around age 26. The brain physically matures from the bottom up, and from the back to front, beginning with the brain stem at the base of the skull and ending with the frontal lobes, which sit behind the forehead. This chronology is important to understand because the last part of the brain to develop, the frontal lobes, enables people to plan, think abstractly, be self-aware, make judgments, choose between various courses of action, and control impulses [30]. And this maturation happens well after US law has declared someone an adult, at age 18.

Different parts of the brain also begin changing at different times throughout adolescence and young adulthood. That the limbic system of the brain becomes more easily aroused before the frontal lobes are fully developed is one facet of what makes this developmental period so challenging for young people and the adults who try to protect and care for them. In adolescence, since the frontal lobes have not yet achieved the capacity to manage the hyper-aroused limbic system, risky behavior is best addressed by helping youth develop self-regulation skills; they are more successfully motivated with the promise of a reward rather than punishment [34, 35]. Behaviors like explosive emotional outbursts are, in fact, more likely due to an underdeveloped regulatory system in the brain than a teenager *choosing* to act out. Furthermore, when children have been exposed to adverse childhood experiences, as many trafficked children are, their limbic systems can be more easily aroused before the changes of puberty occur [36–38].

Another aspect of adolescence is related to a third part of the brain undergoing major developments during this developmental period: *the relationship system*. The frontal lobes are where the brain maps the world and makes meaning of how a person experiences themselves, other people, and interpersonal relationships. Influenced by the social milieu and the preponderance of neuro-circuits being formed and developed in adolescence, the relational experiences during this time have the chance to lay down either strong or unstable foundations for understanding and relating to others. People are constantly relating to others, interpreting the internal states of others through use of what are called *mirror neurons* in the brain. These changes occur in the brain during adolescence and make youth especially sensitive to the emotional states of others [24]. When any person senses an emotional state in another that may warrant a defensive reaction—such as anger—the emotional center of the brain becomes hyper-aroused and the rational brain center becomes less active. This occurs to a greater degree for adolescents whose brain regions are especially sensitive to others [30]. Finally, the heightened state of the social reward center in the brain during adolescence makes them very easily influenced by peers during this period of development. Such influence can be a great asset if it takes the form of a positive peer environment or a great danger in peer settings that encourage potentially harmful behaviors [19].

13.2.1.3 Trauma and the Brain

The brain is extremely sensitive to stress during periods of developmental plasticity and can ironically become hardwired to seek out more trauma in response to stress. As noted above, when the limbic system, particularly the amygdala, senses a threat in the environment it causes the body to route energy toward the anticipated need to fight, flee, or freeze. Since the frontal lobes are not priority areas for this need, executive functions such as planning, reasoning, and impulse control are not activated during a period of perceived threat [39, 40]. When young children are exposed to stress for prolonged periods of time, their brains have a more frequent need to fight, flee, or freeze, resulting in an overdeveloped amygdala and an underdeveloped frontal lobe [41]. Stress produces a stress hormone called cortisol and when levels of cortisol stay elevated over long periods of time it is toxic to the brain's development and a person's ability to respond to stress throughout their lifetime [37, 38]. Due to the developmental plasticity of the brain in adolescence and young adulthood, exposure to threatening environments can result in a chronically elevated cortisol level. Consequently, a person's baseline state is that of constantly scanning the environment for dangers and maintaining readiness to respond to threats. This state of constant arousal makes people less able to function well in daily life, and to form and maintain healthy relationships [24].

The impact of trauma on the brain is not permanent, even after the windows of developmental plasticity have closed. This means there is not a point of "no-return," beyond which, supportive interventions and caring relationships are no longer able to mitigate the impacts of trauma [12]. Still, it is important to note that the greatest chance to overcome the neurobiological impacts of trauma is during periods of developmental plasticity like adolescence. The functions of the mid-prefrontal cortex are housed in the frontal lobe, which is maturing during adolescence and these functions create the foundation for emotional well-being: bodily regulation,[1] attuned communication, emotional balance, response flexibility, fear modulation, empathy, insight, moral awareness, and intuition [24]. New, positive experiences in adolescence therefore have the potential to help a person overcome trauma on a neurobiological level. New experiences can also help build a foundation that will help ensure the ability to protect the self from future harm.

13.2.2 Preventing Sex Trafficking of Adolescents

Eliminating trafficking requires not only a focus on preventing and stopping the actions of individual exploiters, but also altering the fundamental attitudes and practices at the relationship, community, and society levels [42]. Risk factors for trafficking include individual (e.g., substance use as a means to treat trauma), relationship (e.g., isolation from loved ones and lack of social supports), community (e.g., lack of employment opportunities that limit financial freedom), and societal factors (e.g., marginalization and disenfranchisement of social or racial/ethnic groups) [42]. Strategies aimed at effecting an overall reduction of risk factors must be developed and strengthened in the USA.

In this chapter, from a public health, socioecological perspective, the authors will suggest two methods of preventing the trafficking of youth: development of healthy relationships and development of healthy communities. Neurobiology explains the importance of human connection in building psychological and emotional safety. The power of relationships is critical to creating an individual's sense of belonging, which facilitates the prevention of trafficking. And if trafficked, such relationships are integral to survivor healing. Second, the health of a community has a major impact on how adolescents behave and respond to their environment. Healthy communities are created when leaders make commitments and take actions toward promoting sustainable strategies that allow people to make healthy choices where they work, live, learn, and play [43]. When adolescents have a general sense of belonging and connection to positive opportunities in the community, this leads to better well-being outcomes, including decreased risk of trafficking [12].

---

[1] Bodily regulation is how the human body self-regulates in areas such as temperature, energy level, blood composition, and sleep to maintain a stable internal environment despite changes in the external environment.

13.2.2.1 Power of Relationships

Often mainstream media tells the stories of white, middle class, sex trafficked youth with well-to-do parents from the suburbs; these parents are shocked to learn their adolescent has been exploited. This scenario often resonates with viewers and emphasizes that no one is safe from this travesty. In reality, adolescents with poor support networks or that are homeless are thought to be at the highest risk of being trafficked in the USA [43]. Despite what the media might show, many trafficking survivors have a background of poverty and are children of color. And in general, prolonged neglect, caregiver substance use disorders or mental illness, physical and/or emotional abuse, and chronic financial burdens change the physical landscape of the brains of youth, causing them to constantly scan for threats [44].

Specific relational determinants found to lead to a greater risk of trafficking include experiencing child maltreatment, dysfunctional relationships with caregivers, dating violence, and being runaway, homeless, and/or street youth [45]. Teen relationship violence is the "physical, sexual, psychological, or emotional violence within a dating relationship." A 2011 nationwide CDC survey found that 23% of females and 14% of males who ever reported an experience of rape, physical violence, or stalking by an intimate partner, first survived a form of intimate partner violence between 11 and 17 years of age [43]. Many teenaged girls involved in trafficking are deceived into believing that their trafficker is their boyfriend [45]. The trafficker then exploits the trust of a romantic relationship, for financial gain. Runaway and homeless youth are young people who have left home and do not have a supportive adult network, or safe, stable, or affordable housing [46]. This population of young people is highly susceptible to trafficking, as many are isolated from caring adults and have been exposed to sexual abuse, underemployment, lack of education, and substance use disorders.

Supporting Healthy Individual Development Adolescence is as vital a phase of human brain development as the early years of childhood. Just as early maltreatment and subsequent trauma can negatively impact brain development, positive experiences during adolescence can fortify healthy neural connections, develop executive function, and stimulate learning and healing. Professionals working with young people must understand the neurobiological impact of trauma, to best provide supports and opportunities to counteract that impact [12].

Evidence shows that even when a young person has experienced complex trauma, neuroplasticity makes the brain capable of overcoming trauma and gaining resiliency. The present views of neuroscience suggest that when energy and information flow within the brain, neural correlates of an experience are generated. The linkage of segregated elements of a system that leads to the flexible, adaptive, and coherent flow of energy and information in the brain, the mind, and relationships is known as *neural integration*. This coherent flow enables the individual to attain an intentionally established state of mindfulness that promotes a growing sense of a dynamic and resilient self [47] and can be leveraged to overcome trauma's effects.

Table 13.1 Middle
prefrontal cortex functions

Nine functions of the middle prefrontal cortex [24]
Body regulation
Attuned communication
Emotional balance
Response flexibility
Empathy (a "you" map)
Insight (a "me" map)
Fear modulation
Intuition
Morality (a "we" map)

Healing Individual Trauma Using the power of the brain to heal from trauma first involves basic brain hygiene, which promotes neuroplasticity: This good hygiene includes consistent exercise, healthy diet, and good quality sleep [48–51]. Aerobic activity releases endorphins in the brain, increasing dopamine and reducing the stress chemical called cortisol. For adolescents in particular—who are driven by changes in their developing brains to seek activities that give them a dopamine rush—exercise, which releases dopamine, can be a powerful tool for healing and prevent harmful behaviors. Avoiding stimulants like caffeine and processed sugar can help reduce mood swings in traumatized individuals. A healthy diet fuels the body and the brain, allowing both to take advantage of their intrinsic healing mechanisms [49]. Finally, even when restful sleep is difficult to achieve, establishing and maintaining a calming routine before bed can be beneficial in allowing the brain to heal (Table 13.1).

Experiences shape brain development but not all people have the optimal experiences needed to help them reach their full potential; these people may fail to fully develop all nine of the functions of the mid-prefrontal cortex that support emotional well-being. *Body regulation* is one of these functions and is the process of the body regulating aspects of the physical self, such as heart rate, breathing, digestion, and immune response. It is this function that allows people's bodies to return to their baseline state of functioning after a stressor has occurred. A second function is called *attuned communication*, which allows people to sense another person's feelings or states of being such as knowing when someone else is happy or angry. A third function of *emotional balance* is being able to regulate one's affect or emotional state, such as the ability to return to a state of ease after an event causes anxiety or anger. Fourth, *response flexibility* is the process that enables people to pause before they act in response to an external or internal experience, allowing them to assess options and choose which may be the best course of action. A fifth function of the mid-prefrontal cortex is *empathy* or the ability to put oneself in someone else's shoes and see events and experiences from their point of view. Sixth in the list is *insight* or the ability to be aware of oneself to accurately and meaningfully understand and link past, present, and future. *Fear modulation* is a seventh function that allows a person to calm themselves in the face of a real or perceived threat. An eighth function of *intuition* enables people to register input from neurons in the heart and intestines, colloquially called "the gut," and incorporate this input into cognitive processes. The final function is *morality* and is what enables people to consider what behaviors are best for the broader social good and act from those considerations even when they are alone [24].

Activities designed to promote development of functions of the mid-prefrontal cortex and neural integration of brain regions can facilitate a path to greater well-being in individuals' lives and help them avoid potentially dangerous situations. Engaging in mindful awareness practices is one such activity that takes advantage of the power of neuroplasticity and helps people who have experienced trauma promote the neural integration that is needed for well-being. Mindfulness-based treatments help people build the skills needed to be able to purposefully pay attention to the present moment. When people are present in the moment they are more aware of themselves and others. This makes them better able to identify harmful thought patterns, behaviors and how the people with whom they interact, and activities in which they engage, may be self-harming. When people interrupt harmful thought patterns or behaviors and engage in healthier ones they build new neural connections that can, over time and with practice, become stronger than the preexisting ones; eventually the healthy patterns of thought and behavior become the natural way of engaging with themselves and others in their environment [47].

Relationship Interventions Data shows that re-wiring of the brain is supported by healthy relationships with a caring adult [52]. Connection to caring, compassionate adults exerts a powerful influence in supporting the brain's healthy adaptations [53]. Positive experiences that contradict a traumatized person's negative expectations are likewise critical to helping the brain transform [54]. Organizations such as *My Life My Choice* are focused on empowering youth and ending exploitation through a range of strategies, with survivor–mentor relationships being a primary technique of healing.

My Life My Choice, located in Massachusetts, is an anti-trafficking organization employing a survivor-led model proven effective in helping young people leave dangerous situations and construct new lives for themselves [55]. The Survivor Mentor Program at *My Life My Choice* links exploited young women and girls at high risk of exploitation with an adult female Survivor-Mentor. The mentors are survivors of sex trafficking, trailblazers in the anti-trafficking field, and specialize in working with survivors of exploitation-related trauma [55]. This mentoring–protegé relationship:

> helps young victims of exploitation build the intangible skills that they need to be successful, healthy adults: self-worth, a positive self-image, the ability to trust, and the tools to know how and where to seek help when they need it. The program is centered on long term, consistent service provision—a model of "recovery" rather than "rescue." *My Life My Choice* offers support which addresses both the immediate needs of victims, as well as the long term needs of belonging and stability. Mentors play a pivotal role in helping their mentees recover from the trauma of exploitation by connecting them with much needed services…: therapy, substance abuse treatment [55].

In an effort to prevent exploitation before it begins with high-risk girls, mentors are assigned to give guidance, helping young girls think through a safer path. All tactics to prevent exploitation and shape brighter futures are created in the context of a trusting relationship. This program would benefit from rigorous evaluation to scale up strategies to benefit the entire country.

An older mentoring program, *Big Brothers Big Sisters* (BBBS), provides one-to-one mentoring for children and youth aged 6–18 years of age facing adversity. The program was founded in 1904 (long before the current anti-trafficking movement), and carefully matches youth with caring adult mentors in a relationship supported by professional staff. A 2015 US Department of Health and Human Services (HHS) report on BBBS showed that after 18 months in the program the youth were less likely to begin using illegal drugs or alcohol, or engage in truancy or physical violence as compared to youth not involved with BBBS [56]. In another impact study, alumni of BBBS reported doing better in school specifically because of their mentor; agreed their mentor helped them reach a higher level of education than they thought possible; and agreed their mentor prevented them from dropping out of high school [57]. This is an example of an organization that is solely funded through local fundraising efforts and relies on communities to support organizational viability. BBBS is not specifically an anti-trafficking organization. Still, by providing a youth with at least one caring adult, they decrease that youth's risk of being trafficked. Importantly, this decreased risk is not yet proven, but inferred, as the 2015 HHS report notes lower rates of baseline risk factors for trafficking among BBBS participants and alumni.

13.2.2.2 Power of Communities

What is the difference between an adolescent that is exploited versus one that is not? In poverty-stricken and frequently exploited areas, why are some adolescents not victimized? How can communities play a role in preventing trafficking and facilitating rehabilitation? There are many programs throughout the USA that provide services to survivors. While there are anecdotal successes described by some of those programs, most lack the evidence to support their effectiveness and this is largely due to funding constraints to conduct evaluations. Interventional programs within communities are necessary, yet a more proactive way of addressing trafficking is by promoting the strength and health of communities to prevent trafficking in the first place.

The prevention of trafficking and the treatment of adolescents that are trafficked requires an approach that is owned by all parts of a community—families, schools, law enforcement, employers, city officials, neighborhood leaders, nonprofit organizations, health professionals and systems, and businesses [58]. Places all across the country are focusing on infusing trauma-informed approaches to build healthy communities.

Building Healthy, Trauma-Informed Communities   Healthy communities are ones that intentionally prioritize developing a culture of neighbors-helping-neighbors in activities of daily living that leads to the fulfillment of every community member's highest potential [43]. Healthy communities focus on the social and physical environments to create this culture of safety, connectedness, and opportunity [59]. Healthy communities improve the quality of life for all people who live and work there because they focus on everything that is external to an individual such as the foods available, air quality, the social strength of a community, resident spirituality, and education. The fostering of healthy communities lends to the development of equity and prevents negative outcomes for all residents. Healthy communities take a *proactive* approach to prevention of illness, social problems, climate change, and mental distress [59].

One type of healthy community is a *trauma-informed community* that focuses on addressing the root causes of the trauma faced, rather than simply concentrating on the symptoms [43]. Often, the root causes are related to issues like domestic violence, joblessness, and substance use disorders. Trauma-informed communities concentrate on building a culture focused on the life circumstances of the individual rather than the person's shortcomings and culpability. These communities understand that past traumas can be triggered by experiences in the present and are committed to supporting people as they heal. These communities create a culture in which multidisciplinary professionals and workers are aware of the role of trauma, and how they can reduce re-traumatization to create healing opportunities. Trafficked persons experience chronic trauma, which interferes with neurobiological development and the capacity to integrate sensory, emotional, and cognitive information into a cohesive whole [60]. An example of a trauma-informed community is Tarpons Springs, Florida, where they have made a commitment

> to engage people in all walks of life – education, juvenile justice, welfare, housing, medical practices, businesses, etc. — in a common goal of less trauma…large and small, immediate and generational. The city of Tarpon Springs brought to its community a concept that is sweeping through the mental health and educational communities, but one that has received little public attention [61].

Community Interventions   There are community interventions across the country that could benefit from rigorous evaluation to show effectiveness in the areas of building holistic well-being. A few examples are highlighted here to demonstrate the diversity of ways in which communities can positively impact and mitigate youths' risk of being trafficked.

Head Start

Head Start started in 1965 (again, long pre-dating the current anti-trafficking movement) as a federal government effort to capitalize on childhood brain plasticity: Head Start supports school readiness of children, from low-income families, from birth to age five by enriching their cognitive, social, and emotional development [62].

Head Start programs arrange for a learning environment that promotes children's growth in many areas such as language, literacy, and social and emotional development [62]. The program underscores the function of caretakers as the child's most significant educator [62]. Head Start's programs engage families and build relationships that support family well-being. Further, it aims to impact the overall well-being of communities by minimizing potential individual victimization and poverty. While it is not specifically a trafficking prevention program, Head Start has access to and serves children and families that are at risk for victimization. In a 1969 analysis, the Head Start program was found to support educational gains until children reached the 3rd grade; but after that, the educational difference between attenders and non-attenders was nearly nil [63]. The results were duplicated in 2010, and in fact educational advantages were not significantly different by the 1st grade [64]. Non-educational results were mixed and did not overwhelmingly indicate the utility of Head Start. But given how enmeshed Head Start is in the national fabric—Head Start is present in cities and rural areas of every state in the USA, Washington DC, and US territories [65]—the program is not giving up yet: Head Start now has to compete with other organizations, with similar aims, to achieve federal funding. With access to some of the most vulnerable members of US communities, Head Start must continue to self-reflect and innovate.

And Head Start may not have to look too far: There are some noteworthy models, using trauma-informed work, that show degrees of effectiveness. The Trauma-Informed Community Building (TICB) model is an approach to community building that recognizes the everyday stresses in the community in which a resident lives. Specifically, TICB examines the pervasive historical and current trauma of community violence, generational poverty, and racism [66]. Desired outcomes of TICB are: (1) to increase the readiness of the community to endure personal and neighborhood change; (2) to promote social interconnectivity and increase resiliency so that residents have the capacity to adapt to changing circumstances; and (3) to recognize the interplay of individual, relational, community, and system level factors on residents' experiences to target each of these levels, in all aspects of community building efforts [66]. Although not currently branded as an anti-trafficking intervention, TICB is a big-picture strategy that supports communities addressing issues of poverty and homelessness [66], which indirectly helps prevent trafficking.

National *Compadres* Network and *La Cultura Cura*

The National *Compadres* Network (NCN) is an organization located in San Jose, California, whose focus is the reinforcement of the positive involvement of Latino males in the lives of their families, communities, and society. NCN's mission is

> to strengthen, rebalance, and redevelop the traditional Compadre extended kinship network by encouraging, supporting and re-rooting the positive involvement of males in their families and community and preventing or reducing the incidence of family and community violence, teen pregnancy, substance abuse, and other oppressive behaviors [67].

Decreasing inter-generational violence and substance use, two problems that many trafficked persons and traffickers experience, may help diminish San Jose youth's risk of being trafficked; of course, program monitoring and evaluation, over many years, would be necessary to determine the utility of this program with respect to anti-trafficking aims.

La Cultura Cura, or Cultural-Based Healing, was developed by NCN. This is a program that recognizes that a path to healthy development, restoration, and life-long well-being exists within individual, family and community cultural values, traditions, and indigenous practices. It leverages a multi-generational method of learning and/or recalling one's affirming cultural values, principles, customs, and traditions. This approach is unique because it includes men, women, young people, and elders together in the healing process. This approach is particularly promising because it is culturally responsive for trafficked persons of Latino or indigenous backgrounds [67].

WSU Center for Combating Human Trafficking

Wichita State University's (WSU) Center for Combating Human Trafficking, led by Dr. Karen Countrymen-Roswurn, offers an array of unique services to prevent exploitation and sex trafficking, as well as support healing. Programs include Men's Demand Reduction™ Groups, the Lotus Prevention for Prosperity™ Model, and the Lotus Victim to Vitality™ Model. The men's groups are intended to decrease the demand for pornography and commercial sex. The Lotus Prevention for Prosperity™ Model is a prevention program for middle and high school-aged youth whose curriculum targets young people's ability to practice healthy relationships; form a developmentally appropriate understanding of abuse and exploitation/trafficking; educate young people about resources in the community; and create opportunities for them to show their ability to combat abuse and exploitation. The Lotus Victim to Vitality™ Model is a prevention and intervention model for young people who are either at risk or have already been involved with trafficking [68].

13.3   Conclusion

The plight of young people being trafficked is a tragedy in the USA. Young people deserve a comprehensive approach of awareness, education, prevention, and treatment. Across the USA, it is challenging to find specific programs that show evidence of effectiveness in preventing trafficking. Still, some communities have taken steps to address toxic stress and trauma at a systematic level with the hope of improving the well-being of young adults and growing healthier communities.

13.4   Recommendations

- Invest equitably to particularly support at-risk families with children undergoing early childhood and adolescent development; and prevent traumatic experiences (toxic stressors) from occurring, especially during particularly sensitive periods of brain development.
- Use information about adolescent brain development and the neurobiology of healing from trauma, to inform governmental policies. Education efforts should be targeted toward guardians, families, youth and young adults, community members, employers, educators, law enforcement and court personnel, health professionals, and policy makers.
- Consider supporting initiatives with specific strategies to address whole community well-being from a trauma-informed perspective as a community-level trafficking prevention strategy.
- Community anti-trafficking programs should prioritize rigorous evaluation of the effectiveness of their work. It is necessary to know what types of programs are effective so they can be reproduced across the country. While the evidence is being developed, programs that are trauma-informed, that emphasize survivors leading their own healing, and that build pathways for economic and financial capacity, should be preferentially implemented.

References

1. Steinberg L. Age of opportunity: lessons from the new science of adolescence. New York, NY: First Mariner Books; 2014.
2. Siegel D. Brainstorm: the power and purpose of the teenage brain. New York, NY: Penguin Group; 2013.
3. Clayton EW, Krugman RD, Simon P. Confronting commercial sex exploitation and sex trafficking of minors in the United States, 2013. The National Academies Press, Washington, DC.
4. Koretz D. How do American Students Measure up? Making sense of international comparisons. Future Child. 2009;19(1):37–51.
5. OECD. Education at a glance 2013: OECD indicators. OECD publishing. doi:10.1787/eag-2013-en.
6. Harvard School of Public Health Obesity Prevention Source. Too many kids are too heavy, too young. 2012. http://www.hsph.harvard.edu/obesity-prevention-source/obesity-trends/global-obesity-trends-in-children/#References. Accessed 28 Apr 2016.
7. National Research Council. U.S. health in international perspective: shorter lives, poorer health. 2013. doi:10.17226/13497. Accessed 28 Apr 2016.
8. Centers for Disease Control and Prevention (CDC). 1991–2013 High school youth risk behavior survey data. 2014. http://nccd.cdc.gov/youthonline/. Accessed 28 Apr 2016.
9. Scheffler RM, Hinshaw SP, Modrek S, Levine P. The global market for ADHD medications. Health Aff. 2007;26(2):450–7.
10. Schwarz A, Cohen S. ADHD seen in 11% of uS children as diagnoses rise. New York Times. 31 Mar 2013.
11. Twenge JM, Gentile B, DeWall CN, Ma D, Lacefield K, Schurtz DR. Birth cohort increases in psychopathology among young Americans, 1938–2007: a cross-temporal meta-analysis of the MMPI. Clin Psychol Rev. 2010;30(20):145–54.

12. Jim Casey Youth Opportunities Initiative. The adolescent brain: new research and its implications for youth transitioning from foster care to adulthood. 2011. http://www.aecf.org/resources/the-adolescent-brain-foster-care/. Accessed 6 Mar 2016.
13. Annie E Casey Foundation. No place for kids: the case for reducing juvenile incarceration. 2011. http://www.aecf.org/resources/no-place-for-kids/. Accessed 6 Mar 2016.
14. Race Matters Institute. Unequal opportunities for youth in transition. 2004. http://viablefuturescenter.org/racemattersinstitute/wp-content/uploads/2015/06/youth.pdf. Accessed 6 Mar 2016.
15. Kaplan D, Kemp K. Domestic minor sex trafficking: an emerging health crisis. Brown Univ Child Adolesc Behav Lett. 2015;31(7):1–6.
16. Finklea K, Fernandes-Alcantara AL, Siskin A. Sex trafficking of children in the United States: overview and issues for Congress. Federation of American Scientists' Congressional Research Service Reports. 2015. https://www.fas.org/sgp/crs/misc/R41878.pdf. Accessed 4 Mar 2016.
17. Saar MS, Epstein R, Rosenthal L, Vafa Y. The sexual abuse to prison pipeline: the girls' story. Center on Poverty and Inequality. 2015. http://www.law.georgetown.edu/academics/centers-institutes/poverty-inequality/upload/2015_cop_sexual-abuse_layout_web-2.pdf. Accessed 4 Mar 2016.
18. Centers for Disease Control and Prevention. Mortality among teenagers aged 12–19 years: United States, 1999–2006. 2010. http://www.cdc.gov/nchs/products/databriefs/db37.htm. Accessed 28 Apr 2016.
19. Cauffman E, Steinberg L. Emerging findings from adolescent development and juvenile justice. Vict Offender. 2012;7:428–49.
20. Juvenile law Center. Promoting normalcy for children and youth in foster care. 2015. http://www.jlc.org/resources/publications/promoting-normalcy-children-and-youth-foster-care. Accessed 28 Apr 2016.
21. Doidge N. The brain that changes itself: stories of personal triumph from the frontiers of brain science. New York, NY: Penguin; 2007.
22. Lillard AS, Erisir A. Old dogs learning new tricks: neuroplasticity beyond the juvenile period. Dev Rev. 2011;31(4):207–39.
23. Greenough WT, Black JE, Wallace CS. Experience and brain development. Child Dev. 1987;58(3):539–59.
24. Siegel D. The developing mind: how relationships and the brain interact to shape who we are. New York, NY: The Guilford Press; 2012:
25. Rothman EF, Edwards EM, Heeren T, Hingson RW. Adverse childhood experiences predict earlier age of drinking onset: results from a representative US sample of current or former drinkers. Pediatrics. 2008;122(2):e298–304.
26. Andersen SL, Tomada A, Vincow ES, Valente E, Polcari A, Teicher, MH. Preliminary evidence for sensitive periods in the effect of childhood sexual abuse on regional brain development. 2008. http://www.ncbi.nlm.nih.gov/pmc/articles/PMC4270804/. Accessed 8 Mar 2016.
27. McEwen BS, Gianaros PJ. Stress- and allostasis-induced brain plasticity. Annu Rev Med. 2011;62:431–45.
28. Shonkoff JP, Garner AS. The committee on psychosocial aspects of child and family health, committee on early childhood, adoption and dependent care, and section on developmental and behavioral pediatrics. The lifelong effects of early childhood adversity and toxic stress. Pediatrics. 2012;129(1):e232–46.
29. Hulme SR, Jones OD, Wickliffe CA. Emerging roles of metaplasticity in behavior and disease. Trends Neurosci. 2013;36(6):353–62.
30. Jensen FE. The teenage brain: a neuroscientists survival guide to raising adolescents. New York, NY: HarperCollins; 2015.
31. Galvan A, Hare TA, Parra CE, Penn J, Voss H, Glover G, Casey BJ. Earlier development of the accumbens relative to orbitofrontal cortex might underlie risk-taking behavior in adolescence. J Neurosci. 2006;26(25):6885–92. doi:10.1523/JNEUROSCI.1062-06.2006.
32. Hoogendam JM, Kahn RS, Hillegers MHJ, van Buuren M, Vink M. Different developmental trajectories for anticipation and receipt of reward during adolescence. Develop Cogn Neurosci. 2013;6:113–24. doi:10.1016/j.dcn.2013.08.004.

33. Alzheimer's Disease Research, a BrightFocus Foundation program. http://www.brightfocus. org/alzheimers/. Accessed 1 Aug 2016.
34. Geier CF, Terwilliger R, Teslovich T, Velanova K, Luna B. Immaturities in reward processing and its influence on inhibitory control in adolescence. Cereb Cortex. 2010;20(7):1613–29. doi:10.1093/cercor/bhp225.
35. Teslovich T, Mulder M, Franklin NT, Ruberry EJ, Millner A, Somerville LH, Simen P, Durston S, Casey BJ. Adolescents let sufficient evidence accumulate before making a decision when large incentives are at stake. Dev Sci. 2014;17(1):59–70. doi:10.1111/desc.12092.
36. McGowan PO, Sasaki A, D'Alessio AC, Dymov S, Labonte B, Szyf M, Turecki G, Meaney MJ. Epigenetic regulation of the glucocorticoid receptor in human brain associates with childhood abuse. Nat Neurosci. 2009;12:342–8. doi:10.1038/nn.2270.
37. De Bellis MD. The psychobiology of neglect. Child Maltreat. 2005;10(2):150–72. doi:10.1177/1077559505275116.
38. Rees CA. Understanding emotional abuse. Arch Dis Child. 2010;95(1):59–67. doi:10.1136/adc.2008.143156.
39. Davis M. The role of the amygdala in fear and anxiety. Annu Rev Neurosci. 1992;15:353–75. doi:10.1146/anurev.ne.15.030192.002033.
40. LeDoux JE. The emotional brain, fear and the amygdala. Cell Mol Neurobiol. 2003;23 (4–5):727–38. doi:10.1023/A:1025048802629.
41. Child Welfare Information Gateway. Understanding the effects of maltreatment on brain development. 2015. https://www.childwelfare.gov/pubPDFs/brain_development.pdf. Accessed 28 Apr 2016.
42. United Nations Entity for Gender Equality and the Empowerment of Women. http://www. endvawnow.org/en/articles/1117-apply-the-ecological-model-to-identify-risk-factors-for-perpetration-of-violence-or-those-that-contribute-to-impunity.html. Accessed 24 Apr 2016.
43. Centers for Disease Control and Prevention. Injury Prevention and Control. 2016. http://www. cdc.gov/ViolencePrevention/intimatepartnerviolence/teen_dating_violence.html. Accessed 2 May 2016.
44. Harvard University, Center for the Developing Child. 2015. Key concepts of toxic stress. http://developingchild.harvard.edu/science/key-concepts/toxic-stress/. Accessed 28 Apr 2016.
45. Countryman-Roswurm KI, Bolin B. Domestic minor sex trafficking: assessing and reducing risk. Child Adolesc Social Work J. 2014;31:521–38. doi:10.1007/s10560-014-0336-6.
46. U.S. Department of Health and Human Services. 2016. http://www.acf.hhs.gov/programs/fysb/programs/runaway-homeless-youth. Accessed 1 May 2016.
47. Siegel DJ. Mindful awareness, mindsight, and neural integration. Humanist Psychol. 2009; 37:137–58.
48. Gorgoni M, Atri AD, Lauri G, Rossini PM, Ferlazzo F, Gennaro LD. Is sleep essential for neural plasticity in humans, and how does it affect motor and cognitive recovery? Neural Plast. 2013;2013:103949. doi:10.1155/2013/103949.
49. Stranahan AM, Arumugam TV, Cutler RC, Lee K, Egan JM, Mattson MP. Diabetes impairs hippocampal function through glucocorticoid mediated effects on new and mature neurons. Nat Neurosci. 2008;11:309–17.
50. Swain RA, Berggren KL, Kerr AL, Patel A, Peplinski C, Sikorski A. On aerobic exercise and behavioral and neural plasticity. Brain Sci. 2012;2:709–44.
51. Van Praag H, Shubert T, Zhao C, Gage FH. Exercise enhances learning and hippocampal neurogenesis in aged mice. J Neurosci. 2005;25(38):8680–5. doi:10.1523/JNEUROSCI. 1731-05.2005.
52. Schneider-Munoz A. Developmental assets as a framework for engaging families in out-of-school. 2011.
53. Schneiderman JU, Villagrana M. Meeting children's mental and physical health needs in child welfare: the importance of caregivers. Soc Work Health Care. 2010;49:91–108.
54. Schwartz JM, Begley S. The mind and the brain: neuroplasticity and the power of mental force. New York, NY: HarperCollins; 2003.
55. My Life My Choice. 2016. http://www.fightingexploitation.org/survivor-mentorship. Accessed 19 May 2016.

56. Herrera C, Grossman JB, Kauh TJ, Feldman AF, McMaken J, Jucovy LZ. Making a difference in schools: the big brothers big sisters school based mentoring. Philadelphia, PA: Public/Private Ventures; 2007.
57. Big Brothers Big Sister. 2016. http://www.bbbs.org/site/c.9iILI3NGKhK6F/b.7721455/k.6CBF/Our_impact_on_education.htm. Accessed 19 May 2016.
58. Biglan A. The nurture effect: how the science of human behavior can improve our lives and our world. Oakland, CA: New Harbinger Publications, Inc; 2015.
59. U.S. Department of Health and Human Services. Healthy People. 2010. http://www.cdc.gov/healthyplaces/about.htm. Accessed 20 Mar 2016.
60. van der Kolk BA. Developmental trauma disorder: towards a rational diagnosis for children with complex trauma histories. Psychiatr Ann. 2005;35(5):401–8.
61. Stevens JE. Tarpon Springs, FL may be the first trauma informed city in the U.S. 2012. https://acestoohigh.com/2012/02/13/tarpon-springs-may-be-first-trauma-informed-city-in-u-s/. Accessed 1 Aug 2016.
62. U.S. Department of Health and Human Services. 2015. http://www.benefits.gov/benefits/benefit-details/616. Accessed June 2015.
63. Westinghouse Learning Corporation, Ohio University. The impact of head start; an evaluation of the effects of head start on children's cognitive and affective development (executive summary). Office of Economic Opportunity. June 1969.
64. U.S. Department of Health and Human Services, Administration for Children and Families. Head start impact study. Final Report. Washington, DC. 2010.
65. U.S. Department of Health and Human Services. Administration for children and families. http://www.acf.hhs.gov/programs/ohs/about. Accessed 1 Aug 2016.
66. Weinsten E, Wolin J, Rose S. Trauma informed community building: a model for strengthening community in trauma affected neighborhoods. 2014. http://bridgehousing.com/PDFs/TICB.Paper5.14.pdf. Accessed 20 Mar 2016.
67. National Latino Fatherhood and Family Institute. Lifting Latinos up by their "rootstraps:" Moving beyond trauma through a healing-informed framework for Latino boys and men. 2012. http://www.nationalcompadresnetwork.com/resources/BrownPaperExecutiveSummary2012.pdf. Accessed 20 Mar 2016.
68. Countryman-Roswurm KI, Shaffer VA. It's more than just my body that got hurt: the psychophysiological consequences of sex trafficking. J Traffick Organ Crime Secur. 2015;1(1):1–8.

Chapter 14
Legal Supports for Trafficked Persons: Assisting Survivors via Certification, State/Federal Benefits, and Compensation

Lennon Moore and Brendan Milliner

14.1 Introduction

The Trafficking Victims Protection Act (TVPA) of 2000 is the first comprehensive United States (US) federal law to address trafficking in persons. The law provides a three-pronged approach that includes prevention, protection, and prosecution. The TVPA was reauthorized through the Trafficking Victims Protection Reauthorization Act (TVPRA) of 2003, 2005, 2008, and 2013. The TVPA defines "severe forms of trafficking in persons" as the recruitment, harboring, transportation, provision, or obtaining of a person for the purpose of a commercial sex act, in which a commercial sex act is induced by force, fraud, or coercion, or in which the person is induced to perform such act is under the age of 18 years (Sex Trafficking (22 USC § 7102 (9–10))); or the recruitment, harboring, transportation, provision, or obtaining of a person for labor or services, through the use of force, fraud, or coercion for the purpose of subjection to involuntary servitude, peonage, debt bondage, or slavery (Labor Trafficking (22 USC § 7102 (9))).

US citizens who are trafficked are eligible for state compensation, as are victims of other crimes. They may receive *compensation*, or the provision of medical and mental health care as well as financial assistance, described as follows by the National Crime Victim Compensation Boards:

> Compensation programs can pay for a wide variety of expenses and losses related to criminal injury and homicide.... While each US state operates under its own law, trafficking

---

The original version of this chapter was revised. An erratum to this chapter can be found at DOI: 10.1007/978-3-319-47824-1_25

L. Moore (✉)
Covenant House, 929 Atlantic Avenue, Atlantic City, NJ 08401, USA
e-mail: lennonmoore@covenanthouse.org

B. Milliner
Department of Emergency Medicine, Mount Sinai Medical Center, Box 1620, 1 Gustave L. Levy Place, New York, NY 10029, USA

© Springer International Publishing AG 2017
M. Chisolm-Straker, H. Stoklosa (eds.), *Human Trafficking Is a Public Health Issue*, DOI 10.1007/978-3-319-47824-1_14

victim compensation programs generally have the same basic criteria to determine survivors' eligibility for benefits. Beyond medical care, mental health treatment, funerals, and lost wages, a number of programs also cover crime-scene cleanup, travel costs to receive treatment, moving expenses, and the cost of housekeeping and child care if a victim is unable to perform those tasks. And states continue to work with victims and advocates to find new ways to help victims with more of the costs of recovery. Maximum benefits available from the states average $25,000, with some states able to offer more, and some states having lower limits. Lower caps within the maximum are common for some types of benefits, like funeral and burial costs, mental health counseling, or lost wages [1].

Foreign-born trafficking victims who are not citizens of the US need to go through an additional process to be eligible for federal and state benefits. This process is referred to as *certification*, and is discussed below.

While elsewhere in this book chapter authors avoid use of the term "victim," it is used in the legal discourse of trafficking to clearly delineate those wronged from those who have committed crimes; the term is used in this chapter in this legal context.

14.1.1 Definitions of Frequently Used Terms

14.1.1.1 Involuntary Servitude

A condition of servitude induced by means of any scheme, plan, or pattern intended to cause a person to believe that if the person did not enter into or continue in such condition, that person or another person would suffer serious harm or physical restraint; or the abuse or threatened abuse of the legal process (22 U.S.C. 7102 (6)).

14.1.1.2 Debt Bondage

The status or condition of a debtor arising from a pledge by the debtor of their personal services or of those of a person under their control as a security for debt, if the value of those services as reasonably assessed is not applied toward the liquidation of the debt or the length and nature of those services are not, respectively, limited and defined (22 U.S.C. 7102 (5)).

Note: In plain language, this can be understood as a person's pledge of their labor or services as repayment for a debt or other obligation.

14.1.1.3 Coercion

(A) threats of serious harm to or physical restraint against any person;
(B) any scheme, plan, or pattern intended to cause a person to believe that failure to perform an act would result in serious harm to or physical restraint against any person; or
(C) the abuse or threatened abuse of the legal process (22 U.S.C. 7102 (3)).

14.1.1.4 Commercial Sex Act

The term "commercial sex act" means any sex act on account of which anything of value is given to or received by any person (22 U.S.C. 7102 (4)).

Note: This can be understood as a sex act involving the exchange of something of value (e.g.: money, gifts, basic needs, drugs).

14.1.1.5 Child

As per the United States' definition, this will include any person who is under the age of 18 years.

14.2 Discussion

14.2.1 Eligibility for Benefits

To be eligible for benefits as a victim of a crime, the victim (regardless of nationality) must report the crime promptly to law enforcement (usually within 3 years), and cooperate with police and prosecutors in their criminal investigation; commonly this entails providing testimony at trial and giving evidence about the perpetrator. Victims must submit a timely application for compensation to the Victims of Crime Compensation Board (generally within the same 3 year timeframe), have a cost or loss not covered by insurance or another government benefit program, and must not have committed a criminal act or some substantive act that led to or contributed to the crime. Exceptions are sometimes made to these requirements, especially in the case of child victims. Although they often have the most valuable knowledge to aid in the prosecution as a first-hand witness, minors are not required to assist in the investigation of their traffickers. Regardless of age, apprehension or conviction of the offender(s) is not required for victims to receive compensation and/or certification.

14.2.1.1 Identifying Victims

Some victims are able to leave their trafficking situation when a friend or concerned citizen makes a report to a law enforcement agency or non-governmental organization; law enforcement conducts a raid; a trafficker abandons a victim when they are no longer useful; they are identified in the healthcare setting; or a loved one's search for a victim puts the trafficker at risk of exposure. For professional service providers, identifying a victim is often hampered by the victim's reluctance to disclose due to fear, shame, attachment to the trafficker, isolation from the public, or constant monitoring by the trafficker [2]. The all-too-common perception of youth trafficking victims as "bad kids" who chose to engage in commercial sex or illegal activities, and deserving of the resultant consequences, further prevents victim recognition. Many professionals lack the time necessary to establish rapport, avoid asking questions about trafficking because of their own discomfort, and may be perceived by victims as judgmental, accusatory, or insensitive. Victims who perceive a professional to be non-receptive are less likely to disclose their traumatic experiences, making it even more difficult to identify some trafficking victims.

14.2.1.2 Barriers to Leaving a Trafficking Situation

Time and again trafficked youth are seen as "not worth the effort" by the legal system because they do not want to return home and may, in fact, return to the trafficker or another trafficking situation. It is important for professionals and advocates to understand that for many trafficked youth "home" was a place of abuse, neglect, dysfunction, shame, and stress [3]. Many youth return to their trafficking life because they are lured or threatened by the trafficker, may be unaware that they are a victim, or feel that home is just as bad or worse than being trafficked. Many sex trafficked victims report a sense of belonging with other sex "workers," and believe that engaging in commercial sex is the only skill they have [4]. Helping trafficked youth to understand the truth and providing viable recovery options for youth victims is the key to facilitating an acceptance of services.

Trafficked adults face challenges as well; for example, the day-to-day physical trauma of engaging in commercial sex is often accompanied by substance use[1] to mask physical and emotional pain [2]. Disordered substance use replaces critical thinking with alterations in consciousness, hopelessness, and acceptance of their exploitation and abuse as never-changing. Poverty, lack of marketable skills, and drug use disorders may make people vulnerable to being trafficked. Often, in the authors' experience, when older trafficking victims become less valuable they are abandoned by the trafficker but continue to engage in commercial sex because of the accumulated effects of trauma, poverty, and substance use disorders. Those victims exploited for labor trafficking face similar challenges to leaving. They are frequently working in an unfamiliar area with significant language and cultural barriers that may isolate them from outside assistance. In addition, many victims of labor trafficking may be undocumented or unfamiliar with US visa regulations; this is easily exploited to produce further insecurity and compel them to continue their involvement with their trafficker [5].

---

[1] Youth may similarly use illicit substances, alcohol, or prescription medications.

14.2.1.3 Challenges in Determining Eligibility

While trafficking victims are eligible for benefits through the standard process discussed above (Sect. 14.2.1), the physical and psychological traumas experienced by trafficked persons may present additional challenges in determining eligibility. Often, survivors can be fearful, hostile, distrustful of authorities, and in many cases loyal to the trafficker(s). Furthermore, trafficking survivors may not see themselves as victims, despite legal determinations [2]. Participating in the legal process in and of itself can be a grueling undertaking. Survivors may have to retell traumatic and embarrassing occurrences, face the perpetrator in open court, be challenged about their credibility and questioned about their life choices. It is not uncommon for many months to pass before justice is served and there is no guarantee the trafficker will be found guilty.

14.2.1.4 Trauma Bonding Can Hinder Eligibility

Traffickers may use extreme violence, constant unpredictability, and severe deprivation to control victims, as well as make declarations of love to reinforce their role as savior, spiritual leader, romantic partner, or parental figure [4]. For lonely, disconnected youth, such manipulation can be particularly effective [3]. Many victims are isolated such that they come to fully rely on the trafficker for basic needs and thereby naturally develop feelings of dependency. Loyalty grows from the notion that the trafficker is taking care of the victim by providing the necessities of life. Coupled with the trafficker's assertion that no one cares about or is looking for the victim, victims adapt to their trauma in that they perceive their situation to be normal and the trafficker as a caregiver. This type of *trauma bonding* can make participation in prosecution difficult for the victim. This can complicate the certification process for non-US citizens, as participation in prosecution is often an important element in the certification decision as discussed below (Sect. 14.2.2).

14.2.2 Certification: Establishing Benefits for Non-US Citizens

Certification as a victim of human trafficking is a legal process that allows adult victims of trafficking who are not US citizens or Lawful Permanent Residents (LPRs) to be eligible for benefits and services under any federal or state program or activity to the same extent as a refugee. Victims of trafficking who are US citizens or LPRs do not need certification to receive benefits because they may already be eligible for many benefits.

To receive certification, a person who is 18 years of age or older must:

- Be a victim of a severe form of trafficking as defined by the TVPA;
- Be willing to assist in every reasonable way in the investigation and prosecution of severe forms of trafficking or be unable to cooperate due to physical or psychological trauma; AND

- Have made a *bona fide* ("in good faith") application for a T visa (a type of visa providing legal status to foreign-born victims of human trafficking) that has not been denied; or
- Have received Continued Presence (CP) from the Department of Homeland Security (DHS) to contribute to the prosecution of traffickers in persons.

Once a person has met the requirements listed above, they may receive a Certification Letter from the US Department of Health and Human Services (HHS) Office of Refugee Resettlement (ORR). The certification process typically takes only a few days after ORR is notified, by DHS, that a person has made an application for a T visa or has been granted CP. Certification Letters do not expire but many benefits are time-limited. Foreign-born child victims of trafficking do not need to be certified to receive benefits and services. ORR will instead issue a letter stating that a child is a victim of a severe form of trafficking and is eligible for benefits and services.[2]

In addition, since April 2015 the Wage and Hour Division (WHD) of the Department of Labor has been directly certifying T visa applications for victims of human trafficking in situations related to labor laws and practices. The WHD will consider certifying applications when the following criteria are met:

- The WHD has detected a severe form of trafficking in persons;
- The trafficking activity arises in the context of a work environment or an employment relationship; AND
- There is a credible allegation of a violation of a law that WHD enforces related to the work environment or employment relationship [6].

Furthermore, the WHD will certify U visas (a visa for any non-citizen who was the victim of a crime) in cases of extortion, forced labor, and fraud in foreign labor contracting, and this may be helpful for victims of trafficking who do not formally qualify for a T visa. The Wage and Hour Division enforces several critical federal workplace laws, including the federal minimum wage and overtime laws. Because many wage and hour investigations take place in industries that employ vulnerable workers, the Wage and Hour Division is often the first federal agency to make contact with these workers and detect exploitation in the workplace. These new efforts on the part of the WHD will help qualifying victims of these crimes receive immigration relief from DHS and access the victim services they need to recover and rebuild their lives.

Certification through the WHD can be requested through one of the WHD local offices. A directory of these offices can be found at https://www.dol.gov/whd/.

---

[2] See the Rescue and Restore Fact Sheet on Child Victims and ORR State Letter #10-05 for more information.

14.2.3 Types of Support for Victims of Human Trafficking

The services available for trafficking victims range from monetary compensation and reimbursement for medical and mental health services to direct provision of medical or mental health care and housing. The type and number of available programs vary widely from state to state.

14.2.3.1 Crime Victim Compensation

Programs to provide compensation for crime victims have been in existence in the USA for decades. As of 2016, compensation programs throughout the country dispense close to half a million dollars to victims annually. These programs are largely funded through fees and fines paid by those convicted of the crimes in question.

Victims of human trafficking, along with victims of rape, assault, domestic violence, and other major crimes, are eligible to apply for compensation. Approximately half of claimants are victims of assault, with a substantial percentage of those being victims of domestic violence. Many victims are unaware that compensation programs exist, and the responsibility for informing them of such programs often falls on professionals in law enforcement, victim services, and health care providers who have close contact with victims. The programs available vary from state to state, and professionals should seek more information about the programs available in their area [1].

14.2.3.2 Federal Assistance Programs

Victims of human trafficking (if US citizens or certified/eligible as victims) are eligible for several federal assistance programs through the Department of Health and Human Services. Non-citizen victims may be eligible for additional benefits through the Office of Refugee Resettlement.

Victims who are not certified or eligible cannot enroll in the programs listed in Table 14.1, with limited exceptions for refugees, asylum seekers, and immigrants from Cuba or Haiti. Providers must be especially diligent in helping to obtain certification or eligibility status on behalf of victims, to ensure they are able to receive necessary services.

Certified adults and eligible minors who are not US citizens may also qualify for Refugee Cash Assistance, Refugee Medical Assistance, Refugee Social Services and Targeted Assistance, and Voluntary Agency Matching Grant Programs as described below.

For further information regarding the certification process for non-citizen adult victims, contact the National Human Trafficking Resource Center at NHTRC@PolarisProject.org or (888) 373–7888. Professionals wishing to request a letter of eligibility for a non-citizen minor who has been a victim of trafficking should contact the ORR Anti-Trafficking Division at childtrafficking@acf.hhs.gov or (202) 205–4582.

Table 14.1 Eligibility for HHS federal benefits (adapted from Department of Health and Human Services)

Group	Temporary Assistance for Needy Families	Medicaid	Children's Health Insurance Program	Health Resources and Services Administration Programs	Substance Abuse and Mental Health Services Administration Programs
US citizen or lawful permanent resident	Yes	Yes	Yes (if a minor)	Yes	Yes
Certified adult	Yes	Yes	No	Yes	Yes
Minor with eligibility letter	Yes	Yes	Yes	Yes	Yes
Non-US citizen *without* certification	No	No	No	Yes	Yes
Refugees, asylees, and Cuban/Haitian entrants	Yes	Yes	Yes (if a minor)	Yes	Yes

For US citizens or Certified/Eligible victims who are not US citizens, these benefits include:

- *Temporary Assistance for Needy Families*: a state-administered program to support the basic needs of children. Specific benefits vary by state.
- *Medicaid*: a federal health coverage for medical expenses. As Medicaid is also administered on a state-by-state basis, victim status does not guarantee coverage. Each person is evaluated by the state Medicaid office prior to initiation of benefits.
- *Children's Health Insurance Program (CHIP)*: provides supplementary coverage for minors who do not qualify for Medicaid.
- *Health Resources and Services Administration (HRSA) Programs*: fund and administer a network of health centers providing well-care checkups, treatment for pregnant women, immunizations, dental care, and mental health and substance use disorder care.
- *Substance Abuse and Mental Health Services Administration (SAMHSA) Programs*: fund local and state-based centers for substance use and mental health disorders. While victims may receive support from these centers, eligibility for care is made on a state, local, or even provider level, and victims are not guaranteed coverage.

Non-US citizen victims may also be eligible for the following programs:

- *Refugee Cash Assistance (RCA)*: provides temporary supplemental income for trafficking victims. Generally RCA beneficiaries must enroll in employment service programs to maintain benefits.
- *Refugee Medical Assistance*: provides temporary medical coverage for foreign-born children ineligible for Medicaid or CHIP. Typically available for 8 months after eligibility determination.
- *Refugee Social Services and Targeted Assistance*: offers services to address barriers to finding employment. Depending on the state, benefits may include job training, English-language education, and social adjustment services. These are available only to foreign-born minors with work authorization.
- *Voluntary Agency Matching Grant Programs*: a state-by-state network of agencies providing more comprehensive employment and housing services. Applications must be made within 31 days from the date of eligibility.
- *Health Insurance Marketplace*. Individuals, including refugees can apply for health insurance through the Health Insurance Marketplace. By completing one application, refugees can learn whether they are eligible for Medicaid or CHIP. At the same time, they can also learn whether they are eligible for private health insurance coverage through the Health Insurance Marketplace; and if eligible, whether they qualify for lower costs on monthly premiums for these plans [7].
- *The Unaccompanied Refugee Minors (URM) Program*, through the Office of Refugee Resettlement, provides specialized foster care for refugees and other special populations of youth. To enter this program, victims must be eligible for foster care, under state law, in their area of residence. This program also provides a degree of additional security for victims as it requires the state of residence to cover the cost of medical care even if the victim is found ineligible for Medicaid or CHIP [8]. To enter the URM Program, a youth must be eligible for foster care and/or independent living services under state law. In states operating URM Programs, if the state's legal responsibility for the minor is not established prior to the child's 18th birthday, the youth is not eligible for foster care and subsequent independent living services. In several states, youth must *arrive* in a URM location 2 to 4 months before turning 18 for the state's legal responsibility to be established. When applications are submitted well before a youth turns 18, there is a better chance of a URM placement being identified [8].

For further information regarding the above programs, professionals should visit the Department of Health and Human Services Administration for Children and Families at www.acf.hhs.gov/programs/.

14.2.3.3 State-Administered Programs

State-based programs for victims vary widely across the country in terms of cost and availability. The following, adapted from the New Jersey Office of Victim Witness Advocacy (OVWA), provides an example of services that may be offered, but should not be considered representative of all states. Of note, state-based programs are not necessarily affected by federal certification or eligibility.

- *Counseling and Support Services*: The County Office of Victim-Witness Advocacy staff is trained to help victims deal with the initial shock of the crime and the difficult emotional times afterward. If a victim wants to talk to someone on a regular basis, the staff can help them identify a mental health counselor, who may or may not charge for services. Several county programs sponsor support groups for sexual assault victims, domestic violence victims, and homicide "survivors" (beneficiaries of homicide victims, often victims' children). Office staff can also assist victims to find a shelter or obtain food and clothing.
- *HIV Testing of Defendants and HIV Information and Referrals for Victims*: If a victim came in contact with any bodily fluid of the trafficker, such as blood, saliva, or semen, the court can order the defendant to be tested for HIV infection; the results of that test are then provided to the victim. This allows the victim to better understand their risk of contracting HIV from the trafficker. Additionally a victim-witness counselor will help the victim find a place that offers free, confidential testing.
- *Criminal Justice Orientation and Information*: Victim-witness counselors of the county office of victim-witness advocacy explain the US criminal justice system so that victims know what will happen and when. Victim-witness counselors may give a victim a tour of the courtroom before the trial or grand jury hearing to help familiarize the victims with the formal, authoritative setting.
- *Victim Information and Impact*: Victims will have several opportunities to tell the prosecutor and the judge about how the crime affected them. The county office of victim-witness advocacy will send a Victim Information and Impact form with the *initial contact letter* (the initial contact from the county office to the victim) and will remain in communication with the victim throughout the legal process. County office staff can help the victim fill out the form and prepare both the oral and written statements.
- *Case Status Notification*: The Office of Victim-Witness Advocacy will inform victims of specific events in their case and possible delays in proceedings. Sometimes this is done by telephone, but most often notification is by postal service.
- *Court Accompaniment and Transportation Services*: When a case comes to trial, staff can accompany a victim to court, to explain courtroom events as well as provide support. If called to testify, victims can be reimbursed by the prosecutor's office for public transport or taxi fare. The OVWA can also help with expenses for a non-testifying witness who wants to be present in court.

- *Child Care to Attend Meetings and Court Proceedings*: The County Office of Victim-Witness Advocacy can help with child care when parent-victims need to come to court.
- *Employer and Creditor Intercession*: The OVWA can help a victim who is having difficulty at work or school because of the crime or has to take time off to be in court. Often, the OVWA will contact school or work officials directly, to explain the situation. They can also contact creditors if the victim is not able to pay bills on time due to their criminal victimization.
- *Assistance with Property Return*: The OVWA can also help victims retrieve personal items that were kept for evidence. However, most items cannot be returned until after the convicted are sentenced.
- *Victim-Witness Waiting Rooms*: The OVWA provides waiting rooms where victims and witnesses can sit while waiting to go to court or meet with an assistant prosecutor or investigator.
- *Assistance in Obtaining Restitution*: Restitution is money the defendant must pay to a victim because of losses the victim incurred consequent to the crime. The OVWA can help complete the Victim Information and Impact form. This form will be used by the assistant prosecutor, the probation department, and the judge to decide how much restitution the defendant (the trafficker) must pay. Restitution cannot be for an amount greater than the actual amount of losses suffered.
- *Parole Eligibility and Release Notification*: The OVWA will notify the victim when the trafficker is being considered for parole or when the trafficker is scheduled for release from prison [9].

14.3 Conclusion

Legal protections for trafficking survivors are critical to the public health response to trafficking. When working with a trafficked person, advocates and legal support professionals should focus on the person's experience and individual needs. Survivors of trafficking need to be supported in understanding that they were a victim of violence and abuse, and in accessing the legal and social remedies necessary to facilitate their healing.

14.4 Recommendations

- As a professional working with victims of human trafficking, it is important to be acquainted with available federal and state services for victims and communicate this information to victims.
- Victims of trafficking, particularly minors, face many social barriers to seeking and maintaining support, and ongoing care should be arranged with a social service professional as well as medical and mental health care clinicians.

- Some survivors may find working with law enforcement therapeutic in their healing process. Providers should encourage victims, who are able, to engage with law enforcement; victims can offer law enforcement valuable information about traffickers and the network of people, places, and things that aid in maintaining traffickers' systems of exploitation.
- For victims who are not US citizens, it is important to initiate the certification/ eligibility process as soon as possible to maximize the benefits to which they have access.

The National Human Trafficking Resource Center operates a national hotline to connect victims and providers with federal and local resources. They can be contacted at 1-888-373-7888 or at NHTRC@PolarisProject.org.

References

1. National Association of Crime Victim Compensation Boards. Crime victim compensation: an overview. 2013. http://www.nacvcb.org/index.asp?bid=14. Accessed 19 Mar 2016.
2. US Department of Health and Human Services. Human trafficking into and within the United States: a review of the literature. 2009. https://aspe.hhs.gov/basic-report/human-trafficking-and-within-united-states-review-literature. Accessed 27 May 2016.
3. Jordan Greenbaum MD. Human Trafficking: Global and Domestic Crises (Oral Presentation with Power Point). Blank Center for Safe and Healthy Children. Children's Center of Atlanta 2013.
4. Raghavan C, Doychak K. Trauma-coerced bonding and victims of sex trafficking: where do we go from here? International Journal of Emergency Mental Health and Human Resilience. 2015. http://www.omicsonline.com/open-access/traumacoerced-bonding-and-victims-of-sex-trafficking-where-do-we-go-from-here-1522-4821-1000223.php?aid=55771. Accessed 27 May 2016.
5. National Human Trafficking Resource Center. Domestic Work. https://traffickingresourcecenter.org/labor-trafficking-venuesindustries/domestic-work. Accessed 27 May 2016.
6. Wage and Hour Division of the US Department of Labor. U and T visa certifications. https://www.dol.gov/whd/immigration/UTCert.htm. Accessed 27 May 2016.
7. Office of Refugee Resettlement. Medical assistance in the unaccompanied refugee minors program. 2015. http://www.acf.hhs.gov/programs/orr/resource/state-letter-15-02. Accessed 19 Mar 2016.
8. Department of Health and Human Services. Services available to victims of human trafficking: a resource guide for social service providers. In: HHS, ed. 2012. https://www.acf.hhs.gov/sites/default/files/orr/traffickingservices_0.pdf2012. Accessed 19 Mar 2016.
9. Office of Victim Witness Advocacy, State of New Jersey. Services Listing. 2016; http://nj.gov/oag/dcj/victimwitness/services-listing.htm. Accessed 19 Mar 2016.

Chapter 15
NGOs and the Anti-Trafficking Movement: Advocacy and Service

Valerie Schmitt

15.1 Introduction

While slavery has existed throughout time, the modern anti-trafficking movement is relatively young. Early activists for the anti-trafficking movement primarily consisted of nongovernmental organizations (NGOs) that served individuals directly impacted by labor or sexual exploitation. These NGOs were assisting victims of crime, who today would classify as human trafficking victims. However, without trafficking-specific laws, they lacked a clear path to comprehensive victim services and protection [1].

In the 1990s, NGOs working on forced labor and sexual exploitation coalesced around the need for laws specific to these forms of modern slavery and ultimately were instrumental in advocating for the passage of the first federal law specific to human trafficking. The United Nation's Palermo Protocol [2] and the United States' Trafficking Victim's Protection Act (TVPA) of 2000 [3] provided the recognition and platform needed for the development of anti-trafficking-specific organizations.

One unique attribute of the anti-trafficking movement in the USA is that it was not initially led by survivors or those most closely impacted by human trafficking, but rather the "helpers" who sought to advocate for reforms on behalf of trafficking survivors. This dynamic differentiated the anti-trafficking movement from most other social movements and facilitated the development of a criminal justice centered approach. This chapter will discuss the various functions of NGOs in the anti-trafficking movement and the challenges they face in comprehensively addressing human trafficking within their communities.

V. Schmitt (✉)
Polaris, PO Box 65323, Washington, DC 20035, USA
e-mail: vkschmitt@gmail.com; vschmitt@polarisproject.org

© Springer International Publishing AG 2017   263
M. Chisolm-Straker, H. Stoklosa (eds.), *Human Trafficking Is a Public Health Issue*, DOI 10.1007/978-3-319-47824-1_15

15.2 Discussion

15.2.1 Types of NGOs Engaged in the Anti-Trafficking Movement

The anti-trafficking movement has grown exponentially since the passage of the TVPA and now includes a vast array of stakeholders, from government entities to corporations and nongovernmental organizations. Every year, new organizations are founded to address human trafficking and existing organizations find ways to open their doors to survivors of trafficking.

NGOs in the anti-trafficking movement are both multi-disciplinary and multi-faceted. Many of the NGOs engaged in this work are dedicated solely to human trafficking, while others entered the movement because of their work in related issues, such as poverty, discrimination, women's rights, criminal justice reform, supply chain transparency, or homelessness. A public health socio-ecological framework recognizes the importance of addressing the root causes of trafficking, while simultaneously working with survivors and their support systems to overcome barriers across all domains of life. As such, NGOs in this space span all social service sectors and often serve multiple functions in their communities.

15.2.2 Functions of NGOs in the Anti-Trafficking Movement

Human trafficking is inherently a complex issue to address and requires intervention at the *micro*, *mezzo*, and *macro* levels to be effective. The public health socio-ecological framework is useful in identifying the opportunities NGOs have to progress anti-trafficking efforts.

On the individual, or *micro*, level, anti-trafficking NGOs may work directly with trafficking survivors, at-risk individuals, or with perpetrators. NGOs may use interpersonal relationships between survivor-mentors and newly identified survivors, for example, to support survivors or reduce trafficking risk through strengthening resiliency and building social supports. At the *mezzo* level, organizations may also work within groups to raise awareness about human trafficking, equip community actors to recognize and respond to human trafficking situations, or to address structural inequities that increase the risk of trafficking. NGOs may also seek to cultivate *macro* or foundational societal change, by creating a cultural shift that yields a decrease in demand for commercial sex acts and in which communities regularly purchase fair trade products and services.

While anti-trafficking NGOs may focus primarily on engagement at one of these levels (e.g., direct service providers or policy-oriented organizations), it is likely that they are, at some point, involved in all of these domains. As such, anti-trafficking NGOs fulfill a number of differing functions within the movement.

15.2.2.1 Policy and Advocacy

The Trafficking Victims Protection Act of 2000 was only the first step in the process of ensuring that strong, comprehensive laws are enacted, implemented, and enforced at the state and federal levels. As of 2016, the TVPA has been reauthorized 4 times since 2000. Human trafficking laws must not only lay out the criminal repercussions for committing the crime of human trafficking, but also must safeguard trafficked persons' rights and protections, while repairing the structural challenges that allow trafficking to go unseen.

Anti-trafficking NGOs may seek to affect public policy at the local, state, and federal levels, either through lobbying or grassroots advocacy. For example, the Alliance to End Slavery and Trafficking (ATEST) is a coalition of anti-trafficking NGOs dedicated to informing and implementing public policies designed to prevent and eliminate human trafficking. ATEST accomplishes this goal by regularly convening a coalition of service providers to advance shared policy priorities [4].

15.2.2.2 Direct Comprehensive Services

Likely the largest functional category for NGOs in the anti-trafficking movement involves working directly with survivors to provide the comprehensive services needed to recover and move forward. NGOs may provide one or more of these services in their mission to support and empower survivors to overcome the trauma faced; navigate the complicated legal and social service landscape in which they now find themselves; and work to build a future where they are free to pursue their own goals and dreams.

Legal Services While leaving a trafficking situation may seem like the end of a horrific experience, it is often just the beginning of a new, challenging chapter. Once out of a trafficking situation, many human trafficking survivors are thrust into complicated criminal justice and legal systems. Trafficking survivors are often called on by law enforcement to testify against their trafficker(s); may have opportunities to file civil suits; or may need legal assistance with immigration relief, custody issues, or vacating prior convictions for forced criminal activity while being trafficked.

Victim Advocacy Understanding and navigating the criminal justice system in the USA can be daunting for any individual especially one who is new to the system. This is especially true for survivors of trafficking who have likely experienced high levels of trauma, may be reluctant or fearful to testify against their trafficker, or who had prior negative experiences with the court system or authority figures. Victim advocacy programs are intended to support survivors through the entire process, which may take several years. Advocates support survivors as they meet with prosecutors; prepare them for the experience of testifying; explain the legal process; accompany them to appointments and hearings; and connect them with service referrals in the community.

Case Management Survivors of trafficking may have contact with numerous service providers, from health care practitioners to child welfare to state agencies. Case managers work with survivors to determine needs, develop goals and service plans, and provide connections to local services and resources. Survivors of trafficking often have ongoing needs, including counseling, transportation, housing placement, medical care, reliable access to food and clothing, document replacement, and crime victim compensation, among others. Case managers often serve as the central coordinator for these service needs, ensuring survivors have access to the full spectrum of available services throughout the continuum of care.

Housing Homelessness has been reported to be a leading risk factor for being trafficked [4, 5] and housing is a critical need for survivors of trafficking. And yet, stable and accessible housing continues to be one of the biggest challenges NGOs face in assisting survivors of human trafficking [6]. Communities across the country have limited bed space and even fewer in housing programs that excel in trauma-informed care and are well trained about human trafficking. When available, trafficking-specific housing programs may be able to provide emergency, transitional, or long-term housing options for survivors of trafficking. When trafficking-specific housing programs are not available, survivors may need to rely on local domestic violence shelters, homeless shelters, or general child welfare placements, which may not be fully equipped to serve trafficking survivors.

Vocational Training Employment is often a primary concern for trafficking survivors. Vocational training, when aligned with the survivor's long-term goals and skills, can be empowering; such training is critical for survivors' self-sufficiency and ability to provide for themselves and their families. Vocational training programs may also be able to assist survivors in applying for jobs and connecting with employers, and support survivors through the initial hiring process. Survivors may also seek further educational opportunities, such as General Educational Development (GED) programs or college.

Health and Mental Health Services A crucial aspect of service provision for trafficking survivors is health and mental health services. Trafficked persons are subjected to physical and psychological abuse, resulting in myriad of acute and long-term health concerns. While some survivors may have contact with health care during their trafficking situation—in fact many survivors do report some health care contact—many are denied consistent access to much needed health care [7, 8]. Trafficking survivors may suffer from medical concerns that have gone chronically untreated, may have injuries resulting from violence and assault by their traffickers, or struggle with substance use disorders [9].

In addition to physical health care, it is important for survivors to have access to mental health services, as human trafficking takes a serious psychological toll on the individual. The traumatic impact of trafficking can be quite complex and difficult for survivors to address on their own. Many survivors of both labor and sex trafficking may feel a continued connection or sense of loyalty to their trafficker, known as "trauma bonding," which can be difficult to overcome. Mental health practitioners trained in trauma-informed care can work with a survivor to help them address the resultant trauma responses. While much research has been done in the field of trauma-informed mental health treatment, there is still a paucity of research determining which behavioral health treatments are best used with human trafficking survivors and what modifications in traditional therapies are necessary.

15.2.2.3 Training and Technical Assistance

Many NGOs also serve a training and technical assistance function: In this role, trafficking-specific NGOs help raise the capacity of the community. They may provide trainings to allied professionals, first responders, and community groups to educate others on human trafficking and build skills in identifying and responding to trafficking situations. Beyond trainings, NGOs may also provide ongoing technical assistance to organizations and service-provision agencies less familiar with anti-trafficking work in the form of consultation and information sharing.

15.2.2.4 Community Organizing and Awareness

A primary function of anti-trafficking NGOs is community organizing and awareness-raising about human trafficking. For trafficked persons to reach assistance, communities must have a strong understanding of human trafficking, how to identify it, and how to respond to potential trafficking situations. NGOs, at their core, are community activators, and therefore it is natural for NGOs to play a key role in community organizing for anti-trafficking causes. NGOs may spend significant time in their communities, and inspire people to learn about trafficking, use their skills and experience to further anti-trafficking efforts, and become strong public advocates for anti-trafficking causes.

Community Awareness Anti-trafficking NGOs have always led the anti-trafficking movement in community awareness events. These awareness activities may be formal awareness campaigns targeting a particular audience to change a behavior; or they may be smaller activities meant to build relationships with specific audiences to educate them about human trafficking. Many NGOs also engage in direct outreach within at-risk communities, build rapport with potentially trafficked persons, inform trafficked individuals of their rights and the services available to them, and provide resources or services as needed.

Task Forces and Coalition Building Early in the anti-trafficking movement, human trafficking task forces and coalitions were developed to offer a platform for diverse stakeholders to come together to address human trafficking. Consisting of law enforcement, service providers, government, and NGOs, task forces became the recommended model for coordinating a community's response to human trafficking.

Most anti-trafficking task forces are co-led by an NGO and a government actor. Anti-trafficking work requires the collaboration of everyone in the community and task forces or coalitions allow for the integration of all stakeholders; identify shared priorities; and encourage sustained action towards strategic goals.

Philanthropic Mobilization NGOs also actively engage in philanthropic mobilization. Not only do NGOs activate their community to understand and identify where human trafficking may be occurring in their community, but they also encourage community members to get involved in anti-trafficking work. NGOs provide community members with the opportunity to donate their time, resources, and money to further anti-trafficking initiatives and assist survivors in rebuilding their lives.

15.2.2.5 Faith-Based Organizations

Finally, the faith-based community is a tremendous asset to the anti-trafficking field. Many faith-based communities, including Catholic, Jewish, Muslim, and Protestant communities, have spearheaded awareness campaigns, trafficking prevention programs, direct service programs, and have advocated for public policy improvements for human trafficking-related causes. Faith-based organizations have deep roots in their community and have the ability to shift culture and drive community priorities.

For survivors of trafficking, alienation from their faith community can be devastating, and having a welcoming faith community to join is an incredible asset on their recovery journey. However, survivors may not feel comfortable reaching out to a faith-based organization if they believe they may be judged for actions taken during their trafficking experience; if social services are contingent on engagement in faith-based activities; or if they cannot access comprehensive reproductive health care services. As such, faith-based organizations should work to reduce barriers to accessing assistance through their programs by partnering within their community and clarifying messaging about their programs and services.

15.2.3   Populations Served by Anti-Trafficking NGOs

Most NGOs in the anti-trafficking field have specific populations they serve. They may specialize in serving US citizen minors, foreign national labor trafficking survivors, or women and girls, for example. A smaller number of organizations are able to serve all trafficking survivor populations and these programs tend to be NGOs working solely on the issue of human trafficking. Services for trafficking survivors have expanded greatly since 2000, but there remains a need to identify underserved populations and build the infrastructure to better assist these survivors.

15.2.3.1 Foreign National Populations

Initially, the primary focus of the anti-trafficking movement was to aid foreign nationals who were trafficked within the USA. The TVPA recognized that foreign nationals were at particular risk for human trafficking due to their immigration status, unfamiliarity with US laws and customs, fear of deportation or arrest, and ineligibility for many public benefits [10]. Therefore, the TVPA created options for immigration relief and directed funding to service providers who assisted foreign national survivors.

Many of the NGOs that began to work on human trafficking already served foreign nationals and therefore had already developed the cultural competency to do this work. In fact, the trafficking in persons program at the US Department of Health and Human Services (HHS) was housed within the Office of Refugee Resettlement (ORR) until 2015. HHS provides limited funding for NGOs working with trafficking survivors. ORR also works, through the Unaccompanied Refugee Minor program, with NGOs to provide services to unaccompanied minors who experienced trafficking. Within this program, eligible minor survivors of trafficking can receive comprehensive services from NGOs across the country, including specialized, culturally competent foster care, case management, education, and financial support.

15.2.3.2 Domestic Populations

Domestic survivors of trafficking include individuals who are US citizens or Legal Permanent Residents (LPR). As the anti-trafficking movement's understanding of human trafficking expanded, it was recognized that trafficking was not just occurring within foreign national circles, but that it was affecting domestic populations as well. As such, organizations serving domestic trafficking survivors have increased over time. Many of these organizations focus primarily on serving youth populations, with the definition of "youth" varying across each organization: Some organizations only serve those under the age of 18, some serve youth up to the age of 21, and even fewer serve young people up to the age of 24.

15.2.3.3 Underserved Populations

Despite the increased attention the issue of human trafficking has seen, gaps still exist in the understanding of whom trafficking affects and this impacts communities' infrastructure development. Currently, enormous gaps persist in the identification of and assistance for survivors who are male; lesbian, gay, bisexual, of a transgender experience, or are queer/questioning (LGBTQ); or from tribal communities. Likewise, fewer specialized services exist for labor trafficking survivors in comparison to those for sex trafficking survivors.

Men and Boys Both sex and labor trafficking affect men and boys, and yet the misconception that sex trafficking only affects females and labor trafficking mainly affects males continues to thrive in the anti-trafficking movement and among lay persons. Human trafficking is a difficult crime to quantify and continues to be highly underreported. The perpetuation of gender-based stereotypes contributes to inaccurate statistics as advocates and authorities tend to see what they expect to see.

According to a 2008 John Jay College of Criminal Justice study, 50 % of sexually exploited children in New York City were male [11]. Another New York study found similar results, with 54 % of the respondents identifying as male [12]. Still, it was not until 2015, that the first anti-trafficking shelter opened to exclusively serve boys in North Carolina [13].

LGBTQ Persons Individuals who identify as lesbian, gay, bisexual, have a transgender experience, or are queer/questioning have long been underrepresented in anti-trafficking discourse. LGBTQ youth comprise a disproportionate percentage of runaway and homeless youth and face higher rates of discrimination, violence, and marginalization [14, 15]. There are organizations in the anti-trafficking movement that do serve LGBTQ survivors and there are LGBTQ organizations that understand human trafficking, but there is much work to be done across the field to ensure services, resources, and campaign materials are inclusive of all populations, regardless of gender or sexuality.

American Indian, Alaskan Native, and Native Hawaiians Tribal communities are another example of an underserved population. American Indian, Alaskan Native, and Native Hawaiian individuals are vulnerable to trafficking due to specific historical, social and structural risk factors [16]. Many Native communities face higher rates of poverty, family violence, generational trauma, and homelessness [17]. Traffickers may target Native youth who leave their communities to seek better opportunities in urban areas. Because many trafficking cases involving American Indian or Alaskan Native survivors cross tribal and non-tribal jurisdictions, it is important for NGOs who work with these populations to build strong partnerships with tribal leadership and facilitate strong collaboration between local and tribal law enforcement. Furthermore, victim advocacy and survivor service programs are needed to better serve trafficking survivors from tribal communities.

Labor Trafficking Survivors Finally, there continues to be a disproportionate amount of attention placed on sex trafficking in the USA. This imbalance may contribute to the underreporting of labor trafficking situations and the disproportionate development of anti-trafficking solutions that are designed only for sex trafficking situations. Without public outreach demonstrating that there is assistance available for workers who have been exploited, labor trafficking survivors continue to suffer without help. In some areas of the country, it can be difficult to identify NGO referrals for labor trafficking survivors, particularly if they are male. When an NGO is not readily accessible, survivors may need to move or travel long distances to receive specialized anti-trafficking assistance.

15.2.4   Funding for Anti-Trafficking Services

The services made available by NGOs are largely reliant on the funding received from donors and governmental agencies. That is to say, because most NGOs in the anti-trafficking movement are also non-profit organizations, they are dependent upon external priorities that guide what can be funded through their programs.

15.2.4.1   Funding Streams

Healthy NGOs have a diverse donor base; they take in funding from various funding streams. Some of these funding sources offer long-term, stable commitments, while others allow for more flexibility and innovation.

Government Funding Streams For much of the history of the anti-trafficking movement, the federal government provided the majority of the funding sources for anti-trafficking work, as directed by the TVPA. HHS provides grants to NGOs serving trafficking survivors, through a per capita system. In the Trafficking Victims Assistance Program, three lead service agencies [United States Conference of Catholic Bishops (USCCB), Tapestri Inc., and United States Committee for Refugees and Immigrants] that manage a network of sub-awardees are able to access financial assistance to serve survivors [18]. HHS also provides grants to NGOs in the Rescue and Restore Coalition program [19]. These NGOs are funded to raise community awareness about human trafficking, engage in capacity building, and lead coalition efforts in their community. HHS also provides funding for the National Human Trafficking Resource Center (NHTRC), the national hotline for human trafficking issues [20]. This NHTRC, operated by the NGO Polaris, offers an avenue for callers to gain information about trafficking and be connected to resources and anti-trafficking organizations in their own area.

The Office for Victims of Crime (OVC) at the Department of Justice (DOJ) also provides funding for NGOs delivering direct services to trafficking survivors [21]. Much of the OVC funding is awarded in conjunction with the Bureau of Justice Affairs (BJA), which affords funding to law enforcement entities. This collaboration is intended to ensure that law enforcement and service providers are partnering to protect survivors and hold traffickers accountable.

NGOs who serve trafficking survivors may also access more general Victims of Crime funding to support their work with survivors. Many trafficking survivors, especially US citizens and LPRs, may be able to access financial assistance through their state's crime victim compensation funds. States may also be able use portions of their Victims of Crime Act (VOCA) funds to add to or expand anti-trafficking-specific programs.

And finally, NGOs may be able to apply for government funding that is tied to special populations or projects. For example, in 2014, HHS's Administration for Children and Families supported five states' child welfare agencies to improve their response to child trafficking [22], and the Family and Youth Services Bureau financed three NGOs to provide services to domestic youth populations [23].

Foundation and Private Donation Funding Streams The second major funding source for NGOs is foundation or private donations. While the number of large-scale foundations that fund anti-trafficking work is small, the number of community foundations that are willing to fiscally support this work is increasing. Private donations may come in the form of small or large-scale gifts. These funds may be restricted, in that they can only be spent on specific activities, or they may be unrestricted, allowing greater flexibility for the NGO to allocate funds as needed.

15.2.4.2   How Funding Affects Anti-Trafficking Services

The source and format of the funding that anti-trafficking NGOs receive greatly impacts the work the NGO pursues and the services that are offered. Funding may affect anti-trafficking services in a variety of ways.

First, funding may limit the populations to be served or the services provided. Some funders may have an interest in supporting services for particular populations. For example, a community foundation that focuses on childhood education and women's interests may focus on the intersection of trafficking and youth prevention programming, or in serving female sex trafficking survivors. Notably, most anti-trafficking funding at the time of this writing is awarded to victim assistance programs rather than to other disciplines such as education and prevention programs.

The scarcity of funding for human trafficking programs makes an already competitive market space even more competitive. This complicates a community's coalition building efforts if funding is not addressed openly and strategically as part of the partnership building process. When approached in a collaborative manner, NGOs can think intentionally about how upcoming grant opportunities might best serve the needs of the community and partner or support each other in the application for various grants.

Consistent across all NGOs is the need for sustainability planning. Most funding streams, whether they are one-time gifts or multi-year grants, are time-limited. In order to avoid the disruption of opening a program, serving clients, and then abruptly closing the program when the funding cycle is over, NGOs must be proactive in creating post-grant plans.

15.3   Conclusion

The anti-trafficking movement has come a long way since the passage of the TVPA. NGOs have come together to advocate for stronger legislation on human trafficking and have conducted countless hours of community outreach and education to provide their communities with information about human trafficking, prevention techniques and efforts, and direct services. Dedicated service providers walk alongside survivors of trafficking, as they overcome horrific traumas, to build brighter futures.

15.3.1   Continued Growth

However, there is still much to accomplish. States continue to have vastly different survivor response networks, with varying degrees of quality and accessibility. NGOs continue to face fiscal challenges, particularly in building sustainable plans to appropriately support their anti-trafficking work. Persistent service challenges involve development and implementation of trauma-informed, culturally competent emergency, transitional, and long-term housing programs, health and mental health services, and substance use treatment facilities that are equipped to serve trafficked persons. The field still needs to cultivate new allies and funders who are willing to fund these programs for people victimized by *all* forms of trafficking. Male, LGBTQ, and Native survivor populations remain grossly underserved. NGOs continue to grapple with how to talk about human trafficking to the public and how to meaningfully engage survivors in shaping the future of the anti-trafficking movement.

15.3.2   Cross-Sectional Collaboration

These challenges pose opportunities for continued growth. Anti-trafficking organizations cannot eradicate human trafficking on their own; they must partner with allied professionals. As the anti-trafficking movement matures, it continues to invite others to join the discussion. NGOs working on related and upstream issues such as poverty, civil rights, homelessness, migration, discrimination, and interpersonal violence all have an integral role to play in the prevention of human trafficking.

15.3.3   Movement Building

In conclusion, the anti-trafficking movement is facing a critical time in which it must evaluate its effectiveness and chart a course forward for the field. If approached with intention and collaboration, the movement can integrate the expertise and specialization of the hundreds of engaged anti-trafficking organizations and related-issues organizations to speak with a unified voice and message. The anti-trafficking field needs to carefully balance efforts against sex trafficking and labor trafficking in all aspects of movement building to ensure that all survivors of trafficking are able to seek assistance and find safety. Ultimately, survivor engagement will be critical in the success of the anti-trafficking movement. While the movement was spurred by NGOs and individuals working on behalf of survivors, there is great potential in the expertise and advice of people who have been most closely impacted by human trafficking.

15.4 Recommendations

NGOs in the anti-trafficking movement have been instrumental in mobilizing their communities to combat human trafficking and to serve survivors. Below are five recommendations for NGOs in the anti-trafficking space.

15.4.1 Shift the Paradigm from a Criminal Justice Approach to a Public Health Focus

The TVPA outlined three paradigms needed to effectively address human trafficking: Prevention, Protection, and Prosecution. The anti-trafficking movement thus far has overwhelmingly prioritized prosecution, and to a lesser extent protection. But human trafficking will never be eradicated until we *prevent* it from occurring. This will take partnerships across all sectors to address the risk factors that are correlated with increased human trafficking incidence. By shifting the paradigm from a criminal justice approach to a public health approach, the anti-trafficking movement can more effectively understand where and why trafficking is occurring and tailor interventions that address these dynamics.

15.4.2 Increase and Diversify Funding Opportunities

In comparison to other issue areas, the human trafficking field remains severely underfunded. NGOs should educate funders about the breadth and complexity of human trafficking and how funding opportunities could be used to address gaps in service. More funding is desperately needed in the areas of housing, health, mental health, and substance use treatment programming.

15.4.3 Expand Services for Underserved Populations

NGOs should expand services for underserved populations, including those who are male, LGBTQ, Native, from rural areas and those who have been labor trafficked. When conducting a landscape analysis of a particular community, NGOs should take a broad perspective to see how current actors in the community might be able to help meet service gaps.

15.4.4 Advance Strong Community Partnerships for Success

Despite the rapid growth of anti-trafficking programs and NGOs, survivors of trafficking still fall through the cracks, unidentified. Trafficked persons may have multiple interactions with various service agencies, but due to poor infrastructure or interagency collaboration, the indicators of trafficking are not recognized. NGOs must continue to advance strong community partnerships for success. Task forces and coalitions that involve all sectors of public life are more likely to identify innovative solutions, gain buy-in for new initiatives, and reduce redundancies.

15.4.5 Evaluate Service Models and Outcomes

Because the anti-trafficking movement is such a young movement, there are few precedents for how and which services or programs should be implemented in a given setting. NGOs should prioritize the evaluation of their programs to improve effectiveness and contribute to a growing repertoire of promising and best practices.

References

1. CdeBaca L. Trafficking victims protection act: progress and promise. 2010. http://www.state.gov/j/tip/rls/rm/2010/141446.htm. Accessed 14 Mar 2016.
2. The protocol to prevent, suppress and punish trafficking in persons especially women and children, supplementing the United Nations convention against transnational organized crime, as adopted by the General Assembly on November 15, 2000. http://www.osce.org/odihr/19223?download=true. Accessed 14 Apr 2016.
3. Trafficking Victim's Protection Act (TVPA) of 2000. http://www.state.gov/j/tip/laws. Accessed 14 Apr 2016.
4. ATEST. About the alliance to end slavery and trafficking. 2016. https://endslaveryandtrafficking.org/about. Accessed 14 Apr 2016.
5. Bigelsen J, Vuotto S. Homelessness survival sex and human trafficking: as experienced by the youth of covenant house New York. 2013. http://center.serve.org/nche/downloads/cov-hs-trafficking.pdf. Accessed 14 Mar 2016.
6. Countryman-Roswurm K, Bolin B. Domestic minor sex trafficking: assessing and reducing risk. Child Adolesc Soc Work J. 2014;31:521–8. doi:10.1007/s10560-014-0336-6.
7. Chisolm-Straker M, et al. Health care and human trafficking: we are seeing the unseen. J Health Care Poor Underserved. 2016. https://preprint.press.jhu.edu/preprints/health-care-and-human-trafficking-we-are-seeing-unseen. Accessed 31 May 2016.
8. Lederer LJ, Wetzel CA. Health consequences of sex trafficking and their implications for identifying victims in healthcare facilities. Ann Health Law. 2014;23:61. http://www.global-centurion.org/wp-content/uploads/2014/08/The-Health-Consequences-of-Sex-Trafficking.pdf. Accessed 31 May 2016.
9. Chon K. Human trafficking and opiod abuse. 2016. http://www.acf.hhs.gov/blog/2016/05/human-trafficking-and-opioid-abuse. Accessed 31 May 2016.

10. USDOJ. Report on the tenth anniversary of the trafficking victims protection act. 2010. https://www.justice.gov/sites/default/files/crt/legacy/2010/12/14/tvpaanniversaryreport.pdf. Accessed 14 Mar 2016.
11. Curtis R, Terry K, Dank M, Dombrowski K, Khan B. Commercial sexual exploitation of children in New York City, Volume One: The CSEC population in New York City: size, characteristics, and needs. 2008. https://www.ncjrs.gov/pdffiles1/nij/grants/225083.pdf. Accessed 14 Apr 2016.
12. Dank M, Yahner J, Madden K, Banuelos I, Lilly Y, Ritchie A, Mora M, Conner B. Surviving the streets of New York: experiences of LGBTQ youth, YMSM, and YWSW engaged in survival sex. 2014. http://www.urban.org/research/publication/surviving-streets-new-york-experiences-lgbtq-youth-ymsm-and-ywsw-engaged-survival-sex/view/full_report. Accessed 14 Mar 2016.
13. Restore One. Why boys? 2016. https://restoreonelife.org/boys. Accessed 14 Apr 2016.
14. Cray A, Miller K, Durso LE. Seeking shelter: the experiences and unmet needs of LGBT homeless youth. 2013. https://cdn.americanprogress.org/wp-content/uploads/2013/09/LGBTHomelessYouth.pdf. Accessed 14 Apr 2016.
15. Clayton E, Krugman R, et al. Confronting commercial sexual exploitation and sex trafficking of minors in the United States: a guide for providers of victim and support services. 2013. https://www.nationalacademies.org/hmd/~/media/Files/Report%20Files/2013/Sexual-Exploitation-Sex-Trafficking/ReportGuide-VSS.pdf. Accessed 14 Apr 2016.
16. Pierce A. American Indian adolescent girls: vulnerability to sex trafficking, intervention strategies. Am Indian Alsk Native Ment Health Res. 2012;19:37–56. doi:10.5820/aian.1901.2012.37.
17. Farley M, Mattews N, Deer S, Lopez G, Stark C, Hudon E. Garden of truth: the prostitution and trafficking of native women in Minnesota. 2011. http://www.prostitutionresearch.com/pdfs/Garden_of_Truth_Final_Project_WEB.pdf. Accessed 14 Mar 2016.
18. U.S. Department of Health and Human Services. Trafficking victim assistance program. 2012. http://www.acf.hhs.gov/programs/endtrafficking/tvap. Accessed 14 Apr 2016.
19. U.S. Department of Health and Human Services. Anti-trafficking in persons programs. 2012. http://www.acf.hhs.gov/programs/endtrafficking/programs/rescue-and-restore/about. Accessed 14 Apr 2016.
20. NHTRC. About the National Human Trafficking Resource Center. 2016. http://www.traffickingresourcecenter.org. Accessed 14 Apr 2016.
21. U.S. Department of Justice, Office for Victims of Crime. Matrix of OVC/BJA-funded human trafficking services grantees and task forces. 2016. http://ovc.ncjrs.gov/humantrafficking/traffickingmatrix.html. Accessed 14 Apr 2016.
22. U.S. Department of Health and Human Services. 2015 Demonstration grants for domestic victims of severe forms of human trafficking. 2014. http://www.acf.hhs.gov/programs/fysb/resource/2015-domestic-victims-severe-trafficking . Accessed 14 Apr 2016.
23. U.S. Department of Health and Human Services. FY children's bureau discretionary grants. 2014. http://www.acf.hhs.gov/programs/cb/resource/discretionary-grant-awards-2014. Accessed 14 Apr 2016.

Chapter 16
The Role of Faith-Based Organizations in the US Anti-Trafficking Movement

Jeffrey Barrows

16.1 Introduction

The value of social services provided by the faith-based community has been estimated at $50 billion per year [1]. These services include those dedicated to survivors of human trafficking. Faith-based organizations currently provide multiple services to survivors of human trafficking, and there is evidence their influence within the anti-trafficking movement is growing [2].

As the anti-trafficking movement matures, efforts to provide effective and comprehensive services will be greatly enhanced through collaboration and coordination among all anti-trafficking organizations. The United States (US) government believes in the positive impact of collaboration and coordination, and included these principles of teamwork within the *Federal Strategic Action Plan on Services for Victims of Human Trafficking in the United States 2013–2017* [3].

Unfortunately, there is sometimes misunderstanding and contention between organizations of various faiths as well as between FBOs and secular organizations in the anti-trafficking movement [2, 4]. Ignorance about the motivation and purpose of faith-based organizations contributes to this misunderstanding. Examining the sacred texts of faiths that are major actors in the US-based anti-trafficking movement can shed light on the motivation and purpose of their anti-trafficking work. In addition, investigating the historical context of faith-based anti-trafficking efforts during the late nineteenth and early twentieth century will elucidate the commitment of FBOs to eliminate human trafficking.

Using the socioecological model as a frame, this chapter will present examples of FBOs involved in anti-trafficking work within the USA at the time of this writing.

J. Barrows (✉)
Gracehaven, Upper Arlington, OH 43220, USA
e-mail: jbarrows@gracehavenhouse.org

© Springer International Publishing AG 2017
M. Chisolm-Straker, H. Stoklosa (eds.), *Human Trafficking Is a Public Health Issue*, DOI 10.1007/978-3-319-47824-1_16

The chapter concludes by offering recommendations to further enhance synchronization and cooperation among FBOs, as the diverse faith-based community in the USA combats human trafficking.

16.1.1   Definitions

16.1.1.1   Faith-Based Organization

The use of the term *faith-based organization* (FBO), in this chapter, refers to a group of individuals organized and motivated in their work on the basis of a particular faith system.

16.1.1.2   Anti-Trafficking Organization

An *anti-trafficking organization* engages in work related to mitigating and/or abolishing human trafficking. Such groups may focus on awareness raising, prevention efforts, training professionals and advocates, advocating for policy change, and/or rehabilitation of trafficked persons, or those who purchase commercial sex products or activities.

16.1.1.3   Rehabilitation

Rehabilitation refers to the restoration of a person's ability to function emotionally, relationally, and vocationally at their maximum capacity in society on interpersonal, community, and societal levels.

16.2   Discussion

16.2.1   Sacred Writings and Their Influence on Anti-Trafficking Efforts

16.2.1.1   The Hebrew Bible's Influence on Judaic and Christian Anti-Trafficking Motivations

The Hebrew Bible[1] (HB) serves as a sacred text for Judaism and only differs from the Christian sacred text in punctuation and canonical order. While the HB does include some examples of human slavery, it, more importantly, frequently

---

[1] To maintain uniformity, the term "Hebrew Bible" will be used throughout this chapter to refer to the Judaic sacred text as well as the Christian sacred text called, The Old Testament.

references God's care of vulnerable populations that in contemporary times are recognized as being at higher risk of being trafficked. These populations are the poor, orphaned, or homeless children, and people from ethnic groups living outside their place of origin. Additionally, the HB expresses concern and explicit commands regarding how to respond to the needs of the oppressed.

The Hebrew Bible addresses these populations from two perspectives. First, the HB describes God's protection and concern for these populations.

Deuteronomy 10:18:

> He [God] doth execute justice for the fatherless and widow, and loveth the stranger, in giving him food and raiment. [Jewish Publication Society (JPS)].

The Hebrew Bible also gives various commands, from God to His people, regarding their responsibilities toward these vulnerable groups:

Deuteronomy 24:17,18:

> Thou shalt not pervert the justice due to the stranger, or to the fatherless; nor take the widow's raiment to pledge. But thou shalt remember that thou wast a bondman in Egypt, and HaShem thy G-d redeemed thee thence; therefore I command thee to do this thing. (JPS)

Psalm 82:3,4:

> Judge the poor and fatherless[2]; do justice to the afflicted and destitute. Rescue the poor and needy; deliver them out of the hand of the wicked. (JPS)

Isaiah 1:17:

> Learn to do well; seek justice, relieve the oppressed, judge the fatherless, plead for the widow. (JPS)

These passages, and others, may motivate Jewish and Christian adherents to provide assistance to vulnerable and oppressed populations, including the trafficked, and those at risk of being trafficked.

16.2.1.2 The New Testament's Influence on Christian Anti-Trafficking Motivations

In addition to the Hebrew Bible, the New Testament is also regarded as a sacred text for Christians and the two are closely connected; the New Testament teachings on social justice often refer back to the Hebrew Bible. For example, in the gospel of Luke, Jesus announces His life mission by quoting from the Hebrew Bible prophet, Isaiah.

Luke 4:17–19:

> And the scroll of the prophet Isaiah was handed to him. Unrolling it, he found the place where it is written: "The Spirit of the Lord is on me, because he has anointed me to proclaim good news to the poor. He has sent me to proclaim freedom for the prisoners and recovery of sight for the blind, to set the oppressed free, to proclaim the year of the Lord's favor. [New International Version (NIV)]

---

[2] Also translated as, "Give justice to the poor and fatherless."

In this verse, Jesus declares that helping the oppressed is a major part of His ministry.

The best-known example of Jesus teaching about human compassion for those in need is the parable of the Good Samaritan. In the story, a man from Samaria encounters a stranger, on the road from Jerusalem to Jericho, who has been beaten and robbed. Jesus uses the parable to illustrate what compassion should look like for His followers.

Luke 10:34,35:

> He went to him and bandaged his wounds, pouring on oil and wine. Then he put the man on his own donkey, brought him to an inn and took care of him. The next day he took out two denarii and gave them to the innkeeper. 'Look after him,' he said, 'and when I return, I will reimburse you for any extra expense you may have.' (NIV)

Finally, a clear command within the New Testament, that touches on human trafficking *vis-a-vis* at-risk populations, is found in the epistle of James.

James 1:27:

> Religion that God our Father accepts as pure and faultless is this: to look after orphans and widows in their distress... (NIV)

The New Testament reinforces the Hebrew Bible's instruction to render care and concern to vulnerable and oppressed populations through the teaching and example of Jesus. Christians, as followers of Jesus, may thus be inspired to participate in the US anti-trafficking movement.

16.2.1.3   The Qur'an's Influence on Muslim Anti-Trafficking Motivations

Similar to the sacred writings of the Judaic and Christian faiths, the Qur'an references human trafficking through its discussion of vulnerable populations and slavery. For instance, the following verse from the Qur'an addresses the virtuous act of freeing a slave.

The Qur'an, *Al-Baqarah* 2:177:

> ...but [true] righteousness is [in] one who believes in Allâh, the Last Day, the angels, the Book and the prophets and gives wealth, in spite of love for it,, to relatives, orphans, the needy, the traveler, those who ask [for help], and for freeing slaves... Sahih International

Further, the Qur'an admonishes its followers to fight oppression:

The Qur'an, *Al-Baqarah* 2:193:

> Fight them until there is no [more] fitnah and [until] worship is [acknowledged to be] for Allâh. But if they cease, then there is to be no aggression except against the oppressors. Sahih International

And the Qur'an warns against failure to fight oppression:

The Qur'an, *An-Nisa* 4:75:

> And what is [the matter] with you that you fight not in the cause of Allâh and [for] the oppressed among men, women, and children who say 'Our Lord, take us out of this city of oppressive people and appoint for us from Yourself a protector and appoint from Yourself a helper?' Sahih International

In fact, some Muslim religious leaders have stated that not helping the oppressed is a greater sin than causing the oppression [5]. Such direction may drive Muslims to actively engage in anti-trafficking efforts.

16.2.1.4   The Bahá'u'lláh's Influence on Bahá'í Anti-Trafficking Motivations

As with the Judaic, Christian, and Muslim faiths, the Bahá'í faith's sacred writings' discussions of slavery and vulnerable populations can be interpreted to call for anti-trafficking work. The following sacred writings prohibit slavery and encourage adherents to consider the welfare of the poor and helpless.

The Kitáb-i-Aqdas, para. 72:

> It is forbidden you to trade in slaves, be they men or women. It is not for him who is himself a servant to buy another of God's servants, and this hath been prohibited in His Holy Tablet. Thus, by His mercy, hath the commandment been recorded by the Pen of justice. Let no man exalt himself above another; all are but bondslaves before the Lord...

Tablets of Bahá'u'lláh, p. 70:

> Blessed is the ruler who succoureth the captive, and the rich one who careth for the poor, and the just one who secureth from the wrong doer the rights of the downtrodden, and happy the trustee who observeth that which the Ordainer, the Ancient of Days hath prescribed unto him.

Tablets of Bahá'u'lláh, p. 84:

> Thou must show forth that which will ensure the peace and the well-being of the miserable and the downtrodden. Gird up the loins of thine endeavour, that perchance thou mayest release the captive from his chains, and enable him to attain unto true liberty. Justice is, in this day, bewailing its plight, and Equity groaneth beneath the yoke of oppression.

These quotations from the sacred writings of the Bahá'í faith reveal that justice is an important component of Bahá'í: All human beings are considered equal before God, and therefore no one is allowed to exploit another. In addition, adherents of Bahá'í are directed to look after the welfare of vulnerable populations and work for the freedom of those who are enslaved.

16.2.2   Examples of Nineteenth and Twentieth Century Faith-Motivated Individuals and Organizational Abolitionists

This section will briefly give an overview of the impact of faith-motivated individuals and organizations on the fight against human trafficking in the USA after 1865. The vast majority of these efforts were in opposition to the sex trafficking of females, initially known as "white slavery." The faith backgrounds of the examples highlighted reflect the overall faith communities involved in the anti-trafficking movement during this era.

16.2.2.1   British and European Faith-Motivated Anti-Trafficking Activists in the Early US Anti-Trafficking Movement

The seeds of the US anti-trafficking movement were planted by the work of activists in England responding to the needs of British trafficking survivors. Josephine Butler, a woman of Christian faith, was one of the early British pioneers helping destitute women laboring in the workhouses of nineteenth century England [6]. After encountering women in the workhouses who had been forced into sexual exploitation, Butler formed the Ladies National Association for the Repeal of the Contagious Diseases Acts (LNA), which eventually became the International Abolitionist Federation (IAF) [6]. The work of these organizations rapidly spread to other countries including the USA; the LNA and IAF ignited the early US anti-trafficking movement by inspiring organizations like the Women's Christian Temperance Union to engage in the fight against sex trafficking [7].

The Salvation Army grew out of the evangelistic work of William and Catherine Booth in London and surrounding areas in the 1860s and 1870s [8]. These ardent volunteers often preached to the poor and homeless, regularly encountering and assisting sexually exploited women and girls. The work of The Salvation Army spread to the USA in 1880 with the arrival of George Railton and his seven co-missionaries [9].

In 1885, Constance Rothschild Battersea learned about the plight of sexually exploited Jewish women in London from a Christian missionary. She responded by founding the Jewish Ladies Society for Preventive and Rescue Work, which later became The Jewish Association for the Protection of Girls and Women (JAPGW) [10]. In addition to their rescue work, the JAPGW advocated within the League of Nations for an international response to the growing problem of the trafficking of women and girls for sexual exploitation [6]. These efforts inspired the US Jewish community to engage in anti-trafficking efforts.

In Europe the Catholic faith-based community responded to the growing problem of sexual exploitation of women and girls in the late 1900s by forming the International Catholic Association for the Protection of Girls (ICAPG) headquartered out of Fribourg, Switzerland [6]. The ICAPG was one of the six nongovernmental organizations to serve on the Advisory Committee on the Traffic in Women and Children (ACTWC), formed under the League of Nations in 1921 at the International Conference on White Slave Traffic. That international conference produced the 1921 International Convention for the Suppression of the Traffic in Women and Children. The Convention included an agreement among member nations to extradite traffickers and for each participating country to provide reports on their efforts to combat traffic in women and children; this Convention removed the racial emphasis of previous legislation[3] [6].

---

[3] An example of previously racialized legislation is the "White Slave Traffic Act of 1910". Text available at: http://legisworks.org/sal/36/stats/STATUTE-36-Pg825a.pdf.

16.2.2.2   Frances Willard and the Women's Christian Temperance Union

The Women's Christian Temperance Union (WCTU) was organized in 1873 in Ohio, originally to advocate against the use of alcohol. However, when the British newspaper, The Pall Mall Gazette, published an article about the white slave trade in England in 1885, Frances Willard led the WCTU to set up a "White Cross" department to focus on social purity. Under the leadership of Willard, the WCTU petitioned US state legislatures to create homes for sexually exploited women and raise the age of consent for sex. At that time, the average age of consent varied between different states and ranged from 10 to 12 years of age [11]. Later the WCTU persuaded President Theodore Roosevelt to appoint female inspectors to screen immigrants coming through Ellis Island for being trafficked into sexual exploitation [12].

16.2.2.3   The Work of the US Salvation Army

After the 1880 arrival of George Railton and his seven co-missionaries in the USA, The Salvation Army soon encountered sexually exploited women and girls, as did their counterparts in England. To respond to the multiple needs of these women and girls, the US branch of The Salvation Army opened their first rescue home, Morris Cottage, in Brooklyn, New York in 1886. In the subsequent 6 years, other similar homes were opened in Oakland, Grand Rapids, Los Angeles, and Cleveland. By the early 1900s, these homes were being called the most effective of their kind because of their design to be small, comfortable, and "homey" [9].

16.2.2.4   Sadie American and the National Council of Jewish Women (NCJW)

Sadie American co-founded the National Council of Jewish Women (NCJW) in the USA in 1893, and served as Executive Secretary until 1914 [13]. In 1906, Sadie and the NCJW established The Home for Wayward Girls on Staten Island, in New York, to assist immigrant Jewish girls who were either abducted for sexual exploitation or drawn into it through promises of legitimate marriage. In addition to establishing the home on Staten Island, Sadie and the NCJW developed a network of advocates across 250 US cities, providing advocates the names of immigrant girls coming to their cities. The advocates were to meet the young women as they arrived and offer a support network, to prevent them from becoming targets of traffickers [14]. The NCJW won recognition from women's groups across the USA and Europe. At the International White Slave Traffic Conference in Madrid in 1910, the King and Queen of Spain honored Sadie American and the NCJW for their anti-trafficking work [15].

16.2.3   Various Roles Faith-Motivated Organizations Perform in the Modern Anti-Trafficking Movement

The organizations listed within this chapter are included specifically because they are operating, within the USA, out of a motivation derived from one of several faiths. Importantly, though the motivation for these groups' anti-trafficking work is derived from their various faiths, the vast majority of faith-based organizations do not limit their work to trafficking survivors of the same religion. The organizations are arranged according to the socioecological framework, a multi-level approach to a public health problem. Please note that many organizations work at many levels, and so, in this chapter, they are categorized according to their major area of work.

16.2.3.1   Organizations Working on Policy at the Societal Level

Faith-based organizations are engaged in changing policy affecting human trafficking through legal advocacy at the local, state, and federal levels. The Tahirih Justice Center (TJC) is a Bahá'í faith-based organization named for a nineteenth century woman persecuted because of her Bahá'í faith and the TJC exemplifies this kind of legal advocacy work. The TJC works on behalf of exploited immigrant women and girls at the local and state levels through their offices in Baltimore, Washington DC, and Houston to promote the fair treatment of trafficked persons who are arrested [16].

Effective advocacy at the federal level is amplified when constituents from multiple geographic locations collaborate for a cause. The Coalition of Catholic Organizations Against Human Trafficking (CCOAHT), formed under the United States Conference of Catholic Bishops (USCCB), uses a national network of Catholic agencies to advocate for federal strategies that advance public education on raise awareness about, and promote grassroots efforts to assist survivors of trafficking [17].

Some FBOs concentrate on a specific issue within the anti-trafficking movement as a means of enhancing their federal and state advocacy. Shared Hope International (SHI) focuses on domestic minor sex trafficking (DMST), which is the terminology they developed. SHI has analyzed and graded every state's legislative efforts on DMST, providing concrete suggestions for improvement. Their legislative action center tracks bills and actions across the country, providing an excellent resource for state and local officials seeking policy change regarding DMST [18].

Advocating that businesses incorporate policies to reduce or prevent exploitation of workers is a promising practice being used by T'ruah, a faith-based organization of rabbis and cantors from all types of Judaism. T'ruah partnered with the Coalition of Immokalee Workers (CIW) to train over 60 rabbis across the country to advocate for food chain accountability [19].

Christian Brothers Investment Services (CBIS) developed a program entitled Catholic Responsible Investing (CRI) to influence the policies and practices of corporations within their investment portfolios. Using proxy ballots and filing shareholder resolutions, they persuade companies to monitor suppliers, thus reducing human trafficking within their supply chains. CBIS also advocates for policies that specifically train staff and suppliers on human trafficking; monitor and audit supply chains; and identify vulnerable workers. Companies impacted by CBIS efforts include Target, Campbell's Soup, Wyndham Worldwide, and Macy's [20].

Similarly, the Interfaith Center on Corporate Responsibility (ICCR) is a coalition of faith and values-driven organizations utilizing their influence as shareholders to mitigate human trafficking within global supply chains through advocacy, dialog, and shareholder resolutions [21]. They have developed a statement of principles and recommended practices to confront human trafficking within corporate supply chains [22]. One of their efforts impacting the agricultural sector is a shareholder resolution sent to Kroger (a retail company) requesting an assessment of human trafficking within their supply chain [23].

16.2.3.2 Organizations Working at the Community and Organizational Levels

Faith-based organizations within the anti-trafficking movement working at the community level are involved in activities such as raising awareness, prevention, demand reduction, and education. Communities may be organized locally, or may consist of adherents of the same faith from a large geographic region.

An example of a faith-based organization educating their faith community is, again, T'ruah. In addition to their partnership with the Coalition of Immokalee Workers, T'ruah has created online educational resources to empower US Jewish communities to efficiently engage in various anti-trafficking efforts at a local level. One resource is a handbook entitled "Fighting Modern-Day Slavery: A Handbook for Jewish Communities." Another online-resource is a *Haggadah* (a book to guide the Passover *seder*, or dinner) that encourages Jews to become involved in local anti-trafficking work [19].

The National Council of Jewish Women trains members to use traditional and social media to raise awareness about sex trafficking through their EXODUS initiative. As of 2016, the NCJW has enabled 79 NCJW chapters in 17 states to undertake local anti-sex trafficking efforts [24].

Some Christian denominations are engaged in the anti-trafficking movement through their member churches. At their 27th General Synod, the United Church of Christ (UCC) formally requested affiliates, to educate local members about human trafficking, empowering them in local anti-trafficking efforts [25]. As a denomination, they actively promote National Human Trafficking Awareness Day (January 11), and helped develop an online interfaith toolkit to enable member churches and groups from other faith traditions to become active in the anti-trafficking movement [26].

My Project USA is engaged in community level prevention through their Muslims Against Human Trafficking initiative, which began after the arrest of 29 gang members that sex trafficked Muslim girls [27]. They educate parents on human trafficking and encourage them to build strong families, a promising practice for prevention that harkens back to NCJW's work with immigrant girls. Additional prevention efforts by Muslims Against Human Trafficking include creating safe and productive social circles for girls within their community [28].

Exodus Cry is engaged in a unique community level intervention using a state-of-the-art facial recognition software program in partnership with law enforcement to locate missing children who are possibly being sex trafficked [29].

The Faith Alliance Against Slavery and Trafficking (FAAST), an alliance of Christian organizations, is educating the general anti-trafficking community with their *Hands that Heal* curriculum. This comprehensive, trauma-informed resource enables trafficking survivor service providers to offer appropriate and effective care, and is available in community based and academic editions [30].

Hope For Justice works with law enforcement organizations through the creation of their Tennessee Investigative Center to train and assist regional law enforcement agencies investigating cases of labor trafficking [31].

16.2.3.3   Organizations Working at the Interpersonal and Individual Level

Faith-based organizations engage in many different forms of anti-trafficking efforts at the interpersonal and individual level, including prevention and direct service. Muslims Against Human Trafficking (MAHT) mentors at-risk groups on prevention strategies. The US Conference of Catholic Bishops (USCCB) offers daylong training programs to raise awareness of human trafficking through their Amistad Movement [32]. On Eagle's Wings Ministries have a 12-lesson curriculum on how to avoid sexual exploitation through their "Youth 4 Abolition" initiative in North Carolina [33].

FBOs may engage directly with actively trafficked persons via educating trafficked individuals on the ways in which they are being exploited; making them aware of alternatives to their current situation; and fostering relationships with workers in locations where some forms of commercial sex have been legalized. For example, Eve's Angels works directly with women actively "stripping" and engaged in other commercial sex activities to facilitate their readiness to leave exploitative circumstances [34].

Another form of direct care to those transitioning out of sexual exploitation entails providing a safe place to receive services in a non-residential setting. The REACH (Restoration, Education, Activities, Community, Home) program of the Door to Grace Day Home provides educational resources, life skills training, and mentorship, in a homelike environment, during daytime hours to girls between the ages of 14 and 17 transitioning out of sexual exploitation [35].

The Tahirih Justice Center works directly with immigrant women and girls to provide expert legal services, on a *pro-bono* (free) basis, such as assistance obtaining a T-visa [16].

Case management is a critical service to survivors, who have left their trafficking scenario, and can help survivors connect to the various service providers in their area. The USCCB provides comprehensive case management to foreign-born trafficked persons through their network of direct service providers within the District of Columbia and the states of Delaware, Maryland, Pennsylvania, Virginia, West Virginia, Arkansas, Louisiana, New Mexico, Oklahoma, and Texas [32]. Faith-based organizations may form partnerships with government agencies to enhance their efforts within the anti-trafficking movement: Working closely with the juvenile court of Franklin County, Gracehaven provides specialized case management to survivors of domestic minor sex trafficking in Central Ohio [36].

Transitional housing for trafficking survivors as they exit the trafficking situation is a critical service that is generally difficult to find within the modern anti-trafficking movement. One faith-based group specializing in this type of service is Out of Darkness, operating as a ministry of the Atlanta Dream Center. They created the Solomon House, a transitional residential facility that provides housing, clothing, initial medical exams, and legal assistance for adult female survivors of sex trafficking waiting for long-term residential treatment opportunities. The average stay at the Solomon House is 3 weeks [37].

A variation of short-term transitional housing evolving within the anti-trafficking movement is medium-term residential facilities with an average stay of approximately 90 days. This type of housing enables assessment of client readiness for long-term rehabilitation so that limited resources can be used with maximum efficiency. Examples include the 90-day transitional program of The Samaritan Women [38] and the Renewed Hope House of Wellspring Living [39].

Many long-term residential rehabilitation centers for trafficking survivors are operated by faith-based organizations. Most residential treatment facilities specialize in serving a particular population of trafficking survivors, usually dedicated to services based upon survivor age and type of trafficking experienced. The majority of residential services provided by FBOs are for survivors of sex trafficking.

Covenant House provides residential treatment for homeless youth, including survivors of trafficking in multiple locations around the USA [40]. However, the majority of FBOs operate residential programs at a single location, typically born of a grassroots movement by people passionate about anti-trafficking work. These organizations usually provide multiple rehabilitative services such as mental health counseling and education programing in addition to long-term housing. Examples of FBOs providing residential treatment to survivors of commercial sexual exploitation of children include the JCCA's[4] Gateways Program [41], Gracehaven [42], Wellspring Living For Girls [43], Courage House [44], Freedom Place [45], The Living Water Center [46], and Anne's House [47].

Faith-based organizations that provide residential treatment to adult survivors of domestic sex trafficking include the Dream Center's multi-state network of homes [48], and The Samaritan Women's Restorative Program [49]. One FBO providing

---

[4]Formerly known as the "Jewish Child Care Association," the organization now simply goes by "JCCA."

long-term residential treatment in association with a unique revenue-generating, job skills program is Magdalene Homes and their social enterprise Thistle Farms [50].

While the majority of faith-based organizations in the USA have specialized in caring for survivors of sex trafficking who are US citizens, an example of an FBO specializing in adult survivors of international sex trafficking is Restore NYC's Safehome program [51].

Though most faith-based organizations providing residential treatment specialize in one particular population of trafficking survivors, there are a few exceptions that serve multiple populations. Dawn's Place, founded by several Sisters of the Archdiocese of Philadelphia, provides residential treatment to both international and domestic survivors of sex trafficking [52]. The Sisters of the Divine Savior serve adult women in their Hope House who are survivors of any form of human trafficking, regardless of whether they are US citizens or foreign-born [53].

In addition to providing crucial housing options, FBOs have historically been integral to the provision of medical care to trafficking survivors. The controversy surrounding the non-provision of comprehensive reproductive services by FBOs to trafficking survivors, exemplified by the 2011 pause of HHS funding to the USCCB for survivor services, is beyond the scope of this chapter [54]. However, it is important that this controversy not splinter the anti-trafficking movement such that current partners are transformed into adversaries. Despite differing fundamental philosophies, workers in the anti-trafficking movement may find innovative ways to comprehensively and compassionately serve trafficked persons [55].

16.3   Conclusion

16.3.1   Summary

Faith-based organizations have been involved in a variety of anti-trafficking efforts since the end of the nineteenth century. They raise awareness of modern human trafficking, engage in strategies to prevent trafficking, and advocate for legislative changes at federal, state, and local levels. FBOs provide a variety of direct services to trafficking survivors; and they respond to survivors' unique and diverse needs, undertaking novel initiatives like the development of medium-term programs to evaluate client readiness for rehabilitation. FBOs also have a unique role within the anti-trafficking movement: They are able to respond to the spiritual needs of survivors.

With such a high degree of engagement in the anti-trafficking movement, it is important to measure the impact of services provided by FBOs. One report, published in 2008, evaluating the effect of FBO-provided services to *non*-trafficked populations found that while the services were linked to beneficial outcomes, the overall evaluative research was basic, preliminary, and often not reproducible [54]. Johnson et al. further found that many FBOs had no future plans to conduct empirical studies to evaluate their effectiveness. And the investigators were unable to locate any report on FBOs work with trafficking survivors [56]. That many FBOs are small and have relatively limited financial resources may contribute to this paucity of impact studies.

Because FBOs are motivated by differing faiths, cooperation and collaboration may be hindered; even FBOs from the same faith, but of different denominations or sects, often fail to work synergistically. Insufficient collaboration of FBOs in the anti-trafficking movement is evidenced by the absence of a national association of anti-trafficking FBOs. Ineffective collaboration among anti-trafficking FBOs leads to competition for funds and recognition; programs operate in silos rather than cohesively. Working together, on a large scale, FBOs could increase knowledge, and assess and develop best practices.

Finally, significant gaps in services exist within the anti-trafficking movement because a majority of US-focused FBOs work exclusively on sex trafficking, and few dedicate their efforts to assist survivors of labor trafficking and international survivors of both sex and labor trafficking in the USA.

16.4   Recommendations

1. Faith-based organizations within the anti-trafficking movement should undertake studies to evaluate the positive and negative impacts of their work.
2. Anti-trafficking FBOs should work collaboratively with similar organizations to collate impact data and develop evidence-based best practices.
3. Faith denominations should encourage and facilitate interfaith and intrafaith collaboration among anti-trafficking FBOs.
4. New and existing US focused anti-trafficking FBOs should consider expanding their services to include those for survivors of international sex trafficking, as well as domestic and international survivors of labor trafficking.

Acknowledgment   The author would like to acknowledge Abby Brockman, for her contributions to this chapter.

References

1. Stritt SB. Estimating the value of social services provided by faith-based organizations in the United States. Nonprofit Volunt Sect Q. 2008;37(4):730–42.
2. Harrelson S. Mavericks or allies: the role of faith-based organizations in the anti-trafficking movement. In: Second annual interdisciplinary conference on human trafficking. 2010. Available online at: http://digitalcommons.unl.edu/cgi/viewcontent.cgi?article=1018&context =humtrafconf2. Accessed 12 Apr 2016.
3. Federal Strategic Action Plan on Services for Victims of Human Trafficking in the United States. 2013–2017. Available online at: http://www.ovc.gov/pubs/FederalHumanTrafficking StrategicPlan.pdf. Accessed 5 Apr 2016.
4. Purekal CL. Christianity and sex trafficking: the role of faith-based service providers in the United States. 2012. Available online at: http://conservancy.umn.edu/bitstream/handle/11299/123580/ Purekal_Christianity%20and%20Sex%20Trafficking%20The%20Role%20of%20Faith%20

Based%20Service%20Providers%20in%20the%20United%20States.pdf;sequence=1. Accessed 12 Apr 2016.

5. Al-Islam.org. The thirtieth greater sin: not helping the oppressed. 2016. http://www.al-islam. org/greater-sins-volume-2-ayatullah-sayyid-abdul-husayn-dastghaib-shirazi/thirtieth-greater-sin-not. Accessed 9 Mar 2016.

6. Limoncelli S. The politics of trafficking: the first international movement to combat the sexual exploitation of women. Stanford: Stanford University Press; 2010.

7. Mathers H. Patron saint of prostitutes: Josephine Butler and a Victorian scandal. Gloucestershire: History Press; 2014.

8. Green R. Catherine booth: a biography of the cofounder of The Salvation Army. Grand Rapids: Baker; 1996.

9. McKinley E. Marching to glory: the history of The Salvation Army in the United States 1880–1992. Grand Rapids: Eerdmans; 1995.

10. Kuzmack LG. Woman's cause: the Jewish woman's movement in England and the United States, 1881–1933. Columbus: Ohio State University Press; 1990.

11. Robertson S. Age of consent laws. 2016. https://chnm.gmu.edu/cyh/case-studies/230. Accessed 5 Apr 2016.

12. Cordasco F, Pitkin T. The white slave trade and the immigrants: a chapter in American social history. Detroit: Blaine Ethridge; 1981.

13. Encyclopedia Judaica. Sadie America. In: Jewish virtual library. 2008. http://www.jewishvirtuallibrary.org/jsource/judaica/ejud_0002_0002_0_00961.html. Accessed 10 Feb 2016.

14. Baum C, Hyman P, Michel S. The Jewish woman in America. New York: Plume; 1975.

15. Las N. White slavery. In: Jewish women: a comprehensive historical encyclopedia. 2009. Available via Jewish Women's Archive. http://jwa.org/encyclopedia/article/white-slavery. Accessed 10 Feb 2016.

16. Tahirih Justice Center. http://www.tahirih.org. Accessed 6 Apr 2016.

17. Coalition of Catholic Organizations Against Human Trafficking. http://www.usccb.org/about/anti-trafficking-program/coalition-of-catholic-organizations-against-human-trafficking.cfm. Accessed 7 Apr 2016.

18. Shared Hope International. The Legislative Action Center can be found at: http://sharedhope.org/what-we-do/bring-justice/legislative-action-center/. Accessed 7 Apr 2016.

19. T'ruah- the rabbinic call for human rights. More information is available at: http://www.truah.org/who-we-are/what-we-do.html. Accessed 7 Apr 2016.

20. CBIS. Human trafficking: the supply chain challenge. Available online at: https://cbisonline.com/us/wp-content/uploads/sites/2/2014/06/HUMAN_TRAFFIC_IR_UPDATE_v3.4.1.pdf. Accessed 6 May 2016.

21. Interfaith Center on Corporate Responsibility. Human trafficking and modern day slavery. Available at: http://www.iccr.org/our-issues/human-rights/human-trafficking-and-modern-day-slavery. Accessed 6 May 2016.

22. Interfaith Center on Corporate Responsibility. Statement of principles & recommended practices for confronting human trafficking and modern slavery. Available at: http://www.iccr.org/sites/default/files/resources_attachments/2013ICCR_HTPrinciplesFINAL112013.pdf. Access 13 May 2016.

23. Assess Human Trafficking/Forced Labor in Supply Chain. Available at: http://www.onlineethicalinvestor.org/eidb/wc.dll?eidbproc~reso~11318. Accessed 13 May 2016.

24. National Council of Jewish Women. EXODUS: NCJW's anti-sex trafficking initiative. Available at: http://my.ncjw.org/trafficking. Accessed 7 Apr 2016.

25. United Church of Christ. Human trafficking. http://www.ucc.org/justice_womens-issues_human-trafficking. Accessed 8 Apr 2016.

26. Washington Inter-Religious Staff Community Working Group on Human Trafficking. Interfaith toolkit on human trafficking. 2016. Available for download at: http://www.uccfiles.com/Interfaith-Toolkit-on-Human-Trafficking-2016.pdf. Accessed 8 Apr 2016.

27. MPR News. Indictment: Somali gangs ran sex ring in 3 states. Available at: http://www.mprnews.org/story/2010/11/08/somali-prostitution-ring. Accessed 5 May 2016.

28. MY Project USA. http://www.myprojectusa.org. Accessed 7 Apr 2016.
29. Exodus Cry. What is intervention? http://exoduscry.com/intervention/. Accessed 7 Apr 2016.
30. A preview of each edition is available at: http://faastinternational.org/hands-that-heal. Accessed 7 Apr 2016.
31. Hope For Justice. http://hopeforjustice.org/united-states-of-america/ Accessed 8 Apr 2016.
32. United States Conference of Catholic Bishops. The Amistad Movement. http://www.usccb.org/about/anti-trafficking-program/amistad.cfm. Accessed 8 Apr 2016.
33. On Eagles Wings. Youth 4 Abolition. http://www.youth4abolition.com. Accessed 8 Apr 2016.
34. Eve's Angels. http://www.evesangels.org. Accessed 8 Apr 2016.
35. Door to Grace. Door to Grace Day Home & REACH program. http://www.doortograce.org/our-program/. Accessed 9 Apr 2016.
36. Gracehaven. Survivor care and support. http://www.gracehavenhouse.org. Accessed 8 Apr 2016.
37. Out of Darkness. Solomon House. http://outofdarkness.org/restore/. Accessed 9 Apr 2016.
38. The Samaritan Women. Transitional program. http://thesamaritanwomen.org/transitional-program/. Accessed 9 Apr 2016.
39. Wellspring Living. Renewed Hope House. http://wellspringliving.org/renewedhopehouse/. Accessed 9 Apr 2016.
40. Covenant House. https://www.covenanthouse.org/homeless-teen-issues/human-trafficking. Accessed 9 Apr 2016.
41. JCCA. Gateways program for commercially sexually exploited children. http://www.jccany.org/site/PageServer?pagename=programs_cottage_splash. Accessed 9 Apr 2016.
42. Gracehaven. Residential House. http://www.gracehavenhouse.org. Accessed 9 Apr 2016.
43. Wellspring Living. Wellspring Living for Girls. http://wellspringliving.org/wellspring-living-for-girls/. Accessed 9 Apr 2016.
44. Courage Worldwide. Courage House. http://courageworldwide.org/courage-house/. Accessed 9 Apr 2016.
45. Arrow. Child sex trafficking recovery/freedom place. http://www.arrow.org/services-programs/residential-services/freedom-place/. Accessed 9 Apr 2016.
46. Circle of Friends. The Living Water Center. http://www.cofcl.org/the-living-water-center/. Accessed 9 Apr 2016.
47. The Salvation Army. Promise: partnership to rescue our minors from sexual exploitation-Anne's House. http://www.sapromise.org. Accessed 9 Apr 2016.
48. The Dream Center. Dream center network members. http://www.thedcnetwork.org. Accessed 9 Apr 2016.
49. The Samaritan Women. Restorative Program. http://thesamaritanwomen.org/restorative-program/. Accessed 9 Apr 2016.
50. Thistle Farms. http://thistlefarms.org. Accessed 9 Apr 2016.
51. Restore NYC. Safehome Program. http://restorenyc.org/our-work/safehome-program/. Accessed 9 Apr 2016.
52. Dawn's Place. http://www.ahomefordawn.org. Accessed 9 Apr 2016.
53. Sisters of the Divine Savior. Hope House. http://www.stopenslavement.org/sdshopehouse.html. Accessed 9 Apr 2016.
54. Winn P. HHS Withholds Grant from U.S. Conference of Catholic Bishops Apparently Because Church Opposes Abortion. CNS News. Available online at: http://cnsnews.com/news/article/hhs-withholds-grant-us-conference-catholic-bishops-apparently-because-church-opposes. Accessed 25 May 2016.
55. Human Trafficking and Reproductive Rights. Freedom Network USA. April 2015. http://freedomnetworkusa.org/wp-content/uploads/2012/05/FINAL-April-2015-HT-and--Reproductive-Rights.pdf. Accessed 22 May 2016.
56. Johnson BR, Tompkins RB, Webb D. Objective hope: assessing the effectiveness of faith-based organizations – a review of the literature. 2008. Available online at: http://www.baylor.edu/content/services/document.php/24809.pdf. Accessed 12 Apr 2016.

Chapter 17
Research Informing Advocacy: An Anti-Human Trafficking Tool

Cathy L. Miller and Michelle Lyman

17.1 Introduction

This chapter will explore the role of research as an anti-trafficking advocacy tool by summarizing public health research that has guided US policy on trafficking in persons (TIP). TIP has been recognized as a pandemic and global public health problem [1, 2] and is a criminal enterprise that capitalizes on the social, political, ethnic, religious, economic, and other vulnerabilities of an individual or population. The violation of the basic human right to freedom and subsequent abuses results in enormous adverse consequences to the trafficked person, community, and society at large [3].

The Office of Trafficking in Persons (OTIP) within the United States Department of Health and Human Services (HHS) notes that recognizing TIP as a public health issue informs which professionals intervene and engage with survivors and in what ways. Such framing also affects how institutions and systems confront entrenched cultural norms around power, equity, gender, and consumer behavior, to advance the health and well-being of trafficked persons [4]. Recognizing TIP as a public health issue increases the urgency and demand for expanded rigorous research [4] on the prevention of trafficking and the provision of trauma informed care.

The original version of this chapter was revised. An erratum to this chapter can be found at DOI: 10.1007/978-3-319-47824-1_25

C.L. Miller (✉)
Texas A&M University-Corpus Christi, College of Nursing and Health Sciences,
6300 Ocean Drive, Island Hall 328G, Corpus Christi, TX 78412, USA
e-mail: cathy.miller@tamucc.edu

M. Lyman
University of South Florida, Morsani College of Medicine,
12901 Bruce B. Downs Boulevard, Tampa, FL 33612, USA

© Springer International Publishing AG 2017
M. Chisolm-Straker, H. Stoklosa (eds.), *Human Trafficking Is a Public Health Issue*, DOI 10.1007/978-3-319-47824-1_17

17.1.1 Research Overview

Public health research is a systematic investigation, including research development, testing, and evaluation, designed to develop or contribute to generalizable knowledge concerned with public health [5]. There are many methodological approaches to research: The two basic methodologies are *quantitative* investigation, which tests hypotheses and is concerned with numerical data; and *qualitative* examination, which is interpretative, exploratory, and designed to understand the lived experiences of research participants regarding the phenomenon of interest. *Mixed-methods* research combines both quantitative and qualitative inquiry and is gaining popularity in health-related disciplines. The increasing esteem of mixed-methods research can be attributed to public health professionals' understanding that neither form of research independently presents a holistic picture of the issue of concern. Qualitative data informs and gives a voice to the statistical and epidemiological findings of quantitative efforts [6].

17.1.2 Research as an Advocacy Tool

Advocacy is defined as the act or process of supporting a cause or proposal [7]. TIP and its public health ramifications engender a desire in many to be abolitionists, raise awareness, contribute time and/or money to anti-trafficking organizations, and lobby legislatures, among other advocacy efforts. Research is a powerful tool in the anti-human trafficking tool belt, which lays an objective evidence foundation for other anti-trafficking efforts. In November of 2015 the American Public Health Association (APHA) adopted its first official position on human trafficking: *Expanding and Coordinating Human Trafficking-Related Public Health Research, Evaluation, Education, and Prevention* [8]. The policy statement was conceptualized and written by a team of clinicians and scholars from HEAL (Health, Education, Advocacy, and Linkages) Trafficking, utilizing the best available research to support the need to recognize trafficking in persons as a public health issue in the USA. The APHA policy statement calls for greater use of rigorous research in informing advocacy efforts.

High-quality research can spur and inform legislative and institutional action, yield dedicated funding and resources from private, state, and federal sources, and guide the prevention and intervention efforts of anti-trafficking stakeholders. Public health research has the potential to not only advance anti-trafficking public policy and legislative actions, but also improve the lives of trafficking survivors.

17.2 Discussion

17.2.1 Historical Evolution of Research and Policy in Human Trafficking and Public Health

In historical terms, the study of TIP is in its infancy with great strides made between the 1990s and 2016. Though human trafficking has existed for centuries, research for the purpose of extinguishing trafficking began in the 1990s; health specific inquiries began in 2003. Starting in 1994 with the International Organization for Migration's (IOM) International Responses to Trafficking in Migrants and the Safeguarding of Migrant's Rights Conference [9], there was an increase of investigations into the trends in human trafficking. Initial investigations explored the extent of trafficking as well as what qualified as trafficking. An international definition was sought for collaboration across borders in studying and stopping acts of human trafficking [9].

In the late 1990s and early 2000s organizations such as the International Labour Organization (ILO), United Nations Children's Rights and Emergency Relief Organization (UNICEF), and the IOM led research and policy formation on human trafficking [10]. With the increase in general research on trafficking came the development of new policies to protect trafficked persons and help with the prosecution of traffickers. Data from these studies were and continue to be used to shape guidelines on best practices and inform lawmakers on the needs of trafficked persons and survivors. In 2000, the United Nations (UN) General Assembly adopted the UN Protocol to Prevent, Suppress, and Punish Trafficking in Persons [11], which solidified definitions of trafficking and essential policies for state members. Also in 2000, the USA formalized its definitions of and planned approach to combatting trafficking with the adoption of the Trafficking Victims Protection Act (TVPA) [12]. Together, these policies carved a path for research into the scale and extent of trafficking.

In 2003, the sentinel exploration of trafficking through a public health lens, *The Health Risks and Consequences of Trafficking in Women and Adolescents: Findings from a European Study* [13], was published. Zimmerman and colleagues documented the common physical and mental health conditions that contributed to and were elicited by trafficking among survivors interviewed (see Table 17.1).

The findings illustrated not only health patterns of trafficking, but also detailed them in each stage of the process. The 2003 study provided qualitative details on trafficking as well as categorized the trafficking process for further examination and more precise understanding of physical and mental health consequences, and the mechanisms of trafficking. This publication, along with the guidelines produced in collaboration with the World Health Organization's (WHO), *Ethical and Safety Recommendations for Interviewing Trafficked Women* [14], opened the doors for subsequent publications reviewing the health conditions associated with trafficking in other populations and geographic areas. Further, research by Zimmerman and other scholars catalyzed the creation of guidelines and publications such as *Caring*

Table 17.1 Abuse, health risks, and potential health consequences associated with human trafficking

Examples of forms of abuse or risk	Examples of potential health consequences
Psychological abuses: intimidation of individuals and threats against loved ones, threats with weapons; lies, deception, blackmail to coerce individuals to remain and discourage seeking help from authorities; unsafe, unpredictable, uncontrollable events, and environment; isolation and forced dependency (see "social restrictions" below)	*Mental health:* suicidal ideation, self-harm, suicide; post-trauma symptoms and syndromes (Post-Traumatic Stress Disorder, depression); somatic complaints; immune suppression; sleep disturbances, including frequent nightmares; memory loss, dissociation, and cognition problems; aggressive behavior, irritability, violent outbursts
Physical abuses: murder, torture (e.g.: cigarette burns, suspension), physical attacks with or without weapon; deprivation (sleep, food, light, and other basic necessities); confinement, physical restraint (rope, chain); withholding medical or other essential care	*Physical health:* death, acute injuries, or chronic physical pain (due to contusions, head/ neck trauma, musculoskeletal damage, for example); physical disabilities (e.g.: nerve or bone damage, dental problems); fatigue, exhaustion, poor nutrition, malnutrition, starvation, pesticide poisoning, asthma; deterioration of pre-existing conditions leading to disability or death
Sexual abuses: forced and coerced sex (vaginal and anal) and gang rape; forced prostitution or sexual exploitation (often with no control of number or type of clients); limited access to sexual or reproductive health products and care (e.g.: condoms, oral family planning); sexual humiliation, forced nakedness, forced pornography; coerced misuse of oral contraceptives or other contraceptive methods	*Sexual and reproductive health:* sexually transmitted infections, including HIV/AIDS, and related complications; reproductive or sexual health complications (urinary tract or kidney infections); acute or chronic pain during sex, tearing, and other damage to vaginal tract or anus; unwanted pregnancy, forced or unsafe termination of pregnancy, complications from unsafe terminations

Forced and coerced substance use: non-consensual administering and coercive use of alcohol, drugs, or other substance in order to: control activities, coerce compliance, decrease self-protection, prevent escape; impose long work hours or greater productivity	*Substance use or misuse:* drug or alcohol use disorders, overdose, self-harm; participation in high-risk activities (e.g.: unprotected sex, dangerous labor crime); needle-introduced infection (HIV hepatitis B. hepatitisC), multi-organ damage; sleep problems (e.g.: insomnia, lethargy), negative coping behaviors, smoking, risk-taking, isolation
Social restrictions and manipulation: restriction of movement and activities (e.g.: confinement, surveillance, scheduling); restriction of interpersonal contact (e.g.: friends, family, ethnic or religious community); favoritism to cause divisiveness between co-workers; denial or control of access to information, health, and other services	*Social health consequences of social abuses:* feelings of isolation, loneliness, helplessness; shame, guilt, loss of self-esteem; mistrust of others, social withdrawal, difficulty developing healthy relationships; re-trafficking, re-entry into high-risk conditions
Economic exploitation and debt-bondage: indentured servitude resulting from inflated debt, resale of individuals or debt; usurious charges/deceptive accounting (e.g.: for travel documents, housing, food, clothing, condoms, health care); money-related punishment for perceived misbehavior, escape attempts; overwork to meet payment demands	*Finance-related problems:* inability to afford basic hygiene, nutrition, safe housing, medical care; heightened vulnerability to infections, work-related injuries; dangerous self-medication or foregoing of medication; rejection by family for not sending or returning with money

(continued)

Table 17.1 (continued)

Examples of forms of abuse or risk	Examples of potential health consequences
Legal insecurity: confiscation of passports, travel, and other vital documents; threats to expose individuals' undocumented status to authorities; concealment of individual's documentation status from the individual; fears that health providers will require identity documents or will report to authorities; restrictive immigration employment laws	*Legal and security problems:* acceptance of dangerous travel and work conditions and obedience to traffickers/employers; arrest, detention, long periods in immigration detention centers or prisons, unhygienic and unsafe detention conditions; difficulty obtaining or denial of health treatment from public clinics and other medical services; traumatic reactions resulting from interrogation or participation in a criminal investigation or asylum proceeding; unsafe deportation or return, risk of re-trafficking and retribution
Occupational hazards and abusive working and living conditions: abusive work hours, practices; dangerous work and living conditions (including unhygienic, overcrowded, or poorly ventilated spaces); poor equipment or machinery training and language barriers; no personal protective equipment; repetitive work motions without rest; quota-related penalties and punishment; exposure to harsh environmental conditions (heat, cold, ocean-water)	*Occupational injuries and disease:* exhaustion and poor nutrition; bacterial and other infections communicable diseases; dermatological infections, chemical burns, rash; injury, including limb amputation, abrasions, lacerations; repetitive motion syndromes; musculoskeletal injury; hypothermia, heat exhaustion, dehydration, starvation

Table provided courtesy of Dr. Cathy Zimmerman

for Trafficked Persons: Guidance for Health Providers [15], Hossain and colleagues' *Recommendations for Reproductive and Sexual Health Care of Trafficked Women in Ukraine: Focus on STI/RTI care* [16], and the IOM's 2004 *The Mental Health Aspects of Trafficking in Human Beings: A set of minimum standards* [17].

With increased understanding and interest in TIP, researchers in the public health sector started investigating the broader health patterns among survivors as a means to promote improved identification and care of trafficked persons by health care practitioners. The TVPA Reauthorization in 2005 reflected public health findings regarding the health and wellness of trafficked persons and survivors, featuring pilot programs aiding survivor-minors and a $5 million pilot program for the treatment of trafficked persons abroad [18]. *Turning Pain into Power: Trafficking Survivors' Perspectives on Early Intervention Strategies* was the first US report outlining the potential for clinician intervention and need for health care programs for survivors [19]. Adding to the previous evidence that trafficked persons incur numerous health risks, this study revealed that trafficked persons interacted with health care professionals during their trafficking experience. The report pointed to these interactions as a potential source for intervention and care citing the need for identification tools and resources, such as the Health and Human Services' anti-trafficking education program and toolkit, *Rescue & Restore*.

During that same year another form of health advocacy emerged with the creation of a landmark healthcare facility, Saban Free Clinic in Los Angeles, California. Created by the Coalition to Abolish Slavery and Trafficking (CAST) and run by Susie Baldwin, MD, MPH, the clinic provided primary care to trafficked persons from 2005 to 2011 [20]. Through those years of service to this population, Baldwin studied the health needs of trafficked patients as well as the most effective types of health services. This review of care included the quality of cultural competency and specific training on trafficking and trauma that staff members received.

In 2008 the IOM, UNODC, and ILO collaborated during a two day research meeting through the UN Global Initiative to Fight Human Trafficking (UN GIFT). Findings from the meeting highlighted the gaps and challenges that existed within human trafficking research [21]. Criticism from trafficking research from the late 1990s and early 2000s centered on the lack of standardization of research methods, creating difficulties in international comparisons; disparities in the ability to accurately gauge the extent of trafficking patterns; and an excessive focus on the supply side of trafficking [9, 21]. These difficulties were compounded by the elusive nature of trafficking, and trafficked persons' and survivors' fear of disclosure making random sampling difficult [22]. Additionally, trafficking research did not reflect the actual representation of trafficked populations, with many studies on women and girls who are sex trafficked, despite the fact that men and boys, and labor trafficked individuals comprise a large proportion of trafficking survivors [22].

Another criticism of trafficking research during this period was a lack of critical evaluation of the resources and services provided to trafficked persons and survivors. In 2007 the US Department of Justice released a three-phase evaluation to determine trafficking services' effectiveness [23]. The study reviewed the sustainability, development, and implementation of the respective initiatives of eight programs and the satisfaction of survivors using them. The Department of Justice (DOJ) additionally measured the degree of access and community outreach in the field, outlined organization models, and suggested answers to common obstacles in the field. One-on-one interviews with survivors revealed that clinical care for trafficked persons should be survivor-centered. That is to say, services and care must be informed by the feedback and collaboration of those who benefit from them.

Federal policy during this time period included the US 2008 Reauthorization Act also known as the William Wilberforce TVPRA. While largely extending protections afforded by the T visa[1] and expanding the definition of trafficking, the law also included initiatives for research and awareness [18]. The law calls for a mechanism for quantifying the extent of trafficking, specifically naming the need for an integrated database within the Human Smuggling and Trafficking Center [24]. New requirements also included actions to increase the awareness of trafficking risks among all individuals applying for work and/or education visas.

Since 2005, the increased quantity and diversity of descriptive research concerned with the mental and physical health needs of trafficked persons has led to advancements in care for trafficking survivors. Further, this research has improved education for health care providers on the provision of comprehensive, holistic, culturally competent, and trauma informed health care for trafficked persons. Additional important findings include, the population's needs for acute and long-term comprehensive physical and mental health care, enabling services, and the efficacy of clinician training. Other reviews investigated the very assessment tools that are employed to assess mental health for TIP research [25]. Public health trafficking research has exploded with many more articles on topics ranging from country-specific trafficking patterns to trends in the mental health needs of and effective treatment modalities for trafficked persons [26]. Mental health and its treatment in the context of the complex trauma[2] resulting from trafficking has become more nuanced [27]. In particular, the paradigm of trauma informed care (TIC)[3] has emerged as critical, with interviews with and experiences of trafficked persons informing these practices. For example, TIC has been included in the recommendations of McNiel and colleagues in *Creating an interdisciplinary medical home for survivors of human trafficking* [28] and the best practices identified by Cole and company in *Sex Trafficking of Minors in Metropolitan, Micropolitan, and Rural Communities* [29].

This increase in understanding of the health needs of trafficking survivors has highlighted the need for training of health care professionals on the topic. Depending on the sample represented, studies have demonstrated 28 % to as much as 100 % of trafficked persons have sought health services at least once while under the influence of trafficker [30–33]. These inquiries have also illuminated the paucity of systematic training and the lack of uniformity among the existing education models [3,

---

[1] A type of visa providing legal status to foreign-born trafficked persons.

[2] Complex trauma is the experience of multiple and/or chronic and prolonged developmentally adverse traumatic events, often of an interpersonal nature [29].

[3] Trauma informed care is the systemic approach that realizes, recognizes, and responds to trauma, in addition to seeking to avoid re-traumatization for patients and providers [29].

34]. Publications have recognized the roles of clinicians in a variety of fields ranging from psychiatry, school nursing, emergency medicine, pediatrics, to dentistry [35–38].

The 2013 TVP Reauthorization Act was part of a Violence Against Women Act amendment and created an emergency response policy to guide federal assistance to vulnerable populations at risk of TIP during humanitarian emergencies and post-conflict situations to prevent the trafficking of susceptible people [39]. The law also outlined collaboration between state and local law enforcement for increased efficiency in prosecuting traffickers [18]. The *2013–2017 Federal Strategic Action Plan on Services for Victims of Human Trafficking in the United States* marked another important milestone in federal policy for the public health response to trafficking. The S.O.A.R. (Stop. Observe. Ask. Respond to Human Trafficking) training, a HHS initiative, was an important byproduct of the strategic action plan. First piloted in 2015 and with an expected release in 2016, S.O.A.R. provides uniform human trafficking training for a spectrum of health care professionals. Other examples of clinician education programs include Polaris's webinar training for health care providers, Shared Hope International's (SHI) First Response program, and the IOM Caring for Trafficked Person's program.

One of the most recent studies on health education and trafficking compiles expertise across multiple disciplines into a framework for the education of health care providers (HCPs). This investigation of best practices led to the development of a tool for standardizing interdisciplinary training for clinicians learning to identify, assess, and care for trafficked persons [30]. The quality and validity of developed HCP education programs, along with screening tools for patient identification, are still evolving. High-quality HCP education should train clinicians on labor and sex trafficking and requires well-trained presenters—preferably medical professionals—and should be survivor-informed, evidence-based, and peer-reviewed. Evaluation should not only focus on knowledge retention, but also on clinician behavior change, and improved patient outcomes.

As research advances and gaps in knowledge are addressed, our understanding of the complexity of the TIP experience increases. Each of the four reauthorizations of TVPA reflects the growing body of research on TIP through refined policy that aids in the reintegration and integration of trafficking survivors.[4] Moreover, early research on the health patterns of TIP informs the contemporary HCP education practices being evaluated and the clinical care provided to survivors.

Done well, research and anti-trafficking legislation form a symbiotic relationship with research informing policy, and policy facilitating high-quality research. As interest in eliminating TIP and delivering quality care to trafficked persons increased with awareness in the early 2000s, TIP research increased. Likewise new policies were formed and revised with new evidence. Table 17.2 outlines the timeline for the pivotal public health-related research and policies discussed in this section.

---

[4] Reintegration and integration both refer to a person entering fully into the cultural, civil, and political life in their country of origin or to their new country, respectively.

Table 17.2 Human trafficking research and legislation

	Research	Policy
1994–1999	*1994*: International Organization for Migration's International Responses to Trafficking in Migrants and the Safeguarding of Migrant's Rights Conference [9]	
2000–2005	*2003*: *The Health Risks and Consequences of Trafficking in Women and Adolescents: Findings from a European Study* [13]	*2000*: Victims of Trafficking and Violence Protection Act (TPVA), Palermo Protocol, and UN Protocol to Prevent, Suppress and Punish Trafficking in Persons *2003*: TPV Reauthorization Act (TVPRA) Prosecutorial Remedies and Other Tools to End the Exploitation of Children Today (PROTECT) Act
2006–2010	*2007*: Evaluation Of Comprehensive Services For Victims Of Human Trafficking: Key Findings And Lessons Learned [23]	*2005*: TPVRA *2008*: TPVRA
2011–2016	*2012*: Recommendations for HCP in specific fields (e.g., emergency medicine [37]) *2013*: Review of existing anti-trafficking medical education [34] *2014*: Comprehensive healthcare services for survivors [4, 28] *2016*: Evidence-based standards on developing anti-trafficking medical education [30] Evaluation of research and assessment tools [25]	*2010*: American Nurses Association (ANA) TIP Policy Statement *2011*: American College of Obstetricians and Gynecologist (ACOG) Committee Opinion on Human Trafficking *2013*: TPV Reauthorization Act and National Defense Authorization Act *2013–2017*: Federal Strategic Action Plan on Services for Victims of Human Trafficking in the United States *2014*: Stop. Observe. Ask. Respond to Human Trafficking HHS Training Program *2015*: American Public Health Association's policy—Public health approach to human trafficking

17.3 Conclusion

Rigorous TIP research is a powerful tool to support and inform advocacy efforts, and ultimately shape policy. In this chapter, we have shown that the evolution of research on TIP and public health has informed and should continue to drive the development of evidence-based policy, service provider education, legislation, and funding. The continued pursuit of knowledge to address current gaps in understanding and to best serve those vulnerable and trafficked must continue to fuel anti-trafficking efforts across disciplines. Policy makers must take a proactive stance, drawing on the latest evidence to produce policies addressing the multitude of TIP vulnerabilities, cultural variables, and potential mental and physical health outcomes, to form a comprehensive approach to prevention, recognition, intervention, and longitudinal survivor services.

17.4 Recommendations

17.4.1 Public Health Research to Inform Anti-Trafficking Policy

As previously noted, there are significant gaps in knowledge about TIP. To date, the majority of human trafficking research has focused on the criminal justice response to trafficking, and specific populations, such as women and girls, and sex trafficking. Funding bodies including, but not limited to local, state, and federal governing bodies, philanthropic organizations and individuals, and institutes of higher learning are encouraged to support public health research with a focus on prevention that uses the socio-ecological framework.

Current gaps in research include:

- *Prevention and health care needs of labor trafficking survivors and marginalized populations* vulnerable to trafficking including, but not limited to, runaway, "throwaway," or otherwise homeless youth; those identifying as lesbian, gay, bisexual, transgender-experienced, or questioning (LGBTQ); immigrants, and refugees; non-white racial and ethnic groups; and the intellectually or physically disabled. A proactive, socio-ecologically grounded research agenda for these vulnerable populations have the potential to develop preventative measures and interventions to stop the cycle of vulnerability, violence, and victimization.
- *Effective methodologies for quantifying the scope and magnitude of the problem.* There have been tremendous efforts to address challenges in methodology; [40] still, procedural obstacles in enumerating those trafficked include a lack of standardized data collection and tracking, and poor interagency information sharing across government and non-government (NGO) agencies engaged in anti-trafficking efforts [40].

Fig. 17.1 Understanding
human trafficking in
relation to other forms of
abuse and/or exploitation

- *Utilization of Community-Based Participatory Research (CBPR) and Individual Community Needs Assessment (CNA) studies.* Just as each trafficked person has a different history and experience; each community is different. Each community has its own strengths, challenges, resources, political structure, and cultural norms, which should be explored and better understood.
- *Immediate and longitudinal mental and physical health outcomes of families of trafficked persons, including their children.* Human trafficking affects communities, not just those trafficked. Time, energy, and resources must be devoted to understanding the long-term effects of trafficking beyond the individuals directly impacted.
- *Quantification of the adverse societal and economic outcomes associated with TIP* such as uncompensated health care, incarceration costs, and resource utilization. Funds for any government, organization, or service provider are finite. Quantifying, to the best of our ability, expenditures will empower stakeholders to allocate resources where most needed and incentivize actors to streamline processes.
- *Efficacy of reintegration tools* including but not limited to enabling services, and educational needs, child care, employment, and long-term mental and physical health care.
- *A broader understanding of migration when exploring foreign national trafficking health needs* [40]. Researchers should include recruitment, travel-transit, exploitation, reintegration, and the subsequent marginalization and stigmatization, which occur across geographic and socioeconomic boundaries, into the understanding of TIP. Drawing on interventions that have proven effective with other vulnerable populations such as those experiencing child maltreatment, intimate partner violence, sexual violence, and gang violence may be helpful [41, 42] (see Fig. 17.1).

- *Implementation and evaluation of mentoring programs.* Use and assessment of these programs can help determine the effectiveness of mentoring as a trafficking prevention tool and a way to increase reintegration success for trafficked persons. The Department of Justice (DOJ) has been a leader in supporting mentoring programs for trafficked persons and those at high risk for trafficking. The additional focus on those at risk for victimization exemplifies a focus on prevention.
- *Multidisciplinary, organization-sponsored research to address the identified gaps in clinician training and health system protocols* on human trafficking identification, care, and response. Clinicians do not work in silos; rather they serve patients and communities as a team, working across specialties to provide health care. More information is needed about how to effectively train clinical teams in the service of trafficked persons, successfully implement protocols, and ultimately understand the impact on survivor outcomes.

References

1. De Chesnay M, editor. Sex trafficking: a clinical guide for nurses. New York: Springer; 2013.
2. Dovydaitis T. Human trafficking: the role of the health care provider. J Midwifery Womens Health. 2010;55(5):462–7.
3. Stoklosa H, Grace AM, Littenberg N. Medical education on human trafficking. JAMA Ethics. 2015;17(10):914–21. doi:10.1001/journalofethics.2015.17.10.medu1-1510.
4. United States Department of Health & Human Services Office on Trafficking in Persons. The power of framing human trafficking as a public health issue. 2016. Retrieved from http://www.acf.hhs.gov/programs/endtrafficking/resource/publichealthlens. Accessed 25 May 2016.
5. Centers for Disease Control. Distinguishing public health research and public health non research. 2010. Retrieved from http://www.cdc.gov/od/science/integrity/docs/cdc-policy-distinguishing-public-health-research-nonresearch.pdf. Accessed 25 May 2016.
6. Streubert HJ, Carpenter DR. Qualitative research in nursing: advancing the humanistic imperative. 5th ed. Philadelphia: Wolters Kluwer Health/Lippincott Williams & Wilkins; 2011.
7. Merriam-Webster. Online. n.d. Web. Accessed 25 May 2016.
8. Chisolm-Straker M, Alter H, Atkinson H, Losonczy L, Miller C, Stoklosa H. Expanding and coordinating human trafficking-related public health research, evaluation, education, and prevention. APHA Policy Statement. 3 November 2015. Available at: http://apha.org/policies-and-advocacy/public-health-policy-statements/policy-database?q=trafficking&y=2015. Accessed 15 Aug 2016.
9. Laczko F. Data and research on human trafficking. Int Migr. 2005;43:1–16.
10. Gozdziak EM, Collett EA. Research on human trafficking in North America: a review of literature. Int Migr. 2005;43:99–128.
11. United Nations. Protocol to prevent, suppress and punish trafficking in persons, especially women and children, supplementing the United Nations convention against transnational organized crime. 2000.
12. United States Department of Health & Human Services Office on Trafficking in Persons. The power of framing human trafficking as a public health issue. 2016. Retrieved from http://www.acf.hhs.gov/programs/endtrafficking/resource/publichealthlens. Accessed 25 May 2016.
13. Zimmerman C. The health risks and consequences of trafficking in women and adolescents: findings from a European study. Trans R Soc Trop Med Hyg. 2003. http://www.lshtm.ac.uk/php/ghd/docs/traffickingfinal.pdf. Accessed 1 Aug 2016.

14. Zimmerman C, Watts C. World Health Organization ethical and safety recommendations for interviewing trafficked women. Geneva: World Health Organization; 2003.
15. International Organization for Migration (IOM). Caring for trafficked persons: guidance for health providers. Geneva: International Organization for Migration; 2009.
16. Hossain M, Zimmerman C, Hawkes S, Watts C. Recommendations for the reproductive & sexual health care of trafficked women in Ukraine: focus on STI/RTI care. 1st ed. Trans R Soc Trop Med Hyg (London) and Int Migr. 2005.
17. Baráth Á, International Organization for Migration. The mental health aspects of trafficking in human beings: a set of minimum standards. Budapest: International Organization for Migration; 2004.
18. Polaris. Policy & legislation. n.d. Retrieved from http://polarisproject.org/policy-legislation. Accessed 25 May 2016.
19. Family Violence Prevention Fund. Turning pain into power: trafficking survivors' perspective on early intervention strategies. San Francisco, CA: Family Violence Prevention Fund; 2005.
20. Fehrenbacher A. First, do no harm: designing a model of trauma-informed care for survivors of human trafficking in Los Angeles county. Los Angeles: University of California Los Angeles Center for the Study of Women Update; 2013. p. 16–24.
21. United Nations Global Initiative to Fight Human Trafficking (UN GIFT). Human trafficking: new directions for research. Cairo: International Organization of Migration; 2008.
22. Andrees B, van der Linden MNJ. Designing trafficking research from a labour market perspective the ILO experience. Int Migr. 2005;43:55–73.
23. United States Department of Justice. Evaluation of comprehensive services for victims of human trafficking: key findings and lessons learned. 2007.
24. 110th Congress of the United States. H.R. 7311 William Wilberforce Trafficking Victims Protection Reauthorization Act of 2008.
25. Doherty S, Oram S, Siriwardhana C, Abas M. Suitability of measurements used to assess mental health outcomes in men and women trafficked for sexual and labour exploitation: a systematic review. Lancet Psychiatry. 2016;3(5):464–71. http://doi.org/10.1016/S2215-0366(16)30047-5.
26. Oram S, Abas M, Bick D, Boyle A, French R, Jakobowitz S, et al. Human trafficking and health: a survey of male and female survivors in England. Am J Public Health. 2016;106(6):1073–8. http://doi.org/10.2105/AJPH.2016.303095.
27. Substance Abuse and Mental Health Services Administration. SAMHSA's concept of trauma and guidance for a trauma-informed approach. (HHS Publication No. (SMA) 14-4884). Rockville, MD: Substance Abuse and Mental Health Services Administration; 2014.
28. McNiel M, Held T, Busch-Armendariz N. Creating an interdisciplinary medical home for survivors of human trafficking. Obstet Gynecol. 2014;124(3):611–5. 5p.
29. Cole J, Sprang G. Sex trafficking of minors in metropolitan, micropolitan, and rural communities. Child Abuse Negl. 2015;40:113–23 [serial online].
30. Miller CL, Duke G. Child sex trafficking-recognition, intervention, and referral: an educational framework to guide the development of health care provider education. J Hum Trafficking. 2016;2:177–200.
31. Baldwin S, Eisenman D, Sayles J, Ryan G, Chuang K. Identification of human trafficking victims in health care settings. Health Hum Rights Int J. 2011;13(1):1–14.
32. Lederer LJ, Wetzel CA. The health consequences of sex trafficking and their implications for identifying victims in healthcare facilities. Ann Health Law. 2016;23(1):61–92.
33. Chisolm-Straker M, Baldwin S, Gaïgbé-Togbé B, Ndukwe N, Johnson PN, Richardson LD. J Health Care Poor Underserved. 2016;27(3):1220-33. doi:10.1353/hpu.2016.0131.
34. Ahn R, Alpert EJ, Purcell G, Konstantopoulos WM, McGahan A, Cafferty E, et al. Human trafficking: review of educational resources for health professionals. Am J Prev Med. 2013;44:283–9.
35. Newby A, McGuinness T. Human trafficking: what psychiatric nurses should know to help children and adolescents. J Psychosoc Nurs Ment Health Serv. 2012;50(4):21–4.

36. Hackett A. The role of the school nurse in child protection. Community Pract. 2013;86(12): 26–9. 4p [serial online].
37. Chisolm-Straker M, Richardson L, Cossio T. Combating slavery in the 21st century: the role of emergency medicine. J Health Care Poor Underserved. 2012;23(3):980–7. 8p [serial online].
38. American Dental Association (JADA). 2012;143(5):498–504. 7p [serial online].
39. 113th Congress of the United States. H.R.898. Trafficking Victims Protection Reauthorization Act of 2013
40. Clawson H, Layne M, Small K. Estimating human trafficking into the United States: development of a methodology. Washington, DC: ICF International; 2006.
41. Zimmerman C, Hossain M, Watts C. Human trafficking and health: a conceptual model to inform policy, intervention, and research. Soc Sci Med. 2011;73(2):327–35.
42. Centers for Disease Control. Understanding sex trafficking. n.d. Retrieved from http://www.cdc.gov/violenceprevention/sexualviolence/trafficking.html. Accessed 25 May 2016.

Chapter 18
Caring for Survivors Using a Trauma-Informed Care Framework

Annie Lewis-O'Connor and Elaine J. Alpert

18.1 Introduction

Health care professionals are becoming increasingly cognizant of the impact that trauma can have on health. This growing awareness has led to the development of a conceptual model of patient care, known as *trauma-informed care* [1–4]. Trauma-informed care is an overarching framework that acknowledges the prevalence of current, recent, and past trauma; emphasizes the range of effects of trauma on survivors' physical and mental health; and guides the tone and process of patient care at the individual as well as at the organizational level [3]. Health care services that are delivered within a trauma-informed framework can be sensitive and responsive to a patient's life experiences, resulting in the delivery of more effective care, enhanced patient engagement, and improved health care outcomes.

As stated by the Substance Abuse and Mental Health Services Administration (SAMHSA), "Traumatic experiences can be dehumanizing, shocking or terrifying, singular or multiple compounding events over time, and often include betrayal by a trusted person or institution and a loss of safety" [2]. Survivors of human trafficking often contend with far more than the trauma that results from direct actions of the traffickers: Individuals who are, or have been, exploited typically grapple with an array of intersecting and compounding individual, cultural, societal, institutional, and historical traumatic experiences (e.g., intimate partner violence, sexual assault, a personal history of child maltreatment, chaotic or unstable family circumstances,

A. Lewis-O'Connor (✉)
Brigham and Women's Hospital, Boston, MA, USA

Harvard Medical School, Boston, MA, USA
e-mail: alewisoconnor@partners.org

E.J. Alpert
Faculty of Medicine, University of British Columbia, Vancouver, BC, Canada, V6T 1Z4
e-mail: ejalpert@massmed.org

© Springer International Publishing AG 2017
M. Chisolm-Straker, H. Stoklosa (eds.), *Human Trafficking Is a Public Health Issue*, DOI 10.1007/978-3-319-47824-1_18

substance use, survival sex, homelessness, poverty, undocumented status, community violence, racial or ethnic bias, structural and system-level inequities, religious intolerance or persecution, and a host of other macro- and micro-aggressions[1]). Gay, lesbian, bisexual, and transgender-experienced individuals, as well as those who identify with other gender and sexual minorities, face these challenges as well as those associated with their sexual orientation, gender identity, gender expression, or lifestyle [5]. The pervasiveness of trauma histories among patients interfacing with health care systems is undeniable. Indeed, 90 % of those accessing mental health care and 75 % of those seeking treatment for substance use report ongoing or past trauma exposure [4].

Clearly, traumatic and abusive events, including those experienced by survivors of human trafficking, can alter a person's emotional and physical growth and development, especially when the onset of exploitation occurred during childhood. These exposures also impact one's sense of hope and optimism, responses to major and even commonplace events, health-seeking behavior, and trust in the health care system.

The complex and often daunting lived experiences of many trauma survivors can be associated with profound stigma and shame; impede one's ability to access needed health care, mental health counseling, and other therapeutic and advocacy services; and interfere with the ability to form trusting, therapeutic relationships with care providers, and others. All of these obstacles serve to compound and magnify the effects of the traumas that trafficked persons experience [6].

Individuals who experience trauma often develop personalized strategies and tactics that enable them to function and manage their daily lives in the face of recurrent and at-times overwhelming trauma. On the surface though, some survivors' coping strategies may appear as dysfunctional behaviors. For example, patients may dissociate, engage in self-harm behaviors, express anger or aggression, or use substances. We now know that many behaviors that appear to be maladaptive or even pathological may, in fact, be used to facilitate survival, serving as strategies to cope with otherwise overwhelming stress. For example, while substance use can lead to abuse and addiction (with its attendant adverse health sequelae), "getting high" can also provide temporary respite from trauma. Similarly, while recurrent hypervigilant behavior can impede relationships with friends, family, employers, health care practitioners, and romantic partners, the accompanying hyperawareness can help one remain alert to avoid or flee from further abuse.

While more traditional health care approaches that emphasize rapid diagnosis and targeted treatment may suffice for those who have never experienced significant trauma, survivors of intentional interpersonal violence, including human trafficking, may perceive the traditional health care setting to be impersonal, unwelcoming, or even frightening. In fact, the health care delivery system itself can re-traumatize

---

[1] Micro-aggression: a subtle but offensive comment or action directed at a non-dominant group member that is often unintentional or unconsciously reinforces a stereotype. Macro-aggression: Large-scale or overt aggression toward those of a different race, culture, gender, etc. (Wikipedia).

patients who are coping with trauma and its myriad effects. Due to the coercive, exploitative, and purposefully disempowering nature of human trafficking, customary procedures that are part of usual medical practice, such as asking a patient to undress for an exam, and carrying out routine physical examinations and procedures, can be anxiety-provoking and may be perceived as threatening. As a result, interactions with health providers can trigger memories of past (or ongoing) experiences that can evoke intense feelings of fear, vulnerability, loss of control. Moreover, providers may be perceived by the patient as being impatient, especially when pressed for time. Unfortunately, individuals who have experienced trauma often encounter clinicians who, while well-intentioned, may not be aware of the different types of trauma individual patients may have experienced, as well as the associated cumulative mental health consequences.

Most clinicians have received little to no meaningful education, training, guidance or mentoring in the field of trauma in general, and about human trafficking in particular. In the face of these educational deficits, patients with histories of complex trauma, including trafficking, may be labeled as "difficult," or "noncompliant," and be felt to be particularly burdensome.

Fortunately, this cycle can be interrupted by the introduction of trauma-informed care as a strategy for individual as well as organizational response. Patients and health care providers alike—and even the health care system itself—can benefit substantively when supportive and empathic trauma-informed responses are instituted throughout the health care setting. In recognition of the emerging awareness of the impact of trauma on health, and of the impact of health care delivery itself on the experience of trauma, trauma-informed care has emerged as a foundational framework from which to approach the delivery of all health care services.

18.2 Discussion

18.2.1 Trauma-Informed Care: Lessons from Two and a Half Millennia

Historical conceptualizations about trauma and its effects on health have evolved significantly over time, informing current understandings about the importance of trauma-informed care. Published accounts in the medical literature of emotional and somatic reactions to various forms of trauma date back at least 2,500 years and initially attributed observed distress, particularly in women, to a variety of physical disorders, malfunctions, spatial "misalignments" (for example, a uterus that has "migrated" to an abnormal location within a woman's body), or other failures or deficiencies of women [7]. Such historical accounts underscore the sexist nature that characterized society at-large and health care delivery in particular. The now discredited term "hysteria," is, in fact, derived from the ancient Greek word for uterus (hystera) [8].

The development of more effective and less biased strategies to address psychological trauma, especially in relation to trafficked individuals, emerged over the twentieth century from insights gleaned from three quite disparate fields: (1) armed conflict, (2) early Freudian psychoanalytic theory, and (3) the feminist movement of the mid-late twentieth century. Evolving recognition of war-related psychological effects observed in returning soldiers produced terms such as "shell shock" (World War I), "battle fatigue" (World War II), and Post-Traumatic Stress Disorder or PTSD (Vietnam) [9, 10]. Sigmund Freud postulated that many so-called hysterical symptoms in women could be due, not to "physical misalignment," but rather to psychic trauma, specifically child sexual abuse [11]. Although Freud ultimately repudiated his own hypothesis, current scholarship contends that his initial theory was, indeed, correct [12].

Feminist theory, which attributes inequalities in women's status in society to deliberate individual and systemic gender bias, emerged in the 1960s during what is described as "second wave feminism" [13, 14]. Feminism has continued to grow, catalyzing major and still-evolving changes in nearly all aspects of Western society. Importantly, the feminist movement catalyzed an expanded conception of trauma, from the simplistic understanding of PTSD as being secondary to the physical effects of war, into a broader *trauma theory* [15].

Trauma theory encompasses all forms of trauma and exploitation that affect all genders and age groups. Trauma theory reframes conditions once thought to be pathologies, abnormalities, deficiencies, or problems (e.g., mental health issues, substance use disorders, and "non-compliance" with medical regimens) as predictable and expected adaptations or coping mechanisms deployed in an effort to cope with overwhelming stress. Moreover, the development of trauma theory has resulted in a considerably less sexist understanding of how trauma affects the brain and body. Prior to the development of trauma theory, people who experienced psychic trauma, and became symptomatic or "ill" as a result, were deemed diseased or deficient in either physical capacity or moral character. As a result, trauma theory and its "action arm" of trauma-informed care have allowed the health care community to shift the focus away from "pathologizing" the physical and mental health consequences of victimization ("What is *wrong with you*?") to one that is more nuanced, contextualized, and survivor-centered ("What *happened* to you?"). This new framework moved causation and accountability to the person or entity that caused the trauma, and away from the individual experiencing victimization [2].

This new conceptualization served as the foundation for the development of the principles of trauma-informed care. It is now clear that physical and psychic trauma, including that experienced as a result of human trafficking, can have dramatic, far-reaching, lifelong, and even intergenerational effects on how one manages commonplace as well as extraordinary challenges to life and health. The Substance Abuse and Mental Health Services Administration took an early and proactive leadership role in incorporating trauma theory into the development and implementation of trauma-informed care. In 1994, SAMHSA hosted a seminal conference called "Dare to Vision," which brought trauma to the foreground as a key determinant in the health status of girls and women. The Dare to Vision Conference was the first time survivors had an opportunity to share their own experiences of trauma with policy experts and health care opinion leaders. Of pivotal importance during this conference was the consistent testimony about how the health care system itself both triggered and re-traumatized so many survivors.

A key outcome from the Dare to Vision Conference was the formation of the Women, Co-Occurring Disorders, and Violence Study in 1998, funded by SAMHSA [2]. The purpose of this study was to stimulate the development, implementation, and evaluation of integrated service approaches for women, with co-occurring mental health and substance use disorders (SUD) that also had histories of physical or sexual abuse. These two initiatives, along with early findings from the Adverse Childhood Experiences (ACE) Study [16–18], demonstrated the need for ongoing research, particularly in regard to the prevalence and effects of traumatic exposures during childhood and the consequences of such exposures on physical and mental health across the lifespan. It also became clear that purely clinical interventions, while necessary for some aspects of care, were wholly insufficient in developing meaningful and effective health-focused responses for those suffering from complex trauma.

A health care facility's organizational climate—the set of cultures, policies, and procedures within a health care organization—was also identified as playing a key role in facilitating or in hindering an effective health care response. Accordingly, in 2001, SAMHSA provided funding for the development of the National Child Traumatic Stress Initiative. The Initiative was founded to increase understanding about child trauma and to develop, implement, and evaluate targeted response strategies across the socioecological spectrum. These developments, the observations of Judith Herman published in the seminal work, *Trauma and Recovery* [19], and insights from pioneering scholars and practitioners in the field such as Karen Saakvitne [20], Candace Schachter [21], Susan Schechter [22], and Carole Warshaw [23], helped further develop the field of trauma-informed care (also known as trauma-sensitive practice). Further underscoring the significant contributions to the field, in 2005, SAMHSA funded the National Center for Trauma Informed Care to improve public and behavioral health services for trauma survivors.

In response to this growing body of evidence, an increasing number of health centers and systems have recognized the importance not only of providing clinical services to trauma survivors in a trauma-informed manner, but incorporating trauma-informed principles into the care of *all* patients, and into the operations of the entire health care organization [20].

18.2.2 Guiding Principles of Trauma-Informed Care

Persons who have been abused, including those who are or have been trafficked, may find medical encounters to be both distressing and anxiety-provoking. Evaluations such as dental, anogenital[2], and gynecological exams, and even seemingly innocuous

---

[2] Anogenital: relating to or involving the genital organs and anus.

encounters such as blood pressure checks and abdominal palpation can trigger intense reactions of unease, dread, and avoidance. Because there is often a paucity of visible signs of or definitive disclosure of human trafficking, clinicians should approach the care of *all* patients using the principles of "trauma-informed care," approaching the care of all patients as if they were potential abuse survivors [23–25]. Also known as trauma-aware care, trauma-informed care is in many respects, the behavioral health equivalent of universal precautions for communicable diseases: Similar to routine precautions to prevent the transmission of bodily fluid-borne infections during medical procedures, clinicians who embody trauma-informed care practices assume the possibility of current or past abuse in *all* patients [26, 27].

The overarching goals of the trauma-informed approach are to:

1. Diminish the likelihood and impact of re-traumatization within the health care setting;
2. Recognize survivor strengths and resilience;
3. Foster healing and recovery; and
4. Support the development of healthy short- and long-term coping mechanisms [1, 2].

Dr. Candice L. Schachter and colleagues developed nine principles of trauma-sensitive practice for the care of *individual patients* [21], all of which contribute to the overarching goal of survivor safety:

1. *Respect* means "acknowledging the inherent value of each individual, upholding basic human rights with conviction and compassion, and suspending critical judgment."
2. *Patience* (or taking time) supports actions geared to creating proactive, individualized, and meaningful interactions with patients. A treatment setting that is rushed and impersonal can feel demeaning to someone who has been victimized, and may result in re-traumatization and disengagement.
3. *Rapport* is vital for a productive and successful therapeutic relationship. Balancing professional efficiency with kind, courteous, and genuine concern will facilitate good communication and sincere engagement in a proactive care plan.
4. *Sharing information* helps mitigate fear and anxiety by keeping survivors appraised about what is transpiring during the medical encounter. Sharing information also provides opportunities for survivors to ask questions of and respond to the health care clinician, thus feeling less like an object (case) and more like an active participant (person) in regard to their own health care.
5. *Sharing control* is critical to developing a successful provider–patient relationship. Clinicians need to understand that a central component of being trafficked is the loss of control over one's own body and life. Providers who acknowledge the inherent power imbalance of the provider–patient relationship can move towards real partnerships with patients. These partnerships will be more likely to engender trust and survivor responsiveness without sacrificing clinical efficiency.

6. *Respecting boundaries* asks providers to reflect on personal habits or office routines that may contribute to practice efficiency, while inadvertently making a survivor feel unsafe. Seeking permission to ask certain questions or to examine certain parts of the body reinforces professional boundaries, and models respectful interaction for a survivor. Allowing patients the right to decline specific actions or portions of the exam can help them feel more empowered and actually facilitate the provision of health care.
7. *Fostering mutual learning* may well be the cornerstone of the trauma-informed survivor–provider relationship. Providers who demonstrate appreciation for learning *from the patient* can learn a great deal not only about the health effects of human trafficking and how to effectively engage with survivors, but also discover that survivors can be their "best teachers." When providers express heartfelt caring, concern, and appreciation to survivors for helping them to become better practitioners, survivors may be better able to tolerate occasional missteps that may occur in the relationship (e.g.: having to wait longer than expected to be seen, or an office staff member speaking less than sensitively, etc.).
8. *Understanding nonlinear healing* affirms that healing does not always occur in a linear fashion, rather it can have ebbs and flows that at times can be difficult to predict. These fluctuations might necessitate adjusting the treatment plan to fit the current, rather than the planned, situation.
9. *Demonstrating awareness and knowledge of interpersonal violence* indicates to a survivor that the provider is both knowledgeable and compassionate; it also signifies the importance of creating a safe environment in which to discuss issues, and to engage in acute and comprehensive care.

The overarching goal of Schachter's trauma-sensitive practice work is to facilitate a sense of safety for survivors. Safety is a central concept because when individuals feel safe, they are more able to engage with a treatment plan and become proactive and deliberate in working towards recovery and health.

On an *organizational level*, health care facilities and systems can promote a trauma-informed care approach by guiding how services are provided by the health care system itself. Further, organizations should recognize, address, and provide opportunities for staff who have experienced trauma, violence, and abuse to seek support and advocacy for their own needs [2, 4, 24, 25, 27]. Health care organizations can proactively support trauma-informed care across the organization by focusing on safety, trust and transparency, peer support, collaboration and mutuality, patient and staff empowerment, and understanding the impact of cultural, historic, and gender-related bias and prejudice.

Specific actions that can be taken to address the safety of the physical environment include [2]:

- Limiting the access of potential abusers by developing policies and procedures that promote patient privacy and confidentiality;
- Assuring good lighting in parking lots, common areas, bathrooms, entrances, and exits;

- Prohibiting people from congregating near entrances and exits;
- Monitoring who is coming in and out of the building;
- Positioning security personnel inside and outside of the building and training security staff to utilize trauma-informed approaches;
- Controlling noise levels in waiting rooms;
- Adopting culturally responsive, welcoming language on all signage; and
- Ensuring that patients have clear access to the door in exam rooms and can easily exit if desired.

On a *health system-wide* level, a trauma-informed approach identifies, acknowledges, and responds to the range of physical, emotional, and environmental safety needs of both patients and staff. A system-wide implementation of trauma-informed care, including education of staff allows health systems to craft and deliver optimal care for all patients, particularly for those who are most vulnerable.

Trustworthiness and transparency must be emphasized across the organization, among staff, administration, and patients. Training staff in trauma-informed care approaches assures that knowledge and skills needed to practice in a trauma-informed manner is fully integrated into the organization. The success of building a trust-based and transparent partnership with patients requires proactive and consistent senior leadership support.

Peer support provides survivors the opportunity to share their stories in a meaningful and supported manner without judgment. Engaging survivors by integrating them into an advisory council helps assure that the voices of survivors are heard, respected, and used to inform policies and procedures throughout the organization.

Collaboration and mutuality recognizes the inherent hierarchy within some relationships, and the inequalities caused by gender differences, culture, ethnicity, religion, and socio-economic status. Collaboration across disciplines and service providers (including community-based partners) recognizes the unique contributions of all members of the health care team and assures that decision-making power is equally distributed.

Patient and staff empowerment creates a system that shifts the paradigm from a predetermined hierarchical model of care to one that represents a dynamic partnership with the patient. Autonomy and one's ability to make informed, independent choices are the fundamental principles in all health care relationships; strength and resiliency are core elements of this foundation.

Clinicians and organizations must understand the impact of *cultural, historic, and gender-related bias and prejudice* on survivors' health and on their ability to access and engage in health care services. In addition to the disempowerment wrought by trafficking trauma, societal inequities caused by gender differences, culture, ethnicity, religion, and socio-economic status contribute to the experiences of survivors. These inequities can, in turn, affect how services are (or are not) accessed and received by trafficking survivors. Health care organizations should consciously and proactively address issues that perpetuate inequality and bias in order to deliver services most effectively.

Incorporating trauma-informed care principles into daily practice and system design enhances the likelihood that trafficked patients will be able to access health care services and engage in actions to improve their health without being re-traumatized. These practices also increase the chance that providers will better address the complex range of health needs faced by trafficking survivors.

18.2.3 Case Study: Using a Trauma-Informed "Translator" to Improve Care

The following case illustrates the application of trauma-sensitive care using a "Trauma-Informed Translator" (Lewis-O'Connor and Grossman. Trauma-informed care translator. 31 May 2016, Personal Communication). The case is of a young woman who is being sex trafficked by a male who portrays himself as her "friend." While the case illuminates many features typical of human trafficking, those experiencing trafficking as well as other forms of exploitation can present with a variety of health care needs. The discussion that follows highlights the potential advantages of using a trauma-informed approach in the emergency department (ED) by comparing it to a more traditional, algorithmic approach.

In the traditional model of care, each patient who presents to an emergency department for evaluation and care is assigned a "level of acuity" (a measure of the

Jane presents to the ED triage area. She is accompanied by a male "friend" named Ray who says she has been having a "bad period" for a couple of days. Ray wants to make sure she gets checked out and gets whatever pain medicine she needs so he can take her back home to rest up; Jane needs to be ready for work that night. Ray insists on remaining with Jane throughout the exam because she is "afraid of doctors." Jane states she forgot her insurance card; Ray apologizes, saying he forgot to bring her purse. Jane's screening assessment and vitals in triage reveal a pale, diaphoretic female who appears somewhat younger than her stated age of 19. Vital signs[3]: T 101.6F, P 108 regular, BP 156/60, RR 24. Jane neither speaks spontaneously nor makes eye contact. Questions posed to her are instead answered by Ray. When she is asked to answer questions directly, she speaks in short phrases and looks at Ray immediately after each response. The patient is triaged with an initial working diagnosis of "suspected pelvic inflammatory disease due to a sexually transmitted infection, and suspected abuse."

---

[3] Jane's vital signs are: temperature of 101.6 F; pulse of 108 with a regular rhythm; blood pressure of 156/60; and respiratory rate of 24. Her temperature, pulse, and respiratory rate are all abnormal but not immediately life-threatening. Her blood pressure is mildly elevated.

need for immediate attention) and goes either directly to a treatment room (those who appear more acutely ill), or is asked to sit in the waiting room if a room is not available (those who appear less acutely ill). Once in a room, the patient may be asked to change into a hospital gown. A number of providers may enter in and out of the room in the course of caring for the patient. Each health care facility has its own policy regarding the extent to which visitors (family members and friends) who accompany the patient are allowed into the treatment area. Some facilities have adopted a family centered focus in which accompanying family members and friends are viewed as welcome additions that can assist in allaying fear and contributing to the patient's well-being. Other facilities prefer to allow those accompanying the patient to remain in the waiting area unless called upon to come in for a brief visit.

In the traditional model, some of the history is obtained using "checklist" type questions rather than engaging in a more open-ended dialogue with the patient. For example, in this case, a traditional approach would ask a series of "yes" or "no" questions about Jane's presenting complaint, such as: "Is the person accompanying you your boyfriend?" and "Do you feel safe with him?" A trauma-informed approach would focus on more open-ended questions such as, "Tell me a bit about the man who came with you. Are you in a relationship with him?", and What do you like most about your relationship with your partner?" or, alternatively, "What would you change if you could?" Asking questions designed to yield "yes" or "no" answers are less likely to provide the nuanced context needed to address sensitive issues. Conversely, open-ended questions allow patients to share their narrative in a way that allows them to feel engaged and in control of the conversation.

In the case of Jane and her presentation to the emergency department, the second column of the table below depicts what is likely to occur using the traditional health care approach, while the third column applies the *Trauma-Informed Translator* to her care. Note, the recommended trauma-informed care wording and approach will vary based on the patient situation, but the translator provides some helpful example language and actions (Table 18.1).

A trauma-informed care approach to the patient history results in Jane disclosing that her "friend" Ray is a pimp and that she is being forced to work in commercial sex. She is not able to leave voluntarily and is afraid that Ray will have her gang raped or killed if he finds out that she disclosed her situation or if she tries to leave him. Evaluation confirms the initial working diagnosis of pelvic inflammatory disease. Jane's condition could theoretically be treated as an outpatient, but because she appears to be in a trafficking situation, she is offered hospitalization as an inpatient for antibiotic treatment. She is also told that she will have an opportunity to meet with an advocate and social worker to develop a safety plan related to her trafficking situation.

Table 18.1 Translating into Trauma-Informed Care

Stage of care	Traditional approach	Trauma-informed care approach
Initial assessment/triage (chief complaint)	"What's going on?", "What is the problem?" or "What is your complaint?"	"Can you share with me what happened to you?" "I'm glad you decided to come in to get checked out."
Initial history/triage	Questions answered by accompanying person (Ray). Jane and Ray asked to take seats in waiting room.	Bring Jane to a treatment room and ask Ray to wait in the waiting room. Refer to organizational policy if questioned or challenged by Ray. When alone with Jane, say: "Please help me understand what is happening, Jane."
Moving patient to a treatment room	Jane is brought to a treatment room, told to change into a gown and told what will happen next.	Jane's reaction to the treatment environment and her potential vulnerabilities are noted. Asking, "What can I do for you right now, Jane, to make you comfortable?" displays a sense of caring and builds rapport. Using the patient's name conveys warmth, respect, and acknowledgement of each person's individuality.
Style and mode of questioning	Different members of the health care team come in separately to obtain what they need from the history.	Jane is asked if she would like a medical advocate (if available) to sit with her during the evaluation to provide support. Jane is asked first for permission if anyone other than the main clinician and advocate need to come in. Jane is offered validation and support: "You are doing a really good job," and "Let us know if you need to take a break."
Evaluation of suspected pelvic inflammatory disease due to a sexually transmitted infection	Jane is asked a number of probing questions related to the suspected working diagnosis: "You may have a sexually transmitted infection. Are you sleeping with more than one person?" "How many partners do you have?" "Are you having unprotected sex or sex with many people for money?"	Health provider asks: "How can we help you Jane?" "What would you like to share about what brought you here today?" "Is someone making you have sex when you don't want to? Are you being made to do sexual things with different people?" "How might what is happening to you be affecting your health and well-being?" "What can we do for you right now to help you feel safe?"

(continued)

Table 18.1 (continued)

Stage of care	Traditional approach	Trauma-informed care approach
Physical examination	Jane is told what will need to be done during the physical examination.	Jane is asked if she would prefer leaving her clothes on to the extent possible; Jane and the clinician work together to evaluate discrete areas of her body without fully undressing, whenever possible.
		The examination should occur at a pace that is comfortable for Jane and she should be offered the option of taking breaks or stopping at any time if she is feeling uncomfortable or overwhelmed.
Treatment plan	Jane is informed of the diagnosis and prescribed a treatment plan. Clinician performs tasks with efficiency and communicates "at" Jane instead of "with" Jane.	The health care team and Jane develop a treatment plan together. The team acknowledges Jane's strengths and supports her autonomous decisions without judgment.
		Jane and her care team work together to build a partnership that builds rapport and is non-judgmental, allowing Jane to voice feelings, preferences, and choices.
		The clinician asks, "Please help me understand what is important to you and what you need for your own health and safety right now." The clinician states, "I am so sorry this is happening to you but I am so glad you came in for care. What has helped you to carry on?"
Visitors/accompanying parties	Ray insists on staying with Jane for all parts of the health care encounter. Jane seems to reluctantly agree.	Proactively having a policy and signs posted that require that all patients over the age of 12 be afforded privacy during their health care visit would take the burden off Jane and providers in separating her from Ray, allow time for the clinician and Jane to build rapport, and provide opportunities for inquiry and disclosure. Example wording for sign: "Thank you for coming in with your loved one today. Our policy is to ensure that all patients have time alone with their provider. Thank you for your cooperation."

18.3   Conclusion

In 2014, a report from the National Center for Trauma, Domestic Violence and Mental Health affirmed that the trauma-informed approach incorporates an understanding of the prevalence as well as the physical and mental health impact of trauma. Further, this report described organizational steps that can be taken to reduce re-traumatization within the health care setting. Universal application of trauma-informed care recognizes that trauma is highly prevalent and that a large proportion of patients have had traumatic experiences in their lives.

A trauma-informed care approach encourages service providers and clinicians to provide optimal care by fostering trust, assuring safe environments, acknowledging client/patient strengths (instead of deficiencies), respecting client/patient autonomy and choices, recognizing the unique attributes and needs of each individual, and providing cultural and language-appropriate services and care. A trauma-informed approach would thank all patients for sharing their narrative; point out coping strategies and strengths that are being utilized; remind discharged patients that they are welcome to return at any time for further care; and partner around a treatment plan that is patient-centered and trauma-informed. While it is understandable that health care settings are inherently busy and that fully embracing a trauma-informed translator may not be possible initially, maintaining the core principles of trauma-informed care should facilitate the development of a foundation from which the paradigm of care delivery can be transitioned to a trauma-informed framework.

As illustrated in the above case, trafficked individuals who are in need of health care may be more likely to disclose and benefit from services and referrals when a trauma-informed approach is utilized. Additionally, care organizations should consider how trauma affects all aspects of the institution's functioning, analyze the effect of the environment on trauma survivors, and take organizational steps to provide trauma-informed services across all departments.

18.4   Recommendations

Evidence supports the recommendation that health care services should be provided within an organizational context that is "trauma-informed." For trafficked persons and survivors of human trafficking, the conceptual framework of trauma-informed care offers opportunities to respond optimally via supportive and productive interactions that can promote and improve their health status. The following are suggested recommendations:

- Clinicians should be provided with opportunities to practice in a trauma-informed manner (utilization of interdisciplinary simulation training offers practical experience that can be transferred to the clinical setting);
- Health care organizations and systems should develop, implement, and sustain trauma-sensitive policy and practice guidelines;

- A dedicated committee or working group should be convened and supported to ensure that the process of implementation of trauma-informed care policies and procedures advances within an organization;
- Health care settings should create a Patient Advisory Council (PAC) or similar body composed of survivors and other stakeholders to inform practice and policy (for guidelines on creating and sustaining a PAC, see the Institute for Patient and Family Centered Care www.ipfcc.org);
- Research and quality improvement efforts should be developed that focus on the impact of trauma-informed care practices on organizations, to determine the extent to which a trauma-sensitive framework affects health outcomes and health care utilization.

References

1. Harris M, Fallot RD. Envisioning a trauma-informed service system: a vital paradigm shift. New Dir Ment Health Serv. 2001;89:3–22.
2. Substance Abuse and Mental Health Services Administration. SAMHSA's concept of trauma and guidance for a trauma-informed approach. HHS Publication No. (SMA) 14-4884. Rockville, MD: Substance Abuse and Mental Health Services Administration; 2014.
3. Hopper E, Bassuk EL, Olivet J. Shelter from the storm: trauma-informed care in homelessness services settings. Open Health Serv Policy J. 2010;3(2):80–100.
4. Jennings A. Models for developing trauma-informed behavioral health systems and trauma-specific services. Alexandria, VA: National Association of State Mental Health Program Directors, National Technical Assistance Center for State Mental Health Planning; 2004.
5. Institute of Medicine (US) Committee on Lesbian, Gay, Bisexual, and Transgender Health Issues and Research Gaps and Opportunities. The health of lesbian, gay, bisexual, and transgender people: building a foundation for better understanding. Washington, DC: National Academies Press (US); 2011.
6. Crane PA, Moreno M. Human trafficking: What is the role of the health care provider? J Appl Res Child Inform Policy Child Risk. 2011;2(1):Article 7. Available at: http://digitalcommons. library.tmc.edu/childrenatrisk/vol2/iss1/7. Accessed 1 Aug 2016.
7. Hanson AE. Hippocrates: Diseases of Women 1. Signs. 1975 Dec 1;1(2):567–84.
8. Oswald J. A dictionary of etymology of the English language: and of English synonymes and paronymes. 9th ed. Edinburgh; 1857. p. 249.
9. Myers CS. A contribution to the study of shell shock. Lancet. 1915;185(4772):316–20.
10. Jones E, Wesseley S. Psychiatric battle casualties: and intra- and interwar comparison. Br J Psychiatry. 2001;178(3):242–7.
11. The Ateiology of Hysteria. Lecture delivered to the Society for Psychiatry and Neurology, Vienna, Austria; 21 April 1896.
12. Robinson P. Freud and his critics. Berkeley, CA: University of California Press; 1993.
13. Shapiro A-L. Introduction: history and feminist theory, or talking back to the Beadle. Hist Theory. 1992;31(4), Beiheft (supplement) 31: History and Feminist Theory:1–14. doi:10.2307/2505412.
14. Evans J. Feminist theory today: an introduction to second wave feminism. London: Sage; 1995. ISBN 978-0-8039-8478-3.
15. Caruth C. Trauma: explorations in memory. Baltimore, MD: JHU Press; 1995.
16. Felitti VJ, Anda RF, Nordenberg D, Williamson DF, Spitz AM, Edwards V, Koss MP, Marks JS. Relationship of childhood abuse and household dysfunction to many of the leading causes

of death in adults: The Adverse Childhood Experiences (ACE) Study. American Journal of Preventive Medicine. 1998 May 31;14(4):245–58.

17. Dube SR, Anda RF, Felitti VJ, Edwards VJ, Williamson DF. Exposure to abuse, neglect, and household dysfunction among adults who witnessed intimate partner violence as children: implications for health and social services. Violence and victims. 2002 Feb 1;17(1):3–17.

18. Dube SR, Anda RF, Whitfield CL, Brown DW, Felitti VJ, Dong M, et al. Long-term consequences of childhood sexual abuse by gender of victim. American Journal of Preventive Medicine. 2005;28:430–438.

19. Herman J. Trauma and recovery. New York, NY: Basic Books; 1992.

20. Saakvitne KW, Gamble S, Pearlman LA, Lev BT. Risking connection: a training curriculum for work with survivors of childhood abuse. Baltimore, MD: Sidran Institute Press; 2000.

21. Schachter CL, Stalker CA, Teram E, Lasiuk GC, Danilkewich A. Handbook on sensitive practice for health care practitioner: lessons from adult survivors of childhood sexual abuse. Ottawa: Public Health Agency of Canada; 2008.

22. Schechter S. Women and male violence: the visions and struggles of the battered women's movement. Boston, MA: South End Press; 1982.

23. Warshaw C. Domestic violence, trauma and mental health. In: Renzetti C, Edleson J, editors. Encyclopedia on interpersonal violence. Thousand Oaks, CA: Sage; 2008.

24. Raja S., Hasnain M., Hoersch M., Gove-Yin S. Rajagopalan, C. Trauma Informed Care in Medicine: Current Knowledge and Future Research Directions. *Fam Community Health.* 2015, 38:3, 216–226.

25. Elliott DE, Bjelajac P, Fallot RD, Markoff LS, Reed BG. Trauma informed or trauma-denied: principles and implementation of trauma-informed services for women. J Community Psychol. 2005;33(4):461–77.

26. National Center for Domestic Violence, Trauma and Mental Health. 2013. http://www.nationalcenterdvtraumamh.org/2016/03/ncdvtmh-launches-a-webinar-series-on-trauma-focused-interventions-for-survivors-of-domestic-and-sexual-violence/. Accessed 1 Aug 2016.

27. Menschner C, Maul A. Key ingredients for successful trauma-informed care implementation. Hamilton, NJ: Center for Health Care Strategies; 2016. Issue Brief.

Chapter 19
Sex Trafficking in One US City: Traditional Policing and Boston's Shift to a Survivor-Centered Response

Donna Gavin and Cassandra Thomson

Abbreviations

BPD	Boston Police Department
HTU	Human Trafficking Unit
HT	Human Trafficking
CEASE	Cities Empowered Against Sexual Exploitation (Atlanta, Boston, Cook County, Dallas, Denver, Houston, Oakland, Phoenix, Portland, San Diego, and Seattle)
DCF	Department of Children and Families
SEEN	Support to End Exploitation Now
CSE	Commercial Sexual Exploitation
BUILD	Roxbury Youth Works' Being United in Leading Our Destiny Program
GIFT	Roxbury Youth Works' Gaining Independence for Tomorrow Program
IPV	Interpersonal violence
MLMC	My Life My Choice
JRI	Justice Research Institute
SCDAO	Suffolk County District Attorney's Office
NGO	Non-governmental Organization
EVA Center	Josephine Butler Education Vision and Advocacy Center

The original version of this chapter was revised. An erratum to this chapter can be found at DOI: 10.1007/978-3-319-47824-1_25

D. Gavin (✉)
Law Enforcement/Boston Police, 989 Commonwealth Avenue, Boston, MA 02215, USA
e-mail: donna.gavin@pd.boston.gov

C. Thomson
University of Michigan Law School, 625 S. State Street, Ann Arbor, MI 48109, USA
e-mail: cjthoms@umich.edu

© Springer International Publishing AG 2017
M. Chisolm-Straker, H. Stoklosa (eds.), *Human Trafficking Is a Public Health Issue*, DOI 10.1007/978-3-319-47824-1_19

19.1 Introduction

In 2001, a 17-year-old girl was murdered in a parking lot located about 20 min from Boston. The Boston Police Department (BPD) arrested her for prostitution the previous year. Upon learning of her death, members of various groups including the BPD and other law enforcement, Probation, service providers, social workers, and the Department of Children and Families (DCF) met to discuss how a child involved with several of their agencies had fallen through the cracks. They formed a working group to address the issues related to what at the time was referred to as "teenage prostitution." In 2005, this group formalized their relationships and formed the SEEN Coalition: Support to End Exploitation Now. They no longer use the term "teen prostitution." Today SEEN is a nationally recognized organization with the shared belief that commercial sexual exploitation of children (CSEC) is child abuse. Since that time, the Suffolk County District Attorney's Office (SCDAO) and the Boston Police Department do not charge children under 18 years of age with "prostitution," but rather treat them as victims of child abuse and human trafficking.

More than 15 years have passed since that young woman's premature and violent death, and while no one has been charged with her murder, a handful of organizations in Boston have emerged to help victims of CSEC and pimp-controlled prostitution. Several of these organizations, including My Life My Choice (MLMC), a program of the Justice Research Institute; The Gaining Independence for Tomorrow (GIFT) and Being United in Leading Our Destiny Program (BUILD), both programs of Roxbury Youth Works; and The Josephine Butler Education Vision and Advocacy (EVA) Center of Boston, are briefly described in this chapter. These organizations provide services for victims of trafficking in the Boston area.

In this chapter, the authors focus explicitly on sex trafficking. This is not due to a belief that labor trafficking is less severe, but because less progress has been made in the investigation and prosecution of labor trafficking cases. The anti-trafficking law enforcement field currently struggles to respond to labor trafficking due to lack of data, the hidden nature of labor exploitation, and the fewer prior prosecutions for precedent. Because much of the work in shifting the paradigm of Boston law enforcement's efforts with trafficked persons has been done in the area of prostitution and sex trafficking, this chapter will highlight successes and lessons learned in anti-sex trafficking work. When appropriate, the authors recommend that law enforcement apply similar practices when investigating labor trafficking cases.

Sex trafficking and prostitution are complex issues. Some believe that prostitution is the "oldest profession" and that its longevity is indicative of its inevitability. Others believe that prostitution should be legalized and regulated when it involves "consenting" adults. Yet those in law enforcement see that the lines between trafficking and prostitution are often blurred, and therefore they often use the terms interchangeably.[1] Many cases of sex trafficking start with reports of prostitution

---

[1] Sex trafficking refers to the recruitment, enticement, harboring, transportation, provision, or obtaining of a person for the purposes of a commercial sex act; any commercial sex act involving a minor, regardless of use of force, coercion, or fraud. Prostitution refers to exchanging the performance of sexual acts for money; a legal term, usually connotes a crime.

activity. Numerous women involved in sex trafficking initially deny being exploited by third party pimps/traffickers for myriad reasons. Please note that language referring to trafficking differs among law enforcement and those involved in the medical and other public health professions. The terminology of this chapter is rooted in the authors' experience and is specifically used because many people involved in prostitution, including the victims/survivors, the buyers, and the pimps, use this language. In line with law enforcement linguistics, in this chapter we will use the word "victim" to refer to people still being trafficked. This is not meant to imply that trafficked persons and those involved in prostitution are not daily survivors, but rather to reflect the oppression and exploitation they often endure at the hands of their exploiters, commonly traffickers and buyers. The authors believe that human trafficking is still an emerging crime and law enforcement and other professionals are only at the tip of the proverbial iceberg in addressing it.

The authors agree that survivors are the true experts in this field and are grateful that in Boston there are several who work closely to inform law enforcement efforts. Some were trafficked as children and some entered the commercial sex industry as young adults. They have taught law enforcement that it is not important how a person enters the commercial sex industry but rather what happens to them during that time and how difficult it can be to exit. These survivors run programs to raise awareness about the harm and violence they endured while in the life of commercial sex work while others provide services and support to young people trying to find a way out. The authors also acknowledge that there are some people engaged in commercial sex that use the term "sex workers." Many of these women report they are willingly involved in commercial sex and find it a lucrative and rewarding career. However, in the authors' experience these women make up an overwhelmingly small number of those encountered in the commercial sex industry. Further, the authors acknowledge this chapter will use gendered language and have a different tone from the others of this book. Law enforcement finds that sex trafficking is largely a crime perpetrated against women and children. Although men and boys are likely significantly undercounted as trafficked [1], Boston law enforcement has not yet encountered a large number of male trafficked persons. In Boston, there have been a handful of cases of boys and transgender-experienced youth being trafficked, but overwhelmingly the cases involve girls and young women. Service providers from BUILD have found that there is additional stigma for boys and men to come forward and disclose victimization. Professionals in various disciplines are therefore less likely to recognize victimized boys and men. Still, it is indisputable that there is an epidemic of girls and young women being brutalized by violent pimps/traffickers. In Boston specifically, nearly all cases, seen by law enforcement, have involved male exploiters although there have been several women charged with trafficking. In fact, there have been a growing number of incidences of women trafficking other women both internationally [2] and domestically [3, 4]. Many of the women charged were former victims of trafficking themselves [5].

The authors will highlight several elements of human trafficking in Boston: legislation; characteristics of the problem, including intergenerational violence; a lack of reliable data; the relationship to the opioid crisis; the current service providers in

Boston who work with sex trafficked individuals; strategies of the Human Trafficking Unit (HTU); and best practices found for serving trafficked persons. The chapter ends with a list of recommendations for health professionals caring for and members of law enforcement working on behalf of trafficked individuals.

19.1.1 Setting the Scene: The Massachusetts Human Trafficking Statute

Massachusetts has a relatively new history of human trafficking-related legislation. Through 2010 Massachusetts was one of three states that did not have a human trafficking statute and therefore law enforcement could only present cases to federal authorities. In 2011, the Act Relative to Commercial Sexual Exploitation was passed by the Massachusetts' Legislature, finally allowing local authorities to prosecute trafficking cases [6]. It went into effect in February 2012. Although it took hard work and many years to pass the law, it is one of the most comprehensive in the country. It includes a Safe Harbor Provision that presumes, as the Boston Police Department and the Suffolk County District Attorney's Office (SCDAO) have for years, that children under 18 engaged in commercial sex are victims of trafficking and child abuse rather than offenders of prostitution laws. The Act provides for stiffer penalties for traffickers and pimps as well as a forfeiture provision to support a victim trust fund [6].

The BPD and the SCDAO successfully prosecuted the first case under the statute. In the case of *Commonwealth v. McGhee*, the traffickers preyed upon, kidnapped, raped, and exploited young women from a Boston methadone clinic [7]. The traffickers were found guilty of sex trafficking but appealed the decision in 2015; they challenged the constitutionality of the law. Further, they argued the statute was overly broad because it did not require force, fraud, or coercion to have occurred, which is required to prove trafficking by the federal law [8]. The case was upheld by the Massachusetts Supreme Judicial Court in a unanimous opinion stating, the Massachusetts law was "sufficiently clear and definite," and that it used terms that were both commonly recognized and simply understood [8, 9]. Since then many Massachusetts pimps have been arrested, charged with, and prosecuted for sex trafficking.

19.2 Discussion

19.2.1 Statement of the Problem

The commercial sex industry is estimated to be a multi-billion-dollar industry fueled by demand [10]. The internet has changed the operationalization of the commercial sex industry, including sex trafficking. The internet provides an easy and anonymous way for pimps to recruit vulnerable young women and for buyers to purchase sex. Strip clubs, streets, motels, illicit massage parlors, and online escort sites are all venues where sex trafficking occurs. The commercial sex industry is appealing to pimps and traffickers because of its high profitability to detectability ratio. In comparison, arms or drug trafficking are riskier and somewhat less profitable: Carrying a firearm without a license and possessing illegal drugs are immediately arrestable offenses. Illegal drugs and firearms are tangible evidence and can only be sold once to end-users. However, pimps sell children and young women repeatedly for sex and often the only evidence available is victim testimony. Therefore, selling sex is less risky than other criminal activities, as victims seldom come forward to law enforcement with complaints of being trafficked because of fear of reprisal; the stigma associated with prostitution; lack of alternative options; or no hope for another way of life [11].

Sex trafficking is largely a hidden crime and often escapes police scrutiny. In many cases, traffickers lure young victims by *grooming,* or befriending, them through the internet [12]. Buyers go to dozens of websites every day where teens and young adults are sold in hotels and apartments in cities and towns across the country. Much like it did for domestic violence cases in the 1980s, law enforcement is now realizing the harm and violence sex trafficking causes not only to its victims but the broader community as well. Law enforcement can no longer work in silos, ignoring the interrelatedness of violent crimes like shootings and homicides, drug sales, and gang-related incidents perpetuated by pimps and traffickers.

Although the BPD Human Trafficking Unit works with all trafficked persons regardless of nationality or age, the overwhelming majority of cases investigated and prosecuted thus far have involved young adult women from the USA. The detectives from the BPD HTU focus their efforts on the most violent pimps, many of whom have histories of vicious assaults, and drug and firearm convictions. In several of cases, the trafficked women suffered brutal beatings. When they became pregnant, and thus unable to earn money for their pimps, they found themselves particularly vulnerable with nowhere to live. Many had aged out of child welfare systems and had no support network.

The BPD HTU investigations of sex trafficking are often based on tips from numerous sources including, but not limited to: other law enforcement agencies and BPD units like Sexual Assault, Gang, Drug, and Domestic Violence Units; the National Human Trafficking Resource Center; service providers; medical personnel in emergency departments and health care clinics; DCF; and juvenile and adult probation officers. Several trafficking cases were identified due to assaults and shootings.

19.2.2   Intergenerational Violence

In Boston, the majority of young people involved in the commercial sex industry experienced intergenerational violence in their homes and were placed in the child welfare system. Many aged out of these systems after having bounced from one home to another with little to no support. The toxic stress of their home environment combined with the child welfare system's inability to fully support them make them particularly vulnerable to being trafficked.

Many pimps charged with sex trafficking are already convicted sex offenders. Many young men who become pimps were also victims of child abuse and neglect; they too have grown up in families where there was domestic violence and sometimes prostitution or sex trafficking [5]. Several studies reveal that children who witness intimate partner violence and trafficking, or are trafficked or otherwise abused themselves, are more likely to be affected by violence as adults—either as victims or perpetrators [5, 13–15].

The Intergenerational Violence Cycle created by Professor David Shim and shown in Fig. 19.1 illustrates this pattern of continued violence. This theory was derived from observation chart review data, and these were the factors reported by the women Professor Shim studied.

This figure illustrates how family dysfunction in childhood, compounded by seeking and coping with unmet needs, leads to vulnerability to commercial sexual exploitation (CSE). It is important to note that the "vulnerability to commercial sexual exploitation" is only one possible risk factor among others. CSE in turn often results in use of drugs, involvement in criminal activities, exposure to violence, and psychiatric issues. When survivors of CSE then have children, their progeny may be exposed to dysfunction in the home from an early age, and the intergenerational cycle repeats.

The EVA Center of Boston, an organization that serves women involved in the commercial sex industry, has collected information examining factors that led these women to being trafficked by exploring Adverse Child Experiences (ACE) [17]. The ACE Scoring system measures three categories including abuse, neglect, and household dysfunction [17, 18]. Points are attributed for each category of exposure to child abuse or neglect; higher scores indicate higher levels of exposure. National research shows higher ACE scores are associated with early initiation of sexual activity, alcohol and drug abuse, depression and suicide, heart and liver disease, experiencing intimate partner violence, and early death [17, 18].

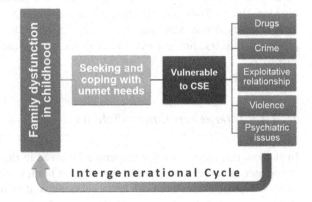

Fig. 19.1 The intergenerational cycle: elements of the flow of children into commercial sexual exploitation. Reproduced with permission from Dr. David Shim [16]

   The original EVA Center study in 2015 involved a cohort of 64 individuals [19]. Due to difficulties obtaining enough categories of ACE information for the entire cohort, the data obtained reflect the ACE scores of 14 individuals. However, the available information suggested that the average ACE score in this population was elevated, between 8 and 10 (see Table 19.1). ACE scores were calculated on a national level with the Centers for Disease Control and Prevention (CDC) and Kaiser [20, 21]. In the CDC-Kaiser ACE Study, ACE scores were examined for the general population of women, and the average ACE score was between 0 and 1. The study investigators for the EVA Center could not test for statistical differences in means (averages) between the two studies because the CDC-Kaiser sample size was much larger, but the difference between the ACE score means suggested that the women at the EVA Center (victims of CSE) experience different traumatic life events in comparison to women in the general population (Table 19.2).

   Further studies in 2016 examined ACE scores and demographics from the EVA Center and two other agencies: My Life My Choice (MLMC) for adult CSE victims and Girls Educational and Mentoring Services (GEMS) serving both minors and adults [21, 22]. These studies identified no significant differences among the groups' ACE scores.

Table 19.1 EVA Center 2015 ACE score distribution, trafficked women[a]

ACE score	Percentage (%)
5 or less	0.00
6	15.38
7	15.38
8	23.08
9	23.08
10	23.08

Reproduced with permission from Dr. David Shim [19]

[a]This data is drawn from a sample of women ($N = 14$) who were served by the EVA Center from 2006 through 2014

Table 19.2 ACE score distribution for CDC-Kaiser ACE Study participants (national percentages)[a]

ACE score	Percentage (%)
0	34.50
1	24.50
2	15.5
3	10.30
4 or more	15.20

Reproduced with permission from Dr. David Shim [19, 20]

[a]These scores are taken from the CDC-Kaiser ACE Study's sample of women ($N = 9367$)

It is also important to note the limitations of ACE's applicability to the CSE population being studied. Some of the ACE questions do not generally apply to the CSE population: In some cases, words were changed to accommodate possible inapplicability to the population (e.g., the word "parents" was changed, with permission, to "primary caretakers" to acknowledge possibly being raised by foster care guardians, extended family members, or other representatives), while question 6 ("Were your parents divorced") was largely inappropriate and thus removed. Additionally, the responses were collated through a chart review at the three sites, and some or a large amount of the ACE questions were not specifically answered. The investigators note that future efforts should directly collect ACE scores from the participants.

Evaluation of the most recent EVA Center sample ($N = 21$) revealed that nearly all participating CSE survivors reported an experience of emotional, physical, *and* sexual abuse in childhood (see Table 19.3). These findings are consistent with existing evidence that it is more common for survivors of CSE to experience multiple types of abuse concurrently than solely experience one type of abuse [21, 22].

19.2.3 Boston Programs

A discussion of Boston law enforcement and human trafficking would not be complete without a reference to the various programs that work with BPD HTU to provide services for survivors and vulnerable youth. Law enforcement relies extensively on the data and guidance provided by these organizations and often works with them to provide services for survivors. These service groups also often work in tandem to determine best practices for law enforcement and health care providers,

Table 19.3 EVA Center "Yes" responses to modified ACE, 2016[a]

ACE question #	CSE survivors reporting experience
1. Emotional abuse	21
2. Physical abuse	21
3. Sexual abuse	19
4. Emotional neglect	14
5. Physical neglect	17
6. *Parents divorced*	*Dropped*
7. Primary female caretaker abuse	5
8. Household substance abuse	10
9. Household abuse or mental illness	6
10. Household criminal background	2

Reproduced with permission from Dr. David Shim [16]
[a]In this study, $N = 21$

address issues related to the commercial sex industry (e.g., substance use disorders), create mentorship opportunities for at-risk individuals, or target demand. Listed below are organizations that work cooperatively with BPD HTU and exemplify survivor-centered practice. They are considered "survivor-centered" because of their trauma-informed[2], non-judgmental approach, and many are survivor-led.

My Life My Choice (MLMC), which accepts referrals for children under 18, provides a set of survivor-led services such as health care practitioner training, prevention groups for vulnerable adolescent girls, survivor mentoring to young victims of CSE, and advocacy and leadership development.

Roxbury Youth Works Gaining Independence for Tomorrow (GIFT) Programs accept referrals for children under 18, and provide life coaches that invoke professional, educational, and personal life experiences to develop relationships with GIFT youth members. They use a non-judgmental, trauma-informed approach to serve survivors with a history or current experience of CSE. These relationships help youth create and sustain positive connections to remain attached to the vital services they need.

Roxbury Youth Works' Being United in Leading our Destiny (BUILD) Program employs an intensive mentoring model to address the complex needs of boys and transgender-experienced youth victimized via CSE.

The Josephine Butler EVA Center, formerly known as *Kim's Project*, serves young women over the age of 18, many of who are referred from law enforcement or the courts. Formed in 2006 by a survivor of the sex trade, this Boston-based program is a survivor-led effort that helps young women exit the commercial sex industry; survivors collaborate with law enforcement throughout New England and provide services to young sex trafficked women.

Project Assert and the After Midnight Program of Boston Medical Center often provides substance detoxification placement and other support for those who have been sex trafficked and struggling with substance use problems.

The CEASE Network is a collaboration of pioneering cities committed to reducing the purchasing of sex by 20 % between 2018 and 2020. This network is dedicated to innovating, testing, and sharing strategies with a promising ability to deter people from buying sex. These techniques have been successful in many major metropolitan areas, including Atlanta, Boston, Chicago, Dallas, Denver, Houston, Oakland, Phoenix, Portland, San Diego, and Seattle [23]. A combination of methods has helped reduce demand at the local level, while also fueling a national movement to end sexual exploitation [24].

---

[2] A trauma-informed approach is one that acknowledges the impact of trauma (e.g.: violence or exploitation) while responding in a way that fully supports without re-traumatizing. A thorough description of this approach is included in Chapter 18 of this book.

19.2.4 Trends in Data from Local Service Providers

Until recently, the lack of data made human trafficking cases nearly impossible to quantify. Trafficking is a crime hiding in "plain sight": Some being trafficked do not realize they are being trafficked; some know they are being exploited but have been manipulated or forced into compliance; service providers and professionals are not systematically trained on how to recognize the signs of trafficking and intervene. As a result, law enforcement leaders on the national, state, and local levels were unable to provide adequate resources to investigate trafficking. But law enforcement officers have begun working with service providers; thus more quantitative data is available. Collaboration across systems reveals human trafficking as not merely an issue of criminality, but a much larger issue of public health.

Though there is not much data available for Boston, the Boston-based MLMC has collected basic statistics on the youth they serve, including trafficking survivors (see Table 19.4). Out of 143 youth served, the majority (76 %) predominantly entered the commercial sex industry between the ages of 13 and 15 though approximately one-fourth entered either at a younger (11–12) or older (16–17) age; most were youth of color (non-white, 77 %). There is a high percentage of child welfare

Table 19.4 MLMC statistics fiscal year 2015

Category	Count (%)
Total youth	
Total youth	143 (100)
Age of entry into commercial sex industry (years)	
11	3 (4)
12	3 (4)
13	16 (20)
14	27 (34)
15	17 (22)
16	7 (9)
17	6 (8)
Gang affiliation	
Yes	29 (23)
No	99 (77)
Systems involved	
Department of Children and Families	107 (80)
Department of Youth Services	23 (17)
Department of Mental Health	9 (7)
Race	
Caucasian	29 (23)
Latina	49 (39)
African American/black	31 (25)
Asian/Pacific Islander	2 (2)
Mixed race	14 (11)

involvement (80 %) and gang involvement (23 %). Though the numbers may vary somewhat on a yearly basis, the demographics tell Boston law enforcement and service providers groups are most affected by CSEC.

19.2.5 Substance Use, the Opioid Crisis, and Sex Trafficking

Substance use has become closely intertwined with the trafficking industry as a means of targeting vulnerable individuals, a method of controlling trafficked persons, or as a coping mechanism for the abuse and trauma suffered [25]. Opioids in particular have become intricately connected to trafficking and coincide with the worsening opioid crisis. A study by Lederer and colleagues found that approximately 22.3 % of 102 survivors surveyed had used heroin; over one-fourth of them said that they had been forced to use a substance (not necessarily opioids) while being trafficked [25]. Many sex trafficking cases have involved young people specifically being targeted by traffickers because of their opioid use disorder [26–28]. While the opioid crisis is newly gaining national attention, this problem is not novel: For many years, opioid addiction was a scourge belonging to inner cities, largely affecting poor families and families of color, and lacking broader public attention and interest. Now that this epidemic has moved into the suburbs and is affecting more middle-class and white families, there has been an outcry for increased services and funding for recovery programs rather than prosecution. This movement has the potential to affect the services and funding provided for survivors of trafficking who suffer from substance use disorders (SUD).

Since 2005, Boston has experienced a surge of people struggling with SUD, particularly the use of opioids [26] and trafficking; the authors are aware of several trafficking survivors and witnesses in sex trafficking cases in Boston who died from overdoses in 2015. In 2006, out of 55 EVA Center referrals, two (3.6 %) were reported to have had a substance use disorder. In contrast, in 2015, from January to September, out of 32 referrals, 22 (68.8 %) needed access to drug treatment programs, and most trafficked clients were between the ages of 17 and 25 years. Between 2009 and 2015, the EVA Center has worked with about 350 young women involved in prostitution and/or sex trafficking, providing them long-term survivor-led peer support. Many of the young women who have been sex trafficked and struggle with SUD also have children, resulting in direct harm to their offspring: According to Carol Erskine of the Worcester[3] Juvenile Court, there has been "a very significant increase in the number of child abuse and neglect cases, and it is clear that parental opioid addiction is a contributing factor" [29]. The public health consequences of trafficking and SUD affect survivors, and their children and families.

---

[3] Worcester is a small city about an hour away from Boston.

19.2.6   Boston Law Enforcement's Approach
to Human Trafficking

19.2.6.1   Challenges to Prosecuting Sex Trafficking Cases

There are a multitude of challenges in prosecuting cases of sex trafficking including the following: reluctance of victims; technological challenges and constantly changing trends; hidden victims; the volume of online advertisements; and jurisdictional issues.

Reluctant Victims/Witnesses Much like those involved in gang and organized crime cases, many victims are unable to cooperate for numerous reasons including fear of reprisal, loyalty and/or love toward the trafficker(s), concern for personal and/or familial safety, and need for housing. Many victims also suffer from complex trauma, or the simultaneous experiences of other types of abuse (e.g., emotional abuse or neglect, sexual abuse, physical abuse, and domestic violence) that are chronic; frequently such trauma begins in early childhood. A history of complex trauma can cause affected persons to have problems in relationships and with authority figures. Often these young people have witnessed police responding to situations where their parents were arrested or those victimized have been arrested for unrelated crimes.

Victimized persons may also have significant difficulties due to the complex trauma of sexual violence, intimate partner violence, and stalking that frequently accompany sex trafficking. Unseen and often misunderstood, these psychological wounds are associated with feelings of "guilt, self-blame, embarrassment, fear… [among] other emotions" [11]. According to Viktoria Kristiansson, JD and Charlene Whitman-Barr, JD, attorneys at AEquitas[4]:

> the trauma caused by…sexual exploitation or trafficking, and intimate partner violence…is often mitigated or overlooked even by experienced professional responders. This disparity can discourage victims from reporting and from seeking help, and can also re-traumatize victims who do come forward if they are blamed for the crimes committed against them or if their disclosures are minimized, criticized, or not believed [11].

Law enforcement officers need to recognize and understand the complexities of trauma to encourage trafficked persons to come forward; the ultimate goal must be healing for the survivor, not prosecution for the state.

Technology Traffickers are constantly up-to-date with new technology and trends that facilitate their criminal enterprises. Unfortunately, law enforcement has limited resources for specialized trainings and tools to keep pace with novel technology [30, 31].

---

[4] AEquitas: The Prosecutors' Resource on Violence Against Women is an organization that aims to improve the quality of justice in human trafficking cases and other abusive and exploitative crimes.

Hidden Victims The commercial sex industry has largely moved inside, to hotels and apartments. Often only the traffickers and buyers know where victims are located.

Jurisdictional Issues Online advertisements such as those on Backpage.com are city-specific but often also extend to other geographical regions and states. Young women are frequently moved from city to city, and state to state. A trafficked person can be moved across several jurisdictional areas in one day. There must be collaboration among law enforcement of varying jurisdictions; they must share resources and intelligence. Although task forces have improved inter-agency and departmental cooperation, there are still often legal and confidentiality concerns as well as "turf battles" and trust issues among investigators [32].

Volume and Nature of Ads The sheer volume of advertisements for commercial sex on the internet makes it impossible for law enforcement to simply "prosecute the problem away." In fact, law enforcement cannot follow up every received tip about possibly under-aged girls in photographs; commonly, images are modified or have only certain body parts showing making identification extremely difficult, if not impossible.

19.2.7   What Works: Working with Survivors and Non-governmental Organizations

Despite the difficulties, there are techniques and methods that allow law enforcement to prosecute offenders, protect civilians, and support survivor healing. Successful officers, agents, and attorneys recognize that reliance on survivor testimony is insufficient for a strong case; these professionals work diligently to uncover evidence and build a well-founded case. They work with survivors and service providers as early as possible to both support the survivor and develop the case.

After shifting to a *survivor-centered* approach to criminal justice, the BPD HTU has been more successful in efforts to curb exploitation. Police in Boston, through a commitment from the top down, are shifting their response to prostitution: More pimps and buyers are being targeted and young women involved in commercial sex are seen as victims rather than criminals. For example:

> In a commonly encountered scenario, BPD detectives meet a woman in a hotel who would have been previously labeled a "prostitute." Detectives explain to the woman why they are concerned she may be a victim of trafficking. They spend time with the survivor and speak with her in a respectful, non-judgmental way. The woman is introduced, to a survivor and if she is interested and willing, and although often challenging, she can begin the journey of leaving the commercial sex industry. Working with a survivor from the EVA Center, she receives assistance to obtain an education, housing, job training, and child care, and makes a plan to become safely self-sufficient.

19.2.8   Learning Best Practices from Other Law Enforcement

Law enforcement must recognize that success is not always measured in arrests and prosecutions but should be about making victims safe. Nonetheless, promising practices and working with law enforcement networks across the country will lead to increased successful prosecutions. Through the CEASE Initiative, law enforcement agencies are sharing best practices in 11 US cities (see Sect.19.2.3). These cities are targeting large-scale trafficking operations, which have crossed state lines. For example, for illicit massage parlors and brothels, they are using the "Capone Theory" similar to the method used to prosecute Al Capone [33]: Prosecutors charge traffickers and property owners with provable criminal offenses like wage, tax, and organized crime code violations when the elements for trafficking cannot be proven. This technique has proved successful in shutting down illegal businesses, seizing associated money and property, and protecting trafficked persons.

Sex trafficking law enforcement investigators are also developing strategic partnerships with hotels and car rental agencies, which are often used by traffickers. Additionally, they are working within their own agencies to build alliances with drug, gang, and homicide investigators as these crimes are often related to trafficking. They have generally learned to be less territorial as these crimes cross city, county, state, and sometimes country borders. They recognize success will only come through collaboration.

Law enforcement has become increasingly aware of how large and intricate human trafficking networks can be. A case with one or two apparent victims often spirals into multiple victims and traffickers: Many traffickers encourage women to bear children. The traffickers then use the children as leverage to coerce the women to work for them. In the incidence of sex trafficking pictured in Fig. 19.2, most of the women and girls were advertised for commercial sex on websites like Backpage. com and trafficked through hotels in several states. In total, in this particular trafficking ring, eight traffickers and ten victims were identified. One of the traffickers is depicted at the center of the diagram below. The red encircled images around him represent his known victims and the children he fathered with them. If the women were not earning money for him through commercial sex, he made them commit other crimes like larceny and credit card fraud. This pimp was sentenced to 30 years in prison after accepting a plea agreement. His attorney reported that he was a victim of child abuse and witnessed domestic violence: His father was murdered when he was a young teenager and his mother had been involved in the commercial sex industry.

This network map depicts one trafficker, his various sex trafficking victims, and their children, in the Boston area. Fathering children with a victim is sometimes used as a form of coercion.

Boston law enforcement has also been discussing ways to address trafficking that occurs in massage parlors and bodywork venues. Many are actually brothels but prosecuting the cases pose unique challenges. Many of the women involved are not from the USA and, because of negative experiences with law enforcement or fear of

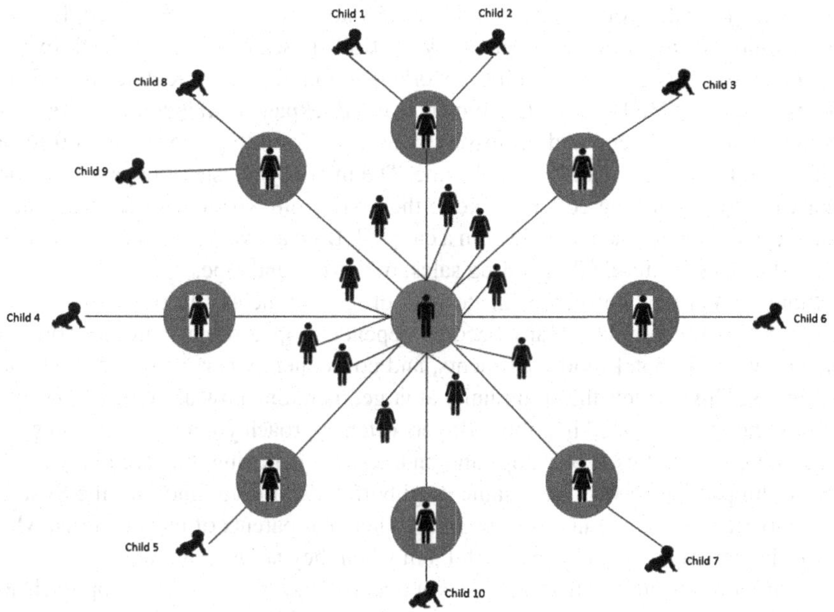

Fig. 19.2 Case example: one trafficker's victim and children network map

deportation, they have an innate distrust of law enforcement. Many are moved from city to city and state to state, so cases may be prosecuted on the federal level. But for a sex trafficking case involving an adult victim to meet the federal standard, the prosecutor must show force, fraud and/or coercion. These women are frequently unwilling to testify or prosecutors do not believe they can meet the burden. Law enforcement entities are thus working together, through the CEASE Network, to determine how to prosecute these cases using different laws. They have also built strong relationships with Polaris, the NGO that operates the National Human Trafficking Hotline. When law enforcement in one jurisdiction has been successful, the information and tools may be shared with other jurisdictions.

19.2.9   Arrest of Buyers Who Fuel the Industry

Law enforcement views sex trafficking and prostitution as a harmful industry that puts countless people and communities at risk. There are still "tracks"[5] of street prostitution in Boston; however, most of the sex trade is conducted behind closed doors using the internet. Many buyers who would not previously seek out commercial sex on the street now feel safe to do so. "The spatial limitations that once

---

[5]A "track" is an area known for street prostitution.

governed the underground commercial sex economy are gone. Now people who once would not have ventured to their city's "stroll" in search of commercial sex are able to anonymously connect with sex workers. Often the new clientele are higher-paying customers" [34]. In Boston, buyers using Backpage.com include professionals like doctors, lawyers, and professors, who can afford to pay $150 to 300 for a half or full hour of "service" at lunch-time. The majority of "street buyers" include men who are often blue-collar workers; they pay from $10 to $40 for a sex act, which usually takes place outside or in a car [35]. Both are venues that often include spin-off crimes including illegal drug sales, robberies, and rape.

Many young women self-medicate with drugs and alcohol in order to sell sex acts to 5 to 10 men a day. Many become dependent upon drugs, can therefore no longer "work" in hotels and apartments, and consequently perform sexual acts on the streets. This impacts the community at large, including how all females in some neighborhoods are treated in public. Buyers often approach young women and girls in certain communities at bus stops and on the street believing they are likely prostitutes. Pimps often "troll" these same neighborhoods. It is common for the Boston police to receive complaints from young women and parents of teenage girls, who report that attempted buyers approach them when they are walking home.

An important, but controversial, component of a comprehensive approach to ending sexual exploitation is to prosecute the buyers, who make sex trafficking possible. To put it simply, "No buyers, no business." While this concept is logical, it has also been postulated that prosecuting buyers will force the commercial sex industry even further "underground." Some have argued this puts trafficked persons at even greater risk and makes it more difficult for service providers and professionals to recognize them and offer aid. From the law enforcement author's perspective this is untrue. Because of the internet and the nature of the online sex trade—which accounts for most sex trafficking cases law enforcement encounters—sex trafficking is already underground. Most commercial sex and trafficking in Boston occur through online escort websites like Backpage and EROS or dating websites like Tinder and Kik. It occurs behind the closed doors of apartments, storefront brothels, and hotels. Men who buy sex do not openly disclose in public that they are doing so. Some post anonymously on sites like USSEXGUIDE. Sex trafficking is still largely ignored and unrecognized: It is inherently underground.

19.3   Conclusion

We are at the tip of the proverbial human trafficking iceberg, much like we were with domestic violence in the 1980s. Both are often hidden crimes because they largely occur behind closed doors and both cause significant physical and emotional harm not only to the victims but also to families and communities. Human trafficking feeds off of and contributes to substance use problems and homelessness. Several survivors have reported that they entered the commercial sex industry because of domestic violence and ultimately became dependent on heroin.

To end exploitation, criminal prosecution of traffickers is simply not enough: To become survivors, victims need viable life options, including safe housing and education. There is no shortage of vulnerable young people that pimps/traffickers are willing to exploit for financial gain. Intergenerational violence, poverty, and systematic oppressions are complex and serious problems that society needs to address to prevent human trafficking. It is crucial to invest in accessible health care, high quality education and housing, and drug rehabilitation. Otherwise, the cycle of violence and exploitation will continue in our most vulnerable communities. Many pimps/traffickers have criminal records and comparatively little to lose; but buyers have jobs and status to protect. Law enforcement should expand their focus to address the demand for commercial sex and invest in the future of at-risk individuals.

19.4 Recommendations

Though much remains to be done to reduce the prevalence of sex trafficking and create a more survivor-centered approach to law enforcement, there are some notable pathways forward.

- *Multi-sector collaboration.* Schools need to teach youth, of all genders, about healthy relationships and the dangers of CSE at an early age, particularly at the middle school level. We must help children identify the signs of unhealthy situations and prevent vulnerable children from becoming victims. Collaborating with survivors, who are the true experts, in all facets of the anti-trafficking response is crucial to reaching trafficked persons and preventing victimization. Working with local organizations will help communities take ownership of the problem and the solutions. Ultimately, law enforcement must acknowledge that we cannot solve the problem of human trafficking by arrest or awareness campaigns alone; that tactic has not worked with attempts to curb illicit substance use and it is not working for trafficking [36]. To truly reduce demand and protect vulnerable individuals, we must work collaboratively, toward a holistic, public health response.
- *Learn from best practices and partnerships.* Law enforcement must work with NGOs, survivors, health care professionals, educators, policy makers and families to develop, evaluate, and promote best practices. The Boston Public Schools in collaboration with SEEN and the BPD HTU have trained school principals, nurses, police officers, and other staff about CSEC. Plans are underway to implement a curriculum for students about healthy relationships; the program will cover prevention of CSEC.
- *Diversion Programs and Safe Harbor Laws.* Diversion programs offer an alternative to the juvenile court system, where first-time offenders (aged 7–18) may have the opportunity to receive services rather than be prosecuted through the traditional court process [37]. This is based on the idea that processing some youth through the formal delinquency system and court hearings may do more harm than good, by stigmatizing and traumatizing them. These are closely related to "Safe Harbor" programs, in which sexually exploited children are treated as

victims of child abuse rather than criminals, and consequently have access to the same resources as victims of child abuse. Massachusetts also includes a "Safe Harbor" provision and directs these victims to NGO or state services rather than to the juvenile court system [38]. Programs like MLMC, GIFT, and BUILD are gender specific [39]. These programs were built because the founders appreciated a need. The Office of Juvenile Justice and Delinquency acknowledges that girls have historically been overlooked in the juvenile justice systems and programs were based on research on boys' programs. Programs specific for girls, boys, and transgender-experienced youth will address the particular risk factors for commercial sexual exploitation each group faces.

- *Survivor-Led Programs.* As is the case for many other victim populations (e.g., survivors of domestic violence and/or sexual assault, and families of homicide victims), survivor-led advocacy and support is necessary to provide services for survivors of human trafficking, including housing. Due to their shared experiences, survivors are more likely to trust survivor-advocates rather than law enforcement or customary social service providers [40].
- *Early Intervention for Children Who Witness IPV and HT.* When children witness relationship conflict (e.g., intimate partner violence or human trafficking), abuse and exploitation, they are at higher risk for becoming involved, as perpetrators or victims, in violence [36]. Breaking this cycle of intergenerational violence is imperative to reducing the number of young men that become pimps and the number of young women that become commercially sexually exploited. Children who witness violence often enter foster care and group homes; some run away. Many age out of systems with little familial support, education, and life skills. In Massachusetts, there has been an effort to increase the number of social workers at the Department of Children and Families. Researchers should identify best practices of education and support for children who enter child welfare systems.
- *Focus on Demand.* Law enforcement should focus on high-frequency buyers and websites that promote human trafficking. Those arrested should include the web host companies that facilitate trafficking. Law enforcement must continue to increase efforts against buyers, but rather than end at arrest, communities must work together to develop relevant interventions. One option, "john schools" is an alternative to criminal conviction for buyers, and may lower the rates of recidivism [41–43].

While progress has been made toward helping sex trafficking victims and at-risk individuals, we have a long journey ahead.

Tips for practitioners in law enforcement in serving survivors:
   Mindset:

- Do not treat survivors as if they are broken
- Understand survivors need empowerment, not "rescue"
- Empathize

- Understand that survivors may experience attachment to their trafficker
- Understand that society, and often law enforcement, have historically treated trafficking survivors poorly, with little respect
- Understand there is no singular or linear path out of a trafficked situation, and sometimes survivors return to a trafficked situation
- Understand need for gender-specific programs (e.g., substance use treatment, housing)
- Recognize some survivors are searching for an escape from their problems, and need love, support, acceptance, and shelter; and, without healthier options, these needs make them vulnerable to being trafficked
- Appreciate that people take pride in having material goods; trafficked persons can feel glamorous when they are able to have things they could not previously afford
- Understand that survivors may feel a range of emotions, including anger, anxiety, fear, shame, and guilt
- At first encounter, let the survivor clean up and offer a jacket or other weather-appropriate clothing, food, and drink
- Be non-judgmental: Recognize the stigma of being trafficked, as well as fears and barriers to leaving

Communication:

- Express appreciation for the survivor's strength and resilience
- Listen to survivors and let them tell their stories at their pace
- Do not interrupt just to get the facts
- Enlist survivor support to develop trust, credibility, and give ongoing support
- Do not talk in public places like hallways
- Build rapport
- Do not make promises
- Do not use a condescending or patronizing tone, even if they are a minor
- Do not make demands
- Be authentic in your concern
- Explain that being trafficked does not define the survivor
- Express concern for their health and safety
- Express they may have other livelihood alternatives to commercial sex
- Give them the choice to have evidence collection and documentation of injuries, explaining why it is important, even if they do not want to press charges
- Explain the limits of confidentiality, including why certain actions are required (e.g., mandated reports for children)
- Explain your role and your goal (the survivor's healing)
- Ask what the survivor wants and how you can help
- Treat someone how you would want your child, mate or friend to be treated.

References

1. ECPAT International. http://www.ecpat.net/node. Accessed 11 May 2016.
2. Bindel J. Women sex trafficking other women: the problem is getting worse. The Guardian. 22 April 2013. http://www.theguardian.com/lifeandstyle/2013/apr/22/women-sex-trafficking-women-problem. Accessed 1 Aug 2016.
3. Buchbinder S. When women traffic other women. The Daily Beast. 7 August 2013. http://www.thedailybeast.com/witw/articles/2013/08/07/when-women-are-found-trafficking-other-women.html. Accessed 1 Aug 2016.
4. Identifying challenges to improve the investigation and prosecution of state and local human trafficking cases. http://www.urban.org/research/publication/identifying-challenges-improve-investigation-and-prosecution-state-and-local-0. Accessed 11 May 2016.
5. Raphael J, Myers-Powell B. From victims to victimizers; interviews with 25 ex-pimps in Chicago. National Human Trafficking Resource Center. 29 September 2014. https://traffickingresourcecenter.org/resources/victims-victimizers-interviews-25-ex-pimps-chicago. Accessed 1 Aug 2016.
6. Session Laws: Chapter 178 of the Acts of 2011. https://malegislature.gov/Laws/SessionLaws/Acts/2011/Chapter178. Accessed 2 May 2016.
7. Commonwealth v. McGhee. Justia Law. http://law.justia.com/cases/massachusetts/supreme-court/2015/sjc-11821.html. Accessed 2 May 2016.
8. Department of State. The Office of Website Management, Bureau of Public Affairs. U.S. laws on trafficking in persons. 3 January 2006. http://www.state.gov/j/tip/laws/. Accessed 1 Aug 2016.
9. The Associated Press. Massachusetts Court affirms anti-human trafficking law. Wbur. 13 August 2015. http://www.wbur.org/2015/08/13/massachusetts-anti-human-trafficking. Accessed 1 Aug 2016.
10. Dank M, Khan B, Downey PM, Kotonias C, Mayer D, Owens C, Pacifici L, Yu L. Estimating the size and structure of the underground commercial sex economy in eight major US cities. Urban Institute. 12 March 2014. http://www.urban.org/research/publication/estimating-size-and-structure-underground-commercial-sex-economy-eight-major-us-cities. Accessed 1 Aug 2016.
11. Kristiansson V, Whitman-Barr C. Integrating a trauma-informed response in violence against women and human trafficking prosecutions. Strategies, no. 13. February 2015. http://www.aequitasresource.org/Integrating-A-Trauma-Informed-Response-In-VAW-and-HT-Strategies.pdf. Accessed 1 Aug 2016.
12. Human Trafficking and the Internet* (*and Other Technologies, Too) | Judicial Division. http://www.americanbar.org/publications/judges_journal/2013/winter/human_trafficking_and_internet_and_other_technologies_too.html. Accessed 2 May 2016.
13. Indermaur D. Young Australians and domestic violence. Pamphlet. http://www.aic.gov.au/publications/current%20series/tandi/181-200/tandi195.html. Accessed 27 Mar 2016.
14. James M. Domestic violence as a form of child abuse: identification and prevention. Child Family Community Australia. https://aifs.gov.au/cfca/publications/domestic-violence-form-child-abuse-identification. Accessed 27 Mar 2016.
15. UNICEF, and The Body Shop International Fund. Behind closed doors: the impact of domestic violence on children. 2006. http://www.unicef.org/media/files/BehindClosedDoors.pdf. Accessed 1 Aug 2016.
16. Gehrenbeck-Shim D, et al. Personal communication. 27 April 2015.
17. Starecheski L. Take the ACE quiz—and learn what it does and doesn't mean. NPR.org. http://www.npr.org/sections/health-shots/2015/03/02/387007941/take-the-ace-quiz-and-learn-what-it-does-and-doesnt-mean. Accessed 2 May 2016.
18. About adverse childhood experiences. http://www.cdc.gov/violenceprevention/acestudy/about_ace.html. Accessed 2 May 2016.

19. Ergas D, Gehrenbeck-Shim D. The precursors for entrance into the sex industry: risk factors and childhood trauma. Unpublished manuscript. Boston, MA: Department of Psychological and Brain Sciences, Boston University; 2015.
20. About the CDC-Kaiser ACE Study|Child Maltreatment|Violence Prevention|Injury Center|CDC. http://www.cdc.gov/violenceprevention/acestudy/about.html. Accessed 2 May 2016; Adverse Childhood Experiences (ACEs). http://www.cdc.gov/violenceprevention/acestudy/index.html. Accessed 2 May 2016.
21. Goncharenko S, Gehrenbeck-Shim DJ. A qualitative analysis of commercial sexual exploitation among adults and minors. Unpublished manuscript. Boston, MA: Department of Psychological and Brain Sciences, Boston University; 2016.
22. Mercer A, Gehrenbeck-Shim DJ. Listening to survivors: a qualitative examination of the traumatic risk factors of commercial sexual exploitation. Unpublished manuscript. Boston, MA: Department of Psychological and Brain Sciences, Boston University; 2016.
23. Cities empowered against sexual exploitation. Cities Initiative. https://www.ceasenetwork.org/. Accessed 15 May 2016.
24. The health consequences of sex trafficking and their implications for identifying victims in healthcare facilities. National Human Trafficking Resource Center. 28 September 2014. https://traffickingresourcecenter.org/resources/health-consequences-sex-trafficking-and-their-implications-identifying-victims-healthcare. Accessed 1 Aug 2016.
25. A look into a destructive cycle of sex work and addiction. MSNBC. 2 December 2014. http://www.msnbc.com/msnbc/Z-and-opioid-abuse. Accessed 1 Aug 2016.
26. Human trafficking and opioid abuse | Administration for children and families. http://www.acf.hhs.gov/blog/2016/05/human-trafficking-and-opioid-abuse. Accessed 3 June 2016.
27. Gibbons P, Stoklosa H. Identification and treatment of human trafficking victims in the emergency department: a case report. J Emerg Med. 2016;50(5):715–9.
28. Opioid and prescription drug abuse. Attorney General of Massachusetts. 4 January 2016. http://www.mass.gov/ago/public-safety/opioids/index.html. Accessed 1 Aug 2016.
29. Levenson M. Concern mounting about the opioid crisis' toll on children - the Boston globe. BostonGlobe.com. 17 October 2015. https://www.bostonglobe.com/metro/2015/10/17/concern-mounting-about-opioid-crisis-toll-children/bbKXGdk4iKry1l6vAcb4hO/story.html. Accessed 1 Aug 2016.
30. DARPA developing ultimate web search engine to police the internet. RT International. https://www.rt.com/usa/darpa-internet-search-engine-788/ Accessed 15 May 2016.
31. Otto G. Memex: law enforcement's answer to searching the dark web. FedScoop. http://fedscoop.com/memex-law-enforcements-answer-to-searching-the-dark-web. Accessed 15 May 2016.
32. Northeastern University Institute on Race and Justice. Understanding and improving law enforcement responses to human trafficking. Final Report. June 2008. http://www.northeastern.edu/humantrafficking/wp-content/uploads/Understanding%20and%20Responding_Full%20Report.pdf. Accessed 1 Aug 2016.
33. Al Capone. FBI. https://www.fbi.gov/about-us/history/famous-cases/al-capone/al-capone. Accessed 2 May 2016.
34. Urban Institute. The hustle: economics of the underground commercial sex economy. 2014. http://apps.urban.org/features/theHustle/index.html. Accessed 1 Aug 2016.
35. Farley M, Golding JM, Matthews ES, Malamuth NM, Jarrett L. Comparing sex buyers with men who do not buy sex: new data on prostitution and trafficking. J Interpers Violence. 31 August 2015. doi:10.1177/0886260515600874.
36. Arkowitz SO, Lilienfeld H. Why 'Just Say No' doesn't work. Scientific American. http://www.scientificamerican.com/article/why-just-say-no-doesnt-work/. Accessed 2 May 2016.
37. Juvenile diversion. Essex District Attorney's Office. 6 November 2011. http://www.mass.gov/essexda/prevention-and-intervention/school-safety/juvenile-diversion.html. Accessed 1 Aug 2016.
38. Representing victims of human trafficking in Massachusetts. Representing Victims of Human Trafficking in Massachusetts. http://www.representingmatraffickingvictims.org/. Accessed 16 May 2016.

39. Chapter 2: What does gender-specific programming look like in practice? http://www.ojjdp.gov/pubs/principles/ch2_6.html. Accessed 3 June 2016.
40. Interagency human trafficking task force. 21 February 2012. http://www.mass.gov/ago/public-safety/human-trafficking/human-trafficking-task-force/. Accessed 1 Aug 2016.
41. 'John Schools' teach lessons from the sex Trade. NOW on PBS. http://www.pbs.org/now/shows/422/prostitution.html. Accessed 2 May 2016.
42. 'Buyer Beware': early success for initiative targeting johns instead of prostitutes. The Seattle Times. 16 May 2015. http://www.seattletimes.com/seattle-news/crime/buyer-beware-early-success-for-initiative-targeting-johns-instead-of-prostitutes/. Accessed 1 Aug 2016.
43. Shively M. San Francisco's 'John School' reduces recidivism among men arrested for soliciting a prostitute. 25 February 2008. http://abtassociates.com/Impact/2008/San-Francisco-s-John-School-Reduces-Recidivism-A.aspx. Accessed 1 Aug 2016.

Chapter 20
The Role of Community Health Centers in Addressing Human Trafficking

Kimberly S.G. Chang and A. Seiji Hayashi

20.1 Introduction

There is growing recognition that human trafficking is a health care and public health issue [1] with severe health consequences affecting some of the most vulnerable members of society. Short- and long-term health harms are caused by the conditions of human trafficking and the way people are controlled for labor or sex. While trafficked, people may be deprived of health care and food, are socially restricted, and are coerced into drug and alcohol use and dependence. They are often forced into dangerous, dirty, and degrading living and working conditions; and they are subject to all forms of abuse (physical, sexual, psychological, emotional, behavioral, and spiritual) [2]. The health harms fall into three categories: physical harms such as sexually transmitted infections (STI), injuries, and malnutrition; mental health harms, such as trauma, depression, and anxiety; and social harms, such as criminalization and stigmatization [2–9]. Viewing human trafficking through a public health lens enables social systems of care and protection to reach more trafficked individuals and prevent human trafficking by strengthening both individuals and communities. A public health approach emphasizes prevention, community outreach, and multidisciplinary collaboration, with a focus on addressing social determinants and preventing harms [10]. Community health centers use this approach for all populations, including those at risk of trafficking and with a trafficking experience. Whereas criminal justice and law enforcement systems reach people in the late stages of trafficking, community health and public health systems

K.S.G. Chang (✉)
Asian Health Services, Oakland, CA, USA
e-mail: ksgchang@gmail.com

A.S. Hayashi
Unity Health Care, Inc., Washington, DC, USA
e-mail: aseijihayashi@gmail.com

© Springer International Publishing AG 2017   347
M. Chisolm-Straker, H. Stoklosa (eds.), *Human Trafficking Is a Public Health Issue*, DOI 10.1007/978-3-319-47824-1_20

have the capacity to extend farther into vulnerable populations, preventing and combating human trafficking earlier, and providing care long after the trafficking ends.

The health care system provides opportunities for interaction and engagement with patients throughout the entire lifespan—from pregnancy, to childhood, through adulthood; from acute emergency care, to long-term, chronic care; from public health community outreach to hospitalizations. All of these points of care are opportunities to prevent, intervene in, start the process of ending exploitation, and begin the healing process for trafficked patients. Studies of trafficked people reveal a wide range of encounters with health care professionals and clinics while being trafficked—between 28 and 87.8 % of survivors had seen a health care professional [2, 11, 12]. As such, primary care professionals and organizations that expand access to care for medically underserved and vulnerable populations play a central role in caring for these patients across lifespans. Examples of these safety net clinics include federally qualified health centers (FQHC), Indian Health Service clinics, free clinics, and others. There are a number of specific types of FQHCs that focus on migrant and seasonal farmworkers, individuals experiencing homelessness, and residents of public housing. This chapter will focus on the variety of FQHCs collectively known as *community health centers* (http://bphc.hrsa.gov).

Community health centers serve a disproportionate share of the nation's poor and uninsured. Most patients are members of racial or ethnic minorities, and millions of health center patients are served in a language other than English [13, 14]. Trafficked persons are often members of society's more vulnerable groups like these [15]. For example, one study found that trafficked individuals in Southeast Asia tended to be poor, young, female, undocumented migrants with low levels of educational attainment [16]. In addition, trafficked persons are more likely to be runaway youth and have a history of trauma or violence [15].

Given that community health centers serve similar populations (and may already unknowingly be serving trafficked patients [17]), developing systems of care within health centers may lead to earlier intervention and prevention efforts. Many health centers have resources and programs in place to care for trafficked persons more effectively than providers in other types of health care settings. For example, many health centers have health care providers and staff that speak the patients' languages or have on site interpreters. Most health centers have social services to connect patients to non-health care resources. Some health centers even have lawyers to assist patients (http://medical-legalpartnership.org). Additionally, health centers have staff to assist patients in navigating the complex health care system with case management and care coordination, a hallmark of a patient-centered medical home. Health centers are now focusing on the integration between primary care and behavioral health, as well as integration of oral health care and primary care, within community health centers.

The United States' vertical organization of the health care system, from a large primary care base to increasingly specialized levels of care, emphasizes the foundational role of community health centers in the prevention, early identification, and acute and long-term treatment of patients who have been labor or sex trafficked. Primary care is the level of a health services system that provides entry into the system for all new needs and problems, provides person-focused (not disease-oriented) care over time, and provides care for all but very unusual conditions. Furthermore, the primary care level coordinates care, regardless of where the care is delivered and who provides it. It focuses on integrating care into a comprehensive treatment plan for patients (e.g., integration of medical and oral health care) and facilitates system optimization and equity of health status (http://www.jhsph.edu/research/centers-and-institutes/johns-hopkins-primary-care-policy-center/definitions.html).

As a large primary care system in the USA, community health centers have multiple opportunities to intercede and identify human trafficking amongst their patients. They are uniquely positioned to be the first point of contact with the health care system for many at risk and trafficked persons. Thus, community health centers can prevent worsening of health issues, but when necessary, refer to specialists, subspecialists, and hospitals. Community health centers also provide many preventative services, health education programs, and community outreach, and therefore, have a great reach into the populations at risk of and affected by human trafficking. Furthermore, community health centers provide continuity of care throughout the lifespan—giving opportunity for long-term engagement with trafficked persons and survivors of human trafficking.

20.2   Discussion

In 2014, 1,278 federally funded community health centers operated almost 10,000 clinics across the USA. These community health centers collectively cared for 22.8 million medically underserved and vulnerable individuals. Of patients served, 71.2% earned an annual income below the federal poverty level (FPL) and 91.4% earned less than 200% of the FPL. Due to the Affordable Care Act, the number of uninsured dropped from 37.5% (2010) to 27.9% (2014). Almost two-thirds (62.2%) of health center patients self-identified as belonging to a racial or ethnic minority group (Black/African American: 23.4%; Asian/Asian American: 3.8%; American Indian/Alaska Native: 1.3%; Native Hawaiian/Other Pacific Islander: 1.2%; and Hispanic/Latino: 34.9%). Nearly a quarter (23.2%) was best served in a language other than English. Individuals experiencing homelessness accounted for 5% (1.1 million) of health center patients, and residents of public housing comprised 1.9%. Additionally, community health centers served 892,000 migrant and seasonal agricultural workers in 2014 [18].

Community health centers grew out of the US civil rights movement to eliminate social inequity and promote social justice. The first federally funded community health centers were founded in Mound Bayou, Mississippi and in Boston, Massachusetts in 1965 by two physicians, H. Jack Geiger and Count Gibson, as part of the Johnson Administration's "War on Poverty" [19]. Increasing health care access was also a prime objective of the civil rights movement as exemplified in this statement by leader Martin Luther King, Jr.: "Of all the forms of inequality, injustice in health care is the most shocking and inhumane." Most health centers continue to see their work as a vehicle for social justice. Human trafficking is a human rights violation, and caring for those trafficked falls squarely within the mission of health centers.

Geiger and Gibson developed the first health centers based on a model called Community Oriented Primary Care (COPC). COPC integrates primary care services with public health approaches. COPC has several distinguishing features that make it especially suitable to care for medically vulnerable populations such as trafficked persons. The first is the use of public health methodologies, such as epidemiology, to define and care for whole populations. Second, patients and community members prioritize health issues and participate in resolving them. Finally, services are not limited to traditional primary care, and may include services aimed at the social determinants of health, such as hunger, housing insecurity, educational attainment, employment, and even environmental justice (http://www.altfutures. org/pubs/leveragingSDH/IAF-CHCsLeveragingSDH.pdf).

Geiger studied COPC in a rural South African village called Pholela in the province of Kwazulu Natal, with Drs. Sydney and Emily Kark. The Karks developed the COPC model to combat community-wide health issues like syphilis. They believed that solutions to health problems should be developed and led by community members themselves [20]. The federal statute authorizing the Health Center Program incorporated this community ownership concept, requiring all FQHCs to have a consumer (patient) majority board of directors [21]. This means that board members with understanding of the cultures, languages, and community can identify issues like human trafficking and guide corresponding health services. Further, this promotes the accountability of health centers to the communities they serve.

In addition to community ownership, a distinguishing hallmark of community health centers is the provision of *enabling services*—services that enable a patient to access care. Trafficked individuals can experience numerous access barriers, such as limited English proficiency, health illiteracy, transportation issues, complex physical, mental health, and social needs, among many others. Many community health centers mitigate these barriers through enabling services. These special, non-clinical services facilitate vulnerable patients' access to care, via outreach, case management, translation/interpretation, referrals, transportation, eligibility assistance, health education, environmental health risk reduction, and health literacy [22] (http:// www.aapcho.org/wp/wp-content/uploads/2014/06/2014-ES-Best-Practices-Report_ FINAL.pdf).

A useful framework to help organize the community health center and health system interface, and the response to trafficked persons, is through a public health prevention model and epidemiologic lens. If human trafficking is considered a disease, and the very real health harms are the symptoms, specific solutions can be crafted to prevent and intervene during different stages of the exploitation [23].

- *Primary prevention* aims to reach people who are not being trafficked, but are at risk.
- Interventions include issue raising awareness in communities, and media or education campaigns.

- *Secondary prevention* tries to reach people in early stages of trafficking, before many health harms may have occurred.
- Interventions include early identification in various settings, like clinics or schools.
- *Tertiary prevention* occurs when a person is being trafficked and is also experiencing physical, mental health, or social harms. This prevention level is late stage and patients usually present in crisis.
- Interventions include acute visits to emergency departments, and are opportunities for an immediate physical intercession, potentially assisting the patient in leaving their trafficked situation.
- And finally, health care presents a unique opportunity to assist and enable *long-term care* for survivors who are no longer being trafficked, or sex trafficked minors who reach 18 years of age and may thereafter be considered sex workers, but may still have serious health consequences from the exploitation. This stage is vital to healing and to preventing revictimization; yet, it is often overlooked in policy and program development of human trafficking organizations.
- Interventions include providing long-term health care and behavioral health care for survivors in the context of primary care (Table 20.1).

There exist models of care for trafficked individuals within community health centers across the country. Because CHCs are grassroots organizations located in the communities they serve, they are well-equipped and informed to create programs specific to the types of human trafficking affecting their patients. As such, there is wide variety in the different programs developed to address human trafficking in health centers;

Table 20.1 Public health model—human trafficking prevention levels [24, 25]

| Prevention levels | | | Health care professional side | |
| | | | Disease: human trafficking (HT) | |
			Absent: a patient is not being trafficked	Present: a patient is being trafficked
Patient side	Illness: Health effects/harms, injuries, impairments	Absent: a patient has not experienced health harms from being trafficked	Primary prevention *HT absent* *Illness absent* Example intervention: raising awareness in communities, media or education campaigns	Secondary prevention *HT present* *Illness absent* Example intervention: early identification in various settings, like clinics or schools
		Present: a patient has experienced health harms from being trafficked	Long-term care *HT absent* *Illness present* Example intervention: providing long-term health care and behavioral health care for survivors (who have a history of being trafficked)	Tertiary prevention *HT present* *Illness present* Example intervention: acute visits to emergency departments

some focus on specific populations, such as domestic minor sex trafficking (DMST) or labor trafficking; and interventions vary from after-care, to prevention and early identification. Five different health center models are discussed below.

20.2.1 Asian Health Services, Oakland, California [26] (www. ahschc.org)

Asian Health Services (AHS) is an FQHC founded in 1974 whose mission is to serve and advocate for the medically underserved, including the immigrant and refugee Asian community, and to assure equal access to health care services regardless of income, insurance status, language, or culture. The issues of commercially sexually exploited children (CSEC) and domestic minor sex trafficking (DMST)[1] first emerged at Asian Health Services (AHS) in Oakland, CA, through its youth program and teen clinic. The AHS youth program was established in 1996 to provide reproductive health education in response to increased Asian and Pacific Islander teenage pregnancies in the county. As a result of increased health education and knowledge of reproductive physiology, youth began requesting health services—in response, a confidential teen clinic was started in 1999. In 2001, AHS youth program staff and teen clinic providers noted that some Southeast Asian adolescent patients repeatedly sought reproductive health services for sexually transmitted infection screening and treatment, reported multiple sexual partners, displayed chronic truancy issues, revealed a history of sexual abuse, and exhibited other high risk factors for sexual exploitation [23, 27]. As staff established rapport and built a therapeutic alliance with their patients, some patients disclosed that they were engaged in the commercial sex industry and talked about their health issues and safety concerns. In an attempt to access resources for patients, AHS staff connected with other community organizers in the education and youth development fields; they realized that several of these organizers were also actively seeking CSEC/DMST resources for their students and clients. Together, they created a CSEC/DMST specific program, *Banteay Srei*, in 2004 [23, 27, 28]. AHS utilizes a programmatic strategy to care for CSEC/DMST across all prevention levels:

- *Primary prevention*: education on healthy relationships for the younger adolescent population; and community health education on commercial sexual exploitation of youth;
- *Secondary prevention*: identification of individuals at high risk for commercial sexual exploitation and sex trafficking; and referrals to local service providers which provide additional prevention resources;

---

[1]The commercial sexual exploitation of children is defined as a range of activities including prostitution, survival sex, child abuse imagery (formerly known as "pornography"), survival sex, sex tourism, mail order brides, stripping or performing in sexual venues. The sex trafficking of domestic minors overlaps with the commercial sexual exploitation of children, but is distinct in referring to exploitation involving a third party exploiter, and in which the child originates from the country in which the exploitation occurs [3].

- *Tertiary prevention*: programming to help trafficked persons and assist them as they transition out of exploitation [3];
- *Long-term comprehensive primary care*: while most support for child-survivors ends once they become adults, AHS continues to care for the patient through adulthood and all life stages, including pregnancy care and pediatric care of children.

AHS' four-pronged programmatic strategy consists of (1) the youth program, (2) a teen clinic, (3) the creation of Banteay Srei, and (4) a school-based health center at Oakland High School. The youth program provides outreach, eligibility assistance, reproductive health education, and navigation of clinical services. The teen clinic provides co-located confidential reproductive clinical services, behavioral health counseling, health education by youth program staff and a peer leader program, and referral resources. The teen clinic routinely and universally screens for sexual exploitation of youth and has implemented a reporting and referral protocol for any youth identified with suspected or disclosed commercial sexual exploitation. Banteay Srei provides youth development and leadership programming specific to at risk or currently sexually exploited girls and young women of Southeast Asian descent; it incorporates programming that highlights and strengthens cultural resiliency. For example, Cambodian interpreters have been included to enable youth to dialogue with mothers, grandmothers, and aunts about the elders' migration and refugee process. For many youth, it is the first time they may hear about their parents' escape from genocide and attendant traumatic experiences; for some, it is the first time they hear the words "I love you" from their mothers in the Cambodian language. *Banteay Srei* also provides case management and care coordination with social services, like reenrolling in school, court advocacy, or connection with shelter support. The AHS school-based health center is at a local high school and health care professionals work with school counselors and educators to identify and help students at risk or suspected of being commercially sexually exploited.

AHS takes their anti-trafficking work further, by conducting research (descriptive investigations of patient population, and development of identification tool); providing trainings for multiple disciplines on human trafficking; and organizing the community to redefine cultural norms, provide resources to at-risk children, and respond to commercial sexual exploitation. AHS also works with local, state, and federal organizations to craft advocacy and policy goals to expand and advance the role of FQHCs in both caring for trafficked persons and preventing trafficking in communities across the country.

20.2.2 Kokua Kalihi Valley Comprehensive Family Services, Honolulu, Hawaii [26] (http://www.kkv.net/index.php/services-and-activities)

Kokua Kalihi Valley Comprehensive Health Services (KKV), an FQHC in Hawaii, has an innovative partnership with the Pacific Survivor Center (PSC). PSC is a Honolulu-based nonprofit organization that focuses on health care and social services for survivors of human trafficking, immigrant domestic violence and torture (http://pschawaii.org/). Since 2012, PSC has been the State of Hawaii subgrantee for the Department of Justice, Office for Victim of Crime's Comprehensive Services for Human Trafficking Victims Grant. PSC provides and coordinates medical, dental, and mental health services for trafficked individuals and survivors of human trafficking, and provides training for health care providers on caring for trafficked persons. Through the unique partnership between KKV and PSC, domestic and immigrant survivors of sex and labor trafficking receive trauma-informed primary medical services (including family medicine, internal medicine, and obstetrics and gynecology), subspecialty services, imaging and laboratory testing, prescription medications, dental care, and mental health services. In addition, PSC clients have access to ancillary KKV services, which includes interpreters, nutritionists, diabetes and renal groups, and insurance eligibility assistance.

Many clients seen through this partnership are trafficked agricultural workers from Southeast Asia, some of whom suffer from chronic illnesses and infections that have never previously been addressed. At the time of this writing in 2016, PSC is conducting research about the health care and access needs of this population. Other clients include domestic survivors of sex trafficking and those actively being sex trafficked, including both minors and adults; they are provided sexually transmitted infection testing and treatment, immunizations, and standard medical care. These clients also have access to sexual assault forensic evaluations, HIV postexposure prophylaxis, and specialized sexual assault counseling through collaboration with the Sex Abuse Treatment Center (SATC) (http://satchawaii.com/).

PSC also provides outreach and medical case management for survivors, prevention programs for at-risk youth, and forensic evaluations for survivors, and works closely with other community partners including SATC, Susannah Wesley Community Center (SWCC), and the Hawaii Immigrant Justice Center at Legal Aid (HIJC) to ensure that actively trafficked persons and trafficking survivors' health care, legal, and social services needs are met. These close collaborations allow clients to receive comprehensive services and seamless continuity of care. All services are provided free to uninsured patients.

20.2.3 Institute for Family Health, New York, New York (http:// www.institute.org/health-care/services/ the-purple-clinic/)

The Institute for Family Health (IFH), among the largest FQHC networks in New York, launched the PurpLE (**Purp**ose: Listen and Engage) Clinic on July 12, 2015. The PurpLE Clinic was created to offer a safe and sensitive primary care health home for people who have experienced sexual trauma, including trafficking and other forms of commercial sexual exploitation. The PurpLE Clinic is held weekly on Sundays, offers extended-hours, and is staffed by a family medicine physician. The clinic is housed in an IFH site in New York City, which is open 7 days a week. The PurpLE Clinic's primary care services mirror the typical primary care services offered through IFH, including routine physical exams, obstetric-gynecologic related care, STI testing and treatment, joint injections, immunizations, hormone therapy, HIV care, and pre-exposure HIV prophylaxis (PrEP).

The PurpLE Clinic also serves as a gateway to IFH's auxiliary services, including mental health care, diabetes team care, case management, dentistry, podiatry, acupuncture, and a prescription assistance program. Additionally, adhering to the FQHC model, the family members, including children of survivors, are also seen at the clinic. All patients meet with case managers for insurance assessment and are placed on a nominal sliding scale fee for clinical care and lab work if they are not insurance eligible. All IFH staff receives education on sexual exploitation and trauma-informed care.

The design and implementation of the PurpLE Clinic was informed by collaborations with local anti-sex trafficking, human rights, domestic violence, and lesbian, gay, bisexual, and transgender (LGBT) focused organizations, and with input from incarcerated sex trafficking survivors on Rikers Island Correctional Facility (New York City's main jail complex). Referrals come primarily from these partners, shelter systems, and through health education and outreach workshops run by PurpLE Clinic staff for community-based organizations. Patients of the PurpLE Clinic have included both sexual violence survivors and their children. Patients have been of all genders, from the USA and abroad, and comprise those currently experiencing or who have previously experienced sexual violence, including human trafficking. Approximately 50% are undocumented and 50% are Medicaid enrolled or eligible.

20.2.4   Citrus Health Network, Hialeah, Florida (http://www. citrushealth.org/CHANCE)

Citrus Health Network was established as a community mental health center in 1979 intended to serve the northwest area of Miami Dade County. In 2004, Citrus Health Network, Inc. (CHN), was established as an FQHC and is the only FQHC to receive the Gold Seal of Approval from the Joint Commission in the state of Florida. Over the years, Citrus has expanded to other areas of the state. Services now include primary care, housing assistance, foster care, and case management services. Staff on site include: psychiatrists, primary care doctors, pediatricians, obstetrics/gynecologists, psychologists, licensed clinical social workers, case managers, and peer support staff.

Citrus Health Network has been providing comprehensive treatment services to youth involved in commercial sexual exploitation since 2013. The Citrus Helping Adolescents Negatively impacted by Commercial Exploitation (CHANCE) Program has provided housing and services to 56 state dependent children in Specialized

Therapeutic Foster Care and treatment services to 125 clients in the Community Response team between autumn 2013 and spring 2016. Clinical and support services offered through the program include: medical and mental health assessment and evaluation, individual therapy, family therapy, group therapy, life coaching, certified behavior analysis, and targeted case management.

Commercially sexually exploited youth benefit from integrated care and a full continuum of treatment options. Some youth have required more intensive clinical services than those offered in a community setting due to the severity of their emotional needs. As such, in the spring of 2016 CHN provided services, to 14 youth who have been involved in commercial sexual exploitation, via Florida's Statewide Inpatient Psychiatric Program (SIPP). The network has worked diligently to create a specialized treatment program within the existing SIPP program to meet the unique needs of this population. In October 2015, CHN opened an independent SIPP designed specifically for youth who have been commercially sexually exploited.

The needs of these trafficked clients are extensive and varied. CHN operates a Children's Crisis Unit (CSU) and a Juvenile Addictions Receiving Facility (JARF). Youth who have been sex trafficked are frequently placed in this facility. CHN developed a 24-h training curriculum for direct care staff members working in the CSU, SIPP, and JARF programs. The curriculum emphasizes the importance of a client-centered and trauma-informed approach for this population. Recognizing the many physical health needs of sex trafficked youth, a pediatrician for CHN received specialized training on commercially sexually exploited youth. The primary care physician provides continuity of care to CSEC clients in both the residential facilities and the FQHC setting.

20.2.5 La Maestra Community Health Centers, San Diego, California (https://www.lamaestra.org/medical-legal-social-services/default.html)

La Maestra Community Health Centers began in 1990 and have grown into an FQHC with 12 sites in underserved communities throughout San Diego County. Its headquarters is in City Heights, the most diverse San Diego community located 16 miles from the USA–Mexico border, and one of the largest centers for refugee resettlement in the nation. The majority of residents live in poverty and experience high rates of health disparities and crime. Inadequate access to legal services, fear of the police, and cultural and linguistic barriers make the already vulnerable population of City Heights more susceptible to trafficking, sexual assault, and violent crime.

La Maestra's Legal Advocacy and Social Services department (LMLASS) was established in 2011, to provide education, assistance, and support to people who face rights violations or who are survivors of crime. The majority of clients are victims of domestic violence and trafficking. The legal advocates do not act as attorneys, but advocate on behalf of survivor clients; they provide information and referrals that help clients in identifying their rights and options as survivors. Between 2011 and 2016 LMLASS has served more than 1,500 clients; 70 (5 %) are survivors of sex or labor trafficking who come from ten different countries. LMLASS' collaborative partners include the US Committee on Refugees and Immigrants, the National Human Trafficking Victim Assistance Program, several law enforcement agencies, and a network of local nonprofits and attorneys providing low-cost legal services, shelter and other assistance.

Trafficked persons are often identified during their clinical visit at La Maestra's health center. Patients may open up to their health care practitioner about issues affecting their health and well-being, or exhibit signs of trauma and exploitation that are recognized by the staff. All clinic personnel are trained by LMLASS to recognize signs of domestic violence and trafficking, maintain confidentiality and safety, and make a sensitive, warm handoff to the LMLASS staff. Moreover, LMLASS' network has helped raise awareness of their services so that trafficked persons, and other agencies, will reach out directly to LMLASS for help. Once a trafficked individual first accesses a service at La Maestra, they are immediately connected to all of the services within the Circle of Care™, including medical, dental, and behavioral health; eligibility assistance; nutritious food and basic necessities; and financial, social, legal, and well-being programs. The Circle of Care™ is a holistic, solution-based approach to providing programs and services; it was created because complete family wellness requires more than just medical services. La Maestra's team works collaboratively to identify the total needs of patients and attend to them through preventative care, education, treatment, and referrals to other needed services. In this way, the Circle of Care™ addresses the social determinants of health, ultimately guiding patients and their families to a state of well-being and self-sufficiency. Thus, La Maestra serves as a "one-stop shop" with many services in a comprehensive health home, preventing the loss of victimized patients before their needs can be addressed, and empowering survivors to rebuild their lives.

20.3   Conclusion

Human trafficking affects the most marginalized members of our communities, both through individual vulnerabilities and social factors facilitating the context for exploitation to occur. Due to historical factors, and the philosophy and mission of health centers, CHCs are located in at-risk communities across the country. As such, community health centers are well positioned to care for people anywhere in the cycle of exploitation and abuse—from primary prevention of trafficking in vulnerable patients and populations, to early identification and urgent treatment of acute health consequences, and to long-term care of sequelae of being trafficked. In many health centers, integration of co-located medical and behavioral health care provides "one-stop" care for patients.

Community health centers utilize a prevention framework, due to their origins as a community-oriented primary care model, breaking down the separation between public health and medical care. They do this through effective provision of enabling services, which help patients to access care. Trafficked persons can benefit from these comprehensive services and this model of care, throughout the stages of exploitation and trafficking. Furthermore, community health centers are located in the neighborhoods where their patients reside and are thus geographically positioned to provide care for exploited patients.

Models of care for trafficked persons in health centers exist and new ones are developing as awareness of human trafficking as a public health and health care issue increases. Models can be comprehensive and include prevention programs, or they may be specialized and tailored to address the multiple health issues of trafficked persons. Regardless of the type of human trafficking care models developed, community health centers also have a unique role and responsibility to identify early, intervene, and help to reframe the issue of trafficking for affected individuals, from a criminal justice framework to a public health perspective. One study showed that using a screening tool in a community health center could help to identify domestic minors who are sex trafficked [17]. Once patients are identified, or suspected of being trafficked, institutional response protocols will vary depending on local and state legislation, and available resources. Community health centers are at the center of care coordination for patients with complex medical, behavioral health, and social needs; CHC's are well positioned to include patients who have been trafficked, in these existing case management and care coordination programs.

While, at the time of this writing, the prevailing criminal justice framework focuses on prosecution and punishment of traffickers, the community health care system focuses on the health and well-being of patients who have been trafficked, and on prevention and early intervention. When the goals of the health and judicial systems align, trafficked patients are willing participants in the prosecution of traffickers; however, sometimes the goals of these systems are at odds. When trafficked patients are not willing or are unable to participate in the prosecution of their traffickers, they can be criminalized, excluded from services, or further traumatized by the very systems meant to help them. A restructuring of system responses, where survivor services and prevention efforts are separate from criminal justice system goals and outcomes, is essential to prevent further marginalization of these patients. For example, when an undocumented survivor of trafficking is unable or unwilling to participate in the prosecution of their trafficker(s), the survivor should not be excluded from services and needed health care. From a health care perspective, this patient would still suffer adverse health consequences from their trafficking experience, so treatment and services should be available, regardless of the case's legal proceedings and outcomes.

In conclusion, a public health framework, which includes a comprehensive primary care health delivery system, and an emphasis on FQHCs as the building blocks of a robust safety net for trafficked persons, provides a system of care and protection that can be both just and effective in healing patients.

20.4 Recommendations

This chapter's recommendations center on facilitating and creating robust programs in community health centers (CHCs) to prevent human trafficking and to care for patients who have been victimized by this crime. It is essential to support CHCs because they are privy to trends and issues affecting their local populations, and human trafficking health care responses require geographically and culturally relevant strategies.

1. Create comprehensive, wrap-around *care teams* in community health centers across the nation focused on reaching out to and providing care for survivors of human trafficking.

   Care teams are essential components of effective community health centers. No longer is health care dependent on a sole health care clinician. As a severely marginalized population, survivors of human trafficking face tremendous barriers in accessing health care. Community health centers have always been at the forefront of addressing those barriers. Care teams would include outreach workers, peer educators, social workers, therapists, case managers, interpreters, and clinical staff like doctors, physician assistants, nurses, nurse practitioners, and medical assistants. Each community health center may develop care teams specific to the needs of their populations, and would utilize different sets of personnel depending on the types of survivors whom they encounter and to whom they provide care. A point person on the care team should be an advocate for the patient, who provides outreach and care coordination, including facilitating communication between law enforcement and social services. Behavioral health and oral health personnel should be included in care teams and programming of services.

2. Create human trafficking specific *programs* within health centers to address the physical, mental health, and social harms that result from being trafficked.

   Community health centers have a track record of developing care programs for specific conditions, such as HIV or diabetes. There are also health centers focused on social conditions affecting health, such as homelessness, or migrant farm work. Public health-framed human trafficking programs, like Banteay Srei of Asian Health Services, should be created for survivors of different types of human trafficking, with an emphasis on culturally relevant strategies to help those affected heal and fulfill their human potential. Programming should address all stages of human trafficking, from primary, secondary, and tertiary prevention, to long-term care.

3. Ensure *language accessibility* for trafficking survivors and *cultural competence* by professionals throughout community health centers.

   Community health centers provide a model for how to care for vulnerable populations. Their history originates in civil rights and health equity work; their emphasis on language access and cultural competency in care models is fundamental to properly serving human trafficking survivors. Language access is critically important for communication with survivors, particularly given survivors' loss of agency, experienced deprivations and restrictions, and the risk that traffickers may attempt to sabotage communications between providers and trafficked patients. The importance of trained interpreters who adhere to principles of confidentiality and trauma-informed care is essential, particularly for minority communities where overlapping social networks between patients and traffickers may exist.

4. Ensure that non-clinical *enabling services* for patients to access care is provided in all community health centers.

   According to the Health Resources and Service Administration's Bureau of Primary Health Care, "enabling services" are defined as non-clinical services that do not include direct patient services but increase a patient's access to health care. Enabling services should be part of a holistic human trafficking health care response model. Enabling services are a hallmark of the community health center model and should be reimbursed by insurance providers.

5. Incorporate *trauma-informed care* training and develop trauma-informed systems, throughout community health centers, and in other sectors.

   All trafficked individuals have experienced some form of trauma. Understanding this is crucial, not only in the design of community health centers, and training of their staff, but also for other non-clinical systems that touch trafficking survivor lives. A robust public health response lies not only in the health care system. Professionals from other sectors working with trafficked persons must be knowledgeable and aware of the physical, mental, emotional, and psychological effects of human trafficking, and how to work with and engage survivors. When professionals appreciate how to partner with those affected and are equipped to approach survivors from a trauma-informed perspective, those survivors will be better supported, and more able to begin a healing process to transition out of the control of the trafficker and dangerous situations.

6. Develop *health care specific funding streams* for comprehensive human trafficking programs in community health centers.

   Funding streams for health care programs should be separate from the criminal justice system. The goals of the two systems are different. Keeping health care provision and maintaining the integrity of health care goals and the needs of the patient at the forefront of health care services is paramount.

References

1. Chon K. The Power of framing human trafficking as a public health issue. Office of Trafficking in Persons, Administration for Family and Children, U.S. Department of Health and Human Services. 2016. Office of Trafficking in Persons: http://www.acf.hhs.gov/programs/endtrafficking/resource/publichealthlens. Accessed 26 Apr 2016.
2. Baldwin S, Eisenman D, Sayles J, Ryan G, Chuang K. Identification of human trafficking victims in health care settings. Health Hum Rights. 2011;13(1):E36–49.

3. Institute of Medicine; National Research Council. Confronting commercial sexual exploitation and sex trafficking of minors in the United States. Washington, DC: The National Academies Press; 2013.
4. Zimmerman C, Yun K, Shvab I, Watts C, Trappolin L, Treppete M, Regan L. The health risks and consequences of trafficking in women and adolescents. Findings from a European Study. London: London School of Hygiene and Tropical Medicine; 2003.
5. Felitti V, Anda R, Nordenberg D, Williamson M, Spitz A, Edwards V, et al. Relationship of childhood abuse and household dysfunction to many of the leading causes of death in adults: the adverse childhood experiences (ACE) study. Am J Prev Med. 1998;14(4):245–58.
6. Dovydaitis T. Human trafficking: the role of the health care provider. J Midwifery Womens Health. 2010;55(5):482–7. doi:10.1016/j.jmwh.2009.12.017.
7. Isaac R, Solak J, Giardino A. Health care providers' training needs related to human trafficking: maximizing the opportunity to effectively screen and intervene. J Appl Res Child. 2011;2(1):1–33.
8. Crane P, Moreno M. Human trafficking: what is the role of the health care provider? J Appl Res Child. 2011;2(1):1–27.
9. Willis B, Levy B. Child prostitution: global health burden, research needs, and interventions. Lancet. 2002;359:1417–22.
10. Todres J. Moving upstream: the merits of a public health law approach to human trafficking. Georgia State University College of Law, Legal Studies Research Paper No. 2011–02. 89 N.C. L. REV. 447. The Social Science Research Network Electronic Paper Collection. 2011. http://ssrn.com/abstract=1742953. Accessed 1 Aug 2016.
11. Lederer L, Wetzel C. The health consequences of sex trafficking and their implications for identifying victims in healthcare facilities. Ann Health Law. 2014;23(1):61–91.
12. Family Violence Prevention Fund. Turning pain into power: trafficking survivors' perspectives on early intervention strategies. San Francisco, CA: Family Violence Prevention Fund; 2005.
13. National Association of Community Health Centers. A sketch of community health centers chartbook 2014. Washington, DC. 2014. http://www.nachc.com/client/Chartbook_2014.pdf. 25 Nov 2015.
14. Lewis VA, Colla CH, Schoenherr KE, et al. Innovation in the safety net: integrating community health centers through accountable care. J Gen Intern Med. 2014;29(11):1484–90.
15. NHTRC: National Human Trafficking Resource Center. 2015. The Victims: https://www.traffickingresourcecenter.org/what-human-trafficking/human-trafficking/victims. Accessed 1 Aug 2016.
16. McGregor Perry K, McEwing L. How do social determinants affect human trafficking in Southeast Asia, and what can we do about it? A systematic review. Health Hum Rights. 2013;15(2).
17. Chang K, Lee K, Park T, Sy E, Quach T. Using a clinic-based screening tool for primary care providers to identify commercially sexually exploited children. J Appl Res Child. 2015;6(1), 6. http://digitalcommons.library.tmc.edu/cgi/viewcontent.cgi?article=1235&context=childrenatrisk. Accessed 1 Aug 2016.
18. US Department of Health and Human Services Health Resources and Services Administration. 2014 Health Center Data. http://bphc.hrsa.gov/uds/datacenter.aspx?year=2014. Accessed 1 Aug 2016.
19. Massachusetts Leaguve of Community Health Centers. History of Community Health Centers. http://www.massleague.org/CHC/History.php. Accessed 17 May 2016.
20. Mullan F, Epstein L. Community-oriented primary care: new relevance in a changing world. Am J Public Health. 2002;92(11):1748–55.
21. USC 254b: health centers. http://uscode.house.gov/view.xhtml?edition=prelim&req=42+usc+254b&f=treesort&fq=true&num=20&hl=true. Accessed 17 May 2016.
22. US Department of Health and Human Services Health Resources and Services Administration. Health center program terms and definitions. 2015. HRSA: http://www.hrsa.gov/grants/apply/assistance/Buckets/definitions.pdf. Accessed 25 Nov 2015.

23. Chang K, Sy E, Vo T, Nguyen S, Thaing M, Lee J, et al. Reframing our response: a new approach to care for commercially sexually exploited children. San Francisco Med. 2014; 87(1): 21–22.
24. Kuehlein T, Sghedoni D, Visentin G, Gérvas J, Jamoule M. Quaternary prevention: a task of the general practitioner. Prim Care. 2010;10(18):350–4.
25. Chang K. Integration of primary care and behavioral health for human trafficking survivors in patient-centered medical homes. Institute of Violence, Abuse & Trauma: 20th international summit & training on violence, Abuse & Trauma across the lifespan. San Diego, CA. 2015.
26. AAPCHO education brief on human trafficking in FQHCs. http://www.aapcho.org/wp/wp-content/uploads/2015/10/AAPCHO-Human-Trafficking-Education-Brief_103015.pdf. Accessed 1 Aug 2016.
27. Sy E, Quach T, Lee J, Yang NI, Thaing M, Chang K. Responding to commercially sexually exploited children (CSEC): a community health center's journey towards creating a primary care clinical CSEC screening tool in the United States. Int J Soc Sci Stud. 2016;4(6):45–51. doi:10.11114/ijsss.v4i6.1576. http://redfame.com/journal/index.php/ijsss/article/view/1576/1627. Accessed 1 Aug 2016.
28. Brown P. In Oakland, redefining sex trade workers as abuse victims. New York Times. 2011. http://www.nytimes.com/2011/05/24/us/24oakland.html. Accessed 1 Aug 2016.

Chapter 21
The Media and Human Trafficking: A Discussion and Critique of the Dominant Narrative

Erin Albright and Kate D'Adamo

21.1 Introduction

Media matters. Whether one is a clinician, judge, teacher, police officer, jury member, or person that has been trafficked, popular media is inescapable. From news networks which stream 24 hours a day, to podcasts or big-budget movies, media is the primary way most people learn about an issue like human trafficking. Not many will read a statute, a law review, or an academic journal article, but most will watch a crime drama, or read a blog or a news article.

This chapter offers a starting point for a deeper discussion about the way the public understands human trafficking in and through media portrayals. It examines the dominant narrative the media has created in contrast to the full picture of trafficking in the United States of America (USA). To be clear, the creation and perpetuation of the narrative is a collective effort: What media writes is informed by its own interests of expanding readership, but is also based heavily on information from press releases, advocacy groups, and journalists' own lived experience. To fully realize the positive potential of the media as a participant in the collective US anti-trafficking movement, we must better understand the human trafficking narrative, its weaknesses and how to construct a more representative media portrayal of human trafficking in the USA.

E. Albright (✉)
e-mail: erin@givewaytofreedom.org

K. D'Adamo
Sex Worker Project, New York, NY, USA
e-mail: kdadamo@urbanjustice.org

© Springer International Publishing AG 2017   363
M. Chisolm-Straker, H. Stoklosa (eds.), *Human Trafficking Is a Public Health Issue*, DOI 10.1007/978-3-319-47824-1_21

This chapter is a discussion and critique of the narrow focus within dominant media narratives about human trafficking. None of the content or critique herein is intended to challenge or undermine the lived experience of any individual, but instead is used to explore the impact of a narrow scope on policy, services, and public understanding, and to expand the dialogue to include a more representative picture of trafficking. The data cited throughout this chapter is used solely for the purpose of demonstrating that the dominant narrative does not reflect the full reality and diversity of human trafficking. None of the data cited should be considered fully representative. Human trafficking statistics have well-described numerous limitations, including the fact that a large portion of research to date has often replicated these media biases in their focus, methodology or analysis.

In addition, with respect to language, this chapter aligns with the rest of the book by using the term "victim" to describe someone actively being trafficked when discussing trafficking in law enforcement terms. Moreover, "victim" will also be used to capture the one-dimensional nature of the media's portrayal of trafficked persons.

21.2 Discussion

21.2.1 Media Creates Knowledge and Priorities

Before delving into the dominant narrative, it is useful to understand the potential and power the media has in shaping both public perception and policy priorities. Humans are, by nature, storytellers. When confronted with new, abstract information, the brain creates narratives to help form the basis for learning, comprehension, and communication. To make sense of and understand this new information, it is filtered through our existing experiences, building on the knowledge we have amassed throughout our lives, both directly and indirectly. It is woven into a story we can understand and relate to, with characters who participate in the classic arc of a beginning, middle, and end.

For particularly foreign concepts or issues, the media often provides these contextualizing stories, thereby shaping the public's understanding of the issue [1] and influencing the public agenda. In the 1960s, Max McCombs and Donald Shaw described this process as "agenda setting" theory. According to this theory "the way an issue or other object is covered in the media…affects the way the public thinks about that object, [and] the way an issue or other object is covered in the media… affects the salience of that object on the public agenda" [2]. Thus the narrative about human trafficking presented by the media is important because it provides the lens through which the general public understands human trafficking, and sets the agenda for which laws are passed, how funding is allocated and what issues are deemed worthy of research and attention [3].

21.2.2   The Dominant Narrative and Its Impact

Turning to the dominant narrative, the majority of the US public, when asked to describe human trafficking, would likely imagine some variation of a young white girl, lured or kidnapped by a nefarious man, forced to engage in sex work. She cannot leave, and endures the violence and injustice of client after client assaulting her. And although the story never quite reaches this far, the implication is usually clear: All she needs is for someone—law enforcement, a service provider, a good Samaritan—to catch the bad guys and rescue her, and return her to the loving home from which she was taken. Many offering such a story would say they came to this understanding because they read a news article, saw a story on a blog or social media, or watched a documentary, TV show, or popular film about trafficking.

This narrative of human trafficking contains elements that most can relate to on some level. And it is these relatable elements that media, advocates, and policy makers rely on to make human trafficking salient and understandable to the public. By connecting the narrative to the collective understanding of good and bad, justice and redemption, and danger and safety, the public is better able to conceptualize trafficking. The difficulty that arises is that too often incredibly complex trafficking stories are shoehorned into black and white paradigms to fit a media cycle or advocacy agenda, distorting public perception of the problem.

What follows is an explanation and critique of five elements of the dominant narrative and their impact on the public's knowledge about trafficking in the USA: (1) the insufficient coverage of all forms of human trafficking; (2) the narrow profile of individuals that have been trafficked; (3) the use of sensationalism to attract readers; (4) the failure to delve into the complexity of the issue; and (5) the singular use of a criminal justice framing. The chapter ends with recommendations for how media consumers, anti-trafficking advocates, and journalists can expand this narrative and find trafficking stories that better reflect lived realities. In this way, we can find a starting point from where the public, the media, and professionals working in the anti-trafficking field can better understand human trafficking, and the media's place in confronting the issue.

21.2.2.1   Type of Trafficking: Sex in the Headlines

Perhaps the biggest criticism of the current US narrative of human trafficking is what it does *not* tell. According to the International Labor Organization (ILO), labor trafficking comprises 68 % of individuals that have been trafficked worldwide [4]. Yet, examining media coverage in the USA one would barely know of the existence of other forms of trafficking outside the sex trade, let alone that other types of trafficking impact far more people. Available data on trafficking in the USA indicates that labor trafficking is a much bigger problem than one would surmise from media coverage. According to the 2014 Attorney General's Annual Report to Congress, 38 % of trafficking survivors that received services through the Department of Justice's Office for Victims of Crime (OVC) anti-trafficking programming, and 74 % of those that received certification from the Department of Health and Human Services (HHS) were trafficked for labor in industries *outside* of the sex trade[1] [5].

There has been some increase in media coverage of labor trafficking, mostly at the behest of service providers and advocates: In 2015, several media outlets published pieces on the subject. The Christian Science Monitor published a series of 14 articles examining labor trafficking and solutions to the problem across the globe [6]. Buzzfeed published a piece on the H-2B[2] visa guest worker program, detailing the exploitation and abuse suffered by workers under the program, and the federal government's continued failure to improve worker protections and hold exploitive employers accountable [7]. In 2016 the Associated Press won a Pulitzer Prize for its series of stories on forced labor in the fishing industry [8].

But these were all long form, investigative stories. They are the exception and do not constitute the vast majority of coverage, especially in the day-to-day, local news that many people rely upon for information. The majority of media coverage—the 600–800 word articles—still disproportionately cover trafficking in the sex trade [9]. This was true 10 years ago, when one study found that 54 % of stories in USA, British, and Canadian print media from 2001 to 2005 focused on human trafficking into prostitution or pornography [10]. Only "20 % referred to the issue in terms of labor exploitation," with the remaining articles discussing it with respect to immigration issues and concerns [10]. More recently, when polled in the spring of 2016, experts in the anti-trafficking field from 20 countries all voiced the same concern: "Asked what they would like journalists to focus *less* on, the answer was an overwhelming chorus: sex slavery. 'Sex sells, but concentrate on economics, debt bondage and sweat shops and enforcement of labour standards,' said one U.S.-based expert [emphasis added]" [9].

A prime example of this disproportionate focus is the coverage of human trafficking before and after large sporting events, most notably the Super Bowl. While media coverage has improved around this event as well, every year there are still stories about a surge in human trafficking. The stories tend to focus exclusively on trafficking in the sex trade and claim that thousands of young girls will be brought into the hosting town to meet the demand for commercial sex [11]. In addition to being unsubstantiated by evidence [12], such media statements propagate untruths about who is trafficked, how, and under what circumstances. Even stories with a

---

[1] Both the HHS and OVC data carry an important caveat: The HHS National Human Trafficking Victim Assistance Program (TVAP) is only for foreign national survivors of trafficking. Hence, numbers of federally recognized labor trafficking survivors, who tend to be foreign nationals, are relatively high in comparison to sex trafficking survivors. The OVC programs serve all survivors, but unlike the TVAP program OVC services are not nation-wide.

[2] The H2-B program allows certain US employers or US agents to hire foreign nationals to work in the USA, to fill temporary nonagricultural jobs.

more measured approach, that do not perpetuate the falsehood and hype, still focus on trafficking in the sex trade by reporting either law enforcement efforts to identify individuals who have been trafficked for sex [13–15]; or whether the Super Bowl is the largest human trafficking event in the USA [16]. Any mention of labor trafficking in this type of story is incidental, included as commentary from experts as one small part in a larger critique of coverage [17]. And yet from concession stands, to hotels, to construction projects and beyond, the potential for labor trafficking surrounds large sporting events. Evidence from outside of the USA draws a clear connection between large-scale events and labor trafficking. For example, the 2022 World Cup will be held in Qatar. The country has invested billions in infrastructure development, an effort that has been routinely criticized for human rights abuses including labor trafficking [18].

Impact The impact of such a disproportionate emphasis on trafficking in the sex trade is a prioritization of policies that disproportionately and sometimes inappropriately target the sex industry. This is often to the detriment and even exclusion of other vulnerable industries and populations. For example, in 2014 only 6% of federal prosecutions were for labor trafficking cases [5]. On the policy front, laws such as the 2014 Strengthening Families and Preventing Sex Trafficking Act also reflect this uneven focus. This law

"directs the Secretary of Health and Human Services (HHS) to report to Congress on information about: (1) children who run away from foster care and their risk of becoming sex trafficking victims, (2) state efforts to provide specialized services, foster family homes, child care institutions, or other forms of placement for children who are sex trafficking victims..." [19].

The ease of adding labor to these provisions is obvious, yet this important piece of federal legislation blatantly left labor trafficking of children out of the law.

21.2.2.2 The Young, White, Female Sex Trafficking Victim

Victims Are Female and Young

According to the dominant narrative, trafficked persons are young and female [20]. It is not uncommon to read that these are "our daughters" [21–23] or "the girl next door": In 2011 Vanity Fair ran an article entitled, *Sex Trafficking of Americans: The Girls Next Door*, accompanied by imagery of a thin, young girl [24]. In 2012, CNN ran a story, *Selling the Girl Next Door*. This emphasis on youth is further illustrated in continued reporting of average age of entry statistics. Depending on the source, readers might see anything from 12 to 14 years old cited as the average age in which girls are first commercially exploited for sex. This statistic has been debunked, and experts have also pointed out the statistical improbability of this claim [25–27]. Nonetheless, it continues to be repeated in story after story, offered by both the media and incautious awareness campaigns.

This hyper-focus on young, female victims is replicated in popular media as well, which highlights young girls as the primary targets of trafficking. In 2004 and 2005, the first appearances of trafficked females on *Law and Order: Special Victims Unit* were young women, but by 2010, the ages had shifted to adolescence, one as young as 14. The 2011 movie *Trade* focused on a 13-year-old girl who was kidnapped, for trafficking, while riding her bicycle. The 2012 film *Eden* also centered on the story of a girl in her teens. Another 2012 film, *Trade of Innocence*, features the story of a couple who set out to rescue "young girls" from the sex trade as a way to cope with the loss of their daughter. While these are just a smattering of the entertainment pieces on the subject, the narrative dominates public understanding: Human trafficking overwhelmingly affects young girls.

This monolithic young female profile is in stark contrast to the observations of those that work directly with survivors and empirical evidence. According to data from OVC anti-trafficking programs, in 2014, 84 % of the survivors served were adults and 16 % were minors; 79 % of served survivors were female, 20 % male, and 1 % transgender experienced [5]. While survivors that make it to service providers are also not necessarily reflective of the full spectrum of those who are trafficked, these service provider reports reflect a more diverse and accurate portrayal of trafficking than the media.

The Victim Is White

It is outside the scope of this chapter to fully capture all the dynamics at play with respect to the inaccurately racialized media coverage of human trafficking. Nonetheless, race is an important part of the dominant narrative, and requires discussion. The race of people who are trafficked has always been a prime element of the way trafficking is conceptualized in the USA. In 1910 Congress passed the "White Slave Traffic Act," one of the first pieces of anti-trafficking legislation that has become known colloquially as the Mann Act [28]. This early precursor to the Trafficking Victims Protection Act (TVPA) highlights the prioritization of white people who are trafficked. Notably absent was any discussion of non-whites who were sex trafficked, and the law does not address labor trafficking at all. The narrative of trafficking in persons in media in the 1980s and 1990s perpetuated this historical "white victim" archetype, emphasizing Eastern European women, who were overwhelmingly fair-skinned and blonde [29]. "These stories heightened public fears about trafficking because White victims of trafficking from Eastern Europe appeared 'as just like the girls next door'...innocent victims who looked like and could be confused with young White women in the U.S." [30].

And yet "[t]hen and today, the majority of victims of trafficking and forced labor are people of color in and from developing countries, not white Europeans. Even within the United States, a significant number of trafficking victims are people of color" [31, 32]. Available data supports this: A study of human trafficking incidents reported by federally funded Human Trafficking Task Forces from 2008 to 2010 found that, of the sex trafficking survivors whose race was known, 40 % were black,

26 % were white, 23 % were Hispanic, 4 % were Asian, and 6 % were other races or ethnicities. Likewise, for confirmed labor trafficking survivors, 56 % were Hispanic, 18 % were other, 15 % were Asian, 10 % were black, and 2 % were white [33].

Impact The impact of this use of a singular archetype—the young, white, female victim trafficked into the sex trade—is that it focuses public sentiment and policy exclusively on one story. When health care providers understand trafficking as always involving coerced sex work among young, white, females they miss the male of color being trafficked. When juries only believe trafficking to involve sexual exploitation, those who traffic people for other forms of labor walk free. This undercuts the ability of individuals who have been trafficked to receive support, find justice, or even be recognized as victimized in the first place.

21.2.2.3 The Sensational

Media is a business, and sex sells. News networks are in constant competition for views and clicks, always seeking the quick sound bite and headline that will bring in more listeners or viewers. As a result, the stories about trafficking—from "Sex Slaves in Suburbia," to "*Your City*! is a Hub for Human Trafficking"—grow increasingly sensational. This drives reporters to search for the most egregious or outrageous stories, or highlight the most sensational details of stories, regardless of how representative the facts may be. Take, for example, a public radio story on the health care response to trafficking. The opening to the otherwise substantive and informative piece tells the story of a survivor identified with a microchip implanted in their side [34]. Although true in that one scenario, anecdotal evidence indicates that such are isolated occurrences: Most trafficked persons do not have microchips.

Similar to the news media, the entertainment industry aims to attract viewers, not necessarily convey a representative truth: In *Taken*, a Hollywood blockbuster film, a father must rescue his teenage daughter from the clutches of an international trafficking ring. There are explosions, frantic phone calls, and a specific timeline in which he must save her or risk losing her forever. In stark contrast, a Covenant House study found that only 9 % of youth trafficked by a third party were exploited by strangers; that is to say, the majority of youth in the study who experienced exploitation knew and trusted their trafficker as a family member, friend, intimate partner, or employer [35]. That the majority of trafficked youth are victimized at the hands of someone they know as opposed to a stranger points to another more subtle method of sensationalism that presents in "narratives about pimp trickery, seduction, captivity, and brutality as the dominant or sole mode of recruitment and management" [36]. Echoing the "stranger danger" sensationalism in *Taken*, in these stories the person trafficked cannot leave without help from outsiders because they have been "brainwashed," or fear violent repercussions if they try to leave.

And while all youth under 18 engaged in commercial sex are trafficking victims under US federal law regardless of third-party involvement, research and interviews with these youth reveal their connections to traffickers to be much more complex than the media conveys. A 2014 study gathered data from three separate studies of active pimps, youth and young adult sex workers in New York and New Jersey and found that, "…recruitment into sex work by pimps is far less common than is presupposed by TVPA institutions and current popular concerns" [36]. Indeed, the study explained that "[t]he conventional narrative of deception, force, or the captive slave—recruited and tied to a pimp through love, debt, addiction, authority, or coercion—did reflect the experiences of some individuals, but for the vast majority this narrative did not resonate" [36]. With respect to recruitment, only 8.1 % of those interviewed indicated that they entered into sex work through a pimp, versus 47 % through peers or friends, and 23 % through customers [36].

Further contradicting the main narrative's emphasis on a controlling third-party forcing young people to engage in sex work, of the 87.2 % of commercially sexually exploited children (CSEC) in New York that expressed the desire to leave the commercial sex industry, "not one of these individuals identified a controlling pimp as an obstacle to leaving". Changes in employment options, educational opportunities, and housing were the most cited "necessary changes" (60.2, 51.4, and 41.4 %, respectively)" [36]. Moreover, for the cases that did reflect the dominant narrative of young girls coerced to engage in commercial sex, the study's findings were consistent with those mentioned previously: The trafficker was often "an informal or legal guardian, or a friend or intimate companion of a parent [and that this] type of pimping (parental) accounted for some of the youngest ages of initiation into sex work, and was the most coercive type of relationship" [36]. The study went on to say that in two of the four cases that fit this profile, "the girls seemed to be staying with their pimp more out of a lack of perceived alternatives than out of love, debt, addiction [imposed], physical might, or authority" [36].

Impact Although there are instances when individuals are abducted and sold for sex, or chained and beaten for labor, the media tends to over-represent such scenarios. "These 'worst of the worst' stories may command attention in the short-term, but at the long-term expense of desensitizing audiences [who may become jurors or service providers], to the more nuanced and at times banal reality of the average human trafficking experience" [37]. This impacts trafficked persons as well. When the perception is tuned to the sensational, trafficked individuals held in debt bondage, or controlled by confiscating identity documents and threatened legal action may not recognize themselves as in an exploitive situation and able to seek help. When society believes that all youth involved in the sex trade are there at the hands of a violent and controlling pimp, it overlooks the systemic failures that contribute to trafficking and continues to pour resources into solutions that may cause more harm than good.

21.2.2.4 An Overly Simplified Narrative

Rarely does trafficking exist in isolation of other complex factors, yet issues of poverty, globalization, race, sexual orientation, gender identity, crime, and systemic biases and failures are seldom examined as part of the human trafficking narrative.

The 2014 study mentioned above, comparing data on youth trading sex,[3] concluded that the public narrative "mask[s] or simplif[ies] the difficult and complex choices and contingencies faced by minors who sell sex" [36]. One 15-year-old girl described her complex circumstances and how she met her trafficker:

> I was in a group home, and I was sittin' on my steps and I was cryin' because they're givin' you allowance—$20 a week—and then you're not allowed to do certain types of jobs because you have a curfew. And if you miss curfew, they ship you somewhere else. So I was just at my rope's end. The things that he was sayin' to me, it sounded good. So, it was like, maybe I can do this. But once I started seein' certain things and certain actions, I might as well have stayed in the hell I was in [38].

Trafficked adults have often also survived complicated histories and complex trauma. In a 2016 article for the Anti-Trafficking Review, authors Kate Mogulescu and Abigail Swenstein described their experience working in the New York Human Trafficking Intervention Courts:

> Many, but not all, of our clients have experienced the levels of force, fraud or coercion that would allow them to be considered "trafficking victims" under the law. Though originally conceived as an anti-trafficking project, framing our work in terms of trafficking has become increasingly problematic as many of our clients' trafficking experiences—while brutal—pale in comparison to the systemic failures and violence they have endured for far longer. The majority are hindered by these daunting obstacles related to their marginalization, even once no longer trafficked [39].

Whether discussing a minor or adult trafficked into any industry, recognizing and understanding complex histories is critical: These are the conditions and root causes that marginalize particular groups of people and make some communities especially vulnerable to exploitation and trafficking. A 2014 study of labor trafficking cases by Northeastern University and the Urban Institute noted that among the study participants "case records and survivor interviews made clear that a lack of upward mobility, economic opportunity, and conflict drove many labor trafficking survivors to seek employment overseas" [40]. The study quotes one person trafficked in the hospitality industry in the USA, who explains how poverty and the need to support her family drove her to seek work abroad through a recruiter in her home country:

> I came from a poor community. We didn't have that much so in our culture, especially where I grew up, everybody is kind of pushed to … work abroad or to have a future. That's how I end up knowing [name of the recruiting agency]. They have an affiliation with my traffickers here in the US [40].

A 2016 survey from the National Survivor Network looked at the role of arrests and their impact on survivor's lives. The survey found that 90% of the survivor respondents had been arrested, with more than 25% reporting between 10 and 20 arrests [41]. "[O]ver half of all respondents believed that 100% of their arrests/

---

[3] The term "trading sex" is used here to reflect the diversity of experiences and ages involved in the study, which included both youth under 18 and youth 18 and over. All youth under 18 involved in commercial sex are victims of trafficking under federal and many state laws.

charges/convictions were directly related to their trafficking experience. Only 26 % believe that the majority of their arrests were not related to their trafficking" [41]. Additionally, 80 % of respondents indicated that their arrest record caused barriers for employment, and 50 % indicated it caused barriers in seeking housing [41]. And lack of housing and employment are two commonly cited risk factors that create vulnerability for trafficking and exploitation [41].

Impact The complexities of an individual's life—before, during, and after the trafficking situation—cannot be ignored. When media miss the true root causes that enable exploitation, the media misses an opportunity to do meaningful work and prevent conditions that enable trafficking from developing in the first place. As Gonzalo Martínez de Vedia, Senior Policy Associate for the Alliance to End Slavery and Trafficking (ATEST) explained,

> Anti-poverty work is anti-trafficking work, worker-rights campaigns are anti-trafficking campaigns. A crime that preys on individuals' lack of options and support cannot be addressed without considering what took those supports away in the first place. Law enforcement interventions might succeed in disrupting individual criminal enterprises, perhaps ending a particular chapter in a person's exploitation, but the socioeconomic groups that are most affected by trafficking can only rise out of recurring victimization through empowerment and education.

Moreover, when the story fails to delve into the difficulty of rebuilding one's life after trafficking, communities end up with short-term, reactionary policies and a lack of resources to support survivor needs [3]. As a consequence, survivors are at risk for returning to the same conditions of poverty, racism, gender discrimination, homophobia, transphobia, and other systemic oppressions, which made them vulnerable to trafficking in the first place.

21.2.2.5 The Story of a Crime

The media's thematic frame of the trafficking narrative is one of a crime. It begins when the perpetrator and the trafficked individual collide, moves to the search for the victim, and ends with her rescue (and sometimes the arrest of a perpetrator). What results is a story, complimenting or often couched in the commonly held but untrue myths of "stranger danger," or predators that lurk in the dark; it is a story about bad things disrupting an individual's otherwise perfect life.

In perpetuating this narrative, the media de-contextualizes trafficking from the life of the trafficked person before and after, and positions criminal justice interventions as the natural solution to human trafficking. The story revolves around the moment of intervention or "rescue," and is punctuated by arrests and prosecutions. For example, the annual FBI Operation Cross Country is framed as a coordinated effort to rescue child victims of sex trafficking [42]. Media coverage focuses heavily on those carrying out the law enforcement operations, detailing the scope of the operation, the numbers of arrests, and the number of "rescued" children. How these children became involved in these situations and how they fare after law enforcement intervention is glaringly absent from media coverage: There is no discussion of how many were involved with coercive third parties, or how many were runaway or homeless youth acting alone or in peer networks to meet survival needs. Many trafficked youth have run from the very systems into which such so-called rescue operations will inevitably place them. After Operation Cross Country VII in 2013, one sergeant from the Bay Area said many trafficked youth often face charges themselves. The sergeant further noted that law enforcement "believe[s] juvenile hall is the immediate safest place for them [trafficked youth]"[4] [43].

This view that the "rescue" is the moment of triumph often stands in glaring contrast to how survivors view their experiences in these operations and raids. In one study of 15 trafficking survivors, the experience is described as "traumatic" and "violent" [44]. Said another survivor in the study, "They were wearing guns and uniforms, and it made me very scared. They didn't tell us anything. They treated us like criminals during the arrest and it was scary" [44]. Another woman described being pistol whipped by an officer in the course of her "rescue" experience [44].

Impact "In the case of trafficking, defining the problem as a crime and national security issue demands criminal justice and national security system responses" [29]. The criminal justice focus is on a small piece of the trafficking picture to the exclusion of a broader, socio-ecological understanding and truth. This disproportionate focus ignores the societal, community, and relational vulnerabilities that need to be addressed to truly decrease trafficking; ignoring these foundational contributors harms the individual and the community's ability to avoid or recover from human trafficking. When public perception centers on a criminal justice solution, it diminishes the funding and political will for the harder battles of true prevention and long-term recovery. Instead, resources and policies focus on a small window of time, and success is based on the number of investigations, arrests, and prosecution—with little consideration for the survivor or what success looks like to them. It allows those in the position to help, such as health care professionals, to imagine their exclusive role to be rescue, and leaves them unprepared for the more complex reality when they encounter real survivors.

21.3 Conclusion

The dominant media narrative impacts individual biases and actions: When a physician only looks for trafficking in young, cisgender[5] girls, they will miss the older trans man who has been forced to trade sex because of increasing debt bondage.

---

[4] In 2008, USA states began passing the so-called Safe Harbor laws, designed to recognize that youth under 18 involved in commercial sex are victims and not perpetrators, and should not be treated as perpetrators with arrest. Despite good intentions, rarely have these laws achieved such outcomes, and many jurisdictions still require arrest or detainment of youth for them to access services.

[5] Cisgender: denoting or relating to a person whose affirmed gender conforms to the gender they were assigned at birth; not transgender.

And when we only conceptualize trafficking as involving the sex industry, we ignore the kitchen workers in the restaurants we frequent and the staff of hotels where we relax and vacation.

And each of these failures compound quickly to solidify and institutionalize these, not as individual biases and short-hand, but as truths supported by government policies and social dialogue. Policies are supposed to solve a problem, and when the policies are based on media fueled biases, resultant laws and actions reflect these biases as well: When a sign with the trafficking help hotline is posted only in adult clubs and not in the many other places where trafficked persons may be, only those in adult clubs will call the hotline, and perception about the industries where people are victimized will be skewed. When money is disproportionately allocated for law enforcement raids to uncover trafficking in the sex industry all other types of trafficking remain underreported and unprosecuted.

The nature of these media stories also shapes the approach to the problem. When savior stories and rescue narratives are prominently featured in the news, such stories beg for legislation to fund and support these efforts. When the story involves kidnapping and clear forms of violence, we predicate services on cooperation with law enforcement without consideration to what that means for most survivors. When a story ends with the trafficked person being saved or returned to their family, viewers give little thought to the complex service and resource needs of survivors. As policies only target one type of victim, those are the victims most identified, and theirs are the stories most told. When articles only celebrate the services for young girls who have been sex trafficked, audiences assume these are the only types of trafficked persons that exist. With every article celebrating a successful raid of massage parlors, audiences assume that this is the most effective tool we have in combating trafficking. Media fuels, finds, and then subsequently sells these narratives.

21.4 Recommendations

For these reasons we have to demand better, more honest, and accurate reporting. We have to demand a more in-depth picture, so that we can develop an understanding of how a youth became homeless and engaged in trading sex to meet basic needs; or how someone who entered the country with a work visa, intending to earn money to support his family, was exploited, and why he did not seek help; or how a history of arrests and systemic racism prevented anyone from seeing the person in front of them as being victimized. This applies to everyone: journalists, advocates, everyone that works in the anti-trafficking field, and the public too. Below are the authors' recommendations for improving the national narrative about trafficking, so that the US public can truly engage with the complexity of trafficking, support all survivors, and ultimately prevent trafficking entirely.

21.4.1 Recommendations for Media Consumers

- *Be critical of the media you are reading and watching.*
- *Seek out community-based media.* Community-based organizations focus on the wider conversation, including solutions focused on root causes and issues which affect all members of the community.
- *Reach out to editors and write letters to the editor to demand more comprehensive coverage.* Frequently, stories are poorly written and unbalanced; some share pictures of actual survivors without their permission or consideration of the ramifications. Demand responsible reporting. Tell editors and authors that pictures of survivors, even with blurred faces, are unacceptable.

21.4.2 Recommendations for Anti-Trafficking Advocates

- *Let survivors lead.* Keeping survivors at the center of advocacy work includes having them direct the work, including the media work that happens. Let them tell *their* story.
- *Get informed consent of every survivor.* And then get it again. Direct service work has an inherent power imbalance. Whenever survivor stories are used, let them make the decision as to how, where, and in what context the story will be used. And make sure they understand the extent to which they can withdraw their consent to share.
- *Do not use pictures or identifying information of minors.* Even with the youth's assent and with their parent or guardian's consent, using pictures and any identifying information for youth survivors is unethical.
- *Survivors should never feel that services are predicated on participation* in a media effort. This may mean not using a story while the survivor is receiving services, having a different individual than the direct provider make the arrangements for consent, or reminding survivors that they do not owe advocates or journalists anything.
- *Protect confidentiality.* When individual stories are shared, anonymize, combine details, and note this to your audience.

21.4.3 Recommendations for Journalists

- *Human trafficking is not just about the arrest or court proceedings.* Trafficked persons existed before being recognized by law enforcement, they were people before they were trafficked. Root causes which create the conditions for exploitation and trafficking existed long before, and continue after survivors exit their trafficking situations. Expand trafficking stories to include those times before they were a "trafficking victim" and follow up on what happened after their trafficking situation.

- *Do not stop at one narrative.* Everyone has a unique experience. While some situations and factors are more common than others, it is essential to paint a larger picture than the youngest victim or the most traumatic violence.
- *Understand the potential impact of your work.* Just because something can be shared does not mean that it should be. Know the impact of media, and communicate to subjects the possible effect of sharing hometowns, names, mugshots, and even blurred out faces. Then and together, decide how to tell the story in the way that will have the least amount of damage and be the most beneficial to survivors and communities.

References

1. Fox RL, Van Sickel RW. Tabloid justice: criminal justice in an age of media frenzy. Boulder, CO: Lynne Rienner; 2001. p. 125–6.
2. McCombs M, et al. Communication and democracy. New York, NY: Routledge; 2013.
3. Sanford R, Martínez DE, Weitzer R. Framing human trafficking: a content analysis of recent US newspaper articles. J Hum Traffick. 2016;2(2):139–55.
4. International Labor Organization. ILO 2012 global estimate of forced labor executive summary. 2012. http://www.ilo.org/wcmsp5/groups/public/@ed_norm/@declaration/documents/publication/wcms_181953.pdf. Accessed 5 May 2016.
5. United States Department of Justice. Attorney general's annual report to congress and assessment U.S. government activities to combat trafficking in persons. 2014. https://www.justice.gov/ag/file/799436/download. Accessed 3 June 2016.
6. Human Trafficking Series, Christian Science Monitor. http://www.csmonitor.com/World/Topics/Human-Trafficking-Series. Accessed 1 Aug 2016.
7. Bensinger K, Garrison J, Singer-Vine J. The New American slavery: invited to the U.S., foreign workers find a nightmare. BuzzFeed. 2015. https://www.buzzfeed.com/jessicagarrison/the-new-american-slavery-invited-to-the-us-foreign-workers-f?utm_term=.sgdVRP7mv#.kiNlej7d8. Accessed 14 Apr 2016.
8. Seafood from Slaves. Associated Press. 2015. http://www.ap.org/explore/seafood-from-slaves/. Accessed 1 Aug 2016.
9. Large T. Sex obsession mars slavery coverage, experts tell journalists. Thomson Reuters Foundation. 2016. http://news.trust.org/item/20160526230336-tzvqd/. Accessed 5 June 2016.
10. Gulati GJ. Media representation of human trafficking in the United States, Great Britain, and Canada. Waltham, MA: Bentley University; 2010.
11. Anderson L. Super Bowl the largest human trafficking event in the country. Desert News National. 2015. http://national.deseretnews.com/article/3412/the-super-bowl-is-the-largest-human-trafficking-event-in-the-country.html. Accessed 6 Feb 2016.
12. Ham J. What's the cost of a rumor? A guide to sorting out the myths and the facts about sporting events and trafficking. Bangkok: Global Alliance Against Traffic in Women; 2011.
13. Thanawala S. FBI tries new approach in Super Bowl sex trafficking fight. The Boston Globe. 2016. http://www.boston.com/sports/new-england-patriots/2016/01/12/fbi-tries-new-approach-in-super-bowl-sex-trafficking-fight?s_campaign=bcom%3Asocialflow%3Atwitter. Accessed 13 Jan 2016.

14. Lybarger J. Massaging the super bowl's sex trafficking stats. SF Weekly. 2016. http://www. sfweekly.com/sanfrancisco/news-super-bowl-sex-trafficking-fbi-sex-work/Content?oid= 4486067. Accessed 26 Feb 2016.
15. Salonga R. Super Bowl 50: human trafficking crackdown yielded dozens of arrests, citations. The Mercury News. 2016. http://www.mercurynews.com/sports/ci_29495319/super-bowl-50-human-trafficking-crackdown-yielded-dozens. Accessed 26 Feb 2016.
16. Carroll L. Does sex trafficking increase around the Super Bowl? Politifact. 2015. http://www. politifact.com/truth-o-meter/statements/2015/jan/29/john-cornyn/does-sex-trafficking-increase-around-super-bowl/. Accessed 6 Feb 2016.
17. Campbell A. Sex trafficking hype surrounding the super bowl does more harm than good. Huffington Post. 2016. http://www.huffingtonpost.com/entry/super-bowl-sex-trafficking-harmful_us_56b4e08be4b08069c7a7068b. Accessed 23 Apr 2016.
18. Plummer C. Slavery at the World Cup? Human Rights Campaign. 2015. http://www.human-rightsfirst.org/blog/slavery-world-cup. Accessed 21 July 2016.
19. Preventing Sex Trafficking and Strengthening Families Act (Public Law 113–183). 2014. https://www.congress.gov/bill/113th-congress/house-bill/4980. Accessed 1 Aug 2016.
20. Johnston A, Friedman B, Sobel M. Framing an emerging issue: how US print and broadcast news media covered sex trafficking, 2008–2012. J Hum Traffick. 2015;1(3):235–54.
21. Moore G, Paulsen E. Exploiting our daughters: fighting sex trafficking, Roll Call. 2014. http:// www.rollcall.com/news/exploiting_our_daughters_fighting_sex_trafficking_commentary-231944-1.html. Accessed 1 Aug 2016.
22. Williams IC. Protecting our daughters from sex trafficking, The Harlem Times. http://the harlemtimes.com/detroit/protecting-daughters-human-trafficking. Accessed 1 Aug 2016.
23. Our daughters are not for sale: congressional resolution. http://rights4girls.org/wp-content/ uploads/r4g/2015/03/Our-Daughters-are-Not-for-Sale-Congressional-Resolution.pdf. Accessed 23 Apr 2016.
24. Fine Collins A. Sex trafficking of Americans: the girls next door. Vanity Fair. 2011. http:// www.vanityfair.com/news/2011/05/sex-trafficking-201105. Accessed 23 Apr 2016.
25. The average age of entry myth. Polaris. 2016. http://polarisproject.org/blog/2016/01/05/aver-age-age-entry-myth. Accessed 1 Aug 2016.
26. Kessler G. Indiana AG touts a debunked and rejected 'fact' on sex trafficking. Washington Post. 2016. https://www.washingtonpost.com/amphtml/news/fact-checker/wp/2016/06/08/ indiana-ag-touts-a-debunked-and-rejected-fact-on-sex-trafficking/. Accessed 8 June 2016.
27. Hall C. Is one of the most-cited statistics about sex work wrong? The Atlantic. 2014. http:// www.theatlantic.com/business/archive/2014/09/is-one-of-the-most-cited-statistics-about-sex-work-wrong/379662/. Accessed 23 Apr 2016.
28. White Slave Traffic Act, Public Law 61–177, 18 U.S.C. § 2421–2424.
29. Fahy S, Farrell A. The problem of human trafficking in the U.S.: public frames and policy responses. J Crim Just. 2009;39:617–26.
30. Fahy S, Farrell A. The problem of human trafficking in the U.S.: public frames and policy responses. J Crim Justice. 2009;39:617–626, p. 620, quoting Finckenauer J, Jahic G. Repre-sentations and misrepresentations of human trafficking, Trends Organ Crime 2005;8(3):24–40, p. 26.
31. Todres J. Human trafficking and film: how popular portrayals influence law and public policy perception. Cornell Law Review. Online, citing International Labor Organization (2012) ILO 2012 Global Estimate of Forced Labor at16. 2015.
32. Javidan P. Global class and the commercial-sexual exploitation of children: toward a multidi-mensional understanding. Colum J Race Law. 2012;1:365–79.
33. National crime victim's right's week: new challenges, new solutions. National Center for Victims of Crime. 2013. pp. 24–25. https://www.ncjrs.gov/ovc_archives/ncvrw/2013/ pdf/2013ResourceGuide-Full.pdf. Accessed 15 Aug 2016.
34. Gorenstein D. Healthcare takes on the fight against trafficking. NPR Marketplace. 2016. http:// www.marketplace.org/2016/03/02/health-care/health-care-takes-fight-against-trafficking. Accessed 1 Aug 2016.

35. Bigelson J. Homelessness, survival sex and human trafficking: as experienced by the youth of covenant house New York. 2013. https://d28whvbyjonrpc.cloudfront.net/s3fs-public/attachments/Covenant-House-trafficking-study.pdf. Accessed 23 May 2016.
36. Marcus A, Horning A, et al. Conflict and agency among sex workers and pimps: a closer look at domestic minor sex trafficking. Ann Am Acad. 2014;653:225–46.
37. Martínez de Vedia G. Beyond the chains: tuning into the full spectrum of human trafficking. 2015. http://freedomnetworkusa.org/food-for-thought-from-fn-policy-co-chair-gonzalo-martinez-de-vedia/. Accessed 14 May 2016.
38. Dank M, et al. Surviving the streets of New York. Urban Institute. 2015. http://www.urban.org/sites/default/files/alfresco/publication-pdfs/2000119-Surviving-the-Streets-of-New-York.pdf. Accessed 1 Aug 2016.
39. Swenstein A, Mogulescu K. Resisting the carceral: the need to align anti-trafficking efforts with movements for criminal justice reform. Anti Traffick Rev. 2016;6:118–22.
40. Dank M, Farrell A, Owens C, et al. Understanding the organization, operation, and victimization process of labor trafficking in the United States. Washington, DC: Urban Institute and Northeastern University; 2014.
41. National Survivor Network. Members survey on the impact of criminal arrest and detention on survivors of human trafficking. 2016.
42. Operation cross country: recovering victims of child sex trafficking. 2015. https://www.fbi.gov/news/stories/2015/october/operation-cross-country. Accessed 14 May 2016.
43. Clark L, Kelly J. Some trafficking victims "rescued" by fbi have been arrested. The Chronical of Social Change. 2013. https://chronicleofsocialchange.org/featured/some-trafficking-victims-rescued-by-fbi-have-been-arrested/3687. Accessed 14 May 2016.
44. Ditmore M, Thukral J. Accountability and the use of raids to fight trafficking. Anti Traffick Rev. 2012 1:140. http://www2.law.columbia.edu/faculty_franke/Gender_Justice/Accountabililty%20and%20the%20Use%20of%20Raids%20to%20Fight%20Trafficking.pdf. Accessed 1 Aug 2016.

Chapter 22
Human Trafficking: Perspectives on Prevention

Elaine J. Alpert and Sharon E. Chin

22.1 Introduction

Q: How do you eat an elephant?
A: One bite at a time.

Q: How do you cross an abyss?
A: In one giant leap.

How does a nation approach preventing a phenomenon as massive, longstanding, ingrained, and seemingly intractable as human trafficking? Should the United States (US) use the "eating the elephant" approach by taking one incremental bite at a time? Or, is nothing short of a giant leap required to make an impact on prevention? Alternatively, might some combination of these approaches—or some other approach altogether—prove best?

22.1.1 Historical Perspectives on Slavery and Trafficking

Human trafficking and its close cousin, slavery, have been part of human history for millennia. Human beings have been obtained, controlled, and exploited for labor, and presumably for sexual services, for at least 5,000 years, when early societies

---

The original version of this chapter was revised. An erratum to this chapter can be found at DOI: 10.1007/978-3-319-47824-1_25

E.J. Alpert (✉)
Faculty of Medicine, University of British Columbia, Vancouver, BC, Canada, V6T 1Z4
e-mail: ejalpert@massmed.org

S.E. Chin
Independent Scholar and Program Evaluation Specialist, Somerset, NJ, USA
e-mail: schin.mph@gmail.com

© Springer International Publishing AG 2017
M. Chisolm-Straker, H. Stoklosa (eds.), *Human Trafficking Is a Public Health Issue*, DOI 10.1007/978-3-319-47824-1_22

began to evolve from ones that were strictly hunter-gatherer communities to those that were less nomadic and more agrarian [1]. More than a thousand years later, circa 1760 BCE, the first known "legal" references to slavery were included in several of the 282 laws of the Mesopotamian Code of Hammurabi, enacted to bring order to the governance of ancient Babylonia. The many mentions of slavery in the Code indicate that the enslavement of human beings was well-established within society by that time [2].

Slavery continued to be legitimized and extensively recorded over the ensuing 3,500 years, as evidenced by numerous references to both indentured servitude and slavery in legal documents, historical accounts, sacred texts, and works of art worldwide [3]. The capture and forced removal of human beings from their homes and communities in Africa, and their subsequent transport to Portugal, Spain, Britain, the Netherlands, France, Denmark, other countries in Europe, and to disparate colonies throughout North America, the Caribbean, and Asia, marked a particularly brutal chapter in human history. The enslavement of human beings became shockingly prevalent; it is estimated that in the space of four centuries (ca 1450–1850), approximately 12 million human beings were subjected to kidnapping and forced migration from Africa to North America and the Caribbean for exploitation as slaves. Among those captured, between 1.5 and 2 million perished from starvation, disease or abuse during their journey across the Atlantic [4].

Although slavery was embedded as a social norm of human civilization for 5,000 years, the last 200 years (1800s on) have seen a relatively rapid shift from slavery existing as a practice that was legal, publically acknowledged, and accepted as a "given" in society, to one that is now illegal, clandestine, and abhorrent, or, in other words, "unacceptable." The transformation of a human condition from the realm of the "given" to one that is "unacceptable" is a cornerstone of public health, and will be discussed later in this chapter [5].

Even though the 13th Amendment to the US Constitution outlawed slavery in 1865, passage of the Trafficking Victims Protection Act (TVPA) in 2000 acknowledged that the commercial exploitation of human beings still existed, both in the US and worldwide. Reauthorized in 2003, 2005, 2008, and 2013, this landmark legislation not only defined "severe forms of human trafficking" as criminal offenses under federal law, but also established "the three Ps" or priorities on which to focus anti-trafficking efforts: *prosecution* of traffickers, *protection* of victims, and development and implementation of *prevention*-focused initiatives [6]. Utilization of the legal provisions available through the TVPA has, to date, been modest in comparison to the estimated number of trafficked persons in the US. Nonetheless, enactment of this legislation and the consequent federal prominence afforded to the issue of human trafficking have served as critically important catalysts for raising awareness about trafficking in persons in the US, and for enabling the development of prevention-focused public health responses.

22.2 Discussion

22.2.1 Public Health: A Catalyst for Prevention-Focused Social Change

The major goal of public health is to improve the health and well-being of populations, for which prevention plays a foundational role. Examining how an existing *status quo* situation becomes newly conceptualized as a public health problem, and thus a focus for prevention efforts, is central to the evolution of the public health approach to addressing human trafficking.

In 1958, Sir Geoffrey Vickers declared that a given situation becomes defined as a "public health problem" when society ceases to view it as "inevitable" and, instead, begins to perceive it as "unacceptable" [5]. For human trafficking, this rather dramatic transformation was marked in 2000 when the United Nations Palermo Protocol to Prevent, Suppress, and Punish Trafficking in Persons was adopted and the TVPA was signed into law [7]. Among other provisions, the TVPA requires the Secretary of State to submit an annual report to Congress detailing the status of "severe forms of trafficking in persons" around the world, as defined in the statute. The first Trafficking in Persons Report was submitted to Congress in 2001 [8]. This annual publication has now become a globally respected assessment of the status of human trafficking worldwide, informing policy, practice, funding, and prevention efforts both in the US and abroad [9].

The programs and remedies made possible by the TVPA, along with substantial attention in the news media, have increased public awareness about human trafficking in the US, moving it relatively quickly into the realm of the "unacceptable." These developments—supported by the efforts, dedication, and visibility of grassroots advocacy and social justice groups as well as the health and public health sector—have helped define human trafficking as a public health problem. Recent statements from the World Health Organization (2014), the American Public Health Association (2015), and the US federal government (2016), respectively, have reaffirmed that human trafficking is a significant public health problem that merits disciplined basic and translational research, trauma-informed practices, and comprehensive prevention-focused responses [10–12].

22.2.2 Basic Principles of Public Health

Public health can be defined broadly as a discipline or set of activities focused on improving and protecting the health and well-being of populations. More specifically, public health can be described as a science-based, prevention-focused, multidisciplinary, collaborative, social ecologically-oriented and culturally-sensitive discipline that promotes the social, emotional, and physical well-being of communities [13].

Fig. 22.1 The CDC public
health model. (Reproduced
with permission from the
US Centers for Disease
Control and Prevention.
http://www.cdc.gov/
violenceprevention/
overview/
publichealthapproach.html)

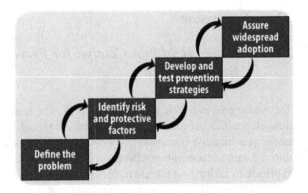

The US Centers for Disease Control and Prevention (CDC-P) describes the public health approach as being comprised of four linked steps, summarized in Fig. 22.1: defining and describing the problem; identifying risk and protective factors; developing and testing prevention strategies; and assuring widespread adoption of promising programs by implementing and scaling successful initiatives [14].

The public health approach to human trafficking has been evolving rapidly; definitions, risk, protective, and promotive (or contributory) factors are becoming better delineated through qualitative and quantitative research efforts. Overall, the field is still in its infancy with respect to developing and testing prevention strategies, as well as in scaling promising practices to achieve maximal effectiveness in at-risk populations.

22.2.3   The Social Ecological Model: A Framework for Understanding Risk Factors

To define and describe a public health issue such as human trafficking, it is essential to understand the individual and environmental factors that contribute to its occurrence and that prevent at-risk and victimized individuals from breaking free. One way to conceptualize these influences is through the social ecological model (SEM), which is a framework for describing the complex interplay among factors that contribute to public health problems [15]. Figure 22.2 illustrates the four main levels of the SEM: individual, relationship, community, and societal.

Using the SEM as an organizing framework, both "push" and "pull" determinants at each level emerge as risk factors for human trafficking. These factors either drive individuals from their current situation into an at-risk one (push factors) or draw individuals into a coercive situation (pull factors) [16–21]. Table 22.1 lists some of the common push and pull factors that contribute to human trafficking at each level of the SEM. Of note, some factors can be categorized into multiple levels or have both "push" and "pull" elements.

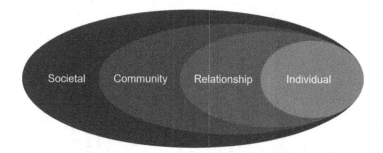

Fig. 22.2 The social-ecological model. (Reproduced with permission from the US Centers for Disease Control and Prevention. http://www.cdc.gov/violenceprevention/overview/social-ecologicalmodel.html)

Careful consideration of behavioral (individual) and social (relationship, community, and societal) determinants can contribute to an enhanced understanding of the complex conditions that contribute to a person's risk of being trafficked, and inform culturally appropriate, prevention-focused interventions.

22.2.4   Public Health Prevention

22.2.4.1   Types of Prevention

As described in Chap. 20: *The Role of Community Health Centers in Addressing Human Trafficking*, prevention strategies are normally classified into one of three categories: *primary prevention, secondary prevention, and tertiary prevention*. Originally conceptualized in the 1950s when public health programs were focused mainly on biological issues related to chronic and infectious diseases, this organizing schema aptly describes initiatives throughout the universe of public health, and is particularly applicable to violence prevention and to addressing all forms of exploitation, including human trafficking [22–24].

In brief, the goal of primary prevention is complete prevention before a phenomenon occurs; the goal of secondary prevention is early intervention and mitigation of risk factors; and the goal of tertiary prevention is intervention and recovery. *Primary prevention initiatives*, when successful, address the root causes of, and risk factors for, a problem before there is any occurrence of the target issue. In human trafficking, primary prevention programs might focus on reducing vulnerabilities and enhancing capacity and resiliency so that coercion and exploitation do not take place at all. *Secondary prevention initiatives* are designed to address existing risk factors or to intervene early once a problem has begun, to prevent, further, more serious, or lasting damage. In anti-trafficking efforts, secondary prevention programs often seek to educate those who are at risk or who may be in early stages of exploitation to mitigate risk factors, provide support, or offer guidance for avoidance.

Table 22.1 Key behavioral and social determinants for human trafficking, organized according to the social ecological model

S-E level	Key behavioral and social determinants	
	Push factors	Pull factors
Individual	• Need for basic necessities (food, shelter, clothing, etc.) • Exposure to violence and abuse • Emotional deprivation • Poor education, illiteracy • Young age (limited life experience, immature prefrontal cortex) • Early socialization as sexual object • Minority gender, ethnicity, race • Experience of discrimination or stigma • Extreme familial poverty	• Lure of a better life • Image of lucrative job opportunities, glamorous lifestyle, fame • Desire for material comforts • Expectation of future love, success
Relationship	• Family instability/abuse by family members • Loyalty, obligation, love, or desire to help family • Sold or persuaded by family • Peer influences • Desire to please an intimate partner • Need to belong, desire for kinship • Extreme familial poverty	• Seduction by an intimate partner • Misplaced trust in others' promises • Deception, "bait and switch" of job promises

Community	• Economic pressures • Political conflict • Natural disasters • Religious persecution • Racial/ethnic discrimination • Bias against marginalized or vulnerable individuals (e.g., homophobia, transphobia) • Sexism • Corruption • Community violence	• Facilitation by corrupt local police and governmental authorities, some of whom are traffickers themselves

Society and environment	• Inequitable distribution of opportunities
	• Gender inequities
	• Sexual objectification of women and children, especially girls, as a social norm
	• Natural disasters
	• Environmental degradation due to:
	  o Climate change
	  o Pesticides and other environmental toxins
	  o Decreased crop and fish yields
		• Societal expectations for children in general, and girls in particular
		• Societal expectation to provide for family
		• Demand for cheap goods and labor
		• TV, radio, Internet messages that promise easy access to desirable lifestyle and consumer goods
		• Corruption
		• Globalization

Secondary prevention programs also educate health care practitioners, teachers, and other intermediaries; these individuals, in turn, can better identify and respond to those who may be at risk. In contrast, *tertiary prevention initiatives* are designed to minimize the impact of, and promote recovery from, situations that have already occurred. Tertiary prevention initiatives against human trafficking intervene to help survivors separate from their trafficking situation and pursue lives free of further exploitation.

22.2.4.2 The "Evolution" of Prevention

When a "new" public health problem is first identified, initial responses tend to be directed toward tertiary prevention. Subsequently, secondary prevention programs emerge to facilitate early identification of at-risk individuals and to address and reduce existing risk factors. Primary prevention programs are usually established last, if at all.

In the case of human trafficking, the initial focus on tertiary prevention-style rapid and emergency responses aimed at capturing traffickers and assisting actively trafficked persons was necessary and understandable. Such efforts are typically visible, identifiable, and frequently covered by news media. Law enforcement raids on suspected trafficking sites based on tips or investigations, trafficking hotlines, and emergency shelters for trafficked persons are all examples of tertiary prevention responses. Since the success of these efforts is generally measurable, outcome data can be supplied to funders and policy makers to support continued emergency response efforts.

Secondary prevention efforts frequently focus on school, community, and health sector-based awareness education, and on educating policymakers, law enforcement personnel, health care professionals, teachers, education administrators, faith leaders, business owners, corporate representatives, and other intermediaries. Clinical education for health care practitioners has become increasingly available, focusing on building knowledge and skills to enhance early identification, trauma-informed assessment and response, risk factor mitigation, and community-based referral of trafficked or at-risk patients. Many secondary prevention programs incorporate elements of tertiary prevention as well, in order to respond more effectively to urgent or crisis situations that may arise during identification or disclosure. In general, while secondary prevention programs can be developed, implemented, and evaluated within a funding cycle, documenting long-term benefits can be challenging unless extended follow-up evaluations are pursued.

Clearly, primary prevention is the "holy grail" of public health. It is generally considered far better and more cost-effective to prevent an adverse outcome, such as trafficking, from occurring at all, than to attempt to ameliorate damage or engage in a "rescue" once it has occurred. Still, it can take years or even generations to demonstrate the efficacy of primary prevention efforts, rather than the hours, days, weeks, or months that are needed to document the impact of secondary and tertiary prevention endeavors. Additionally, and perhaps most vexing, effective primary prevention is normally devoid of media spectacle or fanfare. Trying to generate enthusiasm about something that has *not* happened is far more difficult than proclaiming that something *has* happened, especially when that "something" is a dramatic, life-saving rescue. As such, media accounts, which influence policymakers and funders as well as the general public, are far less likely to cover primary prevention efforts than other initiatives. For these reasons, primary prevention tends to be far less compelling to policymakers and funders, who generally operate on comparatively short funding and election cycles.

22.2.5 The Spectrum of Prevention: A Framework for Conceptualizing Prevention Initiatives

Effective prevention requires developing, implementing, and sustaining a range of strategies that span primary, secondary, and tertiary prevention approaches across each level of the SEM. The "Spectrum of Prevention," developed by Larry Cohen and based on earlier work by Marshall Swift in treating developmental disabilities, is a systematic tool that can be used to conceptualize, implement, and evaluate a wide range of public health prevention efforts, including the prevention of human trafficking [25].

The Spectrum of Prevention identifies six complementary levels that produce a synergistic effect on prevention when used together. Figure 22.3, reproduced with permission from the National Sexual Violence Resource Center (NSVRC), illustrates the six levels along with their definitions, as they apply to sexual violence [26]. In 2006, NSVRC published a summary of specific initiatives that have been developed at each level of the Spectrum of Prevention in regard to the prevention of sexual violence [27]. Similarly, the Spectrum of Prevention can be used to guide the development, implementation, adoption, and evaluation of similar initiatives geared to the prevention of human trafficking.

22.2.6 Safeness: A Framework for Primary Prevention

A new and innovative construct called "safeness" may prove to be an important contributor to the field of public health, and to the prevention of human trafficking. This concept, illustrated in Fig. 22.4, was introduced by Connie Mitchell MD, MPH, Deputy Director of the Center for Family Health, California Department of Public Health, and explained in a January 2016 webinar presentation entitled "New Public Health Strategies for Violence Prevention" [28].

While *safety* can be thought of as a beneficial outcome derived from actions directed toward reducing risk or danger within a physical environment, the construct of *safeness* represents a more internalized and integrated sense of security or well-being. Emerging evidence, including from publications based on insights from the Adverse Childhood Experiences Study, also indicates a likely association

Level of Spectrum	Definition of Level
1 Strengthening Individual Knowledge and Skills	Enhancing an individual's capability of preventing violence and promoting safety
2 Promoting Community Education	Reaching groups of people with information and resources to prevent violence and promote safety
3 Educating Providers	Informing providers who will transmit skills and knowledge to others and model positive norms
4 Fostering Coalitions and Networks	Bringing together groups and individuals for broader goals and greater impact
5 Changing Organizational Practices	Adopting regulations and shaping norms to prevent violence and improve safety
6 Influencing Policies and Legislation	Enacting laws and policies that support healthy community norms and a violence-free society

Fig. 22.3 The spectrum of prevention framework. (Reproduced with permission from the National Sexual Violence Resource Center http://www.preventioninstitute.org/component/jlibrary/article/id-105/127.html)

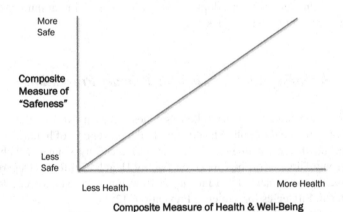

Fig. 22.4 Safeness gradient of health. (Reproduced with permission from Connie Mitchell MD, MPH)

between a compromised sense of safeness and subsequent risk for both victimization and perpetration of violence [29–32]. Understanding safeness, its importance to healthy human development, and the features that lead to its compromise, may help explain the factors that underlie risk for both victimization and perpetration of human trafficking.

Considerations of "safeness" go beyond foundational public health principles that focus on identifying and ameliorating risk factors. A safeness orientation focuses on creating, enhancing, and preserving the capacity of individuals, as well as communities, to remain resilient in the face of existing or even future threats. The building blocks of safeness include not only a family and community environment free from extreme physical danger, but also secure emotional attachment during early childhood; the fulfillment of physiologic needs such as sufficient nutritious food, clean water, and stable housing; the provision of high-quality basic education; and access to loving and supportive social connections or "social capacity" within families, in friend relationships, and in community settings. In many respects, these factors, when absent, compromised, or threatened, resemble the previously described *push* and *pull* factors for human trafficking.

Thus, when developing prevention strategies for human trafficking, reacting exclusively to specific identified risks to safety represents a necessary, but inherently insufficient dimension. Acknowledging the importance of promoting safeness in infant, child, and youth development as a building block for primary prevention may prompt renewed commitment by individuals, families, communities, and society to address the root causes of trafficking.

22.2.7   Existing Human Trafficking Prevention Programs

For the most part, existing trafficking prevention efforts have focused predominantly on tertiary prevention (trafficking intervention and crisis support), or secondary prevention (activities that promote school and community-based awareness, or that provide tools to help trained intermediaries identify, assess, and refer at-risk individuals). Similar to early responses to other public health issues such as HIV-AIDS, domestic violence, and intravenous drug use, most early trafficking prevention programs consisted of either grassroots survivor-led initiatives, or government-initiated programs. Although not intended to be exhaustive in scope, this section describes the characteristics of selected trafficking prevention programs to highlight their noteworthy features, as well as their potential for scaling to a greater geographic reach, to an expanded population of at-risk individuals, or to different types of exploitation.

- The US Department of Health and Human Services Rescue and Restore Campaign and its accompanying National Human Trafficking Resource Center (NHTRC) are examples of federally-led secondary and tertiary prevention initiatives created to help identify and assist labor and sex trafficked individuals in the

US [33]. A major component of the Rescue and Restore Campaign has been the implementation of a non-governmental partnership with the NHTRC (www.traffickingresourcecenter.org) and its accompanying 24-h Hotline (1-888-373-7888). This collaboration provides web and telephone-based resource and referral information to trafficked persons (tertiary prevention), and assists intermediaries, ranging from health care providers to the lay public, in recognizing whether an observed situation may be related to trafficking (secondary and tertiary prevention). NHTRC also offers a free, online resource library as well as web-based trainings for clinicians, educators, and the general public (secondary prevention) [34, 35]. In addition, a variety of toolkits, practice guides, and public education and awareness materials are available free of charge through the Rescue and Restore Campaign [36].

- The Girls Educational and Mentoring Services (GEMS), founded in 1998 by Rachel Lloyd, is one of the oldest community-based programs in the US designed to help sexually exploited girls and young women break free from commercial sexual exploitation (CSE). Geared to the 12- to 24-year-old age group, GEMS has grown from a one-person "kitchen table" endeavor to a well-known and well-respected awareness-raising and comprehensive service delivery program that addresses a range of prevention and intervention needs, focusing predominantly on secondary and tertiary prevention activities. GEMS tertiary prevention activities include short-term, crisis, and transitional residential care for girls and young women who are being actively exploited, as well as court advocacy for at-risk youth in the foster care and correctional systems. GEMS secondary prevention programs focus on peer-led outreach workshops that educate at-risk young women about CSE and other forms of coercive control, such as domestic violence [37].

- My Life My Choice (MLMC) was launched in 2002 in response to the death of a teenage girl who had been commercially sexually exploited. A survivor-led initiative for providers, at-risk adolescent girls, and young people victimized via sex trafficking, MLMC engages mainly in secondary and tertiary prevention activities for commercially sexually exploited girls, boys, and transgender-experienced youth from 12 to 18 years of age [38]. A program of the non-profit Justice Resource Institute in Boston, Massachusetts, MLMC's major tertiary prevention activity matches young people who have been sexually exploited with adult "survivor mentors" to help build resiliency skills focusing on self-worth, trust, help-seeking, and leadership [39]. Secondary prevention activities center around facilitated groups that take part in a 10-session curriculum that teaches participants how to recognize and resist recruitment tactics commonly used by pimps, and to find a path out of exploitation for those who are already trafficked [40]. MLMC offers secondary-prevention training for law enforcement personnel and for a variety of intermediary service providers. MLMC also advocates for legislative reforms and service coordination by serving on a number of governmental and non-governmental coalitions and task forces. Finally, MLMC maintains an active social media presence to raise awareness and change social norms about commercial sexual exploitation of young people.

- ECPAT International, which began in 1990 as an organization (initially but no longer) called End Child Prostitution in Asian Tourism (ECPAT), is now a network of 90 collaborating organizations in 82 countries, including the USA [41]. ECPAT International's prevention-focused work focuses on secondary prevention of child sexual exploitation through a range of legal and social initiatives. Within the USA, one of ECPAT's signature collaborations has been the development of a Tourism Child-Protection Code of Conduct. This initiative enlists the travel and tourism industry, including hotel operators, in efforts to prevent child sex trafficking [42]. ECPAT has helped participating businesses develop business-specific policies and procedures on sexual exploitation prevention, has helped train employees, and has provided information to travelers about children's vulnerabilities and rights.

- Some labor trafficking prevention efforts target members of the general public who may not be aware that food, clothing, gemstones, and other consumer products they purchase might be farmed, mined, or manufactured by exploited or trafficked workers. Some initiatives also work with companies that purchase raw materials for use in their businesses. One of the first worker-based human rights organizations, the Coalition of Immokalee Workers (CIW), was formed in 1993, in response to revelations about the exploitation of farmworkers in Immokalee, Florida [43]. CIW brought national attention to the plight of migrant workers and other individuals forced into involuntary servitude and rapidly became a leader in anti-labor trafficking efforts. Arising from CIW's efforts, the Campaign for Fair Food and its companion Fair Food Program are primary and secondary prevention initiatives aimed at raising awareness among the general public about farm labor exploitation and for ensuring fair wages and humane working conditions for farmworkers on participating farms [44]. To support these efforts, the Fair Food Program formulated a Code of Conduct to enable retail food companies to adopt industry-wide best practices for fair treatment and compensation of farmworkers. Companies that comply with the Code participate in an independent third-party monitoring program by the Fair Food Standards Council so that their products can be designated "Fair Food Certified." This program, therefore, changes organizational practices at the primary prevention level.

- As a primary and secondary prevention-focused initiative, a non-profit organization called "Made in a Free World" builds public and corporate awareness about the role of forced labor in the manufacture of consumer products. Made in a Free World provides tools that businesses can use to monitor supply chains for exploited labor and also produces media awareness campaigns targeted to consumers. In 2011, this organization launched an online tool called "Slavery Footprint" to help members of the general public estimate the number of slaves that may be involved in the production of common consumer items, thereby providing the general public a clear and direct connection to how labor trafficking may be affecting goods they wish to purchase [45]. The goal of campaigns such as these is to persuade corporations to stop purchasing raw materials made by trafficked labor and to promote fair, living wages for all workers.

- The US Department of Labor provides a primary and secondary prevention-focused toolkit to help businesses combat labor trafficking, especially child labor trafficking, by helping companies develop a business-specific "social compliance system" [46]. Elements of the toolkit include guidance on how to engage stakeholders and partners, assess risks and impacts, develop a code of conduct, communicate and train across the supply chain, monitor for compliance, remediate violations, engage in independent review, and report on performance.

- In an effort to raise public awareness (secondary prevention) about the impact of child labor and forced labor on goods that may be purchased by US-based consumers, the US Department of Labor's Bureau of International Labor Affairs (ILAB) maintains a web-based, searchable list of goods, organized by country, that it deems likely to be produced by child labor or forced labor. Efforts such as these not only raise public awareness about forced labor practices but also may help consumers avoid purchasing items that come from exploitative supply chains [47].
- To help communities develop their own secondary and tertiary human trafficking prevention strategies, the United Nations (UN) Office on Drugs and Crime published a Toolkit to Combat Trafficking in Persons in 2008 to increase the capacity of victim service providers, law enforcement personnel, judges, prosecutors, policy-makers and the general public to address the goals of the Palermo Protocol. The UN Toolkit also highlights global examples of promising practices that raise public awareness about human trafficking, including media initiatives that use videos, posters, radio announcements, and theater performances [48].

Effective human trafficking prevention programs need not be designed specifically with trafficking prevention as the exclusive goal. Well thought-out, comprehensive initiatives that focus broadly on increasing safeness and that address the underlying behavioral and social determinants of exploitation can serve valuable prevention functions. Such efforts can decrease vulnerability and build resilience among those at greatest risk of being trafficked. Youth-based programs that model respectful behavior, engage young people with supportive adult mentors, and provide concrete resources and life skills, can deliver essential human trafficking prevention results. Labor programs that advocate for worker safety, fair wages and working conditions, and accountable labor practices, can help prevent labor trafficking and promote economic independence.

22.2.8 Moving Forward: Perspectives on Preventing Human Trafficking Through the Lens of Public Health

The prevention of human trafficking can be incorporated into virtually every aspect of public health research, service delivery, and policy formulation. The programs described in this chapter represent only a small, illustrative sampling of the growing number of prevention-focused anti-trafficking initiatives that exist in the US. While none have undergone rigorous evaluation to date, each embodies innovative and potentially promising elements that should be researched further, applied to a broad variety of public health-focused programs, and translated into policy. The next steps listed below encompass primary, secondary, and tertiary prevention, organized according to the Spectrum of Prevention. These strategies are by no means mutually exclusive—quite often actions at one level of the Spectrum reinforce those at one or more other levels. Thus, complementary approaches promulgated at multiple levels of the Spectrum have the potential to produce a powerful synergistic effect on the prevention of human trafficking.

22.2.8.1   Strengthen Individual Knowledge and Skills

Health care providers, child welfare workers, home care workers, spiritual leaders, law enforcement personnel, social service providers, and virtually everyone else who comes in contact with those who may be at risk of being trafficked can communicate primary prevention-focused messages that strengthen individual knowledge and skills. Even those who are not generally considered formal "public health providers," such as local health inspectors, barbers, hairdressers, shopkeepers, cashiers, locksmiths, hotel employees, and others, can promote prevention by employing techniques that strengthen individual knowledge and skills. Key messages delivered during appointments, support groups, and home visits, can raise awareness about the existence and impact of human trafficking, and about one's right to healthy, non-coercive relationships, non-exploitative labor practices, and a future free from abuse and coercion. Whether delivered interactively during a one-on-one conversation in the context of an appointment or visit, or in the context of a group message such as a sermon, classroom session, or community outreach activity, such messages are often memorable, empowering, and can even be life-changing.

Children already in the child welfare and juvenile justice systems can benefit from well-designed education and awareness programs that incorporate tools developed to promote healthy physical, social, and emotional development of at-risk youth, especially for those aging-out or otherwise exiting the foster care or juvenile justice system. Programs such as YouthThrive, developed more generally to support resilience, social capacity, and social-emotional competence for youth in foster care, can potentially be adapted to support specific trafficking prevention strategies, like those pioneered by GEMS, geared to young people [49, 50].

Teachers can incorporate messages about healthy relationships, resilience, and ways to identify and reach out to trusted adults, throughout elementary, secondary and post-secondary education. Such efforts can help empower and inform students to make age-appropriate decisions about their lives and bodies, and to reach out for guidance, support, and help when needed.

Secondary prevention can be reinforced in the service delivery setting by incorporating sensitive inquiry about all forms of violence across the lifespan, including human trafficking, appropriate to the setting. Tertiary prevention strategies and protocols can be developed for use in emergency settings and urgent response situations.

22.2.8.2   Promote Community Education

Community education about human trafficking can be delivered to groups of people, including the general public, by ensuring that informative and culturally appropriate public education, awareness and outreach materials are developed and distributed widely using print, audio, video, web-based and social media channels. Informational posters, brochures, and tip cards containing basic education and local resource information can be displayed prominently in public areas such as lobbies, waiting rooms, buses, trains, billboards, and signage in shops and restaurants. Messages that increase public awareness about sex and labor trafficking can be made available via articles prepared for traditional print and online news media, and through radio, television, and web-based public service announcements. Awareness and outreach messages can also be communicated using letters to the editor, op-ed pieces, web and social media messages, YouTube and other user-upload modalities, community-based outreach programs, and community viewings of awareness documentaries through community centers, schools, libraries, and houses of worship. To supplement efforts designed to strengthen individual knowledge and skills, complementary information can be made available to individuals in private areas such as consultation rooms, examination rooms, and lavatories, where it might be safer and less stigmatizing for those who may be at risk to read or pick up information.

22.2.8.3   Educate Providers

Professional education meetings, employee orientation and follow-up staff training, and in-service sessions, roll call, and other venues can be used to train office staff and other employees and providers to work as a seamless team to help identify and respond efficiently and compassionately to those who may be experiencing human trafficking, or who may be at risk. Staff training can cover basic education and awareness, office safety procedures, and strategies for self-care. Continuing professional education opportunities can keep providers and staff up to date about new developments in identification, assessment, response and prevention, and about leadership opportunities in the field.

A singular opportunity presents itself regarding priorities for the education of clinically-focused health care professionals, particularly for medical students and physicians in practice. Although emphasized insufficiently in most traditional venues of health professional education, the public health role of the physician as a leader, advocate, and change agent is arguably as important as the more traditional, historical duty that focuses almost exclusively on providing clinical care for individual patients. More broadly, every clinician's job extends far beyond the office, clinic, examining room, or hospital ward. Health care practitioners tend to be highly respected in the communities in which they live and work. Their opinions are sought out and given great credence, and their influence as role models and community leaders is often quite visible. Educating health care providers about the importance of adopting a proactive, prevention-focused public health approach to addressing human trafficking can expand horizons for all forms of prevention-focused responses.

22.2.8.4   Foster Coalitions and Networks

On an organizational level, individual public health providers and the systems in which they work can facilitate the creation, implementation, and evaluation of primary, secondary, and tertiary prevention-focused health promotion collaborations with community-based advocacy agencies. Programs can be developed de novo or through established frameworks such as the social ecological model or the Spectrum of Prevention. System-wide, trauma-informed care and robust, comprehensive referral protocols can be developed in partnership with representatives from within and outside of public health delivery, health, social welfare, faith, education, and law enforcement systems, taking advantage of existing continuous quality improvement mechanisms and existing or new relationships with community-based advocacy organizations.

Similar prevention-focused efforts can be implemented within virtually every sector of society. For example, within the education sector, school systems can collaborate with community-based agencies and with parents and caregivers to promote primary, secondary, and even tertiary prevention within the school setting, extending into the after-school and home environments. Similarly, the health sector can work with community-based agencies to develop ways for community agencies to assure that survivors receiving community-based support services can access trauma-informed health services and social supports. Effective coalitions and networks can assure that referral mechanisms to community-based agencies are in place for survivors who disclose experiences of human trafficking in the context of health care.

Additional ways individuals and organizations can contribute to public health-focused human trafficking prevention efforts, via fostering coalitions and networks, include:

- Joining community coalitions and task forces
- Advocating for improved services
- Volunteering within local communities and at client-serving agencies
- Participating in multidisciplinary or interprofessional trainings
- Consulting for or testifying before legislative bodies
- Responding as an expert, respected voice to media requests
- Modeling respectful, nonviolent behavior within their own families, practices, and communities.

The input of survivors, supportive family members, coworkers, and others directly impacted by human trafficking should be regarded as integral, and arguably essential, to the development of any prevention-focused coalition or network. Their lived experiences and opinions should be solicited and respected.

22.2.8.5   Change Organizational Practices

Every sector of society can contribute to trafficking prevention efforts by creating and ensuring trauma-informed protocols and practices, and by contributing to the development of collaborative processes and organizational strategies that promote identification, assessment, and efficient, yet compassionate, responses to at-risk and trafficked individuals. Creating a trauma-informed organizational environment that recognizes the importance of "safeness" as a key component of public health can become a prevention-focused intervention in and of itself.

Prevention activities targeted to preventing both sexual and labor exploitation can be developed beyond the health care, hotel, tourism and food service industries to the construction industry, the clothing and apparel industry, manufacturing, hair and nail salons, and elsewhere. ECPAT's Tourism-Child Protection Code of Conduct and CIW's Fair Food Code of Conduct are but two examples of how existing initiatives can serve as models for changing organizational practices. In terms of consumer product labeling, the established methodology of certifying "worthy" food products (for example, as "Fair Food Certified" by the Fair Food Program) could be extended to non-food consumer items to ensure that their manufacture was free of coerced labor.

Within every sector of society, organizational practices that ensure a trauma-informed environment can help promote both safety and a sense of safeness for individuals seeking services, as well as for staff. Specifically, the essential elements of safeness, including trust, respect, consistency, and compassion, can be incorporated into the policies and procedures of virtually any program, and to the growing body of basic and translational research that informs prevention-focused program and policy development at every level of prevention. In this way, those receiving services can be helped to feel as safe and well cared for as possible when disclosing their experiences, accessing services, or seeking help or refuge from any type of abuse, including human trafficking. Those providing services, in turn, can feel supported and validated in the course of their work, thus potentially helping to prevent both secondary traumatization and burnout among staff.

Professionally-trained providers should remain mindful of the valuable contributions that can be made by all members of society (for example, local shopkeepers, community-based health promoters, neighbors, active bystanders, and others who lack formal professional training) to the prevention of human trafficking, and should take care to acknowledge and respect the contributions of others, especially survivors. Put simply, the public health community can lead by example, modeling interactions that are engaged, respectful, open, and non-hierarchical, without assuming leadership of a team or other group unless specifically asked. By setting such an example, even individual health care providers can very effectively "teach peace" and work toward the primary prevention of human trafficking in the course of their professional and personal activities [51].

22.2.8.6   Influence Policy and Legislation

Municipal, regional, statewide, and even federal policies that promote safeness for individuals, families, and communities, can promote primary prevention outcomes not only for the prevention of human trafficking, but also for a wide range of additional public health concerns. Although such endeavors take time, resources, commitment, and political will to develop and implement, they can accomplish a broad and lasting beneficial impact. Initiatives can be developed that take full advantage of the provisions of the TVPA and of the increasing number of recently enacted state safe harbor and victim protection laws that serve trafficked persons. Public health-focused individuals can also work closely with legislators and policymakers to improve existing legislation and to introduce new legislation that furthers research, program development and implementation, provider and public education, and evaluation of promising practices geared to the prevention of human trafficking.

22.3   Conclusion

Human trafficking cannot be prevented by a single agency working alone, or by any individual effort, no matter how earnestly conducted. As illustrated in the Spectrum of Prevention, public health professionals in all sectors of society must collaborate actively with others, including health care providers and the practices, organizations, and systems in which they work; grassroots advocates; social workers; child welfare and juvenile justice personnel; law enforcement representatives; legislators and policymakers; faith leaders; community stakeholders, business owners and representatives; survivors; and others. Together, these groups must work together to address the underlying causes of trafficking, such as gender, social and economic inequality; unsafe migration; poverty; and interpersonal violence, including child sexual abuse.

Although the root causes of human trafficking can be traced to thousands of years of deeply ingrained social and economic inequality, underscored by hierarchies of power, control, and political and sexual domination, human trafficking need not become an eternal legacy. Understanding human trafficking as a public health issue highlights its preventable nature. To achieve effective prevention though, a serious commitment to tackling entrenched social norms and addressing the root causes of individual and population vulnerability to trafficking must be made. Such a massive endeavor can best be accomplished using a comprehensive strategy of primary, secondary, and tertiary prevention efforts at each level of the Spectrum of Prevention, keeping the importance of individual and community safeness in the forefront of all efforts.

By practicing prevention, every sector of society can foster an environment in which individuals feel more comfortable disclosing experiences of trafficking and other forms of abuse, and in seeking help when needed. A society where each and every person feels respected and has a sense of safeness can reduce shame, promote safety, and foster autonomy, which can potentially empower even the most vulnerable individuals to take steps toward living free and independent lives.

22.4 Recommendations

Preventing human trafficking is a monumental endeavor that will require "all hands on deck" for primary, secondary, and tertiary prevention. Human trafficking is preventable, but only if a serious commitment is made to addressing entrenched social norms and environmental factors that give rise to trafficking, including poverty, racial, ethnic and gender inequality and discrimination, deficits in girls' education, family violence, and even climate change. The Spectrum of Prevention offers a way forward:

- Strengthen Individual Knowledge and Skills (see Sect. 22.2.8.1)
- Promote Community Education (see Sect. 22.2.8.2)
- Educate Providers (see Sect. 22.2.8.3)
- Foster Coalitions and Networks (see Sect. 22.2.8.4)
- Change Organizational Practices (see Sect. 22.2.8.5)
- Influence Policy and Legislation (see Sect. 22.2.8.6).

References

1. Rammel EC. From Sumerian gods to modern day: the history of slavery. Ancient Origins. 2013. http://www.ancient-origins.net/human-origins/sumerian-gods-modern-day-history--slavery-00442. Accessed 18 June 2016.
2. UShistory.org. Hammurabi's code: an eye for an eye. Ancient civilizations online textbook. 2014. http://www.ushistory.org/civ/4c.asp. Accessed 18 June 2016.
3. Gasciogne B. History of slavery. Historyworld. 2001. http://www.historyworld.net/wrldhis/PlainTextHistories.asp?ParagraphID=cio. Accessed 18 June 2016.
4. Wright DR. Slavery in Africa. Microsoft Encarta Online Encyclopedia. 2000. http://autocww.colorado.edu/~toldy3/E64ContentFiles/AfricanHistory/SlaveryInAfrica.html. Accessed 18 June 2016.
5. Vickers G. What sets the goals of public health? N Engl J Med. 1958;258:589–96. doi:10.1056/NEJM19580320258120.
6. U.S. Department of State. U.S. laws on trafficking in persons. 2016. http://www.state.gov/j/tip/laws/. Accessed 18 June 2016.
7. UN General Assembly. Protocol to prevent, suppress and punish trafficking in persons, especially women and children, supplementing the United Nations Convention against Transnational Organized Crime. 2000. http://www.osce.org/odihr/19223?download=true. Accessed 19 June 2016.
8. U.S. Department of State. Victims of Trafficking and Violence Protection Act of 2000: trafficking in Persons Report: 2001 Trafficking in Persons Report. 2001. http://www.state.gov/j/tip/rls/tiprpt/2001/. Accessed 18 June 2016.
9. U.S. Department of State. 2015 trafficking in persons report. 2015. http://www.state.gov/j/tip/rls/tiprpt/. Accessed 18 June 2016.
10. World Health Organization. A public health approach to human trafficking. 2014. http://www.euro.who.int/en/health-topics/health-determinants/migration-and-health/news/news/2014/12/a-public-health-approach-to-human-trafficking. Accessed 18 June 2016.

11. American Public Health Association. Policy statement 2015–16: public heath approach to human trafficking. 2015. https://www.apha.org/news-and-media/news-releases/apha-news-releases/new-policies-at-apha-2015. Accessed 29 June 2016.
12. U.S. Department of Health and Human Services, Office on Trafficking in Persons. The power of framing human trafficking as a public health issue. 2016. http://www.acf.hhs.gov/programs/endtrafficking/resource/publichealthlens. Accessed 18 June 2016.
13. Alpert E. Personal communication: Introduction to Intervention Planning course material. University of British Columbia College of Health Disciplines, Interprofessional Health and Human Services (IHHS) 410 course entitled "Improving Public Health: An Interprofessional Approach to Designing and Implementing Effective Interventions." 2009-2014.
14. Centers for Disease Control and Prevention. The public health approach to violence prevention. 2016. http://www.cdc.gov/violenceprevention/pdf/ph_app_violence-a.pdf. Accessed 18 June 2016.
15. Centers for Disease Control and Prevention. The social-ecological model: a framework for prevention. 2016. http://www.cdc.gov/ViolencePrevention/overview/social-ecologicalmodel.html. Accessed 18 June 2016.
16. Zimmerman C. Trafficking in women: the health of women in post-trafficking services in Europe who were trafficked into prostitution or sexually abused as domestic labourers. Dissertation, Division of Public Health and Policy, London School of Hygiene and Tropical Medicine, University of London. 2007. https://healtrafficking.files.wordpress.com/2015/03/498767.pdf. Accessed 18 June 2016.
17. Zimmerman C, Hossain M, Watts C. Human trafficking and health: a conceptual model to inform policy, intervention and research. Soc Sci Med. 2011;73(2):327–35.
18. Macias-Konstantopoulos W, Ahn R, Alpert EJ, et al. An international comparative public health analysis of sex trafficking of women and girls in eight cities: achieving a more effective health sector response. J Urban Health. 2013;90(6):1194–204. doi:10.1007/s11524-013-9837-4.
19. Cho S-Y. Modeling for determinants of human trafficking. Economics of Security Working Paper 70, Economics of Security, Berlin. 2012. https://www.diw.de/documents/publikationen/73/diw_01.c.405651.de/diw_econsec0070.pdf. Accessed 29 June 2016.
20. Institute of Medicine and National Research Council. Confronting commercial sexual exploitation and sex trafficking of minors in the United States: a guide for providers of victim and support services. 2013. https://www.nationalacademies.org/hmd/~/media/Files/Report%20Files/2013/Sexual-Exploitation-Sex-Trafficking/ReportGuide-VSS.pdf. Accessed 29 June 2016.
21. London School of Hygiene & Tropical Medicine, Buller AM, Stoklosa H, Zimmerman C, International Organization for Migration, Vaca V, Borland R. Labour exploitation, trafficking and migrant health: multi-country findings on the health risks and consequences of migrant and trafficked workers. International Organization for Migration, London School of Hygiene & Tropical Medicine, and U.S. Department of State. https://publications.iom.int/system/files/pdf/labour_exploitation_trafficking_en.pdf. Accessed 29 June 2016.
22. Commission on Chronic Illness. Chronic illness in the United States, vol. 1. Cambridge, MA: Commonwealth Fund/Harvard University Press; 1957.
23. Last JM, Wallace RB. Maxey-Rosenau-Last public health & preventive medicine. 13th ed. Norwalk, CT: Appleton & Lange; 1992. p. 207–12.
24. Chamberlain L. A prevention primer for domestic violence: terminology, tools, and the public health approach. Harrisburg, PA: VAWnet, a project of the National Resource Center on Domestic Violence/Pennsylvania Coalition Against Domestic Violence; 2008. http://www.vawnet.org. Accessed 05 June 2016.
25. Cohen L, Swift S. The spectrum of prevention: developing a comprehensive approach to injury prevention. Inj Prev. 1999;5:203–7.
26. National Sexual Violence Resource Center. Sexual violence and the Spectrum of Prevention, fact sheet. 2009. http://www.nsvrc.org/sites/default/files/Factsheet_spectrum-of-prevention.pdf. Accessed 18 June 2016.
27. Davis R, Parks LF, Cohen L. Sexual violence and the Spectrum of Prevention: towards a community solution. National Sexual Violence Resource Center. 2006. http://www.nsvrc.org/sites/default/files/Publications_NSVRC_Booklets_Sexual-Violence-and-the-Spectrum-of-Prevention_Towards-a-Community-Solution_0.pdf. Accessed 18 June 2016.

28. Mitchell C. New public health strategies for violence prevention. National Health Collaborative on Violence and Abuse. Webinar. 2016. www.nhcva.org. Accessed 18 June 2016.
29. Mitchell C. Personal communication. 2016.
30. Felitti VJ, Anda RF, et al. Relationship of childhood abuse and household dysfunction to many of the leading causes of death in adults: the Adverse Childhood Experiences Study. Am J Prev Med. 1998;14(4):245–58.
31. Middlebrooks JS, Audage NC. The effects of childhood stress on health across the lifespan. Atlanta, GA: Centers for Disease Control and Prevention; 2008.
32. Raphael J, Myers-Powell B. From victims to victimizers: interviews with 25 ex-pimps in Chicago.2010.https://law.depaul.edu/about/centers-and-institutes/schiller-ducanto-fleck-family-law-center/Documents/interview_ex_pimps.pdf. Accessed 29 June 2016.
33. U.S. Department of Health and Human Services Office on Trafficking in Persons. Rescue and restore victims of human trafficking, resource document. 2015. http://www.acf.hhs.gov/programs/endtrafficking/resource/about-rescue-restore. Accessed 13 June 2016.
34. National Human Trafficking Resource Center. Resource library. 2016. https://traffickingresourcecenter.org/resources. Accessed 18 June 2016.
35. National Human Trafficking Resource Center. Online trainings. 2016. https://traffickingresourcecenter.org/material-type/online-trainings. Accessed 18 June 2016.
36. U.S. Department of Health and Human Services Office on Trafficking in Persons. Rescue & Restore Campaign Tool Kits. 2012. http://www.acf.hhs.gov/programs/endtrafficking/resource/rescue-restore-campaign-tool-kits. Accessed 18 June 2016.
37. Girls Educational and Mentoring Services. Prevention and outreach. 2016. http://www.gems-girls.org/about/what-we-do/our-services/prevention-outreach. Accessed 18 June 2016.
38. My life my choice. http://www.fightingexploitation.org/. Accessed 18 June 2016.
39. My Life My Choice. Survivor mentorship. Undated. http://www.fightingexploitation.org/survivor-mentorship. Accessed 18 June 2016.
40. My Life My Choice. Preventing the exploitation of girls: a groundbreaking curriculum. Undated. http://www.ncjfcj.org/sites/default/files/My%20Life%20My%20Choice%20Description.pdf. Accessed 18 June 2016.
41. ECPAT International. http://www.ecpat.org/. Accessed 18 June 2016.
42. The Code. The code of conduct for the protection of children from sexual exploitation in travel and tourism. Undated. http://www.thecode.org/. Accessed 18 June 2016.
43. Coalition of Immokalee Workers. About CIW. 2012. http://www.ciw-online.org/about/. Accessed 13 June 2016.
44. Fair Food Program. http://www.fairfoodprogram.org/. Accessed 18 June 2016.
45. Made in a Free World. How many slaves work for you? 2011. http://slaveryfootprint.org. Accessed 14 June 2016.
46. U.S. Department of Labor. Toolkit for responsible businesses. 2005. https://www.dol.gov/ilab/child-forced-labor/index.htm. Accessed 14 June 2016.
47. U.S. Department of Labor. List of goods produced by child labor or forced labor. 2016. https://www.dol.gov/ilab/reports/child-labor/list-of-goods/. Accessed 18 June 2016.
48. United Nations Office on Drugs and Crime. Toolkit to combat trafficking in persons. 2008. https://www.unodc.org/documents/human-trafficking/HT_Toolkit08_English.pdf. Accessed 14 June 2016.
49. Center for the Study of Social Policy. YouthThrive. http://www.cssp.org/reform/child-welfare/youththrive. Accessed 20 June 2016.
50. Center for the Study of Social Policy. YouthThrive: protective & promotive factors for healthy development and well-being. Undated. http://www.cssp.org/reform/child-welfare/youth-thrive/Youth-Thrive-PPF-definitions.pdf. Accessed 20 June 2016.
51. Glidden D. Personal communication. 1996.

Chapter 23
Combating Modern Bondage: The Development of a Multi-Disciplinary Approach to Human Trafficking

Laura J. Lederer

23.1 Introduction

23.1.1 An Old Problem in a New Form: The Emergence of Modern Day Slavery

The United States Congress passed the 13th Amendment to the Constitution on January 31, 1865. By year's end, the states had ratified the Amendment, acknowledging that, "Neither slavery nor involuntary servitude, except as a punishment for crime whereof the party shall have been duly convicted, shall exist within the United States…".[1] This document, so formative in the development of US socio-political history, did not anticipate the rise of a new sort of slavery. The enslavement of Africans and blacks in the late eighteenth and nineteenth century was clearly visible in southern agrarian culture; in the early twentieth century new forms of slavery such as *white slavery* emerged slowly from the shadows [1]. *White slavery* was a misnomer, which described the international movement of women and children of many races and ethnicities into prostitution at the turn of the century and through 1920 [2]. The problem was serious enough that the first series of international treaties were drafted in 1904 and again in 1910.[2] Then, at the end of the twentieth century, a few nongovernmental organizations (NGOs) sounded an alarm about a yet another kind of slavery: People

---

[1] Section 1 of the 13th Amendment to the Constitution officially abolished slavery in America, and was ratified on December 6, 1865, after the conclusion of the American Civil War.

[2] International Agreement for the Suppression of the White Slave Traffic, 18 May 1904, 35 Stat. 1979, 1 L.N.T.S. 83, *entered into force* 18 July 1905; http://www1.umn.edu/humanrts/instree/whiteslavetraffic1904.html.

The original version of this chapter was revised. An erratum to this chapter can be found at DOI:10.1007/978-3-319-47824-1_25

L.J. Lederer (✉)
Global Centurion, 5746 Union Mill Road, Suite 514, Clifton, VA 20124, USA
e-mail: llederer@globalcenturion.org

© Springer International Publishing AG 2017   401
M. Chisolm-Straker, H. Stoklosa (eds.), *Human Trafficking Is a Public Health Issue*, DOI 10.1007/978-3-319-47824-1_23

were being stripped of autonomy, sometimes moved vast distances, and compelled to do someone else's bidding for that third party's gain. The earliest reports were about commercial sexual exploitation; next came reports of forced labor and domestic servitude. New NGOs formed to address what they called "human trafficking," later defined as the recruiting, transporting, harboring, buying or selling of human beings for purposes of commercial sexual exploitation or forced labor (see footnote 1).

23.1.2   Noticing the Problem: Early NGO Responses

A number of watershed cases alerted the global community to the crisis of human trafficking. One such case emerged from the work of a wildlife anti-trafficking organization, Global Survival Network (GSN). In pursuit of Russian mafia who were capturing and selling endangered Siberian Tigers, GSN members, wearing tie tack cameras, and hidden sound equipment, posed as buyers to trap the wildlife traffickers. After months of preparation, GSN members met with the Russian traffickers but were told they had no tigers to sell. Instead, the Russian mafia offered to sell them a roomful of young women. Captured in grainy black and white footage, GSN broke a story that ignited the anti-trafficking movement [3]. In the aftermath of this case, hundreds of other reports of human trafficking came from Southeast Asia, Eastern and Central Europe, Africa, South America, and the USA. For the first time, human trafficking was acknowledged as a humanitarian crisis of global proportions.

Another critical report of regional trafficking was written by Human Rights Watch. The report investigated the human trafficking trade routes between Thailand and Japan. This landmark study presented the commercial sex industry as an issue of transnational concern. The report broke a silence about the thousands of young women and children who were being trafficked into Thailand from Burma; it called the traffickers so "efficient and ruthless" that the authors of the study and the survivors interviewed had to remain anonymous for their own safety [4]. The authors chronicled the physical abuse debt bondage; illegal confinement; forced labor; rape; exposure to HIV/AIDS; and murder. The report called upon the Thai government and the world human rights community to take action. The GSN footage and the Human Rights Watch report catalyzed a grassroots response. Subsequent investigations uncovered trafficking rings in dozens of countries around the world. By 1994 a few organizations had begun to track the transnational nature and scope of human trafficking and its terrible effects. One such organization, The Protection Project, contacted over 190 countries and territories around the world. They mapped countries of origin, destination, and transit from cases reported by Ministries of Justice in over a hundred countries, and cataloged the body of law addressing human trafficking including debt bondage, peonage, involuntary servitude, and slavery laws as well as prostitution, pimping, pandering, procuring, brothel usage, and other laws addressing commercial sexual exploitation.[3]

---

[3] The Protection Project, International Mapping of Human Trafficking, Database on Laws Addressing Human Trafficking, Laura J. Lederer, Director, first housed at University of Minnesota Law School (1994–1997) and Harvard University's Kennedy School of Government (1997–2000); https://www.gpo.gov/fdsys/pkg/CHRG-106shrg63986/html/CHRG-106shrg63986.htm.

While new stories erupted globally and grassroots movements formed quickly, domestic judicial responses lagged: Because there were no laws prohibiting human trafficking, those trafficked suffered and traffickers were tried and prosecuted under laws that did not adequately punish the perpetrators. For example, in a 1997 case, young women and children who were trafficked from Thailand to the USA and sold into prostitution were identified as having been "smuggled" into the USA. The defendant, Joseph Morales, was charged with three counts of importing and harboring illegal aliens, and conspiracy to import and harbor illegal aliens (https://www. unodc.org/cld/case-law-doc/traffickingpersonscrimetype/usa/1995/united_ states_v_joseph_morales.html). Because the women were labeled as smuggled rather than trafficking survivors, some of them were imprisoned and others were summarily deported. This case highlights the egregious injustice of survivors being treated like criminals. As this pattern was repeated in countries around the world, it became clear that a new approach was needed—one that punished the perpetrator but protected and assisted trafficking survivors. By 1998, an unlikely coalition of feminists and faith-based organizations formed in the USA to advocate for a change in the law [5]. They worked with visionary legislators who recognized this inadequacy and by 1998, a first draft of what would become the Trafficking Victims Protection Act of 2000 had been introduced in Congress.[4]

23.2 Discussion

23.2.1 The "Three P's" Approach and the Trafficking Victims Protection Act: A Fledgling Infrastructure to Fight Human Trafficking

As the concern of modern day slavery emerged in the late 1990s, the Clinton administration undertook a proactive response. The administration formulated a "3 P" strategy that emphasized the prevention of trafficking, prosecution of perpetrators, and protection of the vulnerable individuals who have been trafficked [6]. This strategy helped shape the approach taken in the groundbreaking Trafficking Victims Protection Act (TVPA) of 2000. The TVPA acknowledged that, "No comprehensive law exists in the United States that penalizes the range of offenses involved in the trafficking scheme," and set forth a legal standard to fill the gap.[5] This legislation, founded on the tripartite "3 P" strategy, became the cornerstone of domestic anti-

---

[4] Representative Christopher Smith, original sponsor, Trafficking Victims Protection Act draft, 1998. Others co-sponsors were the late Paul Wellstone, then Senator Sam Brownback, and Rep. Sam Gjendensen.

[5] See Sec. 102. Purposes and Findings. Trafficking Victims Protection Act of 2000; https://www. govtrack.us/congress/bills/106/hr3244/text.

human trafficking legislation. While it had many provisions, the TVPA accomplished four primary objectives:

1. The TVPA defined severe forms of trafficking in persons as "sex trafficking in which a commercial sex act is induced by force, fraud, or coercion, or in which the person induced to perform such act has not attained 18 years of age" and labor trafficking as the "recruitment, harboring, transportation, provision, or obtaining of a person for labor or services, through the use of force, fraud, or coercion for the purpose of subjection to involuntary servitude, peonage, debt bondage, or slavery."[6]
2. The TVPA strengthened penalties for trafficking to 20 years to life (for aggravated offenses), an indication that the US government took human trafficking as seriously as drug or arms trafficking.
3. The TVPA set up a President's Interagency Task Force on Trafficking, a cabinet level task force, responsible for shaping US government agencies' responses to trafficking; this established political will at the highest level: the White House.
4. The TVPA mandated an annual, comprehensive evaluation of foreign national responses to human trafficking. This mandate is realized in the Trafficking in Persons (TIP) Report, published by the US Department of State. The Report assesses and rates countries on the basis of the progress they are making in addressing trafficking in their own countries.
5. The TVPA established the first "victim-centered" approach to human trafficking, including creating a "T Visa" that allowed non-citizen survivors trafficked in the USA to establish legal residency here and rebuild their lives. The law granted certified survivors a set of benefits including short-term emergency services such as food, clothing, shelter, medical assistance, and legal assistance as well as longer term services such as education and employment assistance.

Importantly, this domestic legislation did not develop in isolation. The United States' pioneering law was paralleled by the United Nation's "Protocol to Prevent, Suppress and Punish Trafficking in Persons, Especially Women and Children," which was signed into force 2 months later in December of 2000. As the USA heightened its attention to modern day slavery, the Protocol urged countries to draft and pass their own laws combating trafficking in persons, and urged a transnational approach to the problem.[7]

---

[6] See Section 103. Definitions. Trafficking Victims Protection Act of 2000; https://www.govtrack.us/congress/bills/106/hr3244/text.

[7] Enacted in December of 2000 as part of the U.N. Convention Against Organized Crime, the Protocol provides an international framework for countries to address the prevention of trafficking, the prosecution of traffickers, and the protection and assistance of trafficked persons. http://www.ohchr.org/EN/ProfessionalInterest/Pages/ProtocolTraffickingInPersons.aspx.

23.2.2   Deeper Dive: The Complexities of Trafficking in Persons

Following the passage of the TVPA, in the USA the main emphasis was on international sex trafficking. The first trafficking cases in Europe, Southeast Asia, and the USA that came to light were gruesome stories of women and children, purchased for a pittance and sold into brothels where they were held against their will, beaten, and forced to sexually service as many as 20 to 30 men a day.[8] Shortly after, NGOs began to uncover flagrant cases of labor trafficking, including children sold to cocoa plantation owners in Africa; men and boys in involuntary servitude in the fishing industries in Southeast Asia; and young women trafficked into garment factories in South America where they languished, locked in at night and laboring 12 to 14 hours a day.[9]

Meanwhile in the USA, the common misconception that trafficking was a problem that happened in poor or underdeveloped countries was put to rest when dozens, then hundreds of cases of sex trafficking of US citizens came to light. In one case in Atlanta, Georgia, a man trafficked girls as young as 12 years old for commercial sex.[10] Public outrage in response to this case and others like it galvanized organizations to take domestic action. Slowly, the international gaze of US policy-makers, law enforcement, and grassroots organizations turned inward, toward our domestic landscape, as trafficking was recognized as a domestic problem too. The scope of the problem was larger than originally thought: It included children and adults, sex and labor trafficking, and international and domestic cases.

23.2.3   Triangle of Activity: Supply, Demand, Distribution

Human trafficking is a business. It occurs in a market driven by supply and demand: The trafficked person is a re-sellable commodity (the supply), the trafficker is a profiteering entrepreneur (the distributor), and the buyer, who pays for

---

[8] For example, U.S. v. Cadena, 1998; 16 defendants were charged with luring hundreds of young women and girls, some as young as 14 years old, from Veracruz, Mexico, to the USA using false promises of legitimate jobs. Once in the USA they imposed a debt for getting them across the border and used brutal physical force and violence, sexual assaults, and threats of death and bodily harm to the victims and their families to compel the victims to engage in prostitution 12 h a day, 6 days a week. Those victimized were made to turn over the proceeds to the defendants to pay down the smuggling debts the defendants imposed. Cadena-Sosa and other family members would also search for victims who had run away from a brothel and subject them to beatings and rape upon capture. The defendants were a ring of 20 brothers and friends. The other 4 traffickers were located and extradited to the USA; they were tried and convicted in 2002, 2008, and 2015. http://www.morelaw.com/verdicts/case.asp?s=FL&d=75732.

[9] US State Department Trafficking in Persons Reports, 2001–2005, documenting early cases of labor and sex trafficking in countries around the world. http://www.state.gov/j/tip/rls/tiprpt/.

[10] United States v. Charles Floyd Pipkins. http://openjurist.org/378/f3d/1281/united-states-v-pipkins.

the commodity, fuels the market [7]. In the decade following the 2000 passage of the TVPA, US government and NGO attention was directed to the rescue and restoration of trafficked persons and to prosecution of traffickers. Such efforts meaningfully respond to the aftermath of trafficking, but they do not prevent the exploitation itself. Moreover, anti-trafficking efforts focused merely on rescue ignore the complex realities of trafficked persons, including the power of trauma bonding.[11] The prosecution of individual traffickers may disrupt the market, but such a disruption does not shut down the market altogether. A critical element in eliminating human trafficking is to eliminate demand. If there is no customer, there is no market. In a large part, human trafficking exists because people are willing to pay for commercial sex or because the consumer wants cheap goods and products, encouraging unscrupulous owners and managers to exploit workers. Eradicating this willingness is critical to ending trafficking. Since 2010, some NGOs have turned to abolishing demand—in both labor and sex trafficking—as the key to ending trafficking [8]. Not all NGOs agree with this approach, and some argue that a singular focus on eliminating demand drives trafficking further underground [9]. Nevertheless, since 2010, several key organizations across the political spectrum have turned their focus to the demand side of one form of trafficking, sexual exploitation.[12]

There are a number of approaches to help reduce and eliminate demand. Most important is awareness-raising. Consumers need to know that they may be creating markets for trafficking by demanding less expensive goods. Transparent supply chains in which consumers can see and track where labor comes from, how much laborers are being paid, and whether their working and living conditions are safe and meet basic standards are key to prevention efforts. Education is also key in preventing trafficking: Age appropriate curricula in which children, adolescents, and young people examine examples of modern slavery, and contrast a culture of exploitation with a culture of caring are critical. In the best-case scenario, trafficking could be abolished as a consequence of the buyer's personal awakening to the injustice of the situation. Although some buyer focused efforts are underway, and some report meaningful progress, sympathy for the plight of the trafficked person is difficult to cultivate. Alternative measures then, include heightening the risk for purchasing sex or penalizing companies with slavery in their supply chains. By enforcing legal consequences for buyers, law enforcement agencies may proactively de-incentivize potential buyers.

---

[11] Trauma bonding is the emotional attachment a survivor of abuse forms with their abuser.

[12] See Demand Abolition, a feminist organization leading efforts to draft and pass legislation in all 50 states to target demand. https://www.demandabolition.org/; see also Exodus Cry, a faith based organization focusing on ending demand. http://exoduscry.com/.

23.2.4 President's Interagency Task Force on Trafficking and SPOG: Creating a Multi-Disciplinary Response in the Executive Branch

The President's Interagency Task Force (PITF) is a cabinet-level task force mandated by the TVPA. It is responsible for creating over-arching comprehensive anti-trafficking policy and programing. PITF consists of 18 US government agencies that play a vital role in the on-going effort to end trafficking in persons and meets once a year to insure implementation of anti-trafficking law and policy. It has coordinated a number of federal initiatives to combat trafficking. For example, in 2012, PITF published the first 5-year Federal Strategic Action Plan on Services to Victims of Trafficking in the USA.[13] The Plan outlined objectives to:

1. Align efforts by promoting strategic and coordinated services for victims[14] at the federal, regional, state, territorial, tribal, and local levels.
2. Improve understanding by expanding and coordinating human trafficking-related research, data, and evaluation to support evidence-based victim services.
3. Expand access to services by providing outreach, training, and technical assistance to increase victim identification and expand availability of services.
4. Improve outcomes by promoting effective, culturally appropriate, trauma-informed services that improve the short- and long-term health, safety, and well-being of victims (http://www.acf.hhs.gov/programs/endtrafficking/initiatives/federal-plan).

Other federal agencies have specific missions and mandates that include human trafficking and over the years they have developed programs building on the three Ps—prevention of trafficking, prosecution of traffickers, and protection of and assistance to trafficked persons. Notable programs include:

- U.S. Department of Homeland Security—Blue Campaign
- U.S. Department of Justice—Human Trafficking Task Forces
- U.S. Department of Labor—Reducing Child Labor and Forced Labor Toolkit
- U.S. Department of Health and Human Services—Look Beneath the Surface Campaign
- U.S. Department of State—Annual Trafficking in Persons Report.

---

[13] Federal Strategic Action Plan on Services to Victims of Trafficking in the USA, co-chaired by the US Department of Health and Human Services and the Department of Homeland Security. http://www.ovc.gov/pubs/FederalHumanTraffickingStrategicPlan.pdf.

[14] The term "victim" is used here (and in other sections of this chapter) in reference to trafficked individuals, to reflect the language and spirit of the law discussed.

23.2.5   The Current State of Progress of NGOs and Governmental Agencies Working Against TIP: Differing and Similar Approaches, and Successes and Failures

As the federal government develops an increasingly comprehensive response to trafficking, the field of anti-trafficking work is evolving. Early grassroots efforts emphasized trafficked persons' rescue and restoration and many NGOs continue to be involved in this kind of work. Since 2005 however, NGOs have increasingly focused efforts on affecting systemic change. This means a focus on law, policy, and institutional frameworks that look "upstream"—to the actual root causes of trafficking, in an effort to stop the growing number of people victimized by both labor and sex trafficking.

In addition, survivors have emerged as leaders in the growing anti-trafficking movement. A few of the first to speak were the late Norma Hotaling, who founded SAGE in San Francisco, California, in 1994. Hotaling advocated tirelessly for wraparound services for survivors to have food, clothing, shelter, medical services, legal advice, and peer-led support groups [10]. In Minnesota, Vednita Carter began Breaking Free at around the same time; Carter focused helping women and girls escape systems of prostitution and sexual exploitation through advocacy, services, housing, and education.[15] These two survivor-led organizations were unique not only in creating services tailored to the needs of trafficked persons, but also in giving a voice and a platform to survivors. The importance of this "survivor-led" and "survivor-centered" approach was first noted in a speech at the first SAGE Graduation Ceremony for survivors in December 2004 [11].

In the early 2000s, NGOs developed platforms for survivors to speak, first to insure that people heard their stories firsthand, and later, as experts and leaders in anti-trafficking movement. As one survivor so aptly said, "We are more than our stories." (http://www.mercyworld.org/mercy_global_action/view-post.cfm?id=838, Ms Rani Hong). Many survivors, like Hotaling and Carter, have formed their own organizations.[16] They have also banded together in survivor networks to give voice to their concerns.[17] As the infrastructure for combating human trafficking is becoming more robust, survivors are playing a leadership role in prevention, prosecution,

---

[15] Breaking Free, established 1996, from the website "Who We Are," http://www.breakingfree.net/default.aspx.

[16] A few of the well-known survivor led organizations are Courtney's House, Breaking Free, Veronica's Voice, More Too Life, GEMS, My Life, My Choice, Rahab's House, Dreamcatcher Foundation, and Treasures. Unfortunately SAGE, founded by the late Norma Hotaling, shut its doors in 2015.

[17] See National Survivor Network, http://www.castla.org/nsn and Survivors for Solutions, http://www.survivors4solutions.com/.

and protection activities. Survivors have also contributed to research facilitating a better understanding all aspects of human trafficking from recruiting and transporting, to buying and selling, to methods of force, fraud, and coercion. These developments in anti-trafficking approaches are recognized as critical to success in fighting trafficking: In 2015, President Obama instituted a US Advisory Council on Human Trafficking consisting of US survivors of labor trafficking and sex trafficking to assist in shaping law and policy in the USA [12]. The Council was several years in the making and is the result of NGOs and members of Congress, who helped draft and pass the Survivors of Human Trafficking Empowerment Act in the 2015 Justice for Victims of Trafficking Act.[18] Speaking at the first meeting, one of the survivors said,

> As a collective group of survivors, we have dedicated a huge part of ourselves to the anti-trafficking movement, to respective advocacy efforts. Together, we are changing perception, fighting for justice, and ultimately, over the years, we are contributing to one shared goal: to end modern slavery everywhere it exists. We are a diverse group. Our individual experience as survivors will add a rich expertise to the council [13].

23.2.6 Health and Human Trafficking: A Missing Piece of the Puzzle

For the first 10 years after the passage of the TVPA, human trafficking was seen mainly as a law enforcement problem and human rights abuse. In 2008, the Bush Administration held a landmark National Symposium called the Health Needs of Human Trafficking Victims, where providers, policy-makers, and practitioners discussed acute infections and illnesses, chronic and long-term physical, mental, reproductive, and other health care issues facing trafficked persons and survivors. Panels examined emerging epidemiological issues, and noted the need for increased attention by health care providers to this important population [14]. Following this conference, in 2011, several researchers began looking at the implications of trafficking for health care and human services professionals.

Trafficked persons and survivors have limited access to health care due to their lack of insurance, and unstable economic, and/or immigration status. Those who are foreign-born have varying access to care, depending on their documentation status, state, and county resources, and on the structure and capacity of local safety net health clinics. Despite these barriers, in one study, 87.8 % of sex trafficking survivors self-reported having sought health care in hospitals, clinics, and from private physicians during their victimization [15]. Yet, a 2012 study of emergency

---

[18] Justice for Victims of Trafficking Act, Sec. 115: Survivors of Human Trafficking Empowerment Act, PL 114–22, May 29, 2015, https://www.congress.gov/114/plaws/publ22/PLAW-114publ22.pdf.

clinicians found that only 4.8 % felt confident in identifying trafficked patients [16]. And, at the time of this writing, research on human trafficking trainings for health professionals has not explored long term behavior change and patient outcomes (http://journals.plos.org/plosmedicine/article?id=10.1371/journal.pmed.1001224). Advocates and government agencies concerned about human trafficking recognize a serious need to develop evidence-based education tools and health protocols for health care professionals, not just as a means to broaden the social understanding of victimization, but as a potential and perhaps singular, opportunity for intervening against an insidious crime [17]. With relatively few systematic protocols for identification of trafficked persons in place in US health care settings, health care professionals are not yet providing proper assistance to trafficked individuals.

The importance of health care as a potential point of intervention cannot be overstated, as many trafficked persons' sole contact with non-exploiting people may be a visit to a health care setting. Recognizing this need, in 2013, some medical providers formed a new NGO, HEAL (Health, Education, Advocacy, Linkage) Trafficking. HEAL is an independent network of multi-disciplinary professionals working, from a public health framework, to combat human trafficking; HEAL serves as a centralized resource on public health for the broader anti-trafficking community. The NGO formed to share best practices, expand the evidence base on human trafficking and health, and unify efforts to combat trafficking. HEAL also aims to bring a public health perspective to multi-system approaches to human trafficking at the local, state, federal, and international levels [18].

In 2015, the US Department of Health and Human services undertook a new effort to create a training that could be used nation-wide. The training, entitled SOAR (Stop. Observe. Ask. Respond) to Health and Wellness states:

> Health care and social service providers may come in contact with victims of human trafficking and not recognize the red flags. When this occurs, it leads to missed opportunities for intervention. The U.S. Department of Health and Human Services has a developed a new training for these first responders called SOAR. The SOAR curriculum is grounded in the public health approach that 1) places human trafficking along a spectrum of inter-related violence 2) understands the ripple effects of trauma and 3) encourages cultural-specific intervention efforts [19].

Clinicians and human service professionals who participate in the training learn about the reality of human trafficking in the USA and how trafficking is relevant to their work; how to recognize possible indicators of human trafficking; how to respond appropriately, including using trauma-informed care approaches to treat trafficked patients and to identify services for them. In addition, thorny issues such as HIPAA[19] and mandatory reporting are addressed. Finally the training encourages providers to share the importance of human trafficking awareness and responsiveness with their colleagues and the institutions in which they work [20].

---

[19] HIPPA is the Health Insurance Portability and Accountability Act, and sets the US health care industry standards for protection of patient medical records and other health information that health institutions, insurance companies, and practitioners receive or can access.

23.3   Conclusion

Since the 1990s, the US response to trafficking has grown significantly. A few small NGOs led the way in the 1990s and by the early 2000s, several large NGOs assisted in establishing a broad grass-roots anti-trafficking movement. The field has begun to address prevention through awareness and education. NGOs act as advocates, offering protection and assistance to trafficked persons through a broad array of services. And these groups act as community watchdogs, offering law enforcement "tips," when they are able.

The USA was the first nation to pass comprehensive legislation to prohibit human trafficking while also establishing a victim-centered approach. Since 2005 and following in the US' footsteps, a worldwide movement to stop human trafficking has developed. Now, experts have begun to explore new approaches to the problem that appreciate the economics of trafficking, and examine the public and individual health implications of human trafficking. While much has been accomplished, there is still much to be done.

23.4   Recommendations

For those who work with human trafficking survivors, there is an urgency to do the work that remains. Survivors tell of the physical, mental, emotional, and spiritual devastation that takes place and some have suggested that no amount of services can give a survivor back their childhood, faith in humanity, physical health, and stamina lost to the traffickers. The work of the future must therefore be focused as much as possible on prevention of all forms of trafficking.

- *Research*
- A critical aspect of the work is more sector-specific research of the problem. With a stronger evidence base, programs can be tailored to meet the needs of all sub-populations of survivors.
- *Survivor Leadership*
- It took almost 20 years for NGOs to understand the importance of survivors in anti-trafficking work. Survivors must be recognized, not just for their stories, but as leaders, as experts, and as visionaries who can help problem-solve the critical issues in the fight against trafficking.
- *Technology-Based Efforts*
- Trafficking has moved online and further underground. Anti-trafficking workers need to use the traffickers' new tools—the internet, social media, and other new technologies—to fight trafficking.
- *Local Responses to a Global Problem*

- Finally, tempting as it may be to centralize solutions, community responses at the local and state level will most certainly be key to eradicating trafficking. Larger NGOs and the federal government must encourage and support local responses, and to nurture their growth and maturity. Local groups best understand the specific ways human trafficking manifests in their communities. These organizations can build the local multi-disciplinary response that connects advocates, service providers, law enforcement, community leaders, and others necessary to address trafficking in a comprehensive, trauma-informed, and methodical way.

References

1. Donovan B. White slave crusades. Chicago: University of Illinois Press; 2006.
2. Hughes D. Combating sex trafficking: a history. 2013. http://www.fairobserver.com/region/north_america/combating-sex-trafficking-history/. Accessed 1 Aug 2016.
3. Global survival network footage, 1995–1997, incorporated into the movie, Bought and Sold. 1998. http://www.lib.utexas.edu/taro/hrdi/00009/00009-P.html; Specter M. Contraband women: traffickers' New Cargo. New York Times. 11 Jan 1998. http://www.nytimes.com/1998/01/11/world/contraband-women-a-special-report-traffickers-new-cargo-naive-slavic-women.html?pagewanted=all. Accessed 1 Aug 2016.
4. Human Rights Watch. A modern form of slavery: trafficking of burmese women and girls into brothels in Thailand. Asia Watch. 1993. https://www.hrw.org/reports/1993/thailand/. Accessed 1 Aug 2016.
5. Hertzke A. Freeing god's children: the unlikely alliance for global human rights. 2004. http://freeinggodschildren.com/. Accessed 1 Aug 2016.
6. President Clinton Directive. Memorandum on steps to combat violence against women and trafficking in women and girls. Weekly Comp Pres Doc. 1998, 11 Mar;34:412; cited in Payne VS. On the road to victory in America's war on human trafficking. In: First annual interdisciplinary conference on human trafficking, Paper 10. http://digitalcommons.unl.edu/cgi/viewcontent.cgi?article=1009&context=humtraffconf. Accessed 1 Aug 2016.
7. Lederer L. Addressing demand: why and how policymakers should utilize law and law enforcement to target customers of commercial sexual exploitation. Regent Univ Law Rev. 2010;23:297.
8. Cities empowered against sexual exploitation. Cities Initiative. https://www.ceasenetwork.org/. Accessed 15 May 2016.
9. Freedom Network. End demand fact sheet. http://freedomnetworkusa.org/wp-content/uploads/2012/05/End-Demand-Final.pdf. Accessed 1 Aug 2016.
10. Tenth United Nations Congress on the Prevention of Crime and Treatment of Offenders. Trauma and drug recovery for abuse and prostitution survivors in the criminal justice system. Speech delivered by Norma Hotaling, SAGE; 14 Apr 2000. https://www.ncjrs.gov/pdffiles1/nij/220773.pdf; May M. Norma Hotaling: former homeless prostitute's programs lauded and imitated around the country. SF Gate. 20 Dec 2008. http://www.sfgate.com/bayarea/article/Norma-Hotaling-dies-fought-prostitution-3180057.php. Accessed 1 Aug 2016.
11. Lederer LJ. Survivor-centered approaches: the key to the future. San Francisco: SAGE Graduation; 2004. http://www.globalcenturion.org/. Accessed 1 Aug 2016.
12. President Obama announces more key administration posts. White House Press Release. 16 Dec 2015. https://www.whitehouse.gov/the-press-office/2015/12/16/president-obama-announces-more-key-administration-posts. Accessed 1 Aug 2016.

13. Matual I. Quoted in Human Rights first announcement, New Survivors Council to advise federal government on anti-trafficking policy. 15 Jan 2016. http://www.humanrightsfirst.org/blog/new-survivors-council-advise-federal-government-anti-trafficking-policy. Accessed 1 Aug 2016.
14. National symposium on health needs of human trafficking victims. Post Symposium Brief, 22–23 Sept 2008. https://aspe.hhs.gov/basic-report/national-symposium-health-needs-human-trafficking-victims-post-symposium-brief. Accessed 1 Aug 2016.
15. Lederer L, Wetzel C. The health consequences of sex trafficking and their implications for identifying victims in healthcare facilities. Ann Health Law. 2014;23(1). Loyola University of Chicago. http://www.globalcenturion.org/wp-content/uploads/2014/08/The-Health-Consequences-of-Sex-Trafficking.pdf. Accessed 1 Aug 2016.
16. Chisolm-Straker M, Richardson LD, Cossio T. Combating slavery in the 21st century: the role of emergency medicine. J Health Care Poor Underserved. 2012;23:980–7. https://healtrafficking.files.wordpress.com/2015/03/23-3-chisolm-straker.pdf. Accessed 1 Aug 2016.
17. Stoklosa H, Grace AM, Littenberg N. Medical education on human trafficking. AMA J Ethics. 2014;17(10):914–21.
18. HEAL Trafficking, Inc. Who we are. Available at: https://HEALtrafficking.org/who-we-are/. Accessed 29 Dec 2016.
19. Office on Trafficking in Persons, U.S. Department of Health and Human Services, Administration for Children and Families. 2016. http://www.acf.hhs.gov/programs/endtrafficking/initiatives/soar. Accessed 1 Aug 2016.
20. S.O.A.R. to health and wellness training: a training for health care and social service providers. 2016. http://www.acf.hhs.gov/programs/endtrafficking/initiatives/soar. Accessed 1 Aug 2016.

Chapter 24
Moving Forward: Next Steps in Preventing and Disrupting Human Trafficking

Katherine Y. Chon and Smitha Khorana

24.1 Introduction

Sixteen years into the fight against human trafficking in the United States,[1] we know more now than we did before about the geographic scale and diversity of modern slavery. Globally, the International Labor Organization (ILO) estimates that 21 million people are survivors of forced labor, including 19 million survivors exploited

---

[1] The United States Congress passed the Trafficking Victims Protection Act (TVPA) of 2000 to combat trafficking in persons, a contemporary manifestation of slavery, to ensure just and effective punishment of traffickers, and to protect their victims. The TVPA of 2000 worked to fill in gaps in legal protections, including the establishment of a comprehensive law to penalize the range of offenses involved in human trafficking schemes; to reflect the seriousness of the crime and its components in sentencing guidelines; and to establish protections for victims, including those without legal documentation status. The TVPA of 2000 also recognized that the international community repeatedly condemned slavery, involuntary servitude, violence against women, and other elements of trafficking through various declarations, treaties, and United Nations resolutions and reports, including the Universal Declaration of Human Rights; the 1948 American Declaration on the Rights and Duties of Man; the 1956 Supplementary Convention on the Abolition of Slavery, the Slave Trade, and Institutions and Practices Similar to Slavery; the 1957 Abolition of Forced Labor Convention; the International Covenant on Civil and Political Rights; the Convention Against Torture and Other Cruel, Inhuman or Degrading Treatment or Punishment; United Nations General Assembly Resolutions 50/167, 51/66, and 52/98; the Final Report of the World Congress against Sexual Exploitation of Children (Stockholm, 1996); the Fourth World Conference on Women (Beijing, 1995); and the 1991 Moscow Document of the Organization for Security and Cooperation in Europe.

The original version of this chapter was revised. An erratum to this chapter can be found at DOI: 10.1007/978-3-319-47824-1_25

K.Y. Chon (✉)
U.S. Department of Health and Human Services, Washington, DC, USA
e-mail: katherine.chon@acf.hhs.gov

S. Khorana
Columbia University, 116th Street & Broadway, New York, NY 10027, USA
e-mail: smithakhorana@gmail.com

by private individuals or enterprises and more than two million by state-imposed forms of forced labor or rebel armed groups. The ILO projects that forced labor in the private economy generates $150 billion in illegal profits per year, particularly among domestic work, agriculture, construction, manufacturing, and entertainment sectors [1]. Human trafficking occurs in nearly every country in the world. The US State Department's 2015 Trafficking in Persons Report provides a global assessment on the nature of human trafficking and government actions in 188 countries based on available information from US embassies, government officials, non-government organizations, published reports, articles, and research [2].

Although the methods for determining rigorous prevalence estimates of human trafficking in the US are still in development, cases of forced labor and commercial sexual exploitation have been reported in all 50 states, the District of Columbia, and US territories and insular areas. Examples of the diversity of cases investigated or prosecuted by the US Department of Justice in Fiscal Year (FY) 2014[2] include [3]:

United States v. Yarbrough (Tennessee): Notorious sex trafficker Terrence "T-Rex" Yarbrough was sentenced to serve over 44 years in prison. During the trial, victims[3] recounted a series of violent acts perpetrated by Yarbrough to coerce them into commercial sex at his direction, including being beaten with belts, wooden coat hangers, crowbars, padlocks, and dog chains; being thrown down stairs; having their heads smashed in car doors; having their legs burned with irons; and being scalded with boiling water.

United States v. Khobragade (New York): Defendant Devyani Khobragade, a Deputy Consul General of the Consulate General of India, was indicted in connection with obtaining a visa for employment of an Indian domestic servant in the US, to provide domestic labor and child care at substandard wages. In March 2014, a federal grand jury returned an indictment charging the defendant with visa fraud and false statements.

United States v. Fields (Florida): Andrew Blaine Fields lured young women, some of whom were already involved in commercial sex or drug use, by offering them shelter, transportation, and protection. He then increased their drug dependency into full-blown addiction, saddled them with insurmountable drug debts, and demanded that they engage in commercial sex and provide him all the proceeds to pay down the drug debts he had imposed. When the victims resisted, he

---

[2] References to Fiscal Year (FY) in this chapter refer to the Federal Fiscal Year, which begins on October 1 and ends on September 30. For example, FY 2014 begins on October 1, 2013 and ends September 30, 2014.

[3] In alignment with the *Federal Strategic Action Plan on Services for Victims of Human Trafficking in the United States, 2013–2017*, this chapter uses the terms "victim" and "survivor" to refer to individuals who were trafficked. The term "victim" has legal implications within the criminal justice process and generally means an individual who suffered harm as a result of criminal conduct. "Victims" also have particular rights within the criminal justice process and Federal law enforcement agencies often use the term "victim" as part of their official duties. "Survivor" is a term used to recognize the strengths it takes to continue on a journey toward healing in the aftermath of a traumatic experience. Both terms are intended to honor those who have suffered, or are suffering, the effects of being trafficked. More information is available at http://www.ovc.gov/pubs/FederalHumanTraffickingStrategicPlan.pdf.

threatened to withhold the narcotics until they eventually relented in order to avoid physically excruciating drug withdrawal symptoms. Fields was sentenced to over 33 years including prison for recruiting vulnerable young women and using addictive narcotics to coerce and compel them into commercial sex for his profit.

United States v. Kalu (Colorado): Kizzy Kalu and a co-defendant lured victims from the Philippines on false promises of good jobs as nursing instructors, and then compelled the victims' labor in nursing homes and other long-term care facilities. The defendants threatened to have the victims' visas cancelled and have the victims deported if they did not comply and did not turn over a significant portion of their earnings. The defendants threatened victims with insurmountable debts if they left before the end of a contract the victims were required to sign. Kalu was sentenced to 130 months in prison following his conviction on multiple counts of forced labor, visa fraud, and money laundering. The defendants were ordered to pay over $3.7 million in restitution to the victims of their forced labor scheme.

United States v. Tran (Minnesota): Tieu Tran was sentenced to serve 1 year in prison followed by 1 year supervised release and was ordered to pay over $50,000 in restitution for labor trafficking arising from her role in compelling a Vietnamese national to work at the defendant's son's restaurant to pay down a smuggling debt. The defendant recruited the victim from Vietnam on false promises of legal immigration status and a high-paying job, but then smuggled the victim and others into the US illegally, imposed a significant smuggling debt on the victim, then compelled the victim's labor by using a scheme of manipulation of debts, isolation, and verbal intimidation to hold the victim in fear, knowing the victim did not speak English, feared losing her family home to creditors, and had no money, legal immigration status, or other means of subsistence.

United States v. Callahan (Ohio): Lead defendants were sentenced to 30 and 32 years, respectively, for holding a woman with cognitive disabilities and her child against their will and forcing the woman to perform manual labor for them. The defendants were convicted, following a 3-week trial in March 2014, of using violence, threats, sexual assaults, humiliation, restraint in a locked room, monitoring, threats to have the child taken away from the mother, intimidation with pit bull dogs and snakes, and confinement in unsafe, unsanitary conditions. These techniques were used to control their victims and compel them to clean the defendants' apartment; care for numerous pit bull dogs and snakes the defendants bred and sold; make purchases for the defendants; and perform other tasks at the defendants' direction.

United States v. Perez-Gumeta (Kentucky): Defendant Pedra Perez-Gumeta was sentenced to 18 months in prison and 1 year of supervised release for harboring an undocumented Mexican migrant for financial gain for labor at a Kentucky tobacco farm, and retaining a portion of the migrant's earnings.

In FY 2015, the National Human Trafficking Resource Center (NHTRC), a 24-h anti-trafficking hotline received reports of 5,418 unique cases of trafficking, a 5 percent increase from the prior year. A total of 756 of these cases referenced situations of potential labor trafficking, 3,998 cases referred to potential sex trafficking, 169 cases involved both sex and labor trafficking, and the type of trafficking was not specified by the individual contacting the NHTRC in 495 cases [4]. The populations affected by human trafficking in the US are diverse—impacting foreign nationals and US citizens; adults and children; and people of all genders, across all socio-economic, religious, and cultural backgrounds.

During FY 2015, the NHTRC received calls, emails, and online reports from all 50 states, Washington, D.C., Guam, the Northern Mariana Islands, Puerto Rico, US Virgin Islands, American Samoa, and more than 30 foreign countries requesting assistance in the US and US territories. The top five states with the highest call volume were (in order starting with highest volume): California, Texas, Florida, Ohio, and New York, which together comprised nearly 45 percent of the calls where the caller's state was known [4].

Given the number and profile of trafficking cases identified through law enforcement investigations, reports from non-government organizations, and testimonies of survivors of trafficking, we now know that human trafficking is not an isolated issue on the periphery of the global human rights agenda. Rather, it is connected to a web of problems related to human rights violations, gender-based violence, international labor practices, and even transnational terrorism (e.g., the Islamic State and Boko Haram trafficking women and children to support their operations). The markets and venues for victimization run the spectrum from trafficking by family members to exploitation via online and offline commercial sex markets, and from criminal enterprises to integration into global supply chains. The US State Department's 2014 and 2015 Trafficking in Persons reports spotlight these interconnections, including the risk of human trafficking in global supply chains and labor recruitment; the link between extractive industries[4] and trafficking; modern slavery as a tactic in armed conflicts; the vulnerability of lesbian, gay, bisexual, and transgender (LGBT) individuals to human trafficking; and the use of forced criminality [5, 6].

When Congress passed the Trafficking Victims Protection Act (TVPA) of 2000, the primary focus was to expand legal tools to prosecute human traffickers and legal protections to assist victims and survivors of human trafficking. However, the findings of Congress in the TVPA of 2000 also recognized that human trafficking exposed victims to serious health risks, including HIV. The TVPA of 2000 also highlighted the Declaration of Independence's recognition for the inherent dignity and worth of all people. The TVPA reinforced the idea that the right to be free from slavery and involuntary servitude was among those unalienable rights described in the Declaration of Independence, and purposefully built on the legal history of the US outlawing slavery and involuntary servitude in 1865.

As the country's understanding about the nature of human trafficking evolved, the legal framework to prosecute human traffickers, protect victims, and prevent modern forms of slavery also swiftly expanded at national and local levels. US Congress

---

[4]Extractive industries involve the removal of non-renewable raw materials such as oil, gas, metals, and minerals from the earth, including mining, drilling, and quarrying activities that often occur in geographically remote areas. The connection between forced labor and extractive industries has been well documented, but the State Department's Trafficking in Persons report highlights increasing concern about the presence of sex trafficking in mining areas.

subsequently reauthorized the TVPA in 2003, 2005, 2008, and 2013 with expanded tools to prosecute perpetrators of, protect those victimized by, and prevent human trafficking. Each of these reauthorizations created new tools for the criminal justice system to hold human traffickers accountable and extend support for survivors of human trafficking. For example, the TVPA Reauthorization of 2003 noted that while the US Government made significant progress in investigating and prosecuting acts of trafficking and in responding to the needs of survivors, survivors still faced unintended obstacles in securing needed assistance. Congress also recognized the need for more research to fully understand human trafficking and determine the most effective strategies for combating trafficking. The TVPA Reauthorization of 2005 represented the government's recognition that human trafficking occurs within the borders of the US (not just transnationally); expressed the need for further research to quantify the problem of child sex trafficking; and signified the government's recognition of populations at disproportionate risk to human trafficking, including runaway and homeless youth [7–11].

The year after Congress passed the TVPA of 2000, Texas and Washington were the first two states to criminalize human trafficking, initiating a wave of efforts to strengthen local capacity to respond to human trafficking [12]. By 2012, all 50 states and the District of Columbia passed state criminal statutes against human trafficking. By 2014, the majority of states added basic provisions to address diverse forms of trafficking by increasing investigative tools, authorizing training for law enforcement, requiring posting of a trafficking hotline, and providing more options for survivors of trafficking to seek assistance and justice.

The establishment of a robust federal and state legal framework to combat human trafficking provided a critical foundation to increase investigations, arrests, and prosecutions of human traffickers. In FY 2014, the US Department of Justice (DOJ) opened 835 human trafficking investigations through the Federal Bureau of Investigation (FBI); opened 1083 investigations through 14 anti-trafficking task forces[5]; initiated 208 federal human trafficking prosecutions and charged 335 defendants through 94 US Attorney's Offices; and secured convictions against 184 traffickers. The US Department of Homeland Security (DHS) opened 987 investigations possibly involving human trafficking and the US Department of Defense (DOD) investigated 14 human trafficking cases involving military personnel [6].

Strong rule of law also enabled a victim-centered[6] framework so that survivors of trafficking can access services to leave exploitative situations and rebuild their lives. For example, the US Department of Health and Human Services (HHS) issues

---

[5] DOJ-funded task forces bring law enforcement and community organizations together to assist survivors and bring cases to justice. The list of human trafficking task forces is available at https://ovc.ncjrs.gov/humantrafficking/traffickingmatrix.html.

[6] The *Federal Strategic Action Plan on Services for Victims of Human Trafficking in the United States, 2013–2017* defines a victim-centered approach as one that seeks to minimize re-traumatization associated with the criminal justice process by providing the support of victim advocates and service providers; empowering survivors as engaged participants in the process; and providing survivors an opportunity to play a role in seeing their traffickers brought to justice. A victim-centered approach supports a victim's rights, dignity, autonomy, and self-determination, while simultaneously advancing the government's and society's interest in prosecuting traffickers.

Fiscal Year	Number of Eligibility Letters Issued to Children	Number of Certification Letters Issued to Adults	Total Letters Issued
2001	4	194	198
2002	18	81	99
2003	6	145	151
2004	16	147	163
2005	34	197	231
2006	20	214	234
2007	33	270	303
2008	31	286	317
2009	50	330	380
2010	92	449	541
2011	101	463	564
2012	103	366	469
2013	114	406	520
2014	219	530	749
2015	240	623	863
TOTAL	1,081	4,701	5,782

Fig. 24.1 Number of certification and eligibility letters issued by HHS by fiscal year

Certification and Eligibility Letters so that foreign victims of trafficking in the US are able to access public benefits and services to the same degree as refugees regardless of their immigration status. In FY 2015, HHS issued 623 Certification Letters to adults and 240 Eligibility Letters to children (see Fig. 24.1). Certification and Eligibility letters were provided to victims or their representatives in 37 states and the District of Columbia. Certified victims came from 61 countries in the Americas, Asia, Africa, and Europe [4].

The federal government significantly increased funding for survivors of human trafficking by appropriating more than $42 million in funding to DOJ and more than $15 million in funding to HHS in FY 2015. Federally funded victim assistance includes case management and referrals for medical and dental care, mental health and substance use disorder treatment, sustenance and shelter, translation and interpretation services, immigration and legal assistance, employment and training, transportation assistance, and other services such as criminal justice advocacy. In FY 2014, HHS supported 153 community and faith-based organizations that provided assistance to a total of 1,137 survivors and their family members, an increase from 915 individuals served the prior year. DOJ provided services by funding 28 victim service organizations, serving more than 2,782 open client cases, including 1,366 newly identified victims, compared with 1,911 open client cases and 1,009 newly identified victims in the previous year. DHS provided 446 survivors of trafficking with assistance, an increase from 330 survivors in the prior year [6].

Defining human trafficking as a violent crime also increases public awareness of the issue. Community members are more alert and more likely to take action when they see potential trafficking. For example, the increase in public attention led to more than 30,000 cases of human trafficking identified through calls into the NHTRC—including 5,400 unique cases of potential trafficking identified in FY 2015, alone [13]. Changes in public understanding about human trafficking are also leading to increased self-identification of trafficking experiences, leading to more requests for assistance. For example, the NHTRC received 3,487 calls directly from survivors of trafficking in FY 2015, a 34 percent increase from the prior year [4]. When US embassies and consulates worldwide provided a "Know Your Rights" pamphlet[7] that included the NHTRC number and confirmed that applicants for temporary work and exchange visas received, read, and understood the pamphlet, the effort subsequently generated 1,056 calls to the national hotline in FY 2014 [3].

24.1.1   Challenges with the Current Anti-Trafficking Response

As much progress as has been made in establishing legal protections and expanding social safety nets, there are several limitations to addressing human trafficking primarily or exclusively through a criminal justice framework. Several key challenges continue to confront the anti-trafficking response.

First, we are better equipped with the knowledge to prosecute traffickers and identify trafficked individuals than we are equipped with the evidence on knowing what works to prevent and disrupt human trafficking. Despite the positive annual increases in the quantitative outcomes of law enforcement investigations, arrests, convictions, and the number of survivors supported through federal funding noted above, there are limited evaluations of the effectiveness of anti-trafficking programs on the long-term health and well-being of survivors, prevention, and re-victimization. For example, the 2014 and 2015 Trafficking in Persons reports indicate persistent concerns from non-government organizations related to the need for the ability to more effectively screen NGO clients for all forms of trafficking; support appropriate housing that ensures safety of survivors; refrain from detaining victims for criminal activity related to their trafficking situation; and change the social norms that drive demand for commercial sex and forced labor. In addition, there is limited research to shed light on effective practices to prevent human trafficking in its myriad forms

---

[7] The State Department's "Know Your Rights" pamphlet was created in 2009 as authorized by the William Wilberforce Trafficking Victims Protection Reauthorization Act of 2008 (Public Law 110-457). The information pamphlet provides information on the legal rights and resources for foreign nationals applying for employment-based or education-based nonimmigrant visas. The pamphlet is available in more than 30 languages. The English version of the pamphlet was updated in April 2016. More information is available at https://travel.state.gov/content/visas/en/general/rights-pro-tections-temporary-workers.html.

or to disrupt the social, economic, and other dynamics that enable human trafficking to exist [5, 6].

Second, we have a good understanding of the diversity of human trafficking and the information to categorize types of human trafficking based on victimology, risk-profile, or venues and markets of exploitation. However, the USA has not yet developed rigorous methodology to determine the prevalence of human trafficking to establish the baselines necessary to sharply target and measure the effectiveness of anti-trafficking interventions according to victimology, risk-profile, or market of exploitation. For example, while we can identify and assist dozens of workers forced into agricultural labor, the anti-trafficking field is not yet equipped with the tools to measure whether the risk to trafficking within agricultural markets is decreasing over time. The lack of consistent and shared terminology and uniform data collection standards across multiple systems of intervention hinder such efforts.

And finally, the changes in the anti-trafficking field to date have largely occurred at the individual level rather than at the community and societal level. Although there is general recognition that each case of victimization has ripple effects, impacting the survivor, their family, and their community, the prevailing locus of change does not fully take these broader consequences into account. The current state of the anti-trafficking field has barely begun to scratch at the surface of the inter-generational impact of violence, socio-economic costs to multiple systems of care, and global supply chain risks to sustainable economic development.

As with any complex and seemingly intractable social problem, the anti-trafficking field must build on and move beyond singular reliance on the criminal justice sector in solving these problems. Human trafficking is a violent crime and also a public health issue; strong rule of law is a necessary foundation for the potency of public health interventions to address the challenges outlined above. As we look ahead to 2030 and beyond, there are at least three ways a public health framework of human trafficking can build on the foundation of progress made.

24.1.2 A Public Health Framework of Human Trafficking

Public health is concerned with protecting the health of individuals, families, and communities. A public health framework seeks to prevent problems from happening or from recurring, and is informed by research and evaluation. A critical component of public health is providing education on behaviors that can ensure and promote positive health outcomes for individuals and communities. HHS integrates public health initiatives through multiple divisions across the Department to prevent epidemics and the spread of disease; protect against environmental hazards; prevent injuries; promote and encourage healthy behavior; respond to disasters; and assure the quality and accessibility of health services.[8] Not only has literature shown a link

---

[8] Three core functions of public health were established in the 1998 Institute of Medicine report, "The Future of Public Health." In 1994, the public health sector defined the purpose of public health in the context of health care reform through the work of a "Core Functions of Public Health

between human trafficking and many other public health issues (e.g., other forms of violence, substance use disorders, psychiatric illness and suicide, sexually transmitted infections, unplanned pregnancies, and communicable diseases), but human trafficking itself hinders the overall well-being and health of those who are trafficked.[9]

Integrating a robust public health framework into anti-trafficking strategies will expand the community of stakeholders who are responsible for creating change, enhance our understanding of how we create change, and help us examine the types of changes we need to make. While there is still much to do to strengthen training and improve responses of law enforcement and service providers, we cannot eradicate human trafficking through arrests alone. Nor can we prevent human trafficking through service provision alone. Despite the annual increases in investigations, arrests, and convictions, only a small percentage of human trafficking cases garner the attention of law enforcement, leaving the majority of trafficked individuals out of reach of justice systems. Similarly, while effective survivor services work to address the aftermath of trafficking, they are not currently designed to deal with the root causes that contribute to victimization or re-victimization.

A public health framework expands the constituents that need to be engaged in anti-trafficking efforts in a crucial way, encouraging a "no wrong doors" approach to identifying diverse points of contact in the community for survivors of trafficking to access services. This allows for individuals at high-risk for trafficking to receive preventative care. Public health recognizes the importance of collectives to address shared social problems and create networks of interventions through coordinated actions (see Fig. 24.2) [14].

For example, a public health framework seeks to empower health care providers and social workers embedded in communities to provide a safe space for individuals to come forward about their experiences. The environment created within the health care system—bolstered by the Hippocratic Oath—can elicit different measures of trust than those found within a criminal justice or legal setting. Equipping educators, parents, and youth workers with the knowledge and tangible resources to understand the risks for trafficking can also improve prevention efforts. Strategically engaging researchers, journalists and media organizations, faith-based organizations, businesses, and philanthropy can leverage the effectiveness of partnerships and non-governmental groups.

Survivors of human trafficking are critical voices to inform the development of community-based programs and government policies to prevent and disrupt human trafficking. Meaningfully engaging survivors of trafficking in participatory and leadership roles will contribute to more effective intervention and prevention strategies.

Steering Committee" involving HHS and key national public health organizations. Learn about the inter-connected components of the US public health system at http://www.cdc.gov/nphpsp/essentialservices.html.

[9] In 2015, the American Public Health Association adopted a new policy statement, "Expanding and Coordinating Human Trafficking-Related Public Health Research, Evaluation, Education, and Prevention," available at https://www.apha.org/policies-and-advocacy/public-health-policy-statements/policy-database/2016/01/26/14/28/expanding-and-coordinating-human-trafficking-related-public-health-activities.

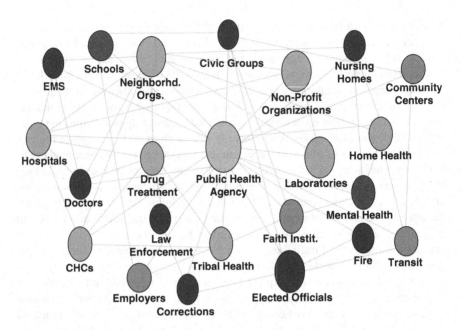

Fig. 24.2 The public health system

Survivors of trafficking are already taking leadership positions as advocates, policy makers, and service providers in community-based and government organizations across the country. In 2015, President Obama appointed 11 survivor leaders to the US Advisory Council on Human Trafficking to provide input and expertise to federal agencies, including the President's Interagency Task Force to Monitor and Combat Trafficking in Persons, on US anti-trafficking policies and programs [15–17].

Although the federal and local legislative landscape on human trafficking in the last 15 years has concentrated action within the criminal justice system, recent Congressional attention has included an expanded circle of stakeholders who have been a critical force in responding to human trafficking. The Preventing Sex Trafficking and Strengthening Families Act of 2014 requires foster care agencies to identify, report, and determine services for those who have been sex trafficked. The legislation places new responsibilities within the child welfare system instead of primarily within juvenile justice and other law enforcement systems [18, 19]. The Justice for Victims of Trafficking Act of 2015 added new requirements for child protective services, runaway and homeless youth programs, and health care providers to increase anti-trafficking engagement through training, victim identification, and service referrals. The Justice for Victims of Trafficking Act also changed the federal definition of child abuse and neglect and of sexual abuse by including children who have experienced trafficking [15].

Federal Executive action has also expanded who is responsible for preventing and disrupting human trafficking. In 2012, President Obama issued an Executive

Order, *Strengthening Protections Against Trafficking in Persons in Federal Contracts*, recognizing the role of the private sector, non-government organizations, and the federal government to work together to prevent and eliminate instances of trafficking-related activities in federal contracts and in private sector supply chains. Related requirements in the Ending Trafficking in Government Contracting Act (as part of the National Defense Authorization Act of 2013) established new safeguards to prevent trafficking in supply chains [20–22].

A public health lens also changes how we create change. In addition to responding to human trafficking crimes and addressing the immediate needs of trafficking survivors, a public health framework recognizes the social, economic, and historical determinants of health and well-being that contribute to the risk for human trafficking. Anti-trafficking interventions must build on the criminal justice and social service response by incorporating prevention strategies, adapted to meet the unique needs and environmental circumstances specific to populations at high risk for trafficking. While human trafficking can impact anyone, some populations are more vulnerable to human trafficking because of experiences of prior violence, stigma and marginalization, and poverty.

A public health-driven approach identifies the particular ecosystem of factors that create risks in different populations and adapts interventions to disrupt those unique set of factors, rather than relying on a one-size-fits-all approach. In the fight against cancer, there are prevention and treatment interventions that are useful for many types of cancer. Similarly, there are anti-trafficking principles that can be useful in a variety of settings. However, not all cancers are alike and each unique form requires a targeted response that fits particular molecular and biological characteristics. And just as health care providers have different approaches to treating lung cancer and skin cancer, anti-trafficking organizations must develop targeted strategies that identify the unique driving factors of each type of trafficking market or system. For example, effective interventions to disrupt the conditions that enable trafficking within the construction industry will be different from those that seek to prevent trafficking in residential brothels.

Finally, a public health paradigm changes what is at stake to truly disrupt the dynamics that facilitate human trafficking. The very existence of modern slavery indicates the presence of normalized and commercialized violence. Deeply rooted cultural norms around power, equity, gender, and consumer behavior shape the social and economic drivers that enable human trafficking. In contrast to a largely legal paradigm, a public health framework is designed to confront entrenched interests and recognize the social norms that create blind spots and barriers to effectively preventing and ending human trafficking. Public health also sees human trafficking along a spectrum of interpersonal violence, understands the generational ripple effects of trauma, and encourages culturally relevant prevention and intervention efforts to reduce barriers to care.

The abolition of chattel slavery in the historical development of the US required a restructuring of the social and economic organization of society and an awakening to normalized injustices. Similarly, the long-term solutions to prevent and eradicate human trafficking will require changes in social norms and other deeply rooted structures. For example, the US must once again clarify its values for justice and equity, including making more informed consumer choices to avoid the purchase of goods and services produced by forced labor; confronting the reality of demand and power dynamics that drive sex trafficking and gender-based violence; and investing government, philanthropic, and research resources to effectively eradicate human trafficking.

24.2 Discussion

"It is easier to build strong children than to repair broken men."

—Frederick Douglass

Human traffickers are ever-evolving in their tactics to control trafficked persons and escape detection. The more we understand the factors they use to their advantage to enable human trafficking, the smarter we can leverage resources to predict and prevent trafficking from occurring and recurring. There are three primary themes of human trafficking risk factors: (1) the existence of other forms of violence that contributes to normalizing the commercialized violence of trafficking; (2) the experience of disconnection, social isolation, shame, and stigma; and (3) the economic dynamics and demand that fuel the profit incentives of trafficking.

24.2.1 The Commercialized Violence of Trafficking Connected to Other Forms of Violence

Human trafficking is not a random, isolated crime. Survivors of one form of violence are more likely to be a victim of other forms of violence: Violence in the personal sphere enables traffickers to transform abuse into a commodity. For example, a Centers for Disease Control and Prevention (CDC) report on the links among multiple forms of violence states that girls who are sexually abused are more likely to experience physical violence, sexual re-victimization; engage in self-harm; and be a victim of intimate partner violence later in life. Youth who were physically abused by a dating partner are more likely to have suffered abuse as a child, been a victim of sexual assault, and witnessed violence in their family [23].

While not all victims of child abuse and maltreatment become victims of human trafficking, child protection professionals are encountering abused and neglected children who are targeted by traffickers and pimps. For example, a survey conducted by the Los Angeles Probation Department revealed that 59 percent of the 174 juveniles arrested on prostitution-related charges in the county were in the foster care system and they were often recruited from group homes. The California Child Welfare Council found between 50 and 80 percent of those who experienced commercial sexual exploitation are or were involved in the child welfare system. The Department of Children and Families in Connecticut reported that 86 out of 88 children identified as child sex trafficking survivors had been involved with child welfare services [24].

Survivors of violence are also at higher risk for behaving violently. Children who experience physical abuse or neglect early in their lives are at greater risk for committing violence against peers (particularly boys), bullying, perpetrating teen dating and intimate partner violence, and committing child abuse and sexual violence later in life [23]. Trafficking is part of a larger cycle of violence that can extend across the life span.

Some state-specific research on the experience of children in the juvenile justice system is beginning to illustrate these connections between experience of past abuse and future criminalized behavior: A 2006 study in Oregon found 93 percent of incarcerated girls had experienced sexual or physical abuse and 76 percent experienced at least one incident of sexual abuse by the age of 13. A 2009 study in South Carolina found 81 percent of incarcerated girls reported a history of sexual violence and a 2014 study in Florida found 84 percent of incarcerated girls experienced family violence [25]. A public health approach can address harmful behavior stemming from trauma prior to engagement in criminal justice institutions.

A separate survey of former male sex traffickers in Chicago found that the majority was abused as children. Eighty-eight percent reported physical abuse, 76 percent reported sexual abuse at an average age of 9.5 years, and 88 percent reported witnessing domestic violence in the home. Sixty percent had family members involved in the commercial sex industry [26]. Public health interventions can work to prevent pathways towards the perpetuation of human trafficking and other violent crimes.

The correlation between human trafficking and other forms of violence is alarming, especially since the CDC estimates that 1 in 4 children experience some form of child maltreatment in their lifetimes in the US [27]. And nearly 1 in 3 women and 1 in 8 men have experienced sexual violence, physical violence, or stalking by an intimate partner [28]. Many of these reports also recognize the underestimation of experienced violence and abuse due to non-reporting by some survivors and compounding trauma from those who experience multiple forms of violence.

We need to work together across health, social services, and criminal justice systems to coordinate local resources and services for anyone affected by violence. We must broaden violence prevention and intervention efforts to address multiple, connected forms of violence to improve public health.

HHS has been actively working to prevent violence across the life spectrum over the last 35 years: The 1979 Surgeon General's Report, *Healthy People*, first recognized violence prevention as a public health issue by emphasizing that "the health community could not ignore the consequences of violent behavior in an effort to improve the health of children, adolescents, and young adults." The report identified violence as one of the 15 priority areas to improve the nation's health. The HHS Healthy People initiative evolved over time through the release of Healthy People 1990, Healthy People 2000, Healthy People 2010, and Healthy People 2020, increasingly integrating the need to address violent and abusive behavior as a public health priority through multi-sector cooperation and integration. In March 2016, HHS started the process to seek nominations for members of the Secretary's Advisory Committee to inform the development of Healthy People 2030, which provides an opportunity to further shape the country's progress to address violence and abuse, including human trafficking [29–31].

In the spirit of Healthy People goals, HHS integrates anti-trafficking responses across multiple health and human service systems, recognizing the linkages of trafficking to other forms of violence across the life spectrum. The Children's Bureau is working with state child welfare agencies to implement new federal legislation to strengthen training, victim identification, and care for youth who experience or are at high risk for human trafficking. The Family and Youth Services Bureau provides a series of trainings on trauma-informed care for survivors of trafficking; the Bureau also supports anti-domestic violence and runaway and homeless youth organizations to work with survivors of trafficking. The Substance Abuse and Mental Health Services Administration is leveraging its National Child Traumatic Stress Network for early intervention and prevention practices. The Health Resources Services Administration is supporting Federally Qualified Health Centers working with underserved communities to identify and serve survivors of human trafficking. HHS is also partnering with more than a dozen federal agencies to implement the 5-year *Federal Strategic Action Plan on Services for Victims of Human Trafficking in the United States, 2013–2017* to coordinate, collaborate, and build capacity across multiple sectors and levels of government [32–36].

24.2.2   The Experience of Disconnection, Social Isolation, Shame, and Stigma

Anyone can be a victim of human trafficking regardless of age, socio-economic status, gender, race, or nationality. However, the 2015 Trafficking in Persons Report notes that particularly vulnerable populations in the US include children in the child welfare and juvenile justice systems; runaway and homeless youth; children working in agriculture; American Indians and Alaska Natives; migrant laborers, foreign national domestic workers in diplomatic households; populations with limited English proficiency; persons with disabilities; rural populations, and LGBT individuals [6]. A common experience among these populations that are disproportionally impacted by human trafficking is the experience of disconnection, social and physical isolation, and shame and stigma.

Many youth are often disengaged from their families or other sources of safety and support due to shame and stigma, violence in the home, or violence in the community. The National Center for Missing and Exploited Children estimates that 1 in 6 endangered runaways were likely sex trafficked in 2014, which is an increase from their estimate of 1 in 7 endangered runaways in 2013 [37].

In a 2016 Street Outreach Study funded by the HHS Family and Youth Services Bureau, homeless youth were asked if they had ever traded sex with anyone for something they needed. About 36 percent had traded sex for money, a place to spend the night, food, protection, or drugs (see Fig. 24.3). Most of the youth who reported trading sex for money did so only after they became homeless. More than half of

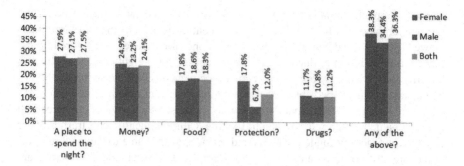

Fig. 24.3 Percentage of surveyed homeless youth who exchanged sex for something they needed

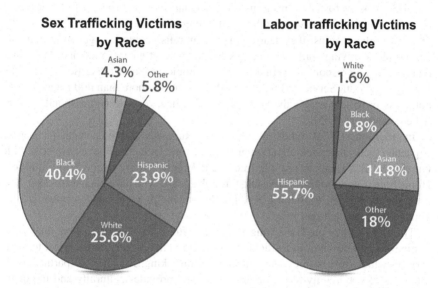

Fig. 24.4 Race of trafficking victims identified in law enforcement investigations when race was known

homeless youth became homeless for the first time because they were asked to leave home by a parent or caregiver. The study surveyed 873 youth in 11 cities [38].

Traffickers take advantage of this social isolation, and lack of stable resources and protection. LGBT youth can be up to five times more likely than heterosexual youth to be victims of human trafficking. LGBT youth are also over-represented among runaway and homeless youth and child welfare populations. Many may be leaving homes where they experienced abuse or were expelled by family members unaccepting of their sexual orientation or gender identity [24].

Human trafficking also disproportionately impacts non-White racial and ethnic groups. For example, the Human Trafficking Reporting System identified the majority of survivors of sex and labor trafficking were Black, Hispanic, and Asian in confirmed cases investigated by state and federal law enforcement between 2008 and 2010 (see Fig. 24.4) [39].

Unaccompanied minors coming to the US from Mexico and Central America are also vulnerable to trafficking. Fifty-eight percent of unaccompanied children interviewed by the United Nations High Commissioner for Refugees were forcibly displaced from their homes due to violence and abuse. Forty-eight percent of children experienced violence by organized crime, 21 percent survived abuse in their homes by caretakers, and 38 percent were recruited into forced criminality [40]. The HHS Office of Refugee Resettlement works with social service providers to screen all unaccompanied children for human trafficking. Children identified as trafficked are eligible for federally funded benefits and services to the same extent as a refugee, without regard to immigration status. For example, child survivors of trafficking are eligible for the Unaccompanied Refugee Minor program, which places children in culturally appropriate and community-based foster care settings [41–43].

HHS works to foster connections for youth survivors to access safe homes, caring adults, and health services. When children grow up in stable environments with nurturing relationships, they learn empathy, impulse control, anger management, and problem solving—all resiliency skills that protect against violence. Programs that prevent and respond to trafficking among homeless youth are critical. The HHS Family and Youth Services Bureau (FYSB) is training more than 400 runaway and homeless programs across the country to recognize, respect, and respond to trafficked persons [44, 45].

In addition, FYSB funds the National Runaway Safeline, which recently expanded their family reunification program, Home Free. They have partnered with Greyhound Bus Lines to provide free bus tickets to reunify over 15,000 families. Home Free is now available to youth, through age 21, who have been trafficked. The program recognizes trafficking risk factors and helps coordinate services at the youth's final destination [46].

The HHS Office on Trafficking in Persons funds the NHTRC, a national 24-h hotline where a survivor of trafficking anywhere in the country can connect to local services which can also prevent recurrence of trafficking. The NHTRC partners with hundreds of community-based organizations and provides culturally and linguistically accessible services to better connect underserved populations. For example in FY 2015, the NHTRC fielded nearly 6 percent of substantive calls in Spanish, 1 percent of calls in 30 other languages, and provided services for hearing and speech-impaired individuals. The NHTRC connected survivors of trafficking for social service referrals in 7,252 cases. Partnerships with local community-based organizations and victim-centered law enforcement can increase help-seeking behavior and reduce social disconnection [4].

24.2.3 The Economic Dynamics and Demand that Fuels Human Trafficking

Compared to relatively simple economic structures and trade systems that existed during the trans-Atlantic slavery period in the eighteenth and nineteenth centuries, modern slavery is integrated into a complex web of domestic and transnational routes than span diverse legal, illegal, and gray markets. Yet, human trafficking today also exists within distinct market systems, operating on specific business models with unique economic and social drivers. There are many different subtypes of human trafficking with varying causes and manifestations. Deconstructing the social problem of human trafficking, rather than grouping distinct forms of trafficking under the same generic banner, will help identify and fine-tune the effectiveness of policy and program interventions.

For example, open and publicaly accessible criminal trafficking networks operate differently from closed and private criminal trafficking networks. Brothels disguised as commercial massage parlors are considered open networks since they publicly advertise their locations in newspapers and online, are likely to operate in downtown and suburban areas accessible to the public, and tend to operate similar to franchise business models across the US. In contrast, residential brothels operating in homes and an on-call basis rely on street-level word of mouth advertising among a specific customer base and tend to have more mobile operations. Other closed criminal trafficking networks operate completely online (e.g., child abuse imagery rings), presenting their own set of challenges in identifying locations of victimization.

Other forms of trafficking are part of both formal and informal economic markets around the world. Global supply chains that contain goods or products produced by slavery and forced labor include the production of cotton from Uzbekistan, shrimp from Thailand, and other raw materials coming from specific countries or geographic areas. The tools to track and monitor slavery in global supply chains differ from the tools required to respond to trafficking in more informal, independent, and non-networked-based markets. For example, the exploitation of domestic servants in homes of diplomats, professionals, and other individuals, or forced begging and street peddling is facilitated by a different set of factors than those that drive supply chain dynamics.

There are also time-bound conditions that can further exacerbate the risk factors and conditions for human trafficking, including natural disasters, war and conflict, and other conditions leading to voluntary migration and involuntary displacement. Thoughtful interventions that can attack the vulnerable nodes of each type of human trafficking market can change the specific high profit, low risk economic dynamic that enables human trafficking to flourish. Likewise, predictive analysis on the likely conditions that could exacerbate human trafficking can guide interventions to reduce the harm and ultimately decrease the scale and scope of human trafficking impacting individuals and communities.

As in any market, consumers contribute to the economic engine of both sex trafficking and labor trafficking in illegal and legal, formal and informal markets. A DOJ-funded study estimated that the worth of the underground sex economy in eight US cities in 2007 was between $39.9 and $290 million. Pimps and sex traffickers interviewed for the study earned between $5,000 and $32,833 a week and perceived their crimes as low risk. Drivers, secretaries, nannies, and others employed by traffickers to support operations also profited from the exploitation. The study found that even feuding gang members would work together in the sex trade to prioritize profit rather than engage in turf wars. The ability to advertise online and through social media to reach a more diverse customer base has enabled the growth of the commercial sex industry. The role of the internet has also increased child pornography[10] and availability of graphic content of younger victims [47].

The majority of consumer-oriented strategies to prevent sex trafficking have focused primarily on criminal justice-driven demand reduction tactics, including reverse stings, vehicle seizures, sending letters home, and "john school" education programs. A DOJ-funded study that examined these types of national demand reduction efforts reported that comprehensive demand-reduction initiatives achieved 40 to 80 percent reduction in commercial sex and sex trafficking markets. The study concluded that there was little evidence that sex trafficking markets substantially changed without demand-reduction strategies and that decreasing supply only had temporary effects or displaced activity to other areas [48].

Proponents of consumer-oriented strategies seek to disrupt the economic drivers that incentivize sex traffickers and to address the normalization of gender-based violence in the commercial sex industry. However, critics of demand-reduction activities note limitations of the approach, including not preventing the more violent or abusive consumers who may have more experience evading law enforcement, masking structural factors that need to be addressed (e.g., poverty and restrictive immigration practices), and increasing stigma for individuals in the commercial sex industry [49].

A public health framework used to examine the demand dynamics that facilitate sex trafficking can help to bridge the concerns to address both the economic and social root causes of commercial sexual exploitation, violence, and trafficking. For example, public health-oriented research can provide additional insight into distinct segments of the demand for commercial sex and sex trafficking, differentiating the motivations and causal factors leading to purchase decisions. Community-based education efforts can work to change public and individual awareness levels that reach buyers or potential buyers through targeted and culturally specific messages to change attitudes and behaviors that contribute to violence and trafficking in the commercial sex industry. Training for mental health and counseling professionals treating substance use disorders, self-harm, and violent behavior can address some of the psycho-social factors that contribute to commercial sexual exploitation and trafficking in non-shaming environments. Age-appropriate, early education efforts focused on healthy relationships can further work to prevent sexual violence and exploitation. Engaging survivors of trafficking and former buyers to develop messages for social campaigns and inform policies can also generate greater action outside of a criminal justice response.

The US government encourages zero-tolerance policies for government employees and contractors, and codes of conduct for businesses to help reduce demand contributing to both sex trafficking and labor trafficking. The zero-tolerance policy in the 2002 National Security Presidential Directive 22 called for Department of Defense agencies to review internal structures, personnel requirements, information systems, and professional education and training to carry out responsibilities to combat trafficking. In 2012, President Obama issued a zero-tolerance policy regarding government employees and contractor personnel from engaging in

---

[10] Now called "child abuse imagery".

human trafficking, including supporting or promoting human trafficking, procuring commercial sex acts, or using forced labor in the performance of a contract or sub-contract [50–53].

Other US government actions to address the economic dynamics of trafficking, include engaging consumers in preventing and disrupting labor trafficking, empowering workers and businesses, conducting research, investigating civil cases, and forming public–private partnerships to spur innovation. The US Department of Labor (DOL) maintains a list of goods and source countries believed to be producing materials via child labor or forced labor. In 2014, DOL identified 136 goods, 74 countries, and 353 line items (combination of a good and country) made by forced and child labor.[11] Many of these goods enter into the products purchased by US consumers on a daily basis, from clothing to food to electronics [54–56]. This type of research provides consumers and businesses with information that can impact purchase decisions to reduce profits made from forced labor.

A Department of Justice-funded study of labor trafficking estimated approximately 38,000 Spanish-speaking survivors of human trafficking work in San Diego County, California. The industries with the highest numbers of violations were construction, food processing, and janitorial/cleaning. Construction had the highest rates (35 percent for reported trafficking violations and 63 percent for abusive labor practices). Agriculture had the lowest rates of both reported trafficking violations (16 percent) and abusive labor practices (27 percent). Examples of reported abuses included inability to leave the workplace, confiscation of identification documents, prohibitions on contacting family members, and physical and sexual violence [57]. Nationally, the top industries reported in cases of labor trafficking identified by the HHS-funded National Human Trafficking Resource Center between 2013 and 2015 were domestic work, traveling sales crews, agriculture, restaurant and food services, and health and beauty services [58]. Reporting on these types of industry-level vulnerabilities to trafficking can equip business leaders with information to reduce risk and assess how they procure labor services to prevent human trafficking.

In addition to investigation of criminal cases, the US government through the Equal Employment Opportunity Commission (EEOC) also investigates civil cases involving human trafficking. The EEOC implements laws prohibiting discrimination

---

[11] Forced labor is defined by the International Labor Organization (ILO) Convention 29 as "all work or service which is exacted from any person under the menace of any penalty and for which the said person has not offered himself voluntarily." Child labor includes minors under age 18 working in the worst forms of child labor as outlined in ILO Convention 182 and children engaged in work that is exploitative and/or interferes with their ability to participate in or complete required years of schooling, in line with ILO Convention 138. ILO Convention 182 defines the worst forms of child labor all forms of slavery or practices similar to slavery, such as the sale and trafficking of children, debt bondage, and serfdom and forced or compulsory labor, including forced or compulsory recruitment of children for use in armed conflict; the use, procuring or offering of a child for prostitution, the production of pornography or for pornographic performances; the use, procuring or offering of a child for illicit activities, in particular for the production and trafficking of drugs as defined in the relevant international treaties; and work which, by its nature or the circumstances in which it is carried out, is likely to harm the health, safety, or morals of children. More information on the definitions of forced and child labor are available at https://www.dol.gov/ilab/child-forced-labor/What-are-Child-Labor-and-Forced-Labor.htm.

on the basis of race, national origin, and sex, including sexual harassment [3, 59]. Examples of EEOC cases related to human trafficking in FY 2014 include:

EEOC v. Global Horizons (including Mac Farms of Hawaii, LLC, Kauai Coffee Co., Inc., Kelena Farms, Inc. and Captain Cook Coffee Co., Ltd.) (Hawaii): EEOC settled its case against four farms for $2.4 million and comprehensive equitable relief for approximately 500 Thai farmworker victims of national origin discrimination and retaliation. The settlement encompasses monetary relief, options for jobs and benefits, housing, other reimbursements of expenses, and sweeping injunctive relief remedies. The total settlement in this case so far is $3.5 million, which includes a prior settlement with Del Monte Fresh Produce for $1.2 million. In addition, the court found the labor contractor, Global Horizons, liable for a pattern or practice of harassing, discriminating, and retaliating against hundreds of Thai workers. The court later entered a default judgment against Global and Maui Pineapple, finding them jointly liable for $8.7 million in damages [60–63].

EEOC v. Signal International, LLC (Mississippi): EEOC alleged that Signal subjected a class of Indian employees to discriminatory treatment and different terms and conditions of employment based on national origin (Indian) or race (Asian). In particular, EEOC alleged that Signal required the Indian employees to live in modular trailers called "man camps," enclosed by fences and built by Signal for the Indian employees, and charged them more than $30 daily for housing and food. EEOC further alleged that the living facilities, food, and overall living conditions were intolerable, demeaning, and unsanitary. In 2015, EEOC announced a $5 million settlement with Signal to resolve the lawsuit, including payment to 476 Indian guest workers and agreement to publicly acknowledge forced labor in the aftermath of hurricanes Katrina and Rita.

The US government has also been empowering technology companies and the private sector to provide tools for businesses and consumers to make empowered buying decisions. In 2015, the US State Department-funded report, *Strengthening Protections Against Trafficking in Persons in Federal and Corporate Supply Chains*, provides a framework and resources on the risk of human trafficking in global supply chains [21]. In 2015, HHS and other federal partners joined Humanity United to launch the *Rethink Supply Chains* challenge competition seeking technological solutions that identify and address labor trafficking in global supply chains, addressing workers voices, recruitment, and traceability. The winning solutions received grants to help seafood suppliers and major retailers to better screen for risks of forced labor, address high-risk zones within their supply chain, and to use mobile technology to improve visibility of trafficked workers by capturing and analyzing worker feedback [64]. In 2015, the White House gave the Presidential Medal for Extraordinary Efforts to Combat Human Trafficking in Persons to the Coalition of Immokalee Workers for pioneering the Fair Food Program to empower agricultural workers and leverage market forces and consumer awareness to promote supply chain transparency [65].

The importance of consumer engagement in the fight against forced labor has also been acknowledged by the international community. In 2014, the Nobel Peace Prize committee awarded the honor to Kailash Satyarthi, the founder of GoodWeave.

GoodWeave is a nonprofit organization that educates consumers on forced labor used in the production of rugs. Consumer awareness eventually led to the RugMark label, a certification system that incentivizes manufacturers to stop exploiting harmful child labor. The growing recognition of the economic dynamics that drive human trafficking are also reflected in other major international actions. For example, when the United Nations adopted the new Sustainable Development Goals (SDG) in September 2015, the 17 goals to address poverty and development also included actions to address sex trafficking and forced labor: Three of the goals focused on gender equality; decent work and economic growth; and peace, justice, and strong institutions [66, 67]. As the international community works to meet these SDG goals by 2030, a public health framework that calls on multiple sectors and institutions to come together, can help move this agenda forward.

24.3 Conclusion

Public health has a history of addressing issues with urgency—like preventing car accidents and reducing tobacco use—even if they directly affect a relative minority of our population. We must broaden public health's role in the fight against human trafficking because the field has a fundamental understanding that life can be improved and societies can be transformed even in the midst of seemingly entrenched interests. The public health field must invest in rigorous research to gather the data to revolutionize public attitudes and behavior to prevent and disrupt human trafficking. Public health approaches must inform policies that recognize human trafficking as an interconnected issue to other forms of violence and systemic inequities. Human trafficking affects us all, directly or indirectly, with broad societal, economic, and multi-generational consequences.

24.4 Recommendations

In 2016 (the time of this writing), as we look to add to the foundation of the previous 15 years' efforts and prioritize actions towards 2030, the anti-trafficking field can apply the public health framework by adapting the National Public Health Performance Standards in ten essential areas to create population-wide impact[12]:

1. *Monitor health status to identify and solve community health problems*: Identify how human trafficking is impacting a specific geographic area or community

---

[12] The National Public Health Performance Standards (NPHPS) provides a framework that can help identify areas for system improvement, strengthen state, and local partnerships, and ensure that a strong system is in place for addressing public health issues. The NPHPS was developed by the American Public Health Association, Association of State and Territorial Health Officials, Centers for Disease Control and Prevention, National Association of County and City Health Officials, National Network of Public Health Institutes, and Public Health Foundation. More information about the NPHPS and its tools are available at http://www.cdc.gov/nphpsp/.

by establishing and promoting use of uniform data collection standards that can be used across sectors and systems of care. Uniform data elements and definitions, combined with innovations in technology, can synchronize data collection efforts, enable data-driven decisions, provide clarity on survivor service needs, identify root causes, protective elements, and risk-factors, improve resource allocation and coordination efforts, and support analysis of trafficking trends and dynamics.

2. *Diagnose and investigate health problems and health hazards in the community*: Conduct community needs surveys to assess how the community (across multiple sectors) is ready to identify the harms and socio-economic consequences of human trafficking; respond to the diverse forms of trafficking; and is able to measure the effectiveness of the response.

3. *Inform, educate, and empower people about health issues*: Identify communication channels to keep diverse stakeholders informed about human trafficking issues; look for opportunities to build knowledge and shape attitudes to promote anti-trafficking initiatives; and promote media advocacy and social marketing to effectively target messages that will develop skills and change behaviors to reduce risk and promote help-seeking behavior among high risk populations and trafficking survivors.

4. *Mobilize community partnerships and actions to identify and solve health problems*: Identify strategic partnerships to screen for trafficked persons in multiple systems of care and in non-institutional settings; connect survivors of trafficking to sustained community resources and engagement; and prevent human trafficking through early interventions for high-risk populations and industries.

5. *Develop policies and plans that support individual and community health efforts*: Identify and communicate government and private sector policies that promote prevention, disruption, and eradication of human trafficking, including the development of multi-sector plans that increase coordination, collaboration, and capacity building.

6. *Enforce laws and regulations that protect health and ensure safety*: Assess whether existing laws, regulations, and policies enable intended prosecution, protection, and prevention goals. Identify whether implementation of policies and programs assure survivors' civil rights, utilize best practices, and connect survivors to the community rather than punish, isolate, or stigmatize them or individuals at risk for trafficking.

7. *Link people to needed personal health services and assure the provision of health care when otherwise unavailable*: Assess whether survivors are able to access the benefits and services available to them and whether individuals at risk for victimization or perpetration are receiving support to prevent human trafficking. Identify populations experiencing barriers to accessing services and facilitate effective entry into culturally appropriate coordinated systems of care, including transportation and other enabling services.

8. *Assure competent public and personal health care workforce*: Provide training to a wide range of health care clinicians, public health professionals, social workers, and other first responders. These trainings should include incentivizing

learning through continuing education credits. Further, disciplines should develop professional, data-driven standards to identify trafficking among patients, community members, or clients, respond to survivor needs, and prevent trafficking among high-risk populations.

9. *Evaluate effectiveness, accessibility, and quality of personal and population-based health services*: Assess the needs and risk factors of populations affected by human trafficking, segmented by type of trafficking and unique geographic and other demographic factors. Invest in quality improvement initiatives, including peer-to-peer networking, survivor-informed anti-trafficking initiatives, provision of technical guidance, and training on performance measurement.

10. *Research for new insights and innovative solutions to health problems*: Provide opportunities to discover and use new tools and processes to accomplish anti-trafficking goals, focusing on outcomes and not just outputs. Fund participatory and community-based research to directly engage stakeholders impacted by trafficking. Identify public–private partnerships to drive innovation, leverage technology, and benefit from user-designed principles to develop products and services. Report on results implementing evidence-based or promising practices.

References

1. International Labour Organization. Profits and poverty: the economics of forced labor. Geneva. 2014. http://www.ilo.org/wcmsp5/groups/public/---ed_norm/---declaration/documents/publication/wcms_243391.pdf. Accessed 23 May 2016.
2. U.S. Department of State. 2015 Trafficking in Persons report. Washington, DC. 2015. http://www.state.gov/j/tip/rls/tiprpt/. Accessed 23 May 2016.
3. US Department of Justice. Attorney General's annual report to congress and assessment of U.S. government activities to combat trafficking in persons fiscal year 2014. 2014. https://www.justice.gov/ag/file/799436/download. Accessed 23 May 2016.
4. US Department of Health and Human Services. Submission to the FY 2015 Attorney General's report to congress. 2015.
5. US State Department. Trafficking in persons report 2014. 2014. http://www.state.gov/j/tip/rls/tiprpt/2014/index.htm. Accessed 23 May 2016.
6. US State Department. Trafficking in persons report 2015. 2015. http://www.state.gov/j/tip/rls/tiprpt/2015/index.htm. Accessed 23 May 2016.
7. US Government Printing Office. Victims of Trafficking and Violence Protection Act of 2000. Public Law 106-386. 2000.
8. US Government Printing Office. Trafficking Victims Protection Reauthorization Act of 2003. Public Law 108-193. 2003.
9. US Government Printing Office. Trafficking Victims Protection Reauthorization Act of 2005. Public Law 109-164. 2005.
10. US Government Printing Office. William Wilberforce Trafficking Victims Protection Reauthorization Act of 2008. Public Law 110-457. 2008.
11. US Government Printing Office. Violence Against Women Reauthorization Act of 2013. Public Law 113-4. 2013.
12. Polaris. A look back: building a human trafficking legal framework. 2014. http://polarisproject.org/sites/default/files/2014-Look-Back.pdf. Accessed 23 May 2016.

13. National Human Trafficking Resource Center. National Human Trafficking Resource Center data breakdown: United State report 1/1/2015–12/31/2015. 2016. http://traffickingresource-center.org/resources/2015-nhtrc-annual-report. Accessed 23 May 2016.
14. Centers for Disease Control and Prevention. National public health performance standards overview: strengthening systems, improving the public's health. http://www.cdc.gov/nphpsp/documents/raudsep-nphps-overview.pdf. Accessed 23 May 2016.
15. US Printing Office. Justice for Victims of Trafficking Act of 2015. Public Law 114-22. 2015.
16. White House. President Obama announces more key administration posts. 2015. https://www.whitehouse.gov/the-press-office/2015/12/16/president-obama-announces-more-key--administration-posts. Accessed 23 May 2016.
17. White House. Fact sheet: president's interagency task force to monitor and combat trafficking in persons. 2016. https://www.whitehouse.gov/the-press-office/2016/01/05/fact-sheet-presidents-interagency-task-force-monitor-and-combat. Accessed 23 May 2016.
18. US Printing Office. Preventing Sex Trafficking and Strengthening Families Act. Public Law 113-183. 2014.
19. Children's Bureau, Administration for Children and Families, U.S. Department of Health and Human Services. Information Memorandum: New legislation—Public Law 113-183, the Preventing Sex Trafficking and Strengthening Families Act. 2014. http://www.acf.hhs.gov/sites/default/files/cb/im1403.pdf. Accessed 23 May 2016.
20. White House. Executive Order—Strengthening protections against trafficking in persons in federal contracts. 2012. https://www.whitehouse.gov/the-press-office/2012/09/25/executive-order-strengthening-protections-against-trafficking-persons-fe. Accessed 23 May 2016.
21. Verite. Strengthening protections against trafficking in persons in federal and corporate supply chains. 2015. http://www.state.gov/documents/organization/237137.pdf. Accessed 23 May 2016.
22. National Archives and Records Administration. Federal acquisition regulation; ending trafficking in persons. 2015. https://www.federalregister.gov/articles/2015/01/29/2015-01524/federal-acquisition-regulation-ending-trafficking-in-persons. Accessed 23 May 2016.
23. Centers for Disease Control and Prevention and Prevention Institute. Connecting the dots: an overview of the links among multiple forms of violence. 2014. http://www.cdc.gov/violenceprevention/pdf/connecting_the_dots-a.pdf. Accessed 23 May 2016.
24. Administration for Children, Youth and Families, U.S. Department of Health and Human Services. Guidance to states and services on addressing human trafficking of children and youth in the United States. 2013. http://www.acf.hhs.gov/programs/cb/resource/human-trafficking-guidance. Accessed 23 May 2016.
25. Human Rights Project for Girls, Georgetown Law Center on Poverty and Inequality, Ms. Foundation for Women. The sexual abuse to prison pipeline: the girls' story. 2015. http://rights4girls.org/wp-content/uploads/r4g/2015/02/2015_COP_sexual-abuse_layout_web-1.pdf. Accessed 23 May 2016.
26. Jody Raphael and Brenda Myers-Powell. From victims to victimizers: interviews with 25 ex-pimps in Chicago. 2010. https://law.depaul.edu/about/centers-and-institutes/schiller-ducanto-fleck-family-law-center/Documents/interview_ex_pimps.pdf. Accessed 23 May 2016.
27. Centers for Disease Control and Prevention. Child abuse and neglect prevention. http://www.cdc.gov/violenceprevention/childmaltreatment/index.html. Accessed 23 May 2016.
28. Centers for Disease Control and Prevention. Intimate partner violence: consequences. http://www.cdc.gov/violenceprevention/intimatepartnerviolence/consequences.html. Accessed 23 May 2016.
29. Centers for Disease Control and Prevention. The history of violence as a public health issue. http://www.cdc.gov/violenceprevention/pdf/history_violence-a.pdf. Accessed 23 May 2016.
30. Office of Disease Prevention and Health Promotion, U.S. Department of Health and Human Services. History & development of healthy people. https://www.healthypeople.gov/2020/about/History-and-Development-of-Healthy-People. Accessed 23 May 2016.

31. Office of Disease Prevention and Health Promotion, U.S. Department of Health and Human Services. Call for nominations: Healthy People 2030 Advisory Committee. http://health.gov/news/past-events/2016/03/call-for-nominations-healthy-people-2030-advisory-committee/. Accessed 23 May 2016.
32. Children's Bureau, Administration for Children and Families, U.S. Department of Health and Human Services. Information Memorandum: New legislation—Public Law 113-183, the Preventing Sex Trafficking and Strengthening Families Act. 2015. http://www.acf.hhs.gov/sites/default/files/cb/im1403.pdf. Accessed 23 May 2016.
33. Children's Bureau, Administration for Children and Families, U.S. Department of Health and Human Services. Program Instruction: New legislation—Public Law 113-183, the Preventing Sex Trafficking and Strengthening Families Act. 2015. http://www.acf.hhs.gov/sites/default/files/cb/pi1507.pdf. Accessed 23 May 2016.
34. National Child Traumatic Stress Network. Human trafficking awareness month. 2016. http://www.nctsn.org/resources/public-awareness/human-trafficking. Accessed 23 May 2016.
35. American Public Health Association. Establishing policies and building capacity of federally qualified health centers to address sex trafficking. 2015. https://apha.confex.com/apha/143am/webprogram/Paper325200.html. Accessed 23 May 2016.
36. Office for Victims of Crime, U.S. Department of Justice. Federal strategic action plan on services for victims of human trafficking in the United States, 2013–2017. 2014. http://ovc.ncjrs.gov/humantrafficking/plan.html. Accessed 23 May 2016.
37. National Center for Missing and Exploited Children. Child sex trafficking. http://www.missingkids.com/1in6. Accessed 23 May 2016.
38. Family and Youth Services Bureau, Administration for Children and Families, U.S. Department of Health and Human Services. Final report—Street Outreach Program data collection study. 2016. http://www.acf.hhs.gov/programs/fysb/resource/street-outreach-program-data-collection-study. Accessed 23 May 2016.
39. Duren Banks and Tracey Kyckelhahn. Characteristics of suspected human trafficking incidents, 2008–2010. 2011. https://www.ncjrs.gov/ovc_archives/ncvrw/2013/pdf/2013ResourceGuide-Full.pdf. Accessed 23 May 2016.
40. UN High Commissioner for Refugees. Children on the run. 2016. http://www.unhcr.org/en-us/about-us/background/56fc266f4/children-on-the-run-full-report.html?query=children%20on%20the%20run. Accessed 23 May 2016.
41. Office of Refugee Resettlement, Administration for Children and Families, U.S. Department of Health and Human Services. Children entering the United States unaccompanied. 2015. http://www.acf.hhs.gov/programs/orr/resource/children-entering-the-united-states--unaccompanied. Accessed 23 May 2016.
42. Office of Refugee Resettlement, Administration for Children and Families, U.S. Department of Health and Human Services. URM eligibility and application. 2015. http://www.acf.hhs.gov/programs/orr/resource/state-letter-15-07. Accessed 23 May 2016.
43. Office on Trafficking in Persons, Administration for Children and Families, U.S. Department of Health and Human Services. Stop. Observe. Ask. Respond to human trafficking: a training for health care and social service providers. 2016. http://www.acf.hhs.gov/programs/endtrafficking/initiatives/soar. Accessed 23 May 2016.
44. Children's Bureau, Administration for Children and Families, U.S. Department of Health and Human Services. Implementation of the Fostering Connections to Success and Increasing Adoptions Act of 2008 Working Document. 2013. http://www.acf.hhs.gov/programs/cb/resource/implementation-of-the-fostering-connections. Accessed 31 May 2016.
45. Family and Youth Services Bureau, Administration for Children and Families, U.S. Department of Health and Human Services. Runaway and Homeless youth Training & Technical Assistance Center: HTR3. http://www.rhyttac.net/technical-assistance/htr3. Accessed 23 May 2016.
46. National Runaway Safeline. Free Greyhound bus tickets to homeless youth "Home Free" program expands. 2016. http://www.1800runaway.org/2016/03/free-greyhound-tickets-to-

homeless-youth-home-free-program-expands/?utm_source=blog&utm_medium=email&
utm_campaign=031116DFHomeFreeExpands. Accessed 23 May 2016.

47. Urban Institute. Estimating the size and structure of the underground commercial sex economy
    in eight major US cities. 2014. http://www.urban.org/sites/default/files/alfresco/publication-
    pdfs/413047-Estimating-the-Size-and-Structure-of-the-Underground-Commercial-Sex--
    Economy-in-Eight-Major-US-Cities.PDF. Accessed 23 May 2016.

48. Abt Associates. A national overview of prostitution and sex trafficking demand reduction
    efforts: final report. 2012. https://www.ncjrs.gov/pdffiles1/nij/grants/238796.pdf. Accessed 23
    May 2016.

49. Global Alliance Against Traffic in Women. Moving beyond 'supply and demand' catch-
    phrases: assessing the uses and limitations of demand-based approaches in anti-trafficking.
    2011. http://www.gaatw.org/publications/MovingBeyond_SupplyandDemand_GAATW2011.
    pdf. Accessed 31 May 2016.

50. US State Department. Prevention: fighting sex trafficking by curbing demand for commercial
    sex acts. 2013. http://www.state.gov/documents/organization/211845.pdf. Accessed 31 May
    2016.

51. White House. National security presidential directive/NSPD-22: combating trafficking per-
    sons. 2002. http://ctip.defense.gov/Portals/12/Documents/NSPD-22.pdf. Accessed 31, May
    2016.

52. White House. Executive Order—Strengthening protections against trafficking in persons in
    Federal Contracts. https://www.whitehouse.gov/the-press-office/2012/09/25/executive-order-
    strengthening-protections-against-trafficking-persons-fe. Accessed 31 May 2016.

53. White House. Fact Sheet: executive Order strengthening protections against trafficking in
    persons in federal contracts. 2012. https://www.whitehouse.gov/the-press-office/2012/09/
    25/fact-sheet-executive-order-strengthening-protections-against-trafficking. Accessed 31 May
    2016.

54. US Department of Labor. List of goods produced by child labor or forced labor. 2014. https://
    www.dol.gov/ilab/reports/child-labor/list-of-goods/. Accessed 23 May 2016.

55. US Department of Labor. List of products produced by forced or indentured child labor. 2014.
    https://www.dol.gov/ilab/reports/pdf/EO_Report_2014.pdf. Accessed 23 May 2016.

56. US Department of Labor. Reducing child labor and forced labor: a toolkit for responsible busi-
    nesses. https://www.dol.gov/ilab/child-forced-labor/. Accessed 23 May 2016.

57. Zhang S. Looking for a hidden population: trafficking of migrant laborers in San Diego County.
    2012.   http://www.nij.gov/topics/crime/human-trafficking/pages/nature-extent-projects.aspx.
    Accessed 23 May 2016.

58. National Human Trafficking Resource Center. Hotline statistics. 2016. http://trafficking
    resourcecenter.org/states. Accessed 23 May 2016.

59. U.S. Equal Employment Opportunity Commission. Human trafficking. https://www.eeoc.gov/
    eeoc/interagency/trafficking.cfm. Accessed 23 May 2016

60. U.S. Equal Employment Opportunity Commission. Judge approves $2.4 million EEOC settle-
    ment with four Hawaii farms for over 500 Thai Farmworkers. 2014. https://www.eeoc.gov/
    eeoc/newsroom/release/9-5-14.cfm. Accessed 23 May 2016.

61. U.S. Equal Employment Opportunity Commission. Del monte fresh produce agrees to settle
    EEOC farmworker national origin lawsuit. 2013. https://www.eeoc.gov/eeoc/newsroom/
    release/11-18-13a.cfm. Accessed 23 May 2016.

62. U.S. Equal Employment Opportunity Commission. Federal judge finds global horizons liable
    for discriminating, harassing, and retaliating against hundreds of Thai farm workers in EEOC
    Suit. 2014. https://www.eeoc.gov/eeoc/newsroom/release/3-24-14.cfm. Accessed 23 May
    2016.

63. U.S. Equal Employment Opportunity Commission. Signal international, LLC to pay $5
    million to settle EEOC race, national origin lawsuit. 2015. https://www.eeoc.gov/eeoc/
    newsroom/release/12-18-15.cfm. Accessed 23 May 2016.

64. Partnership for Freedom. Rehink supply chains. 2016. https://www.partnershipforfreedom. org/rethinksupplychains/#winners-current. Accessed 23 May 2016.
65. U.S. Department of State. Remarks at the white house forum on combating human trafficking in supply chains. 2015. http://www.state.gov/secretary/remarks/2015/01/236950.htm. Accessed 23 May 2016.
66. United Nations. Sustainable Development Goals. 2015. https://sustainabledevelopment. un.org/. Accessed 23 May 2016.
67. UNICEF United States Fund. The sustainable development goals that aim to end human trafficking. 2016. https://www.unicefusa.org/stories/sustainable-development-goals-aim-end--human-trafficking/29864. Accessed 23 May 2016.

ERRATUM

Human Trafficking Is a Public Health Issue
A Paradigm Expansion in the United States

Makini Chisolm-Straker and Hanni Stoklosa

Editors

© Springer International Publishing AG 2017
M. Chisolm-Straker, H. Stoklosa (eds.), *Human Trafficking Is a Public Health Issue*, DOI 10.1007/978-3-319-47824-1

DOI 10.1007/978-3-319-47824-1_25

In **Chapter 5** titled "The Ignored Exploitation: Labor Trafficking in the United States" the affiliation of the author Susie Baldwin has been updated to read as "HEAL Trafficking, P.O. Box 31602, 3001 North Broadway, Los Angeles, CA 90031, USA, e-mail: SBaldwin@healtrafficking.org".

In **Chapter 7** titled "Children at Risk: Foster Care and Human Trafficking" the affiliation of the authors should read as:

Kathryn Martin
"Washington, DC, USA, e-mail: kathryn.p.martin@gmail.com".

Kimberly Caceres
"SUNY Albany, 135 Western Avenue, Albany, NY 12222, USA".

The updated online version of the original book can be found at
http://dx.doi.org/10.1007/978-3-319-47824-1

© Springer International Publishing AG 2017   E1
M. Chisolm-Straker, H. Stoklosa (eds.), *Human Trafficking Is a Public Health Issue*, DOI 10.1007/978-3-319-47824-1_25

In **Chapter 14** titled "Legal Supports for Trafficked Persons: Assisting Survivors via Certification, State/Federal Benefits, and Compensation" the affiliation of the authors should read as:

Lennon Moore
"Covenant House, 929 Atlantic Avenue, Atlantic City, NJ 08401, USA,
e-mail: lennonmoore@covenanthouse.org".

Brendan Milliner
"Department of Emergency Medicine, Mount Sinai Medical Center,
Box 1620, 1 Gustave L. Levy Place, New York, NY 10029, USA".

In **Chapter 17** titled "Research Informing Advocacy: An Anti-Human Trafficking Tool" the affiliation of the authors should read as:

Cathy L. Miller
"Texas A&M University-Corpus Christi, College of Nursing and Health Sciences,
6300 Ocean Drive, Island Hall 328G, Corpus Christi, TX 78412, USA,
e-mail: cathy.miller@tamucc.edu".

Michelle Lyman
"University of South Florida, Morsani College of Medicine,
12901 Bruce B. Downs Boulevard, Tampa, FL 33612, USA".

In **Chapter 19** titled "Sex Trafficking in One US City: Traditional Policing and Boston's Shift to a Survivor-Centered Response" the affiliation of the author Cassandra Thomson has been updated to read as "University of Michigan Law School, 625 S. State Street, Ann Arbor, MI 48109, USA, e-mail: cjthoms@umich.edu".

In **Chapter 22** titled "Human Trafficking: Perspectives on Prevention" the affiliation of the authors should read as:

Elaine J. Alpert
"Faculty of Medicine, University of British Columbia, Vancouver,
BC, Canada, V6T 1Z4, e-mail: ejalpert@massmed.org".

Sharon E. Chin
"Independent Scholar and Program Evaluation Specialist, Somerset, NJ, USA
e-mail: schin.mph@gmail.com".

In **Chapter 23** titled "Combating Modern Bondage: The Development of a Multi-Disciplinary Approach to Human Trafficking" the affiliation of the author Laura J. Lederer has been updated to read as "Global Centurion, 5746 Union Mill Road, Suite 514, Clifton, VA 20124, USA, e-mail: llederer@globalcenturion.org".

In **Chapter 24** titled "Moving Forward: Next Steps in Preventing and Disrupting Human Trafficking" the affiliation of the author Smitha Khorana has been updated to read as "Columbia University, 116th Street & Broadway, New York, NY 10027, USA, e-mail: smithakhorana@gmail.com".

In the **Front Matter**, the author biography of the author Kathryn Martin has been updated to read as:

"**Kathryn Martin, MPH** is a 2016 Mirzayan Science & Technology Policy Graduate Fellow with the National Academies of Sciences, Engineering, and Medicine. In this role, she works on the Innovate to Incubate (i2I) and Forum for Investing in Young Children Globally (iYCG) teams. Martin's research interests span a wide range of issues, including child and adolescent well-being, school-based health centers, nutritional health in adverse conditions, and child trafficking. She received her Bachelor of Science in Foreign Service from Georgetown University and a Master of Public Health degree from Columbia University Mailman School of Public Health."

Correction to: Physical Health of Human Trafficking Survivors: Unmet Essentials

Wendy Macias-Konstantopoulos and Zheng B. Ma

Correction to:
Chapter 11 in: M. Chisolm-Straker, H. Stoklosa (eds.),
Human Trafficking Is a Public Health Issue,
https://doi.org/10.1007/978-3-319-47824-1_11

In Chapter 11 titled "Physical Health of Human Trafficking Survivors: Unmet Essentials" a paragraph of this chapter on page 193 was published with errors. It has been updated in all renditions of the book to read as follows:

Repeated sexual abuse, sexually transmitted infections, and a lack of access to contraception during trafficking are related to high risk of unplanned pregnancy and other gynecological symptoms. In one U.S. study, 63.8% of sex trafficking survivors reported at least one gynecologic symptom such as pain during sex or urinary tract infections. Of those who reported pregnancies, 71.2% reported at least one pregnancy during their exploitation, and 21.2% reported five or more pregnancies. Among those who responded to questions regarding termination of pregnancy, 55.2% reported at least one abortion and 29.9% reported multiple abortions [37].

The updated online version of this chapter can be found at
https://doi.org/10.1007/978-3-319-47824-1_11

Index

© Springer International Publishing AG 2017
M. Chisolm-Straker, H. Stoklosa (eds.), *Human Trafficking Is a Public Health
Issue*, DOI 10.1007/978-3-319-47824-1

Printed in the United States
By Bookmasters